THE GREEN GUIDE

Ph Hurian/MICHELIN

Ireland

Director	Hervé Deguine
Series Editor	Manuela Magni
Editors	Elizabeth Bowen, Michael Ivory
Practical Points	Elizabeth Bowen, Natacha Brumard, Michel Chaput
Mapping	Alain Baldet, Geneviève Corbic, Virginie Bruno, Fabienne Renard, Gaëlle Wachs
Picture Editor	Catherine Guégan
Technical Assistants	Audrey Horne, Titus McCready
Lay-out	Marie-Pierre Rénier, Michel Moulin, Jean-Paul Josset
Graphics	Christiane Beylier
Cover	Agence Carré Noir
Production	Pierre Ballochard, Renaud Leblanc
Marketing	Hervé Binetruy
Sales	John Lewis (UK), Gayle Sparks (USA)
Public Relations	Gonzague de Jarnac, Paul Cordle
Thanks	Dr Peter Harbison, Dr Ríonach O'Hogan
Contact	The Green Guide
	Michelin Travel Publications
	Hannay House
	39 Clarendon Road
	Watford
	Herts
	WD17 1JA
	☏ 01923 205 240
	Fax 01923 205 241
	www.ViaMichelin.com
	TheGreenGuide-uk@uk.michelin.com

THE GREEN GUIDE:
The Spirit of Discovery

Leisure time spent with The Green Guide is also a time for refreshing your spirit, enjoying yourself, and taking advantage of our selection of fine restaurants, hotels and other places for relaxing: immerse yourself in the local culture, discover new horizons, experience the local lifestyle. The Green Guide opens the door for you.

Each year our writers go touring: visiting the sights, devising the driving tours, identifying the highlights, selecting the most attractive hotels and restaurants, checking the routes for the maps and plans.

Each title is compiled with great care, giving you the benefit of regular revisions and Michelin's first-hand knowledge. The Green Guide responds to changing circumstances and takes account of its readers' suggestions; all comments are welcome.

Share with us our enthusiasm for travel, which has led us to discover over 60 destinations in France and other countries. Like us, let yourself be guided by the desire to explore, which is the best motive for travel: the spirit of discovery.

Contents

Practical Points   17

Insights and Images   63

James Joyce in Dublin

H Champollion/MICHELIN

Dingle Harbour

B Pérousse/MICHELIN

SELECTED SIGHTS

Kenmare Horse Fair

Glenveagh Castle garden

Maps and Plans

Companion Publications

A map reference to the appropriate Michelin map is given for each chapter in the Selected Sights section of this guide.

• Michelin map 712 – Ireland:

Scale 1 : 400 000 - 1cm : 4km - 1in : 6.30 miles - covers the Republic of Ireland and Northern Ireland, and the network of motorways and major roads. It provides information on shipping routes, distances in miles and kilometres, town plans of Dublin and Belfast, services, sporting and tourist attractions and an index of places; the key and text are printed in four languages.

• Michelin Tourist and Motoring Atlas Great Britain & Ireland:

Scale 1 : 300 000 - 1cm : 3km - 1in : 4.75 miles (based on 1 : 400 000) - covers the whole of the United Kingdom and the Republic of Ireland, the national networks of motorways and major roads. It provides information on route planning, shipping routes, distances in miles and kilometres, over 60 town plans, services and sporting and tourist attractions and an index of places; the key and text are printed in six languages.

• Michelin map 713 – Great Britain and Ireland:

Scale 1 : 1 000 000 - 1cm : 10km - 1inch : 15.8 miles - covers the whole of the United Kingdom and the Republic of Ireland, the national networks of motorways and major roads. It provides information on shipping routes, distances in miles and kilometres, a list of Unitary Authorities for Wales and Scotland; the key and text are printed in four languages.

• Internet:

Users can access personalised route plans, Michelin mapping on line, addresses of hotels and restaurants listed in The Red Guide and practical and tourist information through the internet:

www.ViaMichelin.com

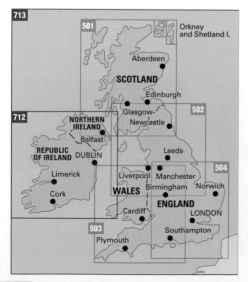

List of Maps and Plans

Town Plans

Plans of Monuments

Local Maps

Key

Selected monuments and sights

	Tour - Departure point
	Ecclesiastical building
	Synagogue - Mosque
	Building
▪	Statue, small building
ɫ	Calvary, wayside cross
◎	Fountain
	Rampart - Tower - Gate
	Château, castle, historic house
	Ruins
⌣	Dam
✿	Factory, power plant
☆	Fort
∩	Cave
	Troglodyte dwelling
	Prehistoric site
	Viewing table
	Viewpoint
▲	Other place of interest

Sports and recreation

	Racecourse
	Skating rink
	Outdoor, indoor swimming pool
	Multiplex Cinema
	Marina, sailing centre
	Trail refuge hut
	Cable cars, gondolas
	Funicular, rack railway
	Tourist train
◇	Recreation area, park
	Theme, amusement park
	Wildlife park, zoo
	Gardens, park, arboretum
	Bird sanctuary, aviary
	Walking tour, footpath
	Of special interest to children

Special symbols

M3	Motorway
A2	Primary route
	Forest, Country Park, National Park

Abbreviations

C	County council offices
H	Town hall
J	Law courts
M	Museum
POL.	Police
T	Theatre
U	University

Highly recommended	★★★
Recommended	★★
Interesting	★

Additional symbols

☒		Tourist information
══ ══		Motorway or other primary route
❶	❶	Junction: complete, limited
⊞═ ═		Pedestrian street
ɪ═══ɪ		Unsuitable for traffic, street subject to restrictions
┉┉ ----		Steps – Footpath
🚆	🚆 S.N.C.F.	Train station – Auto-train station
🚌	🚌 S.N.C.F.	Coach (bus) station
·—·—·		Tram
⊙		Metro, underground
ℙℝ		Park-and-Ride
♿		Access for the disabled
✉		Post office
☏		Telephone
✉		Covered market
·ˣ·		Barracks
⧉		Drawbridge
∪		Quarry
✗		Mine
Ⓑ	Ⓕ	Car ferry (river or lake)
🚤		Ferry service: cars and passengers
⛴		Foot passengers only
③		Access route number common to Michelin maps and town plans
Bert (R.)...		Main shopping street
AZ B		Map co-ordinates
►►		Visit if time permits
⊙		Admission times and charges listed at the end of the guide

Places to stay and places to eat

20 rm	Number of rooms.
€76/100 ☐	Price of single/double room including breakfast.
☐ *€4.50*	Price of breakfast when not included in the room price.
100 beds €19	Number of beds (youth hostel, university residence) and price per person.
€10/26.50	Restaurant prices: minimum and maximum price for a full meal excluding beverages. In many cases the first price refers to a lunch menu. For informal eating places an average price may be given.
⊄	Major credit cards not accepted.
ℙ	Car park for customers.
⊁	No-smoking rooms available Restaurant partly or wholly reserved for non-smokers.
♿	Rooms with wheelchair access.

All prices are given in € in the Republic of Ireland and in £ Sterling in Northern Ireland. Prices quoted include VAT unless otherwise specified. Service charge may be expected.

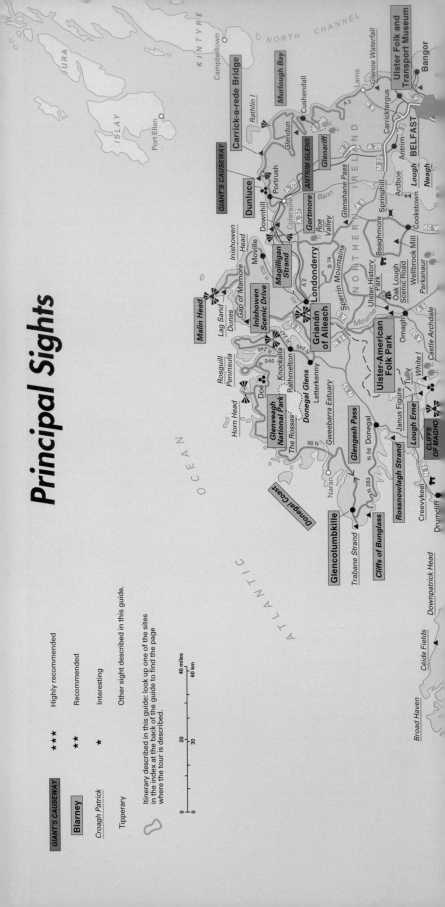

Principal Sights

GIANT'S CAUSEWAY	★★★	Highly recommended
Blarney	★★	Recommended
Croagh Patrick	★	Interesting
Tipperary		Other sight described in this guide.

Itinerary described in this guide: look up one of the sites in the index at the back of the guide to find the page where the tour is described.

0   20   40 miles
0   30   60 km

g Tours

1 Dublin and its Surroundings : 205mi/330km
(one week)

2 Aspects of Ulster : 370mi/590km
(one week)

3 Sights of the Southeast : 305mi/490km
(one week)

4 The Southwest - Counties Cork, Kerry
and Limerick : 505mi/813km (ten days)

5 Glories of Galway, Connemara
and Sligo : 515mi/829km (one week)

6 The Heart of Ireland, the unknown
Midlands : 320mi/515km (one week)

7 Ulster Odyssey : 590mi/950km
(two weeks)

8 Irish Highlights, a grand tour : 1080mi/1738km
(two weeks)

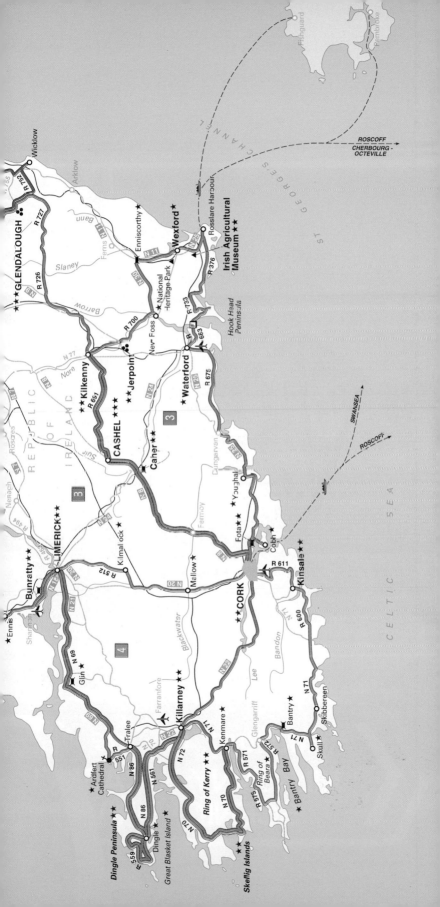

Signpost near Kilkenny

Practical Points

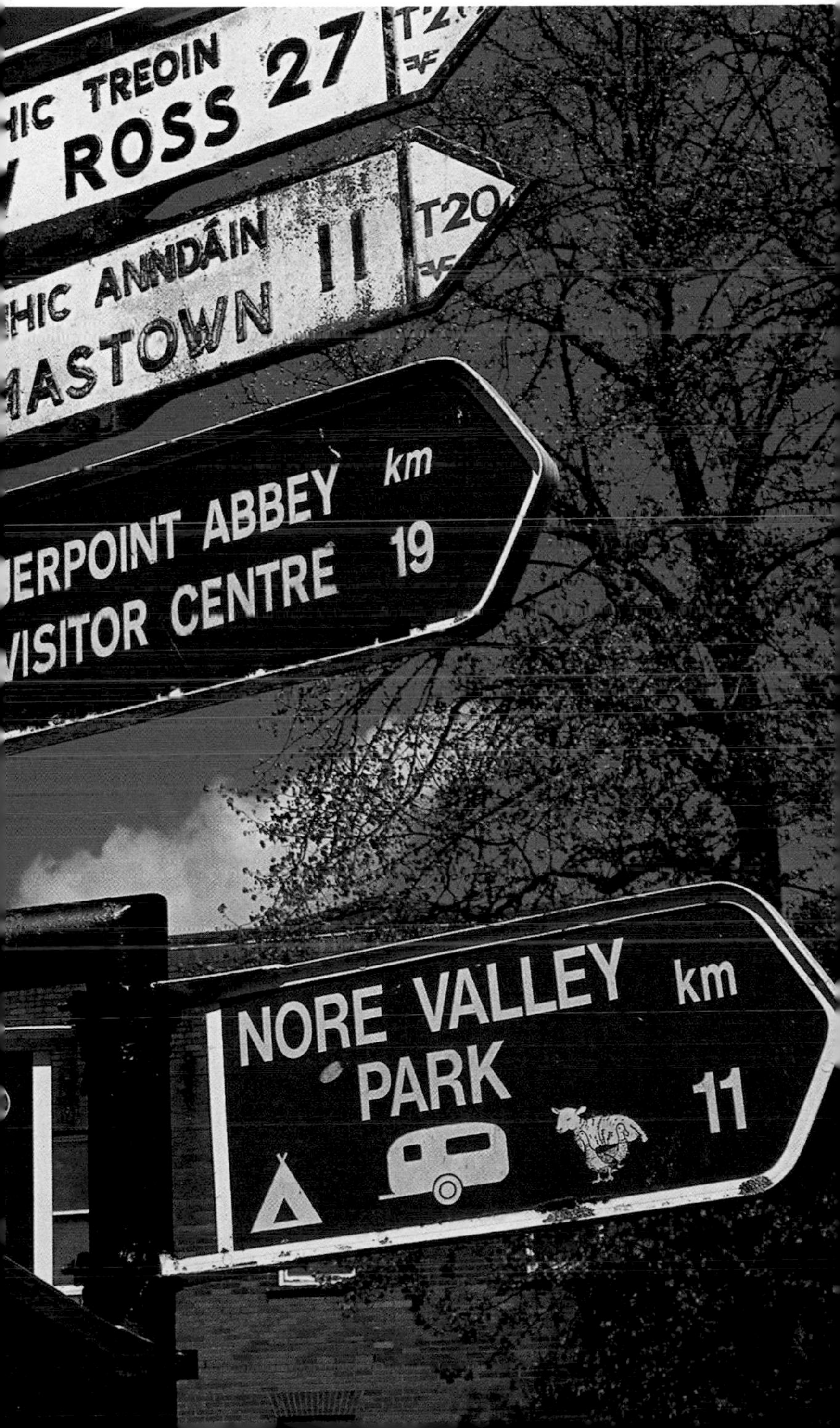

Planning your Trip

Useful Addresses

INTERNET

The internet is a useful source of information to enable you to make the most of your visit.

Republic of Ireland government – www.irlgov.ie

Irish Times – Daily newspaper – www.ireland.com

Irish Radio and TV – www.rte.ie

Irish Language Magazine – www.beo.ie

1 2 Travel – Information on regions, towns, accommodation, tours, helpful tips, interactive maps etc – www.12travel.com

Irish Emigrant Publications, Cathedral Building, Middle Street, Galway. ☎ 091 569 158; Fax 091 569 178; info@emigrant.ie; www.emigrant.ie

TOURIST ORGANISATIONS

For information, brochures, maps and assistance in planning a trip to Ireland contact the following tourist information offices –

IRISH TOURIST BOARD (BORD FÁILTE) OFFICES SITUATED OUTSIDE IRELAND

Australia – 5th Level, 36 Carrington Street, Sydney, NSW 2000. ☎ 029 299 6177, 02 275 0171; info@tourismireland.com.au; www.tourismireland.com

Canada – 2 Bloor Street, Suite 1501, Toronto M4W 3E2. ☎1 866 477 7717 (freephone); info@shamrock.org

Denmark/Norway – Klostergarden, Amagertorv 29,3, 1160 København K. ☎33 15 80 45; Fax 33 93 63 90; www.irland-turism.com; www.visit-ireland.com

Finland – Irlannin Matkailutoimisto, Embassy of Ireland, Erottajankatu 7A PL33, 00130 Helsinki. ☎ 0960 8961; www.irlanninmatkailu.com

Japan – Ireland House 5F, 2-10-7 Kojimachi, Chiyodi-ku, Tokyo 102. ☎03 52 75 16 11; www.traveljapan-ireland.com

New Zealand – 6th Floor, 18 Shortland Street, Private Bag 92136, Auckland 1. ☎(64) 9 977 2255; tourism@ireland.co.nz

Norway – Drammensveien 126A, Pb 295 Skøyen, 0212 Oslo. ☎ 22 56 33 10; Fax 22 12 20 70.

South Africa – c/o Development Promotions, Everite House, 7th Floor, 20 De Korte Street, Braamfontein 2001 Gauteng. ☎ (27) 11 339 4865; Fax (27) 11 339 2474; Helen@dpgsa.co.za

Sweden – Stora Nygatan 40, SE 111 27 Stockholm. ☎ 08 662 8510; info@irlandsinfo.com; www.irlandsinfo.com

United Kingdom – All Ireland Information Desk, Britain Visitor Centre, 1 Regent Street, London SW1Y 4XT *(personal callers and written enquiries only)* ☎ 020 8846 9000 (British Tourist Authority) 150 New Bond Street, London WIY 0AQ *(no callers)*. ☎ 020 7518 0800; Fax 020 7493 9065; info.uk@tourismireland.com James Millar House, 7th Floor, 98 West George Street, Glasgow G2 1PJ, ☎ 0141 572 4030; info@irelandholidays.co.uk; www.tourismireland.com

United States – 345 Park Avenue, New York, NY 10154. ☎ 212 418-0800; ☎ 1800 223 6470 (information line); ☎ 1800 669 9967 (US trade freephone no); info@shamrock.org

B Pérousse/MICHELIN

Liffey River, Dublin

NORTHERN IRELAND TOURIST BOARD (NITB) OFFICES SITUATED OUTSIDE IRELAND

Europe – Büro fur Fremdenverkehr, Westendstr 16-22, D-60325, Frankfurt, Germany. ☎ 069 23 45 04; Fax 069 23 34 80

North America – 551 5th Avenue, Suite 701, New York, NY 10176. ☎ 212 922-0101; Fax 212 922-0099

United Kingdom – All Ireland Information Desk, Britain Visitor Centre, 1 Regent Street, London SW1Y 4XT *(personal callers and written enquiries only)*. ☎ 020 8846 9000 (British Tourist Authority); bvccustomerservices@bta.org.uk; www.visitbritain.com 3rd Floor, 24 Haymarket, London SW1Y 4DG. ☎ 08701 555 250 (info line); Fax 020 7766 9929; info@irelandholidays.co.uk

Irish Tourist Board (Bord Fáilte) –
www.ireland.travel.ie
Baggot Street Bridge, Dublin 2. ☎ 01 602 4000 *(callers within Republic of Ireland only)*; Fax 066 979 2035
53 Castle Street, Belfast BT1 1GH.
☎ 028 9032 7888; Fax 028 9024 0201
44 Foyle Street, Londonderry.
☎/Fax 028 7136 9501

NORTHERN IRELAND TOURIST BOARD (NITB) OFFICES SITUATED IN IRELAND

Northern Ireland Tourist Board (NITB) –
www.discovernorthernireland.com
St Anne Court, 59 North Street, Belfast BT1 1NB. ☎ 028 9024 6609;
infog@nitb.com

Ireland – 16 Nassau Street, Dublin 2.
☎ 01 679 1977; Fax 01 679 1863

REGIONAL TOURISM ORGANISATIONS OFFICES SITUATED IN IRELAND

Dublin Tourism – Dublin Tourism Centre, Suffolk Street, Dublin 2.
www.visitdublin.com

South West Tourism – Grand Parade, Cork. ☎ 021 425 5200;
Fax 021 425 5199;
info@corkkerrytourism.ie;
www.corkkerry.ie

Ireland West Tourism – Victoria Place, Eyre Square, Galway. ☎ 091 537 700, 563 081; Fax 091 537 733, 565 201;
info@irelandwest.ie,
www.irelandwest.travel.ie

East Coast and Midlands East Tourism – Market House, Dublin Road, Mullingar, Co Westmeath.
☎ 044 48650; Fax 044 40413;
info@ecoast-midlandstourism.ie;
www.ecoast-midlands.travel.ie

South East Tourism – 41 The Quay, Waterford. ☎ 051 875 823;
Fax 051 877 388;
info@southeasttourism.ie;
www.southeastireland.com;
www.ireland-southeast.travel.ie

North West Tourism – Temple Street, Sligo. ☎ 071 61201; Fax 071 60360;
irelandnorthwest@eircom.net;
irelandnorthwest@travel.ie;
www.ireland-northwest.travel.ie

Shannon Development – Arthur's Quay, Limerick, Co Limerick.
☎ 061 317 522; Fax 061 317 939;
tourisminfo@shannondev.ie

REGIONAL TOURISM ORGANISATIONS OFFICES SITUATED IN NORTHERN IRELAND

Derry Visitor and Convention Bureau – 44 Foyle Street, Londonderry BT48 6AT. ☎ 028 7137 7577; Fax 028 7137 7992;
www.derryvisitor.com

The Kingdoms of Down – 404 West Street, Newtownards BT23 4EN.
☎ 028 9182 2881; Fax 028 9182 2202;
www.kingdomsofdown.com

Fermanagh Lakeland Tourism –
Wellington Road, Enniskillen BT74 4EF. ☎ 028 6632 3110;
Fax 028 6632 5511;
www.fermanagh-online.com;
www.soeasygoing.com

Causeway Coast and Glens – 11 Lodge Road, Coleraine BT52 1LU.
☎ 028 7032 7720; Fax 028 7032 7719;
www.causewaycoastandglens.com

LOCAL TOURISM ORGANISATIONS

The addresses and telephone numbers of the Tourist Information Centres to be found in most large towns and many tourist resorts in Ireland are printed under the heading **Location** in the chapters in the **Selected Sights** section; some are open only during the summer months. The centres can supply town plans, timetables and information on sightseeing, local entertainment and sports facilities. Many have bureau de change facilities and a hotel reservation service.

FOREIGN EMBASSIES AND CONSULATES IN IRELAND

Australia – Fitzwilton House (2nd floor), Wilton Terrace, Dublin 2.
☎ 01 676 1517; Fax 01 668 5266;
austremb.dublin@dfatgov.au;
www.australianembassy.ie

Canada – Canada House, 65-68 St Stephen's Green, Dublin 2.
☎ 01 478 1988; Fax 01 478 1285;
cndembsy@iol.ie

Denmark – 121-122 St Stephen's Green, Dublin 2. ☎ 01 475 6404 or 01 475 6405; Fax 01 478 4536

Finland – Russell House, Stokes Place, St Stephen's Green, Dublin 2.
☎ 01 478 1344 or 478 1839; Fax 01 478 3727 or 478 1050

Japan – Nutley Building, Merrion Centre, Nutley Lane, Dublin 4.
☎ 01 269 4244 or 269 4033; Fax 01 283 8726

New Zealand – 37 Leeson Park, Dublin 6. ☎ 01 660 4233,
Fax 01 660 4228; nzconsul@indigo.ie

South Africa – Chargé d'Affaires, 2nd Floor, Alexandra House, Earlsfort Centre, Earlsfort Terrace, Dublin 2.
☎ 01 661 5553; Fax 01 661 5590

Sweden – 13-17 Dawson Street, Dublin 2. ☎ 01 671 5822; Fax 01 679 6718

United Kingdom – 29 Merrion Road, Ballsbridge, Dublin 4.
☎ 01 205 3700; Fax 01 205 3885;
bembassy@internet-ireland.ie;
visas@dublin.mail.fco.gov.uk;
www.britishembassy.ie

USA – 42 Elgin Road, Ballsbridge, Dublin 4. ☎ 01 668 8777;
Fax 01 668 9946; www.usembassy.ie

IRISH EMBASSIES

Australia – 20 Arkana Street, Yarralumla, Canberra, ACT 2600.

1 FINGAL   2 SOUTH DUBLIN   3 DÚN LAOGHAIRE-RATHDOWN   O County Towns

☎ 06273 3022; Fax 06273 3741; irishemb@cyberone.com.au

Australia (Consulate General) – Level 30, 400 George Street, Sydney, NSW 2000. ☎ 612 9231 6999; Fax 612 9231 6254; consyd@ireland.com

Canada – Suite 1105, 130 Albert Street, Ottawa, Ontario KIP 5G4. ☎ 613 233 6281; Fax 613 233 5835; embassyofireland@rogers.com

Denmark – Østbanegade 21, I TH.DK-2100 Copenhagen. ☎ 035 42 32 33; Fax 035 43 18 58; irlem_dk@yahoo.com

Finland – Erottajankatu 7A, 00130 Helsinki. Postal Address: PL 33, 00131 Helsinki. ☎ 09 646 006; Fax 09 646 022

Japan – Ireland House 5F, 2-10-7 Kojimachi, Chiyoda-Ku, Tokyo 102-0083. ☎ (03) 3263 0695; Fax (03) 3265 2275

New Zealand – Diplomatic Representation for New Zealand is handled by the embassy in Australia.

Norway – Haakon VIIs gate 1, 0244 Oslo. ☎ (47) 2201 7200; Fax (47) 2201 7201; Hibernia@online.no

South Africa – 1st Floor, Sothern Life Plaza, 1059 Schoeman Street, Arcadia 0083, Pretoria 0001. ☎ (27) 12 342 5062; Fax (27) 12 342 4752; Pretoria@iveagh.irlgov.ie

Sweden – Ostermalmsgatan 97, PO Box 10326, 100 55, Stockholm. ☎ 08 66 18 005; Fax 08 66 01 353; irish.embassy@swipnet.se

United Kingdom – 17 Grosvenor Place, London SW1X 7HR. ☎ 020 7235 2171; Fax 020 7245 6961; eoghan.flood@iveagh.irlgov.ie

United States – 2234 Massachusetts Avenue NW, Washington DC 20008-2849. ☎ 202 462 3939, 462 3940; Fax 202 232 5993; embirlus@aol.com

Formalities

Documents

Visitors entering Ireland must be in possession of a **valid national passport** (except British nationals). In case of loss or theft report to the appropriate embassy and the local police.

Visitors who require an **entry visa** for the Republic of Ireland or Northern Ireland should apply at least three weeks in advance to the Irish Embassy or the United Kingdom Embassy. Useful information for US nationals on visa requirements, customs regulations, medical care etc for international travel is contained in the booklets *Your Trip Abroad* (US$1.25) and *Safe Trip Abroad* (US$1.50), published by the US Government Printing Office.

US Government Printing Office, ☎ 1-202-512-1800; www.access.gpo.gov

Nationals of EU countries require a **valid national driving** licence; nationals of non-EU countries require an **international driving licence**. This is obtainable in the US for US$10 from the National Auto Club, Touring Department, 188 The Embarcardero, Suite 300, San Francisco CA 94105 or from the local branch of the American Automobile Association for US$12 (non-members), US$6 (basic members), free (plus member). ☎ 800 222 4537.

For the vehicle it is necessary to have the **registration papers** (log-book) and a **nationality plate** of the approved size.

Vehicle **insurance cover** is compulsory. Although no longer a legal requirement, the International Insurance Certificate (Green Card) is the most effective proof of insurance cover and is internationally recognised by the police and other authorities.

In the case of loss or theft of any document, report it to the local police or the tourist police.

HEALTH

In Ireland hospital treatment is available in emergencies but is not free of charge except to nationals of the country. Emergency help can be obtained from the Casualty Department of a hospital, from a pharmacy/chemist. For emergency telephone numbers see page 35. Nationals of non-EU countries should take out comprehensive insurance. National of EU countries should apply to their own National Social Security Offices for **Form E111** (not obligatory for UK nationals; proof of identity only necessary) which entitles them to medical treatment under an EU Reciprocal Medical Treatment arrangement, provided treatment is sought from a doctor in Ireland whose name is on the Health Board Panel of Doctors (list available from the local health board).

Information is available from the Aviation Health Institute on precautions to take before and during air travel; on DVT and air travel, on transmission of disease inflight, on radiation and inflight medical incidents; on deaths and incidents of air-related problems.

Aviation Health Institute, 17c Between Town Road, Oxford OX4 3LX, United Kingdom. ☎ 01865 715 999; Fax 01865 715 899; fkahn@aviation-health.org

DOMESTIC ANIMALS

No animals, pets or other, may be brought into the Republic of Ireland, except from the United Kingdom. Domestic animals (dogs, cats) with vaccination documents are allowed into the United Kingdom (Great Britain and Northern Ireland).

Department of Agriculture, Food and Rural Development, Agriculture House, Kildare Street, Dublin 2. ☎ 01 607 2000

CUSTOMS REGULATIONS

Tax-free allowances for various commodities are governed by EU legislation. Details of these allowances are available at most ports of entry to the Republic of Ireland and the United Kingdom, and from customs authorities. It is against the law to bring into the Republic of Ireland firearms, explosives, illicit drugs, all meat and meat products, all plant and plant products (including seeds). It is against the law to bring into the United Kingdom drugs, firearms and ammunition, obscene material featuring children, counterfeit merchandise, unlicensed livestock (birds or animals), anything related to endangered species (furs, ivory, horn, leather) and certain plants (potatoes, bulbs, seeds, trees).

Customs and Excise, Passenger Terminal, Dublin Airport, Co Dublin. ☎ 01 844 5538; Fax 01 844 5420

Customs and Excise, Custom House, Belfast BT1 3ET. ☎ 028 9056 2600 or 028 9023 4466; Fax 028 9056 2972

HM Customs and Excise, Dorset House, Stamford Street, London SE1 9PY. ☎ 0845 010 9000 (National Advice Helpline); ☎ 020 7620 1313 (HQ); 020 7928 3344 (switchboard)

For US nationals returning to the US after travelling abroad there is useful information in the booklet *Know before you go*, published by the US Customs Service (whose offices are listed in the phone book in the Federal Government section under the US Department of the Treasury) and can be obtained by consulting www.customs.ustreas.gov

Seasons

CLIMATE

Extremes of temperature are rare in Ireland but there is the possibility of rain throughout the year. The southeast enjoys the most sun and the east coast is drier than the west. Information about the weather is available in the Republic of Ireland on ☏ 01 842 5555 and in Northern Ireland from the National Meteorological Library and Archive, London Road, Bracknell RG12 2SZ. ☏ 01344 854 841; Fax 854 840; metlib@metoffice.com; www.metoffice.com

Sign of fair weather

THE BEST TIME
The sunniest months are May and June and the warmest are July and August so the best time of year to visit Ireland is in the summer, when most of the festivals take place, although that is when the resorts and hotels are at their busiest.

BANK AND PUBLIC HOLIDAYS
On such days shops, museums and other monuments may be closed or may vary their times of admission. In the Republic of Ireland national museums and art galleries are usually closed on Mondays.
In addition to the usual school holidays at Christmas and in the spring and summer, there are mid-term breaks at Hallowe'en (1 November) and around St Patrick's Day (17 March).

1 January – New Year's Day
17 March – St Patrick's Day (Republic only)
Monday nearest 17 March (Northern Ireland only)
Good Friday (Republic only)
Easter Monday
Monday nearest 1 May – May Day Holiday (Northern Ireland only)
Last Monday in May – Spring Bank Holiday (Northern Ireland only)
First Monday in June – June Holiday (Republic only)
12 July – Orangeman's Day (Northern Ireland only)
First Monday in August – August Bank Holiday (Republic only)

Last Monday in August – August Bank Holiday (Northern Ireland only)
Last Monday in October – October Holiday (Republic only)
25 December – Christmas Day
26 December – (St Stephen's Day/Boxing Day)

TIME DIFFERENCE
In winter standard time throughout Ireland is Greenwich Mean Time (GMT). In summer (mid-March to October) clocks are advanced by one hour to give British Summer Time (BST), which is the same as Central European Time.
Time may be expressed according to the 24-hour clock or the 12-hour clock:

WHAT TO TAKE
Waterproof clothing just in case of rain at any time of year and several layers of clothing as the temperature can vary from day to day. Stout shoes for those intending to go walking in the country.

Budget

In the Republic of Ireland the currency is the euro (€ = 100 cents); in Northern Ireland the currency is Sterling (£1 = 100p = €1.57 at the time of publication), although the euro is widely accepted.
Dublin is more expensive than other parts of the country. Prices may be higher during the summer season (June to September), particularly on the coast and in the west of Ireland, but it is always possible to bargain over hotel prices especially late in the day. See also Services – Concessions and Discounts – page 34.
Most hotels and restaurants, most petrol/gas stations and most shops accept payment by credit card but it is useful to have cash available to pay for local transport, admission charges and budget accommodation.

To the **daily budget for one person** given below (calculated on the basis of a shared double room) add admission charges at €9/£6 on average per day and transport costs (Dublin €1.50 per day; for petrol prices see Getting About below).

Budget Category – For one night's lodging in a guesthouse or cheaper accommodation (€30; £23 in Northern Ireland), a light lunch in a pub or a sandwich in a café (about €20; £9 in Northern Ireland) and an evening meal in a pizzeria, a wine bar or a brasserie (€15; £12 in Northern Ireland) allow an average daily budget of €57; £44 in Northern Ireland.

Moderate Category – For one night's lodging in a comfortable hotel (€45; £35 in Northern Ireland), lunch in a pizzeria, wine bar or brasserie (€15; £12 in Northern Ireland) and dinner in a medium-priced restaurant (€30; £23 in Northern Ireland) allow an average daily budget of €90; £70 in Northern Ireland.

Expensive Category – For one night's lodging in an elegant hotel (over €80; £60 in Northern Ireland) and lunching and dining in gourmet restaurants (over €40; £30 in Northern Ireland) allow a daily budget of €160; £120 in Northern Ireland).

Special Needs

Some of the sights described in this guide are accessible to disabled people – & means full access for wheelchairs; (&) means limited access for wheelchairs.
The **Michelin Red Guide Great Britain and Ireland** indicates hotels with facilities suitable for disabled people.
Information on tourism, accommodation, transport and activity centres is available from several organisations:
Everybody's Hotel Directory – www.everybody.co.uk – On-line directory which gives useful

information about accommodation for disabled and able people in Ireland.
Irish Wheelchair Association, Blackheath Drive, Clontarf, Dublin 3. ☎ 01 818 6400; Fax 01 833 3873; info@iwa.ie; www.iwa.ie
Comhairle, 44 North Great George's Street, Dublin 1. ☎ 01 874 7503; Fax 01 764 7490
Disability Action, Portside Business Park, 189 Airport Road West, Belfast BT3 9AD. ☎ 028 9029 7880, ☎ 028 9066 1252, 028 9029 7882 (textphone); Fax 028 9029 7881; hq@disabilityaction.org; www.disabilityaction.org
Radar, 12 City Forum, 250 City Road, London EC1V 8AF. ☎ 020 7250 3222; Fax 020 7250 0212; minicom 020 73500 4119; radar@radar.org.uk
Holiday Care, Imperial Buildings (2nd Floor), Victoria Road, Horley RH6 7PZ. ☎ 01293 774 535; Fax 01293 784 647, holiday.care@virgin.net; www.holidaycare.org.uk
Tripscope, The Vassall Centre, Gill Avenue, Bristol BS16 2QQ. ☎ 08457 585 641, ☎ 44 117 939 7782 (from outside the UK); Fax 0117 939 7736, Fax 44 117 939 7736 (from outside the UK); enquiries@tripscope.org.uk; www.tripscope.org.uk

Transport

For information on price reductions see Services on p 34.

Getting There

By Air
Dublin airport opened in 1940, its terminal one of the first truly modern buildings in the country; in 1947 a customs-free airport was inaugurated at Shannon, a useful stopping point on the transatlantic route. Shannon has now ceded most of its role as an intercontinental hub to Dublin and there are international flights to and from airports at Cork, Knock, and Belfast (Aldergrove).
Regional and limited international flights are catered for at Carrickfin (Donegal), Bantry, Farranfore (near Killarney), Galway, Londonderry and Sligo, as well as at Belfast City Airport in Belfast's dockland.
Local airlines provide a service to some of the islands – Aran Islands and Tory Island.
All airports are linked by bus to the neighbouring towns.
Aer Lingus is the national carrier, while Ryanair is among the most

dynamic of European low-cost airlines.
Information, brochures and timetables are available from the airlines and from travel agents. Fly-Drive schemes are operated by most airlines.
Aer Lingus – www.aerlingus.ie or www.aerlingus.com
☎ 01 705 333; Fax 01 886 3844; requests@aerlingus.ie
40–41 Upper O'Connell Street, Dublin 1
13 St Stephen's Green, Dublin 2
Jury's Hotel, Ballsbridge
12 Upper George's Street, Dún Laoghaire
Aer Lingus House, 83 Staines Road, London TW3 3JB.
☎ 0845 973 7747 (from within the UK), 020 8234 4333 (Head Office)
British Airways – www.britishairways.com
☎ 1800 626 747 (reservations Dublin - Open daily, 6am-10.15pm (5.15pm Sat; 2.15pm Sun)
UK sales office ☎ 0345 222 111 (from within the UK)
☎ 0845 77 333 77 (reservations), ☎ 0845 77 333 77 (enquiries)
P O Box 365,Uxbridge UP7 0GB

British European – www.british-european.com or www.flybe.com

☏ 08705 676 676 (services to Dublin, Cork, Shannon and Belfast from London City, London Gatwick and London Stansted)
British European, Exeter International Airport, Exeter EX5 2BD

British Regional Air – Book through British Airways

British Midland – www.britishmidland.com or www.flybmi.com

☏ 0870 607 0555; ☏ 0345 554 554 (reservations); ☏ 00 44 1332 854 854 (from outside the UK); Fax 01332 854 105

Easyjet – www.easyjet.com

☏ 0870 600 0000 (services from London to Belfast)
Easyjet, Luton Airport, Luton LU2 9LS

Manx Airlines – www.manx-airlines.com

☏ 08457 256 256; Fax 0151 448 0599 (Liverpool); Fax 01624 826 151 (Isle of Man) (services to Dublin from Manchester and the Isle of Man)

Ryanair – www.ryanair.com

☏ 0541 569 569, ☏ 01 812 1212; Fax 01 609 7081
Corporate Head Office, Dublin Airport, Dublin.
☏ 00 353 94 67222 (Knock International Airport, Co Mayo)
☏ 0871 246 0000, ☏ 0871 246 0004 (accommodation)
☏ 01279 666 200; Fax 01279 666 201
Ryanair, Enterprise House, Stansted Airport, Stansted CM24 1QW

Virgin Express – www.virgin-express.com

☏ 01293 747 747, ☏ 020 7744 0004; Fax 01293 562 345

BY SEA

Details of passenger ferry and car ferry services to Ireland from the United Kingdom and France can be obtained from travel agencies or from the main carriers. Information about

Ferry crossing the Irish Sea

ferries to the offshore islands is given in the Directories in the chapters in the Selected Sights section of the guide.

Brittany Ferries – www.brittany-ferries.com
The Brittany Centre, Wharf Road, Portsmouth, Hants PO2 8RU.
☏ 0990 360 360 (from within UK); Fax 01705 873 237; ☏ 021 427 7801
in Ireland
Millbay Docks, Plymouth, Devon. PL1 3EW. ☏ 0990 360 360;
Tourist House, 42 Grand Parade, Cork. ☏ 021 4277 801; Fax 021 4277 262.

Hoverspeed – ☏ 00 800 1211 1211 (free), www.hoverspeed.co.uk

Irish Ferries – www.irishferries.ie or irishferries.com
2-4 Merrion Row, Dublin 2. ☏ 01 638 3333 (reservations).
Ferryport, Alexandra Road, Dublin 1. ☏ 01 855 2222 (Head Office);
Rosslare Harbour ☏ 053 33158
Bridge Street, Cork ☏ 021 455 1995
Corn Exchange Building, Ground Floor, Brunswick St, Liverpool L2 7TP.
☏ 0870 517 1717 (reservations - from within UK).

Stena Line – www.stenaline.com
Charter House, Park Street, Ashford, Kent TN24 8EX. ☏ 0870 570 7070;
Passenger Terminal, Corry Road, Belfast BT3 9SS. ☏ 028 9074 8748 (Stranraer–Belfast; Liverpool-Belfast)
Ferry Terminal, Dún Laoghaire, Co Dublin. ☏ 01 204 7777 (Holyhead–Dublin, Holyhead–Dún Laoghaire, Fishguard–Rosslare)

P&O Stena-line – www.stenaline.com; www.stenaline.co.uk; www.stenaline.ie
Larne Harbour, Larne BT40 1AQ. ☏ 0870 242 4777 (Cairnryan–Larne); Fax 028 2887 2195

Seacat – www.steam-packet.com
Seacat Terminal, Donegal Quay, Belfast BT1 3AL. ☏ 0990 523 523; Fax 028 9031 4918 (Troon-Belfast, Heysham-Belfast; Liverpool-Dublin)

Swansea Cork Ferries – www.swansea-cork.ie
Harbour Office, Kings Dock, Swansea SA1 1SF. ☏ 01792 456 116; Fax 01792 644 356; scf@iol.ie

BY RAIL

Irish Rail Service (Iarnród Éireann), Northern Ireland Railways and the various British railway companies operate train services between the major cities in Ireland and the United Kingdom.
Despite many closures in the 1950s and 60s, the Republic has a basic network radiating from Dublin and serving most of the main towns, with one cross-country line linking the west

with Waterford and Rosslare. The capital and its coastal suburbs are linked by an efficient electric railway, the DART, part of which is formed by the country's very first railway, the Dublin and Kingstown of 1838. In Northern Ireland the system is even more skeletal; Belfast has a couple of suburban lines and is linked to Londonderry and Dublin. Between Mullingar in the Republic and Derry in the North, a distance of 130mi/210km, there are no railways at all.

Irish Rail – www.irishrail.ie; www.cie.ie; www.cietours.ie (coach tours and fly drive in Ireland, Britain and Europe); www.railtours.ie (day excursions by rail)
Iarnród Éireann Travel Centre, 35 Lower Abbey Street, Dublin 1. ☎ 01 836 6222; ☎ 1850 366 222 (info line); ☎ 01 703 3592 (Customer Services); Fax 01 703 4690
Connolly Station, Dublin 1. ☎ 01 703 2613 (Inter-City Customer Services); 01 836 3333 (enquiries); Fax 01 836 4760.
Heuston Station, Dublin 8. ☎ 01 836 5421 (enquiries); Fax 01 677 1350.
Pearse Station, Westland Road, Dublin 2. ☎ 01 703 3592 (Suburban Rail Customer Services); 01 703 3634 (booking office).
Talking timetables:

Dublin to Ballina	01 8054 299
Dublin to Belfast	01 8054 277
Dublin to Cork	01 8054 200 / 021 504 544
Dublin to Galway	01 8054 222
Dublin to Killarney and Tralee	01 8054 266
Dublin to Limerick	01 8054 211 / 061 413 355
Dublin to Sligo	01 8054 255
Dublin to Waterford	01 8054 233
Dublin to Westport	01 8054 244
Dublin to Wexford and Rosslare	01 8054 288

Northern Ireland Rail, www.translink.co.uk
Central Station, Belfast BT1 3PB. ☎ 028 9089 9400; 028 9089 9411 (enquiries); Fax 028 9035 4090l; feedback@translink.co.uk

BY COACH / BUS
There is a regular coach service between the major Irish towns and the major cities in Great Britain and on the Continent via the car ferry ports at Rosslare, Dublin Ferryport and Larne.
Bus Éireann – www.buseireann.ie; www.infopoint.ie/buse/
Store Street, Dublin 1. ☎ 01 836 6111, 01 830 2222; Fax 01 873 4534
Dublin Bus (Bus Atha Cliath) – www.dublinbus.ie (*see also p 214*) ☎ 01 873 4222

Ulsterbus – www.translink.co.uk
Europa Bus Centre, Glengall Street, Belfast BT12 5AH. ☎ 028 9033 3000 (enquiries), 028 9032 0011 (bus station)
National Express – ☎ 0870 580 8080; www.goby-coach.com
Eurolines – ☎ 0870 514 3219; www.goby-coach.com

BY CAR
For information about driving licence and vehicle insurance see Formalities above
For information about the Highway Code see Motoring below

Getting About

See also Driving Tours Map on p 13.

MOTORING
For the size of its population, the country has a relatively dense road network, much of it the result of government-inspired schemes in the 18C and 19C, some of which were intended to provide work for those rendered destitute by famine. Some stretches of road penetrated remote and difficult country and were epics of construction, among them the Galway to Clifden highway built in the 1820s through the wilds of Connemara. A decade later, William Bald laid out the Antrim Coast Road, one of the finest scenic routes anywhere.
Until recently much of the road system in the South was in poor condition but resurfacing, the widening and realignment of many stretches of main road and the construction of bypasses have transformed the situation, aided in many cases by EU funding. Limited stretches of motorway include the M50 ring road to the west of Dublin and the discontinuous motorway connecting Dublin and Belfast (M1/A1). Many major roads have an inside lane for farm vehicles. In the peatlands the road surface may be undulating and it is necessary to drive at a moderate speed.
The road network in the North was brought up to British standards in the 1960s and 1970s and includes motorways leading west (M1) and northwest (M2) from Belfast.

HIGHWAY CODE
The **minimum driving age** is 16 years old in the Republic of Ireland and 17 in Northern Ireland. Traffic drives on the **left**. Traffic on main roads and on roundabouts has priority.
The driver and front-seat passenger must wear **seat belts.** Rear-seat belts must be worn where they are fitted;

On the Sky Road, Connemara

influence of alcohol are liable to be checked with a breathalyser and to prosecution.

In Northern Ireland – Failure to display a parking paid ticket may result in a fine. Illegal parking is liable to fines and also in certain cases to the vehicle being clamped or towed away.

Drivers suspected of **driving while under the influence of alcohol** are liable to be checked with a breathalyser and to prosecution.

Drivers suspected of **speeding** are liable to prosecution; there are warning signs (camera) beside the road and speed cameras (yellow) which are activated by speeding vehicles.

ROAD SIGNS

The colour code for different types of road sign is

blue for motorways
green for major roads
black on white for local destinations
brown for tourist signs

NATIONAL (REGIONAL) IDENTIFICATION LETTERS

In the Republic of Ireland the vehicle registration number consists of two figures representing the year of registration, a letter indicating the county of registration and the individual registration number (1 or more figures). The international symbol is IRL.

Since 2001 in Great Britain and Northern Ireland the number plates on new vehicles must conform to a standard typeface and size and a British Standard (with GB and EU symbols as permitted options). The individual registration number consists of a two-letter area code, a two-number age code and three letters selected at random.

ROAD TOLLS

The only toll roads are the Dublin East-Link, which spans the Liffey estuary, and the West-Link, which runs north–south on the western edge of the city *(see p 214)*.

PETROL/GAS

Most service stations have dual-pumps; **unleaded pumps** are identified by a green stripe or green pump handles.

children under 12 must travel in the rear seats.

Full or dipped **headlights** should be switched on in poor visibility and at night; use **sidelights** only when the vehicle is stationary in an area without street lighting.

It is obligatory to carry a red warning triangle or to have hazard warning lights to use in the case of a **breakdown** or **accident**.

PARKING

There are multi-storey car parks in towns, disc systems, parking meters and paying parking zones; in the last two cases, small change is necessary and in the last case tickets must be obtained from the ticket machines and displayed inside the windscreen.

In Northern Ireland city centre parking may be restricted and the usual regulations are as follows:

Double red line = no stopping at any time (freeway)

Double yellow line = no parking at any time

Single yellow line = no parking for set periods as indicated on panel

Dotted yellow line = parking limited to certain times only

PENALTIES

In the Republic – Parking offences may attract an on-the-spot fine. Drivers suspected of **speeding** are liable to an on-the-spot fine. Drivers suspected of **driving while under the**

Speed limits		
Republic of Ireland	30mph/48kph	in built-up areas
	60mph/96kph	on country roads
	70mph/112kph	on motorways
Northern Ireland	30mph/48kph	in built-up areas
	60mph/96kph	on country roads
	70mph/112kph	on dual carriageways and motorways

Petrol prices (per litre) in the Republic are:

Unleaded	89.3c
Diesel	78.5c
Super unleaded	99.9c
Lead replacement petrol	108.9c

Petrol prices (per litre) in Northern Ireland vary, being cheaper near the border but the following are a guide:

Unleaded	74.9p
Diesel	75.9p
Lead-free 4 star	77.9p
Lead replacement petrol	82.9p

MAPS AND PLANS

For the maps and plans to use with this guide see pp 6 and 7.
For Route Planning use Michelin Map 712 Ireland and the Michelin Atlas Great Britain and Ireland; both show the major roads (N or A) and many of the minor roads (R/L or B).

MOTORING ORGANISATIONS

In Ireland and the UK accident insurance and breakdown service schemes are arranged by certain motoring organisations for their members. Members of the American Automobile Club should obtain the brochure *Offices to serve you abroad*.

Automobile Association (AA) – www.aaireland.ie
23 Suffolk Street, Dublin 2.
☎ 01 617 9999; Fax 01 617 9900; aa@ireland.ie

Automobile Association (AA) – www.theaa.co.uk
Fanum House, Basingstoke. Hants, RG21 2EA. ☎ 0870 600 0371 (general information), ☎ 00 44 191 223 7071 (international enquiries)

Royal Automobile Club (RAC) www.rac.co.uk
New Mount House, 22–24 Lower Mount Street, Dublin 2. ☎ 01 676 0113
RAC London (Head Office), 89-91 Pall Mall, London SW1Y 5HS. ☎ 020 7930 2345
RAC House, 1 Forest Road, Feltham, TW13 7RR. ☎ 020 8917 2500 (Head Office), 0906 834 7333 (travel information); ☎ 0990 722 722 (Customer Services)

Europ-Assistance –
www.europ-assistance.com
IDA Business Park, Athlumney, Navan, Co Meath. ☎ 046 77333; 046 74396
Sussex House, Perrymount Road, Haywards Heath, West Sussex, RH16 1DN. ☎ 01444 442 442 (Customer Services);
marketing@europ-assistance.co.uk

CAR HIRE / RENTAL

There are car rental agencies at airports, railway stations and in all large towns throughout Ireland. Many airlines operate Fly-Drive schemes with a selected car hire company. European cars usually have manual transmission but automatic cars are available on request. An **international driving licence** is required for non-EU nationals. Many companies do not rent to drivers under 21 or 25.
Before crossing the border between the Republic and Northern Ireland it is important to check that the insurance cover extends to the other country. It is cheaper to return a hire car to its pick-up point than to leave it elsewhere.

BY RAIL, COACH / BUS AND BOAT

For information about these services in Ireland see above
For information about rail services within the Dublin area *see p 214*.

Where to Stay and Where to Eat

Addresses listed in the Guide

Suggestions about where to stay and where to eat are included in the Directory of the chapters which describe popular towns or tourist sites. The places suggested – hotels, guesthouses, B&B's and budget accommodation – have been carefully chosen for their character, convenient location, quality of comfort or value for money (*see also Ideas for Your Visit below*). Although all the places listed have been visited and selected with care, changes may have occurred since our last visit, so if you stay at one of the places suggested, please send us your comments – favourable or otherwise.

Generally speaking, Dublin is more expensive than other towns but offers a wide choice of restaurants ranging from gourmet restaurants to fast-food outlets and accommodation ranging from luxury hotels to B&Bs. In Dublin and other university towns the student halls of residence offer low-priced accommodation in the vacation.

Outside the capital the more popular tourist resorts have a good selection of hotels and restaurants and every town of moderate size has at least one. In the smaller towns and villages there are usually rooms to let in the local bar or the owner will be able to suggest an address. B&B accommodation can be found throughout the country. If you like to experience how the landed gentry used to live, try staying in a country house which offers B&B or a country house hotel, where you may dine at a communal table. If you are intending to stay for a week or more, there is self-catering accommodation in most parts of the country.

In Dublin and in the tourist districts it is advisable to book in advance during the school holidays (Christmas, Easter and June to September). Out of season it is usually possible to find a room without difficulty.

CATEGORIES

Our suggestions are divided into three price categories.

BUDGET CATEGORY

This category comprises the best of the small, simple but well-maintained establishments charging no more than €65 (£45 in Northern Ireland) for a single room. Expect basic service and shared bathrooms for the least expensive room.

The places to eat listed in this category are generally simple, unpretentious places where you can expect to spend no more than €20 (£15 in Northern Ireland).

MODERATE CATEGORY

In this category you can find singles from €65 to €125 (£45-£100 in Northern Ireland) in converted houses or purpose-built hotels and guesthouses. We strongly recommend booking in advance as these small establishments often have a faithful clientele.

This category comprises slightly more formal restaurants where a meal will cost from €20 to €40 (£15 to £30 in Northern Ireland).

EXPENSIVE CATEGORY

In this category (over €125; £100 in Northern Ireland) we recommend a limited number of hotels at the expensive end of the price range; as is to be expected, the rates reflect the outstanding quality of the comfort and service.

The restaurants listed in this category (over €40; £30 in Northern Ireland) are upmarket establishments with a high culinary standard and distinctive ambience. If you would like to eat in a noted but expensive restaurant in town but your budget is limited, consider the excellent-value lunch menus proposed by many of these establishments.

The two rates quoted for each establishment refer to the nightly rate of a single and a double (except for hostel rates, which are quoted per person). One person staying in a double room will generally be given a slight reduction on the double rate, except during major events.

Additional charge for breakfast is noted when applicable. Service and the 17.5% Value Added Tax (VAT) are included in the quoted prices unless otherwise specified. It is always advisable to confirm all details – inclusion of en suite facilities, breakfast and VAT – before making the reservation. A credit card number (and possibly an email or fax for confirmation) will be requested for all reservations.

The two prices given for each restaurant represent a minimum and maximum price for a full meal excluding beverages. Naturally, prices will vary depending on the number of courses and the beverages ordered. Wine can be an expensive item and its inclusion may make a substantial increase in the cost of a meal.

WHERE TO STAY

The different types of accommodation are described below. For details of organisations publishing brochures or supplying information see below – Useful Addresses.

In town centres **parking** can be a problem but many hotels have their own car park on site or a short walk away.

In a small town the only hotel often doubles as the **local disco** and it may be very noisy until the early hours on a Saturday night, especially if there is a wedding party in the house.

At **breakfast** most types of establishment offer a light Continental-style breakfast of coffee and bread and jam as well as the traditional cooked breakfast. In larger establishments there may be a choice for the first course of cereal, porridge, stewed or fresh fruit, yoghurt and fruit juice, followed by a main dish usually of eggs or fish, and ending with toast and marmalade. It is accompanied by tea or coffee.

HOTELS

Traditionally **hotels** tend to be medium to large establishments, where the bedrooms have en suite facilities and a full range of services. The terms **hotel** and **guesthouse** are used fairly loosely, usually at the whim of the proprietors, to apply to a wide variety of accommodation.

GUESTHOUSES

The term **guesthouse** connotes a smaller operation than a hotel with fewer facilities and generally appeals more to visitors on holiday than to those on business. The properties vary from modern purpose-built premises to Georgian and Victorian houses

INNS / PUBS WITH ROOMS

In the smaller towns and villages the local inn often has rooms to let.

BED & BREAKFAST

The distinction between **Bed-and-Breakfast** places and guesthouses is often blurred but the traditional **Bed-and-Breakfast** is a family-run affair, offering one or two bedrooms at a moderate price. This simple form of accommodation is found all over Ireland in properties ranging from a simple bungalow to a great house. Staying in an Irish home provides an opportunity to share in Irish family life.

FARM HOLIDAYS

Being a predominantly agricultural country, Ireland has a great range of

Bord Fáilte, Dublin

A welcome sign in Kenmare

farms, many of which welcome visitors in the summer season.

SELF CATERING

In many parts of the country, particularly the tourist districts, there are purpose-built holiday villages consisting of a cluster of well-appointed cottages.

UNIVERSITY RESIDENCES

Accommodation in **universities** (single rooms and self-catering apartments) is available during the vacations, particularly in Dublin, Cork and Galway.

HOSTELS

There are 50 **youth hostels** in the Republic and six in Northern Ireland. Several companies offer budget accommodation in various towns in Ireland.

CAMPSITES

Ireland has many officially graded caravan and camping parks with modern facilities and a variety of sports facilities.

WHERE TO EAT

Places to eat in Ireland range from the top-class restaurant, offering high quality produce and the latest in the culinary art, through wine bars, bistros, brasseries, to fast food outlets such as pizzerias, cafés and fish and chip shops. In between are the dining rooms of moderate hotels catering for the average family and many pubs. The restaurants of National Trust properties (Northern Ireland only) provide lunch and tea; the one at Mount Stewart is also open for dinner. The restaurants suggested in this guide have been carefully selected for quality, atmosphere, location and value for money.

Cafés and informal eating places and pubs, which keep flexible hours and can provide a light meal in the middle of the day, are listed under **Pubs** and **Light Bite** in the Directories. An average meal in these places will cost under €15 (£12 in Northern Ireland).

We trust you will find places well suited to your specific tastes and budget. Please send us your comments.

Eating Out

Restaurants are usually open in the evening from 6.30pm to 10pm and also at lunchtime from noon to 2.15pm depending on their location. Many close one day a week and they may close early (between 7pm and 8pm on Sundays and Mondays in Northern Ireland).

It is always advisable to book in the evening, particularly at the weekend.

A usual evening meal in a restaurant consists of three courses but in many places it is acceptable to eat only a starter and a main dish or a main dish and a dessert. A meal is usually accompanied by an alcoholic or non-alcoholic drink and followed by tea or coffee. Portions are usually generous but filter coffee is rare in the less expensive restaurants. Most restaurants serve bottled water – still or sparkling – but tap water will be provided on request.

SPECIALITIES

Being an agricultural country, Ireland produces very good home-reared meat, particularly beef and lamb, and excellent dairy products – local cheeses, butter and cream. Near the coast there should be a good choice of fish; salmon is usually available everywhere. In the cheaper restaurants the menu may not offer much in the way of fresh fruit and vegetables but the potatoes are usually very good. Look out for soda bread, for potato cakes (even at breakfast), for oysters and Guinness, for black pudding – a speciality in Co Cork – and for carrageen – a form of seaweed which is used in savoury and sweet dishes.

TIPPING

Tipping is optional but it is very common to leave 10% when the service is particularly pleasing. Usually VAT and service (12.5%) are included in the bill. Some restaurants will leave the total open on a credit card slip so that customers can add a tip to the bill.

and also ...

If you are unable to find suitable accommodation or a pleasing restaurant among the establishments listed in the Directories in the Selected Sights section, consult the **Michelin Red Guide Great Britain and Ireland** which provides a selection of hotels, guesthouses and restaurants.

USEFUL ADDRESSES

Gulliver Call Centre – an **Accommodation Booking Service** operated by Irish Regional Tourism Organisations and by Tourist Information Centres; a small fee is charged for the service and a proportion of the room price is paid direct to the booking service and the balance to the proprietor – ☎ 0800 783 5740; 00 800 6686 6866

Several booklets on accommodation and eating out are published by the Irish Tourist Board (Bord Fáilte) and the Northern Irish Tourist Board (NITB). Other organisations which publish reference books or supply information are:

Irish Hotels Federation, 13 Northbrook Road, Dublin 6. ☎ 01 497 64 59; Fax 01 497 4613; www.beourguest.ie

Northern Ireland Hotels Federation – ☎ 028 9035 1110; www.nihf.co.uk

Manor House Hotels, 1 Sandyford Office Park, Foxrock, Dublin 18. ☎ 01 295 8900; Fax 01 295 8940; info@manorhousehotels.com; reservations@manorhousehotels.com; www.manorhousehotels.com

The Hidden Ireland – Accommodation in historic Irish houses (€5) – P O Box 31, Westport, Co Mayo. ☎ 01 662 7166, 098 66650; Fax 01 662 7144, 098 66651; info@hidden-ireland.com; www.hidden-ireland.com

Ireland's Blue Book – Irish country houses and restaurants – Ardbraccan Glebe, Navan, Co Meath. ☎ 046 23416; Fax 046 23292; mail@irelandsbluebook.com; www.irelandsbluebook.com

Irish Farm Holidays (€4) – 2 Michael Street, Limerick, Co Limerick. ☎ 061 400 700, 400 707; Fax 061 400 771; farmhols@iol.ie; www.irishfarmholidays.com

Northern Ireland Farm and Country Holidays, Greenmount Lodge, 58 Greenmount Road, Omagh BT7 9OYE. ☎ 028 8284 1325; www.nifcha.com

Town and Country Homes Association – publishes *Bed and Breakfast Ireland* (€4.50) – Belleek Road, Ballyshannon, Co Donegal. ☎ 072 22222; Fax 072 22207; admin@townandcountry.ie; www.townandcoutry.ie

Irish Guesthouse Owners' Association, Kathleen's Country House, Killarney, Co Kerry. ☎ 064 32810; Fax 064 32340

Elegant Ireland – Exclusive rented castles, country houses or cottages in Ireland – 15 Harcourt Street, Dublin 2. ☎ 01 475 1632; 01 475 1665; Fax 01 475 1012; info@elegant.ie; www.elegant.ie

Dining in Ireland – List of 400 restaurants – published by Restaurants Association of Ireland, 11 Bridge Court, City Gate, St Augustine Street, Dublin 8. ☎ 01 677 9901; Fax 01 671 8414

Active Ireland Properties Ltd – Short term rentals of upmarket properties including renovated 18C courtyard houses, mills and villages – 19 Harcourt Street, Dublin 2. ☎ 01 478 2045; Fax 01 478 4327; info@activeireland.ie; www.activeireland.ie

Irish Cottages and Holiday Homes Association – Self-Catering Accommodation Guide (€6.50; £5) listing over 5 000 holiday cottages and houses to rent – 4 Whitefriars, Aungier Street, Dublin 2. ☎ 01 475 7596; Fax 01 475 5321; info@irishcottageholidays.com; www.irishcottageholidays.com

Simple **Low-Budget Accommodation** is available in hostels (single, twin and 4/6-bedded rooms) at or from the following addresses:

Independent Holiday Hostels Ireland, 57 Lower Gardiner Street, Dublin 1 ☎ 01 836 4700; Fax 0 836 4710; www.hostels-ireland.com

Kinlay House, 2–12 Lord Edward Street, Dublin 2. ☎ 01 679 6644; Fax 01 679 7437; kinlay-dublin@usitworld.com (also in Cork and Galway)

Barnacles Accommodation Centre, Seville House, New Dock Steet, Galway, Ireland. 091 569 689; Fax 091 561 092; queries@barnacles.ie; http://www.barnacles.ie

Northern Ireland Hostelling International, ☎ 028 9032 4733, www.hini.org.uk

An Óige (Youth Hostel Association), 61 Mountjoy Street, Dublin 7, ☎ 01 830 4555; Fax 01 830 5808; mailbox@anoige.ie; www.irelandyha.org

Usit Accommodation Centres, c/o UCD Village, Belfield, Dublin 4, ☎ 01 706 1071; Fax 01 269 1129; accommodation@usitworld.com; www.iol.ie/usitaccm

Marketing University Summer Accommodation (MUSA), Plassey Campus Centre, University of Limerick ☎ 061 202 360; Fax 061 330 316

Accommodation Office, Trinity College, Dublin 2, ☎ 01 608 1177; Fax 01 671 1267; reservations@tcd.ie; www.tcd.ie/accommodation

Irish Caravan & Camping Council – Publishes a brochure (€2.65) covering the whole country – P O Box 4443, Dublin 2. Fax 098 28237 (brochures); info@camping-irland.ic; www.camping-ireland.ie

Caravan and Camping Ireland (€3) – Published by Bord Fáilte – www.camping-ireland.com

Caravanning and Camping in Northern Ireland – Published by the Northern Ireland Tourist Board; www.discovernorthernireland.com

Where to Stay (€6.20) – Published by the NITB and listing camping and caravan parks in Northern Ireland

Choosing Where to Stay

In choosing a place to stay, the main points for consideration are which part of the country you wish to explore or what activities or sports you would like to pursue, whether you wish to be by the seaside or beside a lake, in a quiet country district or in town near the night spots.

The Driving Tours Map *(see p 13)* and the Places to Stay Map *(see below)* indicate places to stay overnight and seaside resorts and various outdoor activities.

Going Out for the Evening

Traditional Music – The most typically Irish and popular form of evening entertainment is the music and singing performed in the bars in town and country. The instruments played are commonly the violin – called the fiddle by traditional musicians – the flute, the goatskin drum *(bodhrán)* and the free-reed instruments such as the accordion, melodeon and concertina; and also more recently the guitar and banjo.

Conviviality Irish style in a Doolin bar

B Pérousse/MICHELIN

Places to stay

Overnight stop
Sightseeing centre
Resort
Seaside resort
Spa
Marina
Beach
Surf
Nature reserve
Garden
Golf
Racecourse
Greyhound track
Waymarked footpath
Wildlife/Safari park, Zoo
Country park
Forest, Forest park, National park
Airfield
Airport
Tourist or steam railway
Fishing

OCEAN

Aranmore I

Portnoo

Killybegs

ATLANTIC

Belmullet

Rosses Point
Strandhill

Bundora

Killala

Inishcrone

SLIG

Achill I

Ballina
L Conn

Boyle

R Moy

N 17

Newport

Castlebar

REPUBLIC

WESTPORT

Lough Mask

Clifden

Lough Corrib

Tuam

IRELAND

Cashel

Galway

BALLINASLOE

SALTHILL

Aran I

Loughrea

Lisdoonvarna

Ballyvaughan

Lahinch

Lough Derg

Killkee

Kilrush

Killaloe

Nenagh

R Shannon

Limerick ( )

Ballybunnion

Listowel

Adare

Tralee ( )

N 21

Tipperary

Cahe

Dingle

KILLARNEY

Mallow

R   Blackwater

Waterville

Kenmare

Macroom

R Lee

CORK

Youghal

Castletownbere

Glengarriff

N 22

Cobh

Bantry

R Bandon

Bere I

KINSALE

Skibbereen

Clonakilty

Clear I

CELTIC

ROSCOFF   SWANSEA

0   50 km
0   30 miles

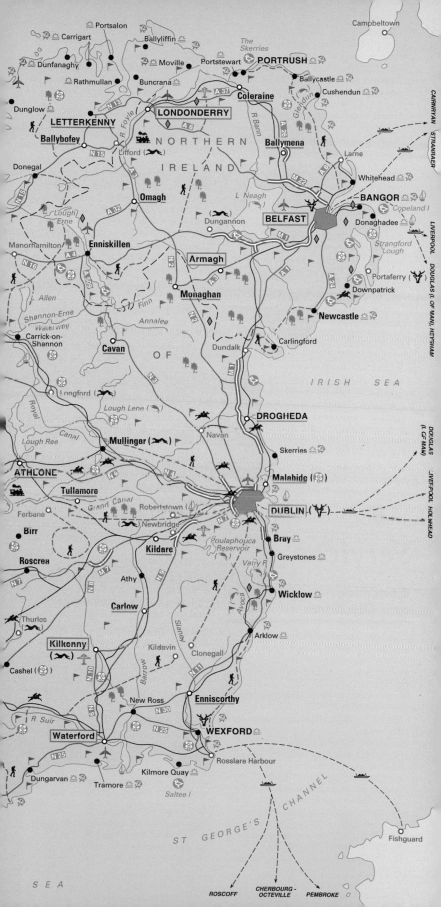

Traditional music has grown in importance in recent years and is played not only at sessions in pubs but also at gatherings known individually as a *céile* and at the weekly and monthly sessions held in the local branches of the national **cultural organisation** – Comhaltas Ceoltóirí Éireann, Cultúrlann na hÉireann, 32 Belgrave Square, Monkstown, Co Dublin, ☎ 01 280 0295. Information also available from Tourist Information Centres.

A feature of Irish traditional music is **dancing**, including individual old-style *(sean-nós)* dancing and particularly **set dancing**, which dates from the 18C and is, for the most part, an adaptation of military dances to existing tunes such as jigs, reels, hornpipes and polkas.

The harp is now rarely played but there are two harp festivals in Keadew *(July–August)* and Nobber *(October)*. The Secretary, O'Carolan Harp Festival Keadew, Co Roscommon ☎ 078 47204; Fax 078 47511; ☎ 046 52115 or 52272.

Cultural Festivals – Ireland hosts a number of literary and musical festivals in honour of individual artists or groups of artists *(see p 57)*. Many are accompanied by bands and parades, horse races and regattas according to the region.

Irish Banquets – For a truly Irish evening entertainment try a medieval banquet accompanied by music and poetry – Knappogue Castle *(see p 253)*;

Bunratty Castle *(see p 311)*; Dunguaire Castle *(see p 133)*; Brú Ború in Cashel *(see p 165)*.

Theatres – Ireland has a lively theatrical scene with theatres in many provincial towns as well as Dublin and Belfast.

In Dublin modern and classic plays are performed at the **Abbey Theatre** and the **Gate Theatre**.

The traditional seasonal festivals and rural way of life are evoked in music, song, dance and mime in the performances of the **National Folk Theatre of Ireland** in Tralee *(see page 346)*, which draw on the local Gaelic tradition.

Productions in the Irish language are put on by the Irish Theatre **(Taibhearc na Gaillimhe)** in Galway *(see page 259)*, which is a state-sponsored body.

Classical Music – In Dublin the **National Concert Hall** (Earlsfort Terrace) has a regular programme of classical and modern orchestral music. Smaller venues offering more specialised music, such as jazz, blues etc, are to be found in Temple Bar in Dublin.

In Belfast the **Waterfront Hall** offers a varied programme of events.

Concerts of **chamber music** *(summer)* are given by Irish and international musicians in some of the great Irish houses; details available from the National Concert Hall in Dublin.

Opera is performed in Dublin and Belfast and also at various **opera festivals** *(see p 57)*.

Services

Concessions and Discounts

If you are intending to apply for a reduced price pass, take some passport-size photos with you as they may be needed for the purchase.

If you intend to claim reductions for senior citizens or students, take the appropriate documents to prove your entitlement.

Many tourist sights offer discount admission charges to families, children, senior citizens, students and the unemployed.

Many hotels offer special prices for short breaks – weekends or stays of at least three days. Out of season or if you arrive late in the day, it may be possible to negotiate a price reduction. The Youth Hostel Association organises packages comprising youth hostel vouchers, rail and bus pass or hostel vouchers, return rail fare and cycle hire.

SEASON TICKETS
The Irish Heritage Service (Dúchas) issues an annual **Heritage Card** (€23), which provides free admission to all Dúchas sites. The card is available from most Dúchas sites or by phone from Dúchas *(see p 50)*.

CHEAP AIR FARES
Several airlines such as Ryanair and Easyjet offer budget fares – see *Getting There*. Prices vary according to how far in advance the booking is made; there are also weekend rates and additional advantages when booking on line.

DISCOUNT RAIL FARES
Special Rover, Explorer and Emerald Card tickets are available, which enable passengers to travel throughout Ireland, by rail only or by

rail and bus; price according to the duration of the ticket

3 days €45
(out of 8 consecutive days)

8 days €100
(out of 15 consecutive days)

15 days €145
(out of 30 consecutive days)

DISCOUNT BUS FARES
Special Rambler, Rover, Explorer and Emerald Card tickets are available, which enable passengers to travel throughout Ireland, by rail only or by rail and bus; price according to the duration of the ticket – *see also Discount Rail Fares above.*

DISCOUNTS FOR STUDENTS
Students with an **International Student Card** can apply for **Student Travelsave** to obtain 50% reduction on Irish Rail and 30% reduction on Bus Éireann.
USIT, 19–21 Aston Quay, Dublin. ☎ 01 679 8833; Fax 01 602 1617; www.usitnow.ie

DISCOUNTS FOR DISABLED PERSONS
Irish Rail Mobility Impaired Liaison Officer ☎ 01 703 2634 **Railcards** are available for disabled people in Northern Ireland on written application together with proof of entitlement and remittance of £14, application forms available from railway stations.
Disabled Persons Railcard Office, P O Box 1YT, Newcastle upon Tyne NE99 1YT. ☎ 0191 269 0303, 0191 269 0304 (textphone)

DISCOUNTS FOR US NATIONALS...
Eurorail Pass, **Flexipass** and **Saver Pass** are options available in the US for travel in Europe and must be purchased in the US, ☎ 212 308 3103; ☎ 1-800-4 EURAIL, 1-888-BRITRAIL and 1-888-EUROSTAR (automated lines for callers within the US only); www.raileurope.com/us

Practical Information

EMERGENCIES
Telephone 999 – for all emergency services (no charge nationwide); ask for Fire, Police, Ambulance, Coastguard and Sea Rescue, Mountain Rescue or Cave Rescue.

CURRENCY
NOTES AND COINS
In the Republic of Ireland the currency is the euro (€1 = 100 cent); in Northern Ireland it is Sterling (£1 = 100 pence = €1.57 at the time of publication).

There is no limit on the amount of currency visitors can import into the Republic of Ireland.

BANKS
Money can be withdrawn from banks using a credit card and a PIN. Since June 2002 there has been no commission charge for EU travellers on cash drawn from Cash Point / ATM machines in the Republic of Ireland.

OPENING HOURS
Banks are open Mondays to Fridays (except public holidays), 10am–12.30pm and 1.30–3pm (3.30pm in Northern Ireland). Exchange facilities outside these hours are available at Belfast, Dublin, Shannon, Connaught and Cork Airports, in some tourist information centres, travel agencies and hotels.

TRAVELLERS' CHEQUES
Some form of identification is necessary when cashing travellers' cheques in banks. Commission charges vary; hotels and shops usually charge more than banks.

CREDIT CARDS
The major credit cards – American Express, Visa/Barclaycard (Carte Bleue), Eurocard (Mastercard/Access) and Diners Club – are widely accepted in shops, hotels, restaurants and petrol stations.

Amex 020 7222 9633

Access/Eurocard 01702 364 364

Barclaycard 01604 230 230

American Express Travel Services – www.americanexpress.co.uk 78 Brompton Road, London SW3 1ER. ☎ 020 7761 7905; Fax 020 7584 7480

POST
Irish postage stamps must be used in the Republic, British stamps in Northern Ireland; they are available from post offices and some shops (newsagents, tobacconists etc).

OPENING HOURS
In the Republic post offices are open Mondays to Saturdays, 8am–5pm or 5.30pm; they are closed on Sundays and public holidays and for 1hr 15min at lunchtime; sub-post offices usually close at 1pm one day a week.
In Northern Ireland post offices are open Mondays to Fridays, 9am–5.30pm, and Saturdays, 9am–12.30pm; sub-post offices close at 1pm on Wednesdays.

CHARGES
Republic of Ireland

Postcards and
Airmail letters up to 25g

Britain	Continental Europe	The rest of the world
€0.38	€0.41	€0.57

Notes and Coins

The euro banknotes were designed by Robert Kalinan, an Austrian artist. His designs were inspired by the theme "Ages and styles of European Architecture". Windows and gateways feature on the front of the banknotes, bridges feature on the reverse, symbolising the European spirit of openness and co-operation.

The images are stylised representations of the typical architectural style of each period, rather than specific structures.

Classical

Baroque and Rococo

Romanesque

19C iron and glass

Gothic

Renaissance

20C modern

Euro coins have one face common to all 12 countries in the European single currency area or "Eurozone" (currently Austria, Belgium, Finland, France, Germany, Greece, Ireland, Italy, Luxembourg, The Netherlands, Portugal and Spain) and a reverse side specific to each country, created by their own national artists.

Euro banknotes look the same throughout the Eurozone. All Euro banknotes and coins can be used anywhere in this area.

£50 note featuring
Sir John Houblon
(1632-1712),
Gatekeeper to the
Bank of England.

£20 note featuring
Michael Faraday (1791-1867),
physicist and inventor of the
Magneto Electric Spark
Apparatus.

£10 note featuring
Charles Dickens (1812-1870),
author of Pickwick Papers,
Oliver Twist, A Christmas
Carol etc.

£5 note featuring
George Stephenson (1781-1848),
engineer, inventor of the Rocket
Locomotive and builder of
the Stockton-Darlington Raiway.

All notes and coins bear an image of the sovereign on one side. A metal strip is threaded through the paper of the bank notes. The reverse side of the £1 coin features different symbols: Royal coat of arms and Three lions rampant (England), Thistle (Scotland), Prince of Wales feathers (Wales) among others.

The Bank of Scotland issues £1 notes which are legal tender throughout the United Kingdom.

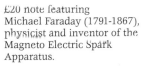

Conversion Tables

Weights and measures

| 1 kilogram (kg) | 2.2 pounds (lb) | 2.2 pounds |
| 1 metric ton (tn) | 1.1 tons | 1.1 tons |

to convert kilograms to pounds, multiply by 2.2

| 1 litre (l) | 2.1 pints (pt) | 1.8 pints |
| 1 litre | 0.3 gallon (gal) | 0.2 gallon |

to convert litres to gallons, multiply by 0.26 (US) or 0.22 (UK)

| 1 hectare (ha) | 2.5 acres | 2.5 acres |
| 1 square kilometre (km²) | 0.4 square miles (sq mi) | 0.4 square miles |

to convert hectares to acres, multiply by 2.4

1 centimetre (cm)	0.4 inches (in)	0.4 inches
1 metre (m)	3.3 feet (ft) - 39.4 inches - 1.1 yards (yd)	
1 kilometre (km)	0.6 miles (mi)	0.6 miles

to convert metres to feet, multiply by 3.28, kilometres to miles, multiply by 0.6

Clothing

Women	EU	US	UK		EU	US	UK	Men
	35	4	2½		40	7½	7	
	36	5	3½		41	8½	8	
	37	6	4½		42	9½	9	
Shoes	38	7	5½		43	10½	10	Shoes
	39	8	6½		44	11½	11	
	40	9	7½		45	12½	12	
	41	10	8½		46	13½	13	
	36	6	8		46	36	36	
	38	8	10		48	38	38	
Dresses &	40	10	12		50	40	40	Suits
suits	42	12	14		52	42	42	
	44	14	16		54	44	44	
	46	16	18		56	46	46	
	36	30	8		37	14½	14½	
	38	32	10		38	15	15	
Blouses &	40	34	12		39	15½	15½	Shirts
sweaters	42	36	14		40	15¾	15¾	
	44	38	16		41	16	16	
	46	40	18		42	16½	16½	

Sizes often vary depending on the designer. These equivalents are given for guidance only.

Speed

kph	10	30	50	70	80	90	100	110	120	130
mph	6	19	31	43	50	56	62	68	75	81

Temperature

Celsius (°C)	0°	5°	10°	15°	20°	25°	30°	40°	60°	80°	100°
Fahrenheit (°F)	32°	41°	50°	59°	68°	77°	86°	104°	140°	176°	212°

To convert Celsius into Fahrenheit, multiply °C by 9, divide by 5, and add 32.
To convert Fahrenheit into Celsius, subtract 32 from °F, multiply by 5, and divide by 9.

Northern Ireland
Postcards

Britain	Continental Europe	The rest of the world
27p	36p	40p

Letters under 60g to Britain

Britain	Continental Europe	The rest of the world

27p (1ˢᵗ class)
19p (2ⁿᵈ class)

Airmail letter under 20g

Britain	Continental Europe	The rest of the world
	36p	65p

TELEPHONE

Mobile telephones can be brought into Ireland.

The telephone service in the Republic of Ireland is organised by Eircom – www.eircom.ie

Pre-paid callcards for internal and international calls from public phones are available from post offices and some shops (newsagents, tobacconists etc). Card phones are cheaper than pay phones.

It is usually more expensive (+ 30%) to make a long-distance telephone call from a hotel than from a telephone box.

To make an **international call** dial 00 followed by the country code, followed by the area code (without the initial 0), followed by the subscriber's number. The codes for direct dialling to other countries are printed at the front of telephone directories and in code books.

```
00 61 ............................... Australia
00 1 ............................... Canada
00 353 ................. Republic of Ireland
00 64 ............................... New Zealand
00 44 ....... United Kingdom (including
           Northern Ireland)
00 1 ....................... United  States  of
           America
```

When dialling from the Republic to Northern Ireland, dial 080 followed by the subscriber's number.

ELECTRICITY

The electric current is 230 volts AC (50 hertz); 3-pin flat or 2-pin round wall sockets are standard.

NEWSPAPERS AND TELEVISION

In the Republic of Ireland the national newspapers on sale are *The Irish Times*, *The Independent* and *The Examiner*. There are 4 television channels – RTE1, RTE2, TV3 and TG4; the last broadcasts in the Irish language.

In Northern Ireland the national newspapers are *The Times*, *The Independent*, *The Daily Telegraph* and *The Guardian*. There are 5 television channels – BBC1, BBC2, ITV, Channel 4 and Channel 5

SHOPPING

Shops in the major cities are open Mondays to Saturdays, 9am–5.30pm (8pm Thursdays). Elsewhere there is all-day or early closing on Mondays or Wednesdays or Thursdays. Some shops may open later and may close for an hour at lunchtime.

Local shops and craft centres are listed in the Directory of the appropriate chapter in the Selected Sights section.

VAT refund is available for non-EU residents. Stores participating in the Tax Back Service must be members of the Retail Export Scheme. Details are available at the information-desk in major department stores.

Sightseeing

As admission times and charges are liable to alteration, the information printed in this guide – valid for 2002 – is for guidance only.

Facilities for the disabled – ♿ means full access for wheelchairs; (♿) means limited access for wheelchairs. As the range of possible facilities is great (for impaired mobility, sight and hearing), readers are advised to telephone in advance to check what is available.

Abbreviations – Dúchas = Department of Arts, Heritage, Gaeltacht and the Islands (formerly OPW = Office of Public Works); HM = Historic Monuments Branch of the Department of the Environment in Northern Ireland; NT = National Trust.

Dates – Dates given are inclusive. The term holidays means bank and public holidays; the term weekend or Sat-Sun means Saturday and Sunday.

Bank and Public Holidays – See p 22.

Admission Times – Ticket offices usually shut 30min before closing time; only exceptions are mentioned. Some places issue timed tickets owing to limited space and facilities.

Charge – The charge given is for an individual adult. Reductions may be available for families, children, students, senior citizens (old-age pensioners) and the unemployed.

Large parties should apply in advance, as many places offer special rates for group bookings and some have special days for group visits.

Prices – Prices are given in the euro currency (€ = 100 cents) in the Republic of Ireland and in Sterling (£ = 100 pence) in Northern Ireland.

Churches – Many Church of Ireland (Anglican) and Presbyterian churches are locked when not in use for services.

Ideas for your Visit

Ireland is a country which invites you to travel slowly, to linger for a drink and a chat. Unfortunately most of us do not have unlimited time at our disposal so the following suggestions are for those who wish to make the most of a brief visit to this beautiful country.

2-day Breaks

DUBLIN CITY

Start with that masterpiece of Irish art, the **Book of Kells** in **Trinity College**. Then make your way up **Grafton Street** and its side streets to enjoy the street musicians and some of the smartest shops in Dublin. Take a stroll in the gardens of **St Stephen's Green** before returning to the streets off the north side to find a place for lunch. In the afternoon visit the **National Museum** or the **National Gallery**, stroll through **Merrion Square** and see how they lived in the Georgian era at **Number Twenty Nine**. Spend the evening exploring **Temple Bar**.

On the second day go to the old town to admire the works of art in the **Chester Beatty Library**. You can take a guided tour of **Dublin Castle** or look into **Christ Church Cathedral** or **St Patrick's Cathedral**. After lunch take the bus out to **Kilmainham Gaol** for a lesson in recent Irish history and then admire the contrast in styles presented by the exhibits in the **Irish Museum of Modern Art** and its context, the **Royal Kilmainham Hospital**.

KILKENNY

Visit **Kilkenny Castle** and its park and go shopping in the **Kilkenny Design Centre**. After lunch drive out to plunge underground into **Dunmore Cave**.

Take the road south down the Nore Valley to visit the magnificent ruins of **Jerpoint Abbey**, to charming **Inistioge** and then drive over Brandon Hill to **Graiguenamanagh** on the River Barrow.

SLIGO

Visit the **Niland Gallery** to see one of the best displays of paintings by Jack B Yeats and stroll through the Abbey ruins. After lunch take a boat trip on **Lough Gill** to see the lake isle of **Innisfree** and **Parke's Castle**.

Take a drive in **Yeats' Country** – to visit the tomb of William Butler Yeats at **Drumcliff** in the shadow of Benbulben and **Lissadell** the home of

Countess Markievicz, before turning inland to **Glencar Waterfall**.

Touring in the traditional way by horse-drawn caravan

3-day Breaks

CORK CITY

Visit the **English Market** and the main streets – **Grand Parade** and **St Patrick's Street**. Admire the exuberant architecture of William Burges at **St Fin Barre's Cathedral**. After lunch cross the river to try your hand at ringing **Shandon Bells** and see how criminals were treated in **Cork City Gaol**.

On the second day take a trip to **Blarney Castle** to kiss the **Blarney Stone** and make a round trip by visiting **Mallow** and **Fermoy** on the beautiful **Blackwater River**.

On the third day drive out to **Fota House** and the **Wildlife Park**, make a lunchtime visit to **Cobh** and end the day sampling whiskey at the **Old Midleton Distillery**.

WESTPORT AND DISTRICT

Stroll round the charming little town and go down to the **Quayside** for lunch. In the afternoon visit **Westport House**.

Drive west to explore the **Murrisk Peninsula** which presents some of the most beautiful landscapes in the west of Ireland – **Croagh Patrick** and **Killary Harbour**.

Take the road north to the **Marian Shrine at Knock** and the **Museum of Country Life** at Turlough near Castlebar.

ENNISKILLEN

Stroll through the town and visit **Enniskillen Castle** and its museums. In the afternoon tour the stately rooms of **Castle Coole**.

Southwest of Enniskillen is another less austere country house, **Florence**

Court with flamboyant plasterwork; nearby are the **Marble Arch Caves**, part of which is visited by boat.
Make a tour round the shores of **Lower Lough Erne** taking in **Devenish Island**, **Castle Archdale** and **White Island**, the **Janus Figure**, **Belleek Pottery**, the **Cliffs of Magho viewpoint** and **Tully Castle**.

LONDONDERRY
Walk round the walls and visit the **Tower Museum**, the **Cathedral** and **Long Tower Church**.
Make a tour in the **Sperrin Mountains** – Roe Valley Country Park, Glenshane Pass, Dungiven Priory, Wellbrook Beetling Mill, Beaghmore Stone Circles, Ulster Plantation Centre in Draperstown, Springhill, Ulster History Park, Sperrin Heritage Centre, Ulster American Folk Park, Gray's Printery in Strabane.
Make a tour north round the **Inishowen (Inis Eoghain) Peninsula** – visiting the many prehistoric and early Christian relics – **Grianán of Aileach**, **Carrowmore High Crosses**, **Clonca Church and Cross** – visit **Malin Head**, famous from the shipping forecasts, and **Fort Dunree Military Museum**.

4-day Breaks

DUBLIN AND DISTRICT
For the first 2 days see Dublin City above.
Drive south into the **Wicklow Mountains** – to **Russborough** or **Powerscourt** – and further south to the monastic ruins at **Glendalough**.
Take the motorway north via Slane to the **Newgrange** prehistoric monuments in the **Boyne Valley** and return via **Trim** and **Tara** or **Malahide** and **Newbridge House**.

KILLARNEY AND DISTRICT
Take a stroll in the town centre and explore the **National Park** on foot – **Knockreer Demesne** and **Ross Castle** – or by car – **Muckross House**, **Muckross Friary** and the **Muckross Peninsula**, and **Torc Waterfall** and **Ladies View**.
Take a guided tour through the **Gap of Dunloe** but choose a fine day.
Drive round the **Ring of Kerry**, providing fine views of the coastline and the mountains.
Drive north to the **Dingle Peninsula**, part of the Gaeltacht, which has many relics of the former way of life in the west of Ireland.

LIMERICK AND DISTRICT
Visit the treasures in the **Hunt Museum** and walk up to the **Castle** and **St Mary's Cathedral**.
Drive northwest into Co Clare to visit **Bunratty Folk Museum and Castle**, **Quin Friary**, **Knappogue Castle** and **Cragganunowen Centre**.
Make a round trip south of Limerick visiting the prehistoric remains at **Lough Gur Interpretive Centre**, the walled town of **Kilmallock** and the childhood haunts of De Valera in **Bruree**, before returning down the Maigue Valley via **Croom**, **Monasteranenagh Abbey** and charming **Adare** with its thatched cottages.
Drive north via Ennis and Ennistimon to the barren landscape of the **Burren** – the **Cliffs of Moher**, **Lisdoonvarna**, **Corkscrew Hill** and **Aillwee Cave**.

BELFAST AND DISTRICT
Visit the city centre and along the waterfront. Try to take in **St Malachy's Church** and the **Oval Church** before lunching in the **Crown Liquor Saloon**. In the afternoon visit the **Ulster Museum** and take a stroll in the **Botanic Gardens** with its two glasshouses.
Drive out east to visit the **Ulster Folk and Transport Museum** at Cultra; after lunch explore the architectural and horticultural splendours of **Mount Stewart** on the east shore of **Strangford Lough**
Drive south up the **Lagan Valley** to learn about one of the traditional Irish industries at the **Irish Linen Centre and Lisburn Museum**. Visit charming **Hillsborough** and the plants and shrubs at **Rowallane**.
Drive north via Ballymena and Ballymoney to marvel at the volcanic columns of the **Giant's Causeway**. In the afternoon drive south along the coast road to see the **coast and glens of Antrim**.

Cruising at Erincurragh in the Fermànagh Lakeland

NITB, Belfast

5-day Break

GALWAY AND DISTRICT

Stroll round the medieval city centre and in the afternoon take the road to **Aughnanure Castle** and the charming fishing village of **Oughterard** on **Lough Corrib**.

Take the road up the east shore of **Lough Corrib** via **Annaghdown** and **Ross Errily Abbey** to **Cong**.

Take the road west through **Connemara** to **Clifden** and return by the coast road.

In Kiltartan country south of Galway visit **Athenry**, a heritage town, **Thoor Ballylee**, once the home of William Butler Yeats, and **Coole Park**, where Lady Augusta Gregory lived.

Take the plane for a one-day visit to **Aranmore**, the largest of the **Aran Islands**, where tourism has softened the once harsh island way of life.

Activity Holidays

The Irish Tourist Board provides information on holidays with the following themes – cruising, horse racing, cycling, golf, walking, gardens, cookery – and summer schools of many kinds such as learning the Irish language.

HORSE-DRAWN CARAVANS

The caravan provides accommodation as well as a leisurely way of exploring the Irish country roads:

Slattery's Horse-drawn Caravans, 1 Russell Street, Tralee, Co Kerry. ☎ 066 26277; Fax 066 25981

Mayo Horsedrawn Caravan Holidays Ltd, Belcarra, Castlebar. ☎ 094 32054

CRUISING

Information on hiring cruisers on rivers, lakes and canals, holiday cruises and short pleasure cruises on the Shannon, barge or waterbus cruises and cruising restaurants is available from a brochure published by the Irish Tourist Board. It is recommended that boat operators be members of the Irish Boat Rental Association (IBRA).

The Inland Waterways Association publishes a guide to the *Grand Canal*. Details of annual waterway rallies and festivals are also available from Tourist Information Centres.

The main waterways for cruising are the River Shannon, the Shannon–Erne Waterway and Lough Erne; canal barges are more suited to the River Barrow, the Grand Canal and the River Shannon. Short daytime canal or river trips are mentioned in the appropriate chapters.

Sailing Holidays in Ireland, c/o Trident Hotel Marina, Kinsale, Co Cork; ☎ 021 772 067; Fax 021 774 170 – for yacht charter.

Waveline Cruisers Ltd, Quigley's Marina, Killinure Point, Glassan, Athlone, Co Westmeath, Ireland. ☎ 0902 85711; Fax 0902 85716; waveline@iol.ie; www.waveline.ie

Celtic Canal Cruisers Ltd, Tullamore, Co Offaly, Ireland. ☎ 0506 21861; Fax 0506 51266

WALKING, CYCLING AND HORSE RIDING

Holidays – chauffeur driven – can be organised around a variety of activities – walking, cycling, horse riding, hunting, shooting, stalking, fishing and tracing ancestors.

Tailormade-Ireland. ☎ 020 7351 5331 ; www.tailormade-Ireland.com

Go-Ireland, Old Orchard House, Market Street, Killorglin, Co Kerry. ☎ 066 976 2094 ; ireland@goactivities.com; www.goactivities.com

IRISH LANGUAGE AND CULTURE

Most of these course are held in the Irish-speaking districts (Gaeltacht) – language courses; language and culture courses with workshops in tin-whistle playing, set-dancing, *sean-nós* singing and hill-walking, and evening events such as lectures on Irish folklore, poetry reading and concerts of traditional music; cultural activity courses on archaeology, marine painting, Celtic pottery, *bodhrán* playing etc.

Oideas Gael, Gleann Cholm Cille, Co Donegal, Republic of Ireland. ☎ 073 30248; Fax 073 30348; oidsgael@iol.ie; www.oideas-gael.com

Making Irish soda bread

Bord Fáilte, Dublin

COOKERY

Dunbrody Abbey Cookery Centre – Campile, New Ross, Co Wexford. ☎ 051 388 933; theneptune@eircom.net; www.cookingireland.com

Driving Tours

While Dublin has become a popular destination for weekenders, Ireland as a country is best explored in a leisurely fashion, taking your time to absorb its unique atmosphere and fall into its unhurried rhythms. The touring programmes outlined below and shown on the map on page 13 offer a choice of itineraries, ranging from short tours from Dublin and Belfast to explorations of the regions of Ireland. For those who really want to see as much as possible in a short time, a tour of the whole country is proposed taking in most of the major sights (see tour 8 below) – but anyone who undertakes it is sure to want to return and explore further!

Itineraries all start and end at a convenient port of entry by air or sea. Overnight stays are shown in bold.

Carnlough in the Antrim Glens

H Champollion/MICHELIN

① DUBLIN AND ITS SURROUNDINGS – ONE WEEK

Conveniently close to the capital, with all its vibrancy and range of attractions, are some of the country's major sights – the stunning prehistoric monuments of the Boyne Valley, great houses and gardens, early Christian Glendalough in its remote valley as well as country towns and charming seaside places.

After two days in **Dublin**, the tour takes you north via the charming harbour town of Howth and the aristocratic desmesne of Malahide to bustling **Drogheda** and the nearby prehistoric grave sites of Newgrange and Knowth and the quiet countryside where the decisive Battle of the Boyne was fought.

Passing to the west of the capital after leaving the vast Anglo-Norman castle at Trim, the route takes in the splendid Palladian mansion of Castletown and the heartland of Irish horse-breeding and racing at the Curragh near **Kildare**. Another superb Great House is visited at Russborough. The road then climbs into the Wicklow Mountains, to their greatest treasure – the monastic remains at Glendalough.

After a night in the seaside town of **Wicklow**, the return to **Dublin** is via the magnificent gardens of Powerscourt and the capital's attractive southern suburbs.

② ASPECTS OF ULSTER – ONE WEEK

Bearing in mind that Northern Ireland comprises only six of Ulster's nine counties, the province's many riches can only really be appreciated in the course of a longer stay (see Tour 7 below). This tour, however, serves as an introduction to the province, its major towns, its wonderful natural landscapes and its array of man-made attractions which include a number of world-class museums.

From **Belfast**, the road leads east past the fascinating Ulster Folk and Transport Museum to the seaside resort of **Bangor**.

The great houses and gardens of Mountstewart and Castle Ward are visited en route to St Patrick's town of Downpatrick and then to the popular seaside resort of **Newcastle**.

The glories of the Mourne Mountains are seen on the way to Ireland's holy city of **Armagh**.

The less grand but equally interesting country houses of Ardress and The Argory are called at on the way to Lough Neagh, Ireland's largest lake. Nearby places of interest include Peatlands Park with its wildlife and demonstrations of turf-cutting, the High Cross at Ardboe, and the archetypal plantation towns of Cookstown and Draperstown. The Ulster-American Folk Park is a must before stopping at the last walled city to be laid out in Europe, **Londonderry**.

The tour continues east along the coast past Portrush and Portstewart to the unique geological formation of the Giant's Causeway and the pretty little seaside resort of **Ballycastle**.

The return to **Belfast** is via the imposing landscapes of the Antrim Glens and the corniche of the Antrim Coast Road.

③ SIGHTS OF THE SOUTHEAST – ONE WEEK

Follow in the footsteps of the Anglo-Normans as they spread across Ireland, building great castles, churches and abbeys, and at the same time get to know one of the great sights of ancient Ireland, the holy hill of Cashel. The Republic's second city, Cork, has an atmosphere all its own, while the southeastern coast has harmonious landscapes and many places of great interest.

On the way to the Viking city of **Wexford**, famous for its opera festival, from the ferry port of Rosslare a visit is made to Johnstown Castle, home of the Irish Agricultural Museum.

The tour continues via the National Heritage Park to the old towns of Enniscorthy and New Ross, then on past the lovely abbey ruins at Jerpoint to medieval **Kilkenny** (2 nights), one of Ireland's most compelling towns.

The Rock of **Cashel** casts its spell on all who visit its hilltop ruins. The road leads south through Caher with its castle and Fermoy with its splendid river crossing to the Republic's second city, **Cork** (2 nights).

From Cork the route heads east along the coast to the maritime town of Cobh overlooking the broad waters of Cork Harbour, then via delightful old Youghal to the southeast's other Viking city of **Waterford**, famous for its lively cultural life.

A ferry crosses Waterford Harbour to the abbeys, gardens, castles and beaches of the Hook Peninsula. The return is then direct to Rosslare.

④ THE SOUTHWEST – COUNTIES CORK, KERRY AND LIMERICK – TEN DAYS

With its rocky peninsulas stretching far into the Atlantic, the country's highest mountains and lush inland landscapes, the far Southwest is perhaps the most alluring region of Ireland for visitors, who have been coming here in number since the beginnings of tourism.

From Shannon Airport the tour passes 15C Bunratty Castle and its Folk Park to the Republic's third largest city, historic **Limerick**.

The country towns of Kilmallock and Mallow are visited on the way to bustling **Cork** (2 nights).

The coastline west of Cork has endearing fishing villages and little maritime towns like **Kinsale**.

More coastal delights include Skibbereen and Skull, and **Bantry** on its great sea-inlet, Bantry Bay.

A splendidly scenic coastal road, the Ring of Beara, winds round the Beara Peninsula, eventually reaching pretty **Kenmare**.

From Kenmare, another panoramic road, the Ring of Kerry, explores the glorious Iveragh Peninsula. There are distant views of the drowned mountain top of Great Skellig Island, once the most austere of monastic retreats, before the world-famous lake and mountain setting of **Killarney** (2 nights) is reached.

From Killarney, the road runs via the Gaelic harbour town of Dingle to the tip of the Dingle Peninsula, with its beehive huts and prospect of the wave-battered Blasket Islands, before turning inland via Tralee, Ardfert Cathedral and Glin Castle to return to **Limerick** and Shannon.

⑤ GLORIES OF GALWAY, CONNEMARA AND SLIGO – ONE WEEK

Connemara sometimes seems to consist more of sky, sea, bog and lake than firm ground, though its mountains, like the splendidly rounded Twelve Bens, are a solid enough presence. In complete contrast are the austere and arid limestone landscapes of the Burren, while Galway city is one of the liveliest places in the whole country.

From Knock airport the route leads first north to the cheerful regional capital of **Sligo** with its many associations with W B Yeats.

To the west of Sligo, north Mayo has vast stretches of bog, the prehistoric monuments of the Ceide Fields, and the cliffs and mountains of **Achill Island**.

An essential detour is made via Castlebar to the state-of-the-art National Museum of Country Life at Turlough, before turning west again to the elegant town of **Westport** and Westport House, one of the finest Great Houses in the West.

Southwest rises St Patrick's holy mountain, Croagh Patrick. The road continues south through the Sheffry Hills, round the end of the fjord-like Killary Harbour and past the opulent 19C country house of Kylemore Abbey to charming little **Clifden**.

Archetypal Connemara landscapes are experienced on the way to Inveran with its air service to Inishmore, the largest of the **Aran Islands**, a fastness of Gaelic speech and traditional ways.

Back on the mainland, vibrant **Galway** is sure to tempt the visitor into a longer stay.

South of Galway lie the strange moonscapes of **The Burren** and the Cliffs of Moher, some of the highest in Europe.

Horse and cart in The Burren

J Malburet/MICHELIN

The tour returns to Knock via Ennis, the miniature capital of Co Clare, the Heritage Town of Athenry and the little cathedral city of Tuam.

6 THE HEART OF IRELAND, THE UNKNOWN MIDLANDS – ONE WEEK

As well as outstanding monuments like the great monastic complex of Clonmacnoise and the enigmatic earthworks around Tulsk, this itinerary for connoisseurs reveals many subtleties sometimes ignored by travellers in a hurry. Among them are castles and country houses, small towns busy with their own affairs, unexpected uplands, the banks of the Shannon, and one of the country's most extensive and well-preserved boglands.

From **Dublin** the route heads northwest to Trim in the shadow of its great Anglo-Norman castle, to the prehistoric burial mounds of Loughcrew and the ancient seat of the Pakenham family at Tullynally, and then on to the workaday midland market town of **Mullingar**.

Co Longford has intriguing features like the delightful estate village of Ardagh. Co Roscommon counters with Strokestown House, which has its own estate village and an authoritative Famine Museum, and with the small town of **Boyle**, graced by its handsome abbey ruins.

The route turns south, to Tulsk, where the Cruachan Ai Visitor Centre gives an insight into the mysteries of the Celtic past, then on to **Athlone** at the southern end of Lough Ree on the River Shannon.

The monastic precinct of Clonmacnoise is one of the great ecclesiastical sights of Ireland, as is the extraordinary little Romanesque cathedral of Clonfert. The tour leaves the Shannon for the little Georgian town of **Birr**, the anteroom to the great house and grounds of the Birr Castle Desmesne.

To the East of Birr rise the green summits of the relatively little visited Slieve Bloom Mountains, and to the northeast, close to little Tullamore, is the vast, strange, and potentially perilous expanse of Clara Bog. From near here there is a straight run back to **Dublin**.

7 ULSTER ODYSSEY – TWO WEEKS

A near-comprehensive tour of the old province of Ulster, taking in not only the six counties of Northern Ireland but also the attractions of the three counties which form part of the Republic, where the quiet countryside of Cavan and Monaghan contrasts with the wild scenery of Donegal's coast and mountains.

From **Belfast** the road to the coast heads for the old town and resort of **Bangor**.

Great houses and desmesnes are visited at Mountstewart and Castle Ward before taking the ferry across the mouth of Strangford Lough to St Patrick's city of Downpatrick, then on to the seaside town of **Newcastle**. The tour winds around the lovely Mourne Mountains before reaching **Armagh**, another holy city, the seat of both Archbishops of Ireland.

From Armagh the road runs southwestward into the Republic through Monaghan and Cavan, before turning northwest to the Fermanagh Lakeland and its little capital, **Enniskillen**.

After Belleek with its famous pottery, Co Donegal is entered, and beyond Donegal town to the west are the dramatic cliffs of Slieve League and the village of Glencolumbkille, still breathing the spirit of its founder, St Columba. The route heads inland to the tweed town of Ardara and then north via Glenveagh National Park to the quiet little resort of **Dunfanaghy** in the lee of Horn Head.

The route now returns past the ancient fortress of Grianan of Aileach to the renowned walled city of **Londonderry** in Northern Ireland. One of many attractions in the **Sperrin Mountains** is the Ulster-American Folk Park.

To the east of the mountains is the typical plantation settlement of Cookstown, a famous High Cross at Ardboe on the shores of the country's greatest lake, Lough Neagh, and the 17C planter's house of Springhill; further north is Draperstown, another plantation settlement. The North's favourite seaside resorts are **Portrush** and Portstewart.

The Giant's Causeway and the Causeway Coast demand a day of anyone's time. A choice of accommodation is to be found in the resort of **Ballycastle**.

The return to **Belfast** is along the Antrim Coast Road through the superlative landscapes of the Glens of Antrim, with a final stop at the great Anglo-Norman castle at Carrickfergus.

8 IRISH HIGHLIGHTS, A GRAND TOUR – TWO WEEKS

The very best that Ireland has to offer to the first-time visitor, guaranteed to whet the appetite for more detailed exploration.

From **Dublin**, the tour visits one of the country's finest mansions, Russborough, penetrates the Wicklow Mountains to the monastic ruins of Glendalough in their deep wooded valley, then continues to the historic city of **Kilkenny** (2 nights).

A whole day is needed to absorb the atmosphere of Ireland's Acropolis, the Rock of **Cashel**.

From the Republic's second city, lively **Cork**, the route heads west to **Killarney** (2 nights) in its incomparable setting of lakes and mountains. The classic drive around the Iveragh Peninsula, the Ring of Kerry, is an experience not to be missed, nor is the Dingle Peninsula, with its ancient stone huts and enclosures and views of the rocky Blasket Islands.

Old **Limerick** is nowadays an up-and-coming place, while Co Clare offers its little capital, Ennis, the mighty Cliffs of Moher and the weird limestone landscapes of The Burren.

North of The Burren is one of the country's most attractive towns, **Galway**, at the head of its great bay. The route to **Clifden** passes through what many regard as the most Irish of landscapes, the bogs, shining lakes, and rounded mountains of Connemara.

More of this wonderful region is experienced on the way to Westport, close to St Patrick's mountain, Croagh Patrick. After Castlebar and the superb new Museum of Country Life at Turlough, the tour continues to the busiest town in the northwest, **Sligo**. Northern Ireland is entered at **Enniskillen**, in the heart of the glorious Fermanagh Lakeland.

An essential stop on the way to the world-renowned walled city of **Londonderry** is the Ulster-American Folk Park.

Northern Ireland has what is perhaps the country's greatest natural attraction, the Giant's Causeway, and there is plenty to see in the province's capital, **Belfast**.

The return to **Dublin** is via the **Boyne Valley** with its battle site and magnificent prehistoric monuments.

Themed Tours

Historic Routes

Sarsfield's Ride – This historical route (70mi/113km signed) makes a wide loop around Limerick passing along byroads through small villages and unspoilt country, following as closely as possible the path taken by General Patrick Sarsfield in August 1690 to intercept an English siege train. King William III of England was encamped at Caherconlish 8 miles east of Limerick waiting for the arrival of heavy siege guns from Dublin, while his army besieged Limerick. Acting on information from a deserter, Sarsfield slipped out of King John's Castle in Limerick with 600 cavalry. His troop headed northeast along the right bank of the Shannon via Bridgetown and forded the Shannon upstream of Killaloe Bridge, which was held by the Williamites. At about this point he was joined by local guides who showed him a route by Kiloscully and Ballyhourigan Wood, where they stopped to rest, before climbing over the Silvermine and the Slievefelim Mountains via Toor and Rear Cross. From Doon they continued south close to the county boundary to Monard, where they turned west. In Cullen they found out that the password for the Williamite camp was Sarsfield. They waited until after midnight to travel the last 2 miles to Ballyneety where they achieved the aim of their excursion – the destruction of the siege train.

Siege of Kinsale – The sites of the various camps and engagements of the opposing forces are marked by a dozen signs erected by the roadsides around Kinsale.

Scenic Routes

Several **Scenic Routes**, designated by the local Tourist Boards, are marked by signs *(Sli)* – **Inis Eoghain Scenic Drive** in Donegal, **Arigna Scenic Drive** around Lough Key near Boyle, **Slea Head Drive** on the Dingle Peninsula, the **Ring of Kerry** round the Iveragh Peninsul west of Killarney, the **Ring of Beara** round the Beara Peninsula west of Glengarriff.

Literary Routes

Those interested in literary affairs may like to see the various places known to **Oliver Goldsmith** during his childhood *(see Athlone)*, visit the different towns where **Anthony Trollope** lived during his residence in Ireland *(see p 141)* or follow the trail of sights associated with **Patrick Kavanagh** *(see 250)*.

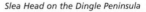

Slea Head on the Dingle Peninsula

Bord Fáilte, Dublin

Other Ways of Exploring the Country

In addition to the ideas listed below, there are many rail and bus trips from the major towns organised by Irish Rail Service (Iarnród Éireann) and Northern Ireland Railways and by Bus Éireann and Ulster Bus (*see Transport p 23*).

By Tourist Train

In recent years there have been a number of ventures to revive branch lines or parts of the main line system. In the early part of the 20C the whole country was covered by a network of railways, run on largely British lines, although the gauge chosen was not the standard European 4ft 8 1/2ins but, idiosyncratically, a broad gauge of 5ft 3ins/1.06m. The more remote districts were served by narrow-gauge systems, each with its own distinctive character like the Donegal Railway or the West Clare *(see p 297)*, the butt of much satire. In those days Irish railways had an old-fashioned charm (and inconvenience!) which was the delight of visiting enthusiasts, though not always appreciated by those who used them day by day. The increase in road traffic in the 1950s and 1960s sounded the death knell, first of the narrow gauge lines, then of much of the rest of the system.

There are occasional excursions by steam trains on the national network and a few tourist railways. The longest is the **Tralee-Blennerville Railway** in Tralee but there are shorter rides on the **Fintown Railway** in Co Donegal, at the **Foyle Valley Railway Centre** in Londonderry, in Downpatrick and on two former peat bog trains – the **Clonmacnoise and West Offaly Railway** near Birr and the narrow gauge railway at **Peatlands Park** between Dungannon and Lough Neagh.

Railway Preservation Society, Ashgrove House, Kill Avenue, Dún Laoghaire, Co Dublin. ☎ 01 280 9147; David461@iol.ie; www.rpsi-online.org

Railway Preservation Society, P O Box 6238, Whitehall, Dublin 9. ☎/Fax 01 837 4533

By Cycle

Irish Cycling Safaris – Guide-led tours with luggage van or self-led tours in all parts of Ireland – Belfield Bike Shop, Belfield House, University College Dublin, Dublin 4, Ireland. ☎ 01 260 0749; Fax 01 716 1168; info@cyclingsafaris.com; www.cyclingsafaris.com

The Táin Trail – The trail (365mi/585km) retraces as closely as possible the route through the midlands from Rathcroghan to the Cooley Peninsula and back taken by Maeve's armies in pursuit of the Brown Bull of Cooley, a tale told in the *Cattle Raid of Cooley (Táin bó Cuailgne)*, one of the great Irish legends.

The circular route can be picked up at any point and passes many historic places of interest – on the northern leg, starting from Rathcroghan, the trail passes through Strokestown, Longford, Fore, Kells, Louth, Dundalk and Omeath to Carlingford; on the southern leg, starting in Carlingford, the trail passes through Monasterboice, Slane, Kells, bypasses Mullingar, and continues through Kilbeggan, Clara, Athlone and Roscommon to Rathcroghan.

Bord Fáilte, Dublin

Cycling in Connemara

On Foot

Ireland has over 30 waymarked routes *(yellow arrow and walking figure)* following disused roads, lanes and forest trails and covering the whole country. As the weather can change quickly and unpredictably it is advisable to let someone know where you are going and when you should return, to be well equipped with suitable clothing, compass, maps and guidebook. In addition to the walks described below, there are others which are described in the appropriate chapter – Beara Way *(see Kenmare)*, Burren Way *(see The Burren)*, Mourne Trail *(see Mourne Mountains)*, Wicklow Way *(see Wicklow Mountains)*.

The Bangor Trail – This is an old drovers' trail (approx 20mi/32km) in the west of Ireland from Newport on the shores of Clew Bay northwards through the Nephin Beg Mountains to Bangor Erris. This area of northwest Connacht consists of hills encircled by a vast area of trackless bog, without trees or houses, nothing between the heather and the sky but the occasional shepherd or farmer.

The Cavan Way – In northwest Co Cavan between Blacklion and Dowra (16mi/26km) over the hills to Shannon Pot, the source of the River Shannon, and then mainly by road to Dowra where it links up with the Leitrim Way *(see below)*.

The Dingle Way – This walk (104mi/168km) starts and finishes in Tralee and takes in the beautiful scenery of the Dingle Peninsula, although the stretch between Tralee and Camp is unexceptional.

The East Munster Way – This walk (44mi/70km) starts from Carrick-on-Suir, passes through Clonmel and finishes in Clogheen in Co Waterford; it includes forest tracks, open moorland and a river towpath.

The Kerry Way *(Slí íbh Ráthach)* – This is the longest walk (133mi/214km) which can be walked clockwise or anti-clockwise, starting and finishing in Killarney. It winds through the Macgillycuddy Reeks before reaching the coast at Glenbeigh and running south and east through Caherciveen, Waterville, Derrynane, Sneem and Kenmare.

The Leitrim Way *(Slí Liatroma)* – Consists of old and new tracks (30mi/48km) from Drumshanbo, along the east shore of Lough Allen at the foot of Slieve Anierin, through Dowra the first town on the River Shannon, up the Owennayle Valley, over a moorland plateau, past Doo Lough (panoramic views), through lowland and forest, over the Tullykeherny Plateau and down a country road into Manorhamilton.

On the Water

Ireland is blessed with many rivers and lakes and is surrounded by the sea. Its once quite extensive system of **canals** and river navigations fell into disuse and dereliction with the coming of the railways and improvements in road transport but, in recent years, some sections have been restored and reopened for cruising, in particular the Ballinamore-Ballyconnell canal,

reopened in 1994 to complete the Shannon-Erne waterway *(see p 160)*; the Grand Canal, linking Dublin with the Shannon, and the Barrow Navigation are also used for cruising holidays aboard canal barges.

The heyday of the canals was in the mid-18C, when they were built with Government funds in the hope that they would promote trade. As well as heavy goods and agricultural produce they carried passengers, who travelled in **flyboats**, towed by teams of galloping horses at an average of 8mph/13kph. A few of the canal hotels, where they stayed overnight, have survived at Portobello in South Dublin, at Robertstown *(see p 276)* and in ruins at Shannon Harbour near Banagher in Co Offaly. Anthony Trollope *(see p 141)* travelled by canal to his first appointment in Ireland; his novel *The Kellys and the O'Kellys* contains a good description of travelling by flyboat.

Some of the many possible boat trips – on the rivers and canals, to the islands in the lakes or offshore – are described in the appropriate chapters of the Selected Sights section.

By Horse-drawn Transport

In country districts and some tourist centres horse-drawn transport is still in use. **Jaunting cars** driven by a jarvie are a popular way of seeing the sights in places like Killarney. The inside and outside cars – the passengers sat face to face in the former and back to back facing the roadside in the latter – are now seen only in museums.

With the Children

Ireland is a great place for children. In addition to the swimming pools and leisure centres in the major towns, there are many bathing beaches on the coast and adventure centres in the Wicklow Mountains and at Westport House.

A number of the old railways are being brought back into service *(see above)*. There are model railways at the **West Cork Model Railway Village** near Clonakilty and the **Fry Model Railway** at Malahide. A great selection of vintage vehicles is on view at the Museum of Transport in Clonmel, the National Transport Museum in Howth Castle north of Dublin, the Museum of Irish Transport in Killarney and the **Ulster Folk and Transport Museum** near Bangor.

Other delights for the mechanically minded are the **Great Telescope at Birr Castle**, which has been restored to working order, and the **Tayto Potato Crisp Factory** near Armagh. Most children enjoy the hands-on experience of making soda bread at the **Life Force Mill** in Cavan or watching the demonstrations of old crafts at the open-air museums – **Muckross Farms** near Killarney, **Ulster Folk and Transport Museum** near Bangor and the **Ulster-American Folk Park** north of Omagh in the Sperrin Mountains.

They are also likely to enjoy seeing how their ancestors lived in earlier centuries at the **Craggaunowen Centre** near Ennis where the *Brendan* is on view, at the **Lough Gur Interpretive Centre** south of Limerick, at the **Irish National Heritage Park** near Wexford and the **Ulster History Park** north of Omagh in the Sperrin Mountains.

Dublin Zoo, **Fota Wildlife Park** and **Belfast Zoo** present a variety of animals to view. Connemara ponies roam wild in the **Connemara National Park** and there are herds of deer in several parks – **Glenveagh National Park** in Co Donegal, **Doneraile Wildlife Park** near Mallow and **Parkanaur Forest Park** near Dungannon. There are many riding schools offering the chance of a **pony ride** or you can take a trip in one of the **jaunting cars** in Killarney.

The action of water on the landmass has produced several caves which can be safely explored – **Aillwee Cave** in The Burren, **Mitchelstown Cave** near Caher, **Dunmore Cave** near Kilkenny, **Crag Cave** near Tralee and **Marble Arch Caves** near Enniskillen.

Other natural features are the breathtaking views from the **Cliffs of Moher** in The Burren, from **Slieve League** in Co Donegal and from the **Cliffs of Magho** overlooking Lough Erne.

Whiterock Beach, Portrush

NITB, Belfast

Tracing Ancestors

For many people of Irish descent a trip to Ireland may be based on or include a search for the birthplace of their ancestors and a visit to relatives still resident in Ireland.

The organisations listed below (some charge fees) can assist in tracing Irish ancestors. Local organisations are listed in the Directory of the appropriate chapter in the Selected Sights section.

Clans of Ireland, c/o Mrs Nuala Cassidy-White, 194 Parkmore, Craigavon BT53 2AQ.

www.irishclans.com – Information about the 243 Irish clans which hold annual **clan gatherings** on ancestral sites

Association of Professional Genealogists in Ireland, 30 Harlech Crescent, Clonskeagh, Dublin 14. http://indigo.ie/~apgi/ – Regulatory body for genealogy in Ireland

Irish Family History Foundation, 1 Clarinda Park North, Dun Laoghaire, Co Dublin. www.irishroots.net

Office of the Registrar General, Joyce House, 11-13 Lombard Street East, Dublin 2 – Open Mon–Fri, 9.30am–12.30pm and 2.15pm–4.30pm. ☎ 01 671 1000; Fax 01 635 4440; www.groireland.ie

National Archives, Bishop Street, Dublin 8 – Open Mon–Fri, 10am–5pm. ☎ 01 4078 2700; Fax 01 4078 2333; mail@nationalarchives.ie; www.nationalarchives.ie

National Library of Ireland, Kildare Street, Dublin 2 (no postal queries) – Open Mon–Fri, 10am–4.45pm, Sat, 10am–12.30pm ☎ 01 603 0022; Fax 01 676 6690; www.nli.ie

Hibernian Research Co Ltd, P O Box 3097, Dublin 6. ☎ 01 496 6522; Fax 01 497 3011

Irish Tourism Service – www.goireland.com/genealogy/ – Genealogy page www.ireland.com/ancestor/ – Extensive collection of Irish genealogy

General Register Office, Oxford House, 49-55 Chichester Street, Belfast BT1 4HL. ☎ 028 9025 2000; Fax 028 9025 2120; www.nisra.gov.uk/gro

Public Record Office, 66 Balmoral Avenue, Belfast BT9 6NY. ☎ 028 0966 1621

North of Ireland Family History Society, c/o Graduate School of Education, The Queen's University of Belfast, 69 University Street, Belfast BT7 1HL.

Ulster Historical Foundation, 12 College Square East, Belfast BT1 6DD. ☎ 028 9033 2288; Fax 028 9023 9885; enquiry@uhf.org.uk; www.ancestryireland.com – Online database of Ulster family records

Sport and Leisure

Ireland is naturally well-endowed with a variety of different physical environments for outdoor **sports and leisure activities**. The long and indented coastline provides facilities for bathing, scuba-diving, windsurfing, sailing, sea-angling and deep-sea fishing. The many inland lakes and waterways are good for cruising, canoeing and water-skiing and attractive to anglers. For golfers there are both inland and links courses. The magnificent mountain ranges which fringe the Atlantic coast from north to south provide exhilarating locations for walking, rambling, orienteering and mountaineering. Hunting and horse racing are concentrated in the flatter, agricultural counties of the south and midlands; pony trekking is country-wide.

Information on all the activities listed below is available from the Irish Tourist Board (Bord Fáilte) and the Northern Irish Tourist Board (NITB) and the two national umbrella organisations.

Irish Sports Council – Frederick Buildings, South Frederick Street, Dublin 2 ☎ 01 662 1444; Fax 01 679 9291

Sports Council for Northern Ireland, House of Sport, 2A Upper Malone Road, Belfast BT9 5LA ☎ 028 9038 1222; Fax 028 9068 2757; info@sportscouncil-ni.org.uk; www.sportni.org

Adventure Sports

Association for Adventure Sports (AFAS), House of Sport, Longmile Road, Dublin 12 ☎ 01 450 9845, 1633; Fax 01 450 2805

CLIMBING AND MOUNTAINEERING

Information on mountaineering, rock-climbing and orienteering is available from the following organisations:

Mountaineering Council of Ireland. ☎ 01 450 7376; Fax 01 450 2805; www.mountaineering.ie or www.climbing.ie

National Mountain and Whitewater Centre – Tiglin, Devil's Glen, Ashford, Co Wicklow. ☎ 040 40169; Fax 0404 40701; mail@tiglin.com; www.tiglin.com - The centre, set in the Wicklow Mountains, offers a variety of courses in climbing, trekking, orienteering, watersports etc

Tollymore Mountain Centre, Bryansford, Newcastle. ☎ 028 4372 2158; Fax 028 4372 6155; admin@tollymoremc.com; www.tollymoremc.com

Airborne Sports

GLIDING

Irish Hang-Gliding and Paragliding Association – ☎ 087 243 6554 (hang-gliding) and ☎ 086 258 5978 (paragliding). www.ihpa.ie or www.uhpc.f9.co.uk (for Northern Ireland)

PARACHUTING

Parachute Association of Ireland – ☎ 1850 260 600

NITB, Belfast

Paragliding at Portrush

Equestrian Sports

HORSE RIDING AND PONY TREKKING

Information on trail riding, based trails, residential centres, horse riding holidays based on hotels is published by the Irish Tourist Board.

Equestrian Holidays Ireland, c/o Clonshire Equestrian Centre, Adare, Co Limerick ☎ 061 396 770; Fax 061 396 726

HUNTING

Information on all the hunts (fox hunting, stag hunting and harriers) in the Republic of Ireland is published by the Irish Tourist Board.

Irish Masters of Foxhounds Association, Thornton, Dunlavin, Co Kildare. ☎/Fax 045 401 294

Heritage

HISTORIC PROPERTIES

Dúchas – The Irish Heritage Service is the State body responsible for the protection and conservation of the natural and built heritage. It offers an **Annual Heritage Card**, providing unlimited admission to all Dúchas sites, which is available at most properties or by phone from Dúchas Visitor Services.

Dúchas Education and Visitor Services, 51 St Stephen's Green, Dublin 2. ☎ 01 647 2453 or 01 647 3000; Fax 01 661 6764, LoCall 1890 47 48 47; info@heritageireland.ie; www.heritageireland.ie

Heritage Towns – Some 25 towns have been designated Heritage Towns because of their architecture and history or particular character, which is illustrated in the local heritage centre.

Historic Monuments – In Northern Ireland many historic monuments are the responsibility of the Department of the Environment.

Environment and Heritage Service : Built Heritage, Department of the Environment, 5-33 Hill Street, Belfast BT1 2LA. ☎ 028 9054 3034; Fax 028 9054 3111.

National Trust – The Trust owns over 200 historic house and gardens and 49 industrial monuments and mills in Northern Ireland, England, Wales and Scotland. Members in Great Britain may use their membership cards to visit NT properties in Northern Ireland. Annual membership (£30), offering unlimited admission to all NT sites, is available at most sites or shops or from The National Trust, Freepost MB 1438, Bromley, Kent BR1 3BR. **Head Office in Northern Ireland**, Rowallane House, Saintfield, Ballynahinch, Co Down BT24 7LH. ☎ (44) 28 9751 0721; www.nationaltrust.org.uk

MUSEUMS AND ART GALLERIES

Museums & Galleries of Northern Ireland. ☎ 028 9038 3000

Northern Ireland Museums Council. ☎ 028 9055 0215; www.nimc.co.uk

NATURE RESERVES AND NATIONAL PARKS

Nature Reserves – Ireland has four **national parks** – Glenveagh, Connemara, Wicklow Mountains and Killarney – in the Republic, many **forest parks** and **country parks** managed for public use and recreation, and numerous **nature reserves** (wildfowl sanctuaries, peat bogs and sand dunes) on both sides of the border.

The Wildlife Service (Dúchas), 51 St Stephen's Green, Dublin 2. ☎ 01 647 3000; Fax 01 662 1767; www.heritageireland.ie

Birdwatch Ireland, Ruttledge House, 8 Longford Place, Monkstown, Co Dublin. ☎ 01 280 4322; Fax 01 284 4407; bird@indigo.ie; www.birdwatchireland.ie

Irish Peatland Conservation Council, Capel Chambers, 119 Capel Street, Dublin 1. ☎/Fax 01 872 2397; ipcc@indigo.ie; www.ipcc.ie

Royal Society for Protection of Birds, Belvoir Park Forest, Belfast BT8 4QT. ☎ 028 9049 1547; Fax 028 9049 1669

Environment & Heritage Service, Natural Heritage, Commonwealth House, 35 Castle Street, Belfast BT1 1GH. ☎ 028 9025 1477; Fax 028 9045 6660; www.ehsni.gov.uk

Land Sports

CYCLING

The brochure published by the Irish Tourist Board suggests several routes. Airlines, ferry companies and the rail network will transport accompanied bicycles. Facilities for cycle hire exist throughout Ireland; a list of shops hiring out cycles in Northern Ireland is available from the NITB.

Irish Cycling Federation, Kelly Roche House, 619 North Circular Road, Dublin 1. ☎ 01 855 1522/3; Fax 01 855 1771

Irish Cycle Hire, Unit 6, Enterprise Centre, Ardee, Co Lough. ☎ 041 685 3772; Fax 041 685 3809, irch@iol.ie; www.irishcyclehire.com

Raleigh Rent-a-Bike Division, Raleigh Ireland Limited, PO Box 3520, Raleigh House, Kylemore Road, Dublin 10. ☎ 01 626 1333; Fax 01 626 1770; raleigh@iol.ie; www.ireland.iol.ie/raleigh/

Rent-a-Bike Ireland, 1 Patrick St, Limerick, Co Limerick. ☎ 061 416 983; emeraldalp@eircom.net; www.irelandrentabike.com; *See also Rambling below.*

GOLF

The Irish Tourist Board publishes *Golfing in Ireland*, a brochure identifying a selection of golf courses, both links and parkland. The NITB publishes a leaflet listing the 80 golf courses in Northern Ireland.

Golfing Union of Ireland, Glencar House, 81 Eglinton Road, Donnybrook, Dublin 4. ☎ 01 269 4111; Fax 01 269 5368; gui@iol.ie; www.gui.ie

Irish Ladies Golf Union, 1 Clonskeagh Square, Dublin. ☎ 01 269 6244

RAMBLING

The Irish Tourist Board publishes brochures on the **national waymarked ways** in the Republic of Ireland; detailed information sheets for individual long-distance walks are available. Waymarked ways are for walking only and are unsuitable for horses and mountain bikes; large groups are also undesirable; dogs should not be brought on ways which cross farmland; any dog seen chasing domestic animals is likely to be shot.

Walking/Cycling Ireland, PO Box 5520, Ballsbridge, Dublin 4. ☎ 01 668 8278; Fax 01 660 5566; wci@kerna.ie; http://kerna.ie/wci/

East–West Mapping, Ballyredmond, Clonegal, Enniscorthy, Co Wexford. ☎/Fax 054 77835; eastwest@eircom. net; www.homepage.eircom.net/ ~eastwest

SHOOTING
In the Republic of Ireland permits are available from the Department of the Environment and Local Government –

National Parks and Wildlife, Dúchas – the Heritage Service, 7 Ely Place, Dublin 2. ☎ 01 647 3000; Fax 01 662 0283; npw@ealga.ie; www.environ.ie

In Northern Ireland permits and walk-up shooting are available on application to the Forestry Service –
District Forest Office, The Grange, Castlewellan Forest Park, Castlewellan BT31 9DU. ☎ 028 4377 2257
District Forest Office, Inishkeen House, Killyhevlin, Enniskillen BT74 4EJ. ☎ 028 6634 3123

WALKING
See Rambling above.

Racing

HORSE RACING
Racecourses are common in almost every part of Ireland. The most well known in the Dublin area are The Curragh, Punchestown, Leopardstown and Fairyhouse.
The most popular festivals are
Fairyhouse *(Easter)*, **Killarney** *(May)*, **Curragh** *(June)*, **Killarney** *(July)*, **Galway**, **Tramore** and **Tralee** *(August)*, **Galway** and **Listowel** *(September)* and **Leopardstown** and **Limerick** *(December)*.
Irish Horseracing Authority, Leopardstown Racecourse, Foxrock, Dublin 18. ☎ 01 289 2888; Fax 01 289 8412; info@irishracing.iha.ie; www.iha.ie/iharace

GREYHOUND RACING
There are 18 race tracks for this popular evening entertainment: Ballyskeagh, Cork, Dublin, Dundalk, Dungannon, Enniscorthy, Galway, Kilkenny, Lifford, Limerick, Londonderry, Longford, Mullingar, Newbridge, Thurles, Tralee, Waterford and Youghal.
Bord na gCon, Irish Greyhound Board, 104 Henry Street, Limerick. ☎ 061 316 788; Fax 061 316 739

Water Sports

CANOEING
The many lakes and rivers provide good sport.

Irish Canoe Union ☎ 01 450 9838, 1633; Fax 01 450 2805; 01 460 4795; office@irishcanoeunion.com, www.irishcanoeunion.com, *See also AFAS above.*

National Mountain and Whitewater Centre, Tiglin, Devil's Glen, Ashford, Co Wicklow ☎ 040 40169; Fax 0404 40701; mail@tiglin.com; www.tiglin.com

FISHING
The Irish Tourist Board publishes several brochures – *Game Angling, Sea Angling* and *Coarse Angling, River Trout Angling, Pike Angling, River Moy Angling, Lough Derg Fishing Guide, Fish Ireland's Shannon Guide* – which provide information on the seasons, fisheries, price of licences and permits, dates of festivals and accommodation. Detailed information is available from the Fisheries Board:

R Holzbachova, Ph Benet/MICHELIN

Fishing at Maam Cross in Connemara

Central Fisheries Board, Balnagowan House, Mobhi Boreen, Glasnevin, Dublin 9. ☎ 01 837 9206; Fax 836 0060; info@cfb.ie; www.cfb.ie

Game fishing permits and licences in Northern Ireland are available from local tackle shops and from the fishery authorities:

Fisheries Conservancy Board for Northern Ireland, 1 Mahon Road, Portadown, Co Armagh, BT62 3EE. ☎ 028 3833 4666; Fax 028 3833 8912; www.fcbni.org

Foyle Fisheries Commission, 8 Victoria Rd, Derry. ☎ 028 7144 2100

SAILING
There are sailing marinas all round the coast of Ireland and on the inland lakes. *Sailing Ireland*, published by the Irish Tourist Board, gives information on **yacht chartering** and **offshore**

Sailing at Carrickfergus

racing, which attracts international teams. All yacht clubs are linked to the Irish Sailing Association:

Irish Sailing Association, 3 Park Road, Dún Laoghaire, Co Dublin. ☎ 01 280 0239; Fax 01 280 7558; info@sailing.ie; isa@iol.ie; www.sailing.ie
Visitor Information (for moorings) ☎ 020 7493 3201

Irish Association for Sail Training, c/o Irish Federation of Marine Industries (IFMI), Confederation House, Kildare Street, Dublin 2. ☎ 01 677 9801

Sub Aqua Diving
Ireland has a beautiful underwater coastline, particularly on the west coast where the Gulf Stream brings an abundant marine life into the clear Atlantic waters.

Irish Underwater Council, 78A Patrick Street, Dún Laoghaire, Co Dublin. ☎ 01 284 4601; Fax 01 284 4602; scubairl@indigo.ie; www.indigo.ie/scuba-irl

Sceilig Aquatics, Caherdaniel, Co Kerry. ☎/Fax 066 947 5277; info@activity-ircland; www.activity-ireland.com

Swimming (and Bathing)
There are swimming pools in the Leisure Centres of most of the larger towns and sea water baths in many seaside resorts.

Water Skiing
Irish Water Ski Federation, Knocknacree Road, Mount Salus, Dalkey, Co Dublin. ☎ 01 450 2122; Fax 01 450 2138; dbk@advance.iol.ie

Surfing
The best conditions are to be found on the northwest and the mid-west coasts; good conditions prevail on the north, the southwest and the south coast; the east coast is practicable only during a storm or strong southerly winds. Surfboards are available for hire.

Irish Surf Association, Easkey House, Easkey, Co Sligo. ☎ 096 49428; Fax 096 49020

Irish Sailing Association – *See Sailing above.*

Windsurfing
Some of the most popular places for windsurfing or sailboarding or boardsailing are in northwest Ireland on the coast of Co Mayo at **Easky**, where the Tiki Cold Water Classic was held in 1997, and on the coast of Co Donegal at **Bundoran**, where the European championships attract many nationalities.

Irish Wind Surfing Association, c/o Moss Veterinary, Naas, Co Kildare. ☎ 087 584 589; Fax 045 879 791

Irish Sailing Association – *See Sailing above.*

Oysterhaven Boardsailing Centre, Kinsale, Co Cork. ☎ 0214 770 738; Fax 0214 477 0776; info@oysterhaven.com; www.oysterhaven.com

Health and Fitness

Spa Resorts

The only active spa in Ireland is **Lisdoonvarna** in The Burren, where you can drink a glass of water from the sulphur spring or go to the health centre for sulphur baths, massage, aromatherapy, reflexology and other treatments.

Thalassotherapy

The abundant supplies of seaweed on the Irish coast are used not only as food but also in hot seaweed baths at Enniscrone west of Sligo and for therapeutic purposes at the outdoor baths in Ballybunnion north of Tralee and at Waterworld in Bundoran in Co Donegal, where you can enjoy various health treatments using heated sea water, local seaweed and sea water drench showers.

What to Buy Locally

Ireland produces a number of articles which have an international reputation, such as **Waterford Crystal**, **Aran sweaters** or **Donegal tweed**. The **Kilkenny Design Centre**, set up in the early 1960s, infused new life into domestic and industrial design in Ireland and markets a good range of craftwork *(see Kilkenny and Dublin)*. Throughout the country there are many less well-known enterprises and individual craftsmen and women producing hand-made articles. Manufacturers of textiles, glass and porcelain usually offer a tour of the factory and have showrooms and shops on the premises; their goods are often available in department stores, specialist shops in the major towns and tourist shops in the popular country districts. The *Linen Homelands Tour* visits the **Irish Linen Centre** as well as various linen manufacturers in and around Lisburn *(see p 431)*.

Some craft workers are grouped in certain regions, such as weavers in Donegal. Others congregate in the special **craft villages**, set up by the Government in Dingle, Donegal town, Blennerville near Tralee or Roundstone in Connemara.

Some Folk Museums and Folk Villages organise demonstrations of traditional crafts.

Glass – The most famous and oldest glass factory in Ireland is in **Waterford**, but since its revival in 1951 several smaller enterprises have started to produce hand-blown lead crystal which is cut, engraved or undecorated – Cavan Crystal, Galway Crystal, Sligo Crystal, Tipperary Crystal, Tyrone Crystal. Most have factory shops where first- and second-quality pieces can be bought and many offer a guided tour of the workshops.

Knitwear – The thick cream-coloured (undyed) knitwear associated with the Aran Islands is the best known of

Aran sweaters to keep out the wind and rain

Irish knitwear and is on sale throughout the country. Ireland produces a great variety of other knitted garments in a variety of textures and colours, particularly thick sweaters to keep out the wind and rain, using the traditional stitches – basket, blackberry, blanket, cable, diamond, moss, plait, trellis and zigzag.

Lace – In the 19C there were many lace-making centres in Ireland but few have survived. In most the skill was fostered by the nuns; the lace-makers of Clones and Carrickmacross have now formed themselves into cooperatives. Kenmare needlepoint lace is the most difficult to make; Clones is a crochet lace but the other centres produce "mixed lace" on a base of machine-made cotton net.

Linen – The demand for bed linen, table linen and tea towels keeps some 20 Irish linen houses in business. The popularity of linen as an apparel fabric has revived in recent years, since blending with synthetic or other natural fibres has reduced its tendency to crease. It is now used by top fashion designers all over the world who appreciate its sheen and interesting texture, its durability and versatility – it is cool in summer and a good insulator in winter; it dyes well in bright clear colours.

Metalwork – Throughout the country, and especially in the craft villages, artists are working in gold, silver, bronze, pewter and enamel to produce dishes and plaques, necklaces, pendants and earrings; the traditional Claddagh rings *(see Galway)* worked in gold show a heart with two clasped hands *(see Mullingar and Timolin)*.

Porcelain and Pottery – The largest porcelain factory is the one at **Belleek** which produces fine translucent Parian ware and specialises in woven basket pieces and naturalistic flower decoration. The Irish Dresden factory *(see p 124)* preserves and develops the tradition of delicate ornamental porcelain figures which originated in Germany. There are many studio potteries in Ireland producing hand-turned articles, such as those in Connemara and the Stephen Pearce Pottery in Shanagarry.

Tweed – The term was first recognised late in the 19C to describe the hand-woven woollen cloth produced in Co Donegal. Donegal tweed is still the most well-known and is now produced, mostly on power looms, by four firms, in Ardara, Donegal town, Downies and Kilcar.

Belleek Pottery – a sample of intricate craftsmanship

Three of these companies also employ out-workers using hand-looms and most have diversified into the production of knitwear and ready-made garments or into weaving other natural fibres – linen, cotton and silk. The original tweeds were made from natural undyed wool – grey, brown or cream; as coloured wool was produced only in small quantities it was introduced as speckles when the wool was carded. The dyes used were obtained from plants, lichens, turf, soot and minerals.

Avoca Weavers *(see p 369)* were founded in 1723 and the Kerry Woollen Mills *(see p 289)* also date from the 18C. Foxford *(see p 304)* and Blarney *(see p 192)* were started in the 19C.

Woodwork – There are a number of craftsmen producing hand-turned articles such as bowls, lamp stands and ornaments; the unique pieces are the graceful and delightful carvings produced by artists from skeletal pieces of **bogwood**. Some wood-turners produce musical instruments such as pipes and drums *(bodhráns) (see Roundstone in Connemara)*.

Food and Drink – The most convenient products to take home with you are Irish whiskey or a bottle of Baileys Irish Cream or Irish Mist, if you are not travelling far, you may also take along Irish cheeses and smoked salmon and other smoked fish or meat.

Books

ART

The Architecture of Ireland from the Earliest Times to 1880 by Maurice Craig (Batsford 1982)

An Introduction to Irish High Crosses, by Hilary Richardson and John Scarry (Mercier Press)

Ireland's Traditional Houses by Kevin Dunaher, Bord Fáilte

Irish Art and Architecture by Peter Harbison, Homan Potterton, Jeanne Sheehy (Thames & Hudson 1978)

The Irish Country House by Peter Somerville-Large (Sinclair-Stevenson 1995)

A Guide to Irish Country Houses by Mark Bence-Jones (1988)

The Painters of Ireland by Anne Crookshank and the Knight of Glin (1978/9)

Exploring the Book of Kells by George Otto Simms (1988)

AUTOBIOGRAPHY

Twenty Years A-Growing by Maurice O'Sullivan (1953, 1992)

Wheels within Wheels by Dervla Murphy (1981)

Woodbrook by David Thomson (1988)

Angela's Ashes by Frank McCourt (1997)

FICTION

Castle Rackrent by Maria Edgeworth (1800)

The Macdermots of Ballycloran, The Kellys and the O'Kellys, Castle Richmond and *The Landleaguers* by Anthony Trollope (1847, 1848, 1860, 1883)

Experiences of an Irish RM by E Somerville and M Ross (1899)

The Playboy of the Western World by JM Synge (1907)

A Portrait of the Artist as a Young Man by James Joyce (1916, 1960)

Ulysses by James Joyce (1922)

The Last September by Elizabeth Bowen (1929)

Troubles by JG Farrell (Fontana 1970) – ISBN 0-000-654046-5

Good Behaviour by Molly Keane (1981, 1988)

Hungry Hill by Daphne du Maurier (1983)

GEOGRAPHY

Geology and Scenery in Ireland by JB Whittow (Penguin Books 1974)

The Book of the Irish Countryside edited by Frank Mitchell (Blackstaff Press 1987)

Reading the Irish Landscape by Frank Mitchell and Michael Ryan (TownHouse 2001) ISBN 1-86059-055-1

The Shannon Floodlands – A Natural History by Stephen Heeny (Tir Eolas – Newtownlynch, Kinvara, Co Galway 1993) – ISBN 1-873821-026

Atlas of the Irish Rural Landscape edited by FHA Aalen, Kevin Whelan and Matthew Stout (Cork University Press 1997) ISBN 1-85918-095-7

The Personality of Ireland - Habitat, Heritage and History by E Estyn Evans (Lilliput 1992) ISBN 0-946640-81-5

Sun Dancing by Geoffrey Moorhouse, Weidenfeld & Nicolson, ISBN 0 297 81595 4 - £18.99 – about the Skellig Isles

HISTORY

Brendan the Navigator by George Otto Simms (O'Brien Press)

The Celts edited by Joseph Raftery (Mercier Press, Dublin 1988)

An Introduction to Celtic Christianity by James P Mackey (T & T Clark, Ltd, Edinburgh 1989)

Ancient Ireland by Jacqueline O'Brien and Peter Harbison

Ireland in Early Medieval Europe edited by Dorothy Whitelock, Rosamund McKitterick, David Dumville (Cambridge University Press 1982)

The Peoples of Ireland by Liam de Paor (Hutchinson 1986)

Citizen Lord by Stella Tillyard (Chatto & Windus) ISBN 0.7011.6538.3 – about Edward Fitzgerald

Huguenot Settlements in Ireland by GI Lee (Longman Green & Co 1936)

The Oxford History of Ireland by RF Foster – ISBN 0-19-285271

The Making of Modern Ireland 1603–1923 by JC Beckett (Faber & Faber 1966)

Citizen Lord by Stella Tillyard (Chatto & Windus) – ISBN 0-7011-6538-3

The Great Hunger by Cecil Woodham-Smith (Penguin Books 1988)

The Identity of Ulster by Ian Adamson (Pretani Press 1982)

Twilight of the Ascendancy by Mark Bence-Jones (1987)

Hungry for Home – a journey from the edge of Ireland – by Cole Moreton (Penguin) ISBN 0-140-27395-6

Fenian Fire – a British Government plot to assassinate Queen Victoria – by Christy Campbell (HarperCollins) ISBN 0-00-710483-9

The Easter Rising by Lorcan Collins and Conor Kostick (O'Brien Press)

The Irish Empire - The Story of the Irish Abroad by Patrick Bishop (Boxtree – MacMillan) ISBN 0 312 26527 1

MYTHOLOGY

A Guide to Irish Mythology by Daragh Smyth (Irish Academic Press)

Fairy and Folk Tales of Ireland by WB Yeats (Colin Smythe 1973)

Irish Folk Tales edited by Henry Glassie (Penguin 1987)

RECIPES

Simply Delicious Recipes by
Darina Allen (1989, 1992)
The Irish Food Guide by Sally and
John McKenna (Anna Livia, Dublin)

TRAVEL

The Road to Roaringwater –
Christopher Somerville (Harper
Collins 1993) ISBN 0 00 638102-2
(1993) – a walk along the west coast
from Malin Head to Cape Clear Island
in Roaringwater Bay

McCarthy's Bar by Pete McCarthy
(Sceptre Lir) ISBN 0 340 76605-0 –
a journey of discovery
in Ireland
The Craic by Mark McCrum (Phoenix
non-fiction) ISBN 0-75380-836-6 – a
journey through Ireland
Literary Tour of Ireland by Elizabeth
Healy (Wolfhound Press Paperbank
2001) ISBN 0-86327-731-4
Round Ireland with a Fridge by
Tony Hawks (Ebury Press)

Events and Festivals

FEBRUARY

All Ireland Dancing Championships – Open to
competitors from Ireland and abroad

**Different town
every year**

MARCH

Horse Ploughing Match and Heavy Horse Show – One of
the three great fairs of Ireland

**Ballycastle,
Fair Head**

*Oul' Lammas Fair, a
traditional horse fair
held in Ballycastle
in the Antrim Glens*

St Patrick's Day Parade – On 17 March in the middle
of a 4-day spectacle of fireworks, carnival, marching
bands and theatre

**Dublin
and all major towns**

Belfast Literary Festival – Celebrates the best of local,
national and international literature

Belfast

Feis Ceoil – Classical music festival for all instruments
including voice

Dublin

APRIL

World Irish Dancing Championships – Competition involving over 4 000 dancers from everywhere in the
world ☎ 01 475 2220 (enquiries)

**Different town
every year**

MAY

Bantry Mussel Fair – Seafood festival promoting the
mussel industry; free street entertainment

Bantry

Fleadh Nua – Folk festival of musicians, singers,
dancers, wrenboys, biddy boys, strawboys, all woven together in a rich cultural pattern

Ennis

Castle Ward Opera *(see p 467)* – Performed in the beautiful grounds of a Georgian country house

Castle Ward

JUNE

Raft Race Weekend – Bands, street theatre, parachute
displays and the Raft Race, raising funds for the RNLI

Portrush

Writers' Week – Literary festival including workshops, exhibitions and a book fair — **Listowel**

National Country Fair – Ireland's premier country sports event and country fair for all the family — **Birr**

Fleadh Amhrán agus Rince – Traditional festival of song, music and dance — **Ballycastle**

Bloomsday – Annual celebration on 16 June of James Joyce's great novel *Ulysses* – readings, re-enactments, music, theatre, street theatre — **Dublin**

Galway Hookers' Regatta *(Crinniú na mBád)* – Annual regatta of traditional Irish sailing vessels on Strangford Lough — **Portaferry**

Northern Ireland Game and Country Fair – General celebration of the countryside, clay pigeon shooting, dog shows — **Ballywalter Park Estate, Co Antrim**

Irish Open Golf Championship — **Different venue each year**

JULY

County Wexford Strawberry Fair – Eating strawberries and cream, arts and crafts exhibition, Irish dancing and mumming, horse and greyhound racing, band recitals — **Enniscorthy**

Willie Clancy Summer School – Major festival of traditional Irish music (particularly *uilleann* pipes) — **Milltown Malbay and other venues**

James Joyce Summer School – Lectures, seminars and social events in Newman House, St Stephen's Green, where Joyce himself studied *(2 weeks)* — **Dublin**

Twelfth of July Parades – Bands, banners and brethren of the Orange Order celebrating the anniversary of the Battle of the Boyne — **Belfast and other venues**

MICHELIN

Lambeg Drums, an impressive sight in the marching season in Northern Ireland

International Rose Week – International rose trials — **Belfast, Dixon Park**

Galway Arts Festival – Theatre, dance, music and street entertainment, Ireland's premier multidisciplinary arts festival *(10 days)* — **Galway**

Loughcrew Opera – Performance in Loughcrew Gardens — **Loughcrew**

Yeats International Summer School – Lectures and seminars — **Sligo**

AUGUST

O'Carolan Harp and Traditional Music Festival – Performance of O'Carolan's works, international harp competition, Irish music, concerts, song and set dancing, many open-air events *(see Boyle)* — **Keadew**

Kerrygold Horse Show – International event with team jumping competitions held at the Royal Dublin Society ground in Ballsbridge; equestrian and social event of the year — **Dublin**

Steam Engine Rally – Held in the grounds of Stradbally Hall next to the Stradbally Steam Museum (*see p 123*) — **Stradbally**

William Carleton Summer School – Annual literary event with lectures, readings, exhibitions and tours, celebrating the life and times of the Clogher Valley 19C novelist, William Carleton — **Clogher Valley**

Pan Celtic International Festival – Inter-Celtic Games with emphasis on sailing, rowing, kayaking and surfing — **Donegal / Sligo**

Kilkenny Arts Festival – Music, visual art, theatre, literature, children's arts and outdoor events — **Kilkenny**

Puck Fair – One of the oldest festivals in Ireland, centred on a billy goat enthroned in a chair, with a traditional horse fair, busking, open-air concerts, parades and fireworks (*3 days*) — **Killorglin**

Gathering of the Boats (*Crinniú na mBád*) – Galway hookers' regatta — **Kinvarra**

All-Ireland Intermediate Road Bowls Finals – Ancient game, played only in Co Armagh and Co Cork, in which competitors used to throw cannonballs — **Armagh**

Connemara Pony Show – Grand showing of the Connemara pony, Ireland's only native pony — **Clifden**

Fleadh Cheoil na hEireann – Traditional Irish music – playing, talking, singing, dancing or listening (*3 days*) — **Different venue each year**

Rosc of Tralee Festival – Bands, parades, dancing, horse racing and other activities, celebrating the art of being Irish (*see Tralee*) — **Tralee**

Oul' Lammas Fair – Oldest traditional Irish fair with horse trading, street entertainment, competitions and market stalls — **Ballycastle**

Lisdoonvarna Matchmaking Festival – Ireland's biggest singles event with music and dance and horse racing (*late August to early October; see The Burren*) — **Lisdoonvarna**

SEPTEMBER

National Heritage Week – Walks, lectures, exhibitions, music recitals, pageants and demonstrations involving many community and national organisations — **Nationwide**

All Ireland Hurling Finals – Annual national hurling championships at Croke Park — **Dublin**

Clarinbridge Oyster Festival – Ladies International Oyster-opening Competition, oyster tasting, good food, good stout, music, dance — **Clarinbridge Map 712 - F 8**

All Ireland Football Finals – Annual national Gaelic Football championship finals at Croke Park — **Dublin**

International Oyster Festival – World Oyster-opening Championships, held in the pubs, oyster tasting, music, song and dance — **Galway**

SEPTEMBER–OCTOBER

Waterford International Festival of Light Opera – Competitive musical festival for amateur musical societies held at the Theatre Royal — **Waterford**

Irish Ancestor Family History Conference – Residential conference between Belfast and Dublin offering practical help in tracing your ancestors (*1 week*) — **Belfast / Dublin**

Dublin Theatre Festival – Best of world theatre and new productions from all the major Irish companies — **Dublin**

OCTOBER

Cork International Film Festival – Ireland's oldest film event established to present the best of international cinema and to serve as a platform for new Irish cinema — **Kinsale**

Kinsale International Festival of Fine Food – The best of fine food and wines in a convivial party atmosphere with music, dance and wine tasting — **Kinsale**

Great October Fair – One of the three great fairs of Ireland for buying and selling horses — **Ballinasloe Map 712 - H 8**

St Patrick's Festival, a week-long celebration of Ireland's national day

O'Carolan Harp and Cultural Festival – Harp and instrumental workshops and competitions, traditional Irish music concerts, step and set dancing, traditional festival Mass in Irish, seminars and lectures *(see p 267)* **Nobber**

Wexford Festival Opera – Production of rare operas and other cultural activities, attracting a large cosmopolitan audience and an international reputation *(1 week)* **Wexford**

OCTOBER–NOVEMBER

Belfast Festival at Queen's – Largest arts festival in Ireland offering music from classical to folk and jazz, together with drama, ballet and cinema **Belfast**

Cork Jazz Festival – One of the most famous places for jazz and an imperative rendez-vous for the greatest names in this genre **Cork**

DECEMBER

Belfast Craft Fair – Large retail craft fair with over 200 exhibitors **Belfast**

Glossary

Certain elements occur very frequently in Irish **place names** and most have a clear meaning.

Alt – cliff
Ard – high, height, hillock
Áth – ford
Bád – boat
Baile – town, townland, homestead
Bán – white, fair; grassland
Beag – little
Béal – opening, entrance, river mouth
Bealtaine – 1 May, month of May
Beann – peak, pointed hill, horn, gable
Beannchair – abounding in peaks or gables
Bearna – gap
Beith – birch tree
Bile – venerated tree
Bó – cow
Boireann – large rock, rocky district
Both – hut, tent
Bóthar – road
Buí – yellow
Bun – end, bottom
Cabhán – hollow
Caiseal – castle, circular stone fort
Caisleán – castle
Caladh – harbour, landing place, marshy
Capall – horse
Carraig – rock
Cath – battle
Cathair – circular stone fort, city
Cealtrach – old burial ground
Céide – hillock
Cill – church
Cillín – little church, children's burial ground
Cliath – a hurdle
Cloch – stone
Cluain – meadow
Cnap – knob, round little hill
Cno – hill
Coinicéar – rabbit warren
Com – mountain recess
Dairbhre – oak-grove
Dearg – red
Díseart – desert, hermitage
Doire – wooded area
Droichead – bridge

Droim – ridge, hillock
Dubh – black
Dún – fort
Eaglais – church
Eas – waterfall
Eiscir – ridge of high land
Eochaill – yew wood
Fear – man
Fearbán – strip of land
Fionn – white, fair-haired person
Fir – men
Gall – foreigner
Gorm – blue
Gort – field
Inbhear – river mouth
Inis – island
Iúr – yew tree
Lár – centre
Leithinis – peninsula
Lios – circular earthen fort, ring
Mór – large
Móta – moat, high mound
Muc – pig
Muirbheach – level stretch of sandy land along the seashore
Muireasc – seaside marsh meadow
Óg – young
Oileán – island
Omhna – tree, tree-trunk
Poll – hole, cave
Ráth – earthen rampart
Rinn – point of land
Sagart – priest
Scéir – sharp rock
Sean – old
Sí – bewitching, enchanting; fairy mound
Slí – route, way
Sliabh – mountain
Sruth – stream
Teach – house
Teampall – church
Tobar – well
Tóchar – causeway
Trá – beach, strand
Túr – tower
Turlach – winter lake
Uachtar – top, upper part

Derryclare Lough, Connemara

H-Champollion/MICHELIN

Insights and Images

Landscape

Visitors cross the seas to Ireland for many reasons – the friendliness and conviviality of the people, the sense of being on the furthest, westernmost edge of the European continent, the Celtic heritage, lively and ever-present folk music – but it is perhaps the landscape which is the country's greatest attraction. Well-deserving of its name of "the Emerald Isle", Ireland does indeed sparkle in endless shades of green, but it is also a land of bare mountains and strange rock formations, stark cliffs and sandy strands, flower-rich boglands and well-tree'd desmesnes. All these elements come together to yield an extraordinary range of landscapes, all within the limited compass of a medium-sized island.

The Shape of the Land

Unlike the archetypal island which is supposed to rise from coastal lowlands to a mountain core, Ireland has a midland heart of mostly low-lying country, protected by highland ramparts around its edge. Only from Dublin northwards is there an extensive opening of the land to the sea, a fifty-mile doorway of fertile land through which successive waves of invaders have entered the country. Overlooking Dublin from the south, the Wicklow Mountains rise to a peak of 3 035ft/925m at Lugnaquilla, but the country's highest point and the most dramatic mountain scenery are to be found in the far southwest, where Carrantuohill (3 414ft/1 038m) and Macgillycuddy's Reeks preside over the glories of the Killarney lakeland and the Iveragh Peninsula. This peninsula is one of several, parts of a much wider set of parallel mountain folds running roughly east-west which were violently folded in Hercynian times and which include the granites of Brittany and the Harz massif in Germany. In Ireland they also include a whole series of ranges dividing the midlands from the island's southern coastline. Their equivalents in the north are the northeast-southwest trending ranges folded in the Caledonian period and which cross to the Atlantic edge in Donegal and Connaught and leap the narrow strait separating Ulster from Scotland.

Bounded by these ancient mountain systems, the central regions of the country are largely underlaid by a much-eroded foundation of Carboniferous limestone. The basis of the rich bone-building pasturelands for which Ireland is famous, it is far from monotonous, producing such famous features as the great escarpment of Benbulben glowering over Sligo or the eerie moonscapes of The Burren in Co Clare. Much of the midland landscape is profoundly marked by the impact of the Ice Ages. The retreating glaciers left unconsolidated deposits of clay, sand and gravel, great tracts of which remain badly drained today, though the worm-like, winding ridges of sandy gravel called eskers – deposited by streams running beneath the glaciers – have always provided dry paths through an otherwise somewhat impenetrable land. The ice sheets also moulded great swarms of **drumlins**, low egg-shaped mounds, most clearly visible when partially submerged as

Invermore River, Connemara

in Clew Bay and Strangford Lough. In the north, a broad band of drumlins extends right across the island, the waterlogged land around them forming a barrier to communication which may well have helped establish Ulster's distinctive identity in ancient times.

Peat Bogs

One of the most intriguing features of the Irish landscape is its peat bogs, the most extensive in Europe, occupying something like a sixth of the land surface, and playing an important role in the country's history, economy, and collective memory. Bogs are of two types, in both of which peat is formed in waterlogged conditions by the accumulation of dead and incompletely decomposed plant material. **Blanket bog** occurs in areas of high rainfall and humidity, mostly in the mountains of the western seaboard, and is mostly composed of dead grasses and sedges. It is usually shallower (6ft/2m to 20ft/6m) than **raised bog**, which is essentially a lowland phenomenon, occurring where rainfall is less, growing above the ground water level, and composed of bog moss (sphagnum) forming a dome. It can reach a depth of 39ft/12m and is scattered over much of the midland area, where it forms a distinctive, open and natural-seeming landscape in contrast to the farmland that usually surrounds it. Raised bogs have developed over time without appreciable human interference, whereas the formation of blanket bog has been affected by such human activities as burning and clearance of scrub and woodland for grazing; peat is an excellent preservative material, and the remains of forests and of Neolithic fields have been uncovered beneath the blanket bogs of the west.

In more recent times, the Irish bogs have played the role fulfilled in other lands by forests, offering a refuge to resisters and outlaws, while their inaccessibility and unfamiliarity made it difficult for invaders to extend their control over the whole country. The early disappearance of Ireland's tree cover and the almost complete lack of coal deposits meant that peat – known locally as turf – became the most important source of fuel. The turfs are traditionally cut with a slane, a narrow spade with a side blade set at a right angle, and laid out to dry. When thoroughly dry, they are stacked into clamps near the house. In a fine summer a family can harvest enough fuel for several years. The cuts sliced deep into the bog and the stacks of drying peat make distinctive patterns in the landscape quite unfamiliar to most visitors from abroad, while the sight, sound and smell of the turf fire glowing in the corner of living room or pub evokes strong emotions in every Irish heart.

Saving the turf, Inishowen

H Champollion/MICHELIN

Since the mid-20C peat has been harvested on an industrial scale in an attempt to provide the country with some of its electric power as well as yielding useful quantities of moss peat for horticultural purposes. The mechanical harvesters of the Bord na Móna (Peat Development Authority) are an impressive sight

as they scrape huge quantities of sun-dried milled peat from a bog that has been drained for a period of five to seven years. The harvested peat is either made into briquettes for domestic use or burned in one of five electricity generating stations.

Climate

Confronting the Atlantic as it does, Ireland has an oceanic climate, tempered by the influence of the warm waters of the Gulf Stream flowing northwards along its western shores. Weather systems blow in one after the other from the southwest, bringing abundant precipitation and ever-changing cloudscapes. The temperature range is limited; it is rarely very hot nor very cold. In the coolest months of January and February temperatures vary between 4° and 7° Celsius, in the warmest months of July and August between 14°C and 16°C. Snowfalls are uncommon except on the highest mountains, where the total annual precipitation can exceed 95in/2 400mm. The southwest is the wettest part of the country, the east the driest, but everywhere it is not so much the amount of rainfall, but its persistence. However, though there may not be many days without rain or a touch of drizzle, it should always be remembered that its occurrence is at least partly responsible for the freshness of the atmosphere and the luminous look of the landscape.

Coast

The country's rock foundation is most dramatically exposed at the interface of land and ocean, particularly in the west, where mountainous peninsulas frequently end in bold headlands, while sea inlets and fjords penetrate far inland. The northern shore of Co Antrim boasts what is surely Ireland's most famous natural wonder, the countless clustered columns of the Giant's Causeway, formed 60 million years ago by violent volcanic disturbances. Few natural ramparts are as spectacular as the bands of shale and sandstone making up the 5mi/8km stretch of the Cliffs of Moher, rising 200m over the Atlantic breakers on the edge of The Burren in Co Clare. The limestones of the Burren leap seaward to form the Aran Islands, where the abrupt cliffs of Inishmore, though less high, are equally awe-inspiring. The discontinuous archipelago along the western coast offers other equally extraordinary sights, none more so than the drowned mountain-top of Skellig Michael, a rocky refuge for a hardy monastic community in the days of

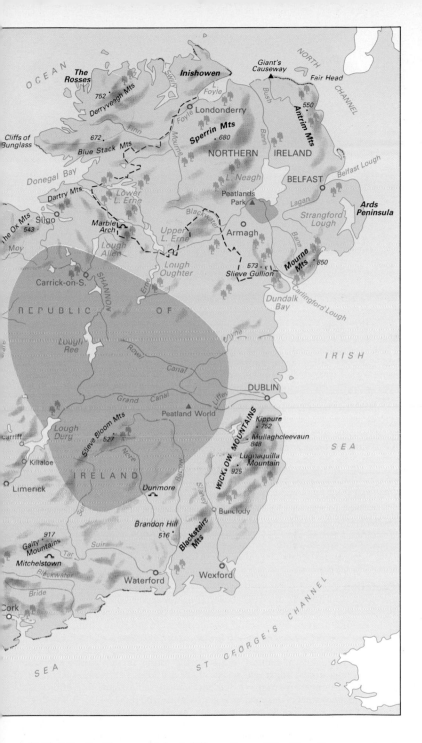

early Christianity. The very highest cliffs are those of the Slieve League peninsula, where a great bastion of quartzite stands no less than 1 972ft/601m above the waves.

In the east of the country, coasts are characterised more by splendid natural harbours formed by drowned valleys, low limestone cliffs and glorious stretches of sandy beach.

Fields and Farms

Despite recent economic trends, Ireland is still very much an **agricultural country**, with more than 80% of the land surface being farmed. Most of this is **pasture**; Ireland has 95% of the best grassland in the European Union,

New Ross, Co Wicklow

but **arable farming** prospers in the drier east, notably in the Ards Peninsular in Ulster and in Co Wexford, where barley is grown on a large scale. As elsewhere in Atlantic Europe, farmland is **enclosed** rather than open, with a variety of field patterns reflecting a complex historical development. The typical field boundary is a hedgebank, topped with native shrubs and trees, often left to grow spontaneously rather than laid to make them stockproof. This leafy growth to some extent makes up for the country's lack of woodland, and gives variety to a landscape which might otherwise tend to monotony. In the rocky peninsulas of the west and elsewhere, stone is used to form boundary walls. Perhaps the most complete development of walled field systems is in the Aran Islands, where tiny enclosures are bounded by drystone walls deliberately built to be permeable to the winds which might otherwise flatten them. In similar areas of poor soil and high rainfall, "**lazy beds**" were made. These were cultivation ridges, created by laying a strip of manure and inverting sods over it from both sides. The raised bed drained easily into the trenches on either side and its soil was warmed by the sun from the side as well as the top, highly advantageous characteristics in a cool, wet country. Lazy beds came into their own with the widespread cultivation of the potato in the pre-Famine years, and whole landscapes are marked by the wrinkled pattern of the subsequently abandoned ridges, sometimes at an elevation where cultivation of any crop would seem doomed to failure.

Vegetation

Most of the country was originally covered in trees, particularly forests of sessile oak. Clearance for agriculture began in Neolithic times and continued until virtually no natural or even semi-natural woodlands were left. One of the last assaults on the native forest was made by the British in the 17C and 18C, on the one hand for building materials and for smelting, on the other to deny refuge to the rebellious Irish. Remnants of natural forest can be found in the southern Wicklow Mountains and around Killarney, where there are also marvellous specimens of the arbutus or strawberry tree. In the 18C considerable replanting efforts were made by many owners of desmesnes eager to landscape their estates in the English manner. Exotic trees like Scots pine, beech, sweet chestnut, monkey puzzle and cedar of Lebanon were introduced to supplement the native species. As some 6% of the land surface was held in desmesnes, the landscape impact was considerable, though it was much reduced subsequently through the break-up and parcelling-out of many estates. The fate of the Anglo-Irish so-called Big House is well known; less familiar is the felling of its heritage of trees and ornamental woodland and their conversion into ordinary farmland or monotonous plantations of conifers. Nevertheless a number of desmesnes have survived, some in the form of **Forest Parks** in public ownership, others in the hands of the National Trust in Northern Ireland.

Gardeners have long taken advantage of the country's favourable, frost-free environment, and Irish gardens are famous for the wide range of plants that are cultivated, particularly when it is possible to provide shelter from the wind. A number of subtropical paradise gardens have been created, among them Garinish Island in Glengarriff Harbour, where flowers bloom all year round. Conditions favour the growth of the rhododendron, which has escaped into woodland where it suppresses other shrubs and trees. It is also seen in hedgerows, as is another garden escapee, the fuchsia. Ireland's botanically most fascinating landscape is perhaps The Burren, where a profusion of acid and lime-loving plants grow in harmonious co-existence.

Rivers and Lakes

Not surprisingly, water is ever-present in the Irish landscape. The country's rivers have a total length of 16 530mi/26 000km and lakes/loughs cover an area of 560sq mi/1 450km². Ireland's low population density and the relative lack of polluting industries means that most of this water is unpolluted and well-stocked with fish and other wildlife.

The watercourses rising on the seaward side of mountains tend to be short and steep, draining straight into the sea. Those that rise inland form slow-moving lowland streams, lined by water-meadows and often widening out into lakes.

Youghal Harbour, Co Cork

The **Shannon**, the country's longest (230mi/370km) river behaves in this way, winding sluggishly through the midland countryside and forming the great expanses of Lough Ree and Lough Derg before discharging into its immensely long estuary below Limerick. In Ulster, **Lough Neagh** is far more impressive than the River Bann which flows through it; though shallow, it is Ireland's largest body of water, covering an area of 153sq mi/400km², and teeming with eels. The country's loveliest lakeland is that which has developed along the course of the Erne, comprising countless lesser lakes as well as island-studded **Upper** and **Lower Lough Erne** themselves.

In the south, rivers rising well inland have cut their way through upland chains to reach the sea; the valleys thus formed by the Blackwater, Nore, Suir, Barrow and Slaney are often of great beauty.

Ireland Today

The prosperous economy of Ireland owes much to forceful government intervention and enthusiastic membership of the European Union in the last decades of the 20C. The effects of new-found affluence, from a high level of car ownership to individual house-building, can be seen everywhere. Social change too has been profound but at the same time many of the characteristics of the Irish way of life which so endear the country to its visitors remain as pronounced as ever, and Irish identity is far from being eroded by the country's whole-hearted entry into the mainstream of contemporary international life.

Jaunting Car

People

Origins

The Irish are commonly thought of as being a Celtic people but this is more of a cultural than ethnic definition. Around 8 000 BC, long before the arrival of the Celts, the coastal areas and river valleys were settled by Mesolithic hunter-gatherers who had moved across the land-bridge which still connected Ireland with Scotland. The dominant Celts seem to have come in several waves during the second half of the last millennium BC, pushed to the western fringe of the Continent by the expansion of the Roman Empire and pressure from Germanic tribes in Central Europe. By the time of the coming of Christianity in the 5C, the population may have amounted to a quarter of a million. Viking attacks began towards the end of the 8C but, although the Norsemen's original objective was pillage, they later settled, founding coastal towns and eventually becoming absorbed into the local population. Subsequent immigration mostly originated from Britain, the Anglo-Norman invaders and their followers being succeeded in the 16C and 17C by a planned influx of settlers and colonists. By the beginning of the 18C, perhaps a quarter of the population of just over two million was of English, Welsh and Scottish origin. Other groups, though far less numerous, added their distinctive flavour; Huguenots in the late 17C, Jews mostly in the late 19C and early 20C. Before the last decades of the 20C, the backwardness of the economy meant that immigration from non-European countries remained statistically insignificant.

Skibbereen, Co Cork

Distribution and Structure

The country has a population of about 5 434 000, of whom 1 689 000 live in Northern Ireland, 3 745 000 in the Republic. This represents a substantial increase over the low point of about 4.5 million, reached in the early 20C, the result of a falling birthrate and continuing emigration. It is largely due to net inward migration but it is still well short of the total of over 8 million in the period immediately preceding the Famine *(see also p 84)*.

The overall density compared with other western European countries is low: 52 people per square kilometre, and a large proportion of the population still live in small towns or the countryside. Villages are relatively few and the isolated family farm is the most typical form of rural settlement; many places which elsewhere in Europe would be classified as villages with a total population of perhaps a few hundred have a full range of urban functions such as a market, shops, pubs, and professional offices. Recent rural building has confirmed the scattered nature of the settlement pattern, with new farmhouses and other homes standing proudly in the middle of fields and a ribbon development of bungalows along the roads. The bigger towns all have a coastal location. Greater Dublin has a disproportionate number of inhabitants, 1 122 600 in total, Greater Belfast some 277 391. No other regional centre in the Republic approaches the capital in population size; Cork has 180 000 inhabitant) and the other cities have under 100 000.

In the Republic birth rates have fallen recently but the population is a relatively young one, with more than 40% under the age of 25 and 24% under the age of 15.

Religious Affiliation and Minorities

In recent years, the power and authority of the Roman Catholic Church may have been sapped by recurrent scandals, but the Republic of Ireland is still a demonstratively Catholic country, with 91% of the population declaring their adherence to the Roman Catholic Church *(see also p 80)*. Attendance at Mass is high, though no longer universal, and much lower in inner city districts of Dublin than in rural areas. The Church's teachings on matters such as abortion continue to command widespread respect; attempts to liberalise restrictions on termination of pregnancy have been defeated when put to referendum. Other Christians, who once formed a quarter of the total population, and almost 50% of the inhabitants of Dublin, have declined in number, either through emigration or intermarriage, and number around 3% of the total population of the Republic, most of them members of the Church of Ireland.

The strength of religious observance is paralleled in Northern Ireland, whose majority Protestant population is split among Presbyterians, Methodists, members of the Church of Ireland and various minor denominations. Roman Catholics form about one third of the Northern population, a proportion which is steadily increasing.

Ethnically indistinguishable from their fellow-citizens, Travellers are perhaps the most visible minority in southern Ireland. Previously known by the now demeaning name of "tinkers", they move their lorries and caravans from one roadside site to another and earn a living mostly from scrap-metal dealing. There are small numbers of Chinese and other Asians in both North and South, and the Republic, especially its remoter western areas, has long attracted individual residents from other European countries, particularly Germany.

Leisure

Music

Music plays a large role in Irish life, not only through the sessions of traditional music played in the bars in the evenings all over the country but also the dancing for which many of the tunes were written. Side by side with this tradition are the modern bands playing every kind of popular music *(see also p 74)*.

Sports

Most forms of sport are played enthusiastically in Ireland, none more so however than those which are uniquely Irish, hurling *(iománaíocht)* and Gaelic football *(peil)*. These, together with **handball** *(liathróid láimhe)* and rounders, are administered by the **Gaelic Athletic Association** *(Cumann Lúthchleas Gael)*, a largely rural movement, founded in 1884 in Thurles.

The national GAA stadium, Croke Park in Dublin, with space for 80 000 spectators, is named after the Association's first patron, Archbishop Croke (1824-1902). The high point of the Gaelic sporting year comes in September, when both the hurling and football national finals are held here. The history of the Association and the exploits of the hurling and football champions are excellently illustrated in the GAA Museums at Croke Park and in Thurles.

Hurling is a fast-moving and high-scoring game of great antiquity, played by two teams each of fifteen players using the long curved stick of the hurley *(camán)* to hit the cork and leather ball into or over the rugby-type goal. Allowing the ball to be handled under certain circumstances increases the excitement of the game, which can seem violent and chaotic to the non-initiated. *Camogie* is a version of hurling adapted for women participants, with a shorter playing time, teams of 12, and a smaller pitch.

Gaelic football is played with a spherical ball, uses the same pitch as hurling and has similar rules; neither game is played outside Ireland to any extent, but Australian Rules football owes much to its Gaelic ancestor.

Horse Racing

The **horse** plays a special part in Irish life and the great Horse Fairs still figure in the Irish calendar. Breeding and racing horses have deep roots in Irish culture; the earliest races were part of pre-Christian festivals. Swimming races, which ceased only recently, also had Celtic origins, in the ritual of immersion. The focal point of Ireland's breeding, racing and training is at the Curragh in Co Kildare. There are about 28 race courses in Ireland; at Laytown Strand, south of Drogheda, the times of races are dictated by the tide and horses are often exercised on the seashore. The first recorded prize is a plate donated in 1640 by the Trustees of the Duke of Leinster. In 1684 King James II presented the King's Plate at Down Royal "to encourage the sport of horse racing". The first steeplechase, a form of race over obstacles invented by Lord Doneraile, took place in 1752 from Buttevant Church to St Leger Church near Doneraile (4.5mi/7km). In the past men challenged one another to pounding matches, in which the participants, accompanied by their grooms, had to follow the leader over any selected obstacle or admit defeat.

Bars and Pubs

More varied and more interesting than its derivatives which have been such a marketing success world-wide, the Irish pub or bar remains the centre of much social life, particularly in the countryside and in small towns, where some still double as general stores. Big-city pubs in both Belfast and Dublin can be places of almost Baroque splendour, redolent with literary or political associations. Drinking and conversation remain the patrons' principal preoccupations, but more and more pubs serve good food and very few

Central Bank, Dublin

Archére

remain an exclusively male preserve. Strangers seeking company are unlikely to remain lonely for long, and the pub is the best place to enjoy fun and good talk, the famous *craic*, as well as music, traditional or contemporary.

Economic Activity

The "Celtic Tiger"

In the 19C, Union with Britain failed for the most part to bring Ireland the benefits, as well as many of the problems, of the Industrial Revolution. The great exception was Belfast, where the existence of the linen and food processing industries stimulated the growth of general engineering. The city joined the ranks of British industrial centres, its role confirmed in the first half of the 20C, when Harland and Wolff built liners like the *Titanic* and Short built famous flying boats. Between 1939-45, the North's economy was further stimulated by the needs of war production and by the presence of British and American military bases.

By contrast, in the years following independence, the Republic concentrated on being self-sufficient rather than on modernising its economy, which remained over-reliant on farming and on the export of agricultural products to Britain. Some stimulation came from government initiatives like the Shannon hydroelectric scheme, but the high level of emigration of people of working age was a fundamental weakness of the economy. The world depression of the 1930s and a trade war with Britain further hindered progress. Ireland's neutral stance during 1939-45 may have made political sense, but brought none of the benefits of intensified production nor of the American aid which helped restore the post-war economies of other European countries. From the 1950s onwards, however, a series of measures were taken to open up the economy and stimulate growth; tax concessions and incentives encouraged export-based, modern industries and attracted foreign investment. A further boost was given when the country joined the European Economic Community in 1972. Together with investment in research and development and the existence of a highly qualified and largely un-unionised workforce, and despite intermittent setbacks, this resulted in an astonishing economic expansion; by the 1990s, the country's growth rate was twice the European Union's average, and modern industries like chemicals and pharmaceuticals, electronics and biotechnology, and information technology constituted 75% of the total industrial output. The strength of the economy of the "Celtic Tiger" meant that Ireland was able to join the single European currency project as one of the few countries complying with the criteria set by the Maastricht Treaty of 1992. The outward migration which had been such a negative feature of Irish life for centuries came to an end and net immigration began, many of the migrants being young professionals bringing with them expertise acquired abroad.

Northern Ireland, once in advance of the South in terms of industry and employment, has suffered like the rest of the United Kingdom from the decline in traditional heavy industries. Government-sponsored initiatives have not always ended in success and the halting progress of the peace process has inhibited the inflow of investment. A mitigating factor is the exceptionally high level of employment in the public sector.

Tourism has become the Republic's second largest indigenous industry. Six million overseas visitors come here every year, drawn by unspoilt landscapes, clean rivers and lakes, peace and quiet, the Celtic heritage, and the friendly welcome extended by local people. Fishing and golf remain major attractions. The once rudimentary visitor facilities are being replaced by state of the art interpretative centres while the previous somewhat carefree attitude to conservation has given way to the meticulous work of Dúchas, the government body charged with preservation of the national heritage.

Modern tourism began with the spread of the railway network in the 19C. The mountain, lake and coastal scenery of the west particularly appealed to Victorian sensibilities. Today, more than half the Republic's visitors still come from Britain, about a million from North America, and many from the over-crowded conurbations of western Europe.

Musical Traditions

Ireland is unusual in having a musical instrument – the harp – as its national emblem. Music plays a very important role in Irish life. Traditional music, song and dance are among the most vibrant aspects of Irish culture. Performances take place frequently and spontaneously in all parts of the country, and it is this very unpredictability which is responsible for much of its attraction. New songs and tunes are constantly being composed.

The harp dominated the musical scene from the Middle Ages until it was proscribed by the English because of its nationalist allure. It was used to accompany the singing or recitation of poetry. Irish harpists, who trained for many years, were admired for their rapid fingerwork and their quick and lively technique; they enjoyed high social status. **Turlough O'Carolan** (Carolan) (1670-1738) started too late in life to reach the highest standard of skill but he was an outstanding composer, much in demand; he left over 200 tunes, which show remarkable melodic invention and are still played.

The first documented mention of mouth-blown pipes in Ireland occurs in an 11C text and the earliest depiction dates from the 15C; these pipes appear to have been primarily for entertainment purposes. The particularly Irish form of pipes, the **uilleann (elbow) pipes**, which have regulators and drones oper-ated by the fingers, emerged in the 18C. These pipes are renowned for the unique sound produced by highly skilled musicians and are closely identified with Irish traditional music, which in recent years has become an important industry.

Traditional Music Today

During the 20C traditional Irish music, which formerly had been played as the accompaniment to dancing, came to be valued in its own right, and is no longer confined to isolated regions. Nowadays, traditional musicians come together in pubs throughout the country for sessions which may be formal, commercial and structured, while others are informal and free of charge. Apart from the pipes, the main instruments used are the fiddle, flute, tin whistle, accordion, concertina, melodeon, banjo, guitar, *bodhrán*, keyboard and the spoons.

Schools and festivals are held throughout the year, though mostly in summer, and people come from many countries to learn an instrument or investigate other aspects of Irish music. Some of the schools celebrate the name of a local musician, the best known of them being the **Willie Clancy Summer School**, which runs over two weekends and is held in the first half of July each year in Milltown Malbay in Co Clare. Specialist classes in regional styles of instrumental playing are also held at many schools, such as the fiddle classes in Glenties, Co Donegal, each October.

Traditional to Pop

Traditional music was popularised through the recordings made by the Irish in America and the formation of *Ceoltóirí Chualann* by Seán O'Riada in the early 1960s. This group of the highest calibre of traditional musicians created a more formalised style and generated an appreciation of Irish music. Out of this group the **Chieftains** were formed and brought Irish traditional music to a worldwide audience. In the same decade in the United States the Clancy Brothers and Tommy Makem achieved the popularisation of the Irish ballad tradition. In subsequent years many traditional music groups emerged including the **Dubliners**, the **Bothy Band**, **De Dannan**, **Planxty** and **Altan**. Members of the Brennan family from the

Irish-speaking region of Donegal penetrated the realm of popular music singing in both Irish and English as the group **Clannad**, while another member of the family, **Enya**, forged a highly successful international career as a solo artist.

During the 1950s and 1960s showbands entertained in ballrooms throughout Ireland. Musicians such as **Rory Gallagher** and **Van Morrison** began their careers in showbands before pursuing solo careers. Today showbands member such as Joe Dolan still have a considerable Irish following among the over-50s age group. Country/Irish music has a large fan base in Ireland. One of the most popular singers is Daniel O'Donnell who has been recording since the mid-1980s.

Traditional Irish music has influenced the bands of recent decades, so much so that Irish rock has often been described as "Celtic Rock". **Thin Lizzy** and **Rory Gallagher** were among the first to gain international celebrity. **Van Morrison** and U2 still continue to maintain their positions on the international stage, entertaining new generations with their brand of Irish music. More recent international celebrities **The Cranberries**, **Sinéad O'Connor** and **The Corrs** have created a worldwide interest in "Celtic" music.

Since 1993, in the wake of similar developments in the UK, a number of Irish bands were created to appeal to the teen pop market. **Boyzone**, **B*witched** and more recently **Westlife** have had huge commercial success. Boyzone members are currently embarking on solo careers; Ronan Keating has the largest following to date. Bands who came to the fore in the 1990s, making the charts in both Ireland and the UK, are Northern Ireland's Therapy, Divine Comedy and Ash. At the forefront of the Club Scene is David Holmes, a DJ turned pop star, who has gained a considerable reputation for his remixing and soundtrack work.

Bands that have not yet entered the charts have loyal fans who flock to their gigs – this underground music scene was brilliantly captured in Roddy Doyle's novel *The Commitments*.

Dance

Set dancing originated in Ireland in the 18C; it consists of figure dances, developed by travelling dancing masters, who adapted the original French dance movements to suit Irish music. Set dancing is very popular and can be seen at many public venues; classes are held on a regular basis at hundreds of places. Although it could not really be described as "traditional", the phenomenon of *Riverdance*, created in 1994 and now seen on five continents, has done for Irish dance what the Chieftains did for Irish music. Other Irish dance shows have followed, including *Lord of the Dance*.

Song

Singing forms part of many of the music festivals held in Ireland, and at least one festival is devoted solely to this art and is held each June in Ennistymon, Co Clare. Traditional singing is usually called old style *(sean-nós)* singing, and is especially closely identified with singing in Irish; songs are also sung in English in this style. Traditional songs in Irish date for the most part from the last two or three hundred years, although some are older and is the style is a good deal older still. Songs in English include recently composed songs and also many songs from the medieval ballad traditions. The style is individual, unaccompanied, free and ornate, with many regional variations. The Irish-speaking area of Rath Cairn, Co Meath, hosts the Irish-language singing festival *Eigse Dharach Uí Chatháin* in October each year.

Flavour of Ireland

Ireland is a sociable and hospitable country where people readily gather in a bar or round a table. There are two culinary traditions: the elaborate meals served in town and country mansions, and the simple dishes of earlier centuries.

Irish Cuisine

Ireland enjoys a reputation for inventive mouth-watering dishes, developed by a wave of talented home-grown chefs, who hold their own with the best in the world. They take advantage of the abundance of fresh produce – vegetables and fruit, meat and dairy products and a wide variety of fresh- and salt-water fish. The Dublin Bay prawn and the Galway oyster have a more than local reputation and the Irish have a great way with the potato, that staple of the national diet, introduced at the end of the 16C. A celebration of this great variety is the **gourmet festival** held in Kinsale.

Breakfast
The traditional **Irish Fry**, known in the north as an "Ulster Fry", consists of fried egg, sausage, bacon, black pudding, potato cakes, mushrooms and tomatoes; it is usually eaten at breakfast but is also served as the evening meal. Other breakfast dishes are kippers and kedgeree.

Fish and Meat
The king of the freshwater fish is the **salmon**, wild or farmed; as a main dish it is usually poached or grilled. Irish smoked salmon is traditionally cured with oak wood. Archaeologists have found evidence by the River Bann of a salmon weir and traces of salmon-smoking dating from 2000 BC.
The other most frequently served freshwater fish is **trout**, farmed or wild. **Shellfish**, such as crab, lobster, scallops, mussels and Dublin Bay prawns (also known as langoustines or scampi) are usually available near the coast, particularly in the southwest. Galway Bay oysters are plump and succulent.
The Irish fishing grounds produce Dover sole (known locally as black sole), lemon sole, plaice, monkfish, turbot, brill, John Dory, cod, hake, haddock, mackerel and herring.
Prime **beef** is raised on the lush pastures in the east and south of Ireland; lamb comes from the uplands. **Pork** is presented in many ways: as joints and chops; as ham or bacon; as pigs' trotters *(crúibíni)*, known in English as crubeens; in white puddings; in black puddings *(drisheen)* flavoured with tansy and eaten for breakfast. The most popular game is rabbit but hare and pheasant are also served.

Traditional Dishes
There is no official recipe for **Irish stew**, which consists of neck of mutton layered in a pot with potatoes, onions and herbs. **Colcannon** is a Harvest or Hallowe'en dish of mashed potatoes, onions, parsnips and white cabbage, mixed with butter and cream. **Champ** is a simpler dish of potatoes mashed with butter to which are added chopped chives or other green vegetables such as parsley, spring onions (scallions), chopped shallots, nettles, peas, cabbage or even carrots (cooked in milk which is added to the purée). Nettles are also made into soup.

Table laid for a Farmhouse Tea

To make **coddle** a forehock of bacon, pork sausages, potatoes and onions are stewed in layers. Collar and cabbage is composed of a collar of bacon, which has been boiled, coated in breadcrumbs and brown sugar and baked, served with cabbage cooked in the bacon stock.

Various sorts of **seaweed**, a highly nutritious source of vitamins and minerals, were traditionally used to thicken soups and stews. **Carrageen** is still used to make a dessert with a delicate flavour. **Dulse** is made into a sweet.

Dairy Products

Irish cookery makes liberal use of butter and cream. Ice cream is particularly popular as a dessert. In recent years many hand-made **cheeses** have appeared on the market: **Cashel Blue** (a soft, creamy, blue-veined cheese made from cow's milk in Tipperary; milder than Stilton), **Cooleeny** (a Camembert-type soft cheese from Thurles in Co Tipperary), **Milleens** (a distinctive spicy cheese from West Cork; as it matures the rind is washed with salt water), **Gubbeen** (soft surface-ripening cheese from Skull in Co Cork).

Bread

A great variety of breads and cakes is baked for breakfast and tea. The most well-known is **soda bread**, made of white or brown flour and buttermilk. **Barm Brack** is a rich fruit cake made with yeast (*báirín breac* – speckled cake).

Beverages

Stout made by **Guinness** or Murphys is the traditional thirst-quencher in Ireland but the drinking of ales (bitter) and lagers is not uncommon. Black Velvet is a mixture of stout and champagne.

Although there are now only three **whiskey** distilleries in Ireland – Bushmills in Co Antrim, which produces the only malt, and Midleton in Co Cork, both owned by the same company, and Cooley in Dundalk – there are many different brands of whiskey. Their distinctive flavours arise from subtle variations in the production process.

For a patriotic drink ask for **The Flag**, a mixture of crème de menthe, tequila and Southern Comfort representing the green, white and orange of the Republican tricolor.

Irish Coffee, a delicious creation, consists of a measure of whiskey, brown sugar and very hot black coffee mixed in a heated glass and topped with a layer of fresh cream.

Myths and Fairies

Some of the best sources for understanding the Celtic mind and imagination are the Irish myths and tales. Most of the earlier stories originated in Ireland and, although many were written by Christian monks, they contain descriptions of gods and goddesses as well as of mortal heroes and heroines.

Religion

The Celts seem to have acknowledged many divinities – gods of war and hunting and goddesses of fertility, harvest and healing. Among those worshipped in Ireland were Brigit and Daghdha; another was Cernunnos, god of animals, plants and forests, whose emblem was antlers. Each tribe had its own tribal god, which varied from tribe to tribe. They believed that certain goddesses lived in sacred wells and that the water goddesses had the power to cure and protect people. They regarded not only wells, but certain springs and rivers – particularly the River Boyne – and trees as sacred. They carved images of their gods on tree-trunks. Assemblies, at which games and races took place, were held at ancient royal or assembly sites, such as Tara and Tullaghoge. The Celts buried their dead, sometimes cremated, with offerings of food and ornaments; they believed that after death they went to join their ancestors, the gods of the Otherworld, who were thought to live in sacred mounds, now known to be prehistoric burial mounds such as at Newgrange, Tara and Rathcrogan.

Fairy Lore

The belief in the **Otherworld** is still an important factor in Irish tradition. This "Otherworld" may exist in a fort or in a mountain, under a lake or under the sea. Hundreds of tales and legends associated with the fairies and their world survive, as the landscape and its placenames bear witness. In Irish the fairies are called *sí* or *na daoine maithe* – the good people, or *na daoine beaga* – the little people. The fairies are said variously to be fallen angels, the ancient gods – the Tuatha Dé Danann – or sometimes the community of the dead. They are believed to be a supernatural community generally invisible to mortals. They inhabit the earth, the air and water and place names indicating fairy involvement of some kind are very common. The earthen tumuli – known as *rath* and *lios* – are often said to be fairy forts and sometimes fairy music can be heard to emanate from them. Many legends are told describing how the fairies "borrowed" or "stole" a mortal to assist them in some task of their own, such as nursing a fairy child or playing music at a fairy wedding. Fairies were also known to remove a mortal child and leave one of their own in its place; parents returning from their chores to find a sick or dying child in the cradle quickly realised that it was a "changeling".

Castlestrange Stone

SLIDE FILE, Dublin

S Allegret/MICHELIN

The giddy little creature depicted here is Ireland's national fairy, the leprechaun. About two feet high – when upright! – and usually of rather wizened appearance, the leprechaun is a cobbler by trade, though he is better known as the crafty guardian of a hidden crock of gold. A mischievous player of tricks on the human race, he steals into their houses at night to create havoc in kitchen and cellar.

Banshee

The Banshee *(Bean Sí)* is a solitary female spirit and when her eerie cry is heard it is a portent of death. Traditions of the banshee are still very strong and many legends are told about her, some depicting her combing her long hair. One legend tells how a man finds her comb and brings it home. The following night he hears wailing and knocking on his window. He catches the comb in a pair of tongs and passes it out of the window. The comb is removed by the banshee and the tongs are broken or damaged; the man then understands that his hand would have met the same fate had he passed the comb with his hand.

The banshee is associated with lamenting, keening and death. The keen *(caoineadh)* was performed by women at funerals and at wakes as part of the lament for the dead. Certain, usually older, women in the community came to the house where the corpse was laid out and took it in turns to perform the keen which was usually composed *ex tempore* and sung to music with a regular refrain during the days of the wake and later at the graveyard. During the wake people also told stories, smoked clay pipes, drank whiskey and played games. The clergy disapproved of many of the wake customs and of the keen.

The Mythological and Historical Cycles

The stories from the four great ancient Irish cycles are arguably among the finest expressions of the Irish imagination and are still a source of artistic inspiration.

The **Mythological Cycle** tells of the heroes or gods who inhabited Ireland before the arrival of the Celts and contains the story of the Battle of Moytura, the Children of Lir and the Wooing of Etain.

The **Ulster Cycle** *(Rúraíocht)* recounts the deeds of the Red Branch Knights of Navan Fort; it includes the **Cattle Raid of Cooley** *(Táin Bó Cuailgne)*, an epic poem which describes how Queen Maeve of Connaught set out to capture the famous brown bull of Cooley and how Ferdia, the Connaught champion, was defeated by the Ulster champion, Cúchulain, which means the hound of Culann.

The **Ossianic Cycle**, also known as the **Fenian Cycle** *(Fiannaíocht)*, is set in the time of Cormac mac Airt, who is said to have reigned at Tara in the 3C, and tells about Fionn mac Cumhaill and the Fianna, whose capital was on the Hill of Allen. The Fenian tales and lore tell of the great deeds of the Fianna or Fenian warriors. Hundreds of Neolithic tombs are called Diarmuid and Gráinne's bed *(Leaba Dhiarmuid agus Ghráinne)* in the belief that these lovers from the Fenian tales slept here during their travels in Ireland.

The **Historical Cycle**, which is also known as the **Cycle of the Kings**, is probably a mixture of history and fiction. Many place names and sites identify with characters and episodes from mythological tales.

A vast number of tales and episodes from these cycles were central to the living storytelling tradition in Ireland until very recently. In addition to their preservation in written literature, the stories were kept alive in oral form, both in Irish and in English, and formed an important part of the repertoire of the storyteller *(seanchaí)*, who was a person of great social importance.

Land of Saints

It is Patrick, Ireland's much-revered patron saint, popularly supposed to have used the shamrock to illustrate the doctrine of the Holy Trinity, who is held responsible for converting the Irish to Christianity. An earlier mission, probably from Roman Britain or Gaul, occurred in the 4C; in 431 Palladius was appointed the first bishop by Pope Celestine I but his efforts met with little success.

The majority (75%) of the population of Ireland is Roman Catholic but most of the country's Roman Catholic churches are of recent date; the traditional religious sites are usually occupied by Anglican churches, a reminder that for many years the Church of Ireland was the country's established church. Many Roman Catholic churches stand in new centres of population though others were built close to a ruined monastery where the faithful heard Mass in the Penal Days and where they continue to be buried.

National Saints

St Patrick – The patron saint of Ireland was born on the west coast of Roman Britain where he was captured as a young man by Irish raiders. After six years of slavery near Sliabh Mis (Slemish in Co Down), he escaped to France and then returned to his birthplace. Inspired by a vision that the people of Ireland were calling him, he went to France to study, possibly at the monasteries of Lérins, Tours and Auxerre. In 432 in middle age he returned to Ireland to convert the people to Christianity. He is thought to have founded his first church at Saul and then travelled to Slane where he challenged the power of the High King and his druids.

In 444, after a visit to Rome, he founded the cathedral church of Armagh, still the ecclesiastical capital of Ireland, as well as many other churches. When he died, probably at Saul in 461, the country was organised into dioceses based on the petty Irish kingdoms.

Patrick is the subject of numerous tales and legends, according to which he banished monsters and drove the snakes out of Ireland.

On St Patrick's day (17 March) people wear a sprig of **shamrock** *(seamróg)*, a custom which is comparatively recent, being first documented in the latter part of the 17C; it is claimed that the saint used this trefoil plant to illustrate the doctrine of the Holy Trinity.

St Bridget – Brigit was a Celtic goddess, whose name means "the exalted person"; it is significant that the same name is given to the most popular female saint in Irish tradition and second only to St Patrick among all the saints. This Leinster saint ("Bríd"), who died c AD 524, established a convent in Kildare *(Cill Dara* in Irish meaning "the church of the oak tree") and this may have been a sacred spot in pre-Christian times. Bridget is perceived to be the protectress of animals and crops, with which she is closely associated.

The most popular legend of St Bridget is associated with Kildare, where she wished to build a convent. The local king refused to grant her more land than could be covered by her cloak, but when she spread her garment it expanded to cover a vast area.

On St Bridget's day (1 February) it is customary to honour the saint by making straw or rush crosses *(Cros Bhríde)*, which have numerous regional variations in design and form.

St Patrick, Bangor Abbey

IRISH MISSIONARY MONKS

The work of monks from Ireland in re-Christianising Europe after the barbarian invasions was so extensive that it has been claimed that the Irish were responsible for saving civilisation. In the late 6C, Columbanus founded monasteries in Luxeuil, Annegray and Fontaines in France and Bobbio in Italy ; his disciple **Gall** gave his name to Switzerland's most renowned monastery, which has preserved a fine collection of Irish manuscripts. **Columba** (Colmcille in Irish) left his native country to found the monastery on Iona ; monks from there moved on to Lindisfarne in the north of England and to the court of Charlemagne. **Fursey** founded a monastery at Lagny near Paris, while **Johanne Eriugena** achieved renown as a philosopher at Laon. Several Irish monks went to Germany and beyond, **Kilian** to Würzburg, Virgil in the 8C to Salzburg, **Marianus Scottus** in the 11C to Cologne, Fulda and Mainz, and a namesake, a member of an important Donegal family, to Regensburg. The most-travelled monk, however, was probably **Brendan** *(see Ennis)*, who may have reached America.

Celtic Church

As continental Europe was overrun by barbarians, the church in Ireland developed a distinctive form of organisation based on monasticism. In the mid-6C and 7C a great many monasteries were founded and by the 8C the administration of the church had been taken over by the abbots. Although bishops continued to perform the sacramental duties and new bishops were consecrated, they were not appointed to particular sees.

Some **monasteries** grew up round a hermit's retreat but many were founded by the head of a clan; members of the family entered the religious life and filled the various offices, as abbot, bishop, priest, teacher or ascetic. The manual work was done either by the monks or by the original tenants of the land, married men with families, whose elder sons usually received a clerical education in the monastery school. Most monasteries were self-sufficient communities providing their own food, clothing, books, tools and horses. Some monasteries seem to have been founded on sites which had pagan religious associations; others were set up by the main highways, often on the boundaries of a kingdom.

The monastic **libraries** contained copies of the Scriptures, the early Fathers, some classical authors and some history; much early Christian scholarship was preserved in Ireland after the fall of the Roman Empire. In the scriptorium the monks made copies of existing texts or wrote their own learned works, using meticulous techniques which are well described and illustrated at the Colmcille Heritage Centre *(see Donegal Glens)*.

Irish monks developed a strong tradition of **asceticism** with a threefold classification of martyrdom. Ascetics seeking to contemplate the presence of God would form small monastic communities in remote places, particularly on islands like the harsh and remote rock of Great Skellig.

Ardagh Chalice (8C)

National Museum of Ireland, Dublin

Romanisation

Following four synods held in the first half of the 12C the Irish church lost its distinctive character and was gradually reorganised on the Roman pattern. Four provinces and 33 new dioceses were created, each with a bishop. Some monastic churches became cathedrals, others were used as parish churches.

Monastic orders from the Continent were introduced. The Augustinians took over earlier monastic centres to be near the people. The Cistercians chose new and remote sites in accordance with their ascetic rule, which attracted many Irish monks; by 1272 there were 38 Cistercian houses in Ireland. The Franciscans settled in the towns in the 13C; in the 15C the Observants spread to the west and north.

The Irish church was further diminished by the Normans with the encouragement of King Henry II and Popes Adrian IV and Alexander III so as "to extend the bounds of the Roman Church". Under the Statute of Kilkenny (1366) Irishmen were forbidden to enter English-run monasteries, and English-speaking clergy were to be appointed to English-speaking parishes.

Reformation

In the 16C the churches in England and Ireland were declared independent of Rome; the monasteries were suppressed. Trinity College in Dublin was founded in 1591 to provide Irish priests for the established church; although Roman Catholics were admitted to degrees in 1793, membership was confined to Anglicans until 1873. The 16C reforms were only intermittently enforced in Ireland; the majority of the people remained faithful to the Roman church and many monasteries continued until suppressed by Cromwell. Early in the 17C the Plantation of Ulster with lowland Scots introduced fervent Presbyterianism.

Penal Laws

Under the repressive measures introduced after the Battle of the Boyne (1690), Roman Catholics were barred from the armed forces, law, commerce, from civic office or office under the crown, and from land purchase; Roman Catholic estates could pass *in toto* to an eldest son if he converted to the established church but otherwise had to be divided among all the sons. No Roman Catholic could attend school, keep a school or go abroad to school. Education was conducted in **hedge schools**, which taught Latin, Greek, arithmetic, Irish, English, history and geography; the masters, who were paid in money or kind, were respected members of the Irish community; several were poets. All Roman Catholic bishops and regular clergy were banished from Ireland, and Roman Catholic worship was forbidden. Roman Catholic priests travelled the country in disguise and said Mass out of doors in remote places or in ruined monastery churches; they used sacramental vessels which could be dismantled to avoid detection.

Dissenters

Roman Catholics were not alone in suffering repression. The Scottish Presbyterians who had migrated to Ulster were frequently regarded with disfavour, though the Protestant Ascendancy could not afford to alienate them completely. The Toleration Act of 1719 granted them freedom of worship, but they continued to endure various disabilities and particularly resented the obligation to pay tithes to the established Church of Ireland; in the 18C many of them emigrated to America, though the majority remained. Their dissatisfaction with the existing order found expression in widespread support for the rebellion of 1798, when a large proportion of the membership of the United Irishmen was composed of Presbyterians. The English Quakers who came to Ireland during the Civil War period also faced discrimination of various kinds, though by the beginning of the 18C this had diminished. Like their counterparts elsewhere, and despite their generally humble beginnings, many Quakers later achieved prominence in commerce and industry.

Denominational Freedom

Under the Catholic Relief Acts of 1791 and 1793, freedom of worship and education were granted. In 1795 **Maynooth Seminary** was established for training Roman Catholic clergy. In 1820 Edmund Rice (1762-1844), a former pupil of a hedge school, obtained papal recognition of the **Christian Brothers** *(see Kilkenny)*, an order which established many boys' schools in Ireland. In 1831 the 18C hedge schools were replaced by the National Schools. In 1869 the Church of Ireland, a member of the Anglican Communion, was disestablished. Apart from Trinity College and two short-lived 16C colleges at Maynooth and Galway, Ireland had no medieval universities. In 1845 charters were issued to incorporate three colleges in Belfast, Cork and Galway but, owing to Roman Catholic opposition, only Queen's College in Belfast thrived. The Catholic University, founded in Dublin in 1854 with Cardinal Newman as Rector, was incorporated as University College when the National University of Ireland was founded in 1908; two years later Maynooth was also recognised as a college of the National University.

Pilgrimages and Patterns

Since the 8C, by which time Ireland was an almost entirely Christian country, the lives of the **saints** have played a major role in popular devotion and also stimulated an entire body of related legends and lore. Saints were seen to be powerful in many spheres of life on earth and in the afterlife; in many instances, they were seen as popular heroes and heroines. Some were said to have had a miraculous birth; others wielded supernatural powers and could triumph against the enemy. Saints had healing powers and even their posessions or relics could effect a cure.

SLIDE FILE, Dublin

Pilgrims climbing Croagh Patrick

Oral tradition has been profoundly influenced by biographies of saints; the lore of saints is widespread throughout Ireland. Thousands of **holy wells**, many associated with local saints, are scattered throughout the countryside; they are said to have curative powers – of a general type or more specific – and are visited frequently, particularly on saints' days.

People still observe the feast days of local saints and the **pattern** (modern Irish *pátrún*; the word is a corruption of patron) when they make a communal visit to a holy well or other religious site under the protection of the local patron saint. In many places holy wells are associated with **rag trees**, named after the hundreds of coloured pieces of cloth attached to their branches, and used to invoke divine assistance, often of a curative kind.

Many traditional religious sites are still visited by pilgrims: Glencolumbkille on St Columba's Day (9 June); Clonmacnoise on St Kieran's Day (9 September); Croagh Patrick in July, when people climb barefoot to the summit. The most rigorous pilgrimage takes place at St Patrick's Purgatory, an island in Lough Derg (southeast of Donegal) where St Patrick spent 40 days in prayer and fasting; during the season (1 June to 15 August) pilgrims spend three days barefoot, take part in an all-night vigil and exist on one meal a day of bread and hot black tea or coffee.

Irish Diaspora

Forty million people of Irish descent live in the USA, 5 million in Canada, 5 million in Australia and unnumbered millions in Great Britain. Estimates suggest that over 60 million people in the world are of Irish origin. The influence of Irish people worldwide is immeasurable and disproportionate to the size of their country of origin.

The imposition of the Anglican Reformation in the reign of Elizabeth I caused a number to leave Munster for Spain and Portugal. The conquest of 1603 caused more departures to Spain and Brittany. Cromwell transported whole regiments, possibly 34 000 men, to Spain and Portugal, while many civilians were shipped to the West Indies where they could be sold as slaves. The Treaty of Limerick in 1691 was followed by the flight of the so-called "Wild Geese", military men who, together with their wives and children, emigrated to France, where they served in the French army until 1697; some of them moved on to Spain, where three Irish regiments were formed. The most famous name among the merchants who settled on the western coast of Europe is that of Richard Hennessy, from Cork, who started the Cognac company.

The first transatlantic emigrants were mostly Presbyterians, the Ulster-Scots (known in the USA as Scots-Irish or Scotch-Irish), descendants of lowland Scots who had settled in Ulster in the 17C. Whole families emigrated early in the 18C owing to religious disability and rising rents. The Roman Catholic Irish tended to emigrate as single young adults, both men and women.

The Scotch-Irish had an influence in America out of all proportion to their numbers, particularly in the War of Independence and in education. The heartland of Ulster settlement was in the Appalachian back country; the name hillbilly derives from King William III. Many of the settlers were involved in pushing the frontier westwards and building the American railways. Over a quarter of the Presidents of the USA have been descended from Scotch-Irish settlers. This Irish-American connection is traced in detail at the Ulster-American Folk Park *(see Sperrin Mountains)* and Andrew Jackson Centre *(see Carrickfergus)* as well as several other family homesteads. Allied military leaders in the Second World War who were of Ulster stock include Alanbrooke, Alexander, Auchinleck, Dill and Montgomery.

Following the Napoleonic Wars emigration recommenced and during the next 25 years over a million Irishmen and women emigrated to Great Britain and the USA.

Emigration reached its peak during the Great Famine when Ireland lost 4 million people, through death and emigration; during the worst years about 1 million fled and another 2.5 million emigrated in the following decade. The great wave of 19C emigrants was largely composed of Roman Catholics from Donegal, Connaught, Munster and Leinster, counties which until then had not seen much emigration. Many landed first in Canada but later crossed the frontier into the USA to escape from British rule. Their descendants include John Fitzgerald Kennedy, Ronald Reagan and William Jefferson Clinton.

ULSTER-SCOTS – SCOTCH-IRISH
Theodore Roosevelt's mother, speaking of her family who came from Co Antrim, described them as "a grim stern people, strong and simple, powerful for good and evil, swayed by gusts of stormy passion, the love of freedom rooted in their very hearts' core ... relentless, revengeful, suspicious, knowing neither ruth nor pity; they were also upright, resolute and fearless, loyal to their friends and devoted to their country".

Emigrant Ship
by E Hayes

The numbers who emigrated to Australia and New Zealand were smaller and included some who were transported to the penal colonies.

The flow of immigrants into Great Britain has waxed and waned since the Irish established colonies in Wales and Scotland in the 5C. Many, particularly those who left Ireland during the Famine in the hope of reaching America but were too weak or penniless to continue, settled in Liverpool and Glasgow. London has a flourishing Irish community, particularly north of the river. Margaret Thatcher, Prime Minister of the United Kingdom (1978-91), is descended from Catherine Sullivan, who emigrated in 1811 from Kenmare and became a washerwoman in England.

In the 18C and 19C many Irishmen, who went to work in Britain on the canals or in agriculture and the building trade, returned home for the winter. Those who went to America or Australasia seldom returned to the mother country. Despite their rural origins most Irish emigrants settled in the big cities rather than on the land of their adopted countries.

Irish emigrants in the late 20C are highly qualified young men and women seeking employment not only in English-speaking countries such as Great Britain and the USA but also throughout the countries of the European Union. In recent years emigration has declined and immigration has increased. In 1997 there was a net inflow of 15 000 people, the highest such figure since the 1970s. Many of these people are the same highly qualified former emigrants, returning to the higher standards of living and new culturally revitalised society of modern Ireland.

Tracing Ancestors

Many people who visit Ireland on holiday, particularly from Australia, New Zealand and the USA, are hoping to trace their grandparents or great-grandparents who left Ireland and settled abroad. This task is more difficult than it could have been owing to the destruction during the Civil War of the the national archives dating from 1174. In the latter years of the 20C a great project was set in motion to collect all the information available from parish records, tombstones and other sources throughout Ireland. Access to these computer records and assistance in tracing ancestors can be obtained through the many regional Genealogical Centres which are listed in the Directories of the appropriate chapters in the Selected Sights section. If you have no idea where in Ireland your ancestors came from, it is best to consult one of the national organisations in Dublin *(see Practical Points – Ideas for your Visit)*.

A good way of exchanging news or meeting long-lost relatives is to attend one of the annual clan gatherings which are held on ancestral sites by some of the 243 Irish clans.

Gaelige

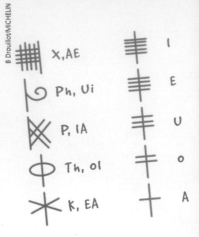

Gaelige, Irish or Gaelic – whichever name is used – is a subtle and extremely expressive language. Although rarely used, it has had a profound influence on the way the Irish use English, which has largely replaced it. Irish is an Indo-European language, one of the Celtic group – Scots Gaelic, the extinct Manx, Welsh, Cornish and Breton – and is closest to Scots Gaelic and Manx. Its wonderfully stylish alphabet, abandoned in the 1960s, can still be seen in old road signs and in other situations where its decorative qualities are appreciated.

Once the natural language of the whole island, Irish has been remorselessly displaced by English, and today is spoken as a first language by only a small minority, some 60 000 in all. Nevertheless it enjoys official status as the first official language of the Republic, remains an important badge of Irish identity and has been consistently promoted by government and cultural organisations since independence; over 40% of adults claim to be able to speak Irish. It has a complex grammar and a pronunciation which most outsiders find difficult to grasp; consonants may remain mute or change their sound according to their position. Even monoglot English speakers have become familiar with the use of the Irish language in official expressions; the prime minister is always referred to as the Taoiseach, the Parliament as Dáil Eireann, the Tourist Board as Bord Fáilte, the national railway as Iarnród Éireann, and all buses heading for the city centre in Dublin bear the direction An Lár.

Ogham Script

The earliest known form of writing in the Irish language is in **Ogham script**. Most of the inscriptions are memorials of the dead and date from the 4C to 7C. The script is based on the Latin alphabet and was probably adapted by poets and wise men before the Latin alphabet became more generally familiar in Christian Ireland. The script consists of 20 characters written as groups of a maximum of five straight lines on either side of, or horizontally or diagonally through, a central line which was usually cut into the vertical edge of a standing stone. Many of these standing stones are found in the southern districts of Ireland.

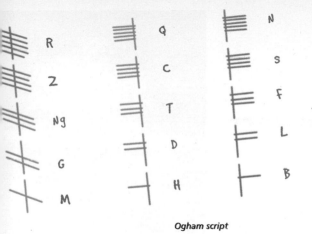

Ogham script

Transition to English

The decline in the use of Irish was caused by the gradual imposition of English law and administration in the 16C and the repressive clauses of the Penal Laws *(see Historical Perspective)* in the 17C. Many Irish people turned to English to achieve a position in society. This trend was accelerated by the teaching of English in the National Schools, which were set up in 1831. During and after the Famine (1845-47) many Irish speakers died or emigrated; in 1835 half the population was estimated to speak Irish; in 1851 one-quarter of the population was recorded as Irish-speaking; by 1911 the number had fallen to one-eighth.

Gaelic Revival

The 19C saw a revival of interest in Ireland's Gaelic heritage, which was closely linked with nationalist politics. Various societies were set up to promote Irish language and culture.

The **Irish Literary Society** was founded in 1892. William Butler Yeats was joined by Edward Martyn and Lady Gregory and in 1899 the society became the **Irish Literary Theatre** (later the Irish National Theatre at the Abbey Theatre); George Moore returned to Dublin especially to take part in the new movement.

In 1893 the **Gaelic League** *(Conradh na Gaeilge)* was founded by Douglas Hyde *(see Strokestown)* for the "de-Anglicisation of Ireland" through the revival of Gaelic as a spoken language and a return to Irish cultural roots. It instituted an annual festival of native culture and campaigned sucessfully for St Patrick's Day (17 March) to be a national holiday.

In 1922 the Constitution stated that Gaelic was an official language and its study was made compulsory in primary schools. The following year it became an obligatory qualification for entry into the Civil Service of the Irish Free State and the Constitution of 1937 named it as the first offical language.

In 1925 in order to foster the use of Irish the new government set up a Commission to investigate conditions in the Gaelic-speaking districts; as a result of its report two organisations – **Gaeltarra Éireann** (1935) and **Údarás na Gaeltachta** (1980) – were established to develop the resources of these areas, collectively known as the **Gaeltacht**. With a total population of over 80 000 (not all of whom are Irish speaking) these are mostly in the most sparsely populated, remote and beautiful western parts of the country – Donegal, Mayo, Galway and Kerry   though there are pockets in the south – near Cork, in Co Waterford and Co Meath. Today, the government's Department of Arts, Heritage, Gaeltacht and the Islands is charged with their social and economic welfare and with the promotion of the Irish language. The radio station *Raidió na Gaeltachta* has broadcast in Irish since 1972, and since 1996 there has been a national television service, *Telefís na Gaeilge*. The summer schools started during the 19C Gaelic revival have become a permanent feature of the Gaeltacht, inspiring and entertaining each new generation.

Letters

Irish men and women of letters have made a significant contribution to English literature through poetry, novels and drama. Poetry was an art form practised by the Celtic bard and medieval monk but theatrical performances were unknown to Gaelic society. To the English language the Irish brought a talent for fantasy, wit and satire and Gaelic speech patterns. Four Irish writers have been awarded the Nobel Prize for Literature: William Butler Yeats in 1923, George Bernard Shaw in 1925, Samuel Beckett in 1969 and Seamus Heaney in 1995.

National Gallery of Ireland, Dublin

Celtic Influence

The Celts may not have left a written literature but their oral tradition has bequeathed a rich legacy of myth and history which inspired later generations.

The work of the monks in the scriptorium of a Celtic monastery was to copy biblical and other religious texts and to write their own commentaries. They decorated their work, particularly the first capital letter of a chapter, with highly ornate Celtic patterns. Several of these **illuminated manuscripts**, of which the most famous is the Book of Kells, are displayed in the Old Library of Trinity College in Dublin.

One account from this early period is *Navigatio*, written in medieval Latin, an account of the voyage from Ireland to America made by St Brendan in the 6C *(see Ennis)*.

Anglo-Irish Literature

The first flowering of Anglo-Irish literature came in the late 17C and 18C when George Farquhar (1678-1707) wrote his stage works, Oliver Goldsmith (1728-74) composed poetry, novels and plays and Richard Brinsley Sheridan (1751-1816) his satirical comedies, including *School for Scandal*.

The major figure of this period was **Jonathan Swift** (1667-1745) *(see also p 229)* who was born in Ireland, studied at Trinity College, Dublin, and spent many years in England before being appointed Dean of St Patrick's Cathedral in Dublin where he stayed until his death. *Gulliver's Travels* is the most famous of his satirical writings on 18C Irish society.

His friend and fellow student, **William Congreve** (1670-1729) wrote witty costume dramas, such as *The Way of the World*, which inspired Wilde and Shaw.

After spending his early childhood among his mother's relatives in Ireland, **Laurence Sterne** (1713-68), made his name in England as an innovator among novelists with *Tristram Shandy* and *A Sentimental Journey*; he is also seen as a forerunner of the stream of consciousness technique practised by James Joyce.

Many Irish writers who achieved success and fame moved to London, where they made a significant contribution to English literature and theatre. The name of the novel *Dracula* is better known than its author, **Bram Stoker** (1847-1912), who worked for several years as an Irish civil servant, writing drama reviews, before moving to London as Henry Irving's manager; only his first novel, *A Snake's Pass*, is set in Ireland. George Moore (1852-1933) described high society in Dublin *(Drama in Muslin)* and introduced the realism of Zola into the novel *(Esther Waters)*. **Oscar Wilde** (1854-1900) achieved huge success in the London theatre with his plays *(Lady Windermere's Fan, The Importance of Being Earnest)* and in society with his distinctive dress and style, and notoriety for his disgrace and prison term in Reading Gaol. **George Bernard Shaw** (1856-1950) commented on the Anglo-Irish dilemma in his journalism and his play *John Bull's Other Island* and explored the contradictions of English society *(Pygmalion)*.

Irish Themes

Several successful authors chose Irish themes for their work. Maria Edgeworth (1767-1849) achieved international fame and the admiration of Sir Walter Scott with her novels *Castle Rackrent* and *The Absentee*; William Carleton (1794-1869) wrote about rural life in County Tyrone. The theme of the novel *The Collegians* by Gerald Griffin (1803-40) was reworked by Dion Boucicault for the stage as *The Colleen Bawn* and by Benedict as an opera, *The Lily of Killarney*. **Anthony Trollope** (1815-82), who began his literary career while working for the Post Office in Ireland, wrote several novels on Irish themes. Canon Sheehan (1852-1913) was admired in Russia by Tolstoy and in the USA for his novels about rural life. Somerville and Ross, a literary partnership composed of **Edith Somerville** (1858-1949) and her cousin, Violet Florence Martin (1862-1915), whose pen-name was **Martin Ross**, produced novels about Anglo-Irish society, *The Real Charlotte* and the highly humorous *Experiences of an Irish RM*, adapted for TV in the 1980s.

Irish Literary Renaissance

In the 19C, as part of the **Gaelic Revival** *(see Gaelige)*, a literary renaissance was taking place in Ireland, based to a large extent in folklore. One of its early influential figures was George Russell (1867-1935), known as AE, mystic, poet and painter, economist and journalist. The leader of this literary movement and the dominant writer of the period was **William Butler Yeats** (1856-1939), who established his name as a poet and playwright and was a founder member of the Abbey Theatre. He lived for a number of years in County Sligo and he recognised the power of the native imagination in Irish oral tradition, especially in the heroic tales and in mythological material, which greatly influenced his writing. His own understanding of the occult influenced his involvement in and interpretations of Irish lore. His *Fairy and Folk Tales of the Irish Peasantry*, first published in 1888, was followed by *Irish Fairy Tales* in 1892. Here he made the distinction between folktale, legend and myth; he was among the first writers to interpret Irish folklore. He admired Douglas Hyde because of Hyde's honest commitment to the Irish language and to native Irish lore. Yeats was part of a group of people who associated Anglo-Irish writing with the revival of a culture which was in danger of disappearing, to a large extent owing to social development. Another leading light in this movement was **Augusta, Lady Gregory** (1852-1932), who lived in County Galway and became friendly with Yeats. They were much influenced by one another and collected folklore together. Among her best-known works is *Visions and Beliefs in the West of Ireland* (1920), which is based on 20 years of work in this area with Yeats. The *Kiltartan History Book* (1909) contained, for the first time, accounts and descriptions of many aspects of historical lore, unchanged from the oral narration of local people. She was one of the first to publish folklore material unedited just as she had collected it. In common with Yeats, she recognised the richness of folklore among the "farmers and potato-diggers and old men" in her own district, the unbroken chain of tradition and the wealth of ballads, tales and lore which was part of the everyday life of the ordinary people around her in County Galway.

Some of the greatest successes written for the **Abbey Theatre** were the plays of **John Millington Synge** (1871-1909), *Riders to the Sea* and *Playboy of the Western World*, inspired by the Aran Islands, and *The Shadow of the Glen*, inspired by the Wicklow Mountains, where language dominates in the bleak landscape; and the pacifist plays of **Sean O'Casey** (1880-1964), *The Shadow of a Gunman, Juno and the Paycock* and *The Plough and the Stars*, written in the aftermath of the First World War.

Literary Exiles

The narrow-mindedness of Irish society is expressed in the drama and fiction of George Moore (1852-1933), who spent part of his early life in Paris, and even more so in the work of **James Joyce** (1882-1941), often considered to be the greatest and certainly the most innovative of 20C writers in English. The appearance of his short story collection, *Dubliners*, was long delayed because of the publisher's attempts to impose cuts. Joyce's anti-clerical and anti-nationalist views led him to leave Dublin in 1904 for exile, first in Trieste, then in Zürich and Paris. His most influential work, the vast novel *Ulysses*, recounts a day in the life of Jewish Dubliner Leopold Bloom as he moves around the city in a strange reprise of the wanderings of Homer's hero. The novel revels in the English language and pushes it to its limits, exploiting the devices of interior monologue and stream of consciousness to extraordinary effect. Dwelling on the most intimate details of everyday life, it was banned not just in Ireland but in Britain and America as well. The even more monumental *Finnegan's Wake* takes these developments even further, exploiting not just the potential of English but of scores of other languages and delighting in word-play and paradox of the utmost complexity.

Much influenced by Joyce, and an associate of his during the older writer's sojourn in Paris, **Samuel Beckett** (1906-89) is remembered mainly as one of the founders of the Theatre of the Absurd. Like Joyce, Beckett found life in Ireland unbearably constricting and spent most of his life in France, being decorated for his work in the Resistance in the Second World War. Unlike Joyce, Beckett honed his language to the bare minimum required to convey his grim vision of human life as an "intolerable existence not worthwhile terminating". His best-known work is the play *En Attendant Godot/Waiting for Godot*, written in French and then translated by the author himself. First produced in 1953 and provoking acclaim and bafflement in equal measure, it is the austere and apparently inconsequential tale of two tramps waiting in vain for a mysterious being who never makes an appearance.

Modern Writing in Ireland

The early 20C produced the bleak realistic poetry of **Patrick Kavanagh** from Monaghan (1904-67 *Ploughman and Other Poems*) – whose influence can be seen in the work of John Montague (b 1929 *The Rough Field*) and Northern poet **Seamus Heaney** (b 1939 *The Death of a Naturalist*) – and of Louis MacNeice (1907-63), who was a member of Auden's circle and an early influence on Derek Mahon (b 1941 *The Hudson Letter*). Novelists included Flann O'Brien (1911-66, real name Brian O'Nolan), who wrote a famous newspaper column as Myles na Gopaleen.

The theme of the Big House survives in the work of Elizabeth Bowen (1899-1973 *The Last September*), **Molly Keane**, writing as MJ Farrell (1905-97 *The Last Puppetstown*), Aidan Higgins (b 1927 *Langrishe, Go Down*), and Jennifer Johnston (b 1930 *The Illusionist*) and in *Woodbrook* (1974) by David Thompson.

Influential writers include **John B Keane** (1928-2002), whose work is firmly set in Co Kerry – his first play *Sive* won the all-Ireland drama festival; *The Field* was made into a film in 1990 and his best novel is *The Bodhran Makers*; also **Edna O'Brien** (b 1932 *The Country Girls*), whose frank accounts of female sexuality in the 1950s were banned in Ireland on first publication and publicly burned in her home village in Co Clare, and the highly acclaimed **John MacGahern** (b 1934 *Amongst Women*), now living in Co Leitrim. *Troubles* by **JG Farrell** (1935-79) brings rare humour to the grim reality of the War of Independence. **Maeve Binchy** (b 1940) writes in lighter vein about episodes in Irish family life. Brendan Behan (1923-64), who was involved in IRA activity at an early age and imprisoned in both Britain and Ireland, made use of these experiences in the vivid and humorous writing of the plays *The Quare Fellow* and *The Hostage* (the latter originally written in Irish) and in his autobiography *Borstal Boy*.

National Gallery of Ireland, Dublin

Northern Irish writers Brian Moore (b 1921 *The Lonely Passion of Judith Hearne*), Patrick McCabe (b 1955 *Butcher Boy*) and Eoin MacNamee (b 1960 *Resurrection Man*) have all seen their work quickly turned into films, as have many writers from the south, including **Roddy Doyle** (b 1958 *The Commitments* and *Paddy Clarke Ha Ha Ha*, which won the Booker prize) and Colin Bateman (b 1962 *Cycle of Violence*), or from outside Ireland such as **Frank McCourt**, who won the Pulitzer Prize in 1997 with *Angela's Ashes* about his childhood in Limerick.

Among the established pillars of Irish drama are **Brian Friel** (b 1929 *Dancing at Lughnasa*, adapted as a film in 1998), Thomas Kilroy (b 1934 *The Secret Fall of Constance Wilde*), Thomas Murphy (b 1935 *Bailegangaire*) and Frank McGuinness (b 1956 *Observe the Sons of Ulster Marching towards the Somme*). Alongside them a new wave of young Irish writers is making an international impact. Encouraged by the Abbey and the Gate Theatres in Dublin, the Royal Court in London and independent theatre companies, such as Rough Magic in Dublin, the Druid Theatre Company in Galway and Red Kettle in Waterford, this new wave includes Martin McDonagh (*The Leenane Trilogy*), Conor McPherson (b 1971 *The Weir*), Marina Carr (b 1964 *The Mai*) and Enda Walsh (*Disco Pigs*).

The Gaelic Revival at the end of the 19C was responsible for the rescue of writing in Irish, which, at the start of that century had fallen to a very low point indeed. An important figure was Peter O'Leary (tAthair Peadar) (1839-1920); his folk-tale *Séadna* of 1910 eschewed archaic literary convention in favour of the vigour of the contemporary spoken language, as did the short stories of Pádraig O'Conaire (1882-1928).

Among the best-known authors is the Connemara-born Máirtín Cadhain, former professor of Irish at Trinity College, whose novel *Cré na Cille* (1949) *(The Clay of the Graveyard)* is the best-known prose writing in recent times. Those who lived and worked on the Great Blasket Island, off the coast of Co Kerry, have produced several works describing island life before the people left in the early 1950s. Modern Irish poetry, composed by Seán O Ríordéin, Máirtín O Direáin and Nuala ní Dhomhnaill among others, has appeared in a number of languages.

Cinema

It was on 20 April 1896 that cinema first appeared in Ireland with a projection of a film by the Lumière brothers in Dublin; by 1909 the Volta in Dublin had been opened by James Joyce himself. Very soon the movies were playing a major role in Irish life. They continue to do so, and in recent years, government support has encouraged cinematic activity; many foreign films have been shot in Ireland and the local industry has produced some memorable works.

In 1904 JT Jameson, a newsreel cameraman, founded the Irish Animated Company (IAC); together with the American cinema, which was anxious to please the many Irish immigrants in the States, it made cinema acceptable in Ireland and launched the local industry. In 1916 and 1917 two more companies were set up – Film Company of Ireland (FCOI) and General Film Supply (GFS). It was not, however, until the founding of the Free State in 1922 that Irish cinema truly flourished in Ireland. Political events supplied the first themes such as the Easter Rising of 1916 in *Irish Destiny* (1926) by Isaac Eppel; incidents in the War of Independence feature in *Guest of the Nation* (1935) by Denis Johnston and *The Dawn* (1936) by Tom Cooper.

Michael Collins *directed by Neil Jordan starring Liam Neeson*

Perhaps the internationally best known film made in Ireland in the 1930s was the documentary *Man of Aran*. The work of an American of Irish descent, Robert O'Flaherty, it presents a compelling and beautiful picture of the harsh traditional life of the people of the Aran Islands, but is more a romantic evocation of humanity's epic struggle against the elements than an accurate record of a particular place, period or people.

One of the earliest non-Irish films to make extensive use of Ireland as a location was Laurence Olivier's *Henry V*. Shot in 1944 as a deliberate wartime morale booster, it used the Powerscourt estate in neutral Ireland as a setting for the large-scale re-creation of the battle of Agincourt. Hundreds of local farmers hired as extras proved themselves more than adequate as stalwart cavalrymen. Plenty of other films have exploited Ireland as a background to films set elsewhere, among them Mel Gibson's *Braveheart* (1996), in which the town of Trim,

its great castle and its surroundings stand in for the Scotland of rebel William Wallace. Earlier, in 1956, the little port of Youghal was transformed into New Bedford, Massachusetts, becoming the harbour town from which in *Moby Dick* Captain Ahab sets out in search of the great whale. More often, however, the cinematic role of Ireland has been as itself, or at least as a version of itself. In what is probably the most celebrated of all films with an Irish setting, *The Quiet Man* (1952), the country appears as a kind of mysterious, pre-industrial rural paradise, inhabited by quaint, stereotypical Irishmen and Irishwomen. The work of the great John Ford, himself of Irish descent, it revolves around the return to his native land of a boxer, memorably played by John Wayne, and features one of the cinema's longest fight scenes, in which Wayne and his rival brawl their way through the village from farmyard to pub. Conflict of another kind was portrayed by David Lean in *Ryan's Daughter* (1970), in which a young married Irishwoman falls for an officer of the British garrison. Its evocation of the wild landscapes and seascapes of the west has never been excelled.

In more recent years, film makers from home and abroad have moved beyond this backward-looking vision of the country, taking their themes from contemporary politics and social questions as well as from history and from literature. Neil Jordan's blockbusting biopic *Michael Collins* (1996), an account of the life and times of the charismatic but doomed Republican leader, was second only to *Titanic* in its success with Irish audiences, not least thanks to the performance of Liam Neeson in the title role. Neeson was only one of several Irish stars like Gabriel Byrne, Stephen Rea and Pierce Brosnan, to emerge in this period with international reputations. Jordan's earlier *The Crying Game* (1992) dealt with the relationship of an IRA gunman and a black British soldier, while his *The Butcher Boy* (1997), in which a young boy from a dysfunctional family descends into madness and murder, has been seen as a metaphor for a country still coming to terms with its troubled history. Jim Sheridan's *The Field* (1991) was equally sombre in its treatment of a farmer's refusal to let his land pass into alien hands. Previously, in 1989, Sheridan had filmed the poignant story of the cerebral palsy victim Christy Brown in *My Left Foot*, in which Daniel Day-Lewis won an Oscar for his extraordinarily moving performance. Day-Lewis also appeared in *In the Name of the Father* (1993), Sheridan's account of the failure of justice following the IRA's bombing of a Guildford pub.

The Oscar-winning *Crying Game* was based on the classic short story by Frank O'Connor, and numerous other works of literature have been translated with varying degrees of success to the screen. Among them are James Joyce's *Dubliners* (1987) by John Huston and, perhaps surprisingly, his *Ulysses* (1967) by Joseph Strick. *Angela's Ashes* (1999), was a not altogether convincing adaptation by Alan Parker of Frank McCourt's best-selling autobiographical memoir of his rain-soaked and wretched Limerick childhood. Roddy Doyle's sensitive and sometimes hilarious novels of contemporary Dublin's low life have inspired *The Commitments* (1991) by Alan Parker and *The Van* (1996) by Stephen Frears.

Mention should also be made of the work of the expatriate director **Ken Loach** – *Hidden Agenda* (1990), *Land and Freedom* (1995), *Carla's Song* (1997) and *Sweet Sixteen* (2002).

Three Irish TV series earned great popularity in the UK – *Father Ted, The Ambassador* starring Pauline Collins and partly filmed in Ely Place in Dublin, and *Ballykissangel*, filmed in Avoca in the Wicklow Mountains.

Architecture

Ecclesiastical Buildings

Romanesque (Norman)

CLONFERT CATHEDRAL, Co Galway – West door – 12C
The inner arch immediately surrounding the door is 300 years later than rest of the doorway, which consists of five rows of columns and five rows of round-headed arches framing the door, surmounted by a hood moulding containing a triangular pediment, the whole capped by a finial.

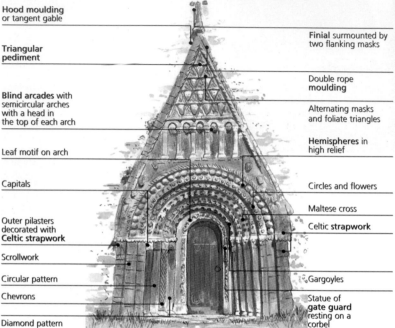

Hood moulding or tangent gable

Triangular pediment

Blind arcades with semicircular arches with a head in the top of each arch

Leaf motif on arch

Capitals

Outer pilasters decorated with **Celtic strapwork**

Scrollwork

Circular pattern

Chevrons

Diamond pattern

Finial surmounted by two flanking masks

Double rope moulding

Alternating masks and foliate triangles

Hemispheres in high relief

Circles and flowers

Maltese cross

Celtic **strapwork**

Gargoyles

Statue of **gate guard** resting on a corbel

Medieval

JERPOINT ABBEY, Co Kilkenny – 12C with 15C tower

Splayed window embrasures

Cloister garth

Cloister arcade

Refectory

Kitchen

Nave

Calefactory (warming room)

North aisle arcade

Screen dividing nave into east end for choir monks and west end for lay brothers

Central tower over crossing with slight battering

Chapter House

String course

Irish crenellations

Double lancet windows

Chancel

Transept

Gothic

ST PATRICK'S CATHEDRAL, Dublin – 13C
Construction begun in the Early English style but extensively restored in the 19C.

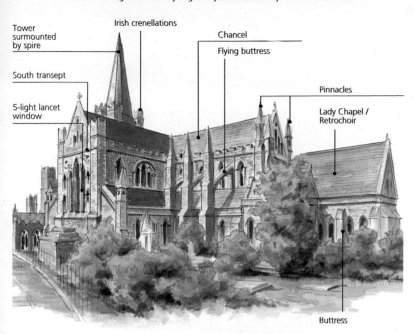

Tower surmounted by spire

Irish crenellations

Chancel

Flying buttress

South transept

5-light lancet window

Pinnacles

Lady Chapel / Retrochoir

Buttress

Neo-Classical

CHRIST CHURCH CATHEDRAL, Waterford – 18C

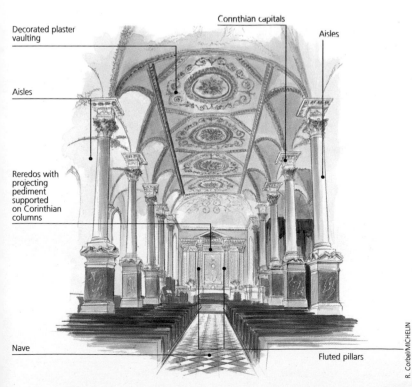

Decorated plaster vaulting

Corinthian capitals

Aisles

Aisles

Reredos with projecting pediment supported on Corinthian columns

Nave

Fluted pillars

R. Corbel/MICHELIN

Neo-Gothic

**CHURCH OF THE MOST HOLY TRINITY (formerly Chapel Royal),
Dublin Castle – 19C**

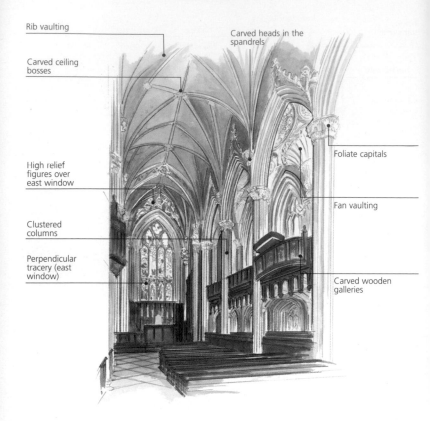

Rib vaulting

Carved ceiling bosses

Carved heads in the spandrels

High relief figures over east window

Foliate capitals

Clustered columns

Fan vaulting

Perpendicular tracery (east window)

Carved wooden galleries

Military Structures

Norman

Motte and bailey

In the immediate post-invasion years, the Normans built timber castles, surmounting a natural or artificial earthern mound (motte). A outer stockaded enclosure (bailey) contained stables, storehouses etc. Later castles were built of stone.

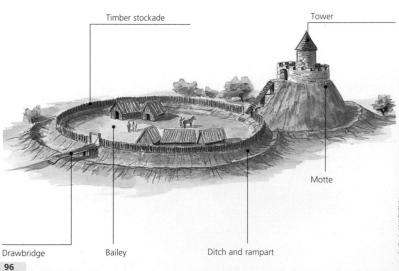

Timber stockade

Tower

Drawbridge

Bailey

Ditch and rampart

Motte

15C-17C

DUNGUAIRE CASTLE, Co Galway – 1520 restored in the 19C

Fortified dwelling, consisting of a **tower house** surrounded by a courtyard, known as a **bawn**, enclosed by defensive wall; the main living accommodation with windows was on the upper floors.

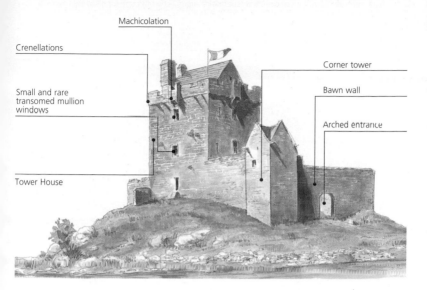

Machicolation

Crenellations

Corner tower

Bawn wall

Small and rare transomed mullion windows

Arched entrance

Tower House

17C

CHARLES FORT, Co Cork   c 1670

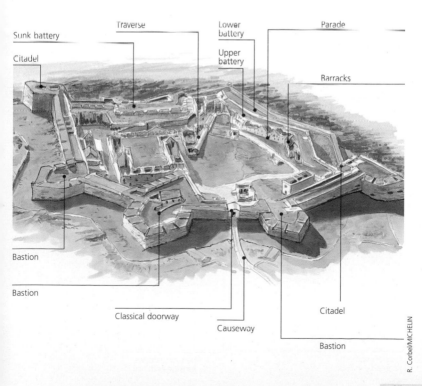

Traverse

Lower battery

Parade

Sunk battery

Citadel

Upper battery

Barracks

Bastion

Bastion

Classical doorway

Causeway

Citadel

Bastion

Secular Buildings

16C

PORTUMNA CASTLE, Co Galway – 1518

Semi-fortified house, with symmetrical fenestration, approached through formal walled gardens.

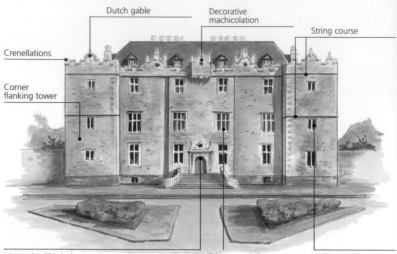

- Dutch gable
- Decorative machicolation
- String course
- Crenellations
- Corner flanking tower
- Mannerist Classical doorcase flanked by gun loops
- Transom window
- Mullion window

17C

SPRINGHILL, Co Tyrone – c 1680 with 18C additions

Unfortified house with symmetrical facade and large and regular fenestration.

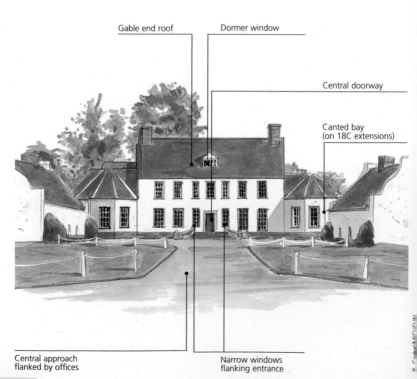

- Gable end roof
- Dormer window
- Central doorway
- Canted bay (on 18C extensions)
- Central approach flanked by offices
- Narrow windows flanking entrance

GEORGIAN URBAN HOUSING

Urban terrace houses built of red brick, with 4 storeys over basement, three bays wide, with regular fenestration, composed of sash windows with wooden glazing bars. The tall windows emphasized the importance of the first floor reception rooms.

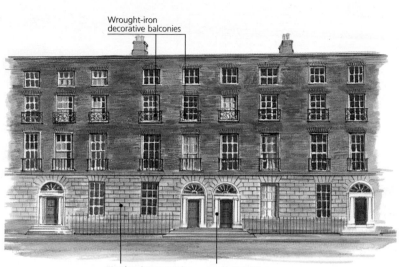

Wrought-iron decorative balconies

Simulated stone work

Doorcase with pillars and fanlight

Doorcases and fanlights (1740s)

Door case capped by a lantern fan light and flanked by pillars with Ionic capitals

Door case capped by a decorated fan light and flanked by pillars with Ionic capitals

Door case capped by a decorative fan light and flanked by pillars with Ionic capitals and by side lights and door scrapers

Door case capped by a decorated fan light and flanked by pillars with Ionic capitals

18C

RUSSBOROUGH, Co Wicklow – 1743-56
House in the **Palladian style** consisting of a main **residential block** linked by curved or straight colonnades to two **flanking service blocks** containing the kitchens and stables.

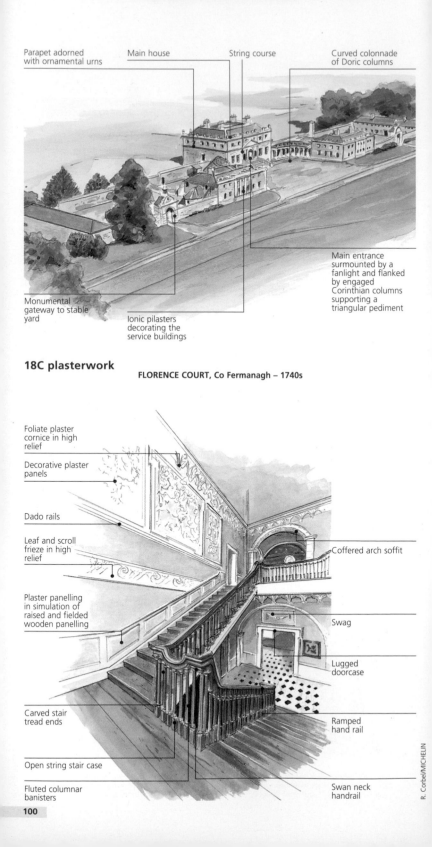

Parapet adorned with ornamental urns

Main house

String course

Curved colonnade of Doric columns

Main entrance surmounted by a fanlight and flanked by engaged Corinthian columns supporting a triangular pediment

Monumental gateway to stable yard

Ionic pilasters decorating the service buildings

18C plasterwork

FLORENCE COURT, Co Fermanagh – 1740s

Foliate plaster cornice in high relief

Decorative plaster panels

Dado rails

Leaf and scroll frieze in high relief

Plaster panelling in simulation of raised and fielded wooden panelling

Carved stair tread ends

Open string stair case

Fluted columnar banisters

Coffered arch soffit

Swag

Lugged doorcase

Ramped hand rail

Swan neck handrail

R. Corbel/MICHELIN

MONAGHAN MARKET HOUSE, Co Monaghan – 1791

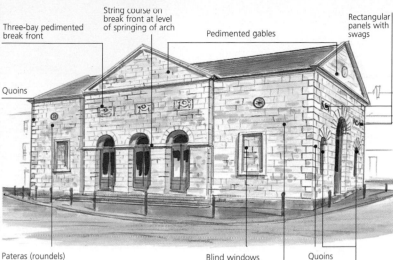

Three-bay pedimented break front

String course on break front at level of springing of arch

Pedimented gables

Rectangular panels with swags

Quoins

Pateras (roundels) with foliated design

Blind windows

Quoins

Rusticated ashlar stonework

Rounded-headed niches

Revival styles

Medieval styles such as Gothic and Norman were revived featuring asymmetric façades and fenestration and varied rooflines.

LISMORE CASTLE, Co Waterford – 19C Neo-Gothic

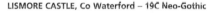

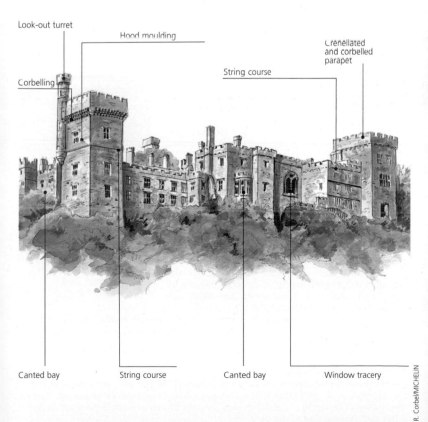

Look-out turret

Hood moulding

Crenellated and corbelled parapet

Corbelling

String course

Canted bay

String course

Canted bay

Window tracery

J Malburet/MICHELIN

Architecture

Although architecture in Ireland has been strongly influenced by stylistic developments originating in Britain or the continent of Europe, usually after some lapse in time, local building has many distinctive features; the medieval round towers with their conical caps have become an emblem of Irishness. Extraordinary is the array of prehistoric monuments and medieval fortified structures... while the Georgian era produced fine building in both town and countryside.

Prehistoric Era

Although the first traces of human habitation in Ireland date from c 7000 BC, the first people to leave structural evidence of their presence were Neolithic farmers, who lived in Ireland from their arrival c 4000 BC to 2000 BC. Traces of their huts have been found at Lough Gur *(see Limerick)*.

Megalithic Tombs

The most visible and enduring monuments of these people are their elaborate **burial mounds**.

The most impressive are the **passage tombs** at Newgrange, Knowth and Dowth in the Boyne Valley, on Bricklieve Mountains, at Loughcrew, at Fourknocks and Knockmany. Each grave consisted of a passage leading to a chamber roofed with a flat stone or a corbelled structure, sometimes with smaller chambers off the other three sides and sometimes containing stone basins. It was covered by a circular mound of earth or stones retained by a ring of upright stones. Passage graves date from 3000 to 2500 BC.

The earliest Megalithic structures, **court tombs**, consisted of a long chamber divided into compartments and covered by a long mound of stones retained by a kerb of upright stones. Before the entrance was a semicircular open court flanked by standing stones as at Creevykeel *(see Sligo)* and Ossian's Grave *(see Antrim Glens)*.

Cardonagh High Cross, Inishowen

H Champollion/MICHELIN

A third style of Megalithic tomb is known as the **portal tomb;** like Proleek *(see Dundalk)*, they are found mostly near the east coast of Ireland. The tomb consisted of two standing stones in front with others behind supporting a massive capstone, which was hauled into place up an earth ramp long since removed. They date from c 2000 BC.

Bronze Age Structures

Stone circles, which date from the Bronze Age (1750-500 BC), are mostly found in the southwest of the country *(see Donegal Glens, Kenmare, Downpatrick, Sperrin Mountains)*. The circle at Drombeg *(see Kinsale)* seems to have been used to determine the shortest day of the year.

Glendalough

Single standing stones probably marked boundaries or the sites of graves. Some were later converted into Christian monuments by being inscribed with a cross or an Ogham inscription *(see Gaelige).*

Of similar antiquity is the cooking pit *(fulacht fiadh)* which was filled with water; hot stones were placed in the water to bring it to boiling point.

Iron Age Dwellings

By the Iron Age, men were living in **homesteads**, approached by a causeway. A ringfort was enclosed by an earth bank *(ráth or dún)* or by a stone wall *(caiseal)* and was surrounded by a ditch. An artificial island *(crannóg)* was formed by heaping up stones in a marsh or lake. Many such dwellings were in use from the Iron Age until the 17C. There is a replica at Craggaunowen *(see Ennis).* Stone forts *(cashels)* like Dún Aonghasa *(see Aran Islands)* and Grianán of Aileach *(see Buncrana),* although restored at various periods, illustrate the type, built on a hill with massive walls and mural chambers. Within the homestead individual huts were built of wattle and daub or of stone with a thatched roof. In the west, beehive huts *(clocháin)* were built entirely of stone using the same technique of **corbelling** inwards to form a roof that was used in the passage graves. Similar stone huts are also found in the monastery on Great Skellig and at Clochan na Carraige on the Aran Islands. They demonstrate the use of dry-stone construction in a treeless land.

At the centre of the homestead there was often an underground stone passage, called a souterrain, used for storage or refuge.

Irish Monastic Settlements

Little remains of most early Christian settlements as the buildings were made of perishable material – wood or wattle and daub. The records describe beautiful wooden churches made of smooth planks constructed with great craft and skill, but none has survived.

Early monasteries consisted of an area enclosed by a circular wall or bank and divided into concentric rings, as at Nendrum *(see Strangford Lough),* or into sectors assigned to different uses. The most important sector was the graveyard, since it was seen as the gateway to heaven.

Round Towers

The slender tapering round towers, just as much a symbol of Ireland as the high crosses, mark the site of early monasteries. Almost unique to Ireland, they were built between about AD 950 and the 12C as bell towers where hand bells, the only kind available, were rung from the top floor to announce the services. The towers were also used to store treasures and possibly as places of refuge; in almost every case the entrance was several feet (10ft/3m) above ground level.

Intact towers vary in height (from 50ft/15m to over 100ft/30m). All were surmounted by a conical cap, sometimes replaced by later battlements. About 65 survive in varying condition, with 12 intact. Most were constructed without foundations and all are tapered.

Tomb Shrines

Some saints' graves are marked by a stone **mortuary house** which resembles a miniature church. These structures, such as St Ciaran's at Clonmacnoise, are among the earliest identifiable stone buildings in Ireland.

Churches

Most early **stone churches** consisted of a single chamber with a west door and an east window; churches with a nave and chancel date from the 12C. None of the surviving churches is very large but there are often several churches on one site. The very large stones employed accentuate the smallness of the churches. The roofs would have been made of thatch or shingles.

The rare **stone-roofed** churches, an Irish peculiarity, employ the corbelling technique. The simplest is Gallarus Oratory; St Doulagh's near Malahide is a 13C church still

Jerpoint Abbey Cloisters

roofed with stone slabs; St Columba's House, St Mochta's House, St Flannan's Oratory and Cormac's Chapel have a small room between the vaulted ceiling and the roof. The earliest examples are devoid of ornament; an exception to this rule is found on White Island in Co Fermanagh, where seven figurative slabs are attached to the walls (which may be later insertions).

Middle Ages

Norman / Romanesque

The first church in the Romanesque style introduced from the Continent in the 12C, was Cormac's Chapel of 1139 at Cashel. In Ireland, Romanesque churches are always small; their typical features, the only elements bearing carved decoration, are round-headed doorways, windows and arches. Ornament includes fantastic animals, human masks and geometric designs such as bosses, zigzags and "teeth". Cormac's Chapel has fine carvings, several series of blind arcades, painted rib vaults and the earliest extant frescoes.

Profusely ornamented west doorways are perhaps unique to Ireland, exemplified by Clonfert (after 1167), Ardfert and St Cronan's in Roscrea.

Norman Castles – The first castles built by Normans were of the **motte and bailey** type. The motte was a natural or artificial mound of earth surrounded by a ditch and usually surmounted by a wooden tower as at Clough in Co Down; the bailey was an area attached to the motte and enclosed by a paling fence. From the start of the 13C, the Normans built more solid stone donjons (keeps) which were square with corner buttresses, as at Trim, Carrickfergus and Greencastle, polygonal as at Dundrum and Athlone or round as at Nenagh. During the 13C entrance towers became more important and barbicans were added for additional defence. In the latter half of the 13C a new symmetrical design was developed consisting of an inner ward with four round corner towers and a combined gatehouse/donjon in the middle of one wall, as at Roscommon.

Gothic Churches

Gothic architecture, introduced to Ireland in the late 12C, is on a much smaller scale than elsewhere and few examples have survived. Most cathedrals show English and Welsh influences, whereas monasteries, founded by Continental monastic orders, are built according to their usual plan of a quadrangle enclosed by cloisters bordered by the church on the north side, the sacristy and chapter house on the east, the refectory and kitchens on the south and the store on the west, with dormitories above the east and south ranges.

Early in the 13C many cathedrals were remodelled; the two Anglican cathedrals in Dublin contain building from this period, although they have been much altered. St Patrick's Cathedral in Dublin, completed in 1254 and to which a tower was added in 1372, is very English in its form and decoration.

A second period of building occurred in the 15C and coincided with the construction of many Franciscan houses in the west. Most existing churches were altered to conform to the new fashion. Broad traceried windows were inserted which let in more light and provided the stonemasons with opportunities for decoration. There is a distinctive Irish character to the capitals and high relief carving in the cloisters at Jerpoint (15C).

Tower Houses

After the Black Death (1348-50) building resumed on a more modest scale. In 1429 a £10 subsidy was offered by Edward VI for the construction of a castle or tower. Over 70% of tower houses, which were erected by native and settler alike, are south of the Dublin–Galway axis.

The most distinctive feature is their verticality, one room on each of four to five storeys, sometimes with a hidden room between two floors.

Defences consisted of corner loop holes, battering at the base, double-stepped merlons, known as **Irish crenellations**, and external machicolations over the corners and the entrance. Most such towers, which were built between 1450 and 1650, were surrounded by a **bawn**, an area enclosed by a defensive wall. Only in the later and larger castles is decoration evident.

Dunguaire Castle

Plantation Period

Plantation Castles

As the country came more firmly under English control in the late 16C, more luxurious rectangular houses were built with square corner towers, as at Kanturk (c 1603), Portumna (c 1618), Glinsk (c 1620) and Ballygally (1625). Often an existing tower house was extended by the addition of a more modern house, as at Leamaneh, Donegal and Carrick-on-Suir. These buildings show a Renaissance influence in plain and regular fenestration with large mullioned windows.

Planter's Gothic

This style was introduced in the early 17C by settlers from England and Scotland who built many parish churches throughout Ireland, a few of which survive unaltered; one of the best examples is St Columb's Cathedral in Londonderry.

Coastal Fortifications

In the Restoration period several important towns were provided with star forts; the most complete surviving fortification is Charles Fort in Kinsale (from 1671). After the French invasion of Bantry Bay in 1796 and Killala in 1798, signal towers were built on the coast. The building of Martello towers began in 1804; about 50 of these squat structures with very thick walls punctuate the coast from Drogheda to Cork and along the Shannon estuary. The so-called Joyce Tower in Sandycove, built of ashlar granite, is typical.

Classical Era

Country Houses

Between the Battle of the Boyne (1690) and the Rebellion (1798) there was a period of relative peace and prosperity during which most of the important country houses were built. While Dutch gables and red brick are attributed to the influence of William of Orange, in general English and French inspiration predominated in the late 17C. In the 18C the influence was mainly Italian sources, often distilled through England and latterly Greek-inspired architects, while in the 19C the English Gothic and Tudor revivalists were influential. Most country houses were built of local stone.

The most popular style in the 18C was the **Palladian villa** which consisted of a central residence – two or three storeys high – flanked by curved or straight colonnades ending in pavilions (usually one storey lower) which housed the kitchens or stables and farm buildings.

The major architect of the first half of the 18C was **Richard Castle** (originally Cassels) (1690-1751), of Huguenot origin. Castle's many houses – Powerscourt, Westport, Russborough, Newbridge – tend to be very solid. He took over the practice of **Sir Edward Lovett Pearce**, who had the major role in designing Castletown *(see Maynooth)* and who built the Houses of Parliament (from 1729), now the Bank of Ireland in Dublin.

The influence of **Robert Adam** (1728-92) arrived in Ireland in 1770, the date of the mausoleum he designed at Templepatrick. Sir William Chambers' work in Ireland is exemplified by Marino Casino (1769-80), a vastly expensive Neo-classical gentleman's retreat cum folly.

James Gandon (1742-1823) was brought to Ireland in 1781 to design Emo Court. His Classical style is well illustrated by the Customs House and the Four Courts in Dublin. The chief work of **James Wyatt** (1746-1813) was at Castle Coole but he also contributed to Slane Castle.

One of the best known Irish architects was **Francis Johnston** (1761-1829), an exponent of both the Classical and the Gothic styles, the former exemplified by Dublin's General Post Office, the latter by Dublin Castle's Chapel Royal.

Interior Decoration

Many interiors were decorated with exuberant stuccowork executed by the Swiss-Italian **Lafranchini** brothers, one of whom executed the stairwell plasterwork at Castletown. Contemporary work of similar quality was carried out by Robert West and at Powerscourt House in Dublin by Michael **Stapleton**, the principal exponent of Adam decor.

Churches

Classical details began to be used in the 17C. St Michan's in Dublin (c 1685) and Lismore (1680) by William Robinson retain some details of 17C work. The early Georgian St Anne's in Shandon in Cork has an imposing west tower with an eastern flavour. The neo-Classical rectangular building with a pillared portico, inspired by the Greek temple, was popular with all the major denominations: St Werburgh's (1754-59), St George's (1812), St Stephen's (1825) and the Pro-Cathedral (finished after 1840) in Dublin, St John the Evangelist (1781-85) at Coolbanagher by Gandon and St George's (1816) in Belfast.

Revival Styles

The Gothic Revival style first appeared in Ireland in the 1760s at Castle Ward and at Malahide Castle. At first Gothic features – crenellations, pointed arches and intricate stuccowork vaulted ceilings – were added to buildings which were basically Classical and symmetrical such as Castle Ward. Kilkenny Castle (c 1826) by William Robertson and Dromoland Castle (1826) by George and James Pain, were enlarged and reworked in Tudor or Gothic style. Johnstown Castle and Ashford Castle are later examples of such Gothicising, which was romantic in flavour, with its accent on asymmetry, but distinctly Victorian in convenience. Trinity College Museum (completed 1857) by Deane and Woodward is a classic of the Venetian Gothic revival; Gosford Castle is neo-Norman; Glenveagh was designed in the Irish Baronial style, whereas Scottish Baronial was used for Belfast Castle and Blarney Castle House.

Gothic Revival Churches

Many early 19C Gothic churches, such as the Church of the Most Holy Trinity (formerly the Chapel Royal) in Dublin Castle, are filled with ornament. Later the influence of Augustus Welby Pugin, who practised widely in Ireland, and JJ McCarthy promoted antiquarian correctness, as at St Fin Barre's in Cork (1862) by William Burges. McCarthy's greatest achievement was probably the completion in Decorated Gothic style of the great new cathedral at Armagh (after 1853). This was only one example, albeit an outstanding one, in the spate of building which followed the Emancipation Act when many Roman Catholic cathedrals and parish churches were constructed in eclectic Gothic variations.

20C

The young Free State restored with admirable promptness the bombed General Post Office, the Four Courts and the Custom House but the record of new design is relatively poor. The Arts and Crafts movement did not find much architectural expression in Ireland; a notable exception is Cavan Town Hall (1908) by William Scott with expressive use of planes and textures. University College Dublin in Earlsfort Terrace (1912), by RM Butler, and the College of Sciences in Upper Merrion Street in Dublin, (1904-13) by Sir Aston Webb, exemplify the Classical revival. Perhaps the most grandiose structure of this period is the huge City Hall (1906) in Belfast, a "great wedding cake of a building" (J Sheehy) with a dome and corner towers.

Modernism

Architectural Modernism was slow to come to Ireland but an early and very striking example was the Church of Christ the King (1927) at Turner's Cross in Cork by Barry Byrne of Chicago. The changes in practice introduced by Vatican II, favouring worship in the round, have inspired many exciting church designs, some of which reflect local physical features – St Conal's Church, Glenties, Co Donegal; St Michael's Church, Creeslough, Co Donegal; Dominican Church, Athy; Prince of Peace Church, Fossa, near Killarney, Holy Trinity, Bunclody. Modern civic architecture arrived in Ireland with the construction of the Ardnacrusha hydroelectric plant in 1929 and the Dublin Airport terminal building of 1940.

Irish Distinction

Towns and Cities

Early Irish villages *(clachans)* were formed of clusters of wattle-and-daub cottages arranged in a haphazard manner. The first towns were founded by the Vikings, invariably on estuaries; among them were Drogheda, Dublin, Waterford and Wexford. Most such places had a Tholsel (toll stall), often an arch or gateway several storeys high, where payment for rights of privilege or passage was made. Norman settlements were mostly confined to the south and east of the country. Towns were often enclosed within town walls, parts of which have survived at Athenry, Kilmallock, Youghal, Fethard and Londonderry. The first widespread foundation of towns occurred in the late 16C and 17C during the plantations of Ulster, Munster and some parts of Leinster; they consisted of timber-framed houses, which have not survived, set out round a green or lining a street. The green was often known as "The Diamond" although rarely a true diamond shape; many such "Diamonds" survive in Ulster. In many Irish towns one of the most elegant buildings is the market and the courthouse, sometimes combined in one structure.

Town Planning – In the 18C and 19C many country landlords indulged in town planning, setting out wide streets as in Strokestown and Moy, tree-lined malls as in Westport, Birr and Castlebar, unusual formal street plans, such as the X-shape in Kenmare, rows of cottages built of local stone as at Glassan, northeast of Athlone, and Shillelagh in Co Wicklow or the picturesque thatched houses of Adare.

In the major towns elegant terraces of houses of Classically inspired design were built of local stone or red brick, some of which was imported from Somerset via Bristol. In 19C Dublin the materials used were grey brick from local clays, local limestone and grey Wicklow granite. Although most terraces were erected piecemeal and lack a unified aesthetic, the influence of the **Wide Streets Commissioners** (in Dublin from 1758) led to distinctly Irish Georgian doorways – usually flanked by columns – and ordered fenestration. The tallest windows are on the principal floor, decreasing in size towards the roofline parapet. Some later terraces by the Wide Streets Commissioners and others were more standardised – Fitzwilliam Street and Square (south side) in Dublin, and Pery Square in Limerick. Internal decoration was often of a very high standard, with Classical motifs common in chimney pieces, plasterwork and timberwork.

In the 20C, town planning in Ireland has had few notable successes. Grandiose plans for the reconstruction of Dublin following the devastation of 1916 were drawn up but never implemented. Many of the close-packed terraced streets of late 19C Belfast have been replaced by planned housing schemes of various kinds, the least succesful of which consisted of brutalist blocks of flats. The attempt to create the "New Town" of Craigavon on the British model, based on the existing urban areas of Lurgan and Portadown, has only been partially realised. In the South, rural prosperity and lax planning controls have led to the abandonment of the picturesque but sub-standard cabin *(see below)* with a scatter of comfortable but visually inappropriate houses and bungalows.

Vernacular Houses

The Irish countryside is full of buildings and other structures of traditional vernacular architecture – not only dwelling houses and outhouses but also structures such as sweathouses and forges.

The small stone sweathouses, were used to treat pleurisy and other ailments and also as a type of "sauna". A fire was lit inside and, when the interior was hot, the ashes were raked out and a layer of rushes placed on the floor to protect the feet from the heat.

The 1841 Census identified four grades of housing, of which the most modest was a windowless one-room mud cabin with a thatched roof *(bothán)*, a type of dwelling which predominated west of a line from Londonderry to Cork. Such houses contained little or no furniture; more windows or rooms meant higher rents. The half door, which is to be found all over Ireland, allowed in light while keeping out animals.

The middle grades of house, single- and two-storey farmhouses, have survived in greater numbers, with glazed windows, hearths and a hierarchy of rooms for distinct social uses.

B Juge/MICHELIN

Merrion Square North

The Irish **long house**, in which all the rooms were interconnecting with the stairs at one end, was a style which lasted from the Middle Ages to the 18C; the one at Cratloe *(see Limerick)* is a rare survivor.

The box-style Georgian house with symmetrical elevation, some Classical detailing such as Venetian or Wyatt windows and a fanlit and columnated doorcase, was very popular with people of more substantial means.

Simple dwellings were often destroyed during evictions or fell into decay. Some have been discovered under layers of modernisation; others, threatened with demolition, have been reconstructed or recreated in Bunratty Folk Park, Glencolmcille Folk Village, the Ulster-American Folk Park and the Ulster Folk Park near Bangor.

Stained Glass

No medieval stained glass has survived in situ in Ireland but there was a revival of interest in this craft in the 1770s with the enamelling work of Thomas Jervais and Richard Hand, much of which was secular. The fashion for the neo-Gothic style of architecture in the 19C for both churches and houses created a great

St Wilfrid and St John Berchmans
(1927) by Harry Clark

The Stained Glass Museum, Ely

demand for stained glass; good examples from this period are St Patrick's Roman Catholic Church in Dundalk, which has glass by Early of Dublin, Hardman of Birmingham and Meyer of Munich, the east window of St Patrick's Anglican church in Monaghan by the German FS Barff, and the altar window of the Cathedral of the Assumption in Tuam by Michael O'Connor (1801-67).

The outstanding contribution made by 20C Irish artists in this field was nurtured by the foundation of **An Túr Gloine** (the Tower of Glass) (1903-63) at the instigation of Edward Martyn and Sarah Purser.

The portrait painter Sarah Purser did designs for several windows including Cormac of Cashel in St Patrick's Cathedral, and another founder member was Michael Healy (d 1941) whose work can be seen in Loughrea Cathedral.

Wilhelmina Margaret Geddes worked for An Túr Gloine from 1912 to 1925 and works by her can be seen in the Municipal Gallery of Modern Art in Dublin – *Episodes from the Life of St Colman* (strong black line used) and in the Ulster Museum – *The Fate of the Children of Lir* (1930).

Evie Hone joined An Túr Gloine in 1934. Her work, which was often inspired by Irish medieval sculpture, includes *The Ascension* (1948) for the Roman Catholic church in Kingscourt, Co Cavan, and *The Beatitudes* (1946) for a chapel in the Jesuit Retreat House at Tullabeg near Tullamore.

Harry Clarke (1889-1931) developed a distinctive personal style as early as 1915, drawing from iconography and legends in a symbolist manner. His first public commission, 12 windows for the Honan Chapel in University College Cork, is one of his greatest works. His "Geneva Window" (1928) is in the Municipal Gallery of Modern Art in Dublin. Just before his death he executed his most important ecclesiastical commission *The Last Judgement with the Blessed Virgin Mary and St Paul* for St Patrick's Church in Newport.

A current revival is headed by James Scanlon and Maud Cotter, both based in Cork.

Irish Art

Constantly receptive to influences from Britain and the rest of Europe and often giving them a specifically local flavour, Irish art was unsurpassed in its originality and creativity in the early Christian era, when sculptors, jewellers, illuminators and others found inspiration in the country's glorious heritage of Celtic arts and crafts. A fainter echo of Celtic achievement came in the paintings and graphic arts associated with the Gaelic Revival of the late 19C and early 20C, but before this, Ireland, quite as much as England, had become a stronghold of the arts and crafts of the Georgian era; the brilliant and sometimes eccentric life of the Anglo-Irish Ascendancy is reflected in the painting of the time as much as in architecture and the decorative arts.

Celtic Art

Tara Brooch (8C)

National Museum of Ireland, Dublin

Circles formed an integral part of Celtic art; the outline of the design was marked out with an iron compass on the piece or page to be decorated. Other decorative motifs were S-and C-shaped curves, spirals and swirls and zigzags, with intricate, interlaced patterns in the interstices. Similar designs, identified by archaeologists as **La Tène**, after the continental Celtic centre found at La Tène in Switzerland which flourished during the last five centuries BC, are found on two granite monuments – at Turoe *(see Athenry)* and Castlestrange *(see Strokestown)* – which date from the 3C BC. They are the only two such monuments to have survived in Ireland and were probably used in religious ceremonies. They resemble the Greek *omphalos* at Delphi, a site raided by the Celts in 290 BC.

Exquisite Craftsmen

The finest Celtic pieces are designed in gold. The beauty of the torc or neckband is well attested. The goldsmith stretched the metal into long narrow strips and then twisted them around each other to make a golden rope; the torc was then shaped to fit around the warrior's neck. The Celts made personal ornaments, such as brooches for fastening clothes, horse harnesses and sword sheaths. They often decorated their goods with enamel, favouring the colour red but also using blue, yellow and green. A regular motif in Celtic design is the triskele, a figure with three arms or legs, symbolising earth, fire and water.

Some early sculptures display a nude female figure with crossed legs, known as *Sheela-na-gig*, which owes much to pagan traditions. Many interpretations have been given to these carvings and it is reasonable to assume that the figure was linked to a fertility cult. Some of them are grotesque and most are to be found in or about churches.

R Holzbachova, Ph Benet/MICHELIN

A Golden Age

A high point in Irish Celtic art is the illuminated manuscript. The first important example is a copy of the psalms dating from around AD 600 and traditionally attributed to St Columba. Compared with later achievements, it is relatively simple, its principal feature being a large decorated initial at the beginning of paragraphs. Its ornamentation of Celtic spirals and stylised animals is further developed in the course of the 7C in the **Book of Durrow**, where a variety of coloured inks is used as well as the black of Columba's manuscript, whole "carpet pages" are given over to decoration rather than text, and the characteristic motif of interlaced bands makes its appearance. Over the next century and a half, the scribes' increasing mastery of their craft resulted in manuscripts of ever greater intricacy and exuberance, culminating in the sublime achievement of the world-famous **Book of Kells** *(see p 268)* dating from around 800. Of equal virtuosity are a number of products of the metalworker's and jeweller's art. The Moylough Belt Shrine (c 700) of silver and enamel has sumptuous ornamentation featuring spirals, interlacing and animal heads, while the almost monumental **Ardagh Chalice** of the same date is a masterpiece of colourful decoration. Its extraordinarily elaborate base, with three friezes in gold around a central rock crystal, would have been only briefly visible when raised during Mass. In a similar way, the splendid ornamentation of the underside of the renowned **Tara Brooch** (also c 700) would have only been seen by its owner when putting on or taking off the cloak it was used to fasten.

Painting

When Gaelic culture waned in the 17C the chief influences on art in Ireland were English and European. A guild of painters was founded in Dublin in 1670 but there was little development until the Dublin Society's Schools were set up in 1746 to promote design in art and manufacture. The first master, Robert West (d 1770), and his assistant, James Mannin (d 1779), had trained in France. The School's most outstanding pupil was probably **Hugh Douglas Hamilton** (1739-1808), who excelled at pastel portraits; in 1778 he visited Italy and while in Rome developed as a painter in oils.

Susanna Drury (fl 1733-70), whose paintings of the Giant's Causeway are in the Ulster Museum, was a member of the Irish school of landscape painting, which emerged in the 18C. **George Barret** (c 1732-84), who moved to England in 1763, introduced the Romantic element into his landscapes. Several Irish artists travelled to Italy. Thomas Roberts (1748-78), a pupil of the Dublin Society's Schools and a brilliant landscape artist, was familiar with Dutch and French painting and exhibited several works in the style of Claude Vernet. The dominant figure of the 18C is **James Barry** (1741-1806), who produced large-scale works in the neo-Classical tradition. He travelled widely, including in Italy, studying painting and sculpture. Joseph Peacock (c 1783-1837) from Dublin was famous for his outdoor fair scenes. Among 18C visitors to Dublin were Vincent Valdré (1742-1814), who painted three panels for the ceiling of St Patrick's Hall in Dublin Castle, and Angelica Kauffmann (1741-1807), who spent seven months in Ireland in 1771 as the guest of the Viceroy, Lord Townshend.

In 1823 the **Royal Hibernian Academy** was incorporated by charter to encourage Irish artists by offering them an annual opportunity of exhibiting their works.

After the Act of Union in 1800 many Irish artists moved to London: Martin Archer Shee (1769-1850), who became President of the Royal Academy in 1830, and Daniel Maclise (1806-70), a popular historical painter. Nathaniel Hone (1831-1917) spent 17 years in France painting out of doors like the painters of the Barbizon school. Roderic O'Conor (1860-1940) from Co Roscommon studied in Antwerp and in France where he met Gauguin, whose influence, together with that of Van Gogh, is obvious in his work. **Sir John Lavery** (1856-1948) from Belfast studied in Paris and is known for his portraits, although he also painted scenes from the French countryside. Another artist who studied abroad is **Sarah Purser** (1848-1943), who was a prolific portrait painter and a founder of *An Túr Gloine*.

The 20C has produced several artists of note. **Jack B Yeats** (1871-1957), brother of William Butler Yeats the poet, painted his views of Irish life with bold brushstrokes in brilliant colours. **Paul Henry** (1876-1958) is known for his ability to represent the luminous quality of the light in the west of Ireland. **William Orpen** (1878-1931), who trained at the Metropolitan School of Art in Dublin and the Slade in London, became a fashionable portrait painter and an official war artist; among his Irish pupils were **Seán Keating** (1889-1977) and **Patrick Tuohy** (1894-1930). Cubism was introduced to Ireland by **Mainie Jellett** (1897-1944) and **Evie Hone** (1894-1955), who is better known for her work in stained glass.

In 1991 the National Gallery and the Hugh Lane Gallery were joined by the Irish Museum of Modern Art at Kilmainham, which is to commission works for its permanent collection and provide a stimulus for future generations.

Sculpture

Cross-slabs and Pillar-stones

Among the earliest stone monuments are the slabs laid flat over an individual grave between the 8C and the 12C. The largest collection is at the monastic site at Clonmacnoise. Of somewhat earlier date are cross-decorated pillar-stones, some set up as grave markers. A number of them may be recycled prehistoric standing stones.

High Crosses

One of the great symbols of Ireland, the free-standing highly-decorated crosses are most numerous in the east of Ireland but they are also found in western and northern Britain. It is thought that high crosses are the successors to small painted or bronze-covered wooden crosses, possibly carved in stone to prevent theft by raiders, and used as a focus for kneeling congregations. They vary in height (6ft/2m-20ft/6m) and most stand on a pyramidal base; the head of the cross is usually ringed and surmounted by a finial often in the shape of a small shrine. The ring probably has a symbolic purpose.

The early carving on late 8C crosses, including some at Clonmacnoise, is mostly decorative consisting of spirals and interlacing. In the 9C and 10C, panels of figures appear illustrating stories at first from the New and then from the Old Testament; such biblical figures or scenes are rare in early Christian art. Animal scenes are often executed on the base. The Cross of Moone *(see Athy)* includes animal and biblical iconography.

The 12C crosses are a fresh batch, not a direct continuation, often lacking a ring *(see Cashel, Glendalough)*. By this date the figure of a bishop or abbot in the Continental style predominates. The best groups of crosses are at Monasterboice, Clonmacnoise, Kells and Ahenny.

Middle Ages to the Renaissance

A distinctive feature of the medieval period is the box tomb found in the chancel of many churches. The lid usually bears a carved effigy of the dead man and sometimes of his wife too. The sides are decorated with figures of the Apostles and saints. In the 15C and 16C, figures and scenes from the Crucifixion were carved in high relief, as on the tomb of Bishop Wellesley (c 1539) in Kildare Cathedral and the Butler effigies in St Canice's Cathedral in Kilkenny. Although predominantly religious, 17C sculpture, such as the Jacobean Segrave or Cosgrave stucco tableaux in St Audeon's Church in Dublin, widened in scope to include stone and timber carved chimney pieces; there are two fine examples of the former in the castles in Donegal and Carrick-on-Suir. On a grand scale are the Renaissance-inspired 17C tombs such as the O'Brien Monument (1600) in St Mary's Cathedral in Limerick, the Chichester Monument (c 1614) in St Nicholas' Church in Carrickfergus and the Earl of Cork's Monument (1620) in Youghal. Carvings from the Restoration period – fine wood relief and stone – survive, especially at the Kilmainham Hospital.

18C to the Present

The spate of building in the 18C provided much work for sculptors. The figures of **Justice** and **Mars** above the gates of Dublin Castle are the work of **Van Nost** as is a statue of George III, now in the Mansion House. **Edward Smyth** (1749-1812), who was a pupil of the Dublin Society's Schools, created the riverine heads on the keystones of the arches and the arms of Ireland on the Custom House and also worked on the Four Courts under James Gandon and on the Bank of Ireland; he had been apprenticed to Simon Vierpyl (c 1725-1810), who worked on the Marino Casino. Vierpyl's work at the Casino includes the urns flanking the external steps; the lions adjacent are the work of the English sculptor Joseph Wilton.

The 19C saw the dominance of Greek Revival detailing; in St Patrick's Church in Monaghan there is a good collection of monuments, especially the monument to Lady Rossmore (c 1807) by Thomas Kirk (1781-1845). John Hogan (1800-58) is acknowledged as a most distinguished sculptor; see his fine plaster *The Drunken Faun* in the Crawford Art Gallery in Cork. Two of his contemporaries, who worked on the Albert Memorial in London, were Patrick MacDowell (1799-1870), who carved the group of Europe on the base of the monument, and John Henry Foley (1818-74), who sculpted the bronze figure of Prince Albert; Foley's best work in Dublin is the O'Connell Monument and the statues of Burke, Goldsmith and Grattan on College Green outside Trinity College in Dublin. The best work of Thomas Farrell (1827-1900) is the Cullen Memorial (1881) in the Pro-Cathedral in Dublin.

On a monumental scale is the Wellington Testimonial (c 1817) in Phoenix Park in Dublin by English architect Sir Robert Smirke; it has bronze reliefs on the base by the sculptors Joseph Robinson Kirk, Farrell and Hogan. The work of Oliver Sheppard (1864-1941) is strongly influenced by the Art Nouveau style.

The Parnell Monument in O'Connell Street in Dublin was designed by Augustus St Gaudens in 1911.

The portrait sculptor **Albert Power** (1883-1945), a resident of Dublin, was elected Associate of RHA in 1911; there are examples of his work in Cavan Cathedral, Mullingar Cathedral and in Eyre Square in Galway. The Belfast sculptor FE McWilliam (1909-92) is represented by a series of bronze figurative sculptures in the Ulster Museum.

More recent work of note includes the *Children of Lir* by Oisin Kelly (1916-81) in the Garden of Remembrance in Dublin. A pleasing aspect of contemporary urban renewal is the placing of sculpture in places where it is readily encountered by the public, who have often responded with affection and amusement. Examples include somewhat quirky statues of Oscar Wilde and James Joyce in Dublin and of WB Yates in Sligo, as well as a famous personification of the Liffey in Dublin's O'Connell Street.

Historical Perspective

More than most European countries, contemporary Ireland remains marked by its troubled history, with the current peace process in Northern Ireland being the latest attempt to reconcile the conflicting traditions and exclusive senses of identity which have marked the country's past.

Marriage of Strong Bow and Eva
by Daniel Mac Lise (1854)

Celtic Ireland

- **6000-1750 BC** – Stone Age; c 3000 BC people turned to farming from hunting and gathering. Construction of passage graves.
- **1750-500 BC** – Bronze Age.
- **500 BC-AD 450** – Iron Age; Celtic tribes arrived from Europe; inter-tribal strife for supremacy and the title of High King (Ard Rí).
- **55 BC-early 5C AD** – Roman occupation of Britain but not Ireland. Trade links proved by finds of Roman coins and jewellery.
- **4C-5C** – Irish Celts (known as Scots) colonised the west of England and Scotland.
- **432-61** – **St Patrick's mission** to convert Ireland to Christianity.
- **6C-11C** – Monastic age; Irish missionaries travelled to the European mainland.
- **795 – Viking Invasions** – Vikings from Norway and Denmark made raids on the monasteries near the coasts and waterways; in 841 they began to settle.
- **1014 – Battle of Clontarf** – **Brian Ború**, King of Munster, gained a Pyrrhic victory against the combined forces of the Danish Vikings and the king of Leinster.
- **1156** – Death of Turlough O'Connor, last powerful native ruler.
- **1159** – Henry II (1154-89) received the title "Lord of Ireland" from Pope Adrian IV and the Pope's blessing to invade Ireland.

Anglo-Norman Ireland

- **1169** – Invited by Dermot, King of Leinster, to oust his opponents, an Anglo-Norman army commanded by "Strongbow", Richard de Clare, landed at Baginbun on the south coast. In 1171, after Dermot's death, Strongbow declared himself King of Leinster, much to the discomfiture of Henry II, who eventually extracted a humiliating declaration of loyalty from his over-ambitious vassal as well as extending English control over much of the country. England's involvement in Irish affairs was now constant, though the interests of the Anglo-Irish frequently diverged from those of the mother country and many settlers became "more Irish than the Irish".
- **1177 – Anglo-Norman** invasion of Ulster under John de Courcy.
- **1185 – Prince John, given the title Lord of Ireland,** visited the country, to which he returned in 1210.
- **1297** – First **Irish Parliament** convened.
- **1315-18 – Bruce Invasion** – Edward Bruce, brother to King Robert of Scotland, landed at Carrickfergus with 6 000 Scottish mercenaries (gallowglasses); he was crowned king in 1316 but died at the Battle of Faughart near Dundalk in 1318.
- **1348-50 – Black Death** – About one-third of the population died.

● **1366 – The Statutes of Kilkenny** promulgated in order to maintain the distinction between Anglo-Normans and native Irish. They prohibited fosterage, bareback riding, hurling, the Irish language and Irish dress and patronage of Irish storytellers and poets but largely failed in their purpose.

● **1394 & 1399 – Richard II** landed in Ireland with an army to re-establish control.

● **1446** – First mention of **The Pale** to describe the area of English influence; by the 15C it was only a narrow coastal strip from Dundalk to south of Dublin.

● **1471** – The Earl of Kildare appointed **Lord Deputy**, marking the rise to power of the Geraldines.

● **1487** – The pretender Lambert Simnel crowned Edward V of England in Dublin by the Earl of Kildare.

● **1491** – Perkin Warbeck, pretender to the English throne, landed in Cork without the opposition of the Earl of Kildare.

● **1494** – Sir Edward Poynings appointed Lord Deputy: under **Poynings' Law** the Irish parliament could not meet or propose legislation without royal consent.

● **1534-40** – Failure of the Kildare (Geraldine) Revolt and the end of Kildare ascendancy.

SPANISH ARMADA

Some 30 ships of the Spanish Armada were wrecked off the Irish coast between Antrim and Kerry. It has been estimated that they contained 8 000 sailors and gunners, 2 100 rowers, 19 000 soldiers and 2 431 pieces of ordnance. Those survivors who were not killed by the Irish were hunted by the English.

Port na Spaniagh on the Giant's Causeway marks the place where the *Gerona*, a galleass, was wrecked without survivors; some of its treasures, recovered by diving on the wreck in 1968, are on display in the Ulster Museum.

On the Inishowen Peninsula at Kinnagoe Bay many interesting military relics were found in the wrecks of *La Duquesa St Anna* and *La Trinidad Valencia*. A map on the clifftop *(at the road junction)* plots the sites of the many ships of the Spanish Armada which were wrecked on the Irish coast.

Three ships – *Juliana, La Levia* and *La Santa Maria de Vision* – were wrecked at Streedagh Point, north of Sligo; over 1 300 men are thought to have died.

One of the survivors who came ashore at Streedagh, Captain Francisco de Cuellar, wrote an account of the shipwreck and of his journey from Sligo through Leitrim, Donegal and Derry to Antrim; from there he sailed to Scotland and returned via Antwerp to Spain.

Reformation and Plantation

● **1539 – Reformation** and **Dissolution of the Monasteries**.

● **1541** – Henry VIII declared **King of Ireland** by the Irish Parliament.

● **1556** – Colonisation of Co Laois (Queen's County) and Offaly (King's County) by English settlers.

● **1579 – Desmond (Munster) Rebellion** severely crushed by Elizabeth I; confiscation and colonisation.

● **1585** – Ireland mapped and divided into counties; 27 sent members to Parliament.

● **1588 – Spanish Armada** – After its defeat in the English Channel, the Spanish Armada, driven by the wind, sailed up the east coast of Great Britain and round the north coast of Scotland. Off the Irish coast stormy weather further depleted its ranks.

● **1598 – Hugh O'Neill,** Earl of Tyrone, leads rebellion and defeats English army at the Battle of Yellow Ford *(see Dungannon)*.

● **1601 – Siege of Kinsale** – 4 000 Spanish troops landed in Kinsale to assist Hugh O'Neill but withdrew when besieged.

● **1603 –** Submission of Hugh O'Neill, Earl of Tyrone, and Rory O'Donnell, Earl of Tyrconnell, at Mellifont to **Lord Mountjoy**, Queen Elizabeth's Deputy.

● **1607 –** The Earls of Tyrconnell and Tyrone sailed from Rathmullan *(see Donegal Coast)* into exile on the Continent. This event, known as the **Flight of the Earls**, marked the final breaking of the political power of Gaelic Ireland.

● **1607-41 – Plantation of Ulster** under James I, in which Protestants from the Scottish lowlands settled in the northern counties of Ireland.

● **1641 – Confederate Rebellion** provoked by the policies of the King's Deputy and the desire of the dispossessed Irish to regain their land; large-scale slaughter of Protestant settlers.

● **1642 – Confederation of Kilkenny** – The Irish and Old English Catholics formed an alliance to defend their religion, land and political rights.

● **1649 – Oliver Cromwell** "pacified" Ireland with great brutality, storming Drogheda and Wexford and transporting thousands of Irish to the West Indies.

● **1653 –** Under the **Cromwellian Settlement** most Roman Catholic landowners judged unsympathetic to the Commonwealth were dispossessed and ordered to retreat west of the Shannon; the proportion of land owned by Roman Catholics dropped drastically.

● **1660 – Restoration** of Charles II and return of some land to Roman Catholic owners.

● **1678 – Oates Conspiracy**, a pretext for the arrest, imprisonment and even the death of various Roman Catholics, among them Oliver Plunkett, Archbishop of Armagh *(see Drogheda)*.

● **1685 –** Revocation of the Edict of Nantes in France caused many **Huguenots** (Protestants) to flee to England and Ireland.

● **1688 – Glorious Revolution** – James II deposed; William of Orange accepted the English throne. 13 Londonderry Apprentice Boys shut the city gates in the face of King James's troops; the following year the city endured a three-month siege by Jacobite army.

● **1690 – Battle of the Boyne** – King William III of England and his allies representing the Protestant interest defeated King James II, who fled to France.

● **1691 – Siege of Limerick** – Following the battles of Athlone and Aughrim *(see Athenry)*, the Irish army retreated to Limerick, where it was besieged. Under the military terms of the **Treaty of Limerick** the Irish defenders were allowed to surrender with honour. Known as the **Wild Geese**, they were permitted to sail for France, where many joined the French army.

Anglo-Irish Ascendancy

● **1695 –** The provisions of the Treaty of Limerick guaranteeing Roman Catholic rights soon ignored and Penal Laws *(see Land of Saints)* enacted imposing severe restrictions on their rights to property, freedom of worship and education.

● **1711 –** Linen Board established to control quality of export of linen, one of many "improvements" (canals, roads, urban planning) which contributed to the country's growing prosperity.

● **1778 – Volunteers** formed to defend Ireland against the French; they supported the demand for an independent Irish parliament.

● **1782 – Repeal of Poynings' Law** and the establishment of an independent Irish Parliament, known as Grattan's Parliament after Henry Grattan who had led the campaign for independence.

● **1791 –** Formation in Belfast of the mostly Presbyterian **United Irishmen**, promoting the ideal of a republican country with no religious distinctions.

● **1791-93 – Catholic Relief Acts** *(see Land of Saints)*.

● **1795 – Rural violence between Protestant Peep O'Day Boys and Catholic Defenders and the** foundation of the **Orange Order** *(see Armagh)*.

● **1796 –** Abortive French invasion in Bantry Bay *(see Bantry)*.

GREAT FAMINE (1845-49)

Potato blight *(phytophthora infestans)* destroyed the potato crop, on which the bulk of the population depended for food; 800 000 people died of hunger, typhus and cholera; hundreds of coffinless bodies were buried in mass graves, Thousands of starving people overwhelmed the workhouses and the depot towns from which the Indian corn imported by the government was distributed; the workhouse capacity was 100 000 but five times that number qualified for relief. The Quakers did most to bring relief to the hungry. Soup kitchens were set up by compassionate landlords and by Protestant groups seeking converts; 50 large cauldrons were imported in 1847 from the Darby works in Coalbrookdale in England. Public works were instituted to provide employment and relief. Some landlords evicted their penniless tenants (in 1847 16 landlords were murdered), others arranged for their emigration. So many died during the voyage or in quarantine that the vessels were known as coffin ships. One million Irish men and women emigrated to England, Scotland, Canada and the USA.

● **1798 – Rebellion of the United Irishmen** launched by Wolfe Tone; the main engagements were in Antrim, Wexford and Mayo; the rising was brutally suppressed and 30 000 rebels died. Tone was captured and committed suicide in prison.

Ireland in the United Kingdom

● **1800 – Act of Union** – Suppression of the Irish Parliament. Ireland was represented at Westminster by 100 seats in the House of Commons and 28 temporal and four spiritual lords in the Upper House.

● **1803   Emmet Rebellion** – An abortive rising led by Robert Emmet (1778-1803), who had been a political exile in France and vainly counted on the invasion of England by Napoleon. Emmet was hanged but his speech from the dock was an inspiration for future generations of nationalists.

● **1823 – Daniel O'Connell** (1775-1847), a Roman Catholic lawyer, known as the Counsellor and the Liberator, elected MP for Clare after campaigning for the recognition of the rights of Catholics and for repeal of the Act of Union.

Daniel O'Connell

● **1829 –** O'Connell's election led to **Roman Catholic Emancipation Act** enabling Roman Catholics to enter Parliament.

● **1848 –** Abortive **Young Ireland Uprising** led by William Smith O'Brien (1803-64).

● **1858 –** Founding of the revolutionary **Irish Republican Brotherhood (IRB)** also known as Fenians.

● **1867 – Manchester Martyrs,** three Fenians who were executed for the murder of a policeman during an attack on a police van in Manchester to release two Fenian prisoners. The doubtful nature of some of the evidence weakened Irish confidence in British justice.

● **1869 –** The anomalous position of the Anglican **Church of Ireland** as the country's "official" church recognised by its disestablishment.

● **1870-1933 – Land Acts –** 17 acts which transferred ownership of large estates from landlords to their tenants.

● **1874 – 59 Home Rulers** elected to Parliament

- **1875-91** – Protestant landowner and MP **Charles Stewart Parnell** (1846-91), leader of the Home Rule party and later of the Land League.
- **1886** – First **Home Rule** Bill, granting Ireland various degrees of independence in domestic matters, introduced by Gladstone but rejected by Parliament.
- **1879-82** – **Land League** formed by Michael Davitt to campaign by passive resistance for the reform of the tenancy laws and land purchase.
- **1891-1923** – **Congested Districts' Board** – Funds from the disestablished Church of Ireland were used in the poorer districts of Ireland to construct harbours and promote fishing, fish curing and modern farming methods; after 1903 the Board was empowered to re-distribute large estates to smallholders.
- **1893** – Second **Home Rule** Bill introduced and rejected by Parliament.
- **1905-08** – **Sinn Féin** (Ourselves) founded to promote the idea of a dual monarchy.
- **1912** – Third **Home Rule** Bill introduced by Asquith. Fierce opposition to Home Rule in Ulster, where three-quarters of the adult population, under the leadership of **Sir Edward Carson**, signed a covenant to prevent it by whatever means necessary. Rival militias were formed and armed with smuggled weaponry, the Ulster Volunteer Force in the north, the Nationalist Irish Volunteers in the south.
- **1914** – **Outbreak of First World War** led to postponement of Home Rule and avoidance of civil war. Irishmen of all persuasions volunteered to fight in the British army.
- **1917** – **Sinn Féin** reorganised under Eamon de Valera as a nationwide movement for the independence of Ireland.
- **1918** – **General Election** at which Redmond's Home Rulers were utterly defeated and Sinn Féin candidates won 73 seats.
- **1919** – **Declaration of Independence** drafted on 8 January and read in Irish, English and French on 21 January at the meeting of the first Irish Assembly (*Dáil Éireann*) in Dublin.
- **1919-20** – **War of Independence** – **Irish Republican Army (IRA)** launched a campaign to make British administration in Ireland impossible; martial law was proclaimed; the Royal Irish Constabulary was reinforced by British ex-servicemen (Black and Tans) who became notorious for their brutal behaviour.
- **1920** – **Government of Ireland Act** providing for partition; six of the nine counties of Ulster remained within the UK, in accordance with the wishes of the majority of the population, with a separate parliament (later referred to as "A Protestant parliament for a Protestant people"; dominion status was granted to the remaining 26 counties, which came to be known as the Free State.

Easter Rising in 1916

The leader of the moderate Nationalists, John Redmond, had hoped that Irish support for the British war effort would swiftly lead to Home Rule at the end of hostilities but the Military Council of the Irish Republican Brotherhood, the more militant nationalists, had secretly organised an uprising. Despite the capture of Sir Roger Casement and a cargo of arms from Germany, and despite a last-minute confusion in orders, the rising was not cancelled. On Easter Monday columns of Volunteers marched into Dublin and took possession of various strongpoints including the General Post Office, where they set up their headquarters; from its steps Patrick Pearse announced the establishment of a republic. The insurgents were hopelessly outnumbered and outgunned and on Saturday they surrendered. Although intended to be a national rebellion, it was confined to Dublin and failed. The insurrection had not enjoyed public support but attitudes changed when the ringleaders were tried by court martial and executed.

Michael Collins

National Library of Ireland, Dublin

David Trimble and John Hume receiving the Nobel Peace Prize

B Sigu/CORBIS-SYGMA

THE TROUBLES

The subordinate position of Roman Catholics in Northern Ireland was challenged by the formation in 1967 of the Northern Ireland Civil Rights Association. A protest march from Belfast to Londonderry in 1969 was attacked by Protestant militants and police, and further unrest led to the deployment of British troops, then to the revival of IRA activity aimed at forcing British withdrawal from the province. In 1972, the Northern Ireland Parliament at Stormont was prorogued and direct rule from Westminster introduced. Successive British attempts in the 1970s and 1980s to construct new forms of governance acceptable to all parties foundered. But in the early 1990s, inter-party talks and the Downing Street Declaration of 1993 made by the British and Irish prime ministers initiated a slow and often difficult "peace process"; an IRA ceasefire was annulled, then reinstated, seemingly permanently, though dissident violence and communal disturbances continued. The Good Friday Agreement of 1998, overwhelmingly endorsed by referendums in both parts of Ireland, led to elections based on proportional representation to a new Northern Ireland Assembly in which Nationalist and Republican interests were represented, notably by members of Sinn Fein. In 2002 the Assembly was suspended.

Partition and Independence

- **1921 – Anglo-Irish Treaty**
- **1922-23 – Civil War** between the Free State Army under the generalship of Michael Collins and Republicans unwilling to accept even the temporary partition of the country. Casualties greater than in War of Independence. Collins assassinated but Republicans defeated.
- **1922 –** Constitution of the **Irish Free State** comprising the 26 counties; the two-tier legislature consisted of the Senate and *Dáil Éireann*.
- **1937 –** New Constitution which changed the official name of the country to **Éire**.
- **1938 –** Three naval bases (Cork Harbour, Bere Island and Lough Swilly) which had remained in British hands under the Anglo-Irish Treaty were returned to Ireland.
- **1939-45 – Second World War** (referred to as the Emergency) in which Éire was neutral but covert aid was given to the Allies.
- **1949 –** Éire became the **Republic of Ireland** and left the Commonwealth.
- **1955** Republic of Ireland joined the United Nations; Irish troops involved in peace-keeping missions.
- **1965 –** Anglo-Irish Free Trade Area Agreement.
- **1973 –** Republic of Ireland, together with Northern Ireland as part of the United Kingdom, became members of the EEC, now the European Union (EU), leading to a period of agricultural prosperity and access to Community funds for development projects.
- **1983 –** Confirmation of ban on abortion in the Republic.
- **1986 –** Confirmation of the ban on divorce in the Republic.
- **1998 – The Republic of Ireland** adopted the Euro as its official currency.
- **2001 – Referendum** in which the electorate of the Republic voted to reject the Treaty of Nice providing for eastward enlargement of the European Union. The treaty was accepted at second referendum in 2002.
- **2002 – Euro coins and banknotes** came into circulation in the Republic. The Royal Ulster Constabulary replaced by the Police Service of Northern Ireland.

A Gyori/CORBIS-SYGMA

Mary Robinson

Custom House, Dublin

Republic of Ireland

Abbeyleix

At the height of the Anglo-Irish Ascendancy in the mid-18C, Viscount de Vesci followed the fashion of the time, demolishing the cottages of his tenants and re-housing the people in a carefully planned new settlement at the gates of his great mansion. Scarcely changed since those days, Abbeyleix is one of the best examples of this type of aristocratic estate development, and is now a designated Heritage Town, but its origins lie much further back in time than the 18C, since it occupies the site of a late-12C Cistercian abbey, itself a successor to an even older monastery.

Location

Population 1 299 - Michelin Atlas p 86 and Map 712 – J 9 – Co Laois.
Abbeyleix *(Mainistir Laoise)* is on N 8 linking the capital and Cork, 61mi/98km SW of Dublin; its broad main street carries a heavy load of through traffic.
Adjacent Sights: See ATHY, CASHEL, KILDARE, KILKENNY, ROSCREA, TULLAMORE.

DIRECTORY
Morrissey's Bar – Many travellers make a point of stopping off at Morrissey's Bar, a wonderful combination of grocer's shop and pub, which, like the town itself, seems little altered since it was built.
Grantstown Lake – *8mi/13km W by R 433* – Woodland walks beside a lake (fishing).

Worth a Visit

Abbeyleix Heritage House

♿ *Open Mar-Sep, Mon-Fri, 9am-5pm; also May-Aug, Sat-Sun, 1-5pm. €3. Parking. Coffee shop.* ☏ *0502 31653; Fax 0502 30059; abbeyleixlaois@hotmail.com*
The exhibition in the old school traces the history of Abbeyleix and its role in the evolution of the region, in which the actions of the de Vescis feature prominently. There is a fine model of the town in its setting as well as one of the Rock of Dunamase.

Abbey Sense Garden

♿ *Open daily, 9am-4pm. Donation.* ☏ *0502 31636 and 31325; Fax 0502 31386; scjmdovehouse@eircom.net*
The old walled garden of a former Brigidine convent has been redesigned with elaborate planting and other features intended to appeal to touch, taste, smell and sound as well as sight.

Excursions

Emo Court★★

15mi/24km NNE of Abbeyleix by N 8, M 7 and R 422. (Dúchas) Gardens: Open daily, daylight hours. Guided tour (1hr): Jul-Aug, Sun at 3pm. House: Guided tour (40min) mid-Jun to mid-Sep, daily, 10.30am-5pm (6pm Sun); last tour 40min before closing. Closed 25-26 Dec. House €2.50. Parking. ☏ *0502 26573; Fax 0502 26573*
This splendid domed Classical mansion was designed by **James Gandon** in 1792 for Lord Portarlington, formerly **John Dawson**, a banker and an architect. After many years of use as a Jesuit seminary, the interior with its rotunda and superb stuccowork has been restored and is furnished with numerous fine pieces as well as varied examples of Wedgwood pottery.
A magnificent avenue of Wellingtonias, the first in Ireland, links the house to the Dublin Road and extensive **gardens** link the house to the lake. The Clucker Garden is planted with azaleas, rhododendrons and Japanese maples; four statues of the Seasons and a ring garden adorn the lawns, and a Grapery planted with trees and shrubs descends to the lakeside walk.

St John the Evangelist

Coolbanagher; from the gates of Emo Court take the road opposite through the village; turn left into R 419 (Portarlington-Portlaoise road). Services: First Sun of month, 10.45am (Matins), other Sun, noon. ☏ *0502 24143 (Rector)*
James Gandon designed this church, his only one, in 1785 for Lord Carlow. The interior is decorated with plaster swags, roundels and garlands.

Rock of Dunamase★

15mi/24km NE of Abbeyleix by R 245, R 247 and N 80 NW.
The rock rising straight from the plain is crowned by the extensive and impressive ruins of the O'More clan fortress, destroyed by Cromwell's army in the mid-17C. Excellent **views★** from the summit (200ft/60m high).

Stradbally Steam Engine Rally

Stradbally Steam Museum*

13mi/21km NE of Abbeyleix by R 245, R 247 and N 80 SE. ⧲ *Museum: Closed for renovation until summer 2003. Trains: In steam Easter-Oct, Bank Hol Sun and Mon. Annual Steam Rally at Stradbally Hall: Aug Bank Hol Sun and Mon.* ☎ *0502 25444; 0502 25513; rallysec@irishsteam.ie; www.irishsteam.ie*

The museum displays a collection of old steam-powered rollers and threshing machines. A narrow-gauge steam railway (1mi/1.6km) runs through the woods. A rally of steam machines is held in the grounds of Stradbally Hall .

In the Stradbally Market Place stands an unusual pagoda-like structure with a red roof which commemorates Dr William Perceval, a local doctor who died in 1899 after 54 years of local practice.

Timahoe Round Tower*

9mi/15km NE of Abbeyleix by R 430 E and a minor road N. This fine example of a round tower (96ft/29m high) was probably built in the 12C and leans slightly (2ft/0.6m) from the vertical; it has a lovely Romanesque double doorway with steps to the interior.

The ruins of a 15C church (*E*) were converted into a castle in the 17C.

Richard Nixon, President of the USA (1969-74), whose ancestors came from the village, visited **Timahoe** in 1970.

Heywood Gardens

Near Ballinakill; 3.5mi/6km SE of Abbeyleix by R 432. (Dúchas) (⧲) Open during daylight hours. Tour: Jul-Aug, Sun 3pm or by appointment. €2.50 Parking. Closed 25-26 Dec. ☎ *056 51863 or 0502 33563 heywoodgardensw@ealga.ie; www.heritageireland.ie*

Although the mansion which they once graced has long since been replaced by a modern college building, these gardens (1906-10) are a fine example of the partnership between the architect **Edwin Lutyens** (1869-1944) and the garden designer **Gertrude Jekyll** (1843-1932). Architectural influences predominate, with terraces, massive retaining walls, gateways, flights of steps, pleached lime walk and hedges of clipped yew. The Italianate sunken garden has a pool and a pavilion; paths and lawns have a prospect of church towers and distant mountains, and a pergola is set high above a pond and wooded ravine.

Adare*

This tiny town in fertile wooded countryside at the tidal limit of the River Maigue is rich in reminders of the Middle Ages but the main reason for the coach parties all stopping in Adare is its picture postcard appearance and its designation as a Heritage town. Giving the place an utterly un-Irish look are rows of pretty, colour-washed cottages, which with their overhanging thatched roofs were built in the mid-19C by the local landowner, the Earl of Dunraven, who succeeded in making his corner of west Limerick resemble something from the English shires.

Directory

WHERE TO STAY

• Budget

Berkeley Lodge – Station Rd -
☎ 061 396 857 - Fax 061 396 857 -
berlodge@iol.ie - ▣ ⵥ⤬ - 6 rm €58/66 ⤋.
Simple, clean accommodation that is
competitively priced and centrally located.
The welcoming owners ensure that guests
have that "home from home" feeling.
Bedrooms at the rear of the house are
quieter.

Carrabawn Guesthouse – Killarney Rd –
0.5mi SW on N 21 - ☎ 061 396 067 -
Fax 061 396 925 -
bridget@carrabawnhouseadare.com - ▣
ⵥ⤬ - 8 rm €65/90 ⤋. A welcoming and
immaculately kept guesthouse, just a 10-
minute walk from the town centre. The
breakfast room overlooks the very pretty
mature garden which the owners have
lovingly established.

• Expensive

Adare Manor – ☎ 061 396 566 - Fax
061 396 124 -
reservations@adaremanor.com - ▣ ⵥ⤬ -
113 rm, 35 suites €375/670 - ⤋ €20 -
Restaurant €52/80. This imposing and
impressive Gothic manor has been
sympathetically extended and lies in
800 acres/323ha, with fishing, golf and
leisure facilities. Grand panelled dining
room with classic menu. Bedrooms in
the main house have the most character.

ENTERTAINMENT

Desmond Hall – Musical evenings round the
fire (see below).

SHOPPING

Irish Dresden – 20mi/32km SW of Adare by
R 515 via Ballingarry and Kilmeedy. The
delicate and elaborate porcelain figures
made in this factory represent musicians and
dancers, ladies in flounced skirts made of
layers of simulated net, angels and figures
for the Christmas crib, and birds and
animals. The original master moulds from
Volkestedt in Germany are still in use
together with new ones of Irish inspiration.
Showroom: Open Mon-Fri, 9am-1pm and
2-5pm. Factory: Guided tour (20min) by
appointment Mon-Fri, 11.15am-noon and
3-4pm. ☎ 063 83030, 83236 (Irish Dresden
Ltd, Dromcolliher, Co Limerick); Fax
063 83192; sales@irishdres.iol.ie

TRACING ANCESTORS

The **Irish Palatine Heritage Centre** in
Rathkeale (see below) provides a
genealogical service for tracing ancestors.

Location

Population 1 042 - Michelin Atlas p 84 and Map 712– F 10 – Co Limerick. Adare (Átha Dara) is 10mi/17km SW of Limerick on the N 21 Tralee road.
🛈 *Adare Heritage Centre. Open Feb-Dec. ☎ 061 396 255; Fax 061 396 610*
Adjacent Sights: See LIMERICK, TRALEE.

Walking About

Adare Heritage Centre
There is more to Adare than picturesque thatched cottages. The historical exhibition tells of Norman invaders, medieval abbeys and the influential Dunraven family. Its highlight is a model which brings to life the town in 1500; there is also an audio-visual presentation (15min).

Church of the Most Holy Trinity (Roman Catholic)
Main Street facing the town park. The square tower and the south wall of the present church were part of a monastery, the only house in Ireland of the **Trinitarian Order**, constructed about 1230 by Maurice Fitzgerald, 2nd Baron of Offaly. The 50 monks were put to death in 1539 at the Dissolution of the Monasteries. The ruins were restored by the 1st Earl of Dunraven and enlarged in 1852. At the rear stands a completely restored 14C **dovecot**.

Adare Parish Church (Anglican)★
The church consists of the nave and part of the choir of an Augustinian priory founded in 1315. The cloisters (north side) were converted into a mausoleum for the family of Quin, the Earls of Dunraven.

Adare Manor
The exuberantly neo-Gothic mansion, now a hotel open to non-residents, was begun in 1832; among the architects involved were James Pain and **Augustus Welby Pugin**. The carved inscriptions state that it was built by the **Earl of Dunraven**. The interior contains an elaborately panelled staircase and a long gallery (132ft/40m). The grounds, which include a maze and a lake, border the River Maigue.

Adare Friary★
Access via Adare Golf Course; ask at the Club House. Beside the River Maigue are the evocative ruins of the Franciscan friary founded by the Earl of Kildare in 1464; extensions were built in the 15C and 16C. The nave, choir, south transept and cloisters are reasonably well preserved. The **Kilmallock Gate** was once the main entrance.

Thatched Cottages, Adare

Desmond Castle

Access via Adare Golf Course; ask at the Club House. The castle had already ceased to be of strategic importance when much of it was demolished by Cromwell's forces. A large square tower stands in the inner ward of the early-14C castle surrounded by a moat. The upper storey of the building in the southwest corner of the outer ward was the **great hall**. Nearby are the remains of **St Nicholas Church** (11C) and the **Desmond Chapel** (14C).

Excursions

Castle Matrix★

7.5mi/13km W of Adare by N 21 at Rathkeale; concealed entrance on north side of busy main road. (&) Guided tour mid-Jun to Sep, daily, 9.30am-6.30pm. €5. Poetry and musical evenings by appointment. Parking. ☎ 087 792 1702; lysard@lycos.com; www.hackertourist.com/talin/trip99
The Norman tower was built in 1440 by the 7th Earl of Desmond; he and his father, the 4th Earl, are the earliest-recorded Norman poets in the Irish language. The Great Hall houses a fine **library** and objets d'art. The castle also houses an **international arts centre** and the **Heraldry Society of Ireland**. It was at Castle Matrix that Edmund Spenser, the poet, and Walter Ralegh, then a captain, met for the first time in 1580 and began a lifelong friendship.

Irish Palatine Heritage Centre★

7.5mi/13km W of Adare by N 21 at Rathkeale. & Open May-Sep, Tue-Fri, 10am-1pm and 2-5pm, Sun, 2-5pm. €2.50. Genealogy service. Parking. Tearoom. ☎ 069 63511 or 64397; Fax 069 63511 or 64220; ipass@eircom.net; www.erin ie/ipa
The centre, housed in an old station-master's house re-erected on a new site, presents an exhibition of photographs, documents, arms, domestic articles and larger

---

IRISH PALATINES

In 1709, following two invasions, a bitter winter, and oppression by their reinstated Catholic ruler, many German Protestants left that part of the Rhineland known as the Palatinate (hence their name), and travelled to England in response to the provision of funds by the English government to enable them to travel to Carolina in the USA. When the money ran out, many were stranded in London until the Dublin government offered to take 500 families; 821 families arrived in Ireland. Landlords were offered subsidies to accept the immigrants; some went to Counties Kerry, Tipperary and Wexford but the majority settled on the estate of Lord Southwell in Rathkeale, where their names – Bovenizer, Corneille, Delmege, Miller, Rynard, Piper, Sparling, Stark, Switzer, Teskey – sounded a foreign note.

They were an industrious people, who introduced new farming techniques, and a pious, God-fearing people, mostly **Lutherans** or **Calvinists**. They responded with great enthusiasm to the preaching of **John Wesley**, who returned to visit them on several occasions after his first visit in 1756.

One of Wesley's preachers, Philip Embury, and his cousin Barbara Heck emigrated to America in 1760. The sermon preached by Philip in his house in New York in 1766 led to the founding of the Methodist Episcopal Church in America.

artefacts, recalling the settlement of German Protestants in the area of **Rathkeale** in the early 18C, their innovative farming methods, their contribution to Methodism and their dispersion throughout the English-speaking world.

Newcastle West★

16mi/26km W of Adare by N 21. This thriving market town, known for its spring water, takes its name from the **castle** (recently restored) in the town square. Originally the castle belonged to the **Knights Templar** but it later passed into the ownership of the **Earls of Desmond**. The banqueting hall, now known as **Desmond Hall**, with an oak minstrel's gallery (restored) and a hooded fireplace (reconstruction), stands over a 13C vaulted stone chamber, lit by ecclesiastical lancet windows. The remains of the castle include the adjoining Great Hall *(Halla Mór)*. *(Dúchas) (&) Guided tour (50min) mid-Jun to mid-Sep, daily, 9.30am-6.30pm (5.40pm last tour). €1.90. ☎ 069 77408*

Askeaton

13mi/20km NW of Adare by N 21 and R 518. On a small island in the River Deel stand the ruins of **Askeaton Castle**, probably founded by William de Burgo c 1199. The tower and walls (15C) are largely intact; the banqueting hall, erected between 1440 and 1459 by the 7th Earl of Desmond, was one of the largest of its kind in Ireland and has a blind arcade in the south wall and finely carved windows.

North of the town centre on the east bank of the river are the ruins of **Askeaton Franciscan Friary**, a 15C foundation. A representation of **St Francis** is to be found in the northeast corner of the cloisters.

Foynes Flying Boat Museum

21mi/34km W of Adare by N 21, R 518 and N 69. & Open end-Mar to Oct, daily, 10am-6pm (5pm last admission); Nov-Apr, by appointment. €4.50. Film and brochure (4 languages). Parking. Refreshments. ☎/Fax 069 65416; famm@eircom.net; www.webforge.net
Before and during the Second World War the small seaport of **Foynes** in the Shannon Estuary, was the operational base for the flying boats which pioneered transatlantic travel by air. The old terminal building now houses a **museum** displaying many models, photographs, log books and technical equipment which evoke the short life of this ancestor of today's busy Shannon Airport; there are screenings of the film *Atlantic Conquest* with original footage linked by a modern commentary.

Glin Castle★

29mi/47km W of Adare by N 21, R 518 and N 69. & Guided tour by appointment. €7. Parking. ☎ 068 34173, 34112; Fax 068 34364; knight@iol.ie; www.glincastle.com
A branch of the famous Fitzgerald family, the Knights of Glin, have lived close to the village of **Glin** for 700 years. Their original stronghold was destroyed by Queen Elizabeth's forces in 1600, though the ruins of its keep still stand, while their present castle was built around 1780-85 and Gothicised around 1820. The **interior** is outstanding, with superb stuccowork, excellent examples of Georgian mahogany furniture, family portraits and other paintings, and a very unusual flying **staircase** with a Venetian window overlooking the formal gardens.

Glin Heritage Centre – *Open May-Sep, Tue-Sun, 10am-6pm. €2.54. ☎ 068 34001*
The neo-Gothic church at the gates of Glin Castle houses an exhibition on the history of Glin and the Fitzgerald family.

Aran Islands★

Keeping watch over the mouth of Galway Bay are the islands of Inishmore, Inishmaan and Inisheer, great slabs of limestone linked geologically to The Burren on the mainland. People have inhabited these lonely isles since ancient times, using the limestone to build great prehistoric forts like Dún Aonghasa and Dún Conor as well as the close-knit network of drystone walls bounding tiny, flower-rich fields. Tellingly evoked in the writings of JM Synge and Robert Flaherty's classic semi-documentary film *Man of Aran*, the islanders' traditional, extremely harsh way of life was led until relatively recently, and the islands remain a stronghold of the Gaelic language.

Location

Population 2 000 - Michelin Atlas p 88 and Map 712 – CD 8 0 Co Galway.
The three Aran Islands extend in an oblique line across the mouth of **Galway Bay**. The smallest, Inisheer, is not far (5mi/8km) from the mainland; the middle island, Inishmaan, is slightly larger; the largest island, Inishmore, is about 7mi/11.3km from the coast of Connemara.

ᛒ *Kilronan, Inishmore. Open Mon-Sat. ☎ 099 61263*
Adjacent Sights: See THE BURREN, CONNEMARA, GALWAY.

Directory

GETTING THERE

There are flights to all three islands from Connemara Regional Airport at Inveran (20mi/32km W of Galway by R 336); they can also be reached by ferry from Galway, from Rossaveel (23mil/37km west of Galway, and from Doolin in The Burren (Inisheer only).

Aran Islands Air Service - Operates May-Aug, daily, 8 flights per day (9min); Sep-Apr, 3 flights per day. ☏ 091 593 034 (reservations); ☏ 099 61109; Fax 091 593 238 (Aer Arann); aerarann@iol.ie; www.aerarannexpress.ie

Galway - Aran Islands Ferry - Operates (2hr) Jun-Sep, Tue, and Thu-Sat at 10.30am (from Galway Docks), at 5pm (from Aran). ☏ 091 567 676 and 091 567 283 (ticket reservations); Fax 091 567 672

Rossaveal – Aran Islands Ferry - Operates (35min) from Rossaveal Apr-Nov, thrice daily to Inishmore (3 times from Inishmaan), twice daily to Inishmore/Inisheer (twice from both); Jun-Aug, extra crossings; Nov-Apr, daily, twice to all 3 islands (twice from all islands). Return €19. Reservation service for minibus, bike hire, walking tours, accommodation, lunch and dinner. Coach service from Galway city. Supervised parking at Rossaveal. ☏ 091 568 903, 561 767, 572 050, 572 273 (after hours); Fax 091 568 538 (Island Ferries Teo); island@iol.ie; www.aranislandferries.com

Doolin (Co Clare) – Aran Islands Ferry - Operates (weather permitting) Jun-Aug. to Inishmore (60min), twice daily; to Inishmaan (45min), twice daily; to Inisheer (30min), 6 times daily (additional sailing Fri only at 6.30pm); from Inishmore, twice daily; from Inishmaan, twice daily; from Inisheer, 5 times daily; Easter-May and Sep; telephone for details. Return €25-€30. ☏ 065 707 4455, 707 4466, 707 4189; Fax 065 707 4417 (Doolin Ferry Co); doolinferries@eircom.net; www.doolinferries.com

GETTING ABOUT

The best way to explore **Inishmore** is on foot or by hired bicycle. There is a regular but infrequent bus service along the island's main road, and minibus operators meet planes and ferries and offer tours of some of the principal sights (€10).

As well as the Tourist Information Centre by the harbour in Kilronan, the Aran Heritage Centre and the visitor centre below Dún Aonghasa are useful sources of information. Understanding of the island's landscape is enhanced by the meticulously detailed Map of the Aran Islands created by Tim Robinson.

SHOPPING

Aran Sweater Market and Museum, Kilronan – Wide range of the famous Aran sweaters with their distinctive family stitches and patterns. Open late-Apr to Oct, daily, 11am-8am; mid-Mar to late-Apr, daily, 11am-5pm, Nov-Mar, daily, 2 hr. ☏ 099 61140; www.aransweatermarket.com

Background

The Aran Islands rise in natural terraces from a flat sandy shores facing Galway Bay to high cliffs confronting the Atlantic; constant sea erosion forms ledges used by fishermen. Rainfall is lower than on the mainland and the islands are never touched by frost. There are over 400 different wild flowers including fuchsias but trees are rare. Natural soil is sparse; the traditional crops of rye and potatoes were grown on an artificial soil created laboriously over the years by depositing layers of sand and seaweed on the bare rock. Traditionally the white cottages were thatched with straw tied down against the wind. Fishing and farming were the main activities; farming has now been displaced in importance by tourism. Cows used to spend the summer grazing in Connemara but returned to Aran where it was dry for the winter; ponies however wintered in Connemara and worked on Aran during the summer months. Illicit whiskey and also peat for fuel were imported by boat from Connemara in exchange for potatoes and limestone.

Despite or because of their remote situation the Aran Islands have been inhabited for centuries. The earliest surviving ruins are the great stone forts which date from the prehistoric era. The later more abundant ruins date from the early and medieval Christian period (5C-16C) when the Aran monasteries were important cultural centres. Traditional crafts are still practised, particularly the production of the distinctive cream-coloured **Aran knitwear** using

WORDS AND IMAGES

The Gaelic speakers of the Aran Islands are great storytellers as well as makers of music. The inhabitants' austere way of life was evoked in great detail by one of their number, Liam O'Flaherty (1896-1984), in his 1924 novel *Thy Neighbour's Wife*. Local stories were the inspiration of JM Synge's play *Riders to the Sea*, set on Inishmaan, and of *The Playboy of the Western World*. Synge had been encouraged by WB Yeats to study the islands and "express a life that has never found expression", an apt enough description both of Synge's *The Aran Islands* (1907) and, despite a highly romanticised approach to its subject, of Robert Flaherty's film of 1934. A deeply felt but more objective account is *Stones of Aran: Pilgrimage* by the Englishman, Tim Robinson (b 1935).

the symbolic stitches which represent elements in nature and the Aran way of life; originally the women spun the wool and the men did the knitting using goose quills for needles.

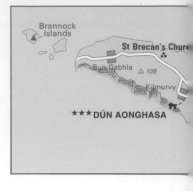

Worth a Visit

INISHMORE (Arainn)

The island (9 x 2.5mi/14.5 x 4km) is served by one road which runs north from the airstrip along the shore of Killeany Bay *(Cuan Chill Éinne)*, to **Kilronan** *(Cill Rónáin)* and then west to the remote hamlet of Bun Gabhla overlooking **Brannock Island** *(Oílean Dá Bhranóg)* and the lighthouse. The old tracks and walls run from northeast to southwest following the natural rifts and the traditional pattern of movement carting seaweed from the shore to fertilise the fields. At the roadside stand square pillars topped by crosses erected in memory of islanders who died abroad or at sea. The Atlantic waves constantly batter the grim, southwestern cliffs and send spectacular spurts of spray through the "puffing-holes" at the island's eastern extremity. Off the quieter, northwestern shore facing Galway Bay, at Port Chorrúch, there is a colony of seals.

Aran Heritage Centre (Ionad Arann)

Kilronan. (&) Open Jun-Aug, daily, 10am-7pm; Apr-May and Sep-Oct, daily, 11am-5pm. €3.50. Café. Craft Shop. Bureau de change. Internet access. ☎ 099 61355; Fax 099 61454; ☎ 091 563 081 (Galway Tourist Office); info@visitaranislands.com; www.visitaranislands.com

Ionad Arann, to give it its Irish name, provides an excellent introduction to the landscape, traditions and culture of the islands. Among the many exhibits there is a *curragh*, the seemingly frail traditional craft made of hide or canvas stretched over a frame of laths and powered by bladeless oars. Regular showings of the documentary film *Man of Aran (75min)* feature unforgettable images of the *curragh* battling against surf and swell and of the seemingly timeless life led by the island's fisherfolk.

St Kieran's Church (Teampall Chiaráin)

1mi/1.7km NW of Kilronan; bear right in Mainistir. Halfway down the slope to the shore stands a small ruined church dedicated to **St Kieran of Clonmacnoise**. Surrounding the church are four cross-inscribed stones and St Kieran's Well.

Dún Aonghasa★★★

4.5mi/7.2km W of Kilronan; 20min there and back on foot from the Visitor Centre in Kilmurvy (Cill Mhuirbhigh). (Dúchas) Visitor Centre: Open daily, 10am-6pm (4pm Nov-Mar). €1.20. Suitable clothing required. Limited parking for cycles. ☎ 099 61008, Fax 099 61009; dunaonghasa@ealga.ie.

A stony path leads uphill to this great drystone fort in its spectacular setting on the very edge of cliffs plunging 200ft/61m to the Atlantic. It is one of the finest prehistoric monuments in Europe and consists of three lines of defence. The ground between the outer and the middle wall is spiked with stone stakes set at an angle to impede attack, an extraordinary sight once described as looking "like infinite headstones of the dead".

Dún Aonghasa

Bord Fáilte, Dublin

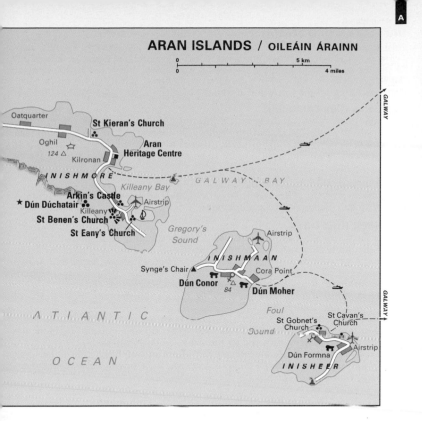

ARAN ISLANDS / OILEÁIN ÁRAINN

A square tunnel in the thickness of the wall leads into the inner compound. The inner wall, which has steps up to wall walks, describes a semicircle beginning and ending on the cliff edge; it is not known whether the fort was originally this shape or whether some of it has collapsed into the sea.

St Brecan's Church (Teampall Bhreacáin)

5.5mi/8.8km NW of Kilronan. Tucked away in a hollow on the north coast overlooking a small bay is an ancient monastic site, also known as Na Seacht d'Teampall, the Seven Churches, though only two of the ruined buildings here are in fact churches. The larger, with massive limestone masonry of early date, was greatly altered in the late Middle Ages and is dedicated to St Brecan whose grave is opposite the west door. The other structures probably served the monastic community or provided shelter for pilgrims. In the southeast corner of the graveyard is a stone inscribed to seven Roman saints.

Dún Dúchatair★

2mi/3km SW of Kilronan. The "Black Fort" is a splendid example of a promontory fort, with a massive curving wall 20ft/6m high and almost as thick, sealing off the much eroded headland.

Arkin's Castle (Caisleán Aircín)

1mi/1.6km S of Kilronan in Killeany. On the south shore of Killeany Bay stand the ruins of a **tower house** which was probably built by John Rawson, to whom the islands were granted by Elizabeth I in 1588. It was fortified by Lord Clanrickard against the Cromwellians who captured it in 1652, lost it and recaptured it in 1653, using stone from St Enda's Church and the nearby friary to strengthen its defences.

St Benen's Church (Teampall Bheanáin)

1mi/1.6km S of Kilronan; in Killeany bear right; 10min there and back on foot. A path climbs the hill past St Eany's oratory (6C or 7C) with a narrow north door and a slim east window. There is a good **view** of Killeany Bay and of the mainland.

St Eany's Church (Teaghlach Éinne)

1.5mi/2.4km S of Kilronan. On the coast south of the airstrip, almost submerged by the surrounding graves, are the ruins of an early church with antae and a round-headed window. **St Enda** is said to be buried here on the site of the monastery, which he founded in about 490. His reputation as a teacher attracted so many famous men to study under him – St Kieran of Clonmacnoise, St Finnian of Moville on Inishowen, St Jarlath of Tuam, St Colman of Kilmacduagh south of Galway – that the island, where 227 saints are buried, became known as Aran of the Saints.

INISHMAAN (Inis Meáin)

Inishmaan (3 x 1mi/5 x 2km) is the bleakest and least visited of the islands, sloping from a bare rocky plateau northeast to a sandy shore. Its houses are strung out in the lee of the high ground. The island exercised a particular fascination for JM Synge, who is said to have favoured a sheltered spot called Synge's Chair (*Cathaoir Synge*) on the western cliffs overlooking Gregory's Sound (*Sunda Ghrióra*).

Dún Conor (Dún Chonchúir)

The huge prehistoric fort (restored) stands on high ground in the centre of the island on the edge of a narrow valley; it consists of a thick stone wall (17.5ft/5.65m), stepped on the inside, round an oval enclosure (227 x 115ft/69 x 35m), which is flanked to the east by an outer court; the entrance is protected by a stone bastion.

Dún Moher or Dún Fearbhaigh

This smaller stone fort (103 x 90ft/31 x 27m) stands on the edge of the high ground overlooking the landing jetty at Cora Point.

INISHEER (Inis Oírr)

Inisheer is the smallest of the islands, with the dwellings of its inhabitants clustering along the north coast. The gentle landscape of the interior is transformed in springtime by countless daffodils. Near the airstrip are the ruins of **St Cavan's Church** (*Teampall Chaomháin*), threatened by the sand; the chancel with its round-headed east window dates from the early 10C; the chancel arch and south door are medieval, probably 14C. The grave of **St Cavan**, the brother of St Kevin of Glendalough, lies nearby (*NE*).

In the centre of the settlements stands **Dún Formna**, a stone fort (170 x 123ft/ 52 x 37m), which contains the ruins of a tower house, probably built by the O'Briens in the 14C and destroyed by the Cromwellians in 1652.

Northwest of the houses are the ruins of **St Gobnet's Church** (*Kilgobnet*); the small medieval oratory has an altar, a round-headed east window and a flat-headed doorway narrowing towards the top.

Athenry

Now a peaceful little market centre and a designated Heritage Town, Athenry was the scene in 1316 of one of Ireland's most savage battles of medieval times, when an Anglo-Norman force massacred a huge army of native Irish. The bloody encounter is commemorated in the town's 14C seal, which features the severed heads of the Irish chieftains displayed on spikes above a gateway. This may well represent Athenry's North Gate, the dominant feature of the walls built to protect the town in the early years of the 13C by its founder, the Anglo-Norman nobleman Meiler de Bermingham.

Location

Population 1 612 - Michelin Atlas p 89 and Map 712 – F 8 – Co Galway.
Athenry (*Baile Átha an Rí*), meaning the town at the river ford, is in South Galway just north of the main road (N 6) between Galway and Loughrea. Park by the Castle.
🛈 *Keller Travel, Ballinasloe. Open Jul-Aug, Mon-Sat.* ☎ *0905 42131*
🛈 *Oranmore. Open May-Sep, Mon-Sat.* ☎ *091 790 811*
Adjacent Sights: See BIRR, CLONMACNOISE, GALWAY, PORTUMNA, STROKESTOWN.

Directory

WHERE TO EAT

• *Budget*
Raftery's – *Craughwell* - ☎ *091 846 004* - 🚳 🅿 *- €15.* Seafood salads and assorted sandwiches are on offer at this well-kept family-run pub in the high street. On colder days, take advantage of the snug bar with its own fireplace.

ENTERTAINMENT

Dunguaire Castle – To recapture the taste of life in the Middle Ages sit down to a medieval banquet and listen to songs, poems and extracts from the writings of Synge, Yeats and Gogarty (*see below*)

EVENTS AND FESTIVALS

Athenry Annual Medieval Festival – *Weekend nearest 15 August.* Open-air play and concert, exhibitions of archery, jousting competitions, a medieval crafts fair and fireworks.

Walking About

Athenry Heritage Centre
♿ *Open Apr-Sep, daily, 10am-6pm. €3.50. Parking at Castle.* ☏ *091 844 661; info@athenryheritagetown.com; www.athenryheritagetown.com*
The display in the former Anglican church traces the history of the town and interprets the medieval monuments (audio-visual show 45min in brief soundbites).

Athenry Castle
(Dúchas) (♿) Open Jun to mid-Sep, daily, 10am-6pm; Apr to May and mid-Sep to Oct, Tue-Sun, 10am-5pm; last admission 45min before closing. €2.50. Audio-visual show (20min). Guided tour by appointment. Parking. ☏ *091 844 797; Fax 091 845 796; athenrycastle@ealga.ie*
The castle, built by Meiler de Bermingham c 1239 but in ruins since 1597, consisted of a central keep, with a vaulted undercroft supported on pillars and a main entrance at first-floor level, enclosed within a stout wall reinforced by two towers.

Dominican Friary
(Dúchas) Key available from Mrs Sheehan in Church Street (€6.35. deposit)
Beside the river on the east side of the town are the ruins of a friary founded in 1241 by Meiler de Bermingham. The choir of the church, which was dedicated to St Peter and St Paul, is 13C with lancet windows, but the pillars and aisle arches date from a 14C rebuilding in which the chancel was extended and a new east window was inserted. The tomb niches date from the 13C to the 15C. The north transept was probably added during repairs after a fire in 1423. In 1574 the friary was confiscated and burned by the Burkes. In 1627 it was returned to the friars, who restored the buildings, and in 1644 it became a university. Eight years later, however, the friars were expelled by the Cromwellians.

Excursions

EAST OF ATHENRY

Loughrea
11mi/18km S by R 348 and R 349. The town lies on the north shore of Lough Rea facing the **Slieve Aughty Mountains**. Its origins lie in a Norman stronghold built in about 1300 by Richard de Burgo, who also founded the **Carmelite Priory**, now in ruins, where General St Ruth, who died at the Battle of Aughrim, is said to be buried under the tower. Part of one of the medieval **town gates** stands on the edge of the cathedral precinct.

St Brendan's Cathedral★ – ♿ *Open daily, 9am-9pm. Audio-guide (€2.54). Guide book.* ☏ *091 841 212; Fax 091 847 367.*
The cathedral of the Roman Catholic diocese of Clonfert *(see p 131)* was designed by William Byrne in the neo-Gothic style in 1897. Of far greater interest than the rather dull exterior of the building is its richly decorated interior, one of the best places in the country in which to appreciate the arts and crafts of the Celtic Revival, with fine examples of stained glass, textiles, sculpture, furnishings, metalwork and woodcarving.
The Clonfert **Diocesan Museum** displays a collection of vestments (15C-20C), chalices (16C-19C), statues, penal crosses, rosaries, crucifixes and missals. ♿ *Open Jun-Aug; if closed, key available from the Cathedral Presbytery. Guided tour by appointment. Parking.* ☏ *091 841 212*

Turoe Stone★
10mi/16km S of Athenry by R 348 and a minor road S from Kiltullagh towards Bullaun; park in gateway. In the middle of a field *(right)* stands a granite boulder (3ft/1m high), presumed to be a Celtic ritual stone. Its domed cap is carved in relief with the finest La Tène decoration in Ireland, a pattern of swelling tendrils "searching like rivulets of a great tidal stream for an outlet" (P Harbison). Other motifs include a stylised bird's head and the **triskele** *(see p 333)*.

Kilconnell Franciscan Friary
15mi/24km E of Athenry by R 348. Plan of layout in the nave.
These extensive ruins are the remains of a monastery founded in 1353 on the site of an earlier monastery begun in the 6C by St Conall. There are two fine tomb niches, one with the figures of six saints

St Joseph *by M Healy in Loughrea Cathedral*

Battle of Aughrim Centre

Aughrim; 5mi/8km S of Kilconnell by minor road. Open Jun-Aug, Tue-Sat and Sun, 10am (2pm Sun) to 6pm (5.15pm last audio-visual show); telephone for confirmation. €4. Parking. Refreshments. ☎ 0905 73939

The Interpretative Centre uses audio-visual, three-dimensional displays and many relics to recreate the bloody battle of Aughrim, based on the account of Captain Walter Dalton, one of the combatants.

BATTLE OF AUGHRIM

Aughrim was the last great battle in the War of the Two Kings *(Cogadh an Dá Rí)* between the exiled King James II of England, supported by Louis XIV of France, and his successor, King William III of England, and his allies. After retreating west following the **Battle of Athlone**, the Jacobite forces, under the French general St Ruth, took up a defensive position at Aughrim against the army of William III, under the Dutchman General Ginkel. On 12 July 1691 45 000 men (20 000 Jacobites composed of Irish, French, Germans and Walloons and 25 000 Williamites composed of Irish, English, Dutch, Germans and Danish) met and fought; 9 000 died. The death of St Ruth at the height of the battle caused disarray among the Jacobites and gave victory to the Williamites. According to legend, the Williamite dead were buried at Clontuskert Priory while the Jacobite dead were stripped and left to rot and their bones were smashed on the walls of Kilconnell Friary.

Clontuskert Augustinian Priory

10mi/16km SE of Aughrim by N 6 to Garbally and S by R 355; 5min on foot from roadside car park (left).

The first monastery on the site was founded by **St Baedán** (d c 809). The **Augustinians**, who arrived in the 12C, had by the end of the 13C established one of the richest monasteries in the diocese. Most of the present ruined building dates from the 15C – east window, rood screen, west door which bears carvings of St Michael, St John, St Katherine and an abbot or bishop.

KILTARTAN COUNTRY

Thoor Ballylee★

23mi/37km S of Athenry by R 348, R 349, N 6 and N 66 (sign). ⚑ (♿) Open Jun-Sep, daily, 10am-6pm. €5. Audio-visual show (17min). Audioguide (7 languages). Guided tour (30min) available. Parking. ☎ 091 631 436 (Jun-Sep), 091 537 700 (Oct-May); Fax 091 537 733; thoorballylee@irelandwest.ie

The 16C **tower house**, which was **William Butler Yeats'** summer house for 11 years, became a powerful symbol in his poetic work, as the inscription on the wall facing the road records. In 1917, the year of his marriage to Georgie Hyde-Lees, he was looking for a property near Lady Gregory's house at Coole Park *(see below)*, where he was a frequent visitor. He spent most of that summer converting the four-storey tower. The local Kiltartan Society has restored the building together with the adjoining miller's cottage and mill wheel, and the tower now houses rare editions of Yeats' works and visitors can enjoy an audio-visual tour.

Kiltartan Gregory Museum

3.5mi/5km W of Thoor Ballylee by minor road and N 18 S. Open Jun-Aug, daily, 10am-6pm; Sep-Oct and May, Sun, 1-5pm. €3. ☎ 091 63106, 632 346; Fax 091 631 482; delourdesfahy@eircom.net; www.gortonline.com/gregorymuseum

The old schoolhouse, built by the Gregory family, displays memorabilia of Augusta, Lady Gregory (1852-1932), co-founder with Yeats of the Abbey Theatre in Dublin; outside are stones commemorating those connected with the Irish Literary Renaissance.

Coole Park

2mi/3km S from Kiltartan by N 18. (Dúchas) ♿ Park: Open daily. Visitor Centre: Open Jun-Sep, daily, 10am-6pm (5pm Sep); Mar-May, Tue-Sun, 10am-5pm; last admission 1hr before closing. Guided tour of exhibition: every 30min. €2. Parking. Coffee shop. ☎ 091 631 804, 563 016; Fax 091 631 653; coolepark@ealga.ie

Coole was the family home of Lady Gregory. In the walled garden stands a great copper beech, the **autograph tree★**, on which many of the significant figures in the Irish Literary Renaissance – William Butler Yeats, George Bernard Shaw, G Russell (AE), John Millington Synge and Sean O'Casey – cut their initials while guests at the house (demolished). The **visitor centre** in the converted stables provides information on the national park – deer enclosure, nature trail; a forest walk *(0.5mi/0.8km)* leads to the lake, where petrified trees protrude from the water.

Kilmacduagh Churches and Round Tower★

3.5mi/5km SW of Gort by R 460; car park.

Set against the strange and stony landscape of The Burren, the extensive ruins of this monastic site straddle the road. The most distinctive feature, visible from far away, is the well-preserved **round tower**, which leans at a slight angle and has preserved its characteristic conical cap. Founded in the 7C by **St Colman**, son of Duagh, the monastery suffered many Viking attacks in the 9C-10C; after the Reformation it became the property of Richard, 2nd Earl of Clanrickard.

The **Glebe House**, a two-storey 13C building, was probably the Abbot's lodging. South of it stands the **Church of St John the Baptist**, a small 12C building with rounded and pointed windows and a later chancel. Beside the **round tower** stands the **cathedral**; its west gable dates from the 11C-12C, the nave from 1200; the south doorway with a bishop's head above it, the two transepts, the west window and the chancel probably date from the 15C; the folk art Crucifixions were moved from the south to the north transept after 1765. **St Mary's Church**, across the road, was built c 1200. **O'Heyne's Church** *(NW)* contains early-13C carving on the chancel arch and east windows.

Dunguaire Castle*

20mi/32km NW of Kilmacduagh by minor road via Tirneevin and Killinny to Kinvarra; car park. Open May to mid-Oct, daily, 9.30am-5.30pm (4.30pm last admission); subject to change; check by telephone. Medieval banquets: daily at 5.30pm and 8.45pm. (subject to demand). Castle €4; banquet €42. Parking. Souvenir shop. ☎ 091 637 108 (Castle), ☎ 061 360 788 (Shannon Heritage central reservations); Fax 061 361 020; reservations@shannondev.ie; www.shannonheritage.com

Facing **Kinvarra**, a charming little port at the head of Kinvarra Bay, stands a four-storey **tower house** with adjoining bawn *(see p 109)*, built in 1520 by the descendants of Guaire, King of Connaught in the 7C. The Martyns of Galway owned it from the 17C to 20C, when it was restored by Oliver St John Gogarty (1924) and by Christobel Lady Ampthill (1954). Traces of the wickerwork support used in its construction are visible on the ground-floor vault. Visitors can climb 76 steps to the top floor for a fine all-round view, or stay longer and participate in a sumptuous "medieval banquet".

Athlone

The county town of Westmeath, straddling the Shannon just to the south of Lough Ree, occupies a strategic position in the very heart of Ireland. Not surprisingly, the important river crossing was soon defended by a fortress; the first castle was built by the Kings of Connacht, while the present stronghold dates from the Anglo-Norman era. Perhaps more surprisingly, Athlone's central location led to its being proposed as a possible capital in the early days of the Free State. Though the town escaped this distinction, it is a hustling place with good rail and road links and easy access to the important visitor attractions of Clonmacnoise and Lough Ree.

Location

Population 7 691 - Michelin Atlas p 90 and Map 712 – I 7 – Co Westmeath.
Athlone *(Baile Átha Luain)* is located on N 6, the Dublin to Galway road, at the junction with N 55 and N 61. There is a **fine view*** of **Lough Ree** from **Ballykeeran Viewpoint** *(4mi/6.4km NE by N 55)*.
🄱 *St Peter's Square, Athlone. Open Jun-Sep, Mon-Sun; Apr-May and Oct. Mon-Sat.* ☎ *0902 04630*

Adjacent Sights: See ATHENRY, BIRR, LONGFORD, MULLINGAR, STROKESTOWN, TULLAMORE.

Background

Siege of Athlone – Its key position meant that Athlone was repeatedly fought over but the town's worst moment came in the course of the Williamite War, when it suffered the most devastating bombardment in Irish history.

Following the Battle of the Boyne *(see p 148)* the Jacobite forces retreated to Athlone. In June 1691 the Williamite army under Ginkel made a determined assault on the bridge; Sergeant Custume, who died a heroic death in its defence, is commemorated in the name of the local barracks. After 10 days of sustained attack the town and the castle fell. Ginkel was made Earl of Athlone. The Jacobites withdrew southwest to Aughrim *(see p 132)*.

> ### JOHN MCCORMACK
> The greatest lyric tenor of his day, John McCormack (1884-1945), was born in Athlone. He sang in the Palestrina Choir of the Pro-Cathedral in Dublin. At 23 he sang a major role at Covent Garden, where he appeared every year until 1914. After achieving fame on the operatic stage in Europe and the USA, he turned to the concert stage. His voice and charisma made him one of the most widely honoured and decorated singers in the world, the only Irish tenor to reach such an international standard. He was made a Count of the Papal Court for his charity work.

Directory

SIGHTSEEING

Athlone Cruises on Lough Ree – *Operate (90min) Jun-Aug, daily, 11am, 2.30pm (times subject to variation). €8. Depart from the Jolly Mariner Marina at Coosan Point on Lough Ree. Taped commentary; bar. Parking. Coffee shop.* ☎ *0902 72892, 72113; Fax 0902 74386 (Athlone Cruisers)*

Viking Tours in a replica Viking longship – *Operate from Strand Fishing Tackle in town centre. Lough Ree Cruises 1hr 30min; Clonmacnoise Cruise (4hr 30min with 1hr 30min at site). Refreshments.* ☎ *0902 73383; Fax 0902 73392; Mob 086 262 1136; vikingtours@ireland.com; www.vikingtoursireland.com*

WHERE TO STAY

• *Budget*

Shelmalier House – *Retreat Rd, Cartrontroy – 1.5mi/2.5km E of Athlone by Dublin rd (N 6) -* ☎ *0902 72245 - Fax 0902 73190 - shelmal@iol.ie - Closed 20 Dec to 30 Jan -* ▣ *- 7 rm €39/60* ☂. Good value purpose-built accommodation in a residential part of the town. The experienced owners run a clean and comfortable house and the bedrooms are decorated to a high standard.

Riverview House – *Summerhill, Galway Rd – 2.5mi/4km W of Athlone on N 6 -* ☎ *0902 94532 - Fax 0902 94532 - riverviewhouse@hotmail.com - Mar to mid-Dec -* ▣ ⳾ *- 4 rm €45/60* ☂. Next to a small tributary of the Shannon, hence the name. Purpose-built guesthouse with a neat garden, bedrooms all ensuite. Good base for fishermen as owners also have a bait and tackle shop.

Glasson Stone Lodge – *Glasson - 5mi/5km NE of Athlone on N 55 -* ☎ *0902 85004 - glassonstonelodge@eircom.net - Mar to Nov -* ⳾ ▣ ⳾ *- 5 rm €45/70* ☂. A guesthouse made all the more welcoming by its charming owner, who provides guests with tea and cakes on their arrival. Breakfast is also particularly impressive. Brightly coloured bedrooms, all with modern power showers.

WHERE TO EAT

• *Moderate*

Wineport Lodge – *Glassan - 5mi/8km NE of Athlone on N 55 and 1mi/1.6km SW of Glassan -* ☎ *0902 85466 - lodge@wineport.ie - Closed 24-26 Dec -* ▣ ⳾ *- €38/46.50.* The more adventurous can arrive at this lough-side timber-built lodge by boat; it has its own landing pier. The modern cooking and impressive winelist are complemented by the stunning views of Lough Ree. Wine-themed bedrooms also available.

EVENTS AND FESTIVALS

The **John McCormack Golden Voice of Athlone** *(late June)* is a competition for young classical singers to pay tribute to John McCormack, to bring good music to the community and to provide assistance to young singers.

TRACING ANCESTORS

Dún na Sí (Fairy Fort) – *Knockdanney, Moate, Co Westmeath. Open Mon-Fri, 10am-4pm (3pm Fri). Genealogy service.* ☎ *0902 81183; Fax 0902 81661; dunnasimoate@tinet.ie; www.core.ie/midlands/projects/mullingar/dunnasi/*

Worth a Visit

Athlone Castle

Market Square. Open May to mid-Oct, daily, 10am-5.30pm. €4.55. Audio-visual show (40min; 3 languages): 4.30pm (last show). ☎ *0902 92912*

Early in the 13C John de Grey, Justiciar of Ireland, built a stone castle on the west bank of the Shannon. The curtain wall and its three fortified towers date from the late 13C. The oldest part of the structure is the central polygonal **keep;** early in the 19C the upper part was greatly altered to accommodate heavy artillery supplemented by new defences, known as the Batteries, west of the town. From the battlements there is a good **view** of the river and the town.

The **Exhibition Centre** has an audio-visual presentation evoking the dramatic days of the Siege of Athlone as well as telling the life story of **John McCormack**. The **Castle Museum**, housed in the keep, covers local history and folk life and displays souvenirs (gramophone and silver cups) of John McCormack. *Open May to early-Oct, daily, 10am-5.30pm (4.30pm last audio-visual show). Visitor Centre and Museum €2.50. Parking.* ☎ *0902 92912 (Castle), 72107 (Urban District Council); Fax 0902 72100*

Church of St Peter and St Paul

Market Square. With its twin towers and cathedral-like proportions, the church almost dwarfs the castle. It was designed by **Ralph Byrne** and consecrated in 1937. There is some striking modern stained glass, most of it from the **Harry Clarke** studios though the one in the priest's sacristy is by **Sarah Purser**, better known as a portrait painter.

Town Centre

From the bridge the main street curves east towards the site of the Dublin Gate. In a side turning *(left)* stand the remains of Court Devenish *(private)*, a Jacobean house (1620) ruined in 1622. The Bawn, a narrow street *(left)*, contains the **birthplace of John McCormack.** The **Franciscan Church** (1931), south of the main street, was built in the Hiberno-Romanesque style inspired by old Irish designs. The **Strand** along the river bank to Burgess Park provides a fine view of the weir, the eel fisheries and the old port on the west bank.

Athy

Little larger nowadays than a big village, Athy is nevertheless a bustling place, the focal point of an extensive rural area and a Heritage town. At the beginning of the Middle Ages it was the largest town in Co Kildare, clustered round a fortified crossing of the river. The Barrow Line, a branch of the Grand Canal, meets the River Barrow here, and visitors come to Athy on boating holidays as well as for the pleasant waterside walks and the good fishing.

Location

Population 5 306 - Michelin Atlas p 86 and Map 712   L 9 – Co Kildare.
Athy *(Baile Àtha)* is on N 78, on the county boundary between Kildare and Carlow.

🛈 *Portlaoise. Open Jun-Sep, Mon-Sat; Oct-May, Mon-Fri. ☎ 0502 2117*
Adjacent Sights: See ABBEYLEIX, KILDARE, KILKENNY, TULLAMORE.

> **DIRECTORY**
> Irish Pewter Mill, Museum and Crafts Centre – For distinctive craftsmanship – *See below*

Walking About

Town Centre

The present bridge, known as Crom-a-Boo Bridge, from the war cry of the Geraldine family, dates from 1796. Beside it stands White's Castle *(private)* which was built in the 16C.

The main square beside the river is graced by the **Courthouse**, built in 1856 as the Corn Exchange. On the opposite side of the square stands the **Town Hall**, which dates from the mid-18C and has housed a market, council chambers and law courts. The brick-vaulted ground floor now houses the **Heritage Centre**; its displays evoke the history of the town and associated personalities and events, such as the Antarctic explorer Ernest Shackleton and the famous Gordon Bennett motor race. *Open daily, 10am (2pm Sun and Bank Hols) to 6pm. €2. ☎ 0507 33075; Fax 0507 33076; athyheritage@eircom.net; www.kildare.ie*

Dominican Church

The striking, fan-shaped modern church is furnished with stained-glass windows and Stations of the Cross by George Campbell (1917-79), a noted North of Ireland artist.

Tour

EAST OF BARROW VALLEY

Drive of 20mi/32km.
From Athy take N 67 E and a minor road (right) via Burtown

Ballitore

The **Quaker meeting house**, built by English Quakers who settled in this area in the 18C, has been converted into a small library and museum describing their sober and industrious lifestyle. One of the most eminent Irishmen of all time, the statesman and political theorist Edmund Burke (1729-97), received part of his education in the village school. The Quaker cemetery with its modest gravestones is on the far side of the village. *Open Jun-Sep, Wed-Sun, noon (2pm Sun) to 5pm (6pm Sun); Oct-May, Tue-Sat, noon-5pm. ☎ 0507 23344; ballitorlib@eircom.net*
Crookstown Mill and Heritage Centre, housed in a converted 1840 cornmill, contains material on the baking and milling industries, items of local historical interest, a graphic/photographic gallery and furniture workshops. *(& to ground floor) Open Apr-Sep, daily, 10am-7pm. Closed Good Fri, 25 Dec. €3.17. Parking. Tearoom. ☎ 0507 23222*
Take N 9 S to Timolin.

Irish Pewter Mill, Museum and Crafts Centre

(&) *Open Mon-Fri, 9.30am-4.30pm. Closed Good Fri to Easter Sun and 25 Dec. Parking. Ramp.* ☎ *050 724 162; timolinpewter@eircom.net; www.kildare.ie/timolinpewter*
There are demonstrations of pewter vessels being cast and a video of the spinning, smithing and polishing. The museum displays moulds, tools and dies used as long ago as the Middle Ages. The building, which is about 1 000 years old, was originally a mill or part of a nunnery.
Continue S by N 9.

Moone High Cross★

The scanty ruins of a 6C monastery founded by **St Columba** enclose an unusual, early 9C high cross (17.5ft/5.3m high). The slender shaft and tapering base carry a wealth of crude but very expressive carved panels of biblical scenes, all worth careful attention. One of the most appealing shows the Feeding of the Five Thousand by means of five loaves, two highly stylised eels, and a pair of smiling fish.
Continue S by N 9 to Castledermot.

Castledermot High Crosses★

9.5mi/16km SE by R 418. The site of a monastery founded by **St Dermot** is marked by two granite **high crosses**, carved with biblical scenes, and a 10C **round tower**, topped by medieval battlements. Ruined chancel walls recall the Franciscan friary founded by Lord Ossory in 1302.
From Castledermot take minor road E; in Graney turn left to Baltinglass.

Baltinglass Abbey

Beside the 19C Anglican church are the ruins of Baltinglass Abbey, which was founded by **Dermot MacMurrough**, King of Leinster, in 1148 and suppressed in 1536. Six Gothic arches flank the nave; the 19C tower and parts of the original cloisters (restored) still stand. Baltinglass, which was started by monks from Mellifont *(see p 148)*, sent out monks in its turn to found Jerpoint *(see p 281)*.
The tiny town of Baltinglass lies at the foot of steep Baltinglass Hill; the main square is dominated by the 1798 memorial, commemorating Michael Dwyer, who was enabled to escape by his faithful comrade Sam MacAllister who drew the fire of the British soldiers on himself.

Bantry★

The market and fishing town of Bantry *(Beanntraí)* stands near the head of the deep-water inlet known as Bantry Bay. Long familiar to mariners as a safe anchorage, the bay was the scene in 1796 of a dramatic episode in British and Irish history, when an attempted French invasion was frustrated by foul weather.

Location

Population 2 777 - Michelin Atlas p 77 and Map 712 – D 12 – Co Cork.
Bantry *(Beanntraí)* is on N 71 between Cork and Killarney on the south shore of Bantry Bay (30mi/48km long) between Skibbereen and Glengarriff.
🅱 *Old Court House, Bantry. Open Apr-Oct.* ☎ *027 50229; www.corkkerry.ie*
Adjacent Sights: See KENMARE, KILLARNEY, SKIBBEREEN.

1796 FRENCH ARMADA

In the winter of this year an expeditionary force of 15 000 French troops, commanded by General Hoche and accompanied by the Irish rebel Wolfe Tone, set sail from Brest intending to invade Ireland and expel the British. But the fleet was dispersed by fog, and a contrary wind meant that only some of the ships were able to enter Bantry Bay. Finally a storm blew up, preventing the troops from landing and eventually forcing the ships to retire. Had the soldiers made their way ashore, the course of history might well have been very different, as facing them was only a scratch force of militiamen led by Richard White, owner of Bantry House.
Ten French warships were destroyed, including the frigate *La Surveillante*, which was scuttled by its crew on 2 January 1797. A 17cwt/863kg French anchor, brought up by a local trawler in 1964, now stands beside the N 17 road south of Bantry, and a captured French longboat is displayed in the National Maritime Museum in Dún Laoghaire.

Directory

SIGHTSEEING

Ferry from Bantry Pier to **Whiddy Island** – *Operates in summer, daily, every hour.*
☎ 00 353 27 50310
There are also scenic cruises of Bantry Bay.

SPORTS AND LEISURE

The inner harbour, with two slipways and safe anchorage, is an ideal location for sailing, water-skiing, windsurfing, canoeing, scuba-diving and swimming. The indoor swimming pool, children's pool and toddlers' pool and leisure centre at the Westlodge Hotel in Bantry are open to the public throughout the year.

EVENTS AND FESTIVALS

The **Bantry Mussel Fair** is held in May each year and the **International Chamber Music Week** in July.

Worth a Visit

Bantry House★

(&) *Open Mar-Oct, daily, 9am-6pm. House and garden €9.50. Brochure (6 languages). Parking. Tearoom; B&B accommodation.* ☎ *027 50047; Fax 027 50795; www.bantryhouse.ie*

This splendidly symmetrical Georgian mansion of 1740 and its **terraced Italianate gardens** stand in superb contrast to the vast scale and wild nature of Bantry Bay. The house is full of tastefully chosen treasures and is intimately connected with the events of 1796, its then owner, Richard White (1767-1851), having been raised to the peerage in recognition of his role as commander of the local militia.

Richard White's son, Viscount Berehaven (1800-68) travelled widely in Europe, bringing back an extraordinary array of items including coloured panels from Pompeii, Savonnerie carpets, Aubusson tapestries once owned by Marie-Antoinette, a Russian travelling shrine with 15C and 16C icons, and Spanish leather with which to clad the sides of the staircase. There are family portraits throughout the house, while the spectacular **dining room** with its royal blue walls is dominated by portraits of King George III and Queen Charlotte, presented by the king at the time of White's ennoblement.

Dining Room, Bantry House

1796 Bantry French Armada

East stables. (&) Open Mar-Oct, daily, 9am-5pm. €4 (includes admission to grounds of Bantry House). ☎ *027 50047; Fax 027 50795*

The converted buildings now house a detailed exhibition on the French Armada *(see above)*. It describes the historical context of the expedition and the composition of the fleet and traces the sequence of events, using a cut-away model of *La Surveillante,* exhibits rescued from the sea and extracts from the journal of Wolfe Tone, who is shown in his cabin on board one of the frigates.

Whiddy Island

The island has had a varied history as the many ruins testify: Kilmore church and graveyard; Reenavanig Castle, the first residence of the White family; fortifications, including three gun batteries, erected as part of the British naval defences in 1801. An American seaplane base was in operation on the island for a few months at the end of the First World War. The oil refinery, built in 1968, ceased operations in 1979 following the disastrous explosion of the tanker *Betelgeuse* in which 50 died.

Excursions

Gougane Barra Forest Park★
23mi/38km – half a day. From Ballylickey take R 584 E inland.
The approach road climbs inland between the vertical rock walls of the **Pass of Keimaneigh** (2mi/3.2km).
West of the lake, which is the source of the **River Lee**, a **forest drive** (3mi/4.8km) makes a loop through the extensive forest park (walks and nature trails) which rises up the steep mountain slopes beside the tumbling mountain stream. St Finbar, the 6C founder of Cork, had a hermitage on the island in the lake. A small causeway leads to the modern island chapel, a popular place of pilgrimage, built in the Irish Romanesque style.

Kilnaruane Inscribed Stone
2mi/3km S of Bantry by N 71; turn left at the Westlodge Hotel (sign). After 0.25mi/0.4km park by the signpost; walk across the field (right). On the hilltop stands a 9C stone pillar, possibly the shaft of a high cross. The stone bears panels of interlacing as well as *(north-east face)* a boat with four oarsmen, possibly a curragh, navigating through a sea of crosses, and *(southwest face)* a cross, a figure at prayer and St Paul and St Anthony in the Desert.

Birr★

With elegant 18C houses lining its shady streets, little Birr is a fine example of a planned Georgian town laid out at the gates of a great house, and now a Heritage town. Tasteful urban development was not the only forte of the local landowners, the Parsons family, later ennobled as the Earls of Rosse. Their vast park contains one of the richest collections of exotic trees and shrubs anywhere, and there are many mementoes of the family's tendency to produce innovators and inventors, among them what for many years was the world's most powerful telescope.

Location
Population 3 355 - Michelin Atlas p 90 and Map 712 – I 8 – Co Offaly.
Birr *(Biorra)* is on N 52 between Tullamore and Nenagh on the country boundary SW of Tullamore in the O'Carroll country. It lies at the confluence of the Little Brosna and Camcor Rivers in the south midlands.
🖪 *Birr. Open mid-May to Sep ☎ 0509 20110; Fax 0509 20660; www.shannondev.ie*
Adjacent Sights: See ABBEYLEIX, ATHLONE, CLONMACNOISE, PORTUMNA, ROSCREA, TULLAMORE.

Background

Birr figures in the early records as the site of an important monastery, which produced the Macregol's Gospels and where the Law of Adamnan was accepted by abbots and chieftains at the Synod of Birr in 697. Owing to its central position in Ireland, Birr was referred to in the Down Survey as Umbilicus Hiberniae.
Until the establishment of the Free State Birr was known as Parsonstown in King's County (the old name of Co Offaly). In 1620 the village was granted to **Sir Lawrence Parsons**, who started weekly markets, set up a glass factory and built most of the castle. In 1642 much of Birr was destroyed by fire during a siege by local clans; in 1690 it was garrisoned by the Williamites and besieged by the Duke of Berwick. During the more peaceful 18C and 19C the town and the castle and demesne were much extended.
The Parsons constantly improved their property and inaugurated some notable "firsts". **Sir William Parsons,** a patron of Handel, enabled the composer to stage the first performance of Messiah in Dublin in 1742. His grandson, another Sir William, the 4th baronet, devoted much time to the late-18C Volunteers. **Sir Lawrence**, the

Directory

SIGHTSEEING

Cruises downstream on the mighty Shannon – *Operate Jun-Sep, Sun at 3.30pm; also Thu at 3.30pm (according to demand); from Banagher Marina downstream to Victoria Lock, Meelick and return (1hr 30min). €8.* ☎ *0509 51112; Fax 0509 51632; silverline@eircom.net; www.silverlinecruisers.com*

WHERE TO STAY

• **Budget**

The Maltings – *Castle St -* ☎ *0509 21345 - Fax 0509 22073 - themaltingsbirr@eircom.net - Closed 24-26 Dec -* 🅿 *- 13 rm €40/70* 🍽 *- Restaurant €7/28.95.* Lovers of the "black stuff" will appreciate the origins; the house was built in 1810 as a maltstore for Guinness. These days it offers spacious, well priced accommodation and has a simple restaurant overlooking the river.

Spinners Town House – *Castle St -* ☎ *0509 21673 - Fax 0509 21672 - spinners@indigo.ie -* ✕ 👌 *- 13 rm €45/90* 🍽 *- Restaurant €18/31.* Lying in the shadow of Birr Castle, the exterior of this Georgian townhouse remains faithful to its origins as a warehouse and mill. The interior is however resolutely hip with modern artwork, polished floors, muted tones and a trendy bistro.

Emmet Guest House – *Emmet Sq -* ☎ *0509 20395 - Fax 0509 21436 - Mar to Oct -* 🍽 *- / rm €45/70* 🍽*.* Those looking for simple, friendly and inexpensive accommodation in the centre of town, will find this Georgian house fitting the bill. The breakfast room overlooks the town square and bedrooms, three of which are attic rooms, are spotlessly kept.

WHERE TO EAT

• **Budget**

The Thatch – *Crinkill – 1.5mi S off N 52 -* ☎ *0509 20682 - thethatchcrinkill@eircom.net - Closed Sun dinner Oct to April -* 🖂 🅿 ✕ *- €16/40.* The current owner is the fifth generation of his family to run this characterful and evocative thatched pub, full of nooks and crannies. Lunchtimes are particularly busy while dinner in the adjoining rustic restaurant is a more formal affair.

ENTERTAINMENT

Concerts are given in the Castle and the park; **exhibitions** are held in the **Castle gallery**.

SPORTS AND LEISURE

Walking in Birr Castle Demesne, on the south bank of the River Camcor, in the Slieve Bloom mountains and beside the Grand Canal.

Boating on the Shannon and the Grand Canal.

Fishing in the Shannon and Brosna rivers for salmon, pike, trout and most coarse species; in the River Suck and the Grand Canal for pike, bream and perch.

EVENTS AND FESTIVALS

Birr Vintage Week is an annual event *(second half of August),* during which there is a Georgian Cricket Match played by men in period costume according to the 1744 rules, and the Irish Independent Carriage Driving Championships are held in the Castle demesne. An **astronomy weekend** takes place in September.

5th baronet, was more nationalist in political sentiment and a friend of **Wolfe Tone** but he retired from politics after the Act of Union in 1800. In the 19C the family genius made **scientific discoveries** and in the 20C was directed towards the collection and propagation of the **rare botanical species** to be found in the gardens.

Walking About

Birr Town★

The principal axis of this little gem of Georgian urban design is **Oxentown Mall,** which runs from the castle gates to the Anglican church between rows of elegant houses and mature trees.

The town centre is formed by **Emmet Square**; prominent among the Georgian houses is Dooley's Hotel (1740). **John's Mall** is graced by a statue of the 3rd Earl of Rosse, while the delightful little Greek temple (1833) is flanked by the **Birr Stone**, a large limestone rock, which may once have marked the supposed meeting place of the mythical Fianna warriors near Seffin. In 1828 it was removed to a mansion in Co Clare to be used for secret celebrations of the Mass but returned to Birr in 1974.

Worth a Visit

Birr Castle Demesne★★

2-3hr. (👌) Open mid-Mar to Oct, daily, 9am-6pm; Nov to mid-Mar, 10am-4pm. €7. Demonstration of the telescope: daily (weather permitting). Brochure (5 languages). Concerts: mid-Jun. Parking. Coffee shop; picnic areas. ☎ *0509 20336; Fax 0509 21583; info@birrcastle.com; www.birrcastle.com*

Gardens – It is sheer delight to follow the many walks threaded through these pleasure grounds (100 acres/40ha) with their rivers, lake, and 1 000-plus species of trees and shrubs. The flora of China and the Himalayas are particularly well represented, and some species are so rare that seeds have been taken from them for the Royal Botanical Gardens at Kew in London. The rich array of plants gives year-round interest, enhanced by the formal planting which includes the world's tallest box hedges.

Extensive herbaceous displays adorn the terraces below the crenellated 17C **castle** (*private*).

Great Telescope★★ – In the 1840s the 3rd Earl of Rosse built a telescope, the **Leviathan of Parsonstown**, which enabled him to see further into space than anyone before; its mirror (72in/183cm) was cast in a furnace built at the bottom of the castle moat and fired with turf from nearby bogs. Astronomers came from as far as Australia, Russia and the USA to see the telescope, which was in use for 60 years until 1908. Its restoration to full working order was completed in 1997.

Birr Scientific and Heritage Foundation

Great Telescope, Birr

Galleries of Discovery – The exhibition set in part of the stable yard celebrates the brilliant activities of the Parsons family – the building of the first-known example of a wrought-iron suspension bridge by the 2nd Earl; the construction of the great telescope and the discovery of distant galaxies by the 3rd Earl; the invention of the steam turbine engine by Charles Parsons in the 1890s; the pioneering work in photography by Mary Countess of Rosse in the 1850s; the world-wide plant-collecting expeditions conducted by the 5th and 6th Earls.

Tours

SLIEVE BLOOM MOUNTAINS★
Round tour of 46mi/73km – half or whole day.
From Birr take R 440 E.

In pleasant contrast to the rather unvarying landscapes of the midlands, and lavishly afforested with pine and spruce, these boggy mountains rise to their highest point at the summit of Arderin (1 728ft/527m). The best way of experiencing them and the fine views they offer is on foot along the 44mi/70km **Slieve Bloom Way**, though drivers will enjoy the route running east from the village of Kinnitty past Forelacka Glen to Drimmo, then north through The Cut to Clonaslee.

The **Slieve Bloom Display Centre** in Kinnitty has good tips on how to tackle the uplands. *Open Apr-Sep, daily.* ☎ 0509 37299 and 0509 37272

AMERICAN CONNECTION
One of the signatories of the American Declaration of Independence in 1776, Charles Carroll of Carrollton, was the grandson of Charles Carroll, who emigrated in 1688 from Letterluna in the Slieve Bloom mountains to the USA, where he was granted land in Maryland.

The village itself has considerable charm; the **Kinnitty Pyramid**, an extraordinary mausoleum modelled on the pyramid of Cheops in Egypt, marks the burial place of the lords of Kinnitty Castle, the Bernard family; it stands in the churchyard just to the south of the village on the Roscrea road.

SHANNON VALLEY

Drive of 20mi/32km. From Birr take R 439 N.

Banagher (Beannchar)

The town is situated on the south bank of the **Shannon** at an important crossing point, defended on the Connacht bank by Cromwell's Castle, a tower house with bastions added around 1650.

The Revd Arthur Nicholls came from Banagher, and when he married **Charlotte Brontë** *(see p 444)*, the couple spent their honeymoon nearby. Another literary resident was Anthony Trollope.

ANTHONY TROLLOPE (1815-82) IN IRELAND

In 1841, having been in the employ of the Post Office since 1834, Trollope was appointed a Surveyor's Clerk in Ireland, where he was based until 1859 when he returned permanently to England.

His first appointment, to which he travelled from Dublin by canal boat, was in **Banagher**, where he took up hunting, a sport he pursued with great enthusiasm for the next 35 years. He was acquainted with Sir William Gregory of Coole Park *(see p 132)*, a contemporary of his at Harrow School. In 1843 during a visit to Drumsna *(see p 161)* he was inspired to begin his first novel, *The Macdermots of Ballycloran*, published in 1847. On 11 June 1844 he married Rose Heseltine, whom he had met two years earlier while on business in Dún Laoghaire (then known as Kingstown).

Later that year they moved to **Clonmel**, where they lived in rented rooms on the first floor of a house in O'Connell Street (then High Street) and there two sons were born – Henry Merivale in March 1846 and Frederic James in September 1847. In 1845 Anthony began his second novel, also on an Irish theme, *The Kellys and the O'Kellys*, which was published in 1848.

The next move took the family to **Mallow**, where they leased a house in the High Street from 1848 to 1851 and Anthony was able to indulge his passion for hunting with the Duhallow, the oldest hunt in Ireland, the Limerick, the Muskerry and the United.

While on secondment in the Channel Islands in 1853, Trollope took up an existing idea and introduced the first **post boxes**, which were painted sage green.

In 1854, after a year in Belfast as Acting Surveyor, he was appointed Surveyor of the Northern District of Ireland but obtained permission to reside in Dublin, where he lived at 5 Seaview Terrace, Donnybrook. As his work involved a good deal of travelling, he created a portable desk *(see p 407)* so that he could write on the train.

His third Irish novel, *Castle Richmond*, in which the action takes place during the Great Famine, was begun in 1859, the year in which he was transferred permanently to England. At the end of his life he began a fourth Irish novel, *The Landleaguers*, about agrarian reform but died in December 1882 before it was finished.

From Banagher take R 356 E ; turn left to Shannon Harbour.

Shannon Harbour

The junction of the **Grand Canal** and the Shannon is now a popular mooring for river cruisers. In its commercial heyday a dry dock, warehousing, a customs post and a hotel (now in ruins) were available beside the lock and canal basin; the local population numbered 1 000, up to 300 000 tons of produce were transhipped annually, and over 250 000 people used the passenger barges, many of them emigrants on their way via Limerick and Cobh to Australia, Canada and America. The locality provides excellent coarse fishing and is a paradise for birdwatchers to see the rare birds, including the corncrake, which visit the wet grasslands known as the Shannon Callows.

Beyond Shannon Harbour in Clonony turn left into R 357 to Shannonbridge.

Clonmacnoise and West Offaly Railway

& *Guided tour by train (50min) Apr-Sep, daily, 10am-5pm, on the hour. €5.50. Craft shop. Parking. Tearoom.* ☎ *0905 74114, 74121; Fax 0905 74210; bograil@bnm.ie; www.bnm.ie*

The narrow-gauge railway takes passengers on a guided tour (45min – 5.5mi/9km) of the **Blackwater Bog**, which is part of the Bog of Allen (20 000 acres/8 090ha), one of the largest unbroken raised bogs in Ireland. The tour includes a view of the various stages in the process of harvesting the peat to fuel the electricity power station at Shannonbridge, and a half-way halt where visitors may step out onto the bog to see and try turf cutting with a *slane*, to study the bog plants and handle a piece of bog wood, 4 000 to 7 000 years old. The railway runs past two trial conifer plantations, established on worked-out bog, and an island farm, which occupies a patch of agricultural land completely surrounded by bog. There are nature trails and a birdwatching hide.

Boyle

On the River Boyle at the foot of the Curlew Mountains (867ft/264m), this pleasant little town has one of the loveliest set of abbey ruins in Ireland and fascinating reminders of one of the most ruthless and ambitious Anglo-Irish landowning dynasties, the King family. The river and the nearby loughs give excellent fishing.

Location

Population 1 695 - Michelin Atlas p 96 and Map 712 – H 6 – Co Roscommon.
Boyle *(Mainistir Na Búille)* lies on N 4, the Dublin to Sligo road, south of the Curlew Mountains between Lough Key and Lough Gara.
🛈 *King House, Boyle. Open May-Sep, daily.* ☎ *079 62145; info@irelandwest.ie*
Adjacent Sights: See CARRICK-ON-SHANNON, KILLALA, KNOCK, SLIGO, STROKES-TOWN.

Directory

SIGHTSEEING
There are boat trips on Lough Key among its many islands.

ENTERTAINMENT
King House – Chamber music and piano recitals and art and heritage exhibitions *(see below)*

EVENTS AND FESTIVALS
O'Carolan Harp Festival – Performance of O'Carolan's works, music, song and dancing, many open-air events – *Late-Jul to early-Aug. Information from the Secretary, Keadew, Co Roscommon.* ☎ *078 47204; Fax 078 47511; ocarolan@eircom.net; www.keadue.HARP.net*

Worth a Visit

King House★

Open May to mid-Oct, daily, 10am-6pm; Apr and late-Oct, Sat-Sun, 10am-6pm; last admission 5pm. €4. Adjacent parking (footbridge over ·river from car park to house). Restaurant. Tourist information office. ☎ *079 63242; Fax 079 63243; kinghouseboyle@ hotmail.com*

King House, Boyle

The Palladian mansion of the King family stands at the east end of the main street. It was built around 1730, probably by an assistant of the eminent architect Sir Edward Lovett Pearce, for a descendant of Sir John King. This Staffordshire gentleman had been sent here a century earlier, charged with subjugating the native Irish. Rewarded for undertaking this task with the lands which once belonged to the local rulers, the MacDermots, the Kings went from strength to strength, eventually acquiring the title of Earls of Kingston, and moving to an even more splendid residence which formed the centrepiece of the vast Rockingham estate *(see below)*.

The mansion has been carefully restored – interesting exhibition on this theme – and now houses well-designed exhibits on the old rulers – O'Connors, Kings of Connaught and MacDermots of Moylurg –

King House, Boyle

and on the exploits of the King family who displaced them. The house was used for many years as a barracks by the Connaught Rangers, who served the Crown well but eventually mutinied in 1920 in protest against government repression during the struggle for independence. Visitors can try their hand at writing with a quill pen and listen to recordings – a Gaelic love poem, the words and even voices of members of the King family.

Frybrook House
Parking in front of the house. Open Jun-Aug, Wed-Sun, 2-5.30pm; Sep-May, by appointment. €3.81. Parking. ☎ 079 63513
More modest altogether than King House, this Georgian dwelling (c 1750) was built for Henry Fry, who was invited to Boyle by the Earl of Kingston *(see above)* and became Chief Magistrate of the area. Among the furnishings, some of which are original, is a postbox designed by John Nash as a model of the gatehouse at Castle Leslie near Monaghan.

Excursions

Boyle Abbey★
2mi/3.2km E of Boyle by N 4. (Dúchas) (&) Open Apr-Oct, daily, 10am-6pm (5.15pm last admission). €1.20. Guided tour (40min): 10am-5pm, hourly. Leaflet (6 languages). Parking ☎ 079 62604; info@heritageireland.ie; www.heritageireland.ie
The ruins belong to a **Cistercian** house founded in 1161 by monks from Mellifont *(see p 148)*. The church is an impressive example of Cistercian architecture, built over several decades and showing the transition from the Romanesque to the Gothic style. Normally frowning on exuberance of any kind, here at Boyle the austere Cistercians gave free rein to their masons, who decorated the capitals with charming carvings of men, beasts and foliage. The abbey buildings were occupied by the Cromwellians who showed them their usual disrespect, and were then used as barracks until the 18C. There is information on the monastic life and a model of the abbey as it once was in the well-preserved **gatehouse**.

Lough Key Forest Park★
2mi/3.2km E of Boyle by N 4. Open daily. €5. Moylurgh Tower: Open Easter-Sep, daily, 8am (11am Sat-Sun) to 4pm (6pm Sat; 7pm Sun) Parking. ☎ 079 62363 (Irish Forestry Board – Coillte Teoranta); seamus.duignen@coillte.ie; www.coillte.ie
With its woodlands, bog garden, ornamental trees and estate buildings, this vast forest park (865 acres/350ha) looks out over the lovely island-studded waters of Lough Key. Until 1959 it was part of the Rockingham estate, the desmesne of the Earls of Kingston, who built themselves a great house here on the site of a MacDermot castle. In the early 19C the house was remodelled by John Nash, while the estate was landscaped by Humphry Repton. In 1959 the house was destroyed by fire, though some outbuildings remain, and a modern structure, the **Moylurg Tower** (132 steps) gives visitors panoramic views over the woods, lakes and hills which formed the setting of one of Ireland's grandest country houses. Nature trails lead through the park, and boat trips on the lough visit islands where there are romantic remains of a MacDermot castle and a medieval monastery.

> **WOODBROOK**
> The name of the house, situated between Lough Key and the main road, which was once the home of the Kirkwood family, is also the name of a charming book by David Thomson, an 18 year-old Oxford student who took a summer job as tutor to Phoebe Kirkwood in 1932 and wrote about the experience.

Tour

MOUNTAINS AND LAKES OF MOYLURG★
Round tour of 50mi/80km.
From Boyle take N 4 N.
As it climbs over the **Curlew Mountains** (867ft/264m) the road provides splendid **views★** of the lakes *(east)*.
In Ballinafad turn left.

Ballinafad Castle
The castle, now in ruins, was built in 1590 to a 13C design with four round corner towers which are square within. It was known as the Castle of the Curlews, as it protected the Curlew Mountain pass.
Continue N on N 4. In Castlebaldwin turn left (sign) to Carrowkeel Cemetery; at the fork bear left. Park at the gate if it is locked; 1hr on foot there and back.

Carrowkeel Megalithic Cemetery

The bleak hilltop in the **Bricklieve Mountains** (1 057ft/321m), which provides a fine **view★★** of the surrounding country, is the site of a megalithic cemetery. The stone mounds, mostly round, contain passage graves dating from the Late Stone Age (2500 to 2000 BC). On a lower ridge (east) are about 50 round huts, probably the dwellings of the people who built the tombs.

From Castlebaldwin take the road along the shore of Lough Arrow. At the end of the lake turn left. In Ballyfarnan turn left onto a steep minor road (narrow entry between two houses) to Altgowlan.

Arigna Scenic Drive (Slí)★

From the **viewpoint** *(right)* there is a superb view of Lough Skean and Lough Meelagh. As the road crosses the watershed another fine view opens up of the steep Arigna Valley and the southern end of **Lough Allen**. The spoil heaps are reminders of the iron industry which once flourished here, its demand for charcoal leading to the clearance of the local oakwoods.

At the T-junction turn right; after 2.5mi/4km turn left into Arigna.

Arigna lies in a narrow river valley between steep mountains which contain some of the rare coal seams in Ireland. The coal, which was first mined to fuel the iron furnaces, later supplied the local power station until it closed in 1990.

In Arigna cross the river and turn left uphill; after 1.5mi/2.4km turn right (sign) onto a very steep and narrow road. At the next junction turn right.

As the road descends from the bare and rugged heights there is an extensive **view★** of Lough Allen, the most northerly of the great Shannon lakes. The river rises in a bog at Shannon Pot *(9mi/14.5km north)*. On the east shore stands Slieve Anierin (1 927ft/586m), the highest point in the Iron Mountains.

At the bottom of the hill turn right onto R 280 to Drumshanbo.

Drumshanbo (Droim Seanbho)

The town at the southern end of **Lough Allen** is a major coarse fishing centre offering anglers not only the waters of the Shannon but also a string of lakes in the drumlin country extending east beyond Ballinamore, which are linked by the Ballinamore and Ballyconnell Canal.

The **Sliabh an Iarainn Visitor Centre** presents an exhibition and an audio-visual presentation on the history of the area – iron and coal mines, the narrow-gauge Cavan and Leitrim Railway *(see p 160)*, sweathouses (an ancient form of sauna bath). *Open Apr-Oct, daily, 10am (2pm Sun) to 6pm. Audio-visual show (30min) €2.* ☎ *078 41522*

From Drumshanbo return N on R 280; turn left onto R 285 and drive through Keadew (Keadue).

The well on the lake shore is named after **St Lasair**, the daughter of St Ronan who founded the monastery.

O'Carolan's Grave

The tombstones *(right)* mark the site of **Kilronan Abbey**, founded in the 6C between Lough Meelagh and the Arigna Mountains. The doorway of the ruined church is 12C-13C. In the transept is the tombstone of **Turlough O'Carolan**.

Return to the last junction; turn right. In Knockvicar turn right to Corrigeenroe; in Corrigeenroe turn left to return to Boyle.

The road provides views of the lake and the mountains as it runs parallel with the Boyle River and skirts the north and west shores of **Lough Key**.

TURLOUGH O'CAROLAN (1670-1738)

The blind harpist (also known as Turlough Carolan) who wrote poetry and music, including the melody of *The Star-Spangled Banner*, was born in **Nobber** in Co Meath. In 1684 his family moved to Carrick-on-Shannon, where Mrs MacDermot Roe became his patron, providing for his education and musical studies. She gave him a horse so that he could perform his compositions at the big houses. After his marriage in 1720 he lived for several years in Mohill, where he is commemorated by a statue in the town centre. He died in 1738 in **Keadew** (Keadue) and his funeral lasted four days. Annual harp festivals *(see p 57)* are held in his honour in Keadew in August and Nobber in October.

Boyne Valley★★

Upstream from Drogheda the River Boyne winds through a fertile and well-wooded landscape marked by an extraordinary concentration of ancient and prehistoric sites. Huge grave mounds, laboriously constructed and enigmatically decorated, testify to the skill and sophistication of the people who thrived here long before work started on the pyramids of Egypt. Much later, in the pre-Christian era, the High Kings of Ireland held court at the Hill of Tara. Christianity was brought to the region by St Patrick himself; the early monastic site at Monasterboice evokes the Irish church before its 12C Romanisation, in contrast to the later, European style of monastery at Mellifont. The clash of arms on the banks of the river in 1690 was an event of European as well as local importance, and the outcome of the Battle of the Boyne is still a factor in contemporary Irish politics.

Location

Michelin Atlas p 93 and Map 712 – M 6 – Co Meath.
The Boyne Valley runs inland from Drogheda; the sights can be reached from N 51 on the north bank of the River Boyne, from M 1 which passes just west of Drogheda or from N 2 which passes through Slane.

▯ *Brú na Bóinne Visitor Centre, Newgrange. Open daily.* ☎ *041 988 0305*
Adjacent Sights: See DROGHEDA, FINGAL, KELLS, TRIM.

> **DIRECTORY**
> Walking   River Boyne towpath, Oldbridge Estate, Townley Hall grounds (nature trail)

Worth a Visit

PREHISTORIC SITES

Built by a farming and stock-raising community in the Neolithic era (3000–2000 BC), on the south-facing slope overlooking the Boyne, then a main artery of communication, the prehistoric burial sites at Knowth, Dowth and Newgrange are the oldest in the British Isles.
There are some 40 graves, consisting of three major graves and many satellites.
Present knowledge suggests that Dowth was built first to align with the setting sun. It was followed by Newgrange where the rising sun penetrates the inner chamber at the winter solstice. Knowth was built later facing east–west to align with the rising sun in March and the setting sun in September.
Only the major graves have been systematically excavated. Sited on the north bank of the river, they have become the subject of intense interest, reflected in the opening of the visitor centre on the south bank and the designation of the area as Brú na Bóinne ("Palace of the Boyne").

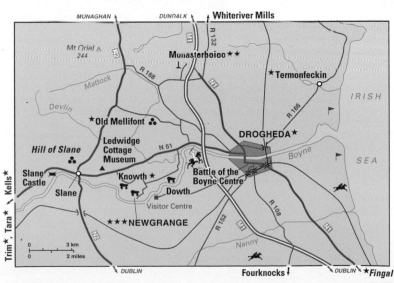

Brú na Bóinne

Brú na Bóinne Visitor Centre – *South bank; footbridge over the river and bus shuttle to graves on the north bank; no other access. (Dúchas) Visitor Centre: Open May-Sep, daily, 9am-6.30pm (7pm Jun to mid-Sep); Mar-Apr and Oct-Feb, daily, 9.30am-5.30pm (5pm Nov-Feb); last admission 45min before closing time. Closed 25-26 Dec. Self-guided tour of centre. Audio-visual show. Burial site: (&) Access via Visitor Centre only (south bank of the River Boyne). Newgrange: Open all year. Knowth: Open May-Oct. Footbridge from Visitor Centre to bus depot; shuttle-bus service to tomb site; last tour 90min before closing of centre. In the high season it is advisable to arrive early at the Visitor Centre as guided tours are on first-come-first-served basis. Leaflet (7 languages). Visitor Centre (1hr) €2.50; Centre and Newgrange (2hr) €5.00; Centre and Knowth (2hr) €3.80, Centre, Newgrange and Knowth (3hr) €8.80. Parking. Tearooms. ☎ 041 988 0300, Fax 041 982 3071; info@heritageireland.com; www.heritageireland.ie*

The well-laid out displays show the site by the river as a dwelling place, and describe the clothing, food and housing of the Neolithic people, their technical knowledge, how the stones were moved on rollers and the different phases of construction and decoration.

Newgrange★★★

Newgrange is one of the best examples of a passage grave in western Europe, its dimensions imposing, the mysterious decoration of its stones a challenge to the imagination.

The **mound** (1.25 acres/0.5ha, 260-280ft/79-85m in diameter and 37ft/11m high) consists of a cairn of medium-sized stones enclosed within a circle of 97 kerbstones, some of which are decorated, set on their long edges, ends touching, surmounted by a facing of round granite boulders.

Newgrange

H Champollion/MICHELIN

Excavations in 1963 made it possible to reconstruct the original south front **revetment** of white quartz stones, except where the entrance has been enlarged to accommodate visitors.

Above the entrance, which was originally closed by an upright slab *(right)*, is the **roof box**, a unique structure with a finely decorated lintel, through which the rays of the rising sun penetrate to the inner chamber for 17 minutes at the winter solstice (21 December).

The passage, which is lined with large standing stones, some decorated and all dressed, leads into a corbelled **chamber** a third of the way into the mound. The three decorated recesses contain stone **basins**, which held the bones of the dead together with funeral offerings of stone and bone beads and pendants, bone pins and small stone balls resembling marbles. The corbelled vaulted roof, completed by a central capstone (4 tonnes), is quite waterproof as the outer faces of the stones are grooved to drain off water.

The mound was surrounded at a distance (39ft/12m x 49ft/15m) by a **great circle** of standing stones. The four opposite the entrance are among the largest; most have been broken off near ground level.

South of the mound are traces of a late-Neolithic – early-Bronze Age **pit circle** which was uncovered in 1982.

Knowth★

Excavations in progress. The mound (40ft/12m high, 220ft/67m in diameter) probably dates from 2500 to 2000 BC. It contains two decorated passage graves discovered in 1967 and 1968; one is simply an enlargement of the passageway but the other is circular and corbelled with side chambers. It is aligned east-west and is surrounded by smaller tombs facing the large central mound. In the early centuries AD the central mound was surrounded by deep defensive ditches.

In about the 8C AD the settlement expanded and several souterrains and rectangular houses were built. From the 12C to 14C the site was occupied by the Normans who constructed a rectangular stone structure on the top of the mound. Excavations conducted since 1962 have made it possible to reconstruct the smaller tombs which had collapsed owing to the passage of time and conversion of the material to other uses.

Dowth

Closed for excavation. The mound, which was raised by man in 3000 BC (1 acre/0.4ha, 280ft/85m in diameter, 50ft/15.24m high), contains two tombs and a souterrain connecting with the north tomb. The base of the mound was enclosed by about 100 kerbstones, many ornamented, although most are covered by landslip.

Other Prehistoric Sites

Tara★

5mi/8km S of Navan by N 3. (Dúchas) (&.) Site: Open all year. Guided tour: May to late-Oct, daily, 10am-6pm (5.15pm last admission). €1.90. Audio-visual show (4 languages). Parking nearby. Coffee shop. ☎ 041 988 0300; Fax 042 982 4798; ☎/Fax 046 25903 (Nov-Apr)

The name of Tara conjures up the spirit of Irish Celtic greatness; the Hill of Tara, also known as Tara of the Kings, played a significant part in Irish legends. Its origin as a religious site is lost in prehistory; it achieved its greatest prestige under the pagan High Kings of Ireland, and even after the introduction of Christianity it retained its significance as the nominal seat of the High King until it was abandoned in 1022.

During the 1798 rebellion a skirmish took place on the hill. In the 19C O'Connell chose it as the site of one of his monster meetings in the cause of Roman Catholic emancipation; 250 000 people came to hear him speak.

The **bare hill** pockmarked with earthworks does not readily suggest a royal palace. An effort of the imagination is required to envisage the many small buildings, of wood or wattle and daub, where the king held his court.

The history of Tara is recounted in an audio-visual presentation in the early-19C **St Patrick's Church,** which incorporates a medieval window.

In the churchyard stands a red sandstone pillar stone, known as **St Adamnán's Cross,** which bears a carved figure which may be the ancient Celtic god **Cernunnos.**

West of the graveyard is the **Rath of the Synods,** a ringfort with three banks. Further south is an Iron Age ringfort, enclosed by a bank and a ditch, known as the **Royal Enclosure.** Within it is the **Mound of the Hostages,** a small passage grave which dates from about 1800 BC. In the centre of the enclosure are two ringforts, known as the **Royal Seat** and **Cormac's House;** at the centre of the latter, beside a statue of St Patrick, is a standing stone known as the **Lia Fáil,** which was moved from its original position near the Mound of the Hostages to be a memorial to those who died in 1798.

South of the Royal Enclosure is part of another earthwork known as **King Laoghaire's Rath.** To the north of the churchyard is a hollow flanked by two long parallel banks, which may have been the grand entrance but which is known as the Banqueting Hall. On the west side are three circular earthworks; the first is known as Gráinne's Fort, the other two as the Sloping Trenches.

South of the hill *(0.5mi/0.8km – visible from the road)* is part of another ringfort, known as **Rath Maeve,** surrounded by a bank and ditch.

Fourknocks

11mi/18km S of Drogheda by R 108; after 10mi/16km turn right; park in the road. Key available from the last house on the right before the stile.

The passage grave, which dates from c 1500 BC, is unusually large compared with the size of the mound. The interior contains stones decorated with zigzags and other prehistoric designs and a human face. It contained over 60 burials.

BATTLE SITE

Battle of the Boyne Centre

(&.) Guided outdoor tour (30-45min) Jun to early-Sep, daily, 9.30am-5.30pm; last admission 45min before closing. Rainproof clothing and stout shoes for uneven ground advisable. Parking. ☎ 041 988 4343; Fax 041 988 4323; battleoftheboyne.ealga.ie

The battlefield site, now part of the Oldbridge estate, granted to the Williamite commander Coddington, is being developed to contain a museum and interpretive centre. The guided tour includes an account of the battle and demonstrations of the cannons and guns used by the opposing armies. There are walks on the estate and beside the river from the Obelisk Bridge.

BATTLE OF THE BOYNE

The battle fought on 12 July 1690 was the decisive engagement in the War of the Two Kings *(Cogadh an Dá Rí)* between **King James II** of England, supported by Louis XIV of France, and King William III of England, **William of Orange**, and his allies, who were engaged in a struggle for the domination of Europe. The soldiers involved – 36 000 in William's army and 25 000 in James's – were of many nationalities: British, Danes, Dutch, Finns, French, Germans, Irish, Poles, Prussians and Swiss.

Whereas the French troops supporting James were under orders to delay William, the latter wished to achieve a speedy victory. As he was making observations on the morning of the battle, he narrowly escaped death from a bullet which tore his coat and grazed his shoulder. He sent some of his force upstream to attack the French left flank and his main force crossed the Boyne at the ford at Oldbridge and attacked the Jacobite army drawn up on the south bank; five crossings were made between 10am and 2pm.

During the battle the **Duke of Schomberg**, once a Marshal of France in Louis XIV's army, who had left France because he was a Protestant and become a soldier of fortune, was killed. William lost 500 men; James lost about 1 000. When he heard that William had crossed the river, James left for Dublin. The following day he rode to Duncannon near Waterford and took ship to Kinsale; from there he sailed to France. In the hope of reversing the Cromwellian land settlement, the Irish fought on until the following year when they suffered a series of defeats at Athlone, Aughrim and Limerick.

The Williamite victory brought about the definitive defeat of the **Stuart** cause and determined the balance of power in Europe.

MONASTIC SITES

Monasterboice**

8mi/13km N of Drogheda by N 1. Overlooked by a half-ruined **round tower**, three **high crosses** of outstanding beauty and interest mark the site of the famous 6C monastery founded by **St Buithe** (Boethius), an important centre of learning closely connected with Armagh.

The **South Cross** was erected by Muiredach in the 9C. The west face shows the Crucifixion, Christ with Peter and Paul, the raised Christ flanked by Apostles and the Mocking of Jesus; on the east face are the Last Judgement, the Adoration of the Magi, Moses striking the Rock, David and Goliath, the Fall of Man, and Cain slaying Abel.

The **West Cross** *(between the two ruined churches)* is unusually tall (23ft/7m) and the subjects of some of the carvings are rare. The west face shows the Crucifixion; on the shaft are the Arrest of Christ, Christ surrounded by Apostles, the Resurrection of the Dead, the Soldiers at the Tomb. The east face shows Christ Militans with *(above)* Christ walking on the water, *(right)* Simon Magus and *(below)* the Fiery Furnace; on the shaft are Goliath, Samuel anointing David, the Golden Calf, the Sacrifice of Isaac, David killing a lion.

The **North Cross** *(northeast corner of the graveyard)* also shows the Crucifixion on the west face. The original shaft is contained in the same enclosure as well as a monastic sundial indicating the hours of the Divine Office.

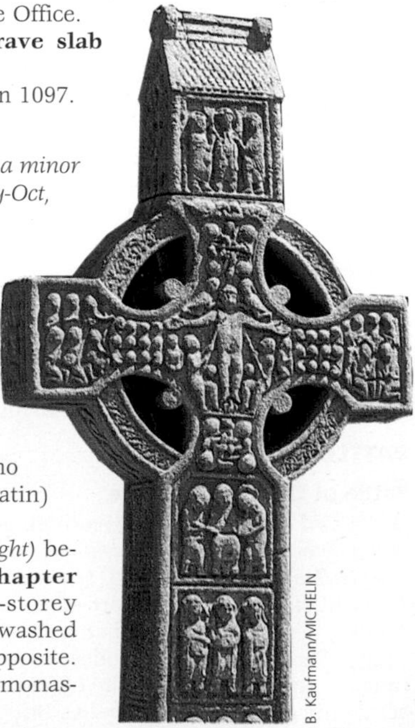

Behind the north church lies an early **grave slab** bearing the name Ruarcan.

The **tower** and its treasures were burned in 1097.

High Cross, Monasterboice

B. Kaufmann/MICHELIN

Mellifont Old Abbey*

6mi/10km W of Drogheda by N 51, R 168 and a minor road west of Tullyallen. (Dúchas) (♿) Open May-Oct, daily, 10am-6pm (5.15pm last admission). €1.90. Guided tour (40min) by appointment. Leaflet (6 languages). Exhibition. Parking. Picnic area. Access by stone stairway. ☎ 041 982 6459, 041 988 0300 (Nov-Apr); Fax 041 982 6053, 982 3071 (Nov-Apr)

On the banks of the **River Mattock**, Mellifont was founded by St Malachy in 1142 with four Irish and nine French monks. The first **Cistercian house** in Ireland, it no doubt owed its name ("Honey fountain" in Latin) to the beauty of its surroundings.

Still standing are the ruined **gatehouse** *(right)* beside the approach road, the vaulted **Chapter House** (14C) and four faces of the two-storey **octagonal lavabo** (12C), where the monks washed their hands before eating in the refectory opposite. Excavation has revealed the outline of the monastic buildings.

The 12C church, which was consecrated in 1157, was designed by one of the Frenchmen; it had a crypt at the west end and three chapels in the transepts – two apsidal chapels flanking a central rectangular one. In 1225 the chancel and transepts were extended. In 1556 the abbey became a private house which was abandoned in 1727.

Hill of Slane

This hilltop with its wide-ranging views is one of the key sites in the story of Irish Christianity. In 433 St Patrick travelled from Saul (in Co Down) by sea and on foot to Slane, where he lit a fire on the hilltop on Easter Eve to challenge the druids who were holding a festival at Tara. As anyone who kindled a fire within sight of Tara did so on pain of death, Patrick was brought before Laoghaire, the High King, to whom he preached the Gospel. Although the king remained a pagan, he allowed his subjects freedom of conscience. One of them, Erc, converted and founded a monastery at Slane; he is said to be buried in the ruined mortuary house in the graveyard.

The church, which was in use until 1723, was part of **Slane Friary**, a Franciscan house, founded in 1512 by Sir Christopher Flemyng, whose arms are on the west wall of the courtyard. The friary, which housed four priests, four lay brothers and four choristers, was suppressed in 1540, occupied by Capuchins in 1631 and abandoned under Cromwell. On the west face of the hill is a motte raised by Richard le Flemyng of Flanders, who arrived in Ireland in 1175.

Termonfeckin★

6mi/10km N of Drogheda by R 167 E or R 166 and a minor road E. (Dúchas) Key available from the cottage opposite. €6.35 deposit for key. Limited parking.

In the graveyard of St Fechin's Church stands a 10C **high cross** depicting *(east face)* the Crucifixion and *(west face)* Christ in Glory; it marks the site of a monastery founded by St Fechin of Fore *(see p 327)*.

Close to the shore stands a 15C or 16C three-storey **tower house** which has an unusual corbelled roof *(45 steps)*: **view** of the coast from Drogheda *(S)* to Clogher Head *(N)*.

SLANE

The centre of the village, known as the "square", was laid out by Viscount Conyngham in the late 18C; it is lit by oil lamps and bordered by four nearly identical Georgian houses, each flanked by two smaller houses.

The Gothic Gate *(S of the crossroads)* was designed by **Francis Johnston** c 1795 as an entrance to Slane Castle. From the bridge over the Boyne there is a **view** of Slane Castle, Slane Mill (1766), the weir and the canal; there is a towpath walk upstream to Navan.

Slane Castle

0.25mi/0.5km W of Slane by N 51. Guided tour mid-May to mid-Aug, Sun-Thu, noon-5pm. Closed 16 June. €7. ☎ 0419 824 163, 207; Fax 0419 824 401; slanecastle@oceanfree.net

The impressive raised **site** overlooking the **River Boyne** is surmounted by an elegant assembly of square turrets, crenellations and artificial machicolations. The present house was built between 1785 and 1821 on the site of a confiscated **Fleming** fortress purchased by the Conynghams in 1641. Only the best architects were employed, among them James Gandon, James Wyatt, Francis Johnston and Thomas Hopper, while Capability Brown designed the stables and landscaped the grounds. Many of the rooms had to be restored after a disastrous fire in 1991.

Ledwidge Cottage Museum

0.5mi/0.8km E of Slane by N 51. ♿ Open daily, 10am-1pm and 2-5.30pm. €2. Parking. ☎ 041 982 4544; 041 982 4244

The cottage displays some of the manuscripts of the poet, **Francis Ledwidge** (1887-1917), whose work, first published through the patronage of Lord Dunsany, reflects his love of the Meath countryside. His childhood home, this four-roomed semi-detached cottage, built under the Labourers' Dwellings Act (1886), has been restored to its original appearance.

Buncrana

With its long sandy beach facing west across Lough Swilly to the mountains of Donegal, Buncrana is a busy seaside resort and the largest town on the Inishowen Peninsula, crowded in summer with holidaymakers from Londonderry, a mere dozen miles away on the far side of the border. Approached by a six-arched bridge spanning the Crana River, O'Docherty's Keep is all that remains of the castle built by the Anglo-Normans and later held by the local lords, the "O'Dochertys tall from dark Donegal" (Benedict Kiely).

Location

Population 3 112 - Michelin Atlas p 101 and Map 712 – JK 2 – Co Donegal. Buncrana *(Bun Cranncha)* is set on the east shore of Lough Swilly, NW of Londonderry. It is a good place from which to make the tour of the Inishowen Peninsula.

🛈 *Buncrana. Open Jun-Aug, Mon-Sat.* ☎ *077 62600*

Adjacent Sights: SEE DONEGAL, DONEGAL COAST, DONEGAL GLENS, LONDONDERRY, SPERRIN MOUNTAINS.

Directory

WHERE TO STAY

• *Budget*

Rossaor House – *Ballyliffin* - ☎ *077 76498 - Fax 077 76498 - rossaor@gofree.indigo.ie - Closed 23 Dec to 2 Jan -* 🅿 *- 4 rm €45/80* ⌧. This comfortably furnished house is surrounded by mature gardens and boasts a welcoming and relaxed atmosphere. Breakfast is served in a conservatory which enjoys wonderful views of Pollan Bay.

WHERE TO EAT

• *Moderate*

The Corncrake – *Millbrae, Carndonagh* - ☎ *077 74534 - Closed Mon and restricted opening in winter -* ⌧ ⤬ *- Booking essential - €27.50/37.* This terraced house on the main street has been converted into a charming little restaurant. The concise and regularly changing menu focuses on fresh, local ingredients to produce simple, tasty dishes.

Tour

INISHOWEN (INIS EOGHAIN) SCENIC DRIVE★★

100mi/160km round trip – 1 day

The drive follows the coast of the Inishowen Peninsula, which terminates in Malin Head, the most northerly point in Ireland. The landscape is composed of rugged mountains covered in blanket bog, fringed by steep cliffs or broad sweeps of sand. Flocks of sheep graze the stony ground. In the fishing villages the traditional cabins are roofed with thatch, tied down with ropes against the wind.

The peninsula is named after Eoghain, a ruler who was a contemporary of St Patrick in the 5C. By the 15C the powerful clan of the O'Dochertys held sway but when their chief was killed in 1608 the whole of the peninsula passed into the possession of the Elizabethan adventurer Sir Arthur Chichester, whose family eventually became the largest landowners in Ireland.

Take the coast road N to Dunree Head.

Fort Dunree Military Museum★

Car park within the military compound. Open Jun-Sep, daily, 10.30am (12.30pm Sun) to 6pm. €4. Guided tour (30min) available. Parking. Refreshments. ☎ *077 61817; dunree@eircom.net; www.dunree.pro.ie*

A drawbridge spans the narrow defile which separates this late 18C fort from the desolate headland of Dunree Head. The fort itself has been converted into a **military museum** containing the original guns; modern interactive technology and a film explain their role in a coastal defence battery; 180 years of records illustrate the evolution of the fort from a fortified earthen embankment, built in 1798 under the threat of French invasion, to an important element in a chain of forts on the shores of Lough Swilly defending a Royal Navy base at Buncrana. In 1914 the entire British Grand Fleet sheltered behind a boom in the Lough. Knockalla Fort is visible across the narrow channel on the opposite shore.

Return to the junction and turn left; at the crossroads turn left.

Gap of Mamore★

The road climbs past rocky outcrops and grazing sheep to the **viewpoint** *(car park – right)* – extensive view north to Dunaff Head.

Turn left past Lenan Strand to Lenan Head.

Lenan Head

The headland, where a gun battery (1895) used to command the entrance to Lough Swilly, is disfigured by a ruined army camp.

Take the road through Dunaff to Clonmany and continue N on R 238.

Ballyliffin (Baile Lifin)

This attractive holiday village is set slightly inland from Pollan Bay and Pollan Strand, a long sandy beach backed by a golf course on Doagh Isle, a flat sandy peninsula.

Continue E on R 238.

Carndonagh High Cross★

At the top of the hill next to the Anglican church stands an 8C **high cross**, decorated with an interlaced cross and a Crucifixion and flanked by two **pillars**, one of which shows David with his harp. In the graveyard stands a **cross pillar**, known as the Marigold Stone, which is decorated with a seven-pointed star, resembling a marigold, on one side and a Crucifixion on the other.

Continue N on R 238 and R 242.

Malin

This 17C Plantation village has kept its original layout, including its central feature, a triangular green.

Lag Sand Dunes★

Massive sand dunes rise up on the north shore of Trawbreaga Bay, the estuary of the Donagh River.

Malin Head★★

The tiny fishing village shelters from the prevailing wind in the lee of the great headland, the most northerly point in Ireland, which figures in the shipping forecasts. On the cliffs stands a tower, originally built in 1805 by the British Admiralty to monitor shipping and later used as a signal tower by Lloyds. North across the sound *(1.5mi/2.4km)* lies Inishtrahull Island, once the site of a hermitage but now deserted. The road circles the headland providing dramatic **views★★** *(southwest)* across the water to Pollan Strand and Dunaff Head.

Take the coast road S via Portaleen to Culdaff. Take R 238 S; turn left into minor road.

Bocan Stone Circle

In a field *(left)* are the remains of a stone circle which originally may have consisted of 30 standing stones.

Return to last junction; turn right into R 238 ; drive towards Culdaff; turn left into minor road.

Clonca Church and Cross

Path across a field. In the 6C St Buodán founded a monastery at Clonca. The ruined church dates from the 17C or 18C but the carved lintel is earlier. Inside is the 16C tombstone of Magnus MacOrristin, who probably came from the Hebrides, showing a sword and a hurley stick and bearing a rare Irish inscription. In the field opposite the church door is **St Buodán's high cross** depicting the miracle of the loaves and fishes *(east face).*

Continue to the next junction, turn left and then right.

Dunagree Point

Carrowmore High Crosses

The site of a monastery founded by Chionais, St Patrick's brother-in-law, is now marked by two **high crosses**, a decorated slab and a boulder inscribed with a cross.

Return to the last junction; turn right; in Gleneely take R 238 S; after 3.5mi/5km turn left to Leckemy and take the minor road NE to Kinnagoe Bay.

Kinnagoe Bay

The sandy beach is sheltered by steep headlands. A map *(at the road junction)* plots the sites of the many ships of the Spanish Armada which were wrecked on the Irish coast; many fascinating military relics were found in *La Duquesa St Anna* and *La Trinidad Valencia*, which were wrecked in the bay. *Clifftop footpath to Inishowen Head.*

Take the minor road S to Greencastle.

The view from the viewpoint *(car park)* embraces open moorland used for turf cutting and sheep pasture extending east to Lough Foyle.

On the edge of Greencastle turn left to Inishowen Head.

Inishowen Head★

The headland (295ft/90m) above the tiny harbour next to the lighthouse on Dunagree Point commands a fine view east along the Antrim coast as far as the Giant's Causeway. *Clifftop footpath to Kinnagoe Bay.*

Take the coast road S past the golf course.

Greencastle

A fine beach makes this a pleasant and popular resort. North of the town on the cliffs opposite Magilligan Point commanding the narrow entrance to Lough Foyle stand the overgrown ruins of a castle built in 1305 by Richard de Burgo, the Red Earl of Ulster, so-called because of his florid complexion. It was captured by Edward Bruce in 1316, fell into the possession of the O'Donnells a few years later and was granted to Sir Arthur Chichester in 1608; the adjoining fort (1812) was used in the defence of Lough Foyle until the end of the 19C.

From Greencastle take R 241 S.

Moville (Bun an Phobail)

Moville (pronounced with the accent on the second syllable), once a bustling port where emigrant ships set sail for the United States, is now a seaside resort. **St Pius' Roman Catholic Church** (1953) is an impressive granite building with a handsome mahogany interior. The cliffs and beaches overlooking Lough Foyle have been incorporated into a landscaped coastal walk, **Moville Green**, interspersed with lawns and shrubberies and sporting facilities.

From Moville take R 241 S; after 2mi/3.2km turn right.

In **Cooley** at the graveyard gate stands a **high cross** (10ft/3m) with a hole in its head through which people clasped hands to seal an undertaking. The graveyard contains a **mortuary house**, a tomb shrine known as the Skull House, a delightful little drystone structure thought to be associated with St Finian, the abbot of the monastery, which was founded by St Patrick and survived until the 12C.

Continue S on R 241. In Muff turn right to Burnfoot; take the minor road to Speenoge.

Grianán of Aileach★★

Car park. This circular stone fort crowning the exposed hilltop and dating from the pre-Christian era is one of the most spectacular structures of its kind in the country, though its present form is speculative and dates from a late 19C reconstruction. It served as the seat of the O'Neill clan from about the 5C to the 11C but even before then was sufficiently famous to have been included in Ptolemy's map of the world

> ### THE WARRIOR COIRRGEND
> This fierce fighter had committed the terrible crime of murdering the son of the king. As punishment, he was ordered to carry the body and a burial stone to Grianán Mountain. The burden killed him and he died crying "Á, leac!" ("Alas, stone!") – the origin of the name of the site.

as a "royal residence". It was destroyed in 1101 by the King of Munster, Murtogh O'Brien, in retaliation for the destruction of his own royal seat at Kincora. A tunnel pierces the stone wall (13ft/4m thick) which contains small chambers and steps to the ramparts and encloses a circle (77ft/23m in diameter). From the ramparts there is an extensive **view★★** *(east)* of Londonderry and the Sperrin Mountains, *(northeast)* of Lough Foyle, *(north)* of the Inishowen Peninsula, and *(west)* of Inch Island, Lough Swilly and Knockalla Mountain.

The circular shape of the stone fort is tellingly echoed at the foot of the hill in **St Aengus Church**, one of the country's finest modern places of worship, designed by Liam McCormick.

Return downhill to N 13; turn left towards Letterkenny.

Grianán Ailigh Centre

Burt; beside N 13. & *Open daily, 10am (noon in winter) to 6pm. €5. Parking. Restaurant.*
☎ 077 68080; Fax 077 68012; www.griananailigh.ie

An exhibition of storyboards and models relating the legends associated with the
site is housed on the upper floor of a redundant Anglican church, which has been
converted into a restaurant. Other displays describe similar Irish stone forts and
the restoration of the church.

Return N on N 13 and minor road to Burnfoot. Take R 238 N to Fahan.

Fahan Cross-Slab

On the south side of the village in the old graveyard beside the Anglican church
stands a 7C **cross-slab**, which is decorated on each face with a cross formed of
interlaced bands; one of them is flanked by two figures. It marks the site of a
monastery which was founded by St Mura in the 7C and survived until at least
1098.

Take R 238 N to Buncrana.

The Burren★★

Covering much of County Clare, the austere limestone plateau of The
Burren ("Place of Rock") is one of Ireland's strangest but most compelling
landscapes. The porosity of the rock means that the rivers have gone
underground, creating extensive cave systems, while much of the surface is
clad in limestone pavement, its surface riven with crevices. Six thousand
years of human occupation have largely denuded The Burren of its trees, but
in spring and early summer, the otherwise desolate scene is enlivened
by an extraordinary variety of flowers, with Mediterranean and Alpine
species flourishing side by side.

Directory

SIGHTSEEING

Aran Islands – *From Doolin there is a
ferry to the Aran Islands (see p 126)
Operates (weather permitting) Jun-Aug: to
Inishmore (60min), twice daily; to Inishmaan
(45min), twice daily; to Inisheer (30min),
6 times daily (additional sailing Fri only at
6.30pm); from Inishmore, twice daily; from
Inishmaan, twice daily; from Inisheer, 5 times
daily; Easter-May and Sep; telephone for
details. Return €25-€30. ☎ 065 707 4455,
707 4466, 707 4189; Fax 065 707 4417
(Doolin Ferry Co); doolinferries@eircom.net;
www.doolinferries.com*
Sea cruises to view the Cliffs of Moher
operate from Liscannor.

WHERE TO EAT

• **Budget**
Linnane's bar – *☎ 065 707 8120 - Closed
lunch Mon and Tue -* 🅿 *- €15.* Perched on
the rocks, looking out over Galway Bay,
where the day can slip by. Simply decorated
with pews and pine tables and a menu that
makes the most of local seafood; from
chowder to mussels, crab cakes and fresh
lobster.

Vaughan's – *☎ 065 708 8004 -
info@vaughanspub.com - Closed 25 Dec -* ✉
🅿 *- €20.* An evening at this pub will
provide all the entertainment you need.
There is live music most nights and set
dancing in the adjacent barn for the more

energetic. The menu ranges from
sandwiches to beef and Guinness
casserole.

ENTERTAINMENT

Irish Traditional Music – **Doolin** has
an international reputation both for the
audience and for the quality of the
musicianship. Other places for sessions
in summer are Ballyvaughan, Kilfenora,
Lisdoonvarna and Ennistimon.

SHOPPING

The **Burren Smokehouse** in Lisdoonvarna
sells craftwork and food – wild and farmed
salmon; eel, mackerel, trout; selection of
cheeses and smoked cheese; gourmet items;
Burren perfumery, jewellery – and operates a
worldwide mail order service. The old kiln
(1989) is still in use for smoking.
For local perfumes visit the **Burren
Perfumery** (see below).

SPORTS AND LEISURE

Seaside Resorts – To the south at
Liscannor, **Lahinch** (long sand beach with
lifeguard on duty) and **Milltown Malbay**;
also to the north at **Fanore**
(S of Black Head) and at **Finavarra**
(NE of Ballyvaughan).
Burren Way – Walking trail *(26mi/42km)*
between Ballyvaughan and Liscannor *(leaflet
from Tourist Information Centre)* passes
through the Caher Valley, mostly on Green

Roads, through Doolin and along the Cliffs of Moher before turning inland to Liscannor.

For **Guided Walks** on botany, archaeology and history ask at the Tourist Information Centre.

There is a pleasant walk from Lisdoonvarna south across the bog at Cnoc na Madre.

The Seaworld Aquarium in Lahinch provides indoor swimming pools, sauna and jacuzzi.

EVENTS AND FESTIVALS

Lisdoonvarna Fair – The Matchmaking Festival takes place from late August to early October – dancing, singsongs, evening pub sessions and walks.

The **Willie Clancy Summer School** *(July)* in Milltown Malbay is a major music festival – all aspects of music, song and dance, particularly of the elbow *(uilleann)* pipes.

An annual summer school is held in **Ennistimon** to celebrate the work of Brian Merriman (b 1749 in Ennistimon), whose poem *The Midnight Court* is unique in Irish Literature.

Location

Michelin Atlas p 88-89 and Map 712 – E 8 – Co Clare.

The Burren *(Boireann)* covers the northern part of Co Clare extending south from Ballyvaughan to Ennistimon and Corofin.

🛈 *Cliffs of Moher, Liscannor, Co Clare. Open Apr-Oct.* ☎ *065 708 1171; TourismInfo@shannondev.ie; www.shannondev.ie/tourism*

Adjacent Sights: See ARAN ISLANDS, ATHENRY, CONNEMARA, ENNIS, GALWAY.

Background

The Burren slopes gently from north to south, its outer limits generally marked by steep escarpments. The classic karstic features of limestone pavements and underground drainage systems are accompanied by sink holes, which, when filled by a rise in the water table, become temporary lakes known as *turlach*. Fissures (grykes) between the slabs (clints) forming the limestone pavements contain enough soil to support a remarkably rich flora, which flourishes in glorious contrast to the stony chaos all around. The human impact on a seemingly empty landscape has been considerable; dry-stone walls define field patterns and enclosures of immense variety, some dating back to neolithic times, and there is an array of tombs, forts and traces of ancient settlements.

The old Celtic practice of booleying is practised in reverse. In winter the cattle are kept on the higher ground, which remains relatively dry and warm not just because of the Gulf Stream but because the mass of limestone acts as a giant storage heater, slowly releasing heat absorbed earlier. In summer, when the uplands may suffer from drought, the animals are kept near the homesteads, where they can be tended and watered.

BOTANISING

The best months to view the 1 000 or so species of flowering plants and ferns in The Burren are May or June but there is something to enjoy in every season. The further you go from the road the more likely you are to be rewarded. The rarer plants favour the more extreme habitats – the sunniest, shadiest, driest or wettest – look for cracks *(grikes)* shallow enough to admit light but deep enough to give shelter. Keep to naked limestone or grassy hill slopes, avoiding the cultivated farmland.

Tour

Round trip of 80mi/128km

Ennistimon (Inis Díomáin)

The **waterfalls** on the River Cullenagh are visible from the seven-arch bridge that spans the river, from the river bank *(through arched entry in the Main Street)* and from the grounds of the Falls Hotel. The town is noted for its shopfronts, many of them in traditional style and with lettering in Irish .

Take N 67 and R 481 N.

Kilfenora High Crosses★

Much shrunken today, Kilfenora was once an important episcopal see. Its cathedral, now in partial ruin, has a number of fascinating features, including superbly carved capitals, crude effiges, and an elegant east window. Outside stand three 12C high crosses. One in particular, the famous Doorty's Cross, is well worth close inspection, despite its eroded condition, with figures of Christ, a bishop, as well as Celtic ornamentation. A fourth cross *(100yd/90m W in a field)* shows the Crucifixion.

The Burren Centre★

& *Open Jun-Sep, daily, 9.30am-6pm; Mar-May and Oct, daily, 10am-5pm. €5. Guided tour (30min; foreign languages). Parking. Restaurant. Bookshop. Tourist information.* ☎ *065 708 8030; Fax 065 708 8102; burrencenter@eircom.net*

In the centre of Kilfenora, the fine displays and audio-visual show of this newly-established and well-laid out centre combine to give visitors an excellent introduction to the natural and human history of the unique landscapes of The Burren. The dramatic diaromas include one of prehistoric bear hunters spearing their fearsome prey and among the informative models is one of Cahercommaun, the only one of the Burren ringforts to have been excavated (by a team of Harvard archaeologists in 1934).

Take R 476 NW.

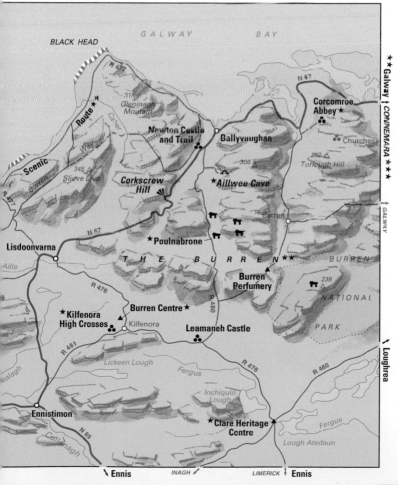

Lisdoonvarna (Lios Dúin Bhearna)

Ireland's only operating spa developed in the 19C round three mineral springs; water from the sulphur spring is served by the glass or the bottle at the Spa Wells; the health centre provides sulphur baths and other treatments. A 17C crucifix adorns the Roman Catholic Church of Our Lady of Lourdes (1878).

Take N 67 N.

BRIDES FOR BACHELORS

Throughout September Lisdoonvarna is the scene of a famous – or notorious – Matchmaking Festival, whose original function was to provide partners for lonely lads living on isolated farms deep in the countryside. For several weeks the little spa town is filled with hordes of merrymakers, less intent nowadays on the serious business of finding a bride than of having a raucously good time.

Corkscrew Hill

There is a fine **view** of the terraced limestone landscape from Corkscrew Hill on the road between Ballyvaughan and Lisdoonvarna (*N 67*).

Newtown Castle and Trail

Open Easter-Sep, Mon-Fri, 10am-5pm (last admission) No charge unguided tour. Guided tour castle and trail €4.44, castle or trail €2.54. Parking. ☎ 065 707 7200; Fax 065 707 7201; admin@burrencollege.com; www.burrencollege.com

The stone spiral staircase of this fine 16C defensive tower house leads to a series of exhibits illustrating the recent restoration of the building and the importance of the region in medieval times as a centre for the study of law. The gallery of the Great Hall beneath the new domed roof leads to a balcony with extensive views over The Burren. A trail on the hillside behind the tower leads to a variety of natural and historic man-made features including an early lime kiln and a Victorian gazebo.

Take R 480 SE.

Aillwee Cave★

Park in the upper car park. (&) Guided tour (35min) daily, 10am-6pm. €7.50. Brochure (5 languages). Parking. Restaurant, tearoom. Disabled by appointment. ☎ 065 707 7036, 707 7067; aillwee@eircom.net; www.aillweecave.ie

Cliffs of Moher

Because of unpredictably fluctuating water levels the underground Burren can be a perilous place, and most of it is inaccessible to the public. This cavern is the only exception, its single tunnel stretching deep into The Burren (0.75mi/1km) adorned with stalactites and stalagmites and a **waterfall★** which is impressively floodlit from below. The bones of a brown bear were found in one of the hibernation pits near the entrance. At the back of the Highway, the largest chamber, there is a vertical drop; even in dry weather the sound of flowing water can be heard.

The **visitor centre**, built in the style of a stone fort in harmony with its surroundings, explains the formation of the cave and its discovery in 1940 by a local herdsman, Jack McCann. Adjacent is the tiny entrance to the extensive cave systems discovered in 1987.

Poulnabrone Portal Tomb★

In a magnificently stony setting on the road between Aillwee and Leamaneh Castle *(R 480)* stands this **dolmen**, the most famous of the many **megalithic tombs** in The Burren.

Leamaneh Castle

For permission to view ask at the modern house beside the castle (left).

Only the shell remains of a four-storey Elizabethan-style fortified house with mullioned windows which was built in the 17C by Conor O'Brien, who was killed in 1651 during the Cromwellian wars. From the top *(88 steps)* of the adjoining 15C **tower house** there is a fine **view**.

Return N on R 480 SE ; bear right into a minor road to Carran.

Burren Perfumery

Open daily, 9.30am (9am Jun-Aug) to 5pm (7pm Jun-Aug); Nov-Feb by appointment. Parking. Tearoom. ☎ 065 708 9102; Fax 065 708 9200

The astonishing diversity of Mediterranean and Alpine flowers living side by side in this seemingly inhospitable landscape are the inspiration for a range of perfumes and soaps made here by traditional methods of distilling and blending. The products of the herb garden are also used for herbal teas. An audio-visual *(9min)* and photographic display give a close-up view of some of the many species of flowers growing nearby.

Turn right into N 67.

H Champollion/MICHELIN

Corcomroe Abbey★

The ruins of this **Cistercian abbey** founded around 1180 blend harmoniously with the limestone of the surrounding Burren. The monks dedicated their abbey to St Mary of the Fertile Rock, perhaps in response to the floristic richness of the stony countryside. There are carved capitals and fine vaulting in the choir and transept chapels. It was here that **William Butler Yeats** set his verse play *The Dreaming of the Bones*. On the north slope of Turlough Hill (925ft/282m) are the ruins of three 12C churches.

Take N 67 W to Ballyvaughan.

Burren eXposure

  Open Mar-Nov, daily, 9.30am-5.30pm. €5. Parking. ☎ *065 707 7277; Fax 065 707 7278; douglasculligan@eircom.net; www.burrenexposure.com*

This interpretation centre occupies a splendid setting overlooking the harbour at **Ballyvaughan**; it uses a series of audio-visual presentations to describe the geology, flora and human history which have combined in the unique landscape of The Burren.

In Ballyvaughan take R 477 W.

Scenic Route★★

The coast road south of Black Head provides a fine view of the huge boulders, deposited at the end of the Ice Age, which rest on the bare limestone pavement; in fine weather the Aran Islands, of similar geological formation, are visible offshore.

W of Lisdoonvarna take N 67 and R 478 S.

Cliffs of Moher★★★

As the cliff edge is extremely dangerous the clifftop path is fenced. The site attracts large numbers of tourist coaches. *Site: Open daily. Visitor Centre: Open Sep-May, daily, 9.30am-5.30pm. O'Brien's Tower: Open (weather permitting) May-Sep, daily, 9.30am-5.30pm; subject to change; check by telephone. Closed Good Fri, 24-26 Dec. Centre no charge; O'Brien's Tower €1.30. Parking. Tearoom.* ☎ *065 708 1565 (Centre),* ☎ *061 360 788 (Shannon Heritage central reservations); Fax 061 236 1020; reservations@shannondev.ie; www.shannonheritagetrade.com*

These great dark sandstone cliffs (600ft/182m high – nearly 5mi/8km long) are among the country's most stunning natural sights. Rising sheer from the Atlantic, they are inhabited by countless screaming seabirds, which throng the ledges or wheel and swoop above the waves. The best view is from **O'Brien's Tower**, built in 1853 by Cornelius O'Brien. The **Visitor Centre** provides much information on the flora and fauna of the area, including examples of local birdlife.

Birchfield House

The ruins of the vast house, built by Cornelius O'Brien, local MP for over 20 years, are dominated by a tall column erected in his honour in 1853.

Caher

In a fine location on the River Suir at the foot of the Galty Mountains, Caher is a busy little crossroads town, designated a Heritage town, benefiting nowadays from the bypass carrying the main Dublin-Cork highway. Dominating the place is its formidable castle, built on a rocky islet in the river, in the 10C/11C the site of a residence of Brian Ború, High King of Ireland. The present stronghold was begun in the 13C, then greatly modified and extended by one of the greatest of Ireland's Anglo-Norman dynasties, the Butlers, who retained possession until it passed into State care in 1961.

Location

Population 2 236 - Michelin Atlas p 85 and Map 712 – I 11 – Co Tipperary.
Caher *(An Cathair)*, also Cahir pronounced Care, marks the junction of N 8 and N 24, S of Cashel and NW of Clonmel.
🛈 *Castle Street, Caher. Open Jul-Aug, daily; May-Jun and Sep, Mon-Sat.* ☎ *052 41453*
Adjacent Sights: See CASHEL, CLONMEL, LISMORE.

Special Feature

Caher Castle★★

(Dúchas) *Open mid-Jun to mid-Sep, daily, 9am-7.30pm; mid-Mar to mid-Jun and mid-Sep to mid-Mar, daily, 9.30am-5.30pm (4.30pm mid-Oct to mid-Mar); last admission 45min before closing. Closed 24-30 Dec. €2.50. Guided tour available. Audio-visual show (4 languages). Leaflet (6 languages).* ☎ *052 41011; Fax 052 42324; cahircastle@ealga.ie*

Though much restored, the castle is one of the largest and finest examples of a late medieval stronghold, with high outer walls embracing outer, middle and inner wards, a barbican, sturdy towers and a splendid keep. The whole ensemble expresses the power and pride of the Anglo-Norman Butlers, Earls of Ormond, who held sway over much of southeastern Ireland, though the castle's defences failed to save it from falling in 1599 to an assault by troops led by Queen Elizabeth I's favourite, the Earl of Essex. More recently, the castle has served magnificently as a set for films requiring a romantic background such as Stanley Kubrick's *Barry Lyndon*, and it is well worth while taking the guided tour around its passageways, spiral staircases, sentry walks and great hall. An **audio-visual presentation** is devoted to the antiquarian delights of the surrounding countryside and there is a splendid illuminated model showing the progress of the 1599 siege.

Walking About

Walk along Castle Street to the Square.

The **Cahir House Hotel**, formerly the family seat of the Butlers after the castle had fallen into disrepair, and the **Market House** (now the library) are part of the 18C transformation of the town centre by the Butlers; the mills also date from this period.

Walk along Old Church Street (N 24 to Clonmel).

The **ruined church**, last used in the 1820s, had a curtain wall, which allowed Roman Catholics and Protestants to worship simultaneously; in the 19C, when Caher was an important garrison town, part of the adjoining cemetery was reserved for military burials. Many Caher men fell in the First World War; they are commemorated by the **Great War Memorial**, a rarity in an Irish town.

Return to the Square and turn right into Church Street (N 8 north towards Cashel).

The Anglican **St Paul's Church** *(Church Street, N 8 north towards Cashel)* was designed in 1820 by John Nash, the famous Regency architect.

Excursions

Swiss Cottage★

1mi/2km S of Caher by R 670 or on foot along the riverbank. (Dúchas) Guided tour (40min) mid-Apr to mid Oct, daily, 10am 6pm; mid-Mar to mid-Apr and mid-Oct to Nov, Tue-Sun and Bank Hols, 10am-1pm and 2-4.30pm; last admission 45min before closing. €2.50 No photography. Parking nearby. Guide book (5 languages). ☎ 052 41144; swisscottage@ealga.ie

While in Caher, John Nash turned his hand to the design of this substantial but wonderfully light-hearted example of a *cottage orné*. The deliciously elaborate two-storeyed thatched cottage was built between 1812 and 1814 as a fishing and hunting lodge for Lord Caher and has been restored with immaculate attention to detail.

Swiss Cottage, Caher

Dúchas, Dublin

In one of the two ground-floor rooms, the hand-painted French wallpaper shows views of the Bosporus. Nearby, the picturesque scene is enhanced by an elegant cast-iron bridge spanning the River Suir.

Burncourt House

8mi/13km W by N 8; in Boolakennedy turn left. Access through farmyard and across a field. The ruined house, with its 26 gables and many chimneys, was built in 1640. A mere ten years later the wife of its owner, Sir Richard Everard, set it on fire rather than let it fall intact into the hands of the hated Cromwellian army.

Mitchelstown Cave

9mi/14.5km W by N 8; in Boolakennedy turn left. Guided tour (35min; 3 languages) daily, 10am-6pm, every 15min. €4.44. Parking. ☎ *052 67246; Fax 052 67943; venglish@oceanfree.net; mitchelstowncave.com*

A flight of 88 steep steps leads into three massive caverns (1mi/2km) containing dripstone formations – stalactites and stalagmites, curtains and pipes. The most impressive is the Tower of Babel, a huge calcite column, in the very straight Kingston Gallery (250ft/76m long). The nearby Old Caves are open only to experienced potholers.

Carrick-on-Shannon★

On the main road and railway between Dublin and Sligo, the county town of Co Leitrim is a major crossing point on the River Shannon. It's a busy boating and cruising centre, its importance enhanced by the restoration and reopening in 1994 of the Ballinamore-Ballyconnell Canal, completing the Shannon-Erne Waterway. Close by are Lough Allen and Lough Key and there is good angling to be had in the area.

Location

Population 1 868 - Michelin Atlas p 96 and Map 712 – H 6 – Co Leitrim.
Carrick-on-Shannon *(Cora Droma Rúisc)* is on N 4, the Dublin to Sligo road, on the east bank of the River Shannon.
🖪 *The Old Barrel Store, The Marina. Open Jul-Aug, daily; Apr-May and Sep, Mon-Sat.* ☎ *078 20170; Fax 078 20089; www.irelandnorthwest.travel.ie*

Adjacent Sights: See BOYLE, CAVAN, KNOCK, LONGFORD, STROKESTOWN.

SHANNON-ERNE WATERWAY

This canal was built (1847-58) as the **Ballinamore-Ballyconnell Navigation** by the engineer John McMahon to join the River Shannon with Lough Erne, the final link in a waterway system which enabled barges to travel between Dublin, Belfast, Limerick and Waterford. Because of railway competition and the lack of industry the hoped-for traffic failed to develop and the canal was abandoned in 1869; by 1880 it was derelict. The waterway (40mi/65km – 13hr) passes through 16 locks and under 34 stone bridges, traverses a chain of lakes – Lough Scur, St John's Lough, Garadice Lough – and follows the course of the Woodford River. The western end joins the River Shannon in **Leitrim** *(4mi/6.5km north of Carrick by R 280).*

Worth a Visit

Costello Chapel

Bridge Street. Open Mar-Oct, daily. Brochure (4 languages). ☎ *078 20251*
The most remarkable thing about this attraction is its size. The mortuary chapel built by Edward Costello as a memorial to his wife who died young in 1877 is tiny, a mere 16 x 12ft/5 x 4m. Mrs Costello was buried in April 1879 under a thick glass slab *(left)* and her husband was interred in 1891.

Directory

SIGHTSEEING
Slieabh an Iarann Riverbus,
Ballinamore – Cruises on the Shannon-Erne Waterway – ☎ *078 44079; Fax 078 45135*
Cavan and Leitrim Railway, Dromod – Narrow-gauge steam railway and tour of engine and work sheds – *Open daily, 10am (1pm Sun) to 5.30pm. Closed Christmas to New Year. €5. Train ride (20min). Tearoom.*

☎/ *Fax 078 38599; dromod@eircom.net; www.cavanandleitrimrailway.com*

TRACING ANCESTORS
Leitrim Genealogy Centre, County Library, Ballinamore, Co Leitrim – *Open Mon-Fri, 10am-1pm and 2-5pm.* ☎ *078 44012; Fax 078 44425; leitrimgenealogy@eircom.net; www.irishroots.net/Leitrim.htm*

St George's Terrace

At the east end of the street stands the **Town Clock**, erected in 1905. The **Market House** and yard *(south side)* were built in 1839 by the local landlord, CM St George, whose elegant house, **Hatley Manor** *(north side)*, was built in the 1830s and named after his ancestral home in Cambridgeshire. Next to it stands the Courthouse of 1821, once linked by underground passage to the neighbouring County Gaol, the site of which is now occupied by a modern **marina**.

Tour

SHANNON VALLEY

Drive of 25mi/40km
From Carrick-on-Shannon take N 4 southeast.

Jamestown

Named after James I, this was a fortified settlement established in 1622 to guard the river crossing downstream from Carrick. The stone arch through which the road enters from the north is all that is left of the **defensive wall**.

Drumsna

It was here, on seeing the ruins of the Jones family mansion and hearing the story of the family's downfall, that **Anthony Trollope** was inspired to write his first novel.

South of Drumsna turn left onto R 201 to Mohill.

At the centre of **Mohill** there is a statue of **Turlough O'Carolan (Carolan)** *(see BOYLE)* seated at his harp; he lived in this village for several years.

Leave Mohill by R 201 which bears right at the end of the main street; at the fork bear right onto L 112; at the next fork bear right; after 0.75mi/1.2km turn left onto a narrow road (sign).

> #### JOHN McGAHERN
> The author of *Amongst Women*, which won the Booker prize in 1991, was brought up in Cootehall, went to school in Carrick-on-Shannon and now lives near Mohill. He is a master at describing provincial life and examining the effect of people's interest in or indifference to their neighbours' lives.

Lough Rynn Demesne*

Open May-Aug, daily, 10am-7pm Grounds €1.59-€4.44 (per car). Guided tour €1.27. Restaurant. Craft shop. Plant sales. ☎ *078 31427; Fax 078 31518*

This extensive domain was acquired by the **Clements** family in 1750 but its picturesque estate buildings and lavish landscaping date mostly from Victorian times and give a vivid picture of the privileged lifestyle led by the Clements, ennobled as the Earls of Leitrim. There are lakes, walled gardens ascending in a series of terraces and an arboretum with a fascinating array of exotic species including a monkey puzzle said to be the oldest in Ireland.

Owing to his hasty temper which was aggravated by a painful war wound, the 3rd Earl was an irascible character, inclined to treat his tenants harshly; his enjoyment of his property was cut short in 1878 when they assassinated him.

On leaving the demesne turn right. At the T-junction turn right; after two side turnings and two crossroads bear right to Dromod.

Dromod and Roosky are two attractive Shannonside villages where river cruisers can moor and replenish their supplies.

From Roosky continue south on N 4; after 3mi/4.8km turn left (sign) to Cloonmorris Abbey (1mi/1.6km).

Cruising on the River Shannon

Bord Fáilte, Dublin

Beside the entrance to the graveyard of the ruined 12C **Cloonmorris church** stands an **Ogham stone** bearing the name Qenuven.

Return to N 4 and continue south; in Newtown Forbes bear right onto a minor road (direction Killashee); turn right onto N 4 and then bear left to Cloondara.

At **Cloondara** the junction of the Royal Canal, the Camlin River and the Shannon is marked by two locks, a picturesque cluster of houses beside the canal basin, a hump-backed bridge, an old watermill and a ruined church.

Rejoin N 5 west of the village and continue to Termonbarry.

The bridge at **Termonbarry** has a lifting section to allow boats to pass and provides a fine view of the lock and weir on the Shannon.

Cashel★★★

Rising like a mirage over the vastness of the Tipperary plain, the Rock of Cashel is Ireland's Acropolis, its ruined buildings wonderfully evocative of the spirit of Celtic Christianity and Irish kingship. From the limestone outcrop (200ft/60m) rises a cluster of structures – castle and fortress, chapel, cathedral and round tower – forming the country's greatest landmark, visible from afar. Seen at close quarters, the Rock reveals a wealth of pattern and texture, the primordial geometry of triangular gable, high-pitched roof, cubes, cones and cylindrical tower set off by battlements, blind arcades, slender window openings and ornate carving.

Location

Population 2 346 - Michelin Atlas p 85 and Map 712 – I 10 – Co Tipperary.
Cashel *(Caiseal)*, a designated Heritage town, is on the main road (N 8) between Cork and Portlaoise.

H Champollion/MICHELIN

Directory

GETTING ABOUT

Public car park beside the Rock.
There is a footpath between the Rock and the gardens of the Cashel Palace Hotel.

ENTERTAINMENT

Brú Ború Theatre – For a **traditional Irish evening** followed by a banquet *(see below)*.

SHOPPING

Farney Castle Visitor Centre, *Holycross, Co Tipperary* – Knitwear and porcelain for sale in the historic castle, built in 1495 and augmented in 1800; the only round tower in Ireland occupied as a family home; home of Irish international designer, Cyril Cullen and the renowned Cullen Harpers – (&) Open Mon-Sat, 9.30am-6pm. Parking. Coffee shop. ☎ 0504 43281; 0504 43357; farneycastle@eircom.net; www.historic.irishcastles.com/farney.htm

SPORTS AND LEISURE

Walking in the Galty Mountains
Greyhound racing in Thurles.

TRACING ANCESTORS

Brú Ború – See Worth a Visit.
Clans Office, *45 West Main Street, Tipperary* – Open Mon-Fri, 9am-5pm. Genealogy service. ☎ 062 33188; Fax 062 33297; tippclan@iol.ie; www.trailblazer.ie/csrc
Tipperary Genealogical Service, *Excel Heritage Centre, Tipperary* – See Excursions.

🄳 *City Hall, Main Street, Cashel. Open Jul-Aug, daily; Apr-Jun and Sep, Mon Sat.*
☎ *062 61333*
There is a footpath up to the Rock from the gardens of the Cashel Palace Hotel.
Adjacent Sights· See ABBEYLEIX, CAHER, CLONMEL, KILKENNY, ROSCREA.

Background

Royal Seat – From about 370 until 1101 the rock was the seat of the kings of Munster, and therefore the provincial capital, and comparable in regal stature to Tara (*see p 147*), home of the High Kings of Ireland. St Patrick visited Cashel in 450 when he baptised King Aengus; there is a legend that during the ceremony, St Patrick accidentally pierced the king's foot with the point of his staff but the king, believing it to be part of the ritual, remained composed. Cashel was a place of much importance during the 10C when it was the stronghold of the holy Cormac MacCullinan, king and bishop

Rock of Cashel

Ecclesiastical Site – In 1101 the site was given to the ecclesiastical authorities whose first building, Cormac's chapel, was consecrated in 1134. The first cathedral was founded in 1169. Three years later it was at Cashel that the country's clergy assembled to honour the claim of Henry II to rule all Ireland.

In 1494 the cathedral was burned down by Gerald Mor, the Great Earl of Kildare. The greatest act of desecration came in 1647, when Lord Inchiquin, seeking the presidency of Munster under the Cromwellian regime, attacked the town of Cashel. Hundreds of people fled to the rock. Lord Inchiquin ordered turf to be piled against the walls of the cathedral and in the subsequent fire many were roasted to death. By the end of that terrible day, most of the population of 3 000 had been killed.

In 1749 the Anglican Archbishop of Cashel, tiring of the climb from his palace to the cathedral, decided to move the cathedral into town. The great storm of 1847 did much damage to the abandoned building. In 1874 the Rock became a National Monument and was subsequently restored.

Worth a Visit

ROCK OF CASHEL★★★

Access to the Rock via the Hall of the Vicars Choral (see below). (Dúchas) (&) Open daily, 9am-7.30pm (5.30pm mid-Mar to mid-Jun; 4.30pm mid-Sep to mid-Mar); last admission 45min before closing. Closed 25-26 Dec. €4.40. Audio-visual show (4 languages). Leaflet (6 languages). ☎ 062 61437; Fax 062 62988; rockofcashel@ealga.ie; www.heritageireland.ie

Cormac's Chapel★★

Cashel's greatest treasure is the chapel, started by Cormac MacCarthy in 1127 and consecrated in 1134. It is a highly ornate Romanesque building, flanked by twin towers and divided into a nave and a chancel. As well as being decorated with some of the earliest frescoes in Ireland, its interior's every stone is adorned with carvings, the most elaborate of their date in Ireland. Among them are human heads and the figures of animals in typically Celtic style, while the interlace carving on a sarcophagus is of Viking inspiration. A centaur aiming his bow at a lion graces the tympanum of the north door.

Round Tower★

In perfect condition, the round tower is built from irregularly coursed sandstone (92ft/28m high). The round-headed doorway (12ft/3.5m above ground level) has an architrave and the four top-storey windows are pointed.

Cathedral

Most of the ruin, including the high-set lancet windows, dates from the 13C. The cathedral was built to a cruciform plan without aisles; the central tower probably dates from the 14C. The transepts have two east chapels each.

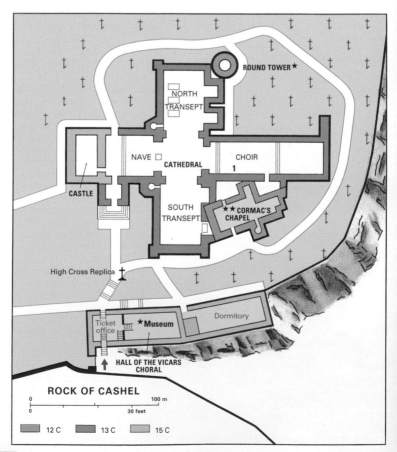

In the south wall of the choir is the tomb (1) of Archbishop Miler MacGrath, the Scoundrel of Cashel, who changed his religious beliefs several times and served as both Anglican and Roman Catholic bishop of Cashel during the reign of Elizabeth I; he died in 1621 at the age of 100.

The west tower (91ft/28m), also called the **castle**, was built as a fortified residence by Archbishop O'Hedigan in 1450. The first three storeys are covered by a pointed vault supporting the principal room.

Museum★

The museum, which is housed in the undercroft of the 15C Hall of the Vicars Choral, displays articles associated with the Rock – the stone cross of St Patrick (12C) which has lost one arm, an evil eye stone, and replicas of the 9C Cashel bell and brooch (originals in the Hunt Museum in Limerick), and of a 17C wine cup and jug (originals in the GPA Bolton Library – see Walking About).

Cormac's Chapel

Hall of the Vicars Choral

The building (extensively renovated in the 1970s) was the clergy residence. The main hall (upstairs) contains a huge 17C stone fireplace and fine items of medieval style furniture made by modern craftsmen. The kitchen has been restored to its original state: butter churns and three-legged stools. A video presentation in the Dormitory sets Cashel in the context of Irish history.

Bru Ború

At the foot of the Rock. & *Open May-Sep, daily, 9am-5pm. Genealogy service. Folk Theatre (music, song, dance): Open mid-Jun to mid-Sep, Tue-Sat at 9pm. Theatre show €13; theatre show and dinner €35. Restaurant.* ☎ *062 61122; Fax 062 62700; bruboru@comhaltas.com; www.comhaltas.com*

A modern village green is a fitting focal point for this cultural centre, which presents performances of native Irish music, song and dance, storytelling and folk theatre. The centre is also home to Celtic Studies and tracing ancestors. Imaginatively presented in the underground chambers beneath the Rock of Cashel, **Sounds of History** traces the milestones and significant characters and events in Irish history.

Walking About

Although dominated by its sublime Rock, the little town of Cashel nevertheless has much of interest to offer.

From the Rock take Bishop's Walk down the hill and through Cashel Palace Hotel Gardens into Main Street.

Cashel Palace Hotel Gardens★

Open daily; Bishop's Walk closed Nov-Good Fri. Parking. Restaurant; bar. ☎ *062 61437; reception@cashel-palace.ie; www.cashel-palace.ie*

The gardens contain a 1702 mulberry tree and hop plants, descendants of those used in 1759 to brew the first **Guinness** dark beer, which was invented by Richard Guinis, agent to the Archbishop of Cashel; his son Arthur founded the world-famous brewery in Dublin.

The Palladian mansion, now a luxury hotel, was built in 1730 as the archbishop's palace, designed by Edward Lovett Pearce for Archbishop Theophilus Bolton. The original panelling and plasterwork in the hall is complemented by the red pine staircase, as impressive as that in the Damer House (see p 333).

Cashel Heritage Centre

Open Mar-Sep, daily, 9.30am-5.30pm; Oct-Feb, Mon-Fri, same times. Commentary (10min; 5 languages). ☎ 062 62511; Fax 062 62068; cashelhc@iol.ie; www.heritagetowns.com

The display traces the history of Cashel with a model of Cashel and commentary – display of royal heirlooms, royal charters and relics of the house of McCarthy Mor.

From Main Street walk up John Street.

GPA Bolton Library★

Open (circumstances permitting) Mar-Aug, Tue-Sun, 9.30am-5.30pm; Sep-Feb, Mon-Fri, 9.30am-5.30pm. €3. Guided tour (30min) available. Parking. ☎ 062 61944 (Library); boltonlibrary@oceanfree.net; www.heritagetowns.com.

This small building, standing in the grounds of the Anglican cathedral, dates from 1836 (renovated in 1986). The oldest of its 12 000 books is a monk's encyclopedia dating from 1168; it also contains two leaves from Chaucer's *The Book of Fame*, printed by William Caxton at Westminster in London in 1483, a note signed by Jonathan Swift *(see p 229)* and a collection of ecclesiastical silver.

Cathedral

Open daily, 9.30am-5.30pm; if closed, key available from Bolton Library in Cathedral grounds. Parking. ☎ 062 61232 (The Dean); boltonlibrary@oceanfree.net

The austere Anglican cathedral, built between 1749 and 1784, has a fine panelled ceiling and stalls for Dean and Chapter; it occupies the site of the old parish church of St John the Baptist and is dedicated jointly to St John and to St Patrick of the Rock.

In the graveyard a number of 13C carved stone coffin lids have been placed against the walls, which are part of 14C town defences; the five gates and two towers were demolished in the 18C.

Walk through to Friar Street.

Parish Church

The Roman Catholic church of St John the Baptist, the oldest RC church in use in Ireland, was opened in 1795, screened by a row of cottages. The mosaics on the façade were added to commemorate the Eucharistic Congress held in Ireland in 1932; another mosaic of Christ the King decorates the baptistery. The interior is unusual in that two galleries run the full length of the building and the ceiling resembles the upturned hull of a ship.

Walk down to the end of Friar Street; turn left into Main Street and right into Dominic Street.

Folk Village

 & *Open daily, 10am-7.30pm (earlier mid-Oct to mid-Mar). €3.50. Brochure (7 languages). Guided tour (1hr) subject to demand. Parking. ☎ 062 62525*

The folk village is a small reconstruction of 18C Irish rural life.

Dominican Friary

The friary was founded by Archbishop David MacKelly *(Dáibhí Mac Ceallaigh)*, a Cork Dominican, in 1243 and suppressed in 1540. The church, which was rebuilt after a fire in 1480, has a long narrow nave and choir; the chancel walls and tower are in a good state of preservation.

Excursions

Holy Cross Abbey★★

9mi/16km north of Cashel by R 660. Open daily, 10am-6pm. Guided tour: Jun-Sep. ☎ 0504 43241 or 43124; frtjbrian02@eircom.net

For long a roofless ruin but now a flourishing parish church, Holy Cross is one of the finest examples of 15C church architecture in the country. It was originally founded for the **Benedictines** by Donal O'Brien, King of Munster, in 1168. Fourteen years later it was transferred to the **Cistercians** and became a major place of pilgrimage, as it was reputed to contain a relic of the True Cross. After the Dissolution it passed to the Earls of Ormond, under whose benevolent dispensation the monks were able to continue in residence into the 17C.

The popularity of the abbey as a centre of pilgrimage made it rich, allowing the 15C rebuilding to be carried out to an unusually high standard. There are windows with stained glass, fine original stonework, and a rare **wall-painting**, showing hunters about to kill a stag beneath an oak tree.

The west range of the restored **cloisters** contains an exhibition and audio-visual presentation and a tourist information office. There is a mill wheel in the adjacent outbuildings.

The **grounds** contain a replica of the Vatican gardens, including the Stations of the Cross and an altar, commemorating the Italian stigmatist Padre Pio.

The eight-arch **bridge** spanning the River Suir, a copy of the original, was constructed in 1626 by James Butler, Baron of Dunboyne, and his wife, Margaret O'Brien; it is ornamented with their arms and carries a short prayer: "May the two who built it escape the pit of hell".

Lár na Páirce

14mi/23km north of Cashel by R 660 to Thurles; Slievenamon Road. Open Mon-Sat, 10am-4.45pm. €4 ☎ 0504 22702; www.tipperarygaa.ie

An elegant 19C building now houses a detailed display tracing the history of the Gaelic Games. The GAA *(see p 72)* was formed, at a meeting held on 1 November 1884 in Miss Hayes' Commercial Hotel in Liberty Square in Thurles, not only to revive Gaelic games but also to give active support to the Irish language, traditional dancing, music and song. Here one can learn that hurling (the men's game) and camogie (the women's game) are played with a hurley, study the rules of Gaelic football and handball, gaze at souvenirs of former champions or look up information about current players and teams on the computer.

Hore Abbey

0.5mi/0.8km west of Cashel by N 74. The last Cistercian house to be founded in medieval Ireland, Hore Abbey was established by monks from Mellifont *(see p 148)* in 1272. Most of the present extensive ruins date from the late 13C. The church was built in cruciform shape, with a chancel, two eastern chapels to each transept and an aisled nave.

Athassel Priory★

5mi/8km west of Cashel by N 74 and minor road south from Golden, across two fields. This was one of the most extensive and flourishing establishments of its kind in Ireland, in its time surrounded by a town of which no trace now remains. The priory was destroyed in 1447 but the central tower of the main church, the nave and chancel walls are reasonably preserved. In the church is a tomb, believed to be that of the Norman, William de Burgh, the founder of the priory.

Tipperary

10m/16km west of Cashel by N 74. A pleasant small county town with enough old buildings and 19C shopfronts to merit Heritage Town status, Tipperary owes much of its fame to what was probably the most popular of all the marching songs of the First World War:

> It's a long way to Tipperary, it's a long way to go
> It's a long way to Tipperary, to the sweetest girl I know
> Goodbye Piccadilly, Goodbye Leicester Square,
> It's a long, long way to Tipperary but my heart lies there.

In the late 19C the town was a centre of Land League agitation and later the headquarters of the 3rd Tipperary Brigade of the IRA which fought many battles in the War of Independence, which are evoked in the **Old IRA Exhibition**. *Open daily, 10am-10pm (7pm in winter). Parking.*

Other aspects of local history are traced in the multi-media interactive show in the **Tipperary Excel Heritage Centre**. *Open daily, 9.30am-5.30pm. Closed Good Fri, 25 Dec. Parking. Restaurant. ☎ 062 80520; Fax 062 80550; info@tipperary-excel.com; www.tipperary-excel.com*

Glen of Aherlow★

2m/3.2km S of Tipperary by R 664. This lovely vale runs for 16m/26km between the conifer forests of the Slievenamuck ridge to the north and the Galty Mountains, Ireland's highest inland range, to the south. The glen was once occupied by the great Wood of Aherlow but has long since been converted into lush and prosperous farmland. The scene is revealed in all its glory from the **viewpoint★★** above Newtown. A gleaming white statue of Christ the King looks southward across the close-knit pattern of hedged fields to the Galtees, their splendid swooping ridge line reaching its highest point (3 018ft/919m) at the summit of Galtymore. The Galty Mountains offer challenging walking among rushing streams, bare slopes and corrie lakes.

Cavan

The little capital of Co Cavan lies in drumlin country – a tranquil, undulating, well-wooded landscape, scattered with countless small lakes which provide extensive coarse fishing and boating facilities. Nearby is Lough Oughter, the largest lake in Co Cavan, fed by the River Erne.

Location

Population 3 509 - Michelin Atlas p 97 and Map 712 – J 6 – Co Cavan.
Cavan *(An Cabhán)* is set at the junction of N 3 with N 54 and N 55 in the heart of angling country.
🗓 *1 Farnham Street, Cavan. Open Apr-Sep, Mon-Sat.* ☎ *049 433 1942; cccb@eircom.net; www.cavan.tourism.com*
Adjacent Sights: See CARRICK-ON-SHANNON, ENNISKILLEN, LONGFORD, MONAGHAN.

Directory

WHERE TO STAY
• *Budget*
Rockwood House – *Cloverhill, Belturbet -* ☎ *047 55351 - Fax 047 55373 - jbmac@eircom.net -* 🅿 ✕ *- 4 rm €40/60* ⌑. Recently built house in a clearing in the woods. The bright conservatory overlooks the attractive garden and the bedrooms are simply, yet pleasantly, furnished. Hospitable owners and good value.

Lacken Millhouse – *Lacken Lower, Bellananagh - 5mi/8km SW of Cavan on N 55 and 2.5mi/4km W of Bellananagh by N 55 off Arva road -* ☎ *049 433 7592 - info@lackenmillhouse.com - Closed at Christmas and New Year -* 🅿 ✕ *- 5 rm €50/77* ⌑ *- Meals €30.* Ideal for those in search of peace and tranquility. This 19C stone house lies on the banks of the River Erne, with 4 acres/1.62ha including the remains of two corn mills. Attractively decorated throughout. A daily changing four-course dinner is provided.

WHERE TO EAT
• *Budget*
The Oak Room – *Cavan Crystal Building, Dublin Rd - 1mi/1.6km E of Cavan on N 3 -* ☎ *049 436 0099 - Closed 1 week Nov, 24-28 Dec and Mon -* 🅿 *- €18.50/39.* The pillars and beams are still very much in evidence at this converted crystal factory, now a sizeable and contemporary restaurant. The menu mixes the modern with a healthy respect for the traditional.

SHOPPING
Cavan Crystal – *Dublin Road -* ☎ *049 43 31 800 - www.cavancrystaldesign.com - Mon-Fri, 9.30am-6pm, Sat, 10am-5pm, Sun, 12am-5pm.* Craftsmanship handed down the generations is displayed at this large development displaying the original designs of Cavan Crystal. Works from top design artists are available to buy and there is always an engraver on hand. Shipping can be arranged.

Carraig Craft Centre – Hand-made baskets of all sorts, particularly made of rushes gathered each summer from Lough Sheelin – *See below.*

SPORTS AND LEISURE
Lough Oughter, consisting of many small lakes interlinked by short, slow-moving rivers, provides sport for **boating** and **canoeists**.

There is also good **coarse angling** here and on the long stretches of the Annalee, a tributary of the Erne, for roach, bream, hybrids, pike, perch; Lough Annagh for trout; also **game angling** for salmon and trout.

Watersports available in and around Cavan are swimming, canoeing, windsurfing and water-skiing.

EVENTS AND FESTIVALS
Belturbet Festival of the Erne – Coarse and trout angling festival, outdoor music, river activity, activities for all age groups incorporating the annual huzzar "Lady of The Erne" pageant *(late July to early August)*

TRACING ANCESTORS
Cavan Genealogy Centre *(Cana House, Farnham Street)* – Open Mon-Fri, 9.30am-4.30pm. ☎ *049 436 1094; Fax 049 433 1494; canahouse@iol.ie; www.irishroots.net/cavan.htm*

Walking About

At the north end of the town stands the Roman Catholic **cathedral** (1942) designed by **Ralph Byrne**, and variously described as "sham Renaissance" or "the last flamboyant fling of historicism". It benefits from examples of work by the distinguished sculptor **Albert Power** (1883-1945). South stands the **Anglican Church**, an aisleless, galleried church with crenellations, a west tower and steeple, by John Bowden, who also designed the Classical **Courthouse** *(opposite).*

Literary Associations

Several famous penmen are connected with County Cavan. The playwright, **Richard Brinsley Sheridan**, was the grandson of Dr Thomas Sheridan, headmaster of Cavan Royal School and a good friend of Jonathan Swift, who often stayed at his home, Quilcagh House near Mullagh. An ancestor of **Edgar Allan Poe** (1809-49) emigrated to America from Killeshandra in the mid-18C. William James, a native of Baillieborough, who emigrated to America because he was a Presbyterian, was the grandfather of **Henry James** (1843-1916). Though born at Cloonyquin (west of Strokestown) **Percy French** (1854-1920), a famous songwriter and gifted painter, is celebrated in Cavan, where he worked for seven years as inspector of loans to tenants. It was while studying engineering at Trinity College in Dublin that he began to write the songs which capture the humour and spirit of his native land. He died in Formby in Lancashire, having moved to England in 1908.

Life Force Mill

Open May-Sep, Mon-Sat, 9am-5pm; otherwise guided tour (1hr) by appointment. Video 25min. €5.08. ☎ *049 436 2722; Fax 049 436 2923; lifeforce.mill@oceanfree.net*

An amusing hands-on experience can be enjoyed in this old flour mill which ceased production in the early 1950s and has been restored to working order. After watching a video presentation on the history of the mill and its restoration, visitors can mix the dough for a loaf of soda bread, inspect the milling machinery in action, then return to the kitchen when the bread is baked.

Life Force Mill, Cavan

Source: Fáilte, Dublin

Excursions

Ballyjamesduff

10mi/16km S of Cavan by N 3, N 55 and a minor road via Cross Keys. The town is named after Sir James Duff, who commanded British troops during the 1798 uprising. It clusters round the Market House (1813) at the junction of five broad streets; during the 18C, it was a lively place on the main coach road between Cavan and Kells, with a weekly market, nine fairs a year and a reputation for selling black cattle.

Cavan County Museum – *Open Tue-Sat, 10am-5pm; also Jun-Oct, Sun, 2-6pm. €2.* ☎ *049 854 4070; Fax 049 854 4332; ccmuseum@eircom.net; www.cavanmuseum.ie*

The museum traces the history of County Cavan with archaeological finds from the Stone Age to the Middle Ages including a three-faced pre-Christian Corleck Head and a 1 000-year-old dug-out boat. There is also a display of 18C, 19C and 20C costume from the **Pighouse Collection**, a gallery on folk life, one on the Gaelic Athletic Association *(see p 72)* and, perhaps most fascinating of all, a gallery hung with the colourful banners and sashes of various orders like the Apprentice Boys of Derry and the Ancient Order of Hibernians. The building is a converted 19C convent set in a typical conventual garden.

Carraig Craft Centre and Basketry Museum

15mi/24km S of Cavan by N 3, N 55 and R 154 to Mount Nugent. Open Apr-Oct, Mon-Fri, 10am-6pm, Sat-Sun, 10am-2pm; Nov-Mar, by appointment. €3. Coffee shop. ☎ *049 8540179; info@meathtourism.ie; www.meathtourism.ie*

This unusual little museum displays baskets of every sort – donkey creels (panniers), baskets for pigeons, eggs,

Basketry

In past centuries in Ireland there was a willow tree – there are 260 sorts of willow – outside each house, mostly in Donegal, Mayo and Galway, to provide material for making baskets. The trees were coppiced to produce long straight shoots, known as withies. Natural withies are dark, stripped withies are white; boiled and stripped withies have a red tinge. Different patterns of weaving and design developed in different parts of the country.

169

turf, potatoes, fish, salmon and eel traps, egg laying, hens and ducks, bee skeps, flower baskets, potato sieves and serving dishes – made from straw and reed as well as from willow.

Kilmore Cathedral

2mi/3.2km W of Cavan by R 198. Open by appointment. Key available from the Deanery, Danesfort. Guided tour by appointment. Parking. ☎/*Fax 049 433 1918; dean@kilmore.anglican.org*

Standing isolated in rolling parkland, the neo-Gothic Anglican cathedral is dedicated to **St Felim** *(Fethlimidh)*, who brought Christianity to the region in the 6C; it is also known as the Bedell Memorial Church.

It incorporates *(north side)* a splendid example of a 12C Romanesque doorway which may have belonged to an earlier church or to the abbey on Trinity Island in Lough Oughter. On display in the chancel is a copy of the Old Testament (printed in 1685) translated into Irish by Bishop William Bedell (1571-1642), whose memorial is over the west door; he is buried in the neighbouring grave-yard.

> ### WILLIAM BEDELL (1571-1642)
> William Bedell was born in Sussex, studied at Cambridge and travelled widely in Europe, before being appointed Provost of Trinity College in Dublin in 1627. In 1629 he became Bishop of Kilmore and tried to introduce reforms. During the 1641 Rebellion he was imprisoned for two years by the Confederates in Clogh Oughter Castle.

Killykeen Forest Park★

5mi/8km W of Cavan by R 198. In two sections linked by a footbridge, the Forest Park (600 acres/243ha) invites visitors to explore part of the patchwork landscape of land and water so characteristic of the River Erne in counties Cavan and Fermanagh. There are three marked nature trails *(maximum 2mi/3.2km)* which follow the shore, identifying the trees and the habitats of birds and animals, and a wildfowl sanctuary in Sally Lake.

On Trinity Island at the southern end of **Lough Oughter** there is the ruin of a Premonstratensian Priory, established in 1250 by monks from Lough Key *(see p 143)*. On an island in the northeast arm of the lake stands Clogh Oughter Castle, a 13C or 14C tower house.

Clonmacnoise★★★

Founded in 545 by St Kieran (Ciarán), Clonmacnoise was not only one of the foremost monastic sites in Ireland, second only to Armagh, but also the burial place of the Kings of Connaught and Tara. With its churches, cathedral, high crosses, ancient grave slabs and round towers, it continues to draw visitors by the thousand, most of them tourists rather than pilgrims, though on 9 September (St Kieran's Day), the faithful still make the pilgrimage here.

Location

Population 1 695 - Michelin Atlas p 90 and Map 712 – I 8 – Co Offaly. Clonmacnoise *(Cluain Mhic Nóis)* is situated on the east bank of the River Shannon 13mi/21km S of Athlone by N 6 and N 62. The monastery's position beside the Shannon now seems remote and inaccessible but in earlier centuries transport was easier by water than over land. The old Pilgrims' Road approached from the north along the esker. 🚩 *Clonmacnoise. Open Apr-Oct, daily.* ☎ *0905 74134; midlandseasttourism@ eircom.net; www.midlandseastireland.travel.ie*

Adjacent Sights: See ATHENRY, ATHLONE, BIRR, PORTUMNA, TUL-LAMORE.

Background

As the monastery's reputation grew the settlement expanded from an original wooden oratory to a cluster of stone churches, numerous monks' dwellings and a round tower within an earth or stone enclosure. None of the surviving ruins is earlier than the 9C. The monastery was plundered many times

> ### ST KIERAN
> St Kieran, a native of Roscommon, went to train under St Finnian at Clonard in Co Meath and then to study under St Enda on Inishmore, one of the Aran Islands; there he had a vision of a great tree growing in the centre of Ireland which St Enda interpreted as a church founded by St Kieran on the banks of the Shannon. After spending some time on Hare Island in Lough Ree, St Kieran with seven companions settled at Clonmacnoise, the field of the sons of Nos, where he died only seven months later of the plague at the age of 33.

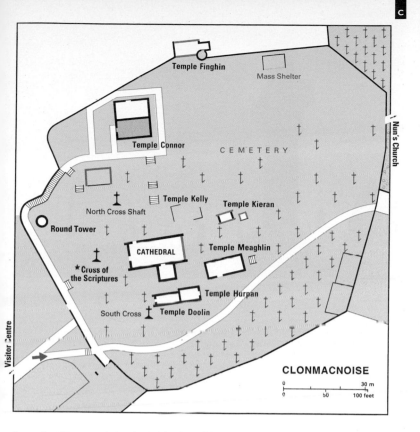

from the 9C onwards by the Irish, the Vikings and the Anglo-Normans, until it was finally reduced to ruin in 1552 by the English garrison from Athlone. A castle built by the Normans c 1212 on the river bank was slighted in the Cromwellian period.

Walking About

Visitor Centre

(Dúchas) ⅙ *Open Jun to mid-Sep, daily, 9am-7pm; mid-Mar to mid-May and mid-Sep to mid-Mar, daily, 10am-6pm (5.30pm Nov to mid-Mar); last admission 45min before closing. Closed 25 Dec. €4.40. Audio-visual show (22min; 4 languages). Parking.* ☎ *0905 74195; Fax 0905 74273; clonmacnoise@ealga.ie; www.heritageireland.ie*

The **Visitor Centre** displays the original **high crosses**, which have been replaced on site by replicas, and a collection of **grave slabs★** uncovered at Clonmacnoise which must have been an important stone-carving centre from the 8C to 12C.

South Cross

The cross (12ft/3.6m), which dates from the early 9C, bears a carving of the Crucifixion on its west face. The decorative spirals and interlacing are similar to those on the crosses at Kells *(see p 268)* and to those at Iona and Kildalton in Scotland.

Temple Doolin

The church, which is named after Edward Dowling, who restored it in 1689 to serve as a mausoleum, is probably pre-12C with antae and a round-headed east window. In the 17C **Temple Hurpan** was added to the east end.

Temple Meaghlin or Temple Rí

The east windows of this church, which dates from about 1200, are similar to those at Clonfert *(see Portumna)* and O'Heyne's Church at Kilmacduagh *(see Athenry)*; there was once a wooden gallery at the west end.

Temple Kieran

Parts of this tiny church, which is said to contain the grave of St Kieran, are pre-12C. From the south side a stone path leads out of the enclosure to the Nun's Church *(see below)*. On the north side is the outline of **Temple Kelly** (12C).

North Cross Shaft

The shaft (c 800) is decorated with lions biting their tails, and a cross-legged figure thought by some to be the Celtic god **Cernunnos**.

Clonmacnoise

Cathedral
The simple rectangular building has been modified many times. The oldest parts probably date from the 10C, when the original wooden church was replaced with a stone structure. The Romanesque west doorway dates from the 12C, the two-storey sacristy may be 13C; in the 15C the elaborate north doorway, surmounted by three plaques depicting St Dominic, St Patrick and St Francis, was constructed by Dean Odo and the chancel was divided into three vaulted chapels.

Cross of the Scriptures★
The cross, which is made of sandstone and is related to the crosses at Monasterboice *(see p 148)*, was erected in the 10C possibly by King Flann (d 916). It is unusual in that its arms protrude upwards from the circle, the west face of which depicts the Crucifixion, the east face the Last Judgement. Other carving shows scenes from the Passion (the soldiers resting on their spears), while the lowest panel on the east face may represent Abbot Colman and King Flann founding the monastery.

Round Tower
This is a fine example of a round tower although it has lost its conical cap. It may have been built in the 10C by Fergal O'Rourke and been repaired in 1120 by Abbot O'Malone, but the arched doorway is most likely 12C.

Temple Connor
Services: May-Aug, last Sun in the month.
The church may date from 1010, when it was endowed by Cathal O'Connor; the small window in the south wall is original. The building was restored in 1911 and is used by the Church of Ireland (Anglican) for services.

Temple Finghin
The 12C church consists of a nave and chancel. The Romanesque chancel arch was modified and strengthened in the 17C. It is unusual in having a south door and a mini round tower incorporated into the chancel.
From the centre of the enclosure follow the old path E across the extended graveyard and along the road; 10min there and back on foot.

Nun's Church
The ruined church consists of a nave and chancel and according to the Annals of the Four Masters *(see p 200)* it was completed in 1167 by Dervorgilla. The west doorway and the chancel arch are beautifully decorated in the Irish Romanesque style.

Excursion

Clonfinlough Stone
2mi/3km E by the minor road and 0.5mi/0.8km S by the minor road; park by the church; 10min there and back on foot up the path and over the stile. Near the edge of the field stands a large boulder which bears symbols similar to the Bronze Age rock art of Galicia in Spain. The natural indentations in the rock have been modified to suggest human figures.
To the south there is a **view** of the Brosna and Shannon river valleys where peat extraction is conducted on a large scale.

Clonmel★

The principal town of Co Tipperary, attractive Clonmel stands in a central position in the fertile and lovely valley of the River Suir. Directly to the south in Co Waterford rise the Comeragh Mountains, providing an impressive back-drop to the many historic buildings of the town which evoke its great period of prosperity in the 18C and 19C.

Location

Population 15 215 - Michelin Atlas p 80 and Map 712 – I 10 – Co Tipperary. Clonmel *(Cluain Meala)* is on N 24 between Waterford and Limerick, on the boundary between Co Tipperary and Co Waterford.

🛈 *Community Office, Clonmel. Open daily.* ☎ *052 22960; www.ireland-southeast.travel.ie*
🛈 *Heritage Centre, Carrick-on-Suir. Open daily.* ☎ *051 640 200*
🛈 *Tierry Centre, Fethard. Open daily.* ☎ *052 31000*
Adjacent Sights: See CAHER, CASHEL, KILKENNY, YOUGHAL.

Directory

SHOPPING

Tipperary Crystal – *Ballynoran* - *10mi/16km E by N 24* - ☎ *051 641 188* - *Mon-Sat, 9am-6pm.* All of the crystal is hand-crafted on the premises, using virtually the same process for the last 200 years. After a demonstration of the manufacturing process, visitors move to the showroom which features a huge selection from tableware to trophies.

EVENTS AND FESTIVALS

Greyhound racing Monday and Thursday evenings. Major annual **coursing** festival in February.
Annual **Writers' Weekend** in September particularly for short story writers and poets.

Background

The town is believed to pre-date the Vikings; its name comes from the Irish words for "a meadow of honey", an Early Christian reference to the great fertility of the Suir valley. Viking longships sailed up the River Suir from Waterford in the early 10C and, according to tradition, a battle was fought at Clonmel in 916 or 917 between the local O'Neill clan and the Vikings. Edward I granted the town a charter and the **walls** were built in the early 14C. The town became an important stronghold of the Butler family, the Earls of Ormond *(see Kilkenny)*. The garrison at Clonmel put up more resistance to Cromwell in the mid-17C than any other Irish town.

Four major figures in English literature had close associations with Clonmel. **Anthony Trollope** *(see Birr)* wrote his first two novels while living in the town from 1844 to 1848. **George Borrow**, who was at school in Clonmel, mentioned the town in two chapters of *Lavengro*. **Marguerite Power**, the Countess of Blessington, a noted early-19C literary figure, was born at Suir Island in 1789; she died in Paris in 1849. **Laurence Sterne** (1713-68), author of *Tristram Shandy*, was born in Mary Street; his family lived at Suir Island.

CLONMEL

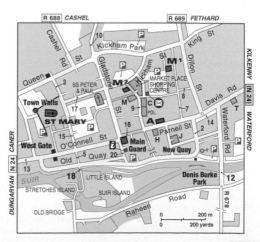

BIANCONI CARS

Charles Bianconi (1786-1875), son of an Italian immigrant from Lombardy and twice Mayor of Clonmel, began a horse-drawn car service in 1815 linking Clonmel to Limerick and Thurles. Following the battle of Waterloo, horses were in plentiful supply at about £10 each; by 1844 he had over 100 in his stables. By 1851 his open long cars, known as Bians, operated in 22 counties with central depots in Clonmel, Galway and Sligo. At its peak the service employed 1 400 horses and 100 vehicles, painted crimson and yellow. It created a nationwide revolution in the carrying of mail, freight and passengers, which was superseded only by the building of the railway network in the later 19C.

Bianconi retired in 1865 but one of his horse-drawn mail cars was used between Clonmel and Dungarvan as late as the 1920s. A coach-horn from a Bianconi mail coach, together with the clock, now handless, by which the departures were timed, are displayed in the foyer of Hearn's Hotel, from where the great entrepreneur ran his extraordinarily successful business.

Walking About

St Mary's Church★

Open daily, 9am-5pm. Services: Sun, 11am. ☎ 052 26643 (Vicar), 087 284 2350 (mobile)
The present Anglican church, with its unusual octagonal tower, was built in the 19C, incorporating parts of earlier 14C buildings. Written references suggest the existence of a building as early as the 13C. In the grounds there are extensive sections of the town walls.

West Gate

In 1831 Clonmel's civic pride and prosperity was symbolised by this mock-Tudor gateway, built on the site of the medieval west gate marking the division between the Anglo-Norman borough and its suburb, Irishtown.

Riverside

Clonmel has an intimate and interesting relationship with the River Suir. The 17C **Old Bridge** crosses the river three times from Little Island and Suir Island *(downstream)* to Stretches Island *(upstream)*, derived from the name of 16C Italian immigrants called Stroccio.The north bank between the Old Bridge and the 18C **Gashouse Bridge** (named after the nearby gas-works) forms the town **quay**, where ships used to unload their cargoes; it is marked by a memorial to the Manchester Martyrs *(see Historical Perspective)* of 1867 and is lined by terraces of **Georgian** houses and tall warehouses.

Main Guard

(Dúchas) Opening arrangements to be confirmed. Regular tour available. Parking nearby. ☎ 01 647 2453
Cromwell's troops destroyed Clonmel's original courthouse during the 1650 siege. It was replaced in 1674 by this handsome three-storeyed structure bearing the town's **coat of arms** and crowned by a cupola.

Worth a Visit

Museum of Transport

Open Mon-Sat, 10am-6pm; also Jun-Aug, Sun, 2.30-6pm. Coffee shop. ☎ 052 29727
Two floors of a stately six-storey mill building now house some two dozen vintage, veteran and classic cars as well as much motoring memorabilia.

County Museum★

Open Tue-Sat, 10am-5pm. Closed Bank Hols. ☎ 052 34550; Fax 052 80390; museum@southtippcoco.ie
The display depicts the history of the region from the Stone Age to the 20C. Coins found locally evoke links with the Roman Empire and there are fascinating memorabilia associated with a famous trial of 1848 rebels as well as with the Royal Irish Regiment, based here until it was disbanded in 1922 after the signing of the Anglo-Irish Treaty. There is also a choice collection of paintings by Irish artists.

Excursions

Nier Valley Scenic Route★★

Round tour of 40mi/64km. From Clonmel take R 678 S. After 5mi/8km turn right; after 4mi/6km make a detour left to a viewpoint. In Ballymacarbry turn right onto R 671 to return to Clonmel.
This tour is an excellent introduction to the dark green forests, moorland and imposing escarpments of the **Comeragh Mountains** which culminate in Knockanaffrin at 2 478ft/753m.

Carrick-on-Suir

13mi/21km E by N 24. This bustling town has an enviable location on the tidal Suir between Slievenamon *(NW)* and the Comeragh foothills *(S)*. Its 15C Old Bridge is evidence of its former importance as the lowest crossing point of the river before the estuary. The **Heritage Centre** traces local history. *(&)* *Open May-Aug, daily, 10am-5pm; Sep-Apr, Mon-Fri, 10am-5pm.* €2.54. Parking. Picnic area. Shop. ☎ 051 640 200; cosda@iol.ie

Ormond Castle★ – The great treasure of Carrick is the partially ruined 15C castle and adjoining Elizabethan mansion which stand in a wooded park. The restored mansion, a very fine example of its type, was built about 1568 by the 10th **Earl of Ormond**, known as Black Tom, to receive his cousin, Queen Elizabeth, who however never visited Ireland. The exterior has fine mullioned windows and gabled roofs; the interior is noted for its **ornamental plasterwork** and long gallery, while an extraordinary collection of charters traces the rise to power and status of the Ormond family. *(Dúchas) (&) Guided tour (40min) mid-Jun to early Sep, daily, 9.30am-6.30pm (5.45pm last admission). €2.50. Leaflet (6 languages). Public parking nearby.* ☎ 051 640 787

Ormond Castle, Carrick-on-Suir

Kilkeeran High Crosses

17mi/27km E by N 24 and R 697. The three crosses, which probably date from the 9C, mark the site of an early monastery. There are eight horsemen on the base of the **West Cross** which otherwise is decorated with interlacing and bosses. It bears an unusual cap, as does the East Cross which was probably not finished as it is undecorated.

Ahenny High Crosses★

19mi/31km E by N 24 and R 697. The decorative interlacing and spirals so characteristic of the Book of Kells are here repeated in stone, which may mean that the two crosses with their unusual caps may date from as early as the 8C. The figures on the base represent seven clergy carrying croziers, led by a clerical cross-bearer.

Fethard★

8mi/13km N by R 689. Little Fethard seems to be dreaming of its long-vanished status as an Anglo-Norman town of some importance; most sections of the late-14C **town walls** remain intact. **Fethard Castle** in the town centre is one of three keeps probably dating from the 15C. The **church**, which has a late-15C crenellated tower, includes earlier buildings much restored between 1400 and 1600. The huge roof-span of the nave is a notable architectural feature and the east window is copied from Kilcooley Abbey. There are many 16C and 17C tombs among the ruins of the 12C Augustinian priory.

The town lost its railway line long ago but the old station has been made into a **museum** with numerous items illustrating the rural and domestic life of earlier centuries. *& Open Sun and Bank Hol Mon, 11.30am-5pm; otherwise by appointment. Sunday €1.50; other days €3. Guided tour (30min). Brochure (2 languages). Collectors' market and car boot sale. Playground. Parking. Café. Picnic area.* ☎ 052 31516

Cobh★

Facing the vast expanse of sheltered water of Cork Harbour, Cobh (pronounced Cove) was destined to be one of Ireland's great outlets to the ocean. The town began to expand in the late 18C, when ships of the Royal Navy assembled here for operations in the American War of Independence and later against France. A period as a health resort in the 19C left a fine legacy of Italianate buildings and neo-Gothic villas, which merit the title Heritage town, but Cobh was famous above all for its role in shipping emigrants to faraway places and as a port of call for transatlantic liners.

Location

Population 6 468 - Michelin Atlas p 78 and Map 712 – H 12 – Co Cork.
Cobh *(An Cóbh)* is on the south side of Great Island, linked by road and by rail to Fota Island and then to the mainland, where R 624 joins N 25.
🛈 *Old Royal Yacht Club, Cobh.* ☎ *021 813 301; tourism@cobharbourchamber.ie; www.cobharbour.chamber.ie*
Adjacent Sights: See CORK, KINSALE, MIDLETON, YOUGHAL.

Directory

GETTING ABOUT

Cork Harbour Car Ferry across the River Lee between Carrigaloe *(east bank)* and Glenbrook *(west bank)* – Operates daily, 7am-12.15am. Time 5min. Capacity 28 cars. There and back €4.50 (car), €1.25 (pedestrian). ☎ 021 481 1223

Cork Harbour Cruises – Operate from Kennedy Pier (1hr – harbour forts, Spike Island, Naval base and major harbour industries) early-Jun to early-Sep, daily at noon, 2pm, 3pm, and 4pm; otherwise by appointment. €5. Parking (5-10min walk). ☎ 021 481 1485 (Marine Transport Services Ltd); mtsirl1@eircom.net

Rail Service
– Operates between Cobh and Cork via Fota Island, daily. ☎ 021 506 766 (Cork Railway Station); www.irishrail.ie

WHERE TO EAT

• *Moderate*

Robin Hill House – *Rushbrooke - 1 mi NE by R 624 -* ☎ *021 481 1395 - robinhillhouse@eircom.net - Closed 25 to 27 Dec, 7 Jan to 7 Feb and Bank Hols -* 🅿 ✸⊷ *- €40.* An unexpectedly contemporary interior lies behind the 19C façade of this converted rectory. The peach-hued restaurant features work by local artists and the menu has a distinct seasonal feel. Regular wine tastings are held in the cellar.

Background

The world's first yachting fraternity, the Water Club, was founded in Cobh as early as 1720. Its successor, the Royal Cork Yacht Club, is now based at Crosshaven *(see Cork)*, but its old headquarters still stands, an elegant waterfront pavilion designed in 1854 by the architect Anthony Salvin. In 1849, Queen Victoria disembarked at Cobh on her first visit to Ireland, and the place was renamed Queenstown in her honour. The Royal Navy continued to use the facilities here even after Independence in 1922, though Cobh, along with the other "Treaty Ports", was handed back to the Free State in 1938.

Until the 1960s, Cobh was a port of call for the *Queen Mary*, the *Queen Elizabeth* and other great ships from lines such as Hamburg Atlantic and North German Lloyd; photographs and paintings of that period hang in the bar of the Commodore Hotel. The traffic was not all tourist class; Cobh was also the point of departure for hundreds of thousands of Irish emigrants who sailed to North America in the late 19C and early 20C, and many of the multitude transported to Australia passed through the port. Their passage is commemorated in the statue of Annie Moore, the first emigrant to pass through the Ellis Island immigration reception centre in New York.

Worth a Visit

St Colman's Cathedral★

Open daily, 7.30am-8pm (earlier winter). Brochure (6 languages). Parking. ☎ *021 813 222; Fax 021 4813 488; cobhpari@iol.ie*
Cobh's steep streets rise from the waterfront to the neo-Gothic Roman Catholic cathedral, designed by Pugin and Ashlin and built between 1868 and 1915. Its tall **spire**, which houses a carillon of 47 bells, is a landmark for miles. The interior is decorated with columns of polished marble, mosaic flooring and a detailed marble reredos.

Lusitania Memorial★

Casement Square. The 1 500 victims of the *Lusitania*, which was torpedoed in 1915 *(see Kinsale)*, are commemorated by an elaborate carving of an angel flanked by two sailors; it was designed by Jerome Connor (1876-1943), a Cork sculptor, and completed after his death by Seamus Murphy.

In nearby Pierce Square a more modest memorial recalls the victims of the *Titanic*; the supposedly unsinkable liner made her last call at Cobh on 11 April 1912 before setting off on her fateful maiden voyage.

Cobh Harbour and Cathedral

Cobh Heritage Centre: The Queenstown Story

& *Open daily, 10am-6pm (5pm Nov-Mar); last admission 1hr before closing. €5. Audio-visual show (5min). Brochure (5 languages). Café* ☎ *021 481 3591; Fax 021 481 3595; cobhher@indigo.ie; www.cobhheritage.com*

Dating from the great days of the ocean liners, but now only serving the suburban line to Cork, Cobh's railway terminus was built on a grand scale. Part of it now houses an exhibition recalling the days when Cobh was a major port. There are fascinating displays on the evolution of the port and its strategic naval role, life aboard ship for convicts and emigrants, the sinking of the *Titanic* and *Lusitania*, and the heyday of the liners between the wars.

Cobh Museum

Open Easter-Oct, Mon-Sat, 11am-1pm and 2-6pm; Sun, 3-6pm. €1.50. Brochure (4 languages). ☎ *021 481 4240, Fax 021 481 1018; cobhmuseum@eircom.net*

A former Presbyterian Church houses a collection of local artefacts with a strongly maritime theme.

Excursion

Fota Island★

4mi/6km N by R 624.

Until 1975 the 780 acre/316ha island in Cork Harbour remained in the possession of the descendants of its 12C Anglo-Norman lord Philip de Barri. In the early 19C the family's hunting lodge was converted by John Smith Barry into a fine neo-Classical gentleman's residence to plans by the leading architects Richard and William Vitruvius Morrison. The estate was thoroughly taken in hand, with harmoniously designed sea defences, walls, lodges, workers' cottages and outbuildings, landscaped parkland and a famous arboretum. Much of the island is now given over to one of the country's finest wildlife parks, while the house has been triumphantly restored after falling into a state of near-dereliction.

Fota House★★ – *Open daily, 10am (11am Sun) to 4.45pm (last admission). Closed at Christmas. €5. Touch panels.* ☎ *021 481 5543; Fax 021 481 5541; info@fotahouse.com; www.fotahouse.com*

Looking out across the savannah-like landscape browsed by the animals of the wildlife park, Fota House presents a symmetrical facade of restrained, almost severe elegance, beyond which are important interiors of outstanding grace and craftsmanship, their appeal enhanced by a few, carefully selected items of fine furniture. The Morrisons' masterly manipulation of space is particularly evident in the entrance hall, with its ochre scagliola columns and vistas terminated by giant vases. Equal attention was given to the humdrum activities which supported the Smith Barrys' lifestyle; the servery, kitchen and scullery are models of their kind, as is the fascinating larder, with realistic-looking game hung on a carousel occupying the centre of a space which could almost be the chapter house of a great abbey. The rounded bays of the house's garden front face a broad lawn rising gently to a delightful little **orangery**; to the left are walled formal gardens, still under restoration.

To the right, paths lead through the silvicultural treasures of the **arboretum★**. John Smith Barry was a prominent plant collector, and his acquistion of rare species were continued by his successors into the 20C. With its brown earth soils and mild climate favouring specimens from northwestern America, Chile, Australasia, Japan and China, the arboretum remains a classic example of a Victorian tree and shrub collection, with individual plants allowed space to develop fully. *(Dúchas) (&)* *Open daily, 10am (11am Sun) to 6pm (5pm Nov-Mar). Closed 25-26 Dec. Guided tour by arrangement. Parking €2. Picnic area. ☎/Fax 021 482 2728*

Wildlife Park★ – & *Open daily, 10am (11am Sun) to 5pm. €7. Park train: single €0.70, round trip €1.40. Parking €2. Children's playground. Restaurant. ☎ 021 481 2678, 481 2736; Fax 021 481 2744; info@fotawildlife.ie; www.fotawildlife.ie*

The park (70 acres/28ha) was established by the Zoological Society of Ireland in 1983 with the main aim of conserving endangered species, like the cheetah which is one of its main attractions. Fota is one of the most popular establishments of its kind in Ireland, with a fine array of creatures, many of them wandering freely around the park. A grassy plateau in the centre of the island provides a natural-looking habitat for giraffes, zebras and antelopes. Various species of monkey disport themselves on a series of islands on the lower part of the site, while flamingoes, pelicans, penguins and other waterfowl are accommodated on and around the surrounding pools. A "train" helps footsore visitors experience the whole of the extensive grounds and there is a playground for children.

Cong★

Once the seat of the kings of Connaught and with the ruins of a famous abbey, attractive little Cong stands on the narrow neck of land (*conga* in Irish) separating Lough Corrib and Lough Mask. It is a popular place to stay, with access not just to the lakes but to the mountains of Connemara and the Joyce Country to the west. The famous Wilde family had a holiday house on the shore of Lough Corrib; in 1867 Oscar's father Sir William Wilde wrote an antiquarian guide book *Lough Corrib, its Shores and Islands,* still in print today and of great interest to the more leisured visitor. Cong was put on the 20C map by the 1952 film *The Quiet Man,* made here and starring John Wayne in one of his best roles as Sean Thornton, a prize fighter returned to his native Ireland after making his name in the USA.

Directory

SIGHTSEEING
Lough Corrib Cruises – *Operate daily at 11am and 2.45pm (30min to Inchagoil Island + 30min on island + 30min to Cong or Oughterard); also at 6pm (1hr with Irish ballad singing). Daytime €13; evening €15. ☎ 092 46029 or 46292 (Cong); 091 552 808 or 091 552 170 (Oughterard); Fax 092 46568; info@corribcruises.com; www.corribcruises.com*

WHERE TO EAT
• *Budget*
John J Burkes – *☎ 092 46175 - tibhurca@eircom.net - Closed 1 week at Christmas - €17.45/43.70. The pretty exterior of this family-run village centre pub gives little indication of its huge interior. A simple lunchtime menu is served in the bar, with the dining room offering a comprehensive menu in the evening. Traditional music at weekends.*

Location

Population 197 - Michelin Atlas p 89 and Map 712s – E 7 - Co Mayo.
Cong *(Conga)* is accessible by N 84 and R 334 from Galway, Castlebar and Westport.
🏛 *Cong. Open Mar-Oct, Mon-Sat.* ☎ *092 46542*
Adjacent Sights: See ATHENRY, CONNEMARA, GALWAY, KNOCK, WESTPORT.

Walking About

Cong Abbey

Car park. (Dúchas) Open dawn-dusk; when closed key available from the caretaker, Michael Collins, Abbey Street, Cong, Co Mayo. ☎ *092 46068*

In its riverside setting, the **Augustinian abbey** was founded in the 12C, probably by Turlough O'Conor, King of Connaught and High King of Ireland, on the site of an earlier monastic foundation (6C or 7C). Among the remains are the chancel, a lovely Romanesque doorway, part of the **cloisters** (c 1200), fine carved stonework in the **chapter house**, and the Guest Refectory with a twisted chimney stack. West of the abbey grounds on an island in the river is the **monks' fishing house** (12C); when a fish was caught in the net which was lowered through a hole in the floor, a bell rang in the kitchen.

> ### DRY CANAL
> **Lough Mask** and **Lough Corrib** are linked by the River Cong, which runs mainly through caves and underground channels in the limestone. The idea of creating a navigable waterway between the two great lakes seemed about to come to fruition, when men doing relief work during the famine laboured for six years to dig a canal (4mi/7km) with three locks. In March 1854 work was suspended; costs had risen, new railways threatened competition and attempts to fill the canal came to nothing when the water drained away into the porous limestone rock. No vessel has ever floated on Cong's dry canal.

Quiet Man Heritage Centre

Open mid-Mar to Oct, daily, 10am-5pm. Guided tour. €3.75. ☎ *092 46009, Fax 092 46448*

The interior is furnished as a replica of the cottage used in the film which brought international fame of a kind to the village, and which is celebrated every year with a John Wayne look-alike contest and other events.

Ashford Castle

Pedestrian entrance south of the Abbey; vehicle entrance on R 346 east of Cong. Grounds and gardens, 9am-6pm, €5.08. ☎ *092 46003; Fax 092 46260; www.ashford.ie*
Boat trip on Lough Corrib: daily (weather permitting). €12.70 per person (min 6). ☎ *092 46029*

In the mid-19C the Guinness family transformed the old 13C castle, built by the de Burgos *(see PORTUMNA)* in its lovely lakeside setting into a huge baronial residence of great sumptuousness; renamed Ashford Castle, it is now a luxury hotel, with grounds open to the public. The grounds include a stone bridge leading to the castle, formal gardens with a terraced walk *(N)*, the Joyces Tower in a woodland setting *(E)* and a series of underground caves known as the Pigeon Hole *(NE)*.

Excursion

Ross Errilly Abbey★

10mi/16km SE of Cong by R 346 and R 344. Although in ruins, Ross Abbey on the south bank of the Black River is one of the best-preserved Franciscan friaries in Ireland, and gives an exceptionally complete picture of the framework of monastic life. It was probably founded in 1351 and greatly extended in 1496, at a time when the Franciscans felt compelled to take over much of the activity of an idle and corrupt official church. After the Reformation the friars continued in residence until 1753, albeit with interruptions; in 1596 the English used the complex as a barracks and in 1656 it was looted by the Cromwellians.

Among the friary's fascinating features are the buildings surrounding the **cloisters** *(entrance at the foot of the tower)* which have survived in part to

> ### CAPTAIN BOYCOTT
> From Lough Mask House (on the eastern shore of the lake) Captain Charles Boycott administered the estates of Lord Erne with a severity that made him extremely unpopular with his tenants. In 1880, after he had evicted a number of them for non-payment of rent, Parnell's Land League made him the first victim of the process that subsequently bore his name. The wretched man and his family were shunned by all around them; no-one would speak to them, shops refused to serve them, and the land could only be worked by a band of Ulstermen protected by troops. Forced to end this intolerable situation by fleeing to England, Boycott nevertheless achieved lexicographical immortality.

Ross Errily Abbey

first-floor level, a second courtyard with a postern gate for entry after dark, and the **kitchen** with its big round **fish tank** and huge fireplace backing onto a large circular oven in the adjoining **bakery**.

The **central tower** (70ft/21.5m), probably added in 1498, provides a fine **view**★ *(76 narrow wooden spiral steps)*.

Connemara★★★

The largest "Gaeltacht" in Ireland, with many road-signs in Gaelic only, Connemara is a wild and beautiful region of mountains, lakes, tumbling streams, undulating bog, sea-girt promontories, unspoilt beaches and panoramic views. Its beauty and remoteness, together with its traces of a traditional way of life, have attracted many artisans, who can be visited at work in their studios – handweaving, knitting, screen printing and carving, making marble inlay, jewellery and pottery.

Location

Michelin Atlas p 88 and Map 712 – C 7 – Co Galway.
Connemara is a sparsely inhabited area, bisected by the Galway-Clifden road (N 59) and a few minor roads which cannot be taken at speed owing to their undulating surface.
🖪 *Galway Road, Clifden. Open Mar-Sep, Mon-Sat.* ☎ *095 21163; Fax 095 21887; info@ irelandwest.ie*
Adjacent Sights: See ARAN ISLANDS, CONG, GALWAY, WESTPORT.

Background

The centre of Connemara is composed of mountain peaks, the **Twelve Bens** or **Pins**, which culminate in Benbaun (2 388ft/728m). The sharp grey peaks of quartzite rock, which is resistant to weathering, are too steep and hard to be clothed in blanket bog. The Bens are drained by mountain streams and ringed by a chain of lakes where trout are plentiful.

Between the foot of the Twelve Pins and the southern coastline extends the level **Connemara Bog**, dotted with innumerable tiny lakes. On a bright day the stretches of water act like mirrors reflecting the sun; in the rain the whole environment seems to be made of water.

Its remoteness, unyielding soils and harsh climate mean that most of the inhabitants of Connemara lived in settlements clinging to the deeply indented coastline, although in the years before the Famine the population was more numerous than now. More than most regions it resisted invaders and colonisation. For centuries the ferocious O'Flaherty clan held sway, until dislodged by Cromwell, whose men exercised a brutal rule from their stronghold on Inishbofin. The area suffered grievously in the Famine, losing many of its people, but its Irish-speaking, peasant culture survived, exercising great fascination on Gaelic revivalists and on nationalists like Patrick Pearse.

Connemara has occasionally benefited from the efforts of enterprising individuals determined to overcome its backwardness and inaccessibility by a variety of development schemes. One such was John D'Arcy, a member of a long-established

Directory

GETTING ABOUT

Ferries from Cleggan to Inishbofin *(see below). Operate (weather permitting) Apr-Oct, daily, from Cleggan at 11.30am, 6.45pm (also 10am, 2pm, 5.45pm Jul-Aug), from Inishbofin at 9am, 5pm (also 10.45am, 1pm, 6.15pm Jul-Aug); winter, Sun, Tue, Fri-Sat, times by phone.* ☎ 095 45903, 44750 *Fax 095 44327; inishbofinferry@eircom.net; www.inishbofinferry.com*

Ferry to St MacDara's Island *(see below). No regular sailings. Passage offered (weather permitting) by local fishermen on Festival Day (16 July) and other days.* ☎ *095 32758 (Matt Corbett).*

SIGHTSEEING

Maritime Wildlife cruises and sea angling cruises from Letterfrack.

WHERE TO STAY

• Budget

Diamond Lodge – *Kylemore Rd - On N 59 -* ☎ *095 41380 - Fax 095 41205 - paulineconroy@eircom.net • 10 March to Oct - ⊡ ✕ - 4 rm €50/76 ⬙.* Built in the 1840s as a hunting lodge, Diamond Lodge is two miles from Kylemore Abbey. It has a bright, attractive sitting room overlooking the pretty garden and the 4 bedrooms, one of which has a four-poster bed, are immaculately kept.

• Moderate

Dolphin Beach Country House – *Lower Sky Rd - 3.5mil/5.6km W by Sky Rd -* ☎ *095 21204 - Fax 095 22935 - dolphinbeach@iolfree.ie – Mid-Mar to mid-Nov - ⊡ ✕ - 8 rm €80/150 - Restaurant €35/37.* A modernised farmhouse whose secluded location really sets it apart; it overlooks the bay and a walk through the garden leads to a sandy beach. Bedrooms are wooden floored and stylish and the dinner menu features local produce.

The Quay House – *Beach Rd -* ☎ *095 21369 - Fax 095 21608 - thequay@iol.ie – Mid-Mar to Oct - 14 rm €85/155 ⬙.* Built in 1820 as the harbour master's house, it has also been a monastery and a convent. Now a handsomely restored town-house hotel, it has its own sense of style and originality coupled with a relaxing atmosphere.

• Expensive

Ballynahinch Castle – *Ballynahinch -* ☎ *095 31006 - Fax 095 31085 - bhinch@iol.ie - Closed Feb and 1 week at Christmas - ⊡ - 37 rm, 3 suites €126/290 ⬙ - Restaurant €24/42.* The castle lies in a vast estate of 350 acres/142ha, providing numerous scenic walks while keen fishermen can take advantage of bountiful salmon and trout. Log fires, quiet reading rooms, hearty dinners and comfortable beds await you.

WHERE TO EAT

• Budget

O'Dowds – *Roundstone -* ☎ *095 35923 - ⊟ - €20.* Choose the rustic bar and a chance to chat with the locals or the adjacent restaurant where the emphasis is on local seafood. A popular spot for weekend family lunches. Internet access available at the "Espresso Stop'"next door.

SHOPPING

For crafts try the IDA craft village at **Roundstone** *(see below)*, the craft shop at **Kylemore Abbey** *(see below)* and, for woollen goods, the **Leenane Cultural Centre** *(see below)*.

Connemara Pony

SPORTS AND LEISURE

Beaches – There is a long sandy beach on the north shore of Clifden Bay west of the harbour *(car park)*.

Scubadive West, Renvyle *Open daily, 10am and 2pm.* ☎ *095 43922; Fax 095 43923; scuba@anu.ie*

Sea Angling – In Clifden, at Letterfrack and at the **Roundstone Sea Angling Centre**

Freshwater Fishing –In Lough Corrib, Lough Mask, Lough Nafooey, in the Joyce River, at Maam Cross and Recess.

Rambling – Visitors intending to walk in the hills should be properly equipped (map and compass, stout waterproof footwear, warm clothes and food) and should advise someone, preferably the **National Park Visitor Centre** *(see below)*, of their route and expected time of return; no one should walk alone.

There is a guided walk up to *(2hr)* and through *(2-4hr)* the **Pass of the Birds** *(first Sunday* in *August)* from Recess northeast up Owentooe River Valley, southeast of Maumeen Peak, through the Pass of the Birds, past St Patrick's Bed and Holy Well, down into Failmore and Joyce River valleys. For a description of the road see North Connemara below.

EVENTS AND FESTIVALS

The **Connemara Pony Show** is held annually in August in Clifden.

Galway family which had originally settled in Ireland in the reign of Elizabeth I. In 1815, having inherited the family estates in Connemara, he moved here, devoting the rest of his life to the development of the new harbour town of Clifden, constantly importuning the authorities for funds to build roads to link his new settlement to Galway and Westport. The Galway road was built in the 1820s; its alignment through uninhabited countryside between the Twelve Bens and the Connemara bog meant that the labourers working on it had to be supplied with tents and cooking utensils. The road has proved a greater success than the railway, opened in 1895 and closed only forty years later, in 1935.

Another reformer nurtured in this wild land was Richard Martin, also known as "Humanity Dick", who founded the Society for the Prevention of Cruelty to Animals and who was adored by his tenants, despite his feudal lifestyle in the family home, **Ballynahinch Castle**, now a hotel, on the south shore of Ballynahinch Lake.

Tours

The two tours described below start from Clifden but they can also be made from Cong or Galway, although it may be necessary to read the descriptions in reverse.

NORTH CONNEMARA
Round trip of 60mi/96km – 1 day

Clifden
Well-sited at the head of a long sea-inlet and still consisting mainly of John d'Arcy's original triangle of broad streets, little Clifden is the unofficial capital of Connemara, crowded with tourists in season and especially lively in August during the famous Connemara Pony Show. Ireland's native pony breed gets its due at the **Station House Museum**, with a plethora of pony memorabilia. Other exhibits in what used to be the locomotive shed of the old railway terminus deal with local history and with two early 20C events which put Connemara "in the forefront of communications technology"; the first was the opening of the Marconi radio station in 1905 at nearby Derryginlagh, the second the first transatlantic flight, which concluded, triumphantly if somewhat ignominiously, with Alcock and Brown's crash-landing in Derryginlagh bog. (&) *Open May-Oct, Mon-Sat, 10am-5pm, Sun, noon-6pm.*
  2. ☎ *095 21494; Fax 095 22112*
From Clifden take the cliff road W.

Sky Road★★
A steep and narrow road climbs along the cliffs on the north side of Clifden Bay past the site of Clifden Castle, John D'Arcy's house. To the south across Clifden Bay rises the round hump of Errisbeg (987ft/300m).

As the road bears northwest over the ridge, a magnificent **view**★★ unfolds *(NW)* of the indented coastline and the islands offshore *(viewing point car park)*. The road descends in a curve to the head of Kingstown Bay and then continues inland along the south shore of Streamstown Bay.

At the T-junction turn left onto N 59. To visit Inishbofin make a detour (4mi/6.5km) W to Cleggan.

Inishbofin
Ferry from Cleggan (see Directory). The island of the White Cow, where St Colman of Lindisfarne founded a monastery in the 7C, is inhabited by farmers and fishermen. The fort was used by **Grace O'Malley** *(see p 362)*, whose ancestors seized the island from the O'Flahertys in the 14C, then by Cromwell, who expelled or imprisoned the monks and converted the place into an internment centre for Catholic priests.

Connemara National Park (Páirc Náisiúnta Chonamara)★
1.5mi/2.4km to car park. (Dúchas) & Park: Open daily. Visitor Centre: Open early-Mar to mid-Oct, daily, 10am (9.30am Jul-Aug) to 5.30pm (6.30pm Jun-Aug); last admission 45min before closing. €2.50. Audio-visual show (15min). Leaflet (7 languages). Self-guiding trails. Guided nature walks (Jul-Aug, 2-3hr; rainwear and boots required). Special events for younger visitors (Jul-Aug). Parking. Coffee shop; indoor and outdoor picnic areas. ☎ *095 41054, 41006; Fax 095 41005*
The park (4 942 acres/2 000ha) has been designated to conserve some of the finest scenery in the Twelve Bens range of mountains and consists of heath, blanket bog and grassland with some natural woodland of oak and birch. The flora ranges from Mediterranean species to alpine and arctic plants on the upper slopes. The **red deer**, once native to Connemara, and the **Connemara pony**, Ireland's only native pony, are established in the park.

The **Visitor Centre**, housed in old farm buildings, provides information on guided walks and nature trails, an audio-visual film and an excellent interpretative exhibition about the Connemara landscape.

Rising behind the Visitor Centre is Diamond Hill (1 460ft/445m), the highest point, which provides a good view. At the foot of its east face the Polladirk River flows north from a large valley, Glanmore, and through a spectacular gorge.

Continue N on N 59. In Letterfrack make a detour left to Rinvyle.

Rinvyle Peninsula

At the end of the peninsula, which is dominated by Tully Mountain, stands **Rinvyle (Currath) Castle**, a ruined tower house, belonging to the O'Flaherty clan. The northeast corner has collapsed revealing a spiral stair, a vaulted third storey and a huge fireplace. There is a fine view of the Mweelrea (Muilrea) Mountains *(NE)* and of the islands offshore – Inishbofin *(W)*, Inishturk and Clare Island *(N)*. The Rinvyle House Hotel was once the home of the Dublin wit and socialite, the surgeon-turned-writer Oliver St John Gogarty, who loved his "long, long house in the ultimate land of the undiscovered West".

Return to N 59 and continue E.

Kylemore Abbey★

(&) Visitor Centre and Abbey: Open daily, 9am-6pm. Closed Good Fri and Christmas. Walled garden: Easter-Oct, 10.30am-4.30pm. Closed Good Fri. Abbey and garden €10; garden €6.50; Abbey, Gothic church, lake walk and video €5. Audio-visual show (4 languages). Leaflet (6 languages). Parking. Restaurant. ☎ 095 41146; Fax 095 41145; info@kylemoreabbey.ie; www.kylemoreabbey.com

The name, *Coill Mhór* in Irish, which means the big wood, refers to the lush wood-land growing on the north shore of Lough Pollacappul at the foot of Doughrough Mountain. The turreted and crenellated neo-Gothic castle, built (1860-67) of Dalkey granite, now houses a community of Irish Benedictine nuns and a convent school. **Kylemore pottery** is made and decorated by hand in the Craft Centre, which sells a wide variety of goods.

The lavish mansion was commissioned by the Manchester financier and MP, Mitchell Henry (1826-1901), who with his wife Margaret Vaughan of Co Down entertained on a grand scale until her death in 1874. The history of the castle and convent is traced in photographs and text and an audio-visual presentation in three rooms of the castle, including the entrance hall with its magnificent staircase and ceiling.

A walk *(10min there and back on foot)* along the wooded shore past rushing streams leads to the **Gothic church** (1878), a replica of Norwich Cathedral, which is used for ecumenical services and concerts.

Victorian Walled Garden★ – *Separate entrance 1mi/1.5km W of Abbey.* Within its high brick walls, this magnificent 6acre/2.5ha garden has been rescued from dereliction and is well on the way to being restored to its late-19C state, when it was one of the most admired in Ireland. It is divided into two distinct sections by a stream and a belt of fine trees; a flower garden with meticulously re-created

Kylemore Abbey

geometrical parterres and a vegetable garden with flourishing crops in exemplary lazybeds. There is a castellated bothy and head gardener's house and the spectacular glasshouses are being rebuilt.

E on N 59.

Killary Harbour★

Car park. There is a fine view of the deep fjord which is the drowned estuary of the Erriff River. *(See also p 363).*

Leenane Cultural Centre

Open Apr-Oct, daily, 9am-6pm. €3. Audio-visual show (13min; 5 languages). Brochure. Café. Shop. ☎ 095 42323, 42231; Fax 095 42337; noeot@eircom.net; www.leenane-connemara.com/shop.htm

The Centre houses a demonstration of the processing of wool – from the fleece to the finished product – carding, spinning, dyeing with natural plant dyes and weaving. There is a selection of hand-made goods on sale in the shop. Outside, several different breeds of sheep, some very ancient, graze on the turf.

Take R 336 S; after 4.5mi/8km turn left onto a steep and narrow mountain road.

Joyce Country★

This area takes its name from a Welsh family which settled in the mountains between Lough Mask and Lough Corrib after the Anglo-Norman invasion in the 12C. The route provides many beautiful perspectives of lake and mountain.

Lough Nafooey★

East of the watershed there is a superb **view** of Lough Nafooey at the foot of Maumtrasna (2 207ft/671m). From the north shore there is a view of the waterfall at the west end of the lake.

Lough Mask

From the Ferry Bridge the full extent of Lough Mask is revealed stretching north at the foot of the Partry Mountains *(W)* towards the Plains of Mayo.

At the T-junction turn left; in Clonbur turn right onto R 345.

Lough Corrib★★

The wooded shore road provides a **view** of this vast and lovely lake, nearly 30mi/48km long, the second largest in Ireland. Its surface is studded with countless islands; on one of them, in the lough's northwestern arm, stands the ruin of **Hen's Castle**, an O'Flaherty stronghold, which was twice defended by Grace O'Malley *(see p 362)*. In 1570 the Joyces, who had murdered her husband, Donal O'Flaherty, tried in vain to gain possession of the castle. Several years later, when it was besieged by English troops from Galway, Grace drove them back by pouring melted roof-lead on their heads and summoned help by sending a man through the underground passage which linked the castle with the shore, to light a beacon on Doon Hill, a promontory on the north shore.

At the T-junction turn left onto R 336. In Maam Cross turn right onto N 59.

Galway–Clifden Road

Maam Cross *(An Teach Dóite)* and **Recess** *(Sraith Salach)* are two popular angling villages. Beyond Recess the many islands of **Derryclare Lough** come into view. North of this lake in the glaciated valley between the Maumturk Mountains *(E)* and two of the Twelve Pins, Bencorr and Derryclare *(W)*, lies **Lough Inagh** *(picnic places)*; the bog is dotted with turf stacks and sheep.

Connemara Heritage and History Centre

3mi/4.8km E of Clifden on N 59 in Lettershea. Open Apr to late-Oct, daily, 10am-6pm. A/v (4 languages). 6. Craft shop. Tearoom. ☎ 095 21246 or 21808; Fax 095 22098

The Centre introduces visitors to the history and landscapes of the region with a small exhibition, a video film, convincing reconstructions of a

> ### ALEXANDER NIMMO (1783-1832)
> Alexander Nimmo was a Scot who came to Ireland in 1809 to assist in surveys into the economic potential of bogland. Fortunately for the natural beauty of the area, his elaborate scheme for converting the bogs of Connemara into productive farmland by means of an elaborate system of canals was never implemented. In 1822 he was appointed engineer of the Western District and his great legacy to the area is its highway network and a number of piers and harbours. While work was in progress on the Galway to Clifden road, Nimmo lived at Corrib Lodge at Maam Cross.

crannog, ringfort, and oratory, and demonstrations of turf winning. Tucked away on the mountain slope above is an authentically rebuilt homestead which may have been the residence of the near-legendary Dan O'Hara, a Famine emigrant.

SOUTH CONNEMARA
Round trip of 75mi/121km – 1 day

Clifden *(see above)*
From Clifden take R 143 S.

Owenglin Cascade
On the southern edge of the town the Owenglin River plunges over a waterfall before entering Ardbear Harbour.
Continue S on R 341 for 2mi/3.2km.

Alcock and Brown Monument
The monument on the hill *(NW)* commemorates the first non-stop transatlantic flight by Alcock and Brown who crash-landed in Derryginlagh Bog *(S)* on 15 June 1919.
Continue S on R 341.

Errisbeg
The outcrop of dense gabbro rock (987ft/300m) shelters two lovely beaches of fine white sand.

Roundstone (Cloch na Rón)★
Now a delightful little resort, Roundstone was laid out as a harbour village by Alexander Nimmo *(see above)*, who populated it with fisherfolk from his native Scotland. On the south side of the town is a **craft village**, one of those established by the Industrial Development Authority. It is best known for the workshop of Malachy Kearns who makes the traditional goatskin drum (*bodhrán* pronounced "borawn") which accompanies folk music.
In Toombeola turn right onto R 342.

Cashel★
This attractive little place, a good angling and shooting centre, nestles at the foot of a hill overlooking Bertraghboy Bay.
Turn right onto R 340.

Carna Peninsula
A string of villages punctuates the shoreline.

Offshore *(S)* lies **St MacDara's Island** where the 6C saint founded a monastery. The little church (c 10C, restored) is built of huge blocks of stone; it has a unique feature in that the projections on the gable ends known as *antae* bend inwards and meet at the roof ridge, possibly in imitation of cruck construction in timber. Fishing boats passing the island used to dip their sails in veneration of **St MacDara**. The island can be reached by boat *(see Directory)* from **Carna**, a lobster-fishing village, where, on the saint's feast day (16 July) a pattern takes place; local people and visitors journey to St MacDara's island for Mass and other prayers; later in the day there are boat races and celebrations.

Kilkieran *(Cill Chiaráin)* on the east coast offers a fine view of the patchwork of islands and peninsulas which lie offshore.
7mi/11.3km N of Kilkieran, turn right (sign) to Patrick Pearse's Cottage.

Patrick Pearse's Cottage
Car park. (Dúchas) (&) Open mid-Jun to mid-Sep, daily, 9.30am-6.30pm; Easter Sat-Mon, 10am-5pm; mid-Sep to late-Sep, Sat-Sun, 10am-6pm; last admission 45min before closing. €1. Parking. ☎ 091 574 292
Nestling against a rocky outcrop on the west shore of **Lough Aroolagh** is the three-roomed thatched cottage built by **Patrick Pearse** *(see p 245, 311)* where he spent his holidays and studied the Irish language.
Return to R 340; Continue E. At the T-junction EITHER turn left onto R 386 and left again in Maam Cross onto N 59 to return to Clifden OR turn right onto R 386 to take the coast road to Galway.

Cork★★

The Republic of Ireland's second city, Cork is a major port and commercial centre, with a university, a distinct historical and cultural identity, and a vibrant and welcoming atmosphere.

The city centre is built on reclaimed marshland between two arms of the River Lee, whose estuary, Cork Harbour, forms the largest natural harbour in Europe. Until the 19C many of the streets were open waterways where ships moored; in 1780, Arthur Young compared Cork to the towns of the Netherlands. To the north of the river the land rises steeply; on the heights is Montenotte, the city's most exclusive residential district.

Location

Population 127 187 - Michelin Atlas p 78 and Map 712 – G 12 – Co Cork.

Cork *(Corcaigh)* is a meeting point of several major road in the national road network: N 25 east to Waterford, N 8 northeast to Cashel, N 20 northwest to Limerick and N 22 west to Killarney. For a magnificent **panorama** of the city go to the **Church of Christ the King★** *(1mi/1.6km S of city centre at Turner's Cross)*, a striking modern church (1937) with a Cubist-style sculpture of Christ on the façade.

🛈 *Grand Parade. Open Jul-Aug, daily; Sep-Jun, Mon-Sat.* ☎ *021 425 5100; Fax 021 425 5199; info@corkkerrytourism.ie; www.corkkerry.ie*

🛈 *Cork Airport* ☎ *Freephone in Arrivals Terminal*

🛈 *Blarney. Open daily.* ☎ *021 438 1624*

🛈 *Castle Gates, The Square, Macroom. Open Jun-Sep, Mon-Sat.* ☎ *028 43280*

Adjacent Sights: See COBH, KINSALE, MALLOW, MIDLETON, YOUGHAL.

Background

A Marshy Place – Cork derives its name from the Irish for a "marshy place", where St Finbar founded a church in 650 on the banks of the River Lee near the present site of University College. Its early development was disrupted in 860 by Viking raids, and in 1172 by the invasion of the Anglo-Normans who eventually broke the Danish hold on the city.

Rebel Cork – Owing to its commercial strength Cork early developed a political independence which has survived to the present day. In 1492 **Perkin Warbeck**, the pretender to the English throne, arrived in Cork; he won the support of the mayor and some leading citizens who accompanied him to England, where he proclaimed himself Richard IV, King of England and Lord of Ireland. Warbeck and his Cork supporters were hanged at Tyburn.

In the 1640s Cork supported the royal cause. Cromwell entered the city in 1649 causing much damage. Cork's humiliation was complete in 1690 when, after a five-day siege, the army of William III entered the city and the walls and other fortifications were destroyed.

In the early 18C Cork received many of the Huguenots who fled from religious persecution in France; their presence is recalled in the name of French Church Street. In the 19C the city lived up to its reputation of rebelliousness by being a stronghold of Fenian agitation. The *Cork Examiner*, the city's daily newspaper, was founded in 1841.

The War of Independence and the subsequent Civil War were bitterly fought in and around Cork. In 1920 the Black and Tans set fire to a substantial portion of the city centre, which was later rebuilt in anonymous modern style. The political unrest was aggravated by the deaths of two Lord Mayors of Cork. Terence McSwiney died on hunger strike in Brixton Prison; Tomás McCurtain was shot in his bed by Crown Forces in the presence of his wife and children.

Commercial and Industrial Centre – Cork began its involvement in trade in the 12C exporting hides and cloth and importing wine from Bordeaux.

By the 18C the city had extended its commercial activities through the production and sale of butter to Great Britain, Europe and America.

In 1852 Cork staged Ireland's first national Industrial Exhibition, modelled on the Great Exhibition held in London the year before. In 1917 the Ford car company set up its first overseas factory at the Marina in Cork; **Henry Ford**, the founder of the American firm, was born at Ballinascarty, north of Clonakilty. The Ford factory closed

> ### ARTISTIC CORK
> Among those sons of Cork who made their mark in the world are **John Hogan** (1800-58) a sculptor whose work is found not only in Cork but elsewhere in Ireland, **Frank O'Connor**, who penned short stories, and **Frank Browne**, a Jesuit and photographer extraordinaire of life in Ireland at the beginning of the 20C but especially of the first stages of the fatal maiden voyage of the *Titanic*.

Directory

GETTING ABOUT

Cork International Airport –
☎ 021 431 3131

Bus Travel – Bus Éireann Travel Centre,
Parnell Place ☎ 021 508 188;
www.infopoint.ie/buse/

Rail Travel – Iarnród Éireann, Travel Centre,
65 Patrick Street ☎ 021 504 888;
www.club.ie/RailNet/

Car Ferry across **Cork Harbour** from
Glenbrook *(southeast of the city centre)*
to Carrigaloe near Cobh on Great Island –
*Operates daily, 7am-12.15am. Time 5min.
Capacity 28 cars. There and back €4.50 (car),
€1.25 (pedestrian).* ☎ 021 481 1223.

Parking – Multi-storey car parks and disc
parking in the street; parking discs available
at the Tourist Office and other outlets in Cork.
Taxis wait for hire in the centre of the main
street.

SIGHTSEEING

Cork City Bus Tour – *Operates early-May to
early-Oct, 10.20am-4.57pm. €11. Tickets
available from the bus tour bus driver or the
Tourist Information Office (see above).*
☎ *Dublin 01 676 5377;
cork@guidefriday.com; www.guidefriday.com*

Day Coach Tours by Easy Tours Cork –
*Operate all year. Depart from customer's
Cork address. €25 (6hr), €30 (8hr)*
☎ *021 436 2484; www.easytourscork.com*

Literary Walking Tours – *in the footsteps
of O'Connor, Joyce, O'Faoláin, Lynch and
Bowen –* ☎ *021 488 5405 or 429 1649.*

Cork Lough – A large grass-fringed lake which
is a thriving bird sanctuary inhabited by many
species, including Mandarin duck, mallard,
moorhen and a large population of swans.
Railway buffs will be interested in a splendid
example of an early Irish steam **locomotive**,
a 2-2-2 built in 1848 and withdrawn in 1874
after 30 years of service, which stands in the
railway station entrance hall.

WHERE TO STAY

• Budget

Aaran Isle Inn – *14 Dyke Parade -*
☎ *021 278 158   16 rm €40/50* ☒. *Good*
location on the western edge of the city
centre, big yellow-painted and tastefully
renovated building.

Busker in Cork City

SLIDE FILE, Dublin

Island House – *Morrison's Quay -*
☎ *021 271 716 -* ▯ *- 51 rm €40/50*
☒. Modern and comfortable, Island
House is located on one of the canals,
very close to the city centre but in a quiet
situation. The rooms are modern and the
kitchen can be used by guests. Favourable
rates for family rooms and 3-bed rooms.
Parking available.

Acorn House – *14 St Patrick's Hill -*
☎ *021 450 2474 - Fax 021 450 2474 -
info@acornhouse-cork.com - Closed 22 Dec
to 16 Jan - 9 rm €55/100* ☒. A Georgian house
in the heart of the city decorated with sympathetic
period charm. The high ceilings lend the
bedrooms that extra airiness and some modern
touches and facilities complement the comfort.

Achill House – *Western Rd -*
☎ *021 427 9447 - Fax 021 427 9447 -
info@achillhouse.com -* ▯ *- 6 rm €50/100*
☒. In a street bulging with a plethora of
guesthouses, this one has a discernibly
contemporary feel with its wood flooring and
pastel shades. Clutter-free with a good level
of mod cons.

• Moderate

Hotel Isaacs – *48 McCurtain Street*
☎ *021 500 011 - 36 rm €65/90* ☒. Next to
the hostel of the same name, close to the
bus and railway stations and the city centre,
at the end of a covered passageway with a
fountain, this is a good place to stay, albeit
on the expensive side. Comfortable 2-3 room
apartments are available too, by the night or
week, at relatively favourable rates (€70-80
per night depending on the number of rooms
and the season).

WHERE TO EAT

• Budget

Blair's Inn – *Cloghroe, Blarney –
3.5mi/5.6km from Blarney via R 617 to
Tower, then via R 579 -* ☎ *0214 381 470 -*
☒ *- €15.* This friendly pub boasts a charming
and secluded wooded setting by the
Owennageara river. Traditional pub fare
during the day, a more elaborate menu
in the evening. Live music on Monday nights.

Isaacs   *48 MacCurtain St -* ☎ *021 450 3805 -
isaacs@iol.ie - Closed 1 week at Christmas and
Sun lunch - Booking essential - €15.85/30.90.*
Bustling converted warehouse with bare brick
walls and vibrant modern art work. A lively
atmosphere is guaranteed and the menu
features modern brasserie-style cooking,
with extra lunchtime specials.

Cafe Paradiso – *16 Lancaster Quay,
Western Rd -* ☎ *021 427 7939 -
dpcolter@eircom.net - Closed 4 days at
Easter, 2 weeks late August, 1 week at
Christmas, Sun and Mon - Booking essential -
€20/35.* Scrubbed pine tables, vivid colours
and cherubs on the walls add to the buzzing
atmosphere, helped by the pleasant and
efficient service. The well-priced vegetarian
food is perennially popular.

• Moderate

Jacques – *Phoenix St -* ☎ *021 427 7387 -
jacquesrestaurant@eircom.net - Closed 23
Dec to 2 Jan, Sun, Sat lunch, Mon dinner*

and Bank Hols - €20.90/39.90. One of the older restaurants in the city, located in a colourful little side street in the centre. Always busy with locals yet retaining an intimate atmosphere. Modern menu with the emphasis on locally sourced ingredients from small producers.

Jacobs on the Mall – *30A South Mall -* ☎ *021 425 1530 - kingsley@eircom.net - Closed 25 Dec, 1 Jan, Sun and lunch Bank Hols - Booking essential - €22.30/36.20.* This former 19C Turkish baths has been converted into one of the city's most stylish restaurants, with a substantial collection of modern Irish art. Attentive service, modern cooking using the best local ingredients and some original combinations.

No 5 Fenn's Quay – *Sheares St -* ☎ *021 427 9527 - polary@eircom.net - Closed Sun - €26.50/38.* Converted from a mews house, bright and informally run. Open all day serving snacks, a fairly light lunch menu and more substantial dishes in the evening. Freshly prepared and correctly priced.

TAKING A BREAK

Culturlann na hEireann – *Belgrave Sq, Monkstown -* ☎ *01 280 02 95 - enquiries@comhaltas.com* – *Open 9.30am-5.30pm.* Music from Monday to Thursday at 9pm, dancing on Friday and Saturday. Cover charge. Don't miss this cultural centre that is also a pub and dance hall. Friday night is lively in the ballroom. After a short demonstration with partners selected from the crowd, the dance master invites all to have a go at set-dancing to the tune of a traditional orchestra. It's popular with older folks but don't be fooled, they can really shake a leg!

ENTERTAINMENT

Everyman Palace Theatre – *MacCurtain Street -* ☎ *021 501 673.*

Kino Cinema – *Washington Street -* ☎ *021 271 571 - kinocinema@indigo.ie* – *Open daily, 1pm-10pm.* Wide selection of films.

Opera House – *Emmet Place -* ☎ *021 270 022.* Touring theatre companies and local productions.

The Half Moon Club – *Emmet Place -* ☎ *021 427 43 08 - www.halfmoontheatre.ie* – *Open daily 8.30am-11.30pm.* Variety of jazz, blues and rock music acts.

UCC Granary Theatre – ☎ *021 904 275.* Range of amateur and professional productions.

SHOPPING

Most of the well-known brands are to be found in **Patrick Street**, the main shopping street running through Cork City centre. **North Main Street** is one of the oldest shopping streets in Cork. The **English Market** *(just off Patrick Street)* offers market-lovers a wide range of fresh produce to choose from.

For something a little different try the **Huguenot Quarter**, a bohemian district which houses a variety of cafés and boutiques, as well as several antique shops, or the **Shandon Crafts Centre**, housed in the old **Butter Exchange** (1750), where visitors may watch such articles as crystal, jewellery and textiles being made – *Open Mon-Sat, 9am-5pm.* ☎ *021 450 7487*

For woollen goods visit the **Blarney Woollen Mills** *(see below).*

Merchant's Quay Shopping Centre – *Patrick Street -* ☎ *427 54 74 - info@merchantquaycork.com - Open Mon-Thu, 9am-6pm, Fri, 9am-7pm, Sat, 9am-6pm, Sun, 2pm-6pm.*

SPORTS AND LEISURE

Greyhound racing.

EVENTS AND FESTIVALS

Cork International Choral and Folk Dance Festival (April/May)

Cork Folk Festival (September)

Cork Jazz Festival (October) – Annual jazz festival which attracts over 35 000 visitors – ☎ *021 427 8979; Fax 021 427 0463*

Cork Film Festival *(October)* which celebrates the best in world cinema. ☎ *021 427 1711*

TRACING ANCESTORS

Cork Archives Institute, *South Main Street* – Stock of family and private papers, housed by the Institute, among ancient gravestones in Christ Church, which was built in 1726 on the site of a medieval church destroyed in the 1690 siege. *Open by appointment Tue-Fri, 10am-1pm and 2.30-5pm. Closed Bank Hols.* ☎ *021 427 7809; Fax 021 427 4668; cai@indigo.ie; www.corkcorp.ie*

down in 1980 at the same time as the Dunlop tyre plant, set up in the 1930s. Ship-building also came to an end in the 1980s. Commercial activity is now concentrated in computer manufacturing companies.

Walking About

St Patrick's Street★

Cork's main shopping thoroughfare offers a wide variety of departmental and speciality shops, supplemented by a large new shopping centre in Merchant's Quay.

English Market

Off St Patrick's Street. This busy covered market was established in 1610, and until the early 19C its main aisle was a waterway, along which merchandise was brought in by boat. Local specialities like black pudding *(drisheen)* and

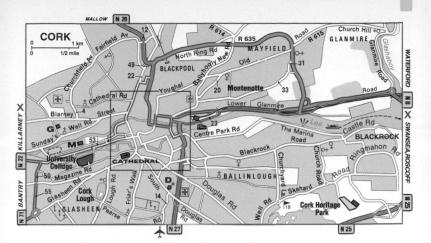

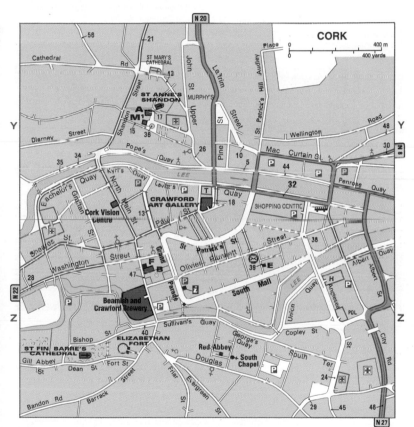

pigs' trotters *(crúibíní – crubeens in English)* are on sale here, and the market is a good place to hear the distinctive Cork accent as the stallholders indulge in their lively banter.

Grand Parade★

The main business street of Cork contains some handsome late-18C bow-fronted buildings hung with grey slates. Until 1800 the street was an open channel of the River Lee lined by merchants' houses; the steps that led down to the boats can still be seen.

From Grand Parade turn right into Tuckey Street.

Beamish and Crawford Brewery

South Main Street. The attractive old-English half-timbered façade belongs to one of the two local breweries.

Return to Grand Parade; at the south end of the street turn left into South Mall.

South Mall★

The Commercial Rooms, now incorporated in the Imperial Hotel at the eastern end of South Mall were built in 1813 for the merchants who ran the Butter Exchange; directly opposite, at the corner of Pembroke Street, is a doorway with the inscription *Cork Library*, the city's first major library, funded by private subscription.

From the east end of South Mall turn right along Morrison's Quay, walk over Trinity Bridge, turn right along George's Quay and left into Dunbar Street.

South Mall, Cork

South Chapel

The chapel (1766) contains a sculpture of the Dead Christ, beneath the high altar; it is the work of John Hogan (1800-58), who spent his boyhood in nearby Cove Street.

Turn right and right again into Mary Street.

Red Abbey

The square tower is all that remains of Cork's oldest building, an Augustinian friary founded in 1300. During the siege of 1690, a cannon was mounted on top of the tower, then outside the city, to batter Cork's eastern walls.

At the south end of the street turn right into Douglas Street; at the T-junction turn left into Barrack Street and right into Fort Street.

Elizabethan Fort★

Originally built in the 1590s for "overawing the citizens of Cork", the fort was rebuilt on its present lines in about 1624 and was converted to a prison in 1835. It was burned down in 1922 by the Anti-Treaty forces before they withdrew from the city. The extensive parapets provide one of the best vantage points in Cork.

Continue west along Fort Street.

St Fin Barre's Cathedral (Anglican)★★

♿ *Open Mon-Sat, 10am-5.30pm (5pm Oct-Apr). Services: Sun, 8am, 11.15am, 7pm. Closed Bank Hols. Donation. Guided tour available. Leaflet (8 languages). Parking.*
☎ *021 496 3387, 496 4742 (Dean of Cork); sfb@iol.ie; www.goireland.com*

Cork's most exuberant church building (1865) was designed by **William Burges** in an early pointed French Gothic style and built in white limestone. It replaced an earlier church (1735) which was preceded by a medieval structure. The church has three spires, the central one rising to 240ft/73m. The apse is lit by 18 windows of stained glass. A brass plate in the floor marks the burial place of Elizabeth Aldworth; she is said to have hidden in a clock-case during a Masonic lodge meeting in her husband's house in 1712 and was made a Mason to secure her silence.

The **cannonball** hanging south of the altar is said to have been fired at the tower of the 1735 church during the 1690 siege.

Worth a Visit

NORTH OF THE RIVER

Shandon Bells★★

St Anne's Anglican Church. Open Mon-Sat, 9am-6pm (10am-4pm winter). Closed Bank Hols. €5. Parking. ☎ 021 450 5906; info@shandonsteeple.com; www.shandonsteeple.com
The church stands on the rising ground to the north of the Lee. Its tower contains Cork's most famous attraction, the carillon of eight bells hung in 1752; among the tunes which visitors may play by pulling levers is Cork's own "anthem", *On the Banks of My Own Lovely Lee*.
The tower, which is faced in limestone on two sides and sandstone on the other two, is built of four blocks of diminishing size and has the largest clock faces in Cork. The church (1722), which has a wooden ceiling, replaces an earlier building destroyed in the 1690 siege; there has been a religious foundation on this site since 1100. The reward for climbing the 133 steps of the tower is a fine prospect of the city in its setting.

Cork Butter Museum

Open May-Sep, daily, 10am-1pm and 2-5pm. €3. ☎ 021 430 0600; Fax 021 430 9966
From the 18th to the early 20C, Cork thrived on the export of butter, with the world's largest butter market and a unique system of quality control. The little museum puts the trade firmly in the context of Irish farming, diet and communications, and there are displays featuring bog butter and traditional and modern butter-making equipment.

Cork City Gaol

Convent Avenue. & Open Mar-Oct, daily, 9.30am-6pm; Nov-Feb, 10am-5pm; last admission 1hr before closing. €5. Audioguide (8 languages). ☎ 021 4305 022; Fax 021 4307 230; corkgaol@indigo.ie; www.corkcitygaol.com
The fortress-like prison, designed by Sir Thomas Deane, opened in 1825 and closed in 1923. After 1878 it was used for women only, except during the period when Ireland gained its independence, when it housed men and women.
The display recalls the prison diet (porridge) and regime (oakum picking, treadmill, solitary confinement), the sort of crimes the prisoners might have committed, the role of the school (1856-79) and the hospital, the graffiti left by 20C prisoners. The audio-visual presentation provides a dramatic insight into the social conditions of 19C Cork.
The **Radio Museum** shows a film about Marconi, who made some of his early transmissions in Ireland *(see p 388)*, and displays pieces of transatlantic cable and relics of the early days of Cork Radio, which made its first broadcast in 1927 from the prison.

SOUTH OF THE RIVER

Crawford Art Gallery★

& Open Mon-Sat, 10am-5pm. Guided tour by appointment. Restaurant. ☎ 021 427 3377; Fax 021 4805043; crawfordgallery@eircom.net; www.synergy.ie/crawford
Named after its founding benefactor, WH Crawford, the gallery is housed in the Custom House of 1724 (later extended) and has a representative collection of 19C and 20C works by Irish artists such as William Conor, John Keating, Sir William Orpen and Seán O'Sullivan, together with works by John Hogan and Daniel Maclise, two noted 19C Cork artists.
Other exhibits include late-19C Japanese samurai armour and a collection of Classical casts from the Vatican. There are frequent touring exhibitions of contemporary Irish and European art.

Cork Public Museum★

Open Mon-Fri, 11am-1pm and 2.15-6pm (5pm Sep-May); Sun, 3-5pm. Closed Bank Hols. Sun €1.50. Parking. ☎ 021 427 0679; Fax 021 427 0931; museum@corkcorp.ie
The exhibits, which are attractively presented in a house in Fitzgerald Park, trace life in the Cork area since prehistoric times. The entrance hall displays the City Coat of Arms, rescued from the old City Hall which was burned in the 1920 fire,

while the collection of maces and other Corporation regalia includes the 1500 **silver dart**, thrown into the sea by Lord Mayors to assert the limits of the city's jurisdiction. A model of the walled city shows the extent of Cork in 1185.

Local crafts include needlepoint lace made in Youghal and 18C Cork silver. The role of the city in the early 20C struggle for independence is given its due attention, and an unusual item is the **Cork Republican Silver** made early in 1922, when the fighting in the city made it impossible to send silver to Dublin to be assayed. The adjoining park exhibits **sculptures** by five contemporary Irish sculptors.

Cork Vision Centre

North Main Street. Open Tue-Sat, 10am-5pm. ☎ 021 427 9925; Fax 021 427 9927; visioncentre@eircom.net; www.corkvisioncentre.com

This urban information centre, located in the deconsecrated 18C St Peter's Church, has displays on the past, present and future of Cork, arranged around a large model (1:500) of the city.

University College

Walking tour: Operates Jun-Sep, Mon, Wed, Fri at 2.30pm, starting from the main gates in Western Road. ☎ 021 427 6871

University College Cork (UCC), now part of the National University, was founded by charter in 1845, together with two other colleges in Galway and Belfast. The original buildings were designed by Benjamin Woodward (1816-61). A walking tour starting from the main gates includes the Main Quadrangle building with its outstanding Stone Corridor, the Boole Library, the Honan Chapel which is noted for its **stained-glass windows★** by **Harry Clarke**, the Crawford Observatory, the Republican Grave Plot and Gaol.

Cork Heritage Park

2mi/3km E of city centre at Blackrock by Blackrock Road and Church Road. ♿ Open Mar-Sep, daily, 10.30am to 5pm; Oct-Feb, by appointment. €3. Parking. Café, picnic areas. Bus routes 2 and 10 from Cork city centre. ☎/Fax 021 435 8854

The centre is housed in the outbuildings of the Bessboro estate, the home of the Pikes, a local **Quaker family**, originally from Newbury in England. As well as tracing the history of the family, who like many prosperous Quakers were known for their charitable works during the Famine, it has displays of local flora and fauna, Cork Harbour, horse-drawn transport, and Cork City fire brigade.

> ### Road Bowls
> The ancient Irish sport of road bowling is still played on Sundays in Co Cork and Co Armagh. A heavy iron ball (28oz/794g; 7in/18cm) is hurled along a stretch of quiet winding country road in as few throws as possible; the ball may hurtle through the air at shoulder height. Betting is heavy.

Excursions

Blarney Castle★★

5mi/8km NW by N 20 and W by a minor road. (♿) Open Mon-Sat, 9am-6.30pm (7pm Jun-Aug; 6pm/dusk, Oct-Apr); Sun, 9.30am-5.30pm/dusk. Closed 24-25 Dec. €5.50. Brochure (3 languages). Parking. Refreshments. ☎ 021 438 5252; Fax 021 438 1518; info@blarneycastle.ie; www.blarneycastle.ie

The central feature of the castle is the massive keep, a fine example of a tower house. In addition there are halls and dungeons, but the main reason why the castle attracts so many visitors is the presence here of the **Blarney Stone**, said to bestow the gift of eloquent speech on all those who kiss it. This is harder than it sounds since the famous piece of rock is set inside the parapet at the top of the castle and can be reached only by lying upside-down with a guide holding one's legs. The stone is believed to have been brought to Ireland during the Crusades.

Kissing the Blarney Stone

R Holzbachova, Ph Benet/MICHELIN

In the 16C Queen Elizabeth I commanded the Earl of Leicester to take the castle from the head of the McCarthy clan. The Earl was frustrated in his mission but he sent back numerous progress reports which so irritated the Queen that she referred to them as "all Blarney".

Blarney Castle House★ – *Private.* It was built in the 1870s in the Scottish baronial style with fine corner turrets and conical-roofed bartizans; it is surrounded by formal gardens and walks giving extensive views of Blarney lake.

On a druidic site beside the Blarney River is the romantically landscaped dell known as **Rock Close.** Laid out in the 19C, the gardens contain wishing steps, which should be negotiated up and down with one's eyes closed. Two dolmens are sited in the close, which has a Fairy Glade with a sacrificial rock, also said to have druidic connotations.

Blarney Woollen Mills is a 19C woollen factory (restored), the successor to the 13 mills developed around the castle as an industrial enterprise in the 18C. Its enormous ground-floor shop is almost as popular with visitors as the Blarney Stone.
&. *Open daily, 9am-6pm. Closed 25-26 Dec, 1 Jan. Gift catalogue. Licensed restaurant.* ☎ *021 438 5280; Fax 021 498 1547; info@blarney.ie; www.blarneywoollenmills.ie*

Dunkathel House★
3mi/5km E of Cork by N 8; after the Dunkettle/Glanmire roundabout turn left (sign). Open May to mid-Oct, Wed-Sun, 2-6pm. €3. Brochure (4 languages). Guided tour (30min) available. Parking. ☎ *021 482 1014; Fax 021 482 1023*

Still lived in, this Georgian house was built around 1790 and stands on rising ground with a superb prospect of the estuary of the River Lee. The interior is particularly appealing, with fascinating items of furniture including a rare barrel organ of 1800 which may be played. To the rear of the hall, where the ceiling and walls are hand painted, is a bifurcating staircase with a cast of the *Three Graces* on the half-landing. An upper room is profusely hung with attractive watercolours by a daughter of the house, Beatrice Gubbins (1878-1944); some are of local inspiration; others were painted in the course of the travels which took her around the Mediterranean and to the West Indies.

Riverstown House
5mi/8km E of Cork by N 8; at the Dunkettle roundabout turn left onto R 639 to Glanmire; continue for 2.5mi/4km; at the crossroads in Riverstown turn right (sign). Open May-Sep, Wed-Sat, 2-6pm; otherwise by appointment. €4. Guided tour available. Parking. ☎ *021 4821205*

In 1745 Dr Jemmett Browne, the Bishop of Cork, spared no expense in rebuilding the original house of 1602, employing the **Lafranchini brothers** to decorate it with fine examples of their sumptuous **plasterwork**.

Crosshaven
15mi/24km SE of Cork by N 28, R 611 and R 612. This popular little resort, located at the point where the Owenabue River widens to form a sheltered inlet of Cork Harbour, is a yachtsman's paradise and, since 1969, the home of the Royal Cork Yacht Club. Boatbuilders thrive here; among their past achievements are the *Brendan (see p 253)* and the *Gypsy Moth V* in which Sir Francis Chichester sailed round the world in 1971. **Crosshaven House** (mid-18C) looks down on the activity of the waterfront while **Fort Meagher**, a fine example of a coastal artillery fort, commands the approach from the sea.

Tour

LEE VALLEY
Drive of 25mi/40km. From Cork take N 22 W.

Ballincollig Gunpowder Mills
&. *Guided tour (1hr; 3 languages) Apr-Sep, Sun-Fri, 10am-5pm. €3.81. Audio-visual show (15min). Parking. Coffee shop. Craft shop.* ☎ *021 487 4430; Fax 021 487 4836; ballinco@indigo.ie; indigo.ie/~ballinco*

This complex of buildings on the south bank of the Lee spreads over an extensive site and is the largest remaining example of a gunpowder manufactory in Europe. The long and fascinating history of gunpowder production here is brought to life by displays, an audio-visual presentation, and a guided tour of some of the restored buildings.

GUNPOWDER AT BALLINCOLLIG
The mills were started in 1794 by Charles Henry Leslie, a Cork banker. In 1805, under the threat of invasion by Napoleon, the British Board of Ordnance bought the mills for £17 000, increased the production and capacity and dug a canal to provide water power and transport. On Napoleon's defeat in 1815 the demand for gunpowder decreased and the mills closed. In 1833 they reopened and by the mid-1850s Ballincollig was one of the largest industrial establishments in the Cork area, employing about 500 men and boys with a wide range of skills – coopers, millwrights, carpenters – who lived in the workers' cottages nearby. The discovery of dynamite and nitroglycerine made gunpowder obsolete and in 1903 the mills closed.

Continue W by N 22; after 5mi/8km turn right (sign).

Farran Forest Park

The valley of the Lee upstream from Cork has been partly drowned to provide hydro-electric power but here in the forest park the surrounding landscape remains attractive.

Continue W by N 22; 1mi/1.5km before Macroom turn left onto R 584 towards Bantry; after 2mi/3km park in the lay-by (left). It is dangerous to venture off the causeway running from the lay-by without taking local advice; water-levels can change rapidly and many parts of the area are very swampy.

The Gearagh

A great rarity, the post-glacial alluvial oak forest, known as the Gearagh, was also inundated but has recovered and is now protected as a National Nature Reserve. In the distant past, its many-branched stream, treacherous reed-beds, mudbanks and countless islands provided a refuge for fugutives from the law, notably distillers of illicit whiskey *(potheen)*. Today despite its forlorn appearance, with blackened tree-stumps protruding from the surface of the water, it is home to an extraordinary variety of flora and fauna, best visited from October onwards when vast numbers of migrant birds arrive, among them whooper swans and greylag geese, many species of duck, curlew, lapwing and golden plover.

Dingle Peninsula★★

The Dingle Peninsula is extreme western Ireland at its most spectacular and atmospheric, a Gaelic-speaking area with sheer cliffs, harsh mountainsides, an intricate network of tiny stone-walled fields, and an extraordinary concentration of ancient stone monuments – ringforts, beehive huts, and inscribed stones. Brandon Mountain (3 121ft/951m) on the north coast, the second-highest in Ireland, is clothed in blanket bog and takes its name from St Brendan of Clonfert *(see p 251)*, a 6C monk, who is reputed to have set out on a transatlantic voyage from Brandon Creek, the narrow sea-inlet at the west foot of the mountain.

Location

Michelin Atlas p 82 and Map 712 – A, B 11 – Co Kerry.

Dingle *(An Daingean)* is the main town on the Dingle Peninsula reached by N 86 the main road from Tralee either via Anascaul or via a detour over the dramatic Connor Pass.

🅱 *Strand Street, Dingle. Open May-Sep, daily, 10am-1pm, 2.15-6pm, Apr and Oct, Mon-Sat. ☎ 066 915 1188; user@cktourism.ie; www.dingle-peninsula.ie*

Adjacent Sights: See KILLARNEY, TRALEE.

Background

The possibilities of the great natural harbour of Dingle were quickly realised by the Anglo-Normans; in 1257 Henry III of England imposed customs duties on exports. The peak of its commercial importance was reached in the 16C when Dingle had particularly strong trading links with Spain; in 1583 the town received permission to build a wall of enclosure.

In the same year a long period of local rule by the house of Desmond came to an end when Gearóid, the rebel Earl, was killed. Three years earlier 600 Spanish and Italian troops sent to aid the Desmond Rebellion had been massacred by government forces at Dún an Óir on the west side of Smerwick Harbour. Following the rebellion of 1641 and the Cromwellian wars Dingle declined significantly as a port for nearly a century, although during the late 18C it had a substantial linen industry.

Tour

In clockwise order starting in Dingle town

Dingle (An Daingean)★

Dingle, the principal centre of population, is the home port of one of Ireland's largest fishing fleets; when the catch is unloaded, the pier (0.25mi/0.4km long) is a scene of frantic activity; at other times it is ideal for a quiet stroll. The town has developed as a popular tourist resort, with brightly painted houses and numerous pubs, restaurants and places to stay.

Directory

GETTING ABOUT

Blasket Islands Ferry – *Operates from Dunquin Pier (weather permitting) 10am-6pm, every 30min. €20 there and back.* ☎ *066 915 6422, 6188*

WHERE TO STAY

• Budget

Devane's – *Goat St; above Main Street -* ☎ *066 915 1193 -* 🚭 *- 6 rm €45/50* 🛏. Comfortable big pink house in the upper part of town.

The Lighthouse – *High Rd -* ☎ *066 915 1829 -* 🚭 *- 6 rm €45/50* 🛏. Main Street leads west past the hospital to this modern house overlooking the bay. Brightly decorated interior with lots of cheerful fabrics and attractive wooded furniture. Ask for one of the rooms with a view. Model hosts.

Captains House – *The Mall -* ☎ *066 915 1531 - Fax 066 915 1079 - captigh@eircom.net - 16 Mar to Nov -* ✖ *- 9 rm €50/110* 🛏. A warm welcome is guaranteed at this cottagey town centre house with a distinctive homely feel. Breakfast is served in the conservatory which overlooks the lovingly tended garden.

Pax House – *Upper John St - 0.75mi/1,2km NE on John St -* ☎ *066 915 1518 - Fax 066 915 2461 - paxhouse@iol.ie - Closed Dec and Jan -* 🅿 ✖ *- 13 rm €60/160* 🛏. Take in the terrific views of Dingle Bay from the balcony of this detached house, set in an elevated position a short walk from the town centre; it provides clean and roomy accommodation.

• Moderate

Cleevaun – *Lady's Cross, Milltown - 1.25mi/2km W on R 559 following signs for Slea Head Drive -* ☎ *066 915 1108 - Fax 066 915 2228 - cleevaun@iol.ie - Mid Feb to mid Nov -* 🅿 ✖ *- 8 rm €80/92* 🛏. Good value, simply done accommodation on the west side of town where the owner makes that extra effort to make your stay comfortable; tea is offered on arrival and she is always willing to help with travel tips and recommendations.

Greenmount House – *Gortonora - By John St -* ☎ *066 915 1414 - Fax 066 915 1974 - mary@greenmounthouse.com - Closed 20 to 27 Dec -* 🅿 ✖ *- 9 rm €90/150* 🛏. Request one of the superior rooms at the top of this purpose-built hotel in an elevated position above the town. A highlight is the sumptuous breakfast served in the conservatory.

Heatons – *The Wood - .05mi/0.8km W on R 559 -* ☎ *066 915 2288 Fax 066 915 2324 - heatons@iol.ie - Closed 1 to 26 Dec -* 🅿 ✖ *- 16 rm €95/174* 🛏. Overlooking the bay, where bedrooms have a contemporary feel and are decorated to a high standard. The newer rooms are particularly spacious and one has a balcony. Buffet breakfast.

WHERE TO EAT

• Moderate

The Chart House – *The Mall -* ☎ *066 915 2255 - charthse@iol.ie - Closed Tue and restricted opening in winter - €25.50/38.* This stone cottage restaurant has a rapidly well-earned reputation for providing good quality modern cooking matched by keen and well-organised service. The works of local artists cover the walls. Not a huge place so book first.

Doyle's Seafood Bar – *4 John St -* ☎ *066 915 1174 - cdoyles@iol.ie - Mid-Feb to mid-Dec -* ✖ *- €27.80/46.70.* Choose your lobster, the house speciality, from the tank in the bar, then pick one of the kitchen tables. Stone floors and an old kitchen range add to the rustic feel of this renowned seafood bar. Accommodation available in the adjacent town house.

SHOPPING

John Weldon – *Green Street -* ☎ *066 915 522 - www.kerryweb.ie/celticjewellery – Open Mon-Wed, 9am-6pm, Thu, 9am-7pm, Fri-Sat, 9am-6pm.* John Weldon is a jewellery designer who takes his inspiration from Celtic traditions, mythology and heritage. This makes an ideal stop for those looking for an original gift or souvenir of their stay in Ireland and visitors are welcome to see the workshop.

Craft Centre *(Ceardlann na Coille) – Ventry Road -* ☎ *066 915 2039 - Open usually daily, 10am-5pm (earlier in winter).* A cluster of workshops – jewellery, making of elbow (*uilleann*) pipes and violins, knitting, feltwork, leatherwork, hand-weaving, upholstery, wood-turning and cabinet-making.

SPORTS AND LEISURE

Beaches – *At Ventry Harbour, Smerwick Harbour, Stradbally Strand.*

Rambling – *Make the pilgrimage up the* **Saint's Road** *(7mi/12km) from Kilmalkedar up the southwest face of Mount Brandon to the oratory and shrine dedicated to St Brendon on the summit.*

As well as plenty of eye-level displays of marine life, the **Oceanworld Aquarium** has a Perspex tunnel enabling visitors to walk through the largest of the tanks. Special attention is given to Fungi, a friendly dolphin who first took up residence in Dingle Harbour in 1983. ♿ *Open daily, 10am-6pm (8.30pm Jul-Aug, 5pm Oct-Mar). €7.50. Parking (paying). Refreshments.* ☎ *066 915 2111; Fax 066 915 2155; marabeo@iol.ie; www.dingle-oceanworld.ie*

On an elevated site in the upper part of town, **Diseart**, an institution devoted to the study of Celtic culture, is installed in the former Convent of the Presentation Sisters, designed by the architect JJ McCarthy; the **Chapel★** has outstanding stained glass by **Harry Clarke**. *Open Jun-Aug, Mon-Fri, 10am-noon and 2-4pm.*

JJ McCarthy, the successor to Pugin, also designed the adjacent **St Mary's Church**★ (1862). The original roof and columns have been replaced by a bold combination of steel girders and copper sheeting.

In **Dingle Library** (next to St Mary's Church) there is a large display of printed material relating to local history, as well as a permanent exhibition on **Thomas Ashe** (1885-1917), who took a leading role in the 1916 Easter Rising and was born at Lispole (5mi/8km east). Open Tue Sat, 10.30am-1.30pm and 2.30-5pm. ☎ 066 91 51499; library.dingle@eircom.net

The **Holy Stone** beside the pavement (junction of Upper Main Street and Chapel Lane) is a large stone (10ft/3m long) with several deep cup marks on it, which may have been cut in prehistoric times.

From Dingle take R 559 W (signed Ceann Sléibhe).

Dingle

B Perousse/MICHELIN

Slea Head (Ceann Sléibhe)★★

On the steep south-facing slopes of Mount Eagle (1 696ft/516m), both east and west of the ford at Glenfahan (parking in lay-bys), the agricultural landscape of early Christian – possibly even prehistoric – times has been largely preserved in all its multi-layered complexity. Though some have been unthinkingly cleared, drystone walls define a filigree pattern of tiny fields, among which are more than 400 **clocháin** or **beehive huts**★ (privately owned). Some of them are set within ringforts like **Cathair na gConchúireach** (admission charge may be requested), where their superb workmanship can be examined and where there is also a souterrain and an inscribed cross.

After rounding the SW point of Slea Head turn left into a minor road leading to a car park.

From **Dunmore Head** there is a superlative **view**★★ in fine weather taking in the dramatically jagged cliffs, the Blasket Sound and the Blasket Islands (see below).

Blasket Islands★

Accessible by boat from Dunquin (see Directory). Uninhabited since 1953, when the remaining population fled their harsh and demanding life, the group consists of four large and three smaller islands, as well as many rocks and reefs. The largest of the islands is the mountainous **Great Blasket** (4 x 0.75mi/6 x 1.2km), now a national historic park where some of the ruined buildings are being restored. Inishvickillane has monastic ruins, a house and cottage and helicopter landing-pad but for most of the year is accessible only by air; from 1974 to 1997 it was owned by the former Taoiseach Charles Haughey.

In 1586 two ships from the Spanish Armada – San Juan and Santa Maria de la Rosa – foundered in the treacherous waters of the Blasket Sound.

Dunquin

In 1969 the quiet isolation of Dunquin was disturbed by the film crew making Ryan's Daughter. To the north, up in the mountains above Carhoo, David Lean built the fictional village of Kirrary but only the school house still stands.

Great Blasket Centre

Dunquin. (Dúchas) ♿ Open late-Mar-Oct, daily, 10am-6pm (7pm Jul-Aug); last admission 45min before closing. €3.10. Audio-visual show (22min; 6 languages). Guided tour (45min) by appointment. Leaflet (6 languages) Parking.

> **BLASKET ISLAND AUTHORS**
> The early 20C Blasket islanders were literate in both Irish and English, and were encouraged by their visitors to develop their literary talents and evoke their elemental way of life before it vanished. Among the better-known works are three novels translated from Irish: *Twenty Years A-Growing* by Maurice O'Sullivan, *Peig* by Peig Sayers, and *The Islandman* by Tomás Ó'Criomhthain, described by EM Forster as "an account of Neolithic life from the inside". Another fine account, albeit from the point of view of an outsider, is *Western Island* by the Englishman Robin Flower. .

Coffee shop. ☎ *066 915 6444, 6371; Fax 066 915 6446; mdemordha@ealga.ie; ionadanbhlascaidmhoir@ealga.ie*

The stark modern building houses a display celebrating the fine Gaelic literary tradition of the Blasket Islands, based on local folktales, which attracted the interest of Irish and foreign intellectuals and scholars. The centre also illustrates the traditional way of life, based on farming, with spade cultivation and donkey transport, and on fishing in the island boats made of skin stretched over a timber frame.

Take R 550 N to Ballyferriter.

Corca Dhuibhne Regional Museum★

Ballyferriter. Open May-Sep, daily, 10am-5pm; Oct-Apr, by request €1.90. Refreshments in summer. Bureau de change. Bookshop. ☎ *066 915 6100, 915 6333; Fax 066 915 6348*

The centre illustrates many details of life and history on the Dingle peninsula: ancient monuments, Blasket Island literature, 190 folk scenes.

Continue on R 550 N.

Gallarus Oratory★★

Ireland has several examples of early Christian oratories, built like beehive huts with drystone walls corbelled inwards, but none is in as perfect a state of preservation as this delightful specimen, evidently built with exceptional care and probably dating from the 9C. Standing among the fields on its own, it is in the shape of an inverted boat, and unlike beehive huts is rectangular rather then circular in plan, a feature which in every other example has led to collapse, since the resulting walls are inherently unstable.

There are two openings, the west doorway and the east window; the doorway has a double lintel above which project two stones, each pierced with a round hole, indicating that the entrance may have been closed with a wooden door.

Gallarus Oratory

Kilmalkedar★

The ruined Romanesque church, probably built in the 12C, is part of a medieval religious complex and has an alphabet stone and an **Ogham stone**. Similar in style to Cormac's Chapel at Cashel, it has a tympanum on the east doorway and blind arcading in the nave, the walls of which survive to their full height.

The chancellor's house *(404yd/369m south)* was once occupied by the chancellor of the diocese of Ardfert *(see p 349)*. St Brendan's House, a two-storey ruin, may have been a priest's residence in medieval times.

From here an old track, the **Saint's Road** *(7mi/12km)*, runs up the southwest face of **Brandon Mountain** to the summit which is crowned by an oratory and shrine dedicated to St Brendan *(see p 253)*.

Return to Dingle and take the minor road NE (sign) to the Connor Pass.

Connor Pass★★

The road hugs the flank of the mountain to reach the highest pass in Ireland open to vehicles (1 496ft/456m – *car park*). There are superb views *(S)* of Dingle Harbour and *(N)* of Brandon Mountain overlooking Brandon Bay and Tralee Bay separated by the Castlegregory Peninsula.

Brandon Bay

The beautiful horseshoe bay is dominated *(W)* by Brandon Mountain and lined *(S and E)* by **Stradbally Strand★★**, the longest sandy beach (12mi/19km) in Ireland; several trackways link the main road to the beach.

Offshore at the north end of the Strand are the **Magharee Islands**, also known as The Seven Hogs. At low tide it is possible to walk from Illauntannig, the largest island, on which there is an early Christian monastery, to Reennafardarrig Island. *Continue E to Camp; turn right into N 86 towards Dingle; turn left onto a minor road (sign).*

Minard Castle

The ruin *(in a dangerous condition)* occupies an excellent vantage point overlooking Dingle Bay. The great square fortress was built by the Knight of Kerry in the 15C and largely destroyed by Cromwellian forces in the 17C.

Donegal

Centred on The Diamond, its distinctive market square, Donegal is a busy and attractive small town at the mouth of the River Eske. It is a good base from which to explore northwards into the glens and mountains, westwards through dramatic coastal scenery or southwards to the seaside resorts on Donegal Bay.

Location

Population 2 296 - Michelin Atlas p 100 and Map 712 – H 4 – Co Donegal. Donegal *(Dún na nGall)* is situated on the south side of the Blue Stack Mountains, overlooking Donegal Bay on N 15 which links Sligo with Strabane on the border with Northern Ireland.

Directory

GETTING ABOUT

Donegal Airport – ☎ 075 48232

SIGHTSEEING

The Waterbus makes a tour of some 20 sights in Donegal Bay – .Operates daily (70min) from Donegal Harbour. ☎/Fax 073 23666; waterbus@donegaltown.com

WHERE TO STAY

• *Budget*

Ardeevin – *Lough Eske, Barnesmore - 5.5mi/9km NE by N 15 following signs for Lough Eske Drive -* ☎ *073 21790 - Fax 073 21790 - seanmcginty@eircom.net - 18 Mar to Nov -* ⌨ ▣ ✎ *- 6 rm €40/65* ⌷. Peace and quiet are guaranteed here and few will fail to be impressed by the stunning views of Lough Eske. The house itself is pleasantly decorated with antiques and the traditional Irish breakfast provides the ideal start for walkers.

Island View House – *Ballyshannon Rd - 0.75mi/1.2km SW on N 15 -* ☎ *073 22411 - dowds@indigo.ie - Closed 25-26 Dec -* ⌨ ▣ *- 4 rm €42/62* ⌷. A grey-hued purpose-built guesthouse with views of the surrounding countryside and lough. Simply decorated with the emphasis on value for money. The owners provide genuine Irish hospitality.

SHOPPING

The famous woollen **Donegal tweed** is made and sold locally. Magee of Donegal, The Diamond – (&) Open Mon-Sat, 9.45am-6pm (9pm Jul-Aug). Demonstrations given on request. Leaflet (3 languages). ☎ 073 22660; Fax 073 23271; sales@mageeshop.com; www.mageeshop.com

There is a **craft village** on the southern outskirts of the town.

Donegal Parian China, Ballyshannon – Open daily, 9am-5pm. Closed Sun, Oct-May. ☎ 072 51826; Fax 072 51122; declan@donegalchina.ie; www.donegalchina.ie

SPORTS AND LEISURE

Drumcliffe Walk – A pleasant wooded walk from the river bridge in Donegal downstream along the north bank of the River Eske overlooking the estuary.

Rossnowlagh Strand is ideal for bathing, surfing and horse riding.

Bundoran town beach can be dangerous but there are sandy beaches for bathing (up and down the coast).

Indoor facilities at **Waterworld** (Bundoran) – tidal wave, aqua volcano, tornado slide, water rapids, sea-based treatments; sea baths and health suite – Open Jun-Aug, daily, 10am-7pm; Apr-May and Sep, Sat-Sun; also Easter week. €7 (including sauna/steam rooms). Refreshments. ☎ 072 41172; Fax 072 42168; aquamara@eircom.net; www.waterworldbundorran.com

EVENTS AND FESTIVALS

Ballyshannon Folk and Traditional Music Festival – Irish music concerts in marquee; open-air concerts; busking competition and workshops (early August)

🛈 *Quay Street, Donegal. Open Jul-Aug, daily; Jun and Sep, Mon-Sat.* ☎ *073 21148; Fax 073 22762; donegaltourism@eircom.net; irelandnorthwest@eircom.net; www.ireland-northwest.travel.ie*
🛈 *Main Street, Bundoran. Open Jul-Aug, daily; Jun and Sep, Mon-Sat.* ☎ *072 41350; irelandnorthwest@eircom.net; www.ireland-northwest.travel.ie*

Adjacent Sights: See BUNCRANA, DONEGAL GLENS, ENNISKILLEN, LONDON-DERRY.

Background

Donegal (*Dún na nGall* - the fort of the foreigners) was established by the Vikings. It then became the stronghold of the O'Donnell clan for 400 years until the flight of the Earl of Tyrconnell in 1607. In 1610 it was granted by the English Crown to Sir Basil Brooke who rebuilt the O'Donnell castle to suit his own requirements and laid out the new Plantation town round the triangular Diamond.

The Irish mounted an unsuccessful attack during the 1641 rebellion; during the Williamite war the town was burned by the Jacobite Duke of Berwick but the castle held out. In 1798 two French ships, carrying reinforcements for General Humbert's army *(see Killala)*, anchored in Donegal Bay but cut their cables on learning of his defeat. The anchor abandoned by the *Romaine* is now displayed on the quay.

Worth a Visit

Donegal Castle★

Donegal Castle

*The Diamond. (Dúchas) (&)
Open mid-Mar to Sep, daily,
10am (2pm Sun) to 6pm
(5.15pm last admission). Closed
25-26 Dec. €3. Guided tour
(30min) every hour. Leaflet
(6 languages). Parking*
☎ *073 22405; Fax 073 22436*
The castle overlooks the town from a bluff on the south bank of the River Eske. The O'Donnell stronghold consisted of a tower house which was largely destroyed by Hugh Roe O'Donnell in 1604 to prevent it falling into the hands of the English. The remains were incorporated into the splendid five-gabled Jacobean mansion built in the courtyard by Sir Basil Brooke, who also built the gatehouse. Above the original entrance to the O'Donnell tower a large mullioned bay window was inserted to light the great hall on the first floor; its stone chimney piece is carved with the Brooke family coat of arms. The rooms are furnished in the style of the 1650s and present visual histories of the O'Donnell and Brooke families.

SLIDE FILE, Dublin

Donegal Railway Heritage Centre

Open Jun-Sep, daily, 10am (2pm Sun) to 5.30pm; Oct-May, Mon-Fri, 10am-5pm, Sat-Sun by appointment. €3. ☎ *073 22655; Fax 073 23843; www.cdrrs.future.easyspace.com*
An exhibition in the old station house traces the history of the narrow-gauge County Donegal Railway, once an integral and much-loved part of the county's landscape. From 1900 until its closure in 1959 its steam and later diesel trains took market produce, farmers, fishermen, shoppers and schoolchildren along the route from Derry and Strabane to the Atlantic Coast. Displays include photographs, contemporary film footage, timetables and a 1940s model of part of the railway. Carriages are being restored with a view to operating vintage train rides on a reopened stretch of scenic line.

Donegal Friary (Abbey)

On the south bank of the estuary over-looking Donegal Bay are the ruins of a **Franciscan house** founded in 1474 by Red Hugh O'Donnell and his wife Nuala and famous as a centre of learning. The buildings were greatly damaged by an explosion in 1601 when the friary was occupied by the English who had the temerity to use it as an arsenal. The friary church was used for Anglican worship until the present church in cut stone was built in 1828 beside the castle.

> **FOUR MASTERS**
>
> The four masters were Michael O'Cleary (b 1580), a Franciscan from Donegal Abbey, and three lay Gaelic scholars, who compiled the *Annals of the Kingdom of Ireland*, an account of Irish history known as the Annals of the Four Masters; the work was done in the 17C while the authors were in refuge at a Franciscan house by the River Drowes south of Bundoran *(see below)*. They are commemorated by the obelisk erected in 1967 in the Diamond in the town centre, and are also recalled in the dedication of the Roman Catholic church which was built in 1935 in local red granite in the Irish Romanesque style.

Excursions

SOUTH OF DONEGAL

Drive of 22mi/36km – half a day. From Donegal take N 15 S. After 4mi/6.4km in Ballintra turn right onto R 231 to Rossnowlagh.

Rossnowlagh Strand★★

A small village and a large hotel overlook the great sweep of sand (2.5mi/4km) which is excellent for bathing, surfing and horse riding; northwest across Donegal Bay rises Slieve League *(see p 202)*.

Continue S on R 231.

Abbey Assaroe

In the late 12C **Cistercian monks** from Boyle Abbey settled by the Erne estuary. The history of their monastery is retold in an audio-visual presentation at **Water Wheels** in the in the old monastic mill (restored).

Ballyshannon

The town, which was created a Borough by Royal Charter in 1613, is set on a steep slope guarding an important crossing point on the **River Erne** close to its mouth. In 1597 the English under Sir Conyers Clifford *(see Boyle)* were defeated here by Red Hugh O'Donnell. Ballyshannon's contemporary fame is due to its extremely popular Folk and Traditional Music Festival, held in late July/early August.

William Allingham (1824-89), the poet, was born in the Mall and is buried in St Anne's churchyard at the top of the hill. Another famous native was "Speaker" Conolly *(see p 321)*, son of a local publican.

From Ballyshannon take N 15 S.

Bundoran (Bun Dobhráin)

Attracting crowds of holidaymakers from Northern Ireland, Bundoran is one of the country's major seaside resorts with a fine view across Donegal Bay to Slieve League; to the south rises the distinctive square mass of Benbulben north of Sligo. The rocks at the north end of the resort have been fashioned into strange shapes by the waves. On the cliffs above there is a golf course where for many years Christy O'Connor was the professional.

Donegal Coast★★

Facing the full force of Atlantic gales in winter, this remote and rugged coastline of deep sea-inlets, jagged cliffs and sandy beaches is backed by spectacular mountains and blanket bog. Its pristine landscapes are largely intact, hardly disfigured by modern development; on the north coast the land is divided into fields by walls of huge round stones and dotted with tiny white houses, each with its own turf stack; the thatched roofs are roped down against the furious winter weather.

Location

Michelin Atlas p 100 and Map 712 – F, G, H, I 2, 3 – Co Donegal.

The roads along the Donegal Coast are narrow and winding; progress is slow but the views are ample compensation.

🅱 *Dunglow. Open Jun-Aug, daily.* ☎ *075 21297; irelandnorthwest@eircom.net; www.ireland-northwest.travel.ie*

Adjacent Sights: See BUNCRANA, DONEGAL, DONEGAL GLENS, LONDONDERRY.

Directory

Getting About

Ferry to Arranmore – *Operates from Burtonport: Jun-Aug, Mon-Sat, 8 sailings daily (7 in Jun); Sun and church hols, 7 sailings daily (6 in Jun); from Aranmore: Jun-Aug. Mon-Sat, 8 sailings daily (6 in June); Sun and church hols, 7 sailings daily (6 in June); fewer sailings out of season, details by phone. Return €8.89. (pedestrian), €25.39 (car and driver), €35.55. (car and family).* ☎ 075 20532; Fax 075 20750; www.travel.ireland.ie

Ferry to Tory Island – *Operates (weather permitting) Bunbeg - Tory Island (1hr 30min): Jun-Aug, daily, once; Oct, daily, once; Nov-May, once daily; Tory Island - Bunbeg (1hr 30min): Jun-Aug, daily, once. Magheroarty - Tory Island (45min): Jun, twice daily; Jul-Aug, 3 times daily. Tory Island - Magheroarty (45min): Jun, 3 times daily; Jul-Aug, 4 times daily. Return €19.05. Coastal Cruises from Bunbeg: Operate on request. Coastal Cruises from Magheroarty (Meenlaragh): Operate on request.* ☎ 074 35502 and 074 35920 *(accommodation on Tory Island).* ☎ 074 35061 *(Magheroarty Pier Office).* ☎ 075 31991 *(Bunbeg Pier Office); 31320 and 31340; Fax 075 31665 (Donegal Coastal Cruises (Turasmara Teo), Strand Road, Middletown, Derrybeg, Co Donegal).*

Donegal Airport at Carrickfin ☎ 075 48284

Where to Stay

• Budget

Atlantic House – *Main St, Dunglow -* ☎ 075 21061 - *Fax 075 21061 - jcannon@iol.ie - Closed 20-30 Dec - 8 rm €30/60* ⌘. In a conveniently central location, this little hotel offers clean, simple and affordable accommodation. There's a cosy lounge next to the breakfast room and the owners run a friendly house.

• Moderate

Ostan Gweedore – *Bunbeg -* ☎ 075 31177 - *Fax 075 31726 - ostangweedore@ireland.com - Restricted opening in winter -* 🅿 ✕ *- 36 rm, 3 suites €80/150* ⌘ *- Restaurant €19/48.25.* Few will fail to be impressed by the stunning views of Gweedore Bay enjoyed from this well-equipped hotel. It enjoys comprehensive leisure facilities as well as comfortable, modern bedrooms. Traditional menu served in the formal dining room.

Where to Eat

• Moderate

The Mill – *Dunfanaghy - 0.5mi/0.8km SW on N 56 -* ☎ 074 36985 - *themillrestaurant@oceanfree.net - Restricted opening in winter and closed Mon -* 🅿 ✕ *- €33/35.* A converted flax mill in a super location on New Lake, with terrific views of Mount Muckish. Pleasant bedrooms and a pretty restaurant with modern Irish cooking.

Shopping

The famous **Donegal tweed** is on sale in several centres – Donegal, Kilcar, Ardara and Downies; carpets are made in Killybegs (see below).

Sports and Leisure

Beaches at Naran and Portnoo. Angling in Glenties at the confluence of the Owenea and Stracashel Rivers.

Hillwalking in the Donegal Highlands – Daily walks (mid-Jul to mid-Aug) – ☎ 073 30248 ; 073 30348; oidsgael@iol.ie; www.oideas-gael.com

Events and Festivals

International Mary from Dungloe Festival – *Dungloe. One week late-Jul to early-Aug.* Music, dancing, entertainment and craic.

Tracing Ancestors

Donegal Ancestry – *Old Steamboat Store, The Quay, Rathmelton* – Family history research centre – *See Rathmelton below*

Tour

DONEGAL TO LETTERKENNY

Donegal to Naran

Drive of 70mi/113km – 1 day
From Donegal take N 56 W. West of Dunkineely, after the turning to St John's Point, turn left; park beyond the old railway embankment.

Killaghtee Cross

In the graveyard of the ivy-covered ruins of Killaghtee Church (12C) stands a 7C **cross-slab**.
Return to N 56 and continue W. After 3mi/4.8km turn left.

Killybegs

Set on a steep hill where the River Strager enters a deep sea-inlet, this bustling little harbour town is one of the country's foremost fishing ports, especially lively at the end of the day when boats from many nations unload their catch.

Killybegs is also famous for the hand-tufted carpets which were first produced in the middle of the 19C.

Within the gates of St Catherine's Church *(turn right uphill; car park)*, which was designed by JB Papworth in about 1840, stands the **tomb slab** *(left)* of Niall Mor MacSweeney; allies of the O'Neills, the MacSweeneys originally came to Ireland as gallowglasses, and the slab shows several of these hardy Scottish mercenaries.

Continue W on R 263; after 3mi/4.8km turn left onto the Coast Road.

Kilcar (Cill Cárthaigh)

Kilcar is a centre for Donegal tweed; visitors can watch the weaving and buy the cloth. It stands where two rivers meet in a narrow sea-inlet with several sandy beaches in the vicinity.

Continue W. In Carrick turn left to Teelin (Teileann); take the second right to Bunglass, a steep, narrow, gated road (passing places).

Cliffs of Bunglass★★

The road leads to one of the most spectacular sights in the whole country, an awe-inspiring prospect of ocean, mountain, and some of the highest cliffs in Europe. After climbing steeply (over 1 000ft/305m) and skirting Lough O'Mulligan the road reaches the cliff top (car park). The cliffs of Bunglass themselves rise 300m from the sea, but they face the south flank of **Slieve League** (1 972ft/601m) dropping sheer into the water. In winter the cliffs seem dark and menacing but on a fine day the sunlight picks out the different hues of the minerals in the rock face.

Return to Carrick and turn left onto R 263. After 2mi/3.2km bear left to Malin Beg (Málainn Bhig).

Glenmalin Court Cairn

Park in the road; 5min return on foot over the stile and along the concrete path. In marshy ground beside a small stream are the substantial remains of a court tomb, known locally as Cloghanmore, meaning the Big Stone.

Continue to the crossroads; turn left along the coast.

Trabane Strand★

Car park; steep steps. The sheltered sandy bay faces south across Donegal Bay to Benbulben *(see SLIGO).*

Return to the crossroads and go straight ahead to Glencolumbkille.

Glencolmcille Folk Village★★

&. *Guided tour (20min) Apr-Sep, daily, 10am (noon Sun) to 6pm, every 30min. €2.75. Brochure. Nature walk. Tourist information. Bureau de change. Parking. Tearoom. Craft shop.* ☎ *073 30017, 073 39026; Fax 073 30334; folkmus@indigo.ie; www.infowing.ie/donegal/Ad/Fr.htm*

The folk village was one of the many initiatives undertaken by the enterprising Father James McDyer (d 1987). Deeply concerned by the plight of his flock in this poor and remote area, he succeeded in bringing electricity to the area, improving the roads, and also set up a number of cooperative ventures. The three cabins of the folk village, each appropriate to a certain period – the 1720s, the 1820s and the 1920s – are furnished to reflect the local way of life: household utensils, tools for spinning and weaving, items from the dairy, turf spades and fishing tackle. Local history can be traced in the School House. Local preserves are on sale and available for tasting in the **Shebeen**.

The ordinary village of Glencolumbkille *(Gleann Cholm Cille)* lies inland from its sandy beaches guarded by a Martello tower on Glen Head (745ft/227m). In this remote and rugged valley St Columba *(Colmcille* in Irish – *see p 208)* built himself a retreat house for quiet prayer. On his feast day (9 June) pilgrims make a penitential tour (3mi/5km) of the glen between midnight and three in the morning stopping at the Stations of the Cross, which are marked by cairns, boulders, pagan standing stones and early Christian cross-slabs. It makes an attractive walk at any time.

On the edge of the village stands the **Ulster Cultural Institute** *(Foras Cutúir Uladh)*, a centre for Gaelic studies and activities, with a display on local archaeology, an archive of traditional music and a shop selling Gaelic books and tapes. &. *Open Mon-Fri, 9.30am-5pm; also Sat-Sun in summer. Restaurant.* ☎ *073 30248; Fax 073 30348; Oidsgael@iol.ie; www.Oideas-Gael.com*

Take the road to Ardara. After 10mi/16km viewing point (left).

Glengesh Pass★★

Car park at viewpoint. From the head of the pass there is a fine view of the glaciated, green valley, enclosed between steep and rugged mountains. Hairpin bends carry the road down to join the river.

Ardara (Ard an Rátha)

Ardara (pronounced with the accent on the last syllable) is an attractive market town on the Owentocker River at the head of a deep sea-inlet. It is an important centre for the production and sale of homespun Donegal tweed. The **Ardara Heritage Centre** traces the history of the locality and, in particular, of the tweed industry, its devastation by government export restrictions in 1699 and its 19C revival, largely due to the efforts of philanthropists Ernest and Alice Hart. Weaving demonstrations are given and the products – rugs, jumpers etc – are on sale. *Open Easter-Sep, daily, 10am (2pm Sun) to 6pm. Audio-visual show (15min). Tearoom.* ☎ *075 41704*

Take N 56 E.

Glengesh Pass

Glenties (na Gleannta)
Glenties is the home town of Patrick MacGill (1890-1963), known as the "Navvy Poet" because of his uncompromising depictions of the hard life led by migrant labourers; he is honoured in a festival each August.

St Conall's Museum and Heritage Centre is housed partly in purpose-built premises and partly and most unusually in the adjoining Courthouse (1843) which contains the original courtroom, still used once a month, and three basement cells. It gives a thorough account of local history with an array of artefacts of all kinds from all periods. *Open Apr-Oct, Mon-Sat, 10am-1pm and 2-5pm. €2.50. Parking.* ☎ *075 51114*

Opposite the museum stands **St Conall's Church** (Roman Catholic), one of Liam McCormick's masterpieces of modern architecture; beneath the steep pitched roof the windows descend to floor level revealing the surrounding water garden; the detached triangular shingled belfry echoes the sheltering conifers.

Take N 56 west. In Maas take R 261 west; after 3mi/5km turn right.

The twin resorts of **Naran** and **Portnoo**, which face Inishkeel in Gweebarra Bay, provide broad sandy beaches, cliff walks, surfing, sailing, fishing and golf.

Naran to Dunfanaghy
70mi/113km – 1 day
E of Naran take R 261 E. In Maas take N 56 N.
A long bridge spans the beautiful **Gweebarra Estuary★**.
Continue N on N 56.

The Rosses★
Dunglow *(An Clochán Liath)* is an attractive small town, known as the capital of The Rosses, a bleak flat rocky Gaelic-speaking region (100sq mi/2560m²) which is dotted with over 100 tiny lakes.
Take R 259 NW.

Burtonport (Ailt an Chorráin)
This remote and tiny harbour provides a regular ferry service *(2mi/3.2km)* to Arranmore Island *(see Directory)*.

Arranmore Island
The island has an annual festival in August. The scenic attractions are rugged cliffs on the northern and western shores, and several lakes. There are six pubs which hold regular traditional music sessions; local crafts – including Aran knitwear – are on sale.
Continue N on R 259. In Crolly turn left onto N 56. After 1mi/1.6km turn left onto R 258; turn left to Bunbeg.

Bunbeg (An Bun Beag)
Beyond the signal tower on the narrow winding Clady estuary is this lovely little harbour, well protected from the Atlantic storms; old warehouses line the quay. Boats sail from here to Tory Island *(see below)*.
Take R 257 N.

Bloody Foreland Head

The headland owes its name to the reddish colour of the rocks, which is enhanced by the evening sun.

Beyond the headland is a wild and remote area with many abandoned houses. Offshore Inishbofin and its sister islands point north towards Tory Island.

Tory Island (Toraigh)

Access by boat from Meenlaragh (Magheroarty) and Gortahork (see Directory); from Gortahork follow the signs (Bloody Foreshore) and turn right down a steep hill to the pier. Frequently cut off from the mainland, bleak and windswept Tory Island *(7mi/11km from the mainland)* is inhabited by Gaelic-speaking fishermen who have been ruled since time immemorial by their "king". Little is left of the monastery founded in the 6C by **St Columba** *(Colmcille)*: a round tower, a Tau cross and two ruined churches. At the Tory School of Primitive Art islanders produce striking paintings in a "folk" style, including depictions of ships at sea, in strong, simple shapes and colours. Examples can be seen at the Glebe House *(see Donegal Glens)*.

Turn left onto N 56.

Ballyness Bay

This sheltered sea-inlet is overlooked by two Gaelic-speaking villages, **Gortahork** *(Gort an Choirce)* and **Falcarragh** *(An Fál Carrach)*.

Dunfanaghy

This trim little town, sited on a flat isthmus in the shelter of Horn Head, was a busy fishing port until the harbour silted up; it is now a seaside resort, with extensive sandy beaches and facilities for sailing, surfing, water-skiing and fishing. The mock-Tudor **Workhouse** was one of many built all over the country in the 1840s; the displays evoke the Famine and its horrific impact on the locality, all the more effectively by being seen through the eyes of one Hannah Harraty, who survived hunger, a wicked stepmother, a life of beggary, and lived to the age of 90. *(& ground floor only) Open mid-Mar to mid-Oct, daily, 10am (noon Sun) to 5pm. €4. Coffee shop.* ☎ *074 36540; Fax 074 36575; janis@theirishfamine.com; theirishfamine.com*

Horn Head Scenic Route★

30min – viewpoint. The headland, a breeding colony for a great variety of seabirds, rises to high cliffs (over 600ft/183m) on the north coast; there is a blow-hole known as McSwyne's Gun *(SW)*.

The narrow road circles the headland giving magnificent **views**: *(W)* Inishbofin, Inishdooey and Inishbeg, three islands, backed by Bloody Foreland Head; *(NW)* Tory Island further offshore; *(E)* Sheep Haven Bay backed by the Rosguill Peninsula *(see below)*; *(NE)* Melmore Head and Malin Head and on a clear day, Scotland; *(inland)* Muckish Mountain and Errigal Mountain.

Dunfanaghy to Letterkenny

80mi/130km – 1 day
From Dunfanaghy take N 56 E.

Portnablagh

From a scattered fishermen's hamlet Portnablagh began to develop into a seaside resort with the opening of the Portnablagh Hotel in 1923. The golf course is a links course designed in 1905 by Harry Vardon.

Ards Forest Park

The park (1 188 acres/481ha) is based on the extensive and beautiful estate which once belonged to the prominent Stewart family of Scottish descent. It extends along the north shore of the Ards Peninsula, rising to a headland, Binnagorm, overlooking Sheep Haven Bay with its bathing beaches. The many and varied delights of the park, all accessible by waymarked footpaths, include the Derryart River, fenland, sand dunes, salt-marsh, a red deer enclosure, a dolmen, ringforts, viewpoints, and Lough Lilly, where white and yellow water lilies flower in August.

Continue S on N 56.

Creeslough

The village sits in the shadow of Muckish Mountain (2 197ft/670m), which is ingeniously reflected in the shape of **St Michael's Church** (Roman Catholic), another of Liam McCormick's outstanding modern churches, designed in 1971. In the early 20C, artists and writers such as William Butler Yeats, AE Russell, Percy French and GK Chesterton were frequent visitors to Creeslough.

In Creeslough turn left (E) onto a minor road.

Doe Castle★

(Dúchas) Scheduled to reopen during 2004. Parking. ☎ *074 38124 (Caretaker); 074 38445 (Castle)*

The ruined castle stands in a strategic and beautiful position on a promontory in Sheep Haven Bay protected by the sea and a rock-cut moat which was spanned by a drawbridge. A bawn encloses a four-storey keep to which an L-shaped building, two round towers and a Great Hall were added later. It is difficult to date as it was frequently attacked, damaged and repaired until its military importance declined after the Battle of the Boyne (1690). Towards the end of the 18C it was made habitable by General George Vaughan Harte, who had served with distinction in India and who mounted several cannon from the Siege of Serringapatam on the turrets and seafront.

The **tomb slab** standing against the tower near the entrance gate is carved with an elaborate cross, and may have belonged to one of the McSweeneys, sometime lords of the castle; until 1968 it stood in the ruins of the neighbouring Franciscan monastery.

On leaving the castle turn left over a hump-backed bridge; turn left onto R 245.

Carrigart (Carraig Airt)
The village is a popular seaside resort on a deep inlet.
Take R 248 NW.

Rosguill Peninsula Atlantic Drive★
9mi/14.5km. The **Atlantic Drive** is a modern road built to open up the scenic delights of the Rosguill Peninsula. From the great curve of sand dunes flanked by the Rosapenna golf links, the road climbs to **Downies** (*Na Dúnaibh*), a resort and centre for Donegal tweed, and then skirts the high ground overlooking *(W)* the deep inlet of Sheep Haven Bay backed by Horn Head, *(NW)* the sheltered beach of Tranarossan Bay, *(N)* the promontory extending to Melmore Head and *(E)* the sandy coves and islands in Mulroy Bay.
In Carrigart take R 245 E.

The road follows the wooded west shore of Mulroy Bay to **Millford**, a good centre for fishing in Lough Fern and the Leannan River *(2mi/3.2km SW).*
In Millford turn left onto R 246. 2mi/3.2km N of Carrowkeel fork left onto the coast road.

Fanad Peninsula
A string of hamlets lines the east shore of Mulroy Bay and Broad Water. North of Kindrum where iodine was extracted from seaweed in the 19C, grass-covered dunes, dotted with white cottages and small lakes, extend to the sandy shore. The lighthouse on Fanad Head *(no access)* marks the entrance to Lough Swilly. Dunaff Head, the Urris Hills and Dunree Head come into view on the opposite shore. **Portsalon** is a small resort at the north end of Warden Beach.
From Portsalon take R 246; after 1mi/1.6km turn left onto the coast road.

Knockalla Viewpoint★
Car park. The north end of Knockalla Mountain (1 194ft/364m) provides a superb **view**.
At the junction bear left onto R 247.

Rathmullan (Ráth Maoláin)
This pretty little place facing Lough Swilly has witnessed more than its share of key events in Irish history. In 1587, at a time when the old Gaelic order still prevailed here in the north, "Red" Hugh O'Donnell, the future lord of Tyrconnell, was lured aboard an English vessel and spirited off to imprisonment in Dublin, a treacherous

Rathmelton Bridge

H Champollion/MICHELIN

act which helped precipitate the following years of warfare. Then in 1607 it was from Rathmullan that the "Flight of the Earls" took place, when Hugh O'Neill and Rory O'Donnell went on board ship with their families on their way into permanent exile on the Continent. The departure of these outstanding representatives of the native aristocracy marked the end of an era, opening the door for the Plantation of Ulster by settlers from England and Scotland. In 1798 the attempts by Wolfe Tone to overthrow British rule finally came to an end when he was captured aboard a French warship and brought ashore near Rathmullan.

The old Napoleonic battery beside the pier is now the **Flight of the Earls' Exhibition**, with displays making the most of these stirring encounters with history. (&) *Open daily, 10am (noon Sun) to 5pm. €2.50. 074 58178 or 58131; Fax 074 58458; info@theflightoftheearls.com; www.theflightoftheearls.com*

Continue SW on R 247.

Rathmelton* (Ráth Mealtain)

With the English look of a typical Plantation town about it, Rathmelton stands on a salmon river flowing into Lough Swilly and was founded early in the 17C by a member of the Stewart family. The Mall, an attractive tree-lined street, along the south bank of the river, opens into the Square. Among the 18C warehouses lining the quay is the old Steamboat Store housing the **Rathmelton Story** exhibition and the **Donegal Ancestry** centre. *Open Jul-Aug, daily, 9.30am (2pm Sun) to 6pm; Sep-Jun, Mon-Fri, 9am-4.30pm (3.30pm Fri); last admission 1hr before closing. Genealogy service.* ☎ *074 51266; Fax 074 51702; donances@indigo.ie; www.indigo.ie/~donances*

The ruined 17C church at the top of the hill contains an interesting Perpendicular east window as well as Romanesque carving brought from Aughnish Island further down the creek. The Revd Francis Mackemie, Rector in Rathmelton until he emigrated in 1683 to Virginia in America, where he founded the first Presbyterian church, is recalled in the name of the **Mackemie Hall** *(Back Lane)*, a former **meeting house** which now houses the library.

Take R 245 S to Letterkenny.

Donegal Glens

The centre of County Donegal is mountainous country traversed by long and sometimes serpentine glens: the Barnesmore Gap running south of the Blue Stack Mountains (2 205ft/672m) to Donegal, the Barnes Gap north of Kilmacrenan to the east of Muckish Mountain (2 197ft/670m), and Muckish Gap at the foot of the south face. The most spectacular of the high peaks is Errigal (2 466ft/752m), a cone of white quartzite, which towers over Dunlewy. Although Lifford is the county town, Letterkenny is larger, and, owing to its position, is a good centre from which to tour the county.

Location

Michelin Atlas p 100 and Map 712 – I 3 – Co Donegal – Local map below. Most of the roads follow the course of the rivers through the glens. N 15 runs between Donegal and Letterkenny which is linked by N 13 to Londonderry over the border.

🅱 *Derry Road, Letterkenny. Open Jul-Aug, daily; Jun and Sep, Mon-Sat; Oct-May, Mon-Fri.* ☎ *074 21160; Fax 074 25180; donegaltourism@eircom.net; irelandnorthwest@eircom.net; www.ireland-northwest.travel.ie*

Adjacent Sights: See BUNCRANA, DONEGAL, DONEGAL COAST, LONDONDERRY.

Worth a Visit

Listed in rough clockwise order from Letterkenny

Letterkenny

Large by local standards, and with a good range of local facilities, this otherwise undistinguished town on the River Swilly has the longest main street in Ireland and is the seat of the bishop of the Roman Catholic diocese of Raphoe. The vast Gothic Revival **Cathedral** has an interior with a somewhat uneasy mixture of neo-Celtic carving and Italianate decor.

The **County Museum** *(High Road)*, which is housed in the old 19C workhouse, traces the folk life and traditions of Donegal, its history, archaeology and geology. & *Open Mon-Fri, 10am-12.30pm and 1-4.30pm, Sat, 1-4.30pm.* ☎ *074 24613; Fax 074 26522; museum@donegalcoco.ie; donegalcountymuseums@eircom.net*

Directory

WHERE TO STAY

• Budget

Ballyraine Guesthouse – Ramelton Rd, Letterkenny - 1.75mi/2.8km E by N 14 on R 245 - ☎ 074 24460 - Fax 074 20857 - ballyraineguesthouse@eircom.net - 🖪 ✕ - 8 rm €38/60 ⌷. This recently built house sits in the suburbs of this busy little market town. Wooden floors feature in the well-kept sitting room and breakfast room while the bedrooms are well equipped and generously proportioned.

Villa Rose – Main St, Ballybofey - Closed 25-26 Dec - ☎ 074 32266 - Fax 074 30666 - villarose@oceanfree.net - ✕ 🖧 - 16 rm €60/98 ⌷ - Restaurant €17.20/24.70. Right in the middle of the high street, this privately owned purpose-built hotel provides neat and affordable accommodation and, with just 16 bedrooms, it has a friendly feel. A traditional menu is offered in the evening.

SPORTS AND LEISURE

Fishing – Cod and pollack in Lough Swilly; salmon, sea trout and brown trout in Crana River.

Rambling – Errigal, the highest mountain in Donegal; from the tiny summit almost all of Donegal and much of the neighbouring counties is within view. The "tourist route" to the summit starts off the R 251 at the lay-by before a sign to Altan Farm. There is no regular track on the lower slopes; walkers must climb the lowest part of the southeast ridge and bear left; on reaching the lower screes, follow a faint track winding steeply upwards. It takes about 4hr 30min to climb to the summit and back.

Hillwalking in the Donegal Highlands – Daily walks (mid-Jul to mid-Aug) – ☎ 073 30248 ; 073 30348; oidsgael@iol.ie; www.oideas-gael.com

Greyhound racing – At Lifford.

TRACING ANCESTORS

Seat of Power Visitor Centre – Lifford (see below). Genealogical centre within the Visitor Centre.

Newmills

(Dúchas) Open early-Jun to late-Sep, daily, 10am-6.30pm (5.45pm last admission). €2.50. Parking. ☎ 074 25115
The corn mill and flax mill were operated by the water power of the River Swilly. The tour explains how the corn was dried and milled and how the flax was treated by retting, rolling, scutching and buffering to produce linen thread.

Lake Finn

19mi/31km west of Letterkenny by R 250 to Fintown. From the roadside village, which faces the lovely Aghla Mountains across the lake, a track leads down to the pier, where paddle boats are available for hire. Another entertaining way of exploring the lakeside scenery is by taking a ride on the restored narrow-gauge **Fintown Railway** (30min there and back). The bumpy and noisy vintage snub-nosed railcar, which gives the railway its name, **Black Pig Train** (An Mhuc Dhubh), is somewhat at odds with the serenity of its surroundings. 🖧 Operates May-Sep, daily, 11am-5pm. €2.54. ☎ 075 46280

Colmcille Heritage Centre

Church Hill; car park. 🖧 Open Easter and May to early-Oct, daily, 10.30am (1pm Sun) to 6.30pm; otherwise by appointment. €2. Guided tour (15min) available. Audioguide available. Brochure. Audio-visual show (4 languages). Parking. Tearoom. ☎ 074 37306, 37044
St Columba (**Colmcille** in Irish) was born by Gartan Lough, and the modern building here presents a detailed exhibition on his life and on the evolution of the Celtic church. There are fine examples of modern stained glass showing biblical scenes and a detailed display evoking the devotion and skills which went into the making of illuminated manuscripts.

Glebe House and Gallery★

Church Hill; car park. (Dúchas) (🖧 to ground floor and gallery) Open late-Mar and mid-May to late-Sep, Sat-Thu, 11am-6.30pm (5.30pm last admission). €2.50. Guided tour (35min) available. Parking. Tearoom (summer). ☎ 074 37071; Fax 074 37521
The gallery stands in the attractive lakeside grounds of an old rectory (1828), which was bought by the artist and collector **Derek Hill**, in 1953; he was born in Southampton in 1916 and worked as a stage designer in Munich.
The **gallery** was built in 1982 to house the **Derek Hill Collection** of paintings by 20C artists, consisting of works by important Irish artists and by the inhabitants of Tory Island who paint in a primitive style producing striking "folk" works. Among the artists represented are Braque, Corot, Degas, Picasso, Renoir, Graham Sutherland and JB Yeats.
The **house** is richly furnished with Japanese and Chinese prints, William Morris fabrics, William de Morgan tiles, a Tiffany lamp and Wemyss ware pottery. There is also a bronze bust of Derek Hill by John Sherlock and works by Derek Hill, Victor Pasmore, Basil Blackshaw, Augustus John, Evie and Nathaniel Hone, Sir William Orpen, Oskar Kokoshka, Cecil Beaton and John Bratby.

St Colmcille's Oratory

On the hillside facing southeast over Lough Akibbon are the scanty remains of a monastery associated with St Colmcille: a holy well, two crosses and the ruins of a church in a graveyard.

Glenveagh National Park★★

(Dúchas) (&) Park and Visitor Centre: Open mid-Mar to early-Nov, daily, 10am-6.30pm (5pm last admission). Castle: Guided tour (45min) same days and times. Park €2.50; castle €2.50. Audio-visual show (25min; 5 languages). Leaflet (7 languages). No photography in castle. Parking; minibus between Visitor Centre and Castle (€1 each way). Restaurant; tearoom. Wheelchair access to Visitor Centre, gardens and ground floor of castle. ☎ 074 37090; Fax 074 37072; glenveaghnationalpark@ealga.ie; www.heritageireland.ie

The park (23 887 acres/9 667ha) consists of Lough Beagh and the surrounding wild landscape of bogs, moorland, and rugged mountain clad in natural woodlands of oak and birch; in sharp contrast, on a promontory beside the lake are luxuriant gardens surrounding a romantic castellated castle built of granite hewn from the hillside. The estate was created by John George Adair by the amalgamation of several smaller holdings from which he evicted all the tenants in 1861. In 1937 it was bought by

the Irish-American millionaire Henry McIlhenny, who sold the land to the Irish National Parks Service in 1975 and in 1983 donated the castle and gardens. The **Visitor Centre**, a cluster of grass-topped pavilions, hidden in a depression, traces the history of the park and offers a short audio-visual show about the conservation of the flora and fauna, including the largest herd of **red deer** in Ireland contained by a fence (28mi/45km long).

The beautiful **gardens★★** were begun by Mrs Adair. The planting is designed to provide colour and interest at all seasons; the stone statues and ornaments add a formal note particularly on the **Terrace** (1966) and in the **Italian**

St Columba

St Columba (known in Irish as St Colmcille) (521-597), who was a native of Donegal, was active during the transition from pagan to Christian Ireland. He was born in Gartan of a noble family, the O'Neill, and in accordance with the custom of the times was fostered at Kilmacrenan as a boy. There are several sites in Donegal associated with his life.

Over a period of 15 years he founded monasteries at Tory, Drumcliffe, Kilmore, Swords, Moon and Durrow (553). In c 560 he embraced the white martyrdom by giving up all he loved and left Ireland for Iona off the coast of Scotland, where he established a famous monastic community. He died in 597, the year in which Augustine landed in Kent.

Glenveagh Castle

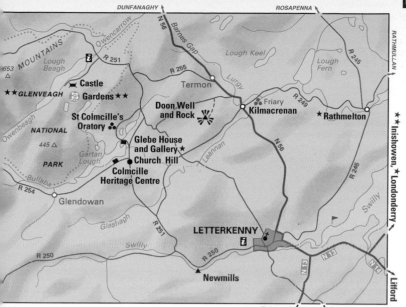

Garden (1958). From the long lawn at the centre of the **Pleasure Grounds**, paths lead up to the **Belgian Walk**, which was constructed during the First World War by convalescent Belgian soldiers staying in the house. The **walled garden** contains an Orangery (1958) designed by Philippe Jullian. From the south end of the gardens there is a long **view** up Lough Beagh to the head of the glen below the peak of Slieve Snaght (2 441ft/683m).

The castellated façade of the **castle** conceals a large Victorian house, designed in 1870 by John Adair's cousin, John Townsend Trench. It was lit by oil lamps until 1957 and heated by a boiler which was fed with turf every three days. The sumptuous furnishings, left by the last American owners, include a carpet woven in Killybegs *(see Donegal Coast)* to match the **drawing room** furnishings; in the Library there are paintings by George Russell, better known as the poet AE.

Dunlewy Centre (Ionad Cois Locha)

Open Easter to early Nov, Mon-Sat, 10.30am-6pm, Sun, 11am-7pm. Guided tour of cottage €4.50. Boat trip with commentary €4.50. Traditional music: Jul-Aug, Tue evening. Restaurant. ☎ *075 31699; Fax 075 31968, dunleweycentre@eircom.net*

On the shore of the lake stands an old weaver's homestead, now this family-oriented visitor centre; it offers weaving displays, a guided tour of the original weaver's cottage, pony treks and special activities such as storytelling boat trips. The restaurant has fine views of Errigal Mountain.

The road from Dunlewy east to Letterkenny *(R 251)* offers wonderful **views** of the lake and its valley, known as the **Poisoned Glen**; a derelict white-stone church forms a striking landmark on the slopes.

Doon Well and Rock

Car park. The rags on the bush show that people still believe in the curative properties long attributed to the well. Until the 16C the **Doon Rock** was the place of inauguration of the O'Donnells, the chiefs of Tirconaill. Its flattened top *(5min there and back on foot)* provides a fine **view** of the surrounding country. It was near here that Sir Cahir O'Docherty *(see p 150)* was shot dead in 1608.

Kilmacrenan

St Columba built the first church here. The site, between the road to Millford and the Leannan River, is now marked by the ruins of a 17C church and traces of Kilmacrenan Friary, which was founded in 1537 by the local chieftain, Manus O'Donnell.

Raphoe

The village of Raphoe (pronounced with the stress on the second syllable) is grouped around its Diamond, an attractive triangular green. In the south corner stands **Raphoe Cathedral**, a Gothic building with 18C tower and transepts, incorporating several carved fragments dating from the 10C to 17C. *Services: Sun, 8am, 12.15pm, 6pm; Wed, 10.30am; Saints' Days, 8pm.* ☎ *074 45226; www.raphoe.com*

The gaunt ruin south of the church was the Bishop's Palace, built in 1636 by Dr John Leslie with flanking towers similar to Kanturk *(see p 319)* and Rathfarnham *(see p 244)* ; it was damaged during the 1641 Rebellion and the Williamite Wars but was repaired, only to be destroyed by fire in 1839.

Beltany Stone Circle

Due south of Raphoe; west up a stone track (sign "Stone Circle"); park at the entrance to The Potato Centre; 10min there and back on foot. Commanding fine views of the surrounding countryside, the stone circle which is about 4ft/1.2m high, dates from the Bronze Age; it consists of 64 stones (150yd/137m circumference) although there were originally many more.

Lifford

The county town's old **courthouse** *(Main Square)*, built in 1746, has been converted into the **Seat of Power Visitor Centre**. This unusually named institution contains a genealogical centre and a display on local history and the evolution of the legal system from the period when the O'Donnell clan held sway, through the Plantation of Ulster to more recent centuries, using models, talking heads, artefacts, audio-visual re-enactments of famous trials and a tour of the prison cells. & *Open Mon-Fri, 9am-4.30pm, Sun, 12.30-4pm. €4.45.* ☎ *074 41733; Fax 074 41228; seatofpower@eircom.net*

Cavanacor House

At Ballindrait, 2mi/3km west of Lifford by N 14; turn left at sign. (&) House: Open Jul-Aug, Tue-Sun and Bank Hols, noon (2pm Sun) to 6pm; also Easter week. €4. Gallery: Open Tue-Sat, noon-6pm. Tearoom. ☎/*Fax 074 41143; joannaok7@hotmail.com; www.b.parsons.edu/~eokane/cavanacorgallery*

This unassuming Plantation house, the oldest dwelling in Donegal, was built c 1611 by Roger Tasker, whose younger daughter Magdalen was the great-great-great-grandmother of James Knox Polk, 11th President of the USA. In 1689, on his way to besiege Derry, **James II** dined under a sycamore in the garden; for this reason he spared the house from destruction when he returned that way in retreat. The outbuildings contain a museum about the history of the house and a display of hand-made pottery.

Drogheda★

Straddling the River Boyne close to its mouth, Drogheda was one of the most important towns of medieval Ireland, with a long and eventful history. It is still a place of some consequence, well located on the Dublin-Belfast road and railway, with varied industries and a harbour. There is an attractive coastline to the north and inland lies the Boyne Valley, with its superlative megalithic tombs and echoes of battle.

Location

Population 24 460 - Michelin Atlas p 93 and Map 712 – M 6 – Co Louth.
Drogheda *(Droichead Átha)*, now bypassed by M 1, is an important bridging point over the River Boyne on the main road north from Dublin (N 1).

Directory

SIGHTSEEING

Walking Tour of Drogheda – See Drogheda Museum below.

WHERE TO STAY

• *Budget*

Tullyesker Country House – *Dundalk Rd - 3.5mi/5.6km N of Drogheda by N 1 -* ☎ *041 983 0430 - Fax 041 983 2624 - mcdonnellfamily@ireland.com - Closed Dec and Jan -* ⌷ ◨ ⤬ *- 5 rm €66* ⌷. This guesthouse enjoys an elevated position on a hillside to the north of the town, providing views of the Boyne Valley. Bedrooms are all a good size and the extensive breakfast served "en famille" allows you to get to know your fellow guests.

Boyne Haven House – *Dublin Rd – 2.5mi/4km SE of Drogheda on N 1 -* ☎ *041 983 6700 - Fax 041 983 6700 - taramcd@ireland.com -* ◨ ⤬ *- 4 rm €50/80* ⌷. A bungalow surroun,ded by a mature garden, just off the main Dublin road. There's a welcoming fire in the pleasant sitting room, and the impressive Irish

breakfast will set you up for the day. Attractively decorated bedrooms.

WHERE TO EAT

• *Moderate*

Keyside Café bar – *The Mall, North Quay -* ☎ *041 984 4878 - Closed Mon - €27/37.* The huge windows of this converted grain warehouse overlook the quay and its wooden floors and exposed brickwork add to its character. The youthful service is enthusiastic and the menu offers modern Irish dishes with some Mediterranean influence.

SHOPPING

Millmount Craft Centre – ☎ *341 984 1960 - Tue-Fri, 10am-5pm.* A group of designers and craftsmen have come together under one roof to celebrate their heritage. In the individual studios one finds original designed jewellery, hand-painted silks, ceramics and knitwear. It's easy to find; it's beneath the 19C Martello Tower.

SPORTS AND LEISURE

Extensive beaches at Bettystown (south)

🏛 *Bus Station, Drogheda. Open daily, May-Sep; Oct, Mon-Sat; 9.30pm-5.30pm.*
☎ *041 983 7070; Fax 041 984 5684; info@drogheda-tourism.ie; www.drogheda-tourism.com*
Adjacent Sights: See BOYNE VALLEY, DUNDALK, FINGAL, KELLS, TRIM.

Background

The town was founded in 911 by the Norsemen, under the Dane Thorgestr. In the late 12C Hugh de Lacy, Lord of Meath, developed it into an important Norman stronghold with two separate parishes, one in the diocese of Armagh and one in Meath. Little remains of the many monasteries which flourished in Drogheda in the Middle Ages and only the **Butter Gate** on Millmount and St Laurence Gate *(see below)* remain of the town walls which were begun in 1234.

Parliament often met in Drogheda and it was during one of these sittings that Poynings' Law *(see Historical Perspective)* was enacted in 1494.

During the Confederate Rebellion Drogheda was twice besieged. In 1641 Sir Henry Tichborne and Lord Moore withstood the forces of Sir Phelim O'Neill until the Earl of Ormond brought relief. When the town was again besieged in 1649 by **Oliver Cromwell** it was stoutly defended by Sir Arthur Aston and 3 000 men. During the siege many people who had taken refuge in St Peter's Church were burned to death when the wooden steeple was set alight. Eventually the city wall was breached on the southeast side of Millmount near St Mary's Church and, according to Cromwell's own estimate, 2 000 died by the sword in the ensuing massacre. Most of the survivors were transported to Barbados.

Walking About

The **town centre** is set on the steep north bank of the river; narrow lanes and flights of steps link the different levels.

St Peter's Church (Roman Catholic)

West Street ♿ *Open daily, 8.30am-7.30pm (9pm Sun-Fri, Jun-Aug; 6pm Sun-Fri, Nov-Feb). Services: Sun, 8am, 11am, noon; Sat, 6.15pm.* ☎ *041 983 8537; Fax 041 984 1351; www.saintpetersdrogheda.ie*

The neo-Gothic building (1881) contains the shrine of Oliver Plunkett (1625-81), Roman Catholic Archbishop of Armagh, who was implicated in the Oates conspiracy, executed for high treason at Tyburn in 1681 and canonised in 1975. As well as his mummified head, there are letters he wrote from Newgate gaol and his cell door.

On leaving the church turn right along West Street; turn left into Old Abbey Lane.

St Mary's Abbey

The roofless nave and crossing tower stand on the oldest monastic site in Drogheda, where, according to tradition, a monastery was founded after St Patrick's visit in 452. In 1206 a Norman settler, Ursus de Swemele and his wife, founded a hospital which was later administered by the Augustinian Friars until the Dissolution in 1543.

From West Street turn right uphill into Fair Street.

Courthouse

On the corner of Fair Street and Bolton Street. The building with its distinctive weather vane was designed by Francis Johnston and completed in 1790.

Walk E along Fair Street and turn left into Magdalene Street.

St Peter's Church (Anglican)

Open by appointment. Services: Mon-Sat 8.30am; Sun, 8.30am and 11.45am. drogheda@armagh.anglican.org; www.drogheda.armagh.anglican.org

This Georgian church of 1753 is the successor to the medieval building burnt by the Cromwellians in the siege of 1649. The porch and spire were added by the

---

OLIVER PLUNKETT (1629-81)

Oliver Plunkett was a member of a notable Anglo-Irish family from Loughcrew *(see p 269)* in Co Meath. He was educated in Rome and trained by his kinsman Patrick, who became Bishop of Meath. In 1670 he was appointed Archbishop of Armagh and Primate of Ireland. Using his family connections with the establishment, particularly Viceroy Berkeley, he began to impose his authority and reverse the effect of years of neglect following the Cromwellian era and the Penal Laws. He travelled extensively in the north of Ireland administering the Sacrament of confirmation; a school was set up for pupils of all ages, priests were ordained, bishops appointed.

In response to a new wave of repression, occasioned by the marriage of Charles II's brother, James Duke of York, to Mary of Modena, a Roman Catholic, Plunkett chose to go into hiding. Anti-monarchists in London accused him of complicity in the "Popish Plot" fabricated by Titus Oates; he was said to have organised an invasion of 40 000 men who would land in Carlingford. Plunkett was arrested in 1679 and brought to trial in Dundalk but no one would give evidence against him. He was later tried in London for treason and condemned to be hung, drawn and quartered at Tyburn. Through the intervention of his friends his body was preserved and eventually various relics were returned to Ireland. He was canonised in 1975.

fashionable architect Francis Johnston in 1793. In the grave-yard, beside the east gate, is a fine example of a cadaver tomb-stone; beyond the gate are three rows of Georgian houses (c 1730) built for clergy widows. *Continue up Magdalene Street and turn right into Upper Magdalene Street.*

Magdalene Tower

The tower (14C) marks the site of a Dominican monastery founded in 1224 by Lucas de Netterville, Archbishop of Armagh, where in 1395 four Irish princes submitted to Richard II. *Continue along Upper Magdalene Street and turn right into King Street; continue into Palace Street and turn left.*

Cadaver tombstone

SLIDE FILE, Dublin

St Laurence Gate★

Uniquely in Ireland, this is a well-preserved three-storey barbican forming part of the 13C gate. The Normans who built it used stone quarried from the walls erected previously by the Vikings. A section of the town wall still stands on the south side. *Walk W along Laurence Street to Shop Street.*

Tholsel

The Tholsel (toll stall) stands at the crossroads in the town centre; a clock tower and a lantern surmount the limestone building (1770) where Corporation meetings and law courts were held until 1889.

Worth a Visit

MILLMOUNT

South Bank.

Generations of rulers left their mark on the eminence dominating the south bank of the Boyne. Quite possibly the site of a passage grave, it was subsequently crowned by an Anglo-Norman motte and then by 18C fortifications. From the Martello Tower there is a fine overall **view** of the town centre on the north bank of the Boyne and of Drogheda's most imposing individual structure, the **railway viaduct** built in 1855 across the Boyne estuary. Until the completion of this splendid structure, passengers travelling between Dublin and Belfast by rail had to leave the train on the south bank and take a coach over the river bridge to join another train on the north side. The point where Cromwell breached the city walls is visible in the churchyard *(SE)* of St Mary's Church (Anglican), which stands on the site of a Carmelite convent.

Drogheda Museum★

(& to ground floor) Open daily, 10am (2.30pm Sun) to 6pm (5.30pm Sun); last tour 1hr before closing. Walking tour on request (approx 1hr - €3). €3.81. Parking. ☎ 041 983 3097; Fax 041 984 1599; info@millmount.net; www.millmount.net

The museum is housed in the old Officers' quarters (1820). The excellent displays cover various aspects of local history: the medieval period; Drogheda's maritime activities; a number of colourful **guild banners**; souvenirs of Friendly Societies and Temperance Groups; Victoriana; domestic utensils set out in a 19C kitchen; obsolete industrial equipment; Battle of the Boyne room; geological collection. The neighbouring Martello Tower was seriously damaged when it was bombarded during the Civil War of 1922; it has now been restored.

Excursion

Whiteriver Mills

Dunleer; 9mi/14.5km north of Drogheda by N 1 and R 132. Open Apr-Sep, daily, 10am (2pm Sun) to 6pm. €3. ☎ 041 685 1141

On the southern edge of Dunleer stands a three-storey 18C mill, which has been lovingly restored to working order; all the processes involved in milling are expertly demonstrated.

Dublin ★★★

Ireland's famous capital – "the fair city" – bestrides the River Liffey and looks seawards to its port and the broad waters of Dublin Bay. The unforgettable outline of the Wicklow Mountains form a magnificent backdrop to the south, while suburbs stretch far inland as well as north to the Ben of Howth and south to Dalkey Headland. Something like a third of the country's population lives in the greater Dublin area, and a disproportionate amount of the country's business is carried out here. Georgian architectural elegance and the increasingly cosmopolitan life of street, café, restaurant and bar make the city an irresistible destination, not just for a weekend, but for longer periods of exploration.

Location

Population 481 854 - Michelin Atlas p 93 and Map 712 – N 7, 8 – Co Dublin.
Dublin *(Baile Átha Cliath)* is set on the east coast, on the estuary of the River Liffey and the shores of Dublin Bay. It forms the hub of the road and rail network and has direct connections with all the major provincial towns. It is served by an international airport (north of the city centre) and by shipping lines from Liverpool, Holyhead and the Isle of Man.
🖪 *For information and accommodation reservations to visitors calling in person:*
Dublin Tourism Centre, Suffolk Street. Open Jul-Aug, daily; Sep-Jun, Mon-Sat.
O'Connell Street, Dublin 1. Open Mon-Sat. Closed Bank Hols.
Dublin Airport, Arrivals Hall. Open daily.
Dún Laoghaire, New Ferry Terminal. Open Mon-Sat.
Dublin 2, Baggot Street Bridge. Open, Mon-Fri. Closed Bank Hols.
Tallaght, The Square, Town Centre. Open Mon-Sat. Closed Bank Hols.
☎ 1850 230 330 (Irish Tourist Board);
☎ 0800 039 7000 (Irish Tourist Board from London);
Fax 020 7493 9065 (from London);
information@dublintourism.ie; www.visitdublin.com
Adjacent Sights: See BOYNE VALLEY, FINGAL, KILDARE, MAYNOOTH, TRIM, WICKLOW MOUNTAINS.

Background

Viking Settlement – The name Dublin is derived from *Dubh Linn*, the Dark Pool at the confluence of the Poddle and the Liffey; the Irish name, *Baile Átha Cliath*, means the city by the hurdle ford. The first permanent settlement beside the Liffey was established at Wood Quay in the 9C by the Vikings, who then spread north of the river where their settlement was known as Oxmantown; at the Battle of Clontarf on the north shore of Dublin Bay in 1014 their power was curbed by Brian Ború *(see p 286)*.

Anglo-Norman Stronghold – After the Anglo-Norman invasion late in the 12C Dublin was granted to the port of Bristol as a trading post by Henry II in 1172. Under constant harassment by the Irish tribes and an unsuccessful invasion (1315-8) by Edward Bruce of Scotland, the extent of the Anglo-Normans' influence waxed and waned but they never lost control of Dublin, which gradually became the seat of Parliament and the centre of government. Early Lord Deputies operated from their own power bases in the Pale – Trim, Maynooth and Kilkenny – but in the 16C Sir Henry Sidney, who was four times Lord Deputy, took up residence in the castle and put it in good repair. Gradually the medieval fortress evolved into an administrative centre and vice-regal court.

Kildare Revolt – The most serious incident occurred in 1534 when Thomas Fitzgerald, known as "Silken Thomas" because of the silk embroidery on his men's apparel, was acting as Vice Deputy during his father's absence in London.

> ### DUBLIN WATERWAYS
> The urban landscape of Dublin is greatly enhanced by the five waterways which traverse the city – **River Liffey**, personified as Anna Livia Pluribella, which flows through the city centre before entering the sea in Dublin Bay; two tributaries, the **River Dodder** on the south bank and the **River Tolka** on the north bank; and two canals, the **Grand Canal** (1757-1803), which passes through the southern suburbs to join the Shannon at Shannon Harbour, north of Birr, and the **Royal Canal** (1790–1817), which passes through the Northside to join the Shannon west of Longford.

Directory

Temple Bar Information Centre, 18 Eustace Street, Temple Bar – Provides a list of interesting things to do and see. & *Open Mon-Fri, 9am-5.30pm.* ☎ *01 671 5717 (24hr Cultureline); 01 677 2255 (office); Fax 01 677 2525; info@temple-bar.ie; www.temple-bar.ie*

GETTING ABOUT

Dublin International Airport – ☎ 01 814 1111.

Aerdart is a bus service from Dublin Airport to the Dart Railway, ☎ *01 849 3016.* Dublin city is served by a bus network and a railway line along the coast.

The **DART** (Dublin Area Rapid Transport) is a **rail service** along the coast (25mi/40km) from Howth in the north to Bray in the south. It serves three stations in central Dublin – Connolly, Tara Street and Pearse. The service operates daily between 6am (9am Sunday) and 11.45pm with trains running every 5–10min during peak times and every 15min off-peak. All-day tickets available at any station – rail only according to distance up to €2.15; rail and bus €7.20. Further details from 35 Lower Abbey Street; ☎ *01 836 6222 (Passenger information); Fax 01 703 4690.*

The **Dublin LUAS System** (scheduled to be in operation by 2003) is a **light rail transit** system with several routes radiating from the city centre – Abbey Street southwest via Drimnagh to Tallaght; St Stephen's Green south via Ranelagh and Dundrum to Sandyford – interlinked with Park and Ride facilities.

Air Link is a bus service operated by Dublin Bus *(see below)* between Dublin Airport and central Dublin; pick-up points – O'Connell Street, Central Bus Station (Store Street); Connolly Railway Station; Parnell Square West.

Dublin Bus (CIE) operates the **bus network** which covers the whole city from the Central Bus Station (Busáras) in Store Street (behind the Custom House); any bus bearing the direction *An Lár* is going to the city centre. The price of a single ticket varies according to the number of stages from €1.65 to 75c. All-day tickets available either exclusively for bus travel or for bus and rail travel combined – bus only €4.50; all-day bus and rail €7.20. All-day tours are available (north along the coast to Howth and Malahide; south along the coast to Bray and Greystones returning inland via Enniskerry. Further details from Dublin Bus, 59 Upper O'Connell Street, Dublin 1; ☎ *01 873 4222; 01 703 3028 (ticket sales); Fax 01 703 3077; www.dublinbus.ie*

Nitelink buses run from the City Centre to the suburbs, every Thursday, Friday and Saturday, at midnight, 1am, 2am and 3am. In the city centre there are **paying car parks**, **parking meters**, **pay and display machines** and **disc parking areas**; an electronic panel, advertising parking spaces, is visible from the west side of St Stephen's Green.

There is **no parking on double yellow lines** at any time; no parking on **single yellow lines** during the hours indicated on the time plate; no parking in **clearways and bus lanes** during the hours indicated on the time plate.

Parking bays for the **disabled** may be used only if a disabled parking permit is displayed. Cars parked illegally may be **clamped**; declamping costs approximately €100 payable by phone by credit card only or at the Parking shop (16 Bachelor's Walk, Dublin 1; ☎ *01 602 2500) by credit card, cash or cheque (with cheque card).*

A system of numbered car parks linked to numbered road junctions on the outskirts of Dublin makes it much easier to find the right route into the city centre.

The only toll roads are the Dublin East-Link (€1), which spans the Liffey estuary, and the Dublin West-Link (€1.20), which runs north–south on the western edge of the city. ☎ *01 668 2888 (East-Link); 01 820 2000 (West-Link).*

SIGHTSEEING

A **Supersaver Card**, available from the Dublin Tourism Centre, provides entry to the following tourist attractions and saves up to 30% on admission prices: Dublin's Viking Adventure, Dublin Writers Museum, James Joyce Museum, Shaw Birthplace, Malahide Castle, Fry Model Railway and Newbridge House.

Several companies organise **circular bus tours** of the city centre on an open-top bus comprehensive tour (2hr 45min) including all the famous sights and a running commentary given by an approved guide; **hop-on-hop-off bus tours** giving unlimited travel throughout the day, with the flexibility of stopping off and visiting various sights and then catching a later bus for no extra charge.

Dublin Bus City Tour – *Operates daily, 9.30am-5pm, every 15min; 5-6.30pm, every 30min. No tour 17 Mar, 30 Oct, 25 Dec. Hop-on-hop-off circular tour (16 stops; minimum 1hr 15min) starting from 59 Upper O'Connell Street. €10.* ☎ *01 873 4222; Fax 01 703 3031 (Dublin Bus); info@dublinbus.ie; www.Dublinbus.ie*

Guide Friday Bus Tour – *Operates daily, 9.40am-5.30pm (4pm in winter), every 10-30min (according to the season). Closed 17 Mar, last Mon in Oct, Christmas. Hop-on-hop-off circular tour (approx 1hr 30min) starting from 14 Upper O'Connell Street and including all main attractions. All-day ticket €12.* ☎ *01 605 7705 (reservations), 676 5377 (office); dublin@guidefriday.com; www.guidefriday.com*

Gray Line Bus Old Dublin Tour – *Operates daily, 9.40am-5.30pm (4pm in winter), every 10-30min (according to the season). Closed 17 Mar, last Mon in Oct, Christmas. Hop-on-hop-off circular tour (approx 1hr 30min) starting from 14 Upper O'Connell Street and including all main attractions. All-day ticket €12.* ☎ *01 605 7705 (reservations), 676 5377 (office); dublin@guidefriday.com; www.guidefriday.com*

Gray Line Tours Ireland – *Operate late-Mar to late-Oct, daily at 10am or 2.30pm returning at 2.30pm or 5pm/6.30pm. Half- or whole-day tours from Dublin to Newgrange, Dublin North Coast, Tara, Powerscourt and Glendalough, Glendalough and Wicklow Mountains. Also 3- and 4-day tours to other parts of Ireland. Half-day tour €19-€24; full-day tour €38. ☎ 01 605 7705 (reservations), 01 676 5377 (office); dublin@guidefriday.com; www.guidefriday.com*

More active sightseers may consider a **bicycle tour** (bicycles provided) of Dublin, accompanied by a guide, who will point out the cultural and historical sights and avoid the busier roads. *Bike hire: €12 per day, €60 per week. Guided tour (3hr): Apr-Oct, Sat-Sun, 10am and 2pm; arrive 15min before start time. €19 (including bike hire, insurance and guide). Book in advance by phone, fax or email, or call into the office at The Harding Hotel, Fishamble Street, next to Christ Church Cathedral. Scenic route descriptions available. Rain gear, helmets and baby seats available. ☎ 01 679 0899; Fax 679 6504; info@dublinbiketours.com; www.dublinbiketours.com*

For sightseers prepared to go further afield there are **steam train excursions**, starting from Dublin and travelling to various provincial towns and cities.

Viking Splash Tours – Sightseeing tour of Dublin by land and water in an amphibious military vehicle starting from Bull Alley Street beside St Patrick's Cathedral and entering the water at the Grand Canal Basin in Ringsend – *Operate (75min) mid-Mar to Oct, daily, 10am (10.30am Sun) to 5pm; Mid-Feb to mid-Mar and Nov, less often. €13.50. 01 453 9185; viking@esatclear.ie; www.vikingsplashtours.com*

Full-day and half-day tours to attractions in the Dublin area are organised by various bus companies: **Dublin Bus** (see above); Irish City Tours (see Dublin Tourism).

Three different **heritage trails**, walking tours with historical themes, are organised by Dublin Tourism; further details from the Dublin Tourism Centre or from the website (see above).

To see the famous Dublin landmarks while learning about key events in Irish history, join a specialised walking tour.

Dublin Historical Walking Tour *Operates May-Sep, daily, 11am, and 3pm; Oct-Apr, Fri-Sun, noon. €10. Departs from Trinity College front gate. ☎ 01 878 0227; Fax 01 878 3787; tours@historicalinsights.ie; www.historicalinsights.ie*

1916 Rebellion Walking Tour *Operates mid-Apr to early-Oct, Mon-Sat, 12.30pm and 2pm; Sun, 1pm. €10. ☎ 01 676 2493; 1916@indigo.ie; www.1916rising.com*

Literary Tour *Operates daily at 7.30pm from The Duke public house, Duke Street. €9. info@dublinpubcrawl.com; www.dublinpubcrawl.com*

The Real Irish Pub Crawl *Operates Jul-Aug, Mon, Wed, Sat, 7pm, Sun, 12.30pm from O'Briens/Mercantile Bar, 28 Dame Street, Dublin 2. €8. ☎ 01 493 2676, 088 510 299, 088 212 2020*

Musical Pub Crawl – Details from Dublin Tourism.

Grafton Street in the rain

WHERE TO STAY

• Budget

Oak Lodge – *4 Pembroke Park - ☎ 01 660 6096 - Fax 01 668 1721 - ⊠ - 3 rm €50/65 ⊡.* In a quiet street of red-brick houses with attractive gardens, this little B&B has spacious and tastefully furnished rooms. Good value for this area.

St Jude's Guesthouse – *17 Pembroke Park ☎ 01 668 0928 - Fax 01 668 0928 - 7 rm €50/65 ⊡.* Classically decorated rooms in a red-brick detached house. Family atmosphere and warm welcome.

• Moderate

Gardiner Lodge – *87 Lower Gardiner St - ☎ 01 836 5229 - Fax 01 836 3279 - 15 rm €65/90 ⊡.* This small Georgian hotel is one of the most appealing in this part of town, with a good level of comfort and rooms attractively furnished with antiques. Prices rise considerably at the weekend and in summer.

Anglesea Town House – *63 Anglesea Rd, Dublin 4 - ☎ 01 668 3877 - Fax 01 668 3461 Closed Christmas and New Year - 7 rm €70/130 ⊡.* Guests enjoy a good level of modern facilities and individually styled bedrooms at this red bricked, ivy-clad house in a smart suburb. Clean and comfortable with a bright conservatory breakfast room.

Aston – *7-9 Aston Quay, D2 - ☎ 01 677 9300 - Fax 01 677 9007 - stay@aston-hotel.com - Closed 24-27 Dec - 27 rm €75/165.* Neat, tidy and friendly house, centrally located. All bedrooms are fully ensuite and half of them have views over the river. There's a small lounge and bar in which to relax after the day's exertions.

Kellys – *36-37 South Great George St - ☎ 01 677 9277 - Fax 01 671 3216 - 27 rm €75/90 ⊡.* Old and partly renovated hotel, one of the few family-run hotels in central Dublin. Level of comfort no more than reasonable, but excellent location and friendly reception.

Morehampton Lodge – *113 Morehampton Rd, Donnybrook -* ☎ *01 283 7499 - Fax 01 283 7595 - 18 rm €90/100* ⌷. Huge and comfortable rooms overlooking the gardens of a lovely house dating from around 1900. All rooms have a fridge, hairdryer and iron. Off-street parking.

Jury Inn Christchurch – *Christchurch Pl, D8 -* ☎ *01 454 0000 - Fax 01 454 0012 - jurysinnchristchurch@jurysdoyle.com - Closed 24-26 Dec -* ✱✕ *- 182 rm €96 -* ⌷ *€8.50 - Restaurant €21.50*. What the hotel may lack in individuality, it makes up for in location and value for money. Functional but perfectly comfortable bedrooms. On the western fringes of Temple Bar so a very short walk into the city centre.

Lynam's – *63-64 O'Connell St, D1 -* ☎ *01 888 0886 - Fax 01 888 0890 - lynamhtl@indigo.ie - Closed 22-26 Dec -* ✱✕ *- 41 rm €95/180* ⌷. A pair of Georgian townhouses on the main shopping road so you cannot get more central than this. Some of the bedrooms are a little compact but all are well-looked after and the owner runs a welcoming establishment.

Trinity Lodge – *12 South Frederick St -* ☎ *01 679 5044 - Fax 01 679 5223 - trinitylodge@eircom.net - Closed 22 to 26 Dec - 10 rm, 3 suites €100/190* ⌷. Benefits not only from its city centre location but by being in one of the quieter streets. A modernised Georgian townhouse with clean, comfortable and well-furnished bedrooms.

• **Expensive**

Brownes Townhouse – *22 St Stephen's Green -* ☎ *01 638 3939 - Fax 01 638 3900 - info@brownesdublin.com - Closed 24 Dec to 4 Jan -* ✱✕ ♿ *- 12 rm €170/225* ⌷ *- Restaurant €29.50/36.50*. It would be hard to beat the location of this sympathetically restored Georgian house which overlooks Stephen's Green in the heart of the city. The original staircase and numerous four-poster beds add to the period atmosphere.

WHERE TO EAT

• **Budget**

The Bad Ass Café – *Crown Alley -* ☎ *01 671 2596 -* ⊟ *- €15*. Those after a flavour of Temple Bar and sensory overload should make this their first stop. It's loud, it's brash and it offers an undemanding menu of assorted grilled dishes and pizza.

Roly's Bistro – *7 Ballsbridge Terr -* ☎ *01 668 2611 - ireland@rolysbistro.ie - Closed 25 and 26 Dec - Booking essential - €17.75/38*. A veritable institution and one of the city's most celebrated restaurants. Tables set close together so you virtually rub shoulders with your neighbour but that's all part of its charm. Modern menu; particularly good value lunch.

The Cellar Bar – *Upper Merrion St (at The Merrion Hotel) -* ☎ *01 603 0631 - info@merrionhotel.com - €20/26*. It's best to book for the very popular lunch at this restored Georgian cellar with its vaulted ceiling and exposed brick walls, and a menu that features classic Irish dishes. At night it reverts to a popular bar, with live music on Tuesday nights.

MacGowans – *16 Phibsborough Rd -* ☎ *01 830 6606 -* ⊟ *- €20*. A very busy pub blending Irish exuberance with American food and perhaps not for those watching the calories. Known for its exceptionally long bar and its late opening hours.

• **Moderate**

Cafe Mao – *2-3 Chatham Row -* ☎ *01 670 4899 - info@cafemao.com - Closed Good Fri and 25-Dec - Bookings not accepted - €22.50/29*. Those looking for a culinary change of pace should head for this authentic South East Asian restaurant. Spread over two floors in a clean, fairly minimalist style with vivid, ersatz Warhol prints. Helpful and attentive service assured.

Dobbin's – *15 Stephen's Lane, off Lower Mount St -* ☎ *01 676 4679 - dobbinswinebistro@eircom.net - Closed 1 week Christmas-New Year, Sun, Mon dinner, Sat lunch and Bank Hols -* ▣ *- Booking essential - €23/50.50*. Almost surreal in its incongruity. An imported Nissen hut with sawdust on the floor plonked in the middle of the financial district. The lively and convivial atmosphere bears testament to its reputation as one of the city's institutions.

Bang Café – *11 Merrion Row -* ☎ *01 676 0898 - www.bangrestaurant.com - Closed 1 week Christmas, Sun and Bank Holiday Mon - Booking essential - €23.65/39.20*. Captures the zeitgeist, with a suitably unstuffy atmosphere that matches the bustle of the surrounding streets. Service is chatty and the open-plan kitchen produces a mix of the classical and the more creative.

Nancy Hands Pub & Restaurant – *30-32 Parkgate St -* ☎ *01 677 0149 -* ⊟ *- €25*. Famed for its vast collection of Irish whiskeys and its mildly schizophrenic décor which lends it a certain Victorian charm. Fairly typical pub fare but generously portioned.

Bistro One – *3 Brighton Rd -* ☎ *01 289 7711 - bistroone@eircom.ie - Closed 25-27 and 31 Dec, 1 Jan, Sun and Mon - Booking essential - €27/41*. Gingham tablecloths and a blackboard menu contribute to the relaxed, informal feel. Somewhat hidden in a residential area to the south of the city. Modern cooking with the occasional added Asian influence.

Chapter One – *18-19 The Dublin Writers Museum, Parnell Sq -* ☎ *01 873 2266 - info@chapteronerestaurant.com - Closed 24 Dec to 9 Jan, Sun, Mon, Sat lunch and Bank Hols -* ▣ *- €27.50/48*. Cavernous room beneath the Dublin Writers's Museum. Contemporary art hangs on the thick granite walls. The cooking is innovative and the service careful. There is an arched alcove available for larger groups.

Bruno's – *30 East Sussex St, Temple Bar -* ☎ *01 670 6767 - www.brunos.ie - Closed 25 Dec to 2 Jan, Sat lunch and Sun - Booking essential - €27.95/36.60*. Its Temple Bar location, wood flooring, mirrors and moody lighting make this another example of the city's new wave of contemporary, yet informal, establishments. The menu features some original touches and the wine list is well-priced.

Patrick Guilbaud – *21 Upper Merrion St -*
☎ *01 676 4192 -*
www.restaurantpatrickguilbaud.eircom.net -
Closed Good Fri, 25 Dec, first week Jan, Sun
and Mon - €28/103. The city's most
renowned restaurant occupies a Georgian
townhouse adjacent to the Merrion hotel.
The superlative cooking, cosmopolitan
surroundings and courteous service all help
to make this one of the ultimate dining
experiences.

La Stampa – *35 Dawson St (at*
La Stampa Hotel) - ☎ *01 677 8611 -*
lastampa@eircom.net - Closed 25 Dec -
Booking essential - €29/50. Look no further
if you're after a true flavour of Dublin's
buzzing restaurant scene. The atmosphere
reverberates around this converted 19C
ballroom with its large mirrors, original
artwork and ornate mosaic ceiling.
Appropriately modern cuisine.

Brownes brasserie – *22 St Stephen's Green*
(at brownes townhouse) - ☎ *01 638 3939 -*
info@brownesdublin.ie - Closed 24 Dec to
4 Jan and Sat lunch - Booking essential -
€29.50/36.50. It is essential to book before
arriving at this ever-popular brasserie with its
distinctive Continental atmosphere and its
"belle époque" feel. The strength of the
European-influenced menu lies in its seafood.

The Tea Room – *6-8 Wellington Quay (at*
The Clarence Hotel) - ☎ *01 670 7766 -*
Closed lunch Sat and Sun - Booking
essential - €30/52. Double-height windows
ensure that this fashionable restaurant is
flooded with light during the day. Cool,
pastel shades add to the understated,
airy feel and the menu offers modern
Irish cooking using top quality
ingredients.

Jacobs Ladder – *4-5 Nassau St -*
☎ *01 670 3865 - www.jacobsladder.ie -*
Closed 17 March, Good Fri, 1 week August,
2 weeks Christmas to New Year, Sun, Mon -
✶ - Booking essential - €31.74/50.45. A
particularly good value lunch is offered at this
first-floor restaurant overlooking Trinity
College park. The chef owner provides
modern Irish cooking in appropriately
modern surroundings, complemented
by a well-chosen wine list.

The Commons – *85-86 Newman House,*
St Stephen's Green - ☎ *01 478 0530 -*
www.thecommons.ie - Closed first 2 weeks
Aug, 24 Dec to 5 Jan, Sat, Sun and Bank
Hols - €32/96. Newman House, former
University College, boasts James Joyce as a
student and the great man is celebrated
through assorted paintings in this basement
restaurant. A discreet and comfortable room,
with detailed and accomplished cooking.

Mermaid Café – *69-70 Dame St -*
☎ *01 670 8236 - info@mermaid.ie - Closed*
Good Fri , 24-26 and 31 Dec, 1 Jan - Booking
essential - €32.20/48.55. Draws in the young
and fashionable with its effervescent
atmosphere as well as its sensibly priced
menu. The food here has an eclectic hue,
drawing influences from all over the world
and also offers daily-changing blackboard
specials.

TAKING A BREAK

Abbey Tavern – *Howth -*
☎ *01 832 20 06 – Open daily from*
10.30am. This pub has existed since
1879 and has charm, a genuine sense of
authenticity and a very convivial atmosphere.
Known for its traditional Irish concerts every
evening from 8.30 with the "Abbey Singers
and Musicians". To the north of the city.

Brazen Head – *20 Lower Bridge St -*
☎ *01 679 5186 - www.brazenhead.com -*
Mon-Sat from 10.30am, Sun, noon-midnight.
Claims to be the oldest pub in the city, being
on the site of a 12C tavern. Although
popular with tourists this doesn't seem to
detract from the atmosphere. Worth getting
there early to get a seat for the music. Has a
pleasant terrace.

Butlers Chocolate Café – *24 Wicklow St -*
☎ *01 671 0599 -*
www.butlerschocolates.com – Open daily,
8am-6pm. The best place to buy chocolates;
for a taste of Ireland try the Jameson Truffle,
filled with Irish whiskey. A useful place to
stop for a mid-morning break but instead of
a tea or coffee try the house speciality a hot
chocolate.

Café Bewley (1) – *Grafton St -*
☎ *635 5470 - Mon-Sat, 7.30am-11pm, Sun,*
8-11am. The essence of café society.
Whether for a coffee and cake or a full meal,
it's worth making a stop here. Particularly
worth seeing the Harry Clarke room as well
as getting tickets for the Café Cabaret in the
evenings.

Café-en-Seine – *40 Dawson Street -*
☎ *01 677 4369 - Mon-Wed, 9am-12.30pm,*
Tue-Sat, 9am-2.30pm. With its fin-de-siècle
Parisian decor, this café represents the new
wave of establishments which combine the
café, bar and brasserie. It's a magnet for the
young and hip with its fashionably long bar.

Cleary's – *36 Amiens St -* ☎ *01 855 2952 –*
Open daily from 11.30am. This is an
authentic old dive, imbued with years of
smoke, fumes, exhortations and the oaths of
working men. Michael Collins roused such
men here and not much has changed since
his day.

Davy Byrne's – *21 Duke Street -*
☎ *01 677 5217 - www.davybyrnes.com -*
Mon-Sat, 10.30am-11pm, Sun, 11am-11pm.
This may be the most famous of the many
pubs associated with James Joyce. Despite
the changes made over the years, Davy
Byrne's is still a pleasant bar with a few
remaining Art Deco touches.

Dohenny & Nesbitt – *5 Lower Baggot St -*
☎ *01 676 2945 – Open daily from 11.30am.*
A classic pub popular with government
workers from the neighbourhood, especially
civil servants from the Ministry of Finance.
Dubliners like to refer to the Dohenny &
Nesbitt School of Economics.

Johnnie Fox Pub – *Glencullen -*
☎ *01 295 5647 - 7nights@johnniefoxs.com -*
Mon-Sat, 10.30am-11.30pm, Sun, noon-
11.30pm. The Fox may look as if it were built
for a film set but it has been in business since
1798. Everything is Irish down to the brass
tacks. Not only is this place for real but you

can enjoy traditional music here every evening.

Kish Fish – *40-42 Bow St* - ☎ *01 872 8211* - *Wed-Fri, 9am-4.30pm.* 100m on the left as you come out of the Old Jameson Distillery is this sweet little fishmonger's shop. Salmon is a particularly popular purchase and much of the produce comes from Galway.

Knightsbridge Bar – *23-25 Bachelor Walk - O'Connell Bridge* - ☎ *01 804 9100 - www.arlington.ie - Open daily from 11am.* In the evenings this vast bar in the heart of the city really comes alive. There's entertainment every night of the week, be it song or dance, and it's all free. Although rather touristy, it's an experience not to be missed.

Magill's – *14 Clarendon St* - ☎ *01 671 3820 - Mon-Sat, 9.15am-5.45pm.* Near Powerscourt Shopping Centre, the delicatessen has smoked salmon at a reasonable price.

Messrs Maguire – *1-2 Burgh Quay – Open daily from 11.30am.* This 19C building facing the Liffey is a good example of the fusion of the old and the new. It has cosy little nooks and crannies, a library bar, restaurant and brasserie. From Wednesday to Sunday a DJ pounds out the music from 9pm.

Mitchell & Son – *21 Kildare St* - ☎ *01 676 0766 - mitchkst@indigo.ie - Mon-Fri, 9am-5.45pm, Sat, 10am-5pm.* This wine merchant's was founded in 1805 and the 6th generation of the family is now at the helm. Celebrated for its famous 'Green Spot' whiskey, aged in sherry casks. They also offer a vast range of wines, rare malts, spirits and cigars.

Mulligan's – *8 Poolbeg St* - ☎ *01 677 5582 - Mon-Wed, 10.30am-11.30pm, Thu, 10.30am-12.30pm, Sun, 1pm-11pm.* You do feel that this celebrated old pub is the genuine article. The Victorian interior with its mahogany and screens is ideal for those looking for more intimacy. It is regularly frequented by journalists and those who take their drinking seriously.

Norseman – *29 East Sussex St.* Locals will tell you this is the best pub in Temple Bar, with a traditional charm all its own. Look for a spot here when the other places are full. Traditional music and jazz every evening.

Oliver St John Gogarthy – *58-9 Temple Bar* - ☎ *01 671 1822 – Open daily from 10.30am.* Located in the heart of Temple Bar, this is always a very popular bar with visitors to the city. There's a first floor restaurant, live music every night until the wee small hours and it acts as the starting point for the 'Musical Pub Crawl'.

O'Donoghue's – *14-15 Merrion Row* - ☎ *01 660 7194 / 676 2807 – Open daily from 10.30am.* Although it is a bit touristy, this pub has excellent traditional Irish music nightly and all day Sunday. The famous group The Dubliners came roaring on the music scene here in 1962. Often crowded, especially weekends.

O'Hooley's – *Gardiner Row - Mon-Fri, 10.30am-11.30pm, Sat, 10.30am-12.30pm, Sun, 10am-11pm.* During the week, this pub is rather ordinary but it comes alive Saturday night when the patrons take over

the entertainment. A country-style band backs up local talent with a traditional song or ballad to share. Having fun is the point here and it is by no means a talent show. The crowd is neither young nor hip but it's an authentic Dublin scene.

Stag's Head – *1 Dame Court* - ☎ *01 679 3701.* Another contender vying for the position of the city's most famous Victorian pub. It's cosy and more intimate than most, with a polished wood bar and mounted stag's head behind it. There's a good choice of draught beers.

Temple Bar – *48 Temple Bar* - ☎ *01 671 2324 - www.temple-bar.ie – Open daily from 10.30am.* A very agreeable pub and a popular choice for a good night out. The musical programme is varied, the acoustics are good and on a summer's day it all moves into the garden. There's even a small shop selling caps and T-shirts.

The Auld Dubliner – *Fleet St* - ☎ *01 677 0527 – Open daily from 10.30am.* Despite its name, this is a relatively recent arrival on the pub scene, and it already has a good reputation for traditional music, Thursday to Sunday nights.

The International Bar – *23 Wicklow St* - ☎ *01 697 9250 – Open daily from 11am.* Cosy little bar in the city centre with a youthful following, no doubt attracted by the upstairs theatre and comedy club which alternates with assorted blues bands. Tickets are available from the bar. Sunday attracts musicians for informal "jams".

The Long Hall – *51 South Great George St* - ☎ *01 475 1590.* This Victorian bar has remained largely unchanged since 1880 and is noted for its very long counter which appears to go on for miles. It's a welcoming and sociable place, attracting visitors from all parts of the globe.

The Madigan's – *25 North Earl St* - ☎ *01 874 5449 - Mon-Sat from 10.30am.* A pub with a bona fide sense of history. Known for its Art Nouveau decoration with period wood and stained-glass windows. Enjoy traditional lunchtime music with the bust of James Joyce looking down at you from behind the bar.

The Porter House – *16 Parliament St* - ☎ *01 679 8847 - Mon-Wed, noon-11.30pm, Tue, noon-12.30pm, Fri-Sat, 1pm-2.30am, Sun, 1pm-11pm.* The city's first micro-brewery has rapidly become a fashionable hangout. It offers a large range of modern beers and thus makes an ideal stop for those wanting a break from the 'black stuff'. Traditional music at weekends, modern during the week.

Zanzibar – *Lower Ormond Quay* - ☎ *01 878 7212 – Open daily, 4pm-3am.* A classic example of the Dublin theme pub with its eccentric Arabic decoration as imagined by Walt Disney. Geared unashamedly to groups out for the night. Queues begin to form later in the evening when it turns into a nightclub.

ENTERTAINMENT

Abbey Theatre – *26 Lower Abbey St* - ☎ *01 878 7222 – Ticket office open daily, 10.30am-7pm.* The building is not very splendid, nonetheless it is a proud symbol of Irish culture. Works by Ireland's best-known authors are performed here regularly (Shaw, Synge, Yeats, O'Casey) as are works by less famous dramatists. The Peacock Theatre, in the same building, specialises in contemporary and experimental work.

Bank of Ireland Arts Centre – *Foster Place.* Recitals.

Gaiety Theatre – ☎ *01 677 1717 - boxoffice@gaietytheatre.com.* Opera and musicals.

Gate Theatre – *1 Cavendish Row - ☎ 01 874 4045 - www.gate-theatre.ie – Ticket office open Mon-Sat, 10.30am-7pm; closed Sun.* Another Dublin institution, founded in the 1920s, this theatre includes non-Irish works in its repertoire.

Irish Film Centre – *Eustace St, Temple Bar - ☎ 01 639 3477.* Film buffs are catered for all year round here. The programme ensures that Irish films as well as the well-known classics are always being shown.

Jurys Irish Cabaret – ☎ *01 660 5000 - May-Oct : Tue-Sat from 11am.* It began in 1960 and today they put on 2 000 shows a year. These 2hr 30min spectaculars incorporate music, singing and dancing in both modern and traditional styles. There are also facilities to have a drink or meal.

National Concert Hall – *Earlsfort Terrace - ☎ 01 417 0077 - risita.wolfe@nch.ie - Mon-Sat, 10am-7pm.*

Olympia Theatre – *72 Dame Street - ☎ 01 677 7744.* Opera and musicals

The Burlington Cabaret – *The Burlington Hotel, Upper Leeson Street - ☎ 01 660 5222 - May-Oct, Mon and Wed-Sat from 6.45pm, Sun from 8pm; closed Thu.* Part of the Burlington hotel, this cabaret venue describes itself as being "a celebration of everything Irish in comedy, music, song and dance" Two ticket prices with or without dinner.

Taylor's Three Rock – *Grange Road, Rathfarnham - ☎ 01 494 2999 - Tue-Sun.* Prepare for audience participation and frenetic music and dance at this large thatched pub. You have a choice of three bars but what draws the crowds is the Music Room where live bands and dance troupes perform virtually nightly.

GOING OUT FOR THE EVENING

La Cave – *28 South Anne Street - ☎ 01 679 4409.* Just off Grafton Street is Dublin's oldest French wine bar serving French food and wine.

Rí-Rá – *11 Dame Court - ☎ 01 670 1220 - www.rira.ie – Open daily, 11pm-2am.* Spread over two floors, this nightclub is loud, funky and popular with the 'in crowd" despite, or because of, being slightly more expensive than others in the city. It's next door to The Globe for those wanting a drink away from the music.

SHOPPING

There is a post office in Suffolk Street opposite the Tourist Information Centre.

The **central shopping** area extends from Grafton Street *(south bank)* to O'Connell Street *(north bank)*. Nassau Street *(parallel with the south side of Trinity College)*

contains several good shops selling a range of **Irish goods** from high fashion to modest souvenirs – clothing, craftwork, pottery, Irish music and instruments, family crests. Bookshops congregate at the north end of Dawson Street. **Cobblestones** *(Smithfield Village)* offers examples of Irish craftsmanship. The **Temple Bar** area offers an eclectic mix of individual little shops and outdoor stalls.

Market-lovers should visit the **Moore Street market** *(Mon-Sat)*, where barrow boys sell fresh fruit and vegetables; **Dublin Corporation Fruit and Vegetable Market** under a cast-iron roof *(Mary's Lane; Sat am)*; **Temple Bar Market** *(Meeting House Square; Sat am)* selling local produce (cheeses, sauces, bread, chocolates, vegetables, drinks, pizzas, pies and sausages). For **antiques** go to Francis Street.

Avoca Mills, *Suffolk Street* – Woollen goods.

Blarney Woollen Mills – *21-23 Nassau St - ☎ 01 671 00 68 - Mon-Fri, 9am-7pm, Sat, 9am-6pm.* There's a huge choice of knitted items and classic Aran sweaters as well as knitwear with more imaginative patterns and designs. They also offer for sale a large choice of crystal, from Waterford, Galway and Tipperary.

Brown Thomas – *Grafton Street* – Dublin's smartest department store.

Celtic Note – *14 Nassau St - www.celticnote.com - Mon-Wed, Fri-Sat, 9am-6.30pm, Thu, 9am-8.30pm, Sun 11am-6pm.* No trip to Ireland is complete without hearing some traditional Celtic music and this is the number one shop for those wishing to take home a musical reminder. There's a vast selection of CDs and cassettes, as well as traditional musical instruments.

Claddagh Records – *2 Cecilia Street, Dublin 2* ☎ 01 677 0262. Specialist folk, traditional and ethnic music.

Dublin Woollen Mills – *41 Lower Ormond Quay - ☎ 01 677 5014 - www.woollenmills.com - Mon-Ssat, 9.30am-6pm, Sun, 1-6pm.* This family firm can lay claim to having once employed James Joyce as an agent during his sojourn in Trieste. A wide selection of authentic knitwear is available, as well as accessories such as scarves, caps and ties.

Powerscourt Centre

House of Ireland – *Nassau Street -* ☎ *01 671 1111 - Mon-Wed, Fri, 9am-6pm, Thu, 9am-8pm, Sat, 9am-6pm, Sun, 11am-6pm.* If it's made in Ireland then it is probably available in this well-known shop. Although perhaps a little expensive the range is vast; from woollens to crystal, porcelain to jewellery.

Kevin & Howlin – *31 Nassau St -* ☎ *01 677 0257 - Mon-Sat, 9am-6pm, Sun, 11am-6pm.* The definitive temple of Donegal tweed in all its forms. The range available at this family firm includes jackets, suits, waistcoats and ties. Alternatively, fabric can be bought by the metre and fashioned into garments by your own tailor.

Kilkenny Shop – *6 Nassau St - Mon-Wed, Fri, 8.30am-6pm, Thu, 8.30am-8pm, Sat, 9am-6pm, Sun, 11am-6pm.* Tweeds, Aran sweaters, lace and Celtic jewellery are just some of the products for sale in this veritable supermarket of traditional Irish products. Wilting shoppers or uninterested partners can refuel in the cafeteria.

National Museum Shop – *Kildare Street, Dublin 2.* Items based on exhibits.

National Museum Shop – *Benburb Street, Dublin 7.* Items based on exhibits.

Market Arcades – *South Great George St.* This covered passage is home to 20-odd shops, some offering second-hand clothing. There are some real bargains to be found, especially in tweed jackets.

Mother's Redcaps Market – *Back Lane - Fri-Sun, 10am-5.30pm.* This emporium has a little bit of everything: old records and second-hand clothes, Aran Island sweaters, lucky charms, dishes, knick-knacks, incense and patchouli.

The **Powerscourt Centre** – *South William Street, Dublin 2.* An 18C townhouse converted into a most attractive shopping centre with a great range of individual shops, including the **Crafts Council Retail Gallery**.

Rory's (Fishing Tackle) – *17A Temple Bar - Fleet St -* ☎ *01 677 2351.* A Dublin institution and a must for fishermen. All the equipment you could ever need is here, including a huge range of flies made at the shop. They are more than willing to help with advice on what to buy and where to fish.

Winding Stair Bookshop & Café – *40 Lower Ormond Quay -* ☎ *01 873 3292 - www.windingstair.ie - Mon-Sat, 9.30am-6pm, Sun, 1pm-6pm -* 🍴 *- €15.* Book-lovers will be in heaven here in this shop which also serves good salads, quiches and fresh pastries. As a bonus, there is a view of Ha'Penny Bridge, so ask for a window seat.

SPORTS AND LEISURE

Croke Park – *Drumcondra.* The stadium where the national finals of the Gaelic games – hurling and football – are held.

Horse Racing at **Leopardstown** (south) and **Fairy House** (north).

Greyhound Racing at Shelbourne Park *(Wed, Thu and Sat, first race at 8pm; €6-8 admission;* ☎ *01 668 3502); Harold's Cross (Mon, Tue and Fri; first race at 8pm; €5 admission, including race card) –* ☎ *01 497 1081*

EVENTS AND FESTIVALS

Bloomsday – Annual celebration (16 June) of James Joyce's great novel *Ulysses* – readings, re-enactments, music, theatre, street theatre

On hearing a false report that his father had been beheaded, he renounced his allegiance to Henry VIII in St Mary's Abbey *(see Worth a Visit)* and launched a rebellion which became known as the Kildare or Geraldine Revolt. He laid siege to the Castle, into which the Constable and his retinue had barricaded themselves, but the citizenry turned against Thomas; the besieged proclaimed the arrival of the

king's army and made a sortie, whereupon the besiegers took fright and scattered. Fitzgerald himself escaped but he was forced to surrender some months later and was executed in London together with his five uncles.

Georgian Dublin – In the relative peace of the 18C, restrictions eased and trade flourished. Buildings were constructed to house public bodies; terraces of fine houses were erected first north and then south of the river; men of property, drawn to the capital on parliamentary and other business, commissioned fine mansions. Under the activities of the Wide Streets Commissioners, established in 1758, Dublin developed into an elegant city, embraced by the Royal and Grand Canals and bisected by the Liffey, now embanked between quays and spanned by several bridges. With the Act of Union (1800) political affairs removed to London and, although known as the "second city of the Empire", Dublin stagnated. Despite many grievous losses, Dublin can still claim to be the finest Georgian city in the British Isles.

Capital of the Republic – There was much destruction during the Easter Rising and the Civil War but key buildings like the Four Courts, the GPO and the Custom House were eventually restored to something like their former glory. The refurbishment projects carried out in the last decades of the 20C mean that Dublin well deserved the title European City of Culture awarded in 1991 by the European Union. Temple Bar has been transformed from a dilapidated district into a network of pedestrian streets, vibrant with pubs, restaurants, hotels, craftshops and cafés. The district of Smithfield west of O'Connell Street has been regenerated under the Harp Project.

> **LITERARY DUBLIN**
>
> Several Nobel Prize winners figure in the long roll of Dublin-born writers who have achieved international fame – Swift, Mangan, Wilde, Shaw, Yeats, Synge, O'Casey, Joyce, Behan, Beckett. Their places of residence are marked with plaques or converted into museums. The major figures are named together with their work in a literary parade in St Patrick's Park. Their literary achievement, past and present, is analysed in the Dublin Writers Museum.

Walking About

The three walks covering the city centre start and finish at O'Connell Bridge or Ha'penny Bridge; they can be altered to suit individual requirements by excluding outlying sections or by amalgamation.

SOUTH BANK

This was the last part of the city centre to be developed, as for many years it was vulnerable to Irish raiding parties swooping down from the Wicklow Mountains. Until the construction of the Old Parliament in 1728 there was little building east of the old town except for Trinity College on the site of All Hallows Monastery.

The district began to develop into a fashionable suburb in the 1750s when the Duke of Leinster built the first nobleman's house south of the river; his prediction that fashionable society would follow soon proved true. Some of the most elegant Georgian terraces are to be found east and south of his mansion. In 1815 the Leinster property

Grand Canal

was bought by the Royal Dublin Society; the National Museum, the National Library and the National Gallery were built in the grounds. After 1922 the mansion was converted to serve as the Parliament *(see Worth a Visit)* of the newly established Free State.

From O'Connell Bridge walk south along Westmoreland Street passing (right) the Bank of Ireland (see Worth a Visit). Traffic negotiating the junction of Westmoreland Street, Dame Street and Grafton Street has increased so greatly that only a slim traffic island remains of **College Green**, formerly known as Hoggen Green, an old Viking burial ground *(haugen)* and meeting place *(thengmote)*.

At the centre stands a statue of **Henry Grattan** by John Foley (1879) and a modern iron sculpture designed by Edward Delaney in memory of **Thomas Davis** (1814-45), poet, leader of the Young Ireland movement and founder of *The Nation*.

Trinity College★★

Entrances in College Green and Nassau Street

Trinity College, Dublin, sometimes known as TCD, was founded in 1592 by Elizabeth I on the site of All Hallows, an **Augustinian monastery** suppressed at the Dissolution. It developed according to the tradition of the Oxford and Cambridge colleges and remained an Anglican preserve until quite recent times. Roman Catholics were excluded until 1873, while the Roman Catholic Church for its part strongly disapproved of the faithful studying here well into the 1960s. Women, of whatever faith, were admitted only in 1903. The College stands in its own grounds, **College Park**, an open space devoted to sports – cricket, rugby, running and hurling – which has diminished as buildings to accommodate the science and medical faculties have been built at the east end. The film *Educating Rita*, starring Michael Caine and Julie Walters, was filmed here.

Beside the entrance gates facing College Green stands an elegant Georgian house built for the Provost in 1758.

Statues by Foley of Oliver Goldsmith and Edmund Burke flank the main gate.

The buildings in **Front Court** date from the mid-18C; the wings terminate in the **Theatre** *(south)* and the **Chapel** *(north)*, both designed by Sir William Chambers with stuccowork by Michael Stapleton. The chapel is mainly lit by high semicircular windows; the organ

DUBLIN

Trinity College

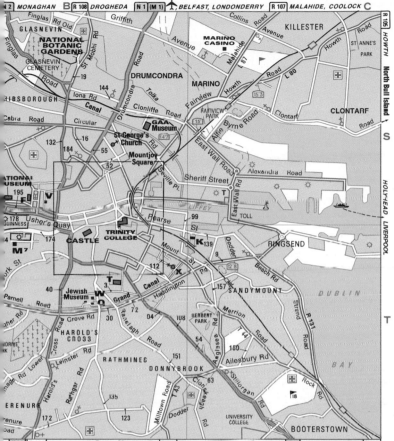

case dates from the 18C. The theatre (1777-91) is used for degree ceremonies, Senate meetings and musical and theatrical performances; it is hung with portraits: Elizabeth I, Edmund Burke, George Berkeley, Jonathan Swift.

Library Court is dominated by the **Campanile** (1853) designed by Charles Lanyon. Among the trees in the centre is a sculpture by Henry Moore, *Reclining Connected Forms* (1969). The area behind the north range is called **Botany Bay**, after the Australian penal colony, possibly because of the students' unruly behaviour. The red-brick range on the east side, known as Rubrics, is the oldest building in the college. The south side is closed by the Old Library and Treasury (*see Worth a Visit*).

The **Museum** (1850) *(south side of New Square)* was designed by Sir Thomas Deane and Benjamin Woodward in the Venetian style promoted by Ruskin; the delightful stone carving of flowers, leaves and animals is by the O'Shea brothers from Cork.

Turn left into Nassau Street.

On the corner with Kildare Street stands the former home of the **Kildare Street Club**, the oldest and most staunchly Unionist of Dublin's gentleman's clubs. The building with its odd floral and animal carvings dates from 1860.

Continue along Nassau Street and Clare Street to Merrion Square.

Merrion Square★

Floodlit at night. The jewel in the crown of Georgian Dublin, the square was laid out in 1762 by John Ensor for the 6th Viscount Fitzwilliam under the policy of the Wide Streets Commissioners. Delicate fanlights surmount the elegant doorways of the

DUBLIN

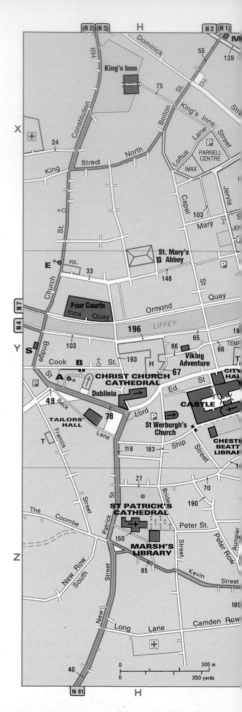

perfectly proportioned red-brick houses; commemorative plaques mark the homes of famous people – Oscar Wilde's father, Sir William Wilde, at no 1, William Butler Yeats at no 82. The mature **gardens** provide a welcome contrast to the busy streets. The west side is graced by the lawns of Leinster House and the National Gallery *(see Worth a Visit)*.

The southeast vista is closed by **St Stephen's Church**, designed in 1821 by John Bowden and completed by Joseph Welland; its Greek façade, surmounted by a domed tower known as the "Pepper Canister", was inspired by three famous Athenian buildings – the Erechtheum, the Tower of the Winds and the Monument of Lysicrates. The Victorian apse (1852) is lit by a stained-glass window depicting the martyrdom of St Stephen. *Open Wed and Sun, as posted on church notice board. Services: Sun, 11am, Wed, 11.30am.* ☎ *01 288 0663 (Vicarage)*

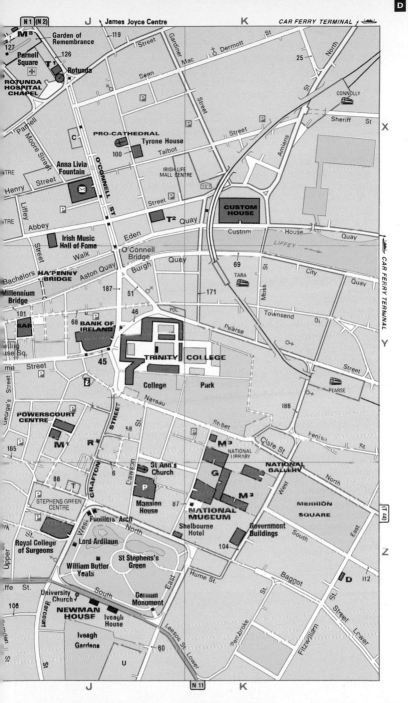

Continue south up Merrion Street passing the Natural History Museum (see Worth a Visit).

Government Buildings

Merrion Street Upper. Guided tour (40min; Taoiseach's Office, Ceremonial Stairs, Cabinet Room) Sat, 10.30am-3.30pm. Tickets (no charge) available same day from National Gallery, Merrion Square West. ☎ 01 619 4116; webmaster@taoiseach.irlgov.ie; www.irlgov.ie/taoiseach

This imposing structure in Edwardian Baroque, opened in 1911 by George V, was the last major public building project carried out in Dublin under British rule. Until 1989 parts of the building were occupied by Trinity College. A major restoration programme, the provision of well-chosen modern furniture and the display of a fascinating range of contemporary artworks make a fine setting for some of the business of government, carried out in committee and conference rooms and in the office of the Prime Minister *(Taoiseach)*.

Among the many handsome Georgian houses are the town house of the Wellesley family, where the Duke of Wellington spent some of his childhood, and the Merrion Street Hotel, its interior restored to its original splendour.

Turn right into the north side of St Stephen's Green.

The **Shelbourne Hotel**, still a centre of Dublin's social life, was built by Martin Burke on the site of Kerry House, residence of the Earl of Shelburne, in 1824; it was rebuilt in 1867 and has an elegant porch flanked by exotic figures.

Turn right into Kildare Street.

Halfway down the street is the National Museum (right) *(see Worth a Visit)* facing the National Library; set back between them is Leinster House, now the seat of the Irish Parliament.

Parliament

Public gallery: Open during parliamentary sessions (Tue-Thu and sometimes Fri, by appointment). Closed Easter (2 weeks), mid-July to early-Oct, at Christmas and during Jan. ☎ 01 618 3296 (Captain of the Guard); info@oireachtas.irlgov.ie; www.irlgov.ie/oireachtas

The two houses **(Dáil Éireann and Seanad Éireann)** meet in **Leinster House**, which was designed in 1745 by Richard Castle for the Duke of Leinster and con-verted to house the Republican parliament in 1922. The public are admitted to the public gallery which overlooks the chamber of the lower house *(Dáil)*. Members of the Dáil take the letters TD after their name.

Turn left into Molesworth Street and left again into Dawson Street.

St Ann's Church

Open Mon-Fri, 10am-4pm. Services: Sun, 8am, 10.45am, 6.30pm; Mon-Fri, 12.45pm. Lunch-hour, evening and weekend concerts. Coffee shop (noon-2.30pm). ☎ 01 676 7727 or 01 288 0663 (vicarage)

St Ann's was one of the earliest Georgian churches in Dublin, an elegant and fash-ionable place of worship designed by Isaac Wills and not really improved by the addition of a Victorian neo-Romanesque west front and stained glass. The bread shelf in the chancel was established in 1723 by a charitable bequest to provide 120 loaves of bread each week for the poor.

Mansion House

The house was built in 1705 by Joshua Dawson, a builder, and bought by the City of Dublin in 1715 as the residence of the Lord Mayor. The spacious Round Room was added for the visit of George IV in 1821; it was here that the first Irish parlia-ment met in 1919 to adopt the Declaration of Independence.

At the top of Dawson Street cross the road into the gardens of St Stephen's Green.

St Stephen's Green

(Dúchas) Open daily, 8am (10am Sun and Bank Hols) to dusk; 25 Dec, 10am-1pm. ☎ 01 475 7816; Fax 01 475 5287

Formerly common land first enclosed in 1663, the beautifully landscaped and well-maintained **gardens** (22 acres/9ha) are a wonderful asset in this densely built-up part of the city. They were laid out in 1880 by Lord Ardilaun, a member of the

St Stephen's Green

B Perousse/MICHELIN

Guinness family; his statue stands on the west side. A bronze sculpture by Henry Moore was erected in memory of **William Butler Yeats** in 1967. The **Fusiliers' Arch** (*northwest entrance*) commemorates those who died in the Boer War and the **German Monument** (*southeast entrance*) expresses the gratitude of the people of the Federal Republic of Germany for help received from the Irish people after the Second World War.

The **Royal College of Surgeons** (*west side*), designed by Edward Parke in 1806, was captured during the Easter Rising in 1916 by a party of insurgents led by Constance Markievicz (*see p 342*).

On the south side are **Newman House** (*see Worth a Visit*) **Iveagh House**, designed by Richard Castle and now the Department of Foreign Affairs, and the **University Church** (1854), designed at the behest of Cardinal Newman by John Pollen in the highly ornate Byzantine and Italian early-Christian style advocated by John Ruskin. ⅙ *Open daily. Services: Sun 11am, noon, 5.30pm; Sat, 7pm; other days, 10am, 1.05pm. Ramp for wheelchairs.* ☎ *01 478 0616*

From the southeast corner of the square turn left into Harcourt Street.

Harcourt Street is lined by elegant terraces of red-brick Georgian houses with handsome door frames and fanlights.

Turn left into Clonmel Street.

Iveagh Gardens

Entrances in Clonmel Street and Earlsfort Terrace. (Dúchas) Open daily, 8.30am (10am Sun and Bank Hols) to dusk (5pm Feb and Nov; 4pm Dec-Jan). Closed 25-26 Dec. ☎ *01 661 3111*

The gardens form an unexpected haven of lawns and tree-lined walks, enhanced by statuesque fountains, a rosarium and a maze. The main axis is terminated by a massive rock-work cascade based on the Bains d'Apollon at Versailles.

Return to St Stephen's Green; walk north and into Grafton Street.

Grafton Street★

Dublin's finest shopping street is now a bustling pedestrian precinct and a favourite haunt of street musicians; in the 19C it was paved with pine blocks to deaden the sound of carriage wheels. In the arcades and lanes on both sides are boutiques and shops of great variety. **Bewley's Oriental Café** (*see Directory*) with its distinctive mosaic façade and stained-glass windows by **Harry Clarke** was opened in 1927, although the business began c 1840. It stands on the site of Whytes School, which was attended by Robert Emmet, Thomas Moore, Richard Sheridan and the Duke of Wellington.

Turn left into Johnson Court.

Powerscourt Centre★

Open Mon-Sat, 9am-6pm. Closed Bank Hols

This 18C town house which contains some fine stucco ceilings was designed in 1771 by Robert Mack for Viscount Powerscourt and is now a most unusual shopping centre occupying the stables and the house (*see Directory*).

To reach the start of the second walk, return to Grafton Street and continue north to College Green and O'Connell Bridge.

OLD DUBLIN

The heart of old Dublin occupies the ridge between the Liffey and its southern tributary, the Poddle River, which now flows underground. Excavations (1974-81) at **Wood Quay**, where the modern Civic Offices of Dublin Corporation now stand, revealed the remains of 150 Viking buildings at 13 different levels (AD 920-1100). The town expanded eastwards along Dame Street to meet the development taking place around Leinster House, and also westwards along the **High Street** into the **Cornmarket**, where vast quantities of grain were sold for export in the Middle Ages. Little remains of the old buildings in **Fishamble Street**, where Molly Malone was born and Handel conducted the first performance of *Messiah* to raise funds for the Rotunda Hospital (*see below*). The **Liberties** was the name given to the area further south and west, which lay outside the jurisdiction of the medieval city; here the buildings vary from 17C high-gable houses built by French Huguenot refugees to 19C mansion flats and 20C modern housing estates.

From the south side of O'Connell Bridge walk upstream along Aston Quay.

Liffey Footbridges

The official name for the delicate cast-iron footbridge, opened in 1816 as the Wellington Bridge, is the **Liffey Bridge** but it is popularly known as the **Ha'penny Bridge★**, because of the 1/2d toll levied until 1919. It now has a companion, the **Millennium Bridge**, opened in 2000, while the north bank of the river has been greatly enhanced by the building of a popular boardwalk with seats and refreshment kiosks.

Opposite the Ha'penny Bridge turn away from the river through the arch.

Liffey Bridge

Merchants' Hall *(Wellington Quay)* was designed by Frederick Darley for the Merchants' Guild, also known as the Fraternity of the Holy Trinity, the first of Dublin's 25 guilds; the arched passage through the building leads into Temple Bar.

Temple Bar

Map of area on corner of Cope Street and Crown Alley.

The area between the river and Dame Street, now known as Temple Bar (28 acres/11ha) takes its name from Sir William Temple, Provost of Trinity (1628-99), who owned land which included a sand bar on the south bank of the river. A stroll through its medieval network of narrow streets and alleys and courts reveals a variety of old buildings – Georgian houses, warehouses and chapels – restored and converted to new uses, interspersed with new purpose-built property. Derelict sites have been converted into open spaces – Temple Bar Square, Meeting House Square and Central Bank Plaza among the banks and insurance offices of Dame Street. This astonishingly successful case of urban renewal, has produced a cultural district with a great variety of places of entertainment as well as "alternative" shops, ethnic restaurants, hotels and public and private residential accommodation. Eustace Street is now home to two national institutions – the Irish Film Centre, the national centre for film in Ireland, and the National Photographic Archive – and also to the **Temple Bar Information Centre** *(see Directory)*.

Walk west up Dame Street. Turn left into Dame Lane, walk past Dublin Castle (see Worth a Visit), past Dubh Linn Garden and the Chester Beatty Library (see Worth a Visit); continue west along Ship Street and turn right into Werburgh Street.

St Werburgh's Church

Werburgh Street. Open by appointment Mon-Fri, 10am-4pm. Services: Sun, 10am. Key available from 8 Castle Street. ☎ 01 478 3710

Built in 1715 on the site of a 12C church, the present building was remodelled in 1759 after a fire and has had one of the city's most elegant Georgian interiors. The British authorities, nervous after the 1798 rebellion, insisted on the removal of the spire, which overlooked the Castle courtyard. One of the most distinguished of the rebels, Lord Edward Fitzgerald, was secretly buried in the vaults; his captor, Major Henry Sirr, is buried in the churchyard.

Walk south down Werburgh Street into Bride Street; turn right into Kevin Street Upper, right into St Patrick Close passing Marsh's Library (see Worth a Visit) and turn right again into Patrick Street.

St Patrick's Cathedral★★

     Open daily, 9am-6pm (5pm Sat Nov-Feb; 3pm Sun Nov-Feb). Closed 24-26 Dec, New Year's Day (except for services). Services: Sun, 8.30am (Holy Eucharist), 11.15am (Sung Eucharist/Matins), 3.15pm (Choral Evensong); Mon-Fri, 5.35pm (Choral Evensong); no sung services Jul-Aug. €3.50. Leaflet (9 languages). Parking. ☎ 01 453 9472 (Office), 475 4817 (Cathedral), 453 5312; Fax 01 454 6374; www.stpatrickscathedral.ie

John Comyn, appointed Archbishop of Dublin in 1181, objected to being subject to the laws and regulations of the City Provosts. He moved his seat out of the city jurisdiction to the site of a holy well used, according to tradition, by St Patrick to baptise converts. His church was promoted to a cathedral and rebuilt in the Early English style in the mid-13C, with a tower added a century later.

The cathedral is for ever associated with **Jonathan Swift**, its Dean from 1713 to 1745. His tomb is marked by a bronze plaque in the floor near the main door, beside it that of his friend "Stella". Swiftian memorabilia his death-mask and a replica of his skull (in the bookcase). Swift wrote his own epitaph, which is inscribed over the door in the south wall next to his bust. He also composed an epitaph for the black marble tomb of the **Duke of Schomberg**, who died at the Battle of the Boyne *(north choir aisle)*, and put up a plaque *(south transept)* to his faithful servant Alexander McGee.

The vaulted **baptistery** in the southwest corner of the nave was probably the entrance to the original church. The 13C floor tiles, transferred from the south transept in the 19C restoration, have been copied throughout the cathedral. The huge and splendid **Boyle Monument** (1632), erected by the great Earl of Cork in memory of his second wife Catherine, is adorned with no fewer than 16 polychrome figures.

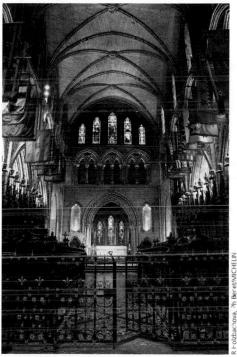

R Holzbachova, Ph Beret/MICHELIN

Saint Patrick's Cathedral

In the north aisle stands a fine statue by Edward Smyth of the Marquess of Buckingham, Viceroy and first Grand Master of the **Order of St Patrick**; until 1871 the cathedral was the chapel of the Order; the knight's banners hang in the choir above the stalls, which are labelled with their escutcheons.

In the north transept stands the old door of the Chapter House; the hole was cut in 1492 so that the Earl of Kildare could "chance his arm" in a conciliatory gesture to Black James Ormond who had taken refuge in the Chapter House; they had quarrelled because Ormond had been appointed Lord Deputy in place of Kildare.

The arches along the east side of **St Patrick's Park** form a literary parade of Dublin-born writers, with their dates and major works; three won a Nobel Prize for Literature.

Continue north up Patrick Street; turn left into Back Lane.

Tailors' Hall★

The Tailors' Hall, built between 1703 and 1707, is the only surviving guild-hall in Dublin; the elaborate entrance gate dates from 1706. The Great Hall has a stage, a handsome marble fireplace and a minute gallery with a wrought-iron railing, approached by an elegant pine staircase. The building is now the head office of *An Taisce*, the Irish equivalent of the British National Trust.

Return to Patrick Street and continue to the north end.

There is a fine view of Christ Church Cathedral and the covered bridge linking it to the old Synod Hall which now houses Dublinia *(see Worth a Visit).*

Christ Church Cathedral★★

&. *Open daily, 9.45am (10am Sat-Sun) to 5pm. Closed 26 Dec. Services: Sun at 11am and 3.30pm, 5pm (Eucharist in Irish 4th Sun in the month). Donation €3; Treasury €3. Self-guided tour with numbered leaflet (10 languages).* ☎ *01 677 8099; Fax 01 679 8991; welcome@cccdub.ie; www.cccdub.ie*

Like the Castle, Christ Church Cathedral became a symbol of the Ascendancy, and the Romanesque/Early English structure is still the seat of the Anglican Bishop of Dublin and Glendalough and the Metropolitan Cathedral of the Southern Province of the Church of Ireland, second only to Armagh.

Largely rebuilt in the 19C by George Scott, it is nevertheless an important link to the city's very earliest days, being the successor to the wooden church built in 1038 by Dunan, the first Bishop of Dublin, on land provided by Sitric, the Viking King of Dublin. Soon after 1170 this building was replaced by a stone church built on the orders of Strongbow, Richard de Clare, Earl of Pembroke.

A number of medieval features survived the 19C rebuilding, among them the elegant **Romanesque south door** overlooking the ruins of the Chapter House, the **brass eagle lectern**, and some of the original encaustic tiles in the Chapel of St Laud; hanging on the chapel wall *(right)* is a casket containing the heart of St Laurence O'Toole, the second Archbishop of Dublin.

In the south aisle is the **"Strongbow" monument;** though the effigy in chain mail is certainly not the great Anglo-Norman commander, the half figure beside it may well belong to the original tomb. "Strongbow's tomb" was frequently specified in legal contracts as the place of payment.

Of all the Cathedral interiors, the 12C Norman **crypt** *(access in the south aisle)* is perhaps the most evocative. It was originally used for services, then let to shopkeepers and afterwards used for burials until the mid-19C; it now houses an exhibition *Treasures of Christ Church*, reflecting 1 000 years of history, architecture and worship in Ireland.

Walk west along High Street.

St Audoen's Church

(Dúchas) (&.) *Open Jun-Sep, daily, 9.30am-5.30pm (4.45pm last admission). €1.90. Guided tour available.* ☎ *01 667 677 0088; Fax 01 670 9431; staudeonschurch@ealga.ie*

The old church (now Anglican) was founded by the Anglo-Normans and dedicated to St Audoen of Rouen in France. The west doorway dates from the 12C; the original 13C nave is lit by 15C windows.

St Audoen's Gate (1275), giving access to the river, is one of the 32 gates which pierced the **Norman city walls**.

Turn right into Cook Street and left into Winetavern Street; walk down to the river and look across to Inns Quay.

Four Courts

The building (1785), which was designed to house four major courts – Chancery, King's Bench, Exchequer and Common Pleas – was begun by Thomas Cooley and

Sunlight Chambers

D

completed by James Gandon; with its six-columned portico and massive, brooding dome it is one of the latter's masterpieces. It was occupied by the rebels in 1916 and again, by anti-Treaty forces, in 1921. On the first occasion it escaped serious damage but in 1921, shelled by the Free State army from across the river and mined by the insurgents, it was virtually destroyed, along with the irreplaceable national archives dating from 1174.

Turn right and walk along Wood Quay and Essex Quay.

On the corner of Essex Quay and Parliament Street stand **Sunlight Chambers**, built as the headquarters of Lever Brothers with coloured terracotta friezes telling the story of soap.

To reach the start of the third walk, continue along the quays to return to the Ha'penny Bridge.

NORTH BANK

In the Middle Ages Oxmantown, the Viking settlement on the north bank of the Liffey, was dominated by **St Mary's Abbey** *(see Worth a Visit)*. In the 17C it was built up on a grid plan around Oxmantown Green, now Smithfield. The Hospital and Free School of King Charles II was founded in 1670 for the education of poor boys who wore a military-style blue uniform; in 1773 the **Bluecoat School**, as it was known, was housed in Blackhall Place in a building designed by Thomas Ivory, now occupied by the Incorporated Law Society.

By the 18C the north bank had become the most fashionable residential district of Dublin, centred on O'Connell Street, then known as Gardiner's Mall. No-one today would describe O'Connell Street as fashionable but it has retained its generous dimensions and remains a vital part of the city centre with its shops, cinemas and fast-food outlets. Further north, the site of Parnell Square was developed by Bartholomew Mosse to raise money for his maternity hospital, which occupied the south side. Many of the once-elegant Georgian terraces in the neighbourhood, particularly **Mountjoy Square**, have passed through neglect and decay to demolition or restoration and conversion. **St George's Church**, where the Duke of Wellington married Kitty Pakenham in 1806, was designed by Francis Johnston in the Greek Ionic style (1802-14) with a marked similarity to St Martin's-in-the-Fields in London.

Two of Dublin's major theatres are located on the north bank. The **Gate Theatre** *(see Directory)* was founded in 1928 by Hilton Edwards and Micheál MacLiammóir. The earlier **Abbey Theatre** *(see Directory)*, now a national institution, was founded in 1904 by Lady Gregory and WB Yeats as part of the Irish literary revival. In 1924 it became the first state-subsidised theatre in the English-speaking world, and for a while its productions continued to cause controversy, even riots, notably with the plays of Sean O'Casey. It is housed in an undistinguished modern building following the destruction by fire in 1951 of the original theatre.

From the north side of O'Connell Bridge walk up O'Connell Street.

O'Connell Street★

The broad and famous street was laid out by Luke Gardiner in the 18C as a tree-lined mall and then converted into a narrow residential square. Renamed **Sackville Street**, it developed into the most important thoroughfare in 18C Dublin; later it was extended south to Carlisle Bridge (1794); the street and the present bridge (1880) were renamed after Daniel O'Connell in 1922.

Down the centre of the street stands a row of **monuments**: *(south to north)* statue by John Foley of Daniel O'Connell; William Smith O'Brien (1803-64), the leader of the Young Ireland Movement who was sentenced to death for treason in 1848; Sir John Gray, who organised Dublin's water supply; James Larkin (1876-1947), founder of the Irish Transport and General Workers' Union (1909); Father Theobald Mathew of the 19C temperance movement.

The **GPO building★** with its Ionic portico was designed by Francis Johnston in 1814. It was the headquarters of the rebels in the **Easter Rising** in 1916 and still bears scars of the fighting.

The **Anna Livia Fountain**, a female personification of the Liffey, soon nicknamed the Floozie in the Jacuzzi, was erected to commemorate Dublin's Millennium in 1988; it occupies the site of Nelson's Pillar (1808), which was damaged by a bomb in 1966 and demolished. It was James Joyce who coined the term Anna Livia out of the Irish for the River Liffey *(Abhainn na Life)*.

Turn right into Talbot Street.

Pro-Cathedral★

Open 8.30am-6.30pm. Services: Sun, 10am, 11am (Sung Latin Mass with Palestrina Choir, except Jul-Aug), noon (Italian Mass, St Kevin's Oratory), 12.30pm, 6.30pm. Guide book. Leaflet. ☎ 01 874 5441; Fax 01 874 2406; www.procathedral.ie

Dublin's most important Roman Catholic place of worship was built in 1821 in the style of a Greek temple with a Doric portico and a dome. Its monumentality contrasts with its rather cramped setting, but Protestant interests kept it away from its intended site on O'Connell Street.

231

In 1851 John Newman made his profession of faith to Cardinal Cullen in this church. The Palestrina Choir was endowed in 1902 by Edward Martyn *(see ATHENRY)*; one of its early members was John McCormack *(see ATHLONE)*.

Opposite the entrance stands **Tyrone House**, an elegant mansion, designed by Richard Castle in 1741 and now occupied by the Department of Education.

Return to O'Connell Street and continue northwards.

Parnell Square

Originally Rutland Square, it was renamed in honour of **Charles Stewart Parnell**, whose statue stands at the road junction.

The south side of the square is filled by the elegant lying-in hospital designed by Richard Castle in 1752 for Dr Bartholomew Mosse (1712-59). The **Rotunda Hospital Chapel★** is an exuberant Rococo creation, decorated with superb stuccowork by Bartholomew Cramillion and carved mahogany woodwork by John Kelly. It is lit by an 18C lantern and a Venetian window which is filled with modern stained glass and surmounted by the Lamb of God on a book with seven seals and the figure of Charity with three children. *Open Wed, 10am-noon; otherwise by written request to Director of Midwifery/Nursing.* ☎ *01 873 0700*

Charles Stewart Parnell

R Holzbachova, Ph Benet/MICHELIN

Funds for the hospital were raised from entertainments given in the **Rotunda**, de-signed in 1764 by John Ensor and now a cinema, and from functions held in the **Assembly Rooms**, designed by Richard Johnston in 1786 and now occupied by the Gate Theatre. More funds were raised from public entertainments held in the walled **pleasure gardens** in the centre of the square, which were laid out with a wilderness, temples of refreshment and a terrace, called the Orchestra, where music was played. The surrounding houses were completed in the 1770s and inhabited by peers and bishops and members of Parliament.

The north end of the square has been converted into a **Garden of Remembrance** designed by Daithí P Hanly. Celtic motifs are incorporated into the design of the gates. The central sculpture by Oisín Kelly echoes Yeats' poem *Easter 1916* with the mythological theme of the transformation of the **Children of Lir** into swans *(see p 327)*. The broken spears in the mosaic reflect the Celtic custom of throwing weapons into water after a battle. *(Dúchas) (&) Open daily, 11am (9.30am May-Sep) to 7pm (8pm May-Sep, 4pm Jan-Feb and Nov-Mar; 1pm 25 Dec). ☎ 01 647 2498 (head office); 01 874 3074 (garden)*

The site is significant; the plans for the Easter Rising (1916) were made in a house *(plaque)* on the north side of the square and the rebels were held prisoner in the square overnight.

On the north side of the square are the Dublin Writers' Museum and the Hugh Lane Gallery (see Worth a Visit). Turn right into Granby Street and pass the Wax Museum (see Worth a Visit). Turn left into Dorset Street and right into Henrietta Street.

Henrietta Street is lined by substantial 18C town houses, awaiting restoration to their former elegance.

King's Inns

The building where barristers used to live as well as study was begun in 1795 and completed in 1827. It is the last great public building designed by James Gandon and the dining room is the only Gandon interior to survive. The west front over-looks an extensive park.

Return to Dorset Street; turn left and right into Dominick Street Lower; turn left into Parnell Street and right into Moore Street.

A lively **street market** is held here at the heart of a busy shoppping district.

PHOENIX PARK★★

West of the city centre on the north bank of the Liffey. Restricted access by car.

The park (1 752 acres/709ha), the largest enclosed urban park in Europe, derives its name from the Gaelic for clear water *(Fionn Uisce)*. The land, confiscated from Kilmainham Priory *(see Worth a Visit)* in 1543 by the Crown, was enclosed in 1662 by the Duke of Ormond who introduced a herd of fallow deer which still roam the Fifteen Acres (actually approximately 300 acres/121ha).

The southeast gate is flanked by the **Wellington Monument**, designed by Sir William Smirke in 1817, and the **People's Garden**, a flower garden sloping to a small lake. From here Chesterfield Avenue, lit by gas lamps, leads to the **Phoenix Monument**, erected by Lord Chesterfield in 1745. To the south stands the residence of the Ambassador of the USA and the **Papal Cross** marking the visit of Pope John Paul II in 1979.

In 1882, at the height of agitation over the Land Act, while walking in the park near the Vice-Regal Lodge the newly appointed Chief Secretary, Lord Frederick Cavendish, and the Under-Secretary, Thomas H Burke, the intended victim, were stabbed to death by the "Invincibles", members of an extremist Fenian sect.

Phoenix Park Visitor Centre

Visitor Centre: (Dúchas) (&) Open Jun-Sep, daily, 10am-6pm; mid-Mar to May and Oct, daily, 9.30am-5pm (5.30pm Apr-May); Nov to mid-Mar, Sat-Sun, 9.30am-4.30pm; last admission 45min before closing. Closed 24-26 Dec. €2.50. Ashtown Castle: Guided tour (20min). Audio-visual show (21min). Nature Trails. Parking. Restaurant; coffee shop. ☎ 01 677 0095; Fax 01 672 6454; phoenixparkvisitorcentre@ealga.ie; www.heritageireland.ie

The history of the park is presented in an old stable block, beside a 17C tower house which was for many years the residence of the park keeper before being incorporated into a private house (now demolished).

Zoological Gardens★

Phoenix Park. Open daily, 9.30am (10.30am Sun) to 6pm (dusk Nov-Feb). €9.80. Play areas. Refreshments. Shops. ☎ 01 474 8900; Fax 01 677 1660; info@dublinzoo.ie; www.dublinzoo.ie

The Zoo, which was founded in 1830, is set in attractive parkland (30 acres/12ha). As well as keeping animals of many types from all parts of the world, it is involved in breeding programmes with other zoos and is under constant development. The **World of Cats** presents snow leopards as well as lions and other felines, while the **World of Primates** with its vivacious monkeys and sad-faced orang-utans exercises a constant appeal. Arctic foxes and snowy owls inhabit **Fringes of the Arctic**, while the lakes and their banks provide a habitat for water fowl, flamingoes, penguins and sealions. **City Farm** and **Pets Corner** are especially popular with children.

Aras an Uachtaráin

Guided tour (1hr) Sat (except 24-26 Dec), 10.30am-4.30pm (3pm winter). Ticket available on the day from Phoenix Park Visitor Centre (☎ 01 677 0095). ☎ 01 670 9155; webmaster@aras.irlgov.ie; www.irlgov.ie/aras

The **official residence** of the President of Ireland, formerly Vice-Regal Lodge, was built (1751-54) as a private house by Nathaniel Clements and in 1815 acquired its Ionic portico by Francis Johnston.

Worth a Visit

COLLEGE GREEN

Trinity College Old Library★★★

Entrances in College Green and Nassau Street. & Open Mon-Sat, 9.30am-5pm, Sun and Bank Hols (17 Mar, Good Fri, Easter Mon and Oct Bank Hol), noon-4.30pm; also Jun-Sep, Sun, 9.30am-4.30pm. Closed 22 Dec-2 Jan. €7; joint ticket with Dublin Experience €10. College Tour (including The Colonnades and the Book of Kells): Apr-Sep, daily, 10am-4pm (last tour), every 30min from the Front Square. €8; joint ticket with the Dublin Experience available. ☎ 01 608 2320; Fax 01 608 2690; www.tcd.ie/library

The austere building (1712-32) was designed by Thomas Burgh, Chief Engineer and Surveyor-General of Her Majesty's Fortifications in Ireland. The library acquired its books by purchase or donation until 1801, when it became a copyright library, receiving copies of every book published in the Commonwealth. Since then the increased pace of acquisition has required new buildings: the Reading Room built in 1937 and the Berkeley Library designed by Paul Koralek in 1967. Until 1892 the ground floor was an open colonnade designed to protect the books from damp; in 1992 part was converted to provide two galleries: The Colonnades for annual themed exhibitions, and the Treasury.

Treasury★★★ – This gallery displays the great treasures of Trinity College Library. The **Book of Kells**, the most famous of them, is an illuminated manuscript of the four Gospels in Latin on vellum, produced c 800; although it was kept at Kells *(see p 268)* until the 17C, it is not known if it was produced in that monastery or elsewhere. The **Book of Durrow** (c 700) is another illustrated manuscript of the Gospels in a simpler style. The **Book of Armagh** (c 807) contains the complete text of the New Testament in Latin, as used by the Celtic Church, as well as the lives of St Patrick and St Martin and the Confession of St Patrick. The **Book of Dimma** contains both the Gospels and some liturgical text; its silver shrine dates from c 1150.

Long Room★★ – Above the entrance door at the top of the stairs are the **arms of Elizabeth I**, a relic of the original college. The **Long Room** (209ft/64m x 40ft/12m) consists of 20 bays lined with bookcases surmounted by a gallery. The original flat ceiling was replaced in the mid-19C by the present higher wooden barrel vault to provide more shelving.

The **Irish harp** (restored), the oldest in Ireland, is at least 500 years old; it was found in Limerick in the 18C; it is made of willow and has 29 strings.

Long Room, Old Library, Trinity College

Dublin Experience

Trinity College, Nassau Street. Open late-May to Sep, daily, 10am-5pm (last show), every hour. €4.20; joint ticket with Old Library €10. Audioguide (4 languages). Refreshments. ☎ 01 608 1688; reservations@tcdie; http: //www.tcd.ie/visitors
Through photography, music and voices the audio-visual presentation *(40min)* gives an entertaining and informative account of a thousand years of Dublin history from the Viking settlement to the modern city.

Bank of Ireland★★

Foster Place. ♿ Open Tue-Fri, 10am-4pm. Closed Bank Hols. €1.50. Charity recitals: Feb-Dec; €9. ☎ 01 671 1488; Fax 01 671 2261
Ireland was governed from this elegant building from 1728, the date of its completion, until 1800, when the Act of Union abolished the country's jurisdiction and transferred it to Westminster. Several eminent architects contributed to its construction, from the original designer, Sir Edward Lovett Pearce, to James Gandon, responsible for the porticoes, and Francis Johnston, who converted it for use by the Bank of Ireland in 1803.

The old House of Commons is now the banking hall. The **House of Lords** is still largely intact, with a magnificent coffered ceiling, a great chandelier of Irish glass, an oak mantelpiece to a design by Inigo Jones, and splendid 17C Flemish tapestries depicting the Battle of the Boyne and the siege of Londonderry. The Mace was taken away as a souvenir by the last Speaker but eventually recovered.

In the **Story of Banking,** an audio-visual presentation *(8min)* and exhibits of currency, bank notes and an old money cart form part of an excellent interpretation of the role of the Bank of Ireland in the commercial development of the country, since its establishment in 1783.

MUSEUM DISTRICT

National Museum★★

Kildare Street. Other collections of the National Museum are displayed at Collins Barracks (see p 241). ♿ *Open Tue-Sun, 10am (2pm Sun) to 5pm. Closed Good Fri, 25 Dec. Audio-visual show (18min; 4 languages). Guided tour (30-45min; €1.27) at frequent intervals. Museum shop. Café.* ☎ *016 777 444; Fax 016 766 116; Marketing@ museums.ie; www.museums.ie*

MUSEUMLINK shuttle service: every 80min; €1.27 one way (National Museum Kildare Street - Natural History Museum Merrion Street - National Museum Collins Barracks).

Access: Buses 7, 7A, 8 (Burgh Quay); 10, 11, 13 (O'Connell Street).

This museum, purpose-built in 1890 with a circular colonnaded portico, domed vestibule and elaborate decoration, concentrates on displaying the riches of the national archaeological collections.

An audio-visual presentation *(15min)* helps put into context the masterpieces of Irish art brought together in **The Treasury★★**. Precious objects range in date from the Bronze Age to the 15C and include: a model boat in gold from the Broighter Hoard (1C); the Lough na Shade Trumpet (1C BC) *(see p 393)*; the Ardagh Chalice (8C); the Tara Brooch (8C); the Shrine of St Patrick's Bell in bronze, gold and silver (c 1100); the "Cathach", a book shrine made to contain the Psalter of St Columba (Colmcille) (12C-15C); the Kavanagh Charter Horn of ivory and brass, the only surviving object associated with Irish kingship (12C-15C).

The section on **Prehistoric Ireland** has a reconstruction of a passage tomb as well as the huge Lurgan Longboat, hollowed from a tree-trunk around 2500 BC. **Ireland's Gold** displays a gleaming array of artefacts, some from hoards preserved for thousands of years in the Irish boglands.

The **Road to Independence** commemorates those involved in the **Easter Rising** in 1916 through photos, MSS, documents, uniforms and death-masks.

Among the objects shown in **Viking Ireland** are artefacts from the Viking settlement at Wood Quay in Old Dublin: iron, bone, wood utensils, clothing and ornaments. St Manchan's Shrine, a spectacular reliquary, is one of several ecclesiastical treasures on display in the section entitled **The Church.**

Small in number but superb in quality, the objects on show from **Ancient Egypt** benefit from their dramatically lit display. **Irish Glass** has fine examples of this craft in which the country has long excelled.

National Gallery★★

Kildare Street/Merrion Street or Clare Street. (Dúchas) ♿ *Open daily, 9.30am (noon Sun) to 5.30pm (8.30pm Thu). Closed Good Fri, 24-26 Dec. Guided tour. Sat, 3pm, Sun, 2pm, 3pm, 4pm. Restaurant.* ☎ *01 661 5133; Fax 01 661 5372; info@ngi.ie; www.nationalgallery.ie*

Ireland's National Gallery has one of the finest collections of art in Europe, housed in a building which has expanded over the years to cope with the collection which has been constantly added to since its inauguration in 1864. By the Merrion Street entrance is a statue of William Dargan (1799-1867); Dargan was a railway magnate and the promoter of the Irish Industrial Exhibition of 1853 which included a Fine Art Hall and which stimulated the foundation of the gallery. Other benefactors have included Sir Hugh Lane, Sir Henry Vaughan, and GB Shaw, whose donation included royalties from *My Fair Lady*. The Milltown Rooms were built to house the Milltown Collection *(see p 372)*. The latest addition is the controversial Millennium Wing, a striking stone-clad edifice providing a spacious new entrance area, first-rate visitor facilities as well as new galleries, some of which are used for changing exhibitions of international significance.

Understandably, the gallery's collection of Irish art is outstanding, ranging from the 17C to the 20C, with fine works by the country's major painters and sculptors together with select items of furniture. There are fascinating topographical pictures, portraits, and a whole room devoted to the work of Jack B Yeats (1871-1957), who was able to evoke much of the flavour of Irish life at the time, painting landscapes, horses, and portraits of friends and family, among them a famous likeness of his brother, WB Yeats.

The gallery's British paintings include canvases by 18C artists like Hogarth, Wilson, Gainsborough, Reynolds and Romney, and there are lovely watercolours by Bonington and Crome. There is an important Italian collection ranging from early altarpieces to pictures by Fra Angelico, Mantegna and Titian and a superbly dramatic Caravaggio, *The Taking of Christ.* French painting is represented by pictures by Claude and Poussin, by several artists of the Rococo, and there are a number of Impressionists. Outstanding among the Dutch paintings is the tranquil *Woman Reading a Letter* by Gabriel Metsu, matched by works by Vermeer, Ruisdael and Hobbema. The Spanish collection is substantial, with pictures by El Greco, Velazquez, Murillo, Zurbaran, and Goya.

Natural History Museum

Merrion Street Upper. (&) Open Tue-Sun, 10am (2pm Sun) to 5pm. ☎ 01 677 7444;
Fax 01 677 7450; Marketing@museum.ie; www.museum.ie.

MUSEUMLINK shuttle service every 80min; €1.27 one way (Natural History
Museum Merrion Street - National Museum Collins Barracks - National Museum Kildare
Street).

Access: Buses 7, 7A, 8 (Burgh Quay).

A barely altered example of a Victorian museum, the building's pillared hall and
galleries are as fascinating as their contents, which include three skeletons of the
Great Irish Deer, now extinct. The specimens, still exhibited in the original display
cabinets cover the full range of mammals, birds, fish and insects ever to have lived
in Ireland.

Heraldic Museum

Kildare Street. & Open Mon-Sat, 10am-8.30pm (4.30pm Thu-Fri; 12.30pm Sat). Closed
Bank Hols, Good Fri, 22 Dec-2 Jan. ☎ 01 603 0311; Fax 01 662 1062; herald@nli.ie;
www.nli.ie

The display presents the banners of the recognised heads of Irish families; the
arms of the provinces, counties, cities and towns; the colours of Irish Regiments
which served in France in the 17C and 18C; various heraldic artefacts.

Number Twenty-Nine★

Guided tour Tue-Sun, 10am (2pm Sun) to 5pm. Closed Good Fri, 2 weeks before
Christmas. €3.15. Brochure (6 languages). Tearoom. ☎ 01 702 6165; Fax 01 702 7796;
numbertwentynine@mail.esb.ie; www.esb.ie/education

Lower Fitzwilliam Street. Occupied from 1794 to 1806 by a widow and her three
children, this 18C terrace house gives an extraordinarily vivid picture of domestic
life in Dublin in the Georgian era. It is furnished throughout with original or
reproduction furniture, carpets and curtains and contemporary furniture and
paintings, and is crammed with the paraphernalia of everyday living. Among the
wealth of objects a wine cistern designed by Francis Johnston and a curved belly-
warmer.

Newman House★★

St Stephen's Green South. Open Jul-Aug, Tue-Sat, noon (2pm Sat) to 5pm; otherwise
by appointment. €4. Guided tour (40min) available. ☎ 01 716 7422, 01 475 7255;
Fax 01 716 7211

The two 18C town houses are named after Cardinal Newman, the first Rector of
University College, which
started here there in 1854.
Relatively little altered,
they enable visitors to experience something of the
atmosphere of the 18C city.
The smaller house was
designed by Richard Castle
in 1738 and among many
original features still has the
glazing bars designed by him.
The Apollo Room has splendid
stucco figures of Apollo
and the Muses by the
Lafranchini brothers, who also
decorated the superb Saloon
on the first floor; two of their
figures were deemed indecent
when the room became a
Jesuit chapel in 1883, and
their nudity was discreetly
covered. The larger house
dates from 1765; the Bishops'
Room has a portrait of Cardinal Newman and his Rector's
Chair, while the staircase is
decorated with lovely Rococo
plasterwork by Richard West
featuring birds and musical
instruments.

Newman House

Civic Museum

William Street South. Open Tue-Sat, 10am-6pm, Sun, 11am-2pm. Closed Bank Hols, Easter and Christmas. ☎ *01 679 4260; Fax 01 6775 954*

The history of Dublin can be traced in the old City Assembly House. The Octagon Room displays maps, prints, postcards, photographs, relics of old buildings and a set of Malton's views of Dublin (1792-99). Early forms of transport are illustrated together with relics of earlier commercial practices.

DUBLIN CASTLE DISTRICT

Dublin Castle** (Hy)

Entrances in Dame Lane and Ship Street. (OPW) (&) Guided tour (45min; including State . Apartments and Undercroft official use permitting) daily, 10am (2pm Sat-Sun and Bank Hols) to 5pm (4 45pm last admission). Closed Good Fri, 24-26 Dec. €4. Guide (5 languages). Restaurant. Wheelchair access (except Undercroft). ☎ *01 677 7129; Fax 01 679 7831; dublincastle@eircom.net; www.historic-centres.com*

For 700 years until 1922 Dublin Castle represented British rule in Ireland. People under suspicion languished in its prisons; traitors' heads were exhibited on spikes over the gate. Embedded within the tight-knit urban fabric of the city, the Castle changed over the centuries from a formidable fortress to an administrative complex of almost domestic character. ByIn the 19C the Lord Deputy usually resided atin Vice-Regal Lodge in Phoenix Park *(see belowabove)*, staying at the Castle only for the few winter weeks of the Castle Season, which was a glittering round of levées, balls and receptions. The Castle is now one of the symbols of Irish statehood, its sumptuous State Apartments used to receive foreign dignitaries and on other important ceremonial occasions.

Its construction – began in 1204, 30 years after the Anglo-Norman landing in Ireland, when King John ordered a castle to be built The site chosen wason the high ground southeast of the existing town, a site and protected to the south and easton two sides by the **River Poddle**. The original structure expanded into a rough quadrangle with a round tower at each corner on the site of the present Upper Yard. In 1604 much of the medieval castle was destroyed by fire. New apartments designed by Sir William Robinson were completed in 1688 but most of them were replaced in the middle of the 18C. The Castle's two courtyards now have an essentially Georgian appearance, with the Powder Tower as the most visible reminder of its medieval origin, even though it too was much altered in the early 19C.

State Apartments – Upper Yard. The upper floor on the south side of the Upper Yard was built between 1750 and 1780 but the interiors have been much modified subsequently.

The **Grand Staircase** and the **Battleaxe Landing** lead to a suite of sumptuously furnished and decorated interiors overlooking Castle Green and the wall named after Queen Victoria, built to protect the royal gaze from the sight of the adjoining stables. In 1916, one room served as a prison for James Connolly, one of the leaders of the Uprising. There is Sheraton, Regency and Louis XIV furniture, fine plaster or painted ceilings, and modern, colourful carpets from Killybegs *(see p 200)*.

Wedgwood Room, Dublin Castle

The **Throne Room** has ovals and roundels of gods and goddesses probably painted by the Venetian Giambattista Bellucci in the early 18C; portraits of Viceroys in the **Picture Gallery** are set off by superb Venetian chandeliers,; and the **Wedgwood Room** has paintings attributed to Angelica Kauffmann (1741-1807) as well as black Wedgwood plaques.

The scene of many a glittering ball in Ascendancy times, **St Patrick's Hall** was built in the mid-18C and named after the Order of the Knights of St Patrick, an order instituted by George III in 1783. Crests, helmets and banners hang above the stall plates recording the names of the members of the Order, while the ceiling painting is a glorification of the relationship between Britain and Ireland. It was the work of Vincenzo Valdré (1742-1814), an Italian who came to Ireland in 1774 with the Viceroy, the Marquess of Buckingham, for whom he had worked at Stowe.

Castle Hall – *Upper Yard*. The dignified attractive two-storey building *(not open)* on the north side of the upper yard was designed c 1750 by Thomas Ivory for the Master of Ceremonies. It incorporates the **Bedford Tower**, which was named after John Russell, Duke of Bedford and Lord Lieutenant, and built on the base of the west tower of the original castle gate. Four days before the state visit of Edward VII and Queen Alexandra in 1907 the Crown Jewels were stolen from the Office of Arms in the Bedford Tower; they have never been recovered.

Flanking Castle Hall are two gates surmounted by statues by Van Nost: *Fortitude* on the west gate and *Justice* on the east gate, which was the sole entrance until the west gate was opened in 1988 and a new bridge built; the fountain and pool recall the old moat. A figure of Justice stands atop the Tower; Dublin wags liked to point out that her back is turned to the city and that her scales dipped unevenly in wet weather; holes were eventually bored in the outer pan to allow the rainwater to drain away.

Powder Tower Undercroft – *Lower Yard*. This is the best place to experience something of the great antiquity of the Castle. Excavations beneath the Powder Tower have revealed parts of the Viking and Norman defences – a 13C arch and relieving arch in the **Old City Wall** which enabled boatmen to enter the moat to deliver goods to the postern gate.

Church of the Most Holy Trinity – *Lower Yard*. This fine example of a Regency Gothick building was designed by Francis Johnston and consecrated in 1814. Before reconsecration as a Roman Catholic place of worship in 1943 it was the Chapel Royal, occupying the site of an earlier, smaller church. The exterior is decorated with over 100 heads carved in Tullamore limestone by Edward Smyth and his son John; the interior plasterwork is by George Stapleton and the woodwork by Richard Stewart. The scenes from the Passion of Christ in the east window are composed of old stained glass from the Continent. The arms of all the Viceroys from 1172 to 1922 are represented in wood on the galleries and chancel walls and in stained glass in the gallery windows.

Chester Beatty Library★★★

Dublin Castle Precinct, Dubh Linn Garden; entrance in Dame Lane or Ship Street. ♿ *Open May-Sep, daily, 10am (11am Sat, 1pm Sun) to 5pm; Oct-Apr, Tue-Sun, 10am (11am Sat, 1pm Sun) to 5pm. Closed Bank Hol Mon, Good Fri, 24-26 Dec and 1 Jan.* ☎ *01 4070 750; Fax 01 4070 760; info@cbl.ie; www.cbl.ie*

This fabulous and beautifully displayed array of Islamic and Far Eastern manuscripts and artworks was bequeathed to the nation by Sir Alfred Chester Beatty (1875-1968), an American businessman who had the distinction of being made the country's first honorary citizen. The large and renowned collection of **Arabic**, **Persian and Turkish manuscripts** includes over 270 copies of the **Koran**, some with illuminations by some of the greatest master calligraphers.

Biblical material consists of Syriac, Armenian, Ethiopian and Coptic texts, also early Western Bibles and Books of Hours. Of international importance are the biblical papyri dating from the early 2C to 4C.

The **Japanese and Chinese collection** includes paintings and prints of the highest quality, including Japanese woodblock prints which influenced 19C European art. In addition, there is , and a large collection of snuff bottles, *netsuke*, jade books and rhinoceros-horn cups.

The **Western European collection** contains many important printed books as well as prints by Dürer, Holbein, Piranesi, Bartolozzi and many others.

City Hall★

Dame Street. Open daily, 10am (2pm Sun) to 5.15pm (5pm Sun). Closed Good Fri and 25-26 Dec. Exhibition. Audioguide (4 languages). €3.81. ☎ *01 672 2204; cityhall@dublincity.ie; www.dublincity.ie/cityhall; www.dublincorp.ie/cityhall*

This magnificent edifice with its dome and portico, built (1769-79) by Thomas Cooley as the Royal Exchange, marked the arrival in Ireland of the neo-Classical style and is one of the finest public buildings in Dublin. When economic activity declined after the 1800 Act of Union, the building lost much of its purpose, and in 1852 it was bought by the City Corporation. During the **Easter Rising** in 1916 it was one of the key points in the city occupied by the insurgents; from the roof they commanded the approaches and main gate of Dublin Castle but after about three hours the regular soldiers regained command of the Upper Yard.

The splendid domed **rotunda** is decorated with early 20C frescoes illustrating aspects of city history. **The Story of the Capital**, a lively introduction to Dublin's past, is housed in the vaulted spaces of the basement. The excellent multi-media exhibition complements Dublinia, not least because of the thoroughness with which it deals with post-medieval history. The array of explanatory panels, plans, photographs, old films, and video screens is supplemented by fascinating artworks and by precious objects like the Civic Sword presented by Henry IV around 1409 *(see also Dublinia below)*.

Dublinia

High Street. (&) Open Apr-Sep, daily, 10am-5pm; Oct-Mar, daily, 11am (10am Sun and Bank Hols) to 4pm (4.30pm Sun and Bank Hols). €5.75. ☎ 01 679 4611; Fax 01 679 7116; info@dublinia.ie; www.dublinia.ie

This entertaining interactive exhibition brings alive the sights, sounds, smells and touch of the medieval city. There are tableaux, live costumed figures, a superb model of the Dublin of around 1500, a mock-up of part of an important archaeological excavation along the Liffey together with some key finds, and a reconstruction of the face of a medieval Dubliner, whose skeleton was found nearby. It is housed in part of the Synod Hall of Christ Church Cathedral to which it is linked by an arch *(see also City Hall above)*.

From the top of St Michael's Tower *(96 steps)* there is a fine **view**.

Marsh's Library★★

St Patrick's Close. Open Mon and Wed-Fri, 10am-1pm and 2-5pm, Sat, 10.30am-1pm. €2.50. Brochure (22 languages). ☎ 01 454 3511; Fax 01 454 3511; keeper@marsh library.ie, www.marshlibrary.ie

The building was designed in 1701 by Sir William Robinson to house the first public library in Ireland. A portrait of the founder, Archbishop Narcissus Marsh, hangs above the stairs. The dark oak bookcases, surmounted by a mitre, divide the long room into seven bays. Beyond the office are three "cages" where precious books can be consulted behind locked wire screens. The total of 25 000 books is composed of four individual collections and contains many rare early works..

O'CONNELL STREET – PARNELL SQUARE

Custom House★★

Custom House Quay; entrance in south front; floodlit at night. Open mid-Mar to Oct, daily, 10am-12.30pm; Sat-Sun and Bank Hols, 2-5pm; Nov to mid-Mar, Wed-Fri, 10am-12.30pm, Sun, 2-5pm. €1. ☎ 01 8882 538

The Custom House, with its long façade and central dome, is one of the great landmarks of Dublin. It was designed by James Gandon and completed in 1791. It was restored after being set on fire by anti-Treaty forces at the beginning of the Civil War in 1921. The **Visitor Centre** occupies the ceremonial vestibules behind the south portico, little altered since Gandon's day. The detailed and fascinating display examines the construction of the building, the fire and restoration, Gandon's career, and the work of the government offices which were housed there – excisemen, roads, canals and railways.

Outside on the quay beside the River Liffey stands the **Famine Memorial**, six bronze figures by Rowan Gillespie, recalling the mixed emotions – ranging from despair through suffering to hope – of the many victims of the Great Famine *(see Historical Perspective)*.

Hugh Lane Gallery of Modern Art★

Parnell Square North. & Open Tue-Sun, 9.30am (11am Sun) to 6pm (5pm Fri-Sun). Closed Good Fri and 25 Dec. Guided tour (40min; €25; book in advance). Bookshop and café. Ramp. ☎ 01 874 1903; Fax 01 872 2182; info@hughlane.ie; www.hughlane.ie

The gallery houses an extensive collection of late-19C and 20C works by Irish and Continental artists including the works collected by **Sir Hugh Lane** (1875–1915), who drowned on the *Lusitania*. The building, a three-storey mansion of Portland stone and granite, flanked by curved screen walls, was designed in 1762 by Sir William Chambers for an earlier connoisseur of art, **James Caulfield**, 1st Earl of Charlemont, who also built the Marino Casino *(see Northside below)*.

The permanent collection includes many fine British and French paintings, among the latter several Impressionists as well as pictures by Corot and Courbet. Contemporary artworks include a characteristic project by Christo for swathing the pathways of St Stephen's Green but the most interesting rooms are perhaps those devoted to works by Irish artists. *Lakeside Cottage* (c 1929) is a typically atmospheric landscape by Paul Henry, while the dramatic canvas *The Rescue of the Prison Van at Manchester* by Maurice MacGonical reconstructs a famous Fenian attack in 1867 *(see Historical Perspective)*. A whole room is devoted to the paintings of Roderic O'Conor (1860-1940), a friend of Gauguin and an important link between artistic life in France and the British Isles; his pictures reflect the influence of his French colleagues, from Seurat to Van Gogh.

Dublin Writers' Museum

Parnell Square North. Open daily, 10am (11am Sun and Bank Hols) to 5pm (6pm, Mon-Fri, Jun-Aug). €5.50; joint ticket available for 3 or all 7 of Dublin Tourism sites. Audioguide (6 languages). Guided tour by appointment. Brochure (7 languages). Restaurant; coffee shop. ☎ 01 872 2077; Fax 01 872 2231; shawhouse@dublintourism.ie; www.visitdublin.com

The museum illustrates the personalities of those Irish writers who were associated with the city of Dublin. On display are personal items, photos, portraits, busts, manuscripts and copies of their major works. The museum also traces the written tradition in Ireland from the illuminated manuscripts of the Celtic Christian church such as the Book of Kells *(see Trinity College Old Library above)* to the present day through Jonathan Swift and his contemporaries, writers who made their names in England such as Oscar Wilde and Bernard Shaw, writers who lived abroad such as James Joyce and Samuel Beckett, the great names who promoted the 19C revival of interest in Irish folklore such as WB Yeats, Synge and O'Casey and those who lived and worked in Dublin such as Flann O'Brien, Brendan Behan and Patrick Kavanagh. Temporary exhibitions are held in the elegant reception rooms, readings and workshops in the children's section.

The museum occupies two Georgian terrace houses with **elegant stucco ceilings★**; the one in the library is by **Michael Stapleton**. Alterations made in 1891-95 by Alfred Darbyshire for George Jameson include stained-glass windows bearing the Jameson monogram, four female figures representing Music, Literature, Art and Science, and, in the first-floor saloon, a series of painted door panels by Gibson and an ornamental colonnade and gilded frieze.

National Wax Museum

Granby Row (northeast corner of Parnell Square). Open daily, 10am (noon Sun) to 5.30pm. €5. ☎ 01 872 6340

The display of waxwork figures combines fantasy and reality. The tableaux on the upper floor illustrate traditional fairy tales. Those on the ground floor are peopled by national figures such as O'Connell, the heroes of the Easter Rising, the Presidents of Ireland, theatrical stars, church leaders, poets and writers, politicians, sportsmen and pop stars.

James Joyce

James Joyce Centre

35 North Great George's Street. Open daily, 9.30am (12.30pm Sun and Bank Hols) to 5pm. €3. Library. Café. ☎ 01 878 8547; Fax 01 878 8488; joycecen @iol.ie; www.james joyce.ie

The centre, which aims to promote an interest in the life and work of **James Joyce**, offers talks, conducted tours of the house and walks through the north inner city. As a boy Joyce lived nearby in Fitzgibbon Street and attended Belvedere College *(Denmark Street)*. The centre is housed in a restored terrace house, which was built in 1784 by Francis Ryan as the town house of Valentine Brown, Earl of Kenmare, the very fine **plasterwork★** is mostly by **Michael Stapleton**. Portraits of members of the Joyce family line the staircase; there are family photographs in the exhibition room.

Irish Music Hall of Fame (IMHF)

Middle Abbey Street. Open daily, 9.30am-6pm (5pm last admission). €7.62. ☎ 01 878 3345; Fax 01 878 3225; www.mcd.ie/hq

Through the visual panels and the sound track on the headphones the story of Irish music unfolds from the presence of Irish harpers at the court of Elizabeth I via traditional Irish music, the showbands of the 1950s, the three years of success in the Eurovision contest to Celtic rock and the 1 000 bands in Dublin at the turn of the Millennium.

FOUR COURTS DISTRICT

St Michan's Church

Church Street. (&) Open Mar-Oct, Mon-Sat, 10am-5pm (1pm Sat); Nov-Mar, Mon-Fri, 12.30pm-3.30pm, Sat 10am-1pm. €3. Guided tour including vaults (30-40min). Gift shop. Wheelchair access to church not vaults. ☎ 01 872 4154 (9.30am-1.30pm); Fax 01 878 2615; stmichan@iol.ie

The first church on the site was probably built by the Danes as St Michan is thought to be a Danish saint. The present church dates from 1095 but gained its present appearance in from 1686.

While the **interior** has many fascinating features, including the early 18C organ played by Handel, it is the **vaults** which attract the majority of visitors with their array of **mummified corpses** preserved for over 300 years by the dry air and constant temperature.

St Mary's Abbey

Mary's Abbey. (Dúchas) Open mid-Jun to mid-Sep, Wed and Sun, 10am-5pm (4.15pm last admission). €1.20. Guided tour available. ☎ 01 872 1490; Fax 01 661 3764; info@heritageireland.ie; www.heritageireland.ie

Founded by Benedictines but taken over by Cistercians, St Mary's was the richest monastery in the Pale as well as being the meeting place for the Council of Ireland. It was here in 1534 that Silken Thomas renounced his allegiance to Henry VIII, thereby setting off the Kildare Revolt. All that remains of the abbey are the **Slype** and the rib vaulted **Chapter House**, which now contains a reconstruction of the 15C cloister arcade (the pieces were recovered in 1975 from a 17C building in Cork Street) and information about the foundation, architecture and history of the abbey and the Cistercian way of life.

NORTHSIDE

See map p 222

National Museum★★

Collins Barracks, Benburh Street. Other collections of the National Museum are displayed at Kildare Street (see p 235). Open Tue-Sat, 10am (2pm Sun) to 5pm. Guided tour (30min-45min) at frequent intervals; €1.27. Parking. Café. Museum shop. ☎ 01 677 7444; Fax 01 677 7450; Marketing@museum.ie; www.museum.ie

MUSEUMLINK shuttle service every 80min; €1.27 one way (National Museum Collins Barracks - National Museum Kildare Street - Natural History Museum Merrion Street).

Access: Buses 90 (Aston Quay), 25, 25A, 66, 67 (Middle Abbey Street).

This great barrack complex, which once housed 3 000 men and 1 000 horses, was built in 1700 on the orders of King William III and designed by Thomas Burgh. It was intended to be "plain and useful, without any unnecessary ornament" and in its day was the largest institution of its kind in the British Isles, a progressive alternative to the contentious practice of billeting soldiers on the population. It has been converted to provide accommodation for several sections of the National Museum including the decorative arts, folk life, history and geology.

As well as space for temporary exhibitions, the **West Block** has galleries devoted to the work of the museum, and an enthralling array of special treasures – 25 highly varied pieces grouped together under the heading of **Curators' Choice;** they include a rare astrolabe from Prague, an elongated late-13C or early-14C wood statue of St Molaise (see p 342) and Bow figurines made by Thomas Frye, some of them modelled on his fellow London Irishmen.

The **South Block** has three floors of galleries: (third floor) Irish country furniture and woodcraft, with period furniture showing the development of furniture from Baroque to Modern, including the fascinating late-19C style unique to Ireland, Neo-Celtic, inspired by objects like the Tara Brooch discovered in 1850; (second floor) scientific instruments; (first floor) Irish silver from the early 17C to the striking work of modern silversmiths.

Marino Casino★★

Off Malahide Road, Marino. (Dúchas) Guided tour May-Oct, daily, 10am-5pm (6pm Jun-Sep); Nov-Apr, Sat-Sun, noon-4pm (5pm Apr); last admission 45min before closing. Closed 25-26 Dec. €2.50. Parking. ☎ 01 833 1618; Fax 01 833 2636; casinomarina@ealga.ie; www.heritageireland.ie

Access: From city centre by bus 20A, 20B, 27, 27B, 42; 123 Imp Bus from O'Connell Street; by DART - Clontarf Road Station.

The charming Palladian villa, designed by Sir William Chambers in 1765, was built in the grounds of Marino House (demolished 1921), the country seat of James Caulfield, Earl of Charlemont *(see pp 239 and 417-418)*, who had met Chambers while making the Grand Tour (1746-54). The casino is built of Portland stone in the French neo-Classical style in the shape of a Greek cross on a rusticated basement; 12 Doric columns support a frieze and cornice topped by pediments, statues and urn-shaped chimneys. The sculpture is by Simon Vierpyl and Joseph Wilton.

The interior contains four state rooms, decorated with elaborate plaster ceilings and inlaid floors using eight different kinds of wood, and four small bedrooms on the upper floor; plans of the building are displayed in the basement service rooms.

National Botanic Gardens★★

Botanic Road, Glasnevin. (Dúchas) (&) Gardens: Open Apr-Sep, daily, 9am (11am Sun) to 6pm; Oct-Mar, daily, 10am (11am Sun) to 4.30pm. Closed 25 Dec. Glasshouses: Open Apr-Sep, daily, 9am (2pm Sun) to 5.15pm (3.15pm Thu, 5.45pm Sat-Sun); Oct-Mar, 10am (2pm Sun) to 4.15pm (3.15pm Thu). Alpine houses: Open Mon-Fri, 10.45am-12.15pm and 2.15-3.15pm; Sun, 2-5.45pm; Bank Hols, 9am-12.45pm and 2-5.45pm. Guided tour (1hr) by appointment €1.90. Leaflet (6 languages). Parking. ☎ 01 837 7596, 837 4388; Fax 01 836 0080

The gardens were established in 1795 on an attractive 48 acre/19ha site beside the Tolka River. The splendid Victorian glasshouses include the **Curvilinear Range** (1843-69), designed by Richard Turner, and the **Great Palm House** (1884).

There is a delightful **walk** along the river bank from the **rose garden,** past the mill-race, through the **peat garden** (walled) and the **bog garden** beside the ornamental pond to the **arboretum.** The specimens in the rock garden, cactus house and fern house are among the 20 000 species grown here.

Glasnevin Cemetery★

Finglas Road, Glasnevin. Guided tour (1hr 30min) from the main gate Wed and Fri at 2.30pm. ☎ 01 830 1133; Mob 086 8911 683 (tour guide); Fax 01 830 1594; www.glasnevin-cemetery.ie

Behind its walls, Europe's largest cemetery (120 acres/49ha) is the resting place of over a million people, nearly all of them of the Roman Catholic faith. As well as anonymous paupers and cholera victims, virtually every personage who has played a role in Ireland's history is buried here, many of them in plots reserved for those of a particular political persuasion. Some graves, like that of President De Valera, are of great simplicity and modesty. By contrast, the the tomb of Daniel O'Connell is a mighty national monument, its vault with its Celtic Revival decor surmounted by a 168ft/51m round tower. The guided tour becomes a fascinating walk through Irish history.

Old Jameson Distillery

Bow Street, Smithfield Village. & Guided tour (1hr; 8 languages) 9.30am-5.30pm (last tour). Closed Good Fri, 25 Dec. €6.28. Gift shop. Restaurant; public bar and tasting bar. ☎ 01 807 2355; Fax 807 2369; ojd@idl.ie; www.whiskeytours.ie

Part of the old distillery, last used as such in 1971, has been converted to show current and earlier methods of production of whiskey. A video *(8min)* is followed by a tour *(20min)* which passes from the centre of a kiln, through the yard where the barley was delivered from the farms to the grain store; the mystery of worts and wash-backs in the process of making and maturing whiskey is explained. The tour ends in the bar where visitors are invited to take part in a whiskey tasting.

Chimney Viewing Tower

Smithfield Village. Open daily, 10am-5pm. €6. ☎ 01 817 3838

The chimney (175ft/5560m), constructed in 1895 as part of the Jameson Distillery, is now flanked by a glass-walled lift and crowned by a glass observation platform – fine views of the city, the bay and the mountains to the south.

GAA Museum

Clonliffe Road. Open May-Sep, daily, 9.30am-6pm; Oct-Apr, Tue-Sun, 10am (noon Sun) to 5pm. Open on match days to Cusack or Canal stand ticketholders. Museum and stadium €8.50; museum only €5. Guided tour available. ☎ 01 855 8176; Fax 01 855 8104; museum@gaa.ie

Croke Park is the home of the national games of Ireland – hurling and Irish football. The museum here traces the development of the **Gaelic Athletic Association** *(see Ireland Today)* and its influence on the sporting, cultural and social traditions of Ireland. Touch-screen technology provides a view of the highlights of past games and the champions in action; visitors can test their speed of reaction and high-jumping ability or try hitting the *sliothar* with a *camán* in the practice nets.

SOUTHSIDE

Kilmainham Gaol Museum★★

Inchicore Road, Kilmainham. (Dúchas) (&) Guided tour (30min) Apr-Sep, daily, 9.30am-4.45pm; Oct-Mar, daily, 9.30am (10am Sun) to 4pm (4.45pm Sun); last tour 1hr before closing; last admission 90min before closing. Closed 24-26 Dec. €4.40. Parking. Tearoom. ☎ 01 453 5984; Fax 01 453 2037; www.visitdublin.ie

The Irish struggle for political independence is excellently presented in the prison where so many Irishmen were incarcerated and some executed for offences against the Crown, among them United Irishmen, Young Irelanders, Fenians, Invincibles, and participants in the Easter Rising.

The exhibition of souvenirs, photographs, letters and press cuttings explains and illustrates the many incidents and rebellions which took place between 1796 and 1924 and their social and political context.

The **tour** includes the Central Hall (1862) containing 100 cells, the chapel with an audio-visual presentation on the history of the prison, individual cells in the 1798 corridor, and the yards where the prisoners took exercise and executions were carried out.

The New Gaol, as it was known for many years, was built in 1792 and consisted of a central range flanked by an east and a west courtyard divided into exercise yards; one contains Erskine Childers' boat the *Asgard (see p 246)*. In 1862, when the east wing was rebuilt, a high outer wall was constructed.

Kilmainham Gaol

Dúchas, Dublin

Irish Museum of Modern Art

Military Road, Kilmainham. Car park. & Open Tue-Sun, 10am (noon Sun, Bank Hols) to 5.30pm (5.15pm last admission). Closed 29 Mar. Guided tour: early-Jun to early-Sep, Wed and Fri at 2.30pm, Sun at 12.15pm. Parking. Café. ☎ 01 612 9900; Fax 01 612 9999; info@modernart.ie; www.modernart.ie

The role of the museum (opened in 1991) is to present 20C Irish and international art and allied theatrical and musical performances, and to establish a permanent collection through purchases and commissions. Its exciting and wide-ranging programme includes exhibitions by some of the 20th century's most influential artists and work by leading young artists from Ireland and abroad. The range of buildings facing the south front of the museum has been converted into artists' studios.

The museum is housed in **Royal Kilmainham Hospital★★**, the earliest-surviving Classical building in Ireland. It was commissioned by the Duke of Ormond, James Butler of Kilkenny, who was appointed Viceroy in 1669 after living in exile in France, and inspired by Les Invalides in Paris. The architect was William Robinson, Surveyor-General since 1670, who designed (1680-84) four ranges of buildings round a courtyard providing accommodation for 300 old soldiers, the last of whom left in 1929. *(Dúchas)* & *Guided heritage tour early-Jun to early-Sep, Tue-Sun, 10am (noon Sun and Bank Hol) to 5.30pm. €3.20. Audio-visual show. Parking. Coffee shop.* ☎ *01 612 9900; Fax 01 612 9999; info@modernart.ie; www.modernart.ie*

In the north range is the **Great Hall**, once the soldiers' dining and recreation room and now a fine setting for concerts and government receptions and the **Chapel,** with a replica papier mâché ceiling replacing the Baroque original the more elaborate parts of which – fruit and vegetable motifs up to (max 12in/30cm long) – had begun to fall off.

Rathfarnham Castle★

3mi/5km south of Dublin by N 81 and R 115. (Dúchas) (&) *Guided tour, May-Oct, daily, 9.30am-5.30pm; last tour 1hr before closing. Conservation in progress. €1.90. Leaflet. Tearoom.* ☎ *01 493 9461, 9462; rathfarnhamcastle@ealga.ie; info@heritageireland.ie; www.heritageireland.ie*

The magnificent but forbidding exterior gives no hint of the elegant 18C interior designed by Sir William Chambers and James "Athenian" Stuart. The rectangular central keep with four flanker towers was built c 1593 by Adam Loftus, a Yorkshireman who became Archbishop of Dublin. The castle was abandoned in the early 20C, then used as a Jesuit seminary; its splendid interiors, remodelled in the 1770s for Henry Loftus, are currently undergoing painstaking restoration.

Guinness Storehouse★

Crane Market Street, off Thomas Street. & *Guided tour (1hr) daily, 9.30am-5pm. Closed Good Fri, 24-26 Dec, 1 Jan. €12.* ☎ *01 408 4800; 01 453 8364 (Infoline); Fax 01 408 4965; guinness-storehouse@guinness.com; www.guinness-storehouse. com*

A free glass of the famous dark stout with the creamy head is served in the visitors' bar in the **old hop store**, at the end of a fascinating survey of the Guinness production process. The history of the **Guinness** family firm is traced through 140 years by means of a film *(20min)* supplemented by text, pictures and obsolete machinery.

In Thomas Street, next to the main gate of the brewery where the new date is painted up every year, is the house built by Arthur Guinness in the 18C. The brewery takes its name from St James' Gate, which pierced the old city wall at this point.

Drimnagh Castle

Long Mile Road. (&) *Guided tour Apr-Sep, Wed, Sat-Sun, noon-5pm; Oct-Mar, Sun, 2-5pm; last tour 4.15pm; other times by appointment. €3.50. Limited wheelchair access to gardens.* ☎ *01 450 2530; Fax 01 450 8927*

Drimnagh is a 13C moated castle consisting of a medieval Great Hall over a vaulted undercroft, flanked by a battlemented tower. It has been restored to its medieval appearance with a formal 17C garden – box hedges, lavender bushes and herbs – at the rear.

Shaw Birthplace

33 Synge Street. Open May-Sep, daily, 10am (11am Sun and Public Hols) to 1pm and 2-5pm. €5.50; joint ticket available for 3 or all 7 Dublin Tourism sites. Audioguide (30min; 7 languages). Brochure (7 languages). ☎ *01 872 2077; Fax 01 872 2231; shawhouse@dublintourism.ie; www.visitdublin.com*

The modest house, where **George Bernard Shaw** (1856-1950) was born and spent his early years, is furnished in the style of the mid-19C.

Waterways Visitor Centre

Grand Canal Quay. (Dúchas) (& *to ground floor) Open Jun-Sep, daily, 9.30am-5.30pm; Oct-May, Wed-Sun, 12.30-5pm; last admission 45min before closing. Closed 25–26 Dec, 1 Jan. €2.50.* ☎ *01 677 7510; Fax 01 677 7514; www.heritageireland.ie*

The modern building, which stands on an island in the **Grand Canal** basin, houses a display explaining canal engineering and the history of the countrywide network of canals which was established in the 18C. The flat roof provides a view of the warehouses lining the canal basin.

Jewish Museum

Walworth Road. Open May-Sep, Sun, Tue and Thu, 11am-3pm; Oct-Apr, Sun, 10.30am-2.30pm or by appointment. Donation. ☎/Fax 01 676 0737; www.visit.dublin.com

The museum was opened in 1985 by Chaim Herzog, President of Israel and son of the first Chief Rabbi of Ireland, in the old Walworth Road Synagogue (1917-c 75). The showcases on the ground floor display material on the history of the Jews in Ireland from the 11C to the 20C. In the kitchen, which is fitted with separate sinks for meat and milk, the table is laid for the Sabbath evening meal.

The **synagogue** upstairs retains all its ritual fittings; the women's gallery has been converted to display religious artefacts.

Pearse Museum

4.5mi/7.2km south of Dublin by N 81. In Terenure fork left. In Rathfarnham bear left (direction: Bray); turn first right onto Grange Road; after 0.5 mile/0.8km turn right onto Sarah Curran Avenue. 10min there and back on foot from the car park by the footpath parallel with the road. (Dúchas) (&) Park: Open daily, 10am-7pm (8pm May-Aug, 5.30pm Feb-Mar, 4.30pm Nov-Jan). Museum: Open daily, 10am-1pm and 2-5.30pm (5pm Sep-Oct; 4pm Nov-Jan); last admission 45min before closing. Closed 25-26 Dec. Audio-visual show (20min). Guided tour (30min) by appointment. Open-air concerts (summer). Parking. Tearoom (May-Sep, daily, Oct-Apr, Sat-Sun). ☎ 01 493 4208, ☎ 01 493 3053 (tearoom); Fax 01 493 6120

Through pictures and manuscripts the museum traces the life of Patrick and William Pearse, founder members of the Irish Volunteers (1913), who were executed in 1916 for their leading role in the **Easter Rising**.

The house (1797) was acquired by the Pearse brothers in 1910 for their boys' school, named after **St Enda** of Aran *(see p 129)*. Their desire to encourage Irish culture and to allow children to develop their talents free from the pressure of exams was reflected in the curriculum, which included Gaelic language, literature and history, theatrical performances, nature study and games.

The **grounds** contain an avenue of trees, called Emmet's Walk in memory of Robert Emmet who courted Sarah Curran in the grounds; a walled garden, where the pupils grew vegetables; a nature walk, called *The Wayfarer*, which follows the river from the lake where the pupils used to swim, to the car park.

PATRICK PEARSE (1879-1914)

He was the second of four children born to Margaret Brady, whose family had moved to Dublin from County Meath during the Great Famine, and James Pearse, a stone carver from England, who came to Ireland in the 1850s, during a boom in church building. From his father's library he acquired a love of English literature and from his maternal great-aunt, Margaret, a love of the Irish language. In 1895, aged sixteen, he joined the Gaelic League and in 1903 became editor of the League's newspaper. Two years later he went to Belgium to study bilingualism in the schools. He wrote many articles proposing the same policy for Ireland and set up his own school for boys. Great names – William Butler Yeats, Patrick MacDonagh and Padraic Colum – took an interest in the pupils' theatrical productions. Pearse spent his holidays in Rosmuc *(see p 185)* in order to study Gaelic. Over the years his original intention simply to promote a pride in things Irish evolved into more active political engagement. In November 1913 he joined the Irish Volunteers to campaign for Home Rule and in February 1914 he joined the IRB. He took a prominent part in the Easter Rising and was executed at Kilmainham Gaol on 2 May 1916, not knowing that his brother was to be executed the following day.

Excursions

THE BEN OF HOWTH★

North side of Dublin Bay by the DART (Raheny Station for North Bull Island) or by the coast road and R 105.

The Ben of Howth is a steep rounded peninsula of rock rising from the sea on the north side of Dublin Bay. Sheltering in the lee is North Bull Island, originally only a sandbank covered at high tide, which has grown to its present size (3mi/4.5km long) and continues to increase in width seawards, since the Bull Wall was built in the late 18C to protect Dublin harbour from silting up.

North Bull Island Interpretive Centre

At the end of the central causeway. Open daily, 10.15am-1pm and 1.30-4pm; closed Fri afternoon. Audioguide (2 languages). Brochure (3 languages). Parking. ☎ 01 833 8341.

The **Interpretive Centre** houses an exhibition on the wildlife and natural habitats of the island which is an important **nature reserve** where many wildfowl and wading birds spend the winter; at high tide the 30 000 shore birds which feed in Dublin Bay all roost on North Bull Island. The island, which consists of sand dunes, salt marshes and mudflats, also accommodates two golf links and attracts many summer visitors to its sandy beaches. For many years the only link with the mainland was a plank bridge to the southern end of the island.

Continue by road or rail to Howth

Howth Harbour

From the high point on the east side of the headland *(car park)* there are two **cliff walks**: south past the Baily Lighthouse on the point and along the cliffs for a fine **view★** over Dublin Bay; or north past the Nose of Howth and Balscadden Bay to the picturesque village of **Howth**, which clings to the steep north face of the headland. At its heart are the ruins of **St Mary's Abbey**; in the chancel is the splendid tomb of a late-15C knight and his lady. *Key from Mrs O'Rourke, 13 Church Street, Howth.*

Below is the harbour (1807-09), which now shelters sailing craft and fishing boats; for 20 years from 1813 it was the packet boat station until Dún Laoghaire (then Kingstown) took over in 1833. Offshore lies **Ireland's Eye**, now a bird sanctuary, where the early Christians built a church (in ruins) in the 6C. *Operates from East Pier, Howth Harbour daily (weather permitting), 11am-6pm, on demand. There and back €8. ☎ 01 831 4200*

West of the village is Howth Castle Demesne. In the grounds is the **National Transport Museum**, a varied and comprehensively labelled collection of commercial and military vehicles, horse-drawn or motorised, neatly parked in a large shed. *(&) Open Jun-Sep, daily, 10am (2pm Sat) to 5.30pm; May and Oct, Sat-Sun and Bank Hols, 2-5.30pm; 26 Dec to 1 Jan, daily, 2-5.30pm. €2.50. Parking. ☎ 01 848 0831; info@nationaltransportmuseum.org; www.nationaltransportmuseum.org*

The castle *(private)*, a medieval keep with a 15C gatehouse, contains work by Morrison and Lutyens. Legend has it that when Grace O'Malley *(see p 362)* was refused hospitality on her return journey from visiting Elizabeth I in London, she abducted the Earl of Howth's son and returned him only when the Earl promised always to keep his door open to her family at mealtimes.

DÚN LAOGHAIRE

South side of Dublin Bay by the DART or by N 31.

Dún Laoghaire, which is the main port of entry to Ireland from Great Britain, is now one of the more attractive residential areas in the greater Dublin region as well as a seaside and boating resort. It grew from a small fishing village into a busy port through the growth of trade with Britain in the 18C and is named after Laoghaire (pronounced Leary), the High King of Ireland in the 5C, who built a fort here.

The **harbour** (251 acres/101ha) was designed by John Rennie and begun in 1817; the main work, built of Dalkey stone, was complete by 1842.

For 100 years the port was known as **Kingstown** in honour of **George IV**, who landed here in September 1821; an **Obelisk**, erected in memory of the king's visit to Ireland, stands on the waterfront south of the harbour.

National Maritime Museum of Ireland

Haigh Terrace, Dún Laoghaire. (&) Closed indefinitely for structural repair. Open previously May-Sep, Tue-Sun, 1-5pm. ☎ 01 280 0969 (24hr); Fax 01 275 0019; www.visitdublin.com

The museum is housed in the Mariners' Church (1835-60) on the south side of Moran Park. The exhibits include a cannon from the Spanish Armada; a French longboat, painted red, white and blue, captured during an attempted landing in Bantry Bay in 1796; the lamp from the Baily lighthouse *(see p 246)* in working order; the chart used by the Commander of the German U-boat which landed Roger Casement on Banna Strand; models of a Guinness barge, Irish coastal *curraghs*, a Rosslare cot (a sea-going flat-bottomed boat), Galway and Donegal hookers (sailing ships – *see p 259*), an Arklow schooner, racing skiffs, ferries, cargo ships, the first transatlantic steam ship *Sirius* (1838); the Halpin Collection, including a model of the *Great Eastern*, and the Cornelissen Collection of model ships showing the evolution from a Greek trireme to the fighting ships of the Second World War.

James Joyce Museum

0.5mi/0.8km east of Dún Laoghaire by the coast road to Sandycove. Open Apr-Oct, daily, 10am-1pm and 2 5pm (2pm-6pm Sun and Bank Hols); Nov-Mar, by appointment. €3; joint ticket available for 3 or all 7 of Dublin Tourism sites. Brochure (8 languages). ☎ 01 280 9265, 872 2077; Fax 01 280 9265; www.visitdublin.com

The Martello Tower (1804) on the point at Sandycove now houses a **Joyce Museum**: first editions, letters, photos, his death-mask, piano, guitar, cabin trunk, walking stick, wallet and cigar case. Joyce stayed there for six days in 1904 as the guest of the writer Oliver Gogarty, who had rented the tower from the government. The upper room, which was the location of the breakfast scene in *Ulysses*, is furnished appropriately, while the **view** from the roof embraces Dún Laoghaire Harbour *(northwest)*, the coast to Dalkey Island *(southeast)* and the Wicklow Mountains *(southwest)*.

Dalkey Village

1mi/1.6km south of Dún Laoghaire by the coast road

Dalkey (pronounced Dawkey), now designated a Heritage town, was once a walled town with seven fortified buildings. **Bulloch Castle** by the shore was built in the 12C by the monks of St Mary's Abbey in Dublin to protect the harbour. Two late-medieval tower houses survive in the heart of the village. **Archbold's Castle** stands opposite the graveyard of the ruined **St Genet's Church**, which may date from the 8C. Next door is the **Goat Castle**, which now houses the **Dalkey Heritage Centre** with excellent displays on local history and a splendid all-round view from the battlements. &

Dalkey Island and Vico Road

Bord Fáilte, Dublin

Open Apr-Dec, Mon-Fri, 9.30am-5pm; Sat-Sun and Public Hols, 11am-5pm. €4. Parking. Craft shop. ☎ 01 285 8366; 01 284 3141; diht@indigo.ie; www.dalkeyhomepage.ie

Many writers, among them LAG Strong, Lennox Robinson, James Joyce and Hugh Leonard, have associations with Dalkey; as a child (1866-74) George Bernard Shaw (1856-1950) lived in Torca Cottage on Dalkey Hill and learnt to swim at Killiney beach. Offshore lies **Dalkey Island**, which is now a bird sanctuary.

From the coast road south of Sorrento Point there is a magnificent **view★★** of Killiney Bay extending south to Bray Head.

Killiney Hill Park

Entrance and car park on the northwest side of Dalkey Hill. The park, which covers the south end of Dalkey Hill, was once the property of Col John Mapas who lived in Killiney Castle, now a hotel; it was opened to the public in 1887 to celebrate Queen Victoria's Jubilee. A **nature trail** winds through the trees and over the heath to the **obelisk**, which was built by John Mapas in 1742 to provide work for his tenants. panoramic **view**.

Dundalk

At the head of Dundalk Bay, midway between Dublin and Belfast, the old county town of Louth is one of the country's largest urban centres, with a harbour and a range of industries. In medieval times Dundalk was fortified by the Anglo-Normans, who used it as a base for incursions into the Gaelic strongholds of Ulster; subsequent repeated attacks and sieges have left little of its early heritage intact. Nevertheless it makes a good centre for exploring the many attractions of the nearby coast and countryside.

Location

Population 25 762 - Michelin Atlas p 98 and Map 712 – M 5, 6 – Co Louth.
Dundalk *(Dún Dealgan)*, situated on the main road (N 1) N up the coast to the border with Northern Ireland, is now bypassed by the motorway (M 1).
🖪 *Jocelyn Street, Dundalk. Open Jun-Sep, Mon-Sat; Oct-Jun, Mon-Fri.* ☎ *042 933 5484; Fax 042 933 8070; dundalktourismoffice@eircom.net.*
Adjacent Sights: See BOYNE VALLEY, DROGHEDA, KELLS, MOURNE MOUNTAINS, NEWRY.

Walking About

Dundalk was comprehensively replanned in Georgian times by its then owner, James, 1st Earl of Clanbrassil.
To the south of the bridge over the Castletown River *(Church Street)* stands one of the few reminders of the place's medieval past, the 14C tower of **St Nicholas' Church** (Anglican); the body of the church was rebuilt in 1707 and later given a spire by Francis Johnston.
The **Courthouse** *(south)* is a formidably austere neo-Classical structure with a Doric portico, designed by Park and Bowden in 1813. An elaborate porch-screen *(Roden Place – east)* leads to **St Patrick's Cathedral** (Roman Catholic), which is modelled on King's College Chapel in Cambridge; the sanctuary and the side chapels are richly decorated with mosaics.
A restored 18C warehouse *(in Jocelyn Street)* houses the **Louth County Museum**, a clear and comprehensive review of local history (archaeological finds, farming and industry, the port and railway) through audio-visual presentations, touch-screens, films and graphics. *Open May-Sep, Mon-Sat, 10.30am-5.30pm, Sun and Bank Hols, 2-6pm. €3.81.* ☎ *042 932 7056/7; Fax 042 932 7058; dlkmuseum1@eircom.net; www.goireland.com*

Directory

SIGHTSEEING

Historical walking tour – *Operates Thu, 7pm.* ☎ *087 288 1191, 042 932 5484 (Dundalk TIC); Fax 042 933 8070; dundalktouristoffice@eircom.net; www.louthholidays.com*

Carlingford Lough Cruises – *Sea-angling and cruising on Carlingford Lough on MV Slieve Foy (35ft); licensed and insured; fast off-shore 105 turbo; fully equipped with latest electronics.* ☎ *042 937 3239 (Peadar/Peter Elmore)*

SHOPPING

Carlingford Craft Gallery – *Next to Carlingford Heritage Centre.*
Contemporary design – *Open Tue-Fri, 11am-noon and 1-5pm, Sun and Bank Hols, noon-6pm.* ☎ *042 937 3005; carlingford@ccoi.ie*

SPORTS AND LEISURE

Táin Trail – Long-distance footpath *(19mi/30km)* encircling the Cooley Peninsula starting and finishing in Carlingford.
Greyhound racing.
Beaches – South at **Blackrock**, north at **Clogherhead** (Long Strand) and northeast on the Cooley Peninsula at **Giles Quay**, facing south, and at **Omeath**, on the shore of Carlingford Lough.
The salt marshes and mudflats *(E)* are a vast **bird sanctuary**.

EVENTS AND FESTIVALS

Annual Patrick Kavanagh Weekend – A celebration of the poet Patrick Kavanagh, held at the Patrick Kavanagh Centre in Inniskeen *(late November – see below)*

Tours

COOLEY PENINSULA

The Cooley Peninsula is a mountainous granite promontory, which provides magnificent land- and seascapes – *(south)* over Dundalk Bay and – *(north)* over Carlingford Lough to the glorious outline of the Mourne Mountains in Northern Ireland. Excellent walking country, it features in many a legend, particular those associated with the figure of Cuchulain, the hero of the epic tale *The Cattle Raid of Cooley (Táin bo Cuainlge)*. Fine sandy beaches stud the edge of Carlingford Lough.
From Dundalk take N 1 N and R 173 E.

Proleek Dolmen★

Park in the grounds of the Ballymascanlon Hotel; 20min there and back on foot through the yard and along the tarmac path between the fields. The massive capstone (40 tons/40.6 tonnes) on its two supports dates from 3000 BC; according to legend the wish will be granted of anyone who can make three pebbles land on the top. Nearby is a wedge-shaped gallery grave.
Continue E and turn left into the mountain road north to Omeath.

Windy Gap★

The road climbs towards Carlingford Mountain (1 932ft/587m). Beyond the site of the Long Woman's Grave *(plaque)* the road enters the aptly named **Windy Gap**, a narrow pass between rocky crags; fine view south over Dundalk Bay. Further north there is a **viewpoint** *(car park)* overlooking the mouth of Newry River at Warrenpoint and the Mourne Mountains rising from the eastern shore .

Omeath

Once a Gaelic-speaking fishing village, Omeath is now a little resort with a rocky shoreline, where one can savour freshly caught seafood. In summer jaunting cars carry fares to the outdoor Stations of the Cross at the monastery of the Rosminian Fathers, and the Carlingford Lough Ferry plies across the border to Warrenpoint.
From Omeath take the coast road R 173 S.

Carlingford★

Viking and Norman monuments add to the charm of this attractive resort, set at the foot of the Cooley Mountains and facing the Mourne Mountains across Carlingford Lough (marina and boat trips). Carlingford Oysters are a local delicacy with a more than local reputation.

Local history from the Vikings to the present day is traced on great triptychs in the **Carlingford Heritage Centre**, housed in the deconsecrated Anglican church, which is the starting point for a guided tour of the town centre. *Open Mar-Oct, 10am-5pm, telephone for details. €2. Video (12min).* ☎ *042 937 3888; Fax 042 937 3882; Carlingfordloughheritagetrust@eircom.net*

Spanning the main street is a gateway, once three storeys high, known as the **Tholsel**, where Parliament is said to have promulgated laws for the Pale *(see TRIM)*. South of the town square stands a 15C fortified house *(right)* with Celtic-style designs on the door and window mouldings; although it is known as the **Mint**, there is no proof that the local mint, founded in 1467, ever operated there.

Overlooking the harbour is **Taaffe's Castle**, a late-15C square tower fortified with machicolations, crenellations, arrow slits and murder holes; the vaulted basement may have been a boat-house since the tide used to reach the foundations. It was built by the Taaffe family, created Earls of Carlingford in 1661.

The ruins of **King John's Castle** stand on a bluff on the north side of the harbour commanding the entrance to Carlingford Lough; the western bailey was probably built by Hugh de Lacy, before King John's visit in 1210; the eastern apartments were added in 1261.

BETWEEN THE FANE AND THE DEE

Inland from Dundalk the undulating countryside is watered by several small rivers flowing east to the coast.
From Dundalk take R 171 SW to Louth.

St Mochta's House★

It is hard to believe that little Louth, which gave its name to the county, was once a capital, the centre of the 11C/12C Kingdom of Oriel. In a field behind the ruins of a Franciscan friary (14C-15C) stands a stone oratory with a **corbelled** roof. Between the steep roof and the vaulted ceiling is a tiny chamber reached by a steep stone stair. The oratory, which has been much restored, probably dates from the second half of the 12C; it is said to have been built in a night as a resting place for St Mochta who died in 534.

From Louth take the minor road N via Chanonrock to Inniskeen.

Inniskeen

The village is the birthplace of Patrick Kavanagh (1904-67), poet, author and journalist, who is buried in the old churchyard; his life and work are sympathetically presented in the **Patrick Kavanagh Centre**, housed in the old church, as well as local history. The remains of a round tower mark the site of a 6C monastery founded by St Daig beside the Fane River. *Open Mon-Fri, 11am-5pm; mid-Mar to Jun, Sun and Bank Hol, 2-6pm; Jun-Nov, Sat-Sun, 2-6pm. Closed 25 Dec to 1 Jan. €4. ☎/Fax 042 937 8560; info@pkc@eircom.net; www.patrickkavanaghcountry.com*

Patrick Kavanagh

Patrick Kavanagh Centre

From Inniskeen take the road W to Carrickmacross.

Carrickmacross

The town, a good angling centre, grew up round a castle built by the Earl of Essex, to whom the land was granted by Elizabeth I. For nearly 200 years it has enjoyed a well-deserved reputation for hand-made lace. **Carrickmacross Lace Gallery** *(Market Square at the north end of the main street)* displays examples of the local work, which is a "mixed lace", composed of cambric patterns applied to machine net and embellished with point stitches and loops; both traditional and modern designs are executed. *Open mid-Apr to Oct, Mon-Tue and Thu-Fri, 9.30am-12.30pm and 1.30-5pm. ☎ 042 966 2088*

The Roman Catholic church (1866) was designed by JJ McCarthy, with stained glass (1925) by Harry Clarke.

From Carrickmacross take R 179 SW to Kingscourt.

Dún A' Rí Forest Park★

The forest park, until 1959 part of the Cabra estate, is set in a valley beside the Cabra River. Its many enticing features can be experienced by following the **nature trail** and four sign-posted **walks; they include** a red deer enclosure; a waterfall downstream from Cromwell's Bridge; a wishing well; Cabra Cottage, the Pratt family mansion until Cabra Castle *(east)* was built in 1814; a ruined flax mill; an ice house; the ruins of Fleming's Castle (1607), named after an Anglo-Norman family who lost their land for supporting James II *(see BOYNE VALLEY).*

From Kingscourt take R 165 SE via Drumcondra; at the crossroads turn left into N 52.

Ardee (Baile Átha Fhirdhia)

The name means the Ford of Ferdia, who fought in the *Cattle Raid of Cooley*. On the east side of the main street stand two fortified buildings: **Hatch's Castle**, a late-medieval fortified house, and **Ardee Castle**, built in 1207 by Roger de Peppard, although much of the present building dates from the 15C. In the 17C the castle was granted to Theobald Taaffe, Earl of Carlingford.

Ennis

Known as the "Banner County", Clare has a long history of dogged nationalism, and it is also famous as the heartland of Irish traditional music. There is evidence of both in the little county town with its narrow winding streets and colourful shopfronts.

Harriet Smithson, the wife of Hector Berlioz, was born in Ennis; her father was the manager of the first theatre built in the town in the late 18C.

Location

Population 15 333 - Michelin Atlas p 83 and Map 712 – F 9 – Co Clare.

Ennis *(Inis)* bestrides the junction of N 8, N 85 and N 68 midway between Limerick and The Burren.

🄳 *Arthurs Row, Ennis. Open daily.* ☎ *065 682 8366; Fax 065 682 8350; touristofficeennis@shannondev.ie; www.shannon.ie/tourism*

Adjacent Sights: See ADARE, THE BURREN, KILLALOE, KILRUSH, LIMERICK, TRALEE.

Directory

ENTERTAINMENT

For a taste of Ireland in the Middle Ages, sit down at a **medieval banquet** in **Knappogue Castle** *(see below)* accompanied by a pageant on the role of women in Irish history.

Demonstrations of **Traditional Folk Music and Dancing** in **Cois na h'Abhna**, a modern circular building on the Galway road *(N 18)*.

TRACING ANCESTORS

Clare Heritage Centre – *See below.*

Background

Royal Origins – Ennis is proud of its distinguished beginnings. Its origin can be traced back to the 13C, when the O'Brien family, kings of Thomond and descendants of the great Brian Ború, built their royal residence nearby.

Because of its central position Ennis became the county town of Clare during the shiring of Ireland in the reign of Elizabeth I. In 1610 the town was granted permission to hold fairs and markets; two years later it received a corporation charter from James I.

Famous Statesmen – Two of the outstanding figures in Irish political history are commemorated in the town. In 1828, the election by an overwhelming majority of **Daniel O'Connell** as MP for Clare led directly to Catholic emancipation the following year. The great man is honoured by a big Doric column in the square named after him. Nearly a century later, his successor was **Eamon de Valera**, who was elected to Parliament for the first time in 1917, and served as Member for the county until 1959. A modern statue to him stands in front of the old Courthouse (1850), a neo-Classical building with a pedimented Ionic portico *(Galway Road N 18)*.

Worth a Visit

Ennis Friary★

(Dúchas) (&) Open late-May to Oct, daily, 9.30am-6.30pm (5.45pm last admission). Closed 25-26 Dec. €1.20. Guided tour on request. Leaflet. Parking. ☎ */Fax 065 682 9100; ennisfriary@ealga.ie; www.heritageireland.ie*

The Friary was founded by an O'Brien in the 13C, and by the 14C had become one of Ireland's foremost institutions of learning, with over 600 students as well as hundreds of friars. Now a lovely ruin, it has a superb east window but is most noteworthy for its sculpture.

An **Ecce Homo** shows Christ with the Instruments of the Passion. St Francis is depicted with a cross-staff in his left hand and the stigmata on his right hand, side and feet; The Creagh tomb (1843) in the chancel consists of five carved panels showing the Passion, taken from the MacMahon tomb (1475), and figures of Christ and the Apostles from another tomb.

Clare County Museum

& *Open Jun-Sep, daily, 9.30am-5.30pm; Oct-Mar, Mon-Sat, 9.30am-1pm and 2-5.30pm; Jan-Feb, Mon-Fri, 9.30am-1pm and 2-5.30pm; last admission 1hr before closing. Admission charge.* ☎ *065 682 3382; Fax 065 684 2119; claremuseum@eircom.net; www.clarelibrary.ie*

Housed in an imaginatively redesigned former convent school, the *Riches of Clare Exhibition* traces the history of this particularly distinctive county via four themes – Earth, Power, Faith and Water – using a variety of state-of-the-art techniques to interpret the carefully selected range of items on display. Among them is a *sheela-na-gig (see IRISH ART)*, a gorgeously carved panel from the wreck of an Armada galleon, and a striking banner of 1917 celebrating the election victory which confirmed Sinn Fein as a force to be reckoned with and de Valera as a major political player.

Cathedral

The Roman Catholic Cathedral, dedicated to St Peter and St Paul, was built between 1831 and 1843 in Tau-cross shape; the tower with its spire was added between 1871 and 1874. Rows of pointed arches divide the nave and aisles and support the decorated panelled ceiling.

Railway Locomotive

Railway Station.
On a plinth stands one of the steam engines from the West Clare railway, immortalised by Percy French's song *Are You Right There, Michael, Are You Right?* The railway, which rambled round the county to Kilkee *(see KILRUSH)* closed down in 1961 and the station is now used only for freight and buses.

Excursions

Dromore Wood National Nature Reserve

8mi/13km N by N 18 (signed) to Barefield. (Dúchas) (&) Forest Park: Open daily during daylight hours. Visitor Centre: Open mid-Jun to mid-Sep, 5 days a week (telephone for details), 10am-6pm (5.15pm last admission). Guide book. ☎ 065 683 7166
This nature reserve (1 000 acres/400ha) encompasses an exceptionally varied array of habitats, including lakes, limestone pavement and turloughs, river, fen and semi-natural woodland, together with several examples of human habitation, notably the ruins of the 17C O'Brien castle.

Dysert O'Dea★

6mi/10km N by N 85, R 476; after 4mi/6.4km turn left (sign); after 1mi/1.6km turn right. Open May-Sep, daily, 10am-6pm. €4. Audio-visual show (2 languages). Brochure. Parking. Refreshments. ☎ 065 683 7401; 065 683 7794 (evenings and off season); mobile 086 327 4824
The monastery here was founded by St Tola in the 8C, and the site has a number of evocative remains, albeit of later date. A great battle raged here in 1318, when an O'Brien routed the Anglo-Norman Richard de Clare, thereby delaying English control of Clare for 200 years. There is an **Archaeology Centre** and a small **museum** devoted to the prehistoric and later culture of the neighbourhood *(audiovisual film (20min); leaflet of walks)*, housed in a 15C tower house with a murder hole above the entrance. From the roof there is a fine **view** of the surrounding country and nearby ruins.
In a neighbouring field *(access on foot or by car)* stands the late-12C **White Cross of Tola.** By this date, the exuberant panel ornamentation of earlier crosses had been replaced by large figures standing out in high relief ; this example shows the Crucifixion and a bishop on its east face. The site also has the stump of an 11C **round tower** and much of the chancel arch and outer walls of an 11C **church**; the Romanesque doorway is a reconstruction of the original.

Clare Heritage Centre★

8.5mi/14km N by N 85 and R 476 at Corrofin. & Open daily, 9.30am-5.30pm. Guided tour (30min) available. Brochure (2 languages). Genealogy service. Parking. Tearoom. ☎ 065 683 7955; Fax 065 683 7540; clareheritage@eircom.net; www.clareroots.com
The centre, housed in the former Anglican church, illustrates life and work in Co Clare in the 19C, with emphasis on the hardships which led some 100 000 of the county's inhabitants to emigrate in the aftermath of the Famine. An intriguing section of oak trunk is marked with the dates of historic events which took place during the growth of the tree. The centre also has extensive genealogical records.

Clare Abbey

1mi/1.6km SE by R 469; turn right before the railway station, then left; park at the corner; 0.5mi/0.8km on foot over the level crossing and right. On the west bank of the River Fergus stand the substantial ruins of an Augustinian friary founded in 1189 by Dónall Mór O'Brien, last king of Munster; they include the central tower, much of the nave and a tall chimney stack, part of the domestic buildings, leaning at a steep angle.

Quin Franciscan Friary★

6.5mi/10.5km SE by R 469; in Quin turn left. (Dúchas) Open late-May to late-Sep, daily, 10.30am (11.30am Sat-Sun) to 6pm. ☎ 091 844 084

The extensive ruins of the friary, built about 1430 by Sioda McNamara, include the **cloisters**, the tower and the south transept. The friary was built on top of a ruined Norman castle (1280-86) which had three round towers and was built on the site of an earlier monastery.

Knappogue Castle★

8mi/13km SE by R 469. (&. ground floor only) Open Apr-Oct, daily, 9.30am-5.30pm (4.30pm last admission); subject to change; check by telephone. Medieval banquets: Apr-Oct, daily, 5.30pm, 8.45pm. Castle €4; banquet €44. Parking. ☎ 061 368 103 (Castle), ☎ 061 360 788 (Shannon Heritage central reservations); Fax 061 361 020; reservations@shannondev.ie; www.shannonheritage.com

This massive tower house, the seat of the McNamara family from 1467 to 1815 has been beautifully restored and furnished and is now used for medieval banquets. The gardens and orchards have been replanted.

Craggaunowen Centre★

11mi/18km SE by R 469 (sign). &. Open Apr-Oct, daily, 10am-6pm (5pm last admission); subject to change; check by telephone. €6.65. Guided tour available. Brochure (3 languages). Parking. Refreshments. ☎ 061 367 178 (site), 061 360 788 (Shannon Heritage central reservations), Fax 061 361 020; reservations@shannon dev.ie; www.shannonheritage.com

THE BRENDAN VOYAGE·

St Brendan of Clonfert, also known as Brendan the Navigator, was a seafaring monk, who in the 6C set sail from Brandon Creek, the narrow sea inlet at the west foot of Brandon Mountain (*see p 197*) on the Dingle Peninsula. His account of the voyage, *Navigatio*, written in medieval Latin, was usually thought to be fanciful until Tim Severin built the *Brendan* and set sail with a small crew, to prove that the earlier voyagers could have reached America several hundred years before Christopher Columbus. The exploits of the 20C adventure, which in many respects substantiate the 6C narrative, are recorded in *The Brendan Voyage*.

Aiming to recreate the ambience of ancient Ireland, the medievalist John Hunt set out to reconstruct a variety of prehistoric structures in this lakeside setting through the imaginative use of archaeological material. As well as a ringfort, a *togher* (wooden marsh track) and a cooking site, there is the artificial island of a *crannóg*. Also here is the *Brendan*, a replica of the kind of frail wood and leather *curragh* aboard which St Brendan may have made his crossing of the Atlantic, and which itself was sailed across the ocean in 1976 by Tim Severin; the patch where the leather hull was holed by an ice floe is clearly visible. Hunt restored the nearby **tower house** which is used to display items from his extensive antiquarian collection, most of which is on display in the Hunt Museum in Limerick (*see p 309*).

An enclosure in the woodlands is home to a group of wild boar (*Porcus sylveticus*); other early breeds, such as the goat-like Soay sheep, can be seen grazing in fields near the entrance to *Craggaunowen – the Living Past*.

The Brendan

Craggaunowen, Shannon Heritage

Enniscorthy

Attractively built on the steep slopes of the River Slaney at its tidal limit, the market town of Enniscorthy has a special place in the history of Ireland because of its involvement in the 1798 rebellion.

Castle and cathedral – both of exceptional interest – dominate a townscape scarcely changed since the 19C. Local events are commemorated in the 1798 memorial *(Market Square)* showing Fr Murphy, a leader of the uprising, and a pikeman, and in the 1916 Easter Rising memorial *(Abbey Square)* which portrays Seamus Rafter, a local commander.

The surrounding country is well suited to the growing of soft fruit, and the Strawberry Fair in early July attracts people from miles around.

Location

Population 3 788 - Michelin Atlas p 81 and Map 712 – M 10 – Co Wexford

Enniscorthy *(Inis Córthaidh)* is set at the junction of the N 11, the major road between Dublin and Wexford, and N 30 which links Enniscorthy and New Ross.

🖪 *The Castle, Enniscorthy. Open Apr-Sep.* ☎ *054 34699; www.irelandsoutheast.travel.ie*

🖪 *Main Street, Gorey. Open all year.* ☎ *055 21248*

Adjacent Sights: See NEW ROSS, WEXFORD, WICKLOW MOUNTAINS.

Directory

SIGHTSEEING

Guided Tour of the town (including or excluding Vinegar Hill) in summer. *Guided tour (1hr; 2hr including Vinegar Hill; 5 minimum) Jun-Oct. €4. Departure from Castle Hill Craft, opposite the Castle.* ☎ *054 36800; Fax 054 36628*

SHOPPING

Arts and Crafts Gallery – *Tinnock, Gorey. Open daily, 2-6pm.* ☎ *0402 37474. Wood turning, stained glass, pottery etc.*

Carley's Bridge Potteries *(see below)* – The original clay pot company making earthenware pots.

Hillview Pottery – *Carley's Bridge.*

Badger Hill Pottery – *Enniscorthy.*

Kiltrea Pottery – *Off R 890 to Kiltealy. Open Mon-Sat, 9.30am-5.30pm; also certain Sun in summer and most Bank Hols.* ☎ *054 35107; Fax 054 34690. Hand-thrown pottery and terracotta.*

SPORTS AND LEISURE

Greyhound racing.

Background

Monastic Foundation – The origins of Enniscorthy go back to the 6C, when St Senan arrived from Scattery Island *(see p 297)* to found a monastic settlement at Templeshannon, the part of Enniscorthy on the east bank of the Slaney River. From the 12C the monastery's fortunes were controlled by the Normans, who ruled from their castle in Enniscorthy until some time in the 15C when a local clan, the MacMurrough Kavanaghs, gained control. In the latter part of the 16C Queen Elizabeth I appointed Sir Henry Wallop and Philip Stamp to put an end to local rule.

Commercial Development – Commercial exploitation was started in the 16C by Queen Elizabeth's men. Sir Henry Wallop felled timber in the rich woodlands and exported it to France and Spain through the port of Wexford; Philip Stamp set up an ironworks, which survived until the 1940s, and brought many English families to settle in Enniscorthy, which expanded across the River Slaney. Towards the end of the 18C distilleries and breweries were set up; by 1796 Enniscorthy had 23 malthouses. Today the town is noted for its bacon curing, fruit growing, cutlery and potteries.

Worth a Visit

National 1798 Visitor Centre

Parnell Road; S of town centre. ♿ *Open daily, 9.30am (11am Sun) to 5pm (last admission). €5.08. Audio-visual show (15min). Guide (6 languages). Craft rooms. Tearoom. Parking.* ☎ *054 37596; Fax 054 37198; 98com@iol.ie; www.1798centre.com*

VINEGAR HILL

21 June 1798 is the most famous date in the history of Enniscorthy. Following the rebellion that year, centred mostly in Co Wexford and Co Wicklow, the insurgents, known as the pikemen after their weapons, made their last stand on Vinegar Hill, which they held for nearly a month. The 20 000 insurgents, accompanied by many women and children, were faced by an equivalent number of government troops led by General Lake; the armed men killed in the battle were far outnumbered by the defenceless people killed by the army. The defeat at Vinegar Hill marked the end of the 1798 rebellion.

The centre was opened in 1998 to mark the bicentenary of the 1798 uprising and to study the birth of popular democracy in Ireland. The rebellion, particularly the three weeks of disruption in Co Wexford, is presented in vivid detail via touch screens, sensory-activated displays, and film and storyboards. Its significance is reviewed in the context of events in France and America at that time and of the development of modern political parties in Ireland as a whole. The presentation reaches its climax with a stirring virtual re-creation of the battle of Vinegar Hill.

Enniscorthy Castle★

With its four corner towers, the castle owes its present formidable appearance to a 1586 rebuilding of the original stronghold probably erected by Raymond le Gros, who led the first Anglo-Norman soldiers into the town in 1169. After many years in the hands of the MacMurrough clan, the castle became Crown property; Elizabeth I granted it to her favourite poet, Edmund Spenser, who spent a mere three days here before escaping its chilly walls.

It now houses the **Wexford County Museum★**.with an array of items evoking the 1798 rebellion and the **Easter Rising** of 1916 as well as more peaceful aspects of local history. (&) *Open Jul-Aug, daily, 10am (2pm Sun) to 8pm; Mar-Jun and Sep, daily, 10am-6pm; Oct-Feb, Sun, 2-5pm. €2. Guided tour (1hr) by appointment. Wheelchair access to ground floor.* ☎/Fax 054 35926; wexmus@iol.ie; www.goireland.ie

St Aidan's Cathedral

This fine Gothic Revival structure is one of the many Roman Catholic churches built in Ireland by Pugin$. The foundation stone was laid in 1843 and the building was roofed in 1846. Many of the stones used in its construction came from the ruined Franciscan friary in Abbey Square, dissolved in 1544.

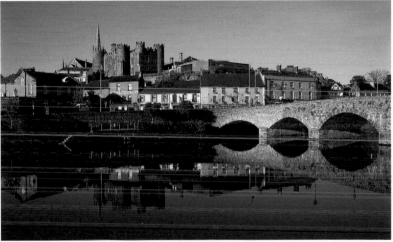

Bord Fáilte, Dublin

Enniscorthy Castle and Bridge

Excursions

Carley's Bridge Potteries

1mi/1.5km W of Enniscorthy past the greyhound track. Open Mon-Fri, 8.30am-5.45pm, Sat-Sun, 11am (2.30pm Sun) to 5pm. Closed Bank Hols. Guided tour (1hr): Mon-Fri. Showroom. Parking. ☎ 054 33512, Fax 054 34360; sales@cbp.ie; www.cbp.ie

Pottery has been made in the Enniscorthy area for hundreds of years. Carley's Bridge Potteries, the oldest in Ireland, were founded in 1659 by two brothers from Cornwall. The local clay is used to make a variety of earthenware pots. It takes three months to make enough pots to fill the kiln and four days for them to be fired and cooled.

Ferns★

8mi/13km NE of Enniscorthy by N 11.

The modest size of the village belies its former role as capital of the province of Leinster and royal seat of the MacMurroughs but the remaining **ruins** are proof enough of the place's ancient importance. The tower and part of the north wall still stand from the abbey founded in the 12C by the King of Leinster, Dermot MacMurrough Kavanagh, supposedly buried in the graveyard of the almost entirely vanished cathedral.

The 13C **castle**, one of the best of its kind in Ireland, has a rectangular keep and circular towers; the first-floor **chapel** has a fine vaulted ceiling. *(Dúchas)* (&) *Opening arrangements to be confirmed. Guided tour available. Tearoom. Parking.* ☎ *0647 2453*

Bunclody

12mi/19km N of Enniscorthy by N 11 and N 80. The town is attractively sited on the River Clody, a tributary of the Slaney, at the north end of the Blackstairs Mountains. The broad central mall is bisected by a stream that falls in steps. The Church of the Most Holy Trinity, consecrated in 1970, is an interesting modern design by EN Smith.

Bunclody was the last bastion in Co Wexford of the Irish language, which was in widespread use in the town until a century ago; even today Gaelic is quite often used in shops, notices and signs.

Mount Leinster★

17mi/28km N of Enniscorthy by N 11 and N 80. In Bunclody take the minor road W, after 4mi/6.4km turn left onto the summit road which ends 0.25 mi/0.4km from the peak.

From the summit (2 602ft/793m) on a clear day there are the finest views in southeast Ireland: not only is there a commanding prospect of much of Wexford and Wicklow, but in exceptional conditions even the Welsh mountains can be seen far off across St George's Channel.

Altamont Gardens

25mi/40km N by N 11 and N 81; turn right (sign) into minor road. (Dúchas) (&) Open mid-Mar to Oct, daily, 9am (10am Sat-Sun) to 5pm (3.30pm Fri, 6pm Sat-Sun); Nov to mid-Mar, Mon-Fri, 9am-5pm (3.30pm Fri). Telephone to check times. Closed 25-26 Dec. Guided tour on request. €2.50. Guide dogs only. Parking. ☎ 503 59444; Fax 503 59510; altamontgardens@ealga.ie

Designed in both formal and informal styles, the gardens have many specimen trees, an arboretum and a small garden with species of flowers normally found growing in Ireland's marshy bogs. The lake was dug out by hand to provide employment during the Famine.

On the horizon rise Mount Leinster *(south)* in the Blackstairs Mountains, and the Wicklow Mountains *(northeast)* across the River Slaney.

Fingal★

The area north of Dublin, which re-adopted the ancient name of Fingal in 1994, consists of rich farmland fringed by a long coastline. The seaside resort of Skerries has several beaches, a colony of grey seals and a fishing harbour where famous Dublin Bay prawns are landed. Portmarnock, another popular resort, is known for its long sandy beach called the Velvet Strand and its championship golf course. In the Middle Ages Fingal formed part of The Pale *(see TRIM)* and contains several historic sites, elegant parks surrounding old stately homes and the charming dormitory town and seaside resort of Malahide.

Location

Michelin Atlas p 93 and Map 712 – N 7 – Co Fingal.

Fingal is the northern sub-division of County Dublin, which includes the city of Dublin and the adjacent suburbs from Balbriggan in the north to Lucan and Brittas in the west and Killiney in the south.

🄱 *For information and accommodation reservations to visitors calling in person:*

Dublin Tourism Centre, Suffolk Street. Open Jul-Aug, daily; Sep Jun, Mon-Sat.
O'Connell Street, Dublin 1. Open Mon-Sat. Closed Bank Hols.
Dublin Airport, Arrivals Hall. Open daily.
Dún Laoghaire, New Ferry Terminal. Open Mon-Sat.
Dublin 2, Baggot Street Bridge. Open, Mon-Fri. Closed Bank Hols.
Tallaght, The Square, Town Centre. Open Mon-Sat. Closed Bank Hols.
☎ 1850 230 330 (Irish Tourist Board);
☎ 0800 039 7000 (Irish Tourist Board from London);
Fax 020 7493 9065 (from London); information@dublintourism.ie; www.visitdublin.com
Adjacent Sights: See BOYNE VALLEY, DROGHEDA, DUBLIN, KELLS, TRIM.

Worth a Visit

Malahide Castle★★

8.5mi/13km N of Dublin by R 107 or by M 1 and R 106. Open Apr-Oct, Mon-Sat, 10am-12.45pm and 2-5pm, Sun and Bank Hols, 11am-12.45pm and 2-6pm; Nov-Mar, Mon-Sat, 10am-12.45pm and 2-5pm, Sun and Bank Hols, 11am-5pm €5.50. Audioguide (8 languages). Brochure (6 languages). Parking. Restaurant, coffee shop; banquets on request. Craft shop. ☎ *01 846 2184, 846 2516; Fax 01 846 2537; malahidecastle@ dublintourism.ie; www.visitdublin.com*

The castle was the home of the Talbot family for nearly 800 years, the great demesne of which it is the crown having been granted to Richard Talbot who came to Ireland with Henry II in 1177. Built around the original 14C tower, the castle has been picturesquely added to over the centuries: the Great Hall (15C), reception rooms (18C), still with some of the original furniture and wonderful **Rococo plasterwork**. Now in public ownership, the castle has lost little of its atmosphere, which is enhanced by the presence of portraits from the National Portrait Collection. The **Great Hall** is dominated by the *Battle of the Boyne* by Jan Wyck; it is said that 14 of the Talbot cousins, all Jacobites, who breakfasted at Malahide on the morning of the battle, were killed in the fighting.

The **Talbot Botanic Gardens** (19 acres/7.5ha with 4 acres/1.5ha of walled garden) were largely created by Milo, the last Lord Talbot, between 1948 and 1973, who indulged his passion for plants from the southern hemisphere. The result is a superb collection of trees and shrubs, set on either side of lovely lawns making a fine setting for the Castle.

Malahide Castle

Fry Model Railway Museum – *Malahide Castle Yard.* The model engines and rolling stock made by Cyril Fry of Dublin are displayed together with information on the development of railways in Ireland and a huge O-gauge model railway incorporating replicas of various railway stations. *Open Apr-Sep, Mon-Sat, 10am-1pm and 2-5pm; Sun and Bank Hols, 2-6pm; €5.50; joint ticket available for any 2 Dublin Tourism sites. Parking.* ☎ *01 846 3779; Fax 01 846 3723; fryrailway@dublintourism.ie; www.visitdublin.com*

Tara's Palace – The grandeur and elegance of three great 18C Irish mansions are recreated in miniature in this magnificent dolls' house. *Open same times as Fry Model Railway (see above). €2.*

Newbridge House★

10mi/16km N of Dublin by M 1 and a minor road E to Donabate. Guided tour (45min) Apr-Sep, Tue-Sat, 10am-1pm and 2-5pm; Sun and Bank Hols, 2-6pm; Oct-Mar, Sat-Sun and Bank Hols, 2-5pm; last tour 1hr before closing. House €5.50; farm €1.50. Playground. Parking. Coffee shop; picnic area. 01 843 6534; Fax 01 846 6535; malahidecastle@dublintourism.ie; www.visitdublin.com

This early-18C Georgian country house, designed by George Semple, stands on the western edge of the little town of Donabate in extensive grounds, one of the finest remaining examples in Ireland of a landscape park.

It has been the home of the Cobbe family since it was built c 1740 for Charles Cobbe, who came to Ireland in 1717 as Chaplain to the Lord Lieutenant, and rose to become Archbishop of Dublin (portrait in the hall).

The **guided tour** of the ground floor and basement reveals interiors which have remained unchanged for decades, even centuries. There is plenty of original furniture, much of it made by Dublin craftsmen, as well as superb 18C and early 19C **stucco** and **plasterwork**. The **Red Drawing Room**, added around 1760 when the Archbishop's son and his wife needed more space to entertain, is particularly fine, still with the wallpaper, curtains and carpet fitted in 1820. A rare and intriguing feature is the the family **museum**, begun in 1790, and decorated in Chinese style. The Cobbes were great travellers, and the museum is crammed with souvenirs, trophies, and exotica brought back from their many trips abroad. The basement **laundry** and the magnificent 18C **kitchen** are fitted with much of their original equipment.

Traditional Farm – A museum of traditional rural life is presented in the buildings round the large cobbled **courtyard** (1790) – dairy (19C), estate worker's dwelling, carpenter's shop, forge, stables and coach house containing a park drag, which could carry 13 passengers, and the Lord Chancellor's State Coach (1790). Domestic animals live in the paddocks; the large walled garden was converted to an orchard during the Second World War.

Ardgillan Castle

22mi/35km N of Dublin by M 1 and a minor road E to Balbriggan. Parking at the entrance to the park and beside the house. Open Jul-Aug, daily, 11am-6pm; Apr-Jun and Sep, Tue-Sun and Bank Hols, 11am-6pm; Oct-Mar, Tue-Sun and Bank Hols, 11am-4.30pm. Closed 23 Dec to 1 Jan. €4. Guided tour available. ☎ 01 849 2212; Fax 01 849 2786

On the coast north of Skerries stands the Georgian country house acquired in 1737 by the Taylor family, descendants of Thomas Taylor, a professional surveyor, who had come to Ireland from Sussex in 1650 to work on the Down Survey.

The interiors include a billiard room, drawing room, dining room, morning room and library, which contain some mementoes and furniture of the Taylor family. Kitchens, larder and scullery occupy the extensive basement, and on the upper floor there is a fascinating exhibition on the **Down Survey**.

Beyond the rose gardens are the walled gardens, laid out with lawns and flowers and vegetables in geometric plots. The west front is screened by a row of 21 Irish yew trees. The great sweep of the grass and woodland down to the shore is a sanctuary for many species of birds and mammals.

> **DOWN SURVEY**
>
> The confiscation and redistribution of almost half the land in Ireland in the course of the Cromwellian Settlement involved the preparation of accurate maps. They were provided by Sir William Petty (*see p 270*) and his team of hastily recruited surveyors in the astonishingly short time of 13 months (1655-56). The operation was known as the Down Survey, not because of any connection with Co Down, but because the results of the survey were set down on maps rather than being shown in tabulated form as was usually the case. The maps were individually drawn and coloured and several sets were made. While at sea between Dublin and London in 1707 the Petty set was captured by the French.

Skerries Mills

20mi/32km N of Dublin by M 1 and R 127. Open daily, 10.30am-5.30pm (4.30pm Oct-Mar). Closed Good Fri, 20 Dec to 1 Jan. €4. ☎ 01 849 5208; Fax 01 849 5213; skerriesmills@indigo.ie

From one mill in the 16C the complex grew to consist of a watermill, two windmills (one with five sails and one with four), mill races, a mill pond and wetlands. This rare survival of 17C-19C industrial technology has been restored to working order.

Swords (Sord)

8mi/14km N of Dublin by M 1.

The bustling county town of Fingal has a history going back to the 6C when St Columba founded a monastery on a low hilltop just to the west of the modern town centre. Its site is marked by the Anglican church, a 9C **round tower** and a 12C **Norman tower**. At the northern end of the town stands **Swords Castle**, the summer palace of the Archbishops of Dublin; the substantial remains include the craggy twin-towered Constable's Tower (fully restored). (&) *Open Mon, Wed, Thu-Fri, 10am-noon and 1-4pm (3pm Fri). ☎ 01 840 0891*

Lusk Heritage Centre

13mi/21km N of Dublin by M 1 and R 127 to Lusk. (Dúchas) Open mid-Jun to mid-Sep, Fri, 10am-5pm (4.15pm last admission). €1.20. Guided tour by appointment (30min). Leaflet (6 languages). ☎ 01 843 7683, 647 2461; Fax 01 661 6764

The centre is housed in the tower of the local Anglican church, which incorporates an earlier round tower. It gives an account of the monastery founded here in the 5C but its star attraction is the magnificent effigy tomb of Sir Christopher Barnewall and his wife Marion Sharl, its Renaissance decoration almost unique in Ireland at this early date (1589).

Galway★★

The largest town in the west of Ireland, Galway bestrides the Corrib River as it enters Galway Bay. It has grown from a medieval core of narrow streets into an exceptionally lively cathedral and university city with many modern industries and a thriving port, and is well placed as a centre for excursions westwards into the wild mountainous country of Connemara; east and south lies the fertile Galway plain. This location, together with the city's own dynamic character, draws cosmopolitan crowds of visitors to its busy streets, which take on an almost Mediterranean air when the summer sun contrives to shine.

Directory

GETTING ABOUT
Galway Airport – *Inveran* – ☎ 091 593 034

SIGHTSEEING
Boat trips to Lough Corrib *(see below)* – ዼ *Operate from Wood Quay, end-Apr to Oct, daily, at 12.30pm (Jul-Aug only), 2.30pm, 4.30pm. Duration 90min. €9. Commentary (various languages). Bar.* ☎ *091 592 447 (Corrib Tours); corribtours@eircom.net* Services to the **Aran Islands** *(see p 126)* by air from the airfield at Inveran *(20mi/32km W of Galway by R 336)* and by sea from Wood Quay.

WHERE TO STAY
• *Budget*
Norman Villa – *86 Lower Salthill, Salthill, 000040 Dublin -* ☎ *091 521 131 - Fax 091 521 131 - normanvilla@oceanfree.net - Mar to Oct -* 🅿 🗶 *- 6 rm €65/110* 😴. *This ivy-clad Victorian house combines period charm, featuring antique beds and original fireplaces, with an eye-catching collection of contemporary Irish art. Meet your fellow guests around the large single breakfast table.*
• *Moderate*
Killeen House – *Killeen Bushypark, 000040 Dublin - 4mi NW by N 59 -* ☎ *091 524 179 - Fax 091 528 065 - killeenhouse@ireland.com - Closed 23-27 Dec -* 🅿 *- 5 rm €100/140* 😴. *Only four miles from the city centre yet this 1840s house has a charming country feel and a very pretty garden. Bedrooms have antique beds and all have a different period theme such as Victorian or Regency, juxtaposed with the latest mod-cons.*
• *Expensive*
Spanish Arch Hotel – *Quay St -* ☎ *091 569 600 - Fax 091 569 191 - emcdgall@iol.ie - Closed 24-25 Dec -* 🅿 *- 20 rm €145/230 -* 😴 *€8 - Restaurant €19/41.50. The original wall of this 16C Carmelite convent provides the backdrop for this hotel's organic restaurant. The wood-panelled Victorian bar is hugely popular with the locals and the bedrooms boast antique beds.*

WHERE TO EAT
• *Budget*
Archway – *Victoria Pl -* ☎ *091 563 693 - archway@indigo.ie - Closed 24 Dec to 10 Jan, Sun and Mon - Booking essential - €20/56. The owners have made the best of the limited space, with a sitting area downstairs and the main restaurant on the first floor. Service is detailed and attentive while the accomplished French-influenced cooking uses first-rate ingredients.*

ENTERTAINMENT
Druid Theatre, *Courthouse Lane* – Specialises in experimental/avant-garde works – ☎ *091 568 617 (Box office); 091 568 660 (Administration); Fax 091 563 109; info@druidtheatre.com; www.druidtheatre.com*
Irish Theatre (An Taibhdhearc na Gaillimhe), *Middle Street* – Stages Irish productions (music, singing, dancing and folk drama) – ☎ *091 563 600 (box office); Fax 091 563 195; taibh@iol.ie; www.taibh.ie*

SPORTS AND LEISURE
Galway Sailing Club – ☎ *091 94527* – Cruiser sailing, dingly sailing, windsurfing and training courses
Greyhound racing.
Angling at Oughterard on Lough Corrib.

EVENTS AND FESTIVALS
The highlights of the traditional **Oyster Festival** *(late September weekend)* are the World Oyster-opening Championship, which is judged on speed, presentation and lack of blood on the plate, and the selection of the Oyster Pearl, whose duties include feeding the mayor an oyster and singing *The Fields of Athenry*; the feasting includes a banquet (Friday), a buffet (Saturday) and a brunch (Sunday).
Commanding as much attention is the **Galway Arts Festival**, held annually *(10 days in July)*.
The **Gathering of the Boats** *(Cruinniú na mBád)*, held in August in Kinvarra Bay, features **Galway hookers**, workboats lovingly restored, a part of Irish heritage.

Irish Hookers

Bord Fáilte, Dublin

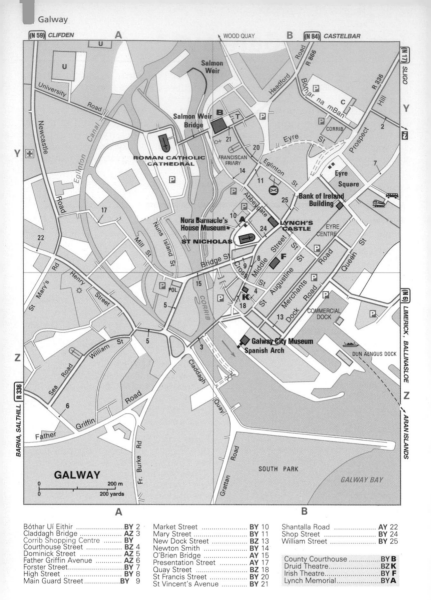

Bóthar Uí Eithir	BY 2	Market Street	BY 10	Shantalla Road	AY 22
Claddagh Bridge	AZ 3	Mary Street	BY 11	Shop Street	BY 24
Corrib Shopping Centre	BY	New Dock Street	BZ 13	William Street	BY 25
Courthouse Street	BZ 4	Newton Smith	BY 14		
Dominick Street	AZ 5	O'Brien Bridge	AY 15		
Father Griffin Avenue	AZ 6	Presentation Street	AY 17	County Courthouse	BY B
Forster Street	BY 7	Quay Street	BZ 18	Druid Theatre	BZ K
High Street	BY 8	St Francis Street	BY 20	Irish Theatre	BY F
Main Guard Street	BY 9	St Vincent's Avenue	BY 21	Lynch Memorial	BY A

Location

Population 57 241 - Michelin Atlas p 89 and Map 712 – E 8 – Co Galway.

Galway *(Gaillimh)* is located on the north shore of Galway Bay at the junction of N 17 from the north, N 6 from the east, N 18 from the south. It is a good centre from which to explore Connemara (R 336 along the north shore of Galway Bay, N 59 and N 84 along the lake shore) and to visit the Aran Islands *(see Directory)*.

🛈 *Forster Street, Galway City. Open Mon-Sat.* ☎ *091 537 700; Fax 091 537 733; info@irelandwest.ie; www.irelandwest.ie*

🛈 *Salthill. Open May-Sep, Mon-Sat.* ☎ *091 520 500*

🛈 *Community Office, Oughterard. Open Mon-Sat.* ☎ *091 552 808; Fax 091 55 2811*

🛈 *Mill Museum, Tuam. Open Jul-Aug, Mon-Sat.* ☎ *093 52486 or 24463*

Adjacent Sights: See ARAN ISLANDS, ATHENRY, THE BURREN, CONG, CONNEMARA.

Background

City of the Tribes – The Anglo-Normans were attracted by the sheltered anchorage strategically located midway along Ireland's western coast. The city was founded on the east bank of the river in the 12C by the de Burgo (later Burke) family *(see p 332)*, who encouraged immigration from England and Wales. Defensive walls were built and, under the control of the 14 leading families, known as the "tribes", Galway prospered on trade, not only with France and Spain but also with the West Indies. As an English enclave in the midst of an often hostile region, the city excluded the native Irish, who occupied their own settlement outside the walls. Prosperity did not, however, survive the religious disputes of the Reformation and their political consequences. After two lengthy sieges – by the Cromwellians in 1652 and by William of Orange's forces in 1691 – Galway went into decline.

The Claddagh – Long before the arrival of the Normans there was a fishing village on the west bank of the Corrib River, an Irish-speaking community which preserved its own traditions and elected its own leader, known as the King. The name derives from the Gaelic word *cladach* meaning a rocky or pebbly shore. The men fished by night while by day the women sold the catch on the Spanish Parade. The picturesque whitewashed thatched cottages sited at random were replaced in the 1930s by a modern uniform housing scheme. The Claddagh finger ring, which bears the device of a heart enclosing two clasped hands, is popular throughout Ireland.

Gaelic Galway – The city adjoins the most extensive Gaelic-speaking region in Ireland: the Aran Islands, Connemara and the Joyce Country. The 19C revival of interest in the language brought many visitors to the region; two of the oldest Gaelic summer schools were founded at the turn of the century at Spiddal *(west)* and Tormakeady on the west shore of Lough Mask.

Since the establishment of the Republic, the Gaelic character of the region has been reinforced: University College, Galway, founded in 1849 as Queen's College, was created a bilingual institution in 1929 and is an important centre for the study of Gaelic language and literature; a state-sponsored Irish Theatre *(Tuibhdhearc na Gaillimhe)* was launched by Micheál Mac Liammóir and his partner Hilton Edwards; in 1969 the offices of the Gaelic Development Authority were moved to Furbogh (Na Forbacha *5mi/8km west of Galway by R 336*) and in 1972 Gaelic Radio began operating from Costelloe (Casla *further west by R 336*).

Literary Galway – Galway city and its environs have produced or fostered several literary personalities. Patrick O'Connor (1882-1928), who wrote short stories in Gaelic, Nora Barnacle (1884-1951), who lived in Bowling Green and married James Joyce, and Frank Harris (1856-1931) were natives of the city. Violet Martin, the second half of the Somerville and Ross partnership, lived at Ross House on the west shore of Lough Corrib. In 1896 Edward Martyn, who lived at Tullira Castle in south Galway, introduced William Butler Yeats to Lady Gregory; together they co-founded the Irish Literary Theatre, which became the Abbey Theatre in Dublin.

Walking About

Eyre Square

The focal point of the modern city between the old town and the docks centres on a small park, named after John F Kennedy, President of the USA, who visited Galway in 1963 *(plaque)*. There are several monuments: the **Browne doorway** removed from the family house in 1906; cannons from the Crimean War presented to the Connaught Rangers; a statue by Albert Power RHA of **Patrick O'Connor** (1882-1928); a statue of **Liam Mellows** who took part in the 1916 Easter Rising and was executed by the Free State army during the Civil War.

On display in the **Bank of Ireland** building are the **sword and mace★** of the city corporation, which was instituted by Richard III in 1484 and abolished in 1841; the sword (1610) bears two Galway silversmiths' marks; the mace, a massive highly decorated piece made in Dublin (1710), was presented by Edward Eyre in 1712. *Open Mon-Fri, 10am-4pm (5pm Thu). Closed Bank Hols. boi19eyresquare@bionet.ie From Eyre Square turn left into William Street.*

Lynch's Castle

This splendid 16C mansion belonged to the most powerful of the 14 tribes. The grey stone façade has some fine carving: gargoyles, hood mouldings over the windows, medallions bearing the lynx, the family crest, and a roundel bearing the arms of Henry VII.
Continue into Shop Street.

St Nicholas' Church★

Open 9am-4.30pm. Services: Sun, 8.30am, 11.30am. Brochure (7 languages).
☎ *091 564 648, 521 914 (Rector), 091 751489 (bookings)*
The medieval church, where Christopher Columbus is said to have worshipped, is dedicated to St Nicholas of Myra, the patron saint of sailors. The **exterior** is decorated with gargoyles and carved mouldings; the **interior** includes a medieval water stoup, a font and numerous tombstones. The south transept was extended to include the Lynch tomb which bears the family crest. The **Lynch Memorial** recalls the legend that in the 15C Judge James Lynch condemned his son Walter to death for murder and acted as hangman since no one else would carry out the sentence.

Spanish Arch, Galway

Walk round to the north side of the Church and into Mary Street.

Nora Barnacle's House
Open mid-May to mid-Sep, Mon-Fri (and occasional Sat), 10am-1pm and 2-5pm. €2.50.
☎ *091 564 743; norabarnaclehouse@eircom.net*
Nora Barnacle, the wife of James Joyce, lived in this two-up-two-down cottage until she left Galway to work in Dublin, where she met Joyce – souvenirs, photos and letters.
Walk south along Mary Street; continue into Cross Street; turn right into Quay Street and left at the end.

Spanish Arch
The name is a reminder of the city's trading links with Spain. The arch itself seems to have been part of a bastion, incorporating four blind arches, one of which was opened in the 18C to give access to a new dock beside Eyre's Long Walk. Part of the medieval **town wall** (20yd/18m long) is visible on the south side of the arch, together with the tidal quays dating from 1270.

Galway City Museum
Open Apr-Oct, daily, 10am-1pm and 2-5pm; Nov-Mar, Mon, Wed-Fri, 10am-1pm and 2-5pm. €2. Guided tour (20min) by appointment. ☎*/Fax 091 567 641*
The buildings adjoining the Spanish Arch house a miscellany of articles illustrating daily life in the area in past centuries. From the rooftop terrace *(open in fine weather only)* there is a fine view of the River Corrib as it enters inner Galway Bay.
Return to the south end of Quay Street; turn left into a narrow lane; turn left into Bridge Street; turn right into Nuns Island Street.

Roman Catholic Cathedral★
The huge neo-Romanesque cathedral, dedicated to Our Lady Assumed into Heaven and St Nicholas, was designed by John J Robinson in 1957 and defies all the precepts of architectural modernism. It is built of black Galway "marble", the local limestone which takes a good polish. Above the altar in St Nicholas' Chapel in the east transept are the early-17C carved stone plaques, depicting the three persons of the Trinity surrounding the Virgin, which were rescued during the Cromwellian period from St Nicholas' Church.

Salmon Weir Bridge
The bridge was built in 1818 to link the old prison (1802-1939), which stood on the cathedral site, with the **County Courthouse**, built (1812-15) on the site of the Franciscan Abbey. Upstream is the **salmon weir**; beyond are the pontoons of the viaduct (1890-1935) of the old Galway-Clifden railway.

Excursions

Annaghdown Church and Priory
12mi/20km N of Galway by N 84; in Cloonboo turn left to Annaghdown.
At Annaghdown St Brendan of Clonfert *(see p 253)* founded a convent for his sister. The 15C building at the southern end of the graveyard is the Cathedral incorporating earlier decorated stonework – a fine doorway and window (c 1200). The middle church is the oldest on the site (11C or 12C). The other ruined building was a parish church. The ruined priory *(turn into the lane west of the graveyard)* is a good example of a fortified monastery (c 1195); there is some Romanesque carving in the church.

Tuam

20mi/32km NE of Galway by N 17.

The tiny city of Tuam, with its two cathedrals, is the ecclesiastical capital of Connaught and the market centre for north Co Galway. In the 12C, when the O'Connor kings of Connaught were High Kings of Ireland, it was virtually the capital of the whole country. Its present layout, with all the streets converging on the central diamond, dates from 1613, when it was given borough status by King James I.

St Mary's Cathedral★ – *W of the town centre.* The Anglican cathedral stands in an enclosure protected by a high wall, the site of a monastery founded late in the 5C by Jarlath. The original cathedral was founded in 1130 but most of the present building, including the hexagonal spire (200ft/61m), dates from the not altogether successful neo-Gothic reconstruction by Sir Thomas Deane in 1860. All that remains of the medieval church is the red sandstone **chancel**; the two windows and the chancel arch with its five rows of moulding are fine examples of 12C Irish-Romanesque architecture. The shaft of a high cross in the north aisle is inscribed with prayers for an O'Connor king. East of the cathedral is a 14C building, which was badly damaged by the Cromwellians and has been restored in its original castellated style to serve as a Synod Hall.

St Jarlath's Churchyard – *W of town centre.* Irish yews grow among the graves surrounding the ruins of the 13C parish church, which was dedicated to the patron saint of Tuam; the west tower contained a lodging for the priest, and after the Reformation Roman Catholic clergy were buried in a side chapel. Some of the tombstones are inscribed with symbols showing the occupation of the deceased.

Mill Museum – *W of North Bridge.* The 17C corn mill on a tributary of the Clare River has been converted into a milling museum; three sets of mill-wheels are driven by an undershot spur wheel. There is an audio-visual presentation on the history of Tuam and its locality.

Cathedral of the Assumption – *E of the town centre.* This cruciform neo-Gothic structure was one of the first major Roman Catholic places of worship to be built in the 19C, its foundation stone being laid in 1827, a year before the Emancipation Act set off a wave of church construction. Funds were subscribed by the local inhabitants regardless of denomination. Such was its profusion of spikes and spires that a 19C tourist (C Otway) said of the cathedral that it put him "in mind of a centipede or a scorpion thrown on its back and clawing at the sky". Inside there are 17C Stations of the Cross, while the 19C stained glass is complemented by later glass from the Harry Clarke Studios.

Knockmoy Abbey★

20mi/32km NE of Galway by N 17 and N 63. In Knockmoy village turn left. After crossing the river turn right and park by the cemetery. 15min there and back on foot by a path and four stiles.

In the fields on the north bank of the River Abbert are the substantial ruins of an abbey which was founded in 1189 for the Cistercians of Boyle by Cathal O'Connor, king of Connaught, and dedicated to the Blessed Virgin Mary.

The church consists of the nave, a transept with two chapels and the **chancel**, which is decorated with some fine stone carving and a 13C tomb niche. Behind a protective grill is a rare **fresco** (1400) of the medieval legend of the Three Live Kings, who are dressed for hawking, and the Three Dead Kings, who bear the inscription "We have been as you are, you shall be as we are". Two partition walls, inserted in the 14C or 15C, have spoiled the east window of the chapter house in the east wing of the conventual buildings; little remains of the refectory in the south wing and even less of the cloisters.

Tour

LOUGH CORRIB★★

17mi/27.5km NW of Galway by N 59.

Lough Corrib, the second-largest lake in Ireland (36mi/58km long), is dotted with numerous islands. These are partly submerged **drumlins**, varying in size from a tuft of grass to Inchagoill island, the site of a 5C monastery.

From Galway take N 59; after 16mi/26km turn right (sign).

Aughnanure Castle★

From car park 5min there and back on foot. (Dúchas) Open May to Sep, daily 9.30am-6.30pm; Apr and Oct, Sat-Sun, 9.30am-6pm (5.15pm last admission). €2.50. Guided tour. Parking. ☎ 091 552 214; Fax 557 244; aughnanurecastle@ealga.ie

The formidable ruins of Aughnanure, a tower house and bawn probably built by Walter de Burgo, stand on an outcrop of rock, defended but also undermined by the Drimneen River. The circular **watchtower** is all that remains of the original bawn

wall. Most of the **Banqueting Hall** has collapsed into the river leaving the east wall with its Decorated windows. The **keep** rises through six storeys from a battered base to Irish-style crenellations with a machicolation on each side. From the roof there is a fine view of Lough Corrib.
Continue NW on N 59.

Oughterard★ (Uachtar Ard)
The attractive town on the west shore of the lake is a famous angling resort and a popular tourist centre.
The shore road north of the village, which ends near the head of the lake at Curraun *(8mi/13km there and back)*, provides an ever more spectacular **view**★★ of the lake and its backdrop of mountains.
Continue NW on N 59.

Glengowla Mine
Guided tour Mar-Nov, daily, 9.30am-6.30pm, every 20min; Dec-Feb, most Sat-Sun. €4.76. ☎ 091 552 360, 552 021, Mobile 087 252 9850; www.iarecordings.org/mineg.html
The silver and lead mine, which contains its original timbers although it closed in 1865, is now open for guided tours down to 70ft/20m.

Glendalough★★★

This once-remote valley among the Wicklow Mountains where St Kevin sought solitude and later founded a great monastery has long been a place of pilgrimage and continues to attract innumerable visitors. The "Glen of the Two Lakes" is one of the most evocative of all Irish monastic sites, both for the beauty of its setting and for the array of buildings, intact or in ruin, which conjure up a vivid picture of the early days of Christianity in Ireland.

Location
Population 1 695 - Michelin Atlas p 87 and Map 712 – M 8 – Co Wicklow.
Glendalough *(Gleann Dá Locha)* is S of Dublin in the Wicklow Mountains and can be reached by the coast route (M 11 and N 11 S to Ashford and R 763 to Annamoe, R 755 S to Laragh and R 756 W or by the inland route (N 7, N 81 and R 756); slower but more scenic routes take the road through the Sally Gap (R 115) or via Enniskerry, Roundwood and Annamore (R 117, R 760, R 755 and R 756).
🄱 *Glendalough. Open daily, 9.30am-6pm (5pm mid-Oct to mid-Mar). ☎ 0404 45352; Fax 0404 45626; info@heritageireland.ie; www.heritageireland.ie*
Adjacent Sights: See ATHY, KILDARE, WICKLOW MOUNTAINS.

DIRECTORY
There is a **bus service** from Dublin via Bray and Roundwood. *Operates 11.30am, 6pm, from Dublin (west side of St Stephen's Green - in front of the Royal College of Surgeons) via Bray and Roundwood. Single P9; return P15. bus@glendalough.com; www.glendaloughbus.com*

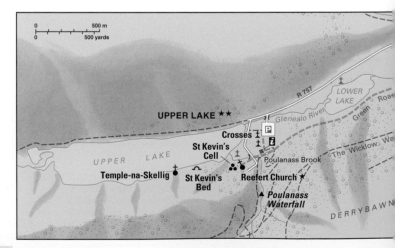

Background

The monastery founded by St Kevin flourished for many years after his death around 617, drawing pilgrims who were deterred from making the journey to Rome by the unstable conditions of the time. Seven pilgrimages to Glendalough were said to be the equivalent of one to far-off Rome. Despite repeated raids and destruction by both Vikings and Irish the monastery enjoyed a golden age in the 10C and 11C, a period of Celtic revival. Glendalough also prospered under the reforming leadership of St Laurence O'Toole (1128-80), who became abbot in 1153 at the age of 25 and was made Archbishop of Dublin in 1163. Decline began in the 13C and an English attack in 1398 caused much destruction. Dissolution followed during the reign of Henry VIII but the pilgrimages continued until the disorderly behaviour of many participants caused their suppression in the 1860s.

ST KEVIN

Probably born around the middle of the 6C, the young Kevin soon attracted attention for his ability to work miracles. He was put into the care of three clerics but he escaped his tutors into the bosom of Nature, supposedly dwelling in the hollow of a tree above the Upper Lake at Glendalough. Though persuaded to take up his studies again, Kevin had fallen under the spell of Glendalough, and it was to the lower part of the valley that he returned with a group of monks to found a monastery. The foundation flourished under his leadership as abbot but, tiring of his fame, he once more retired to the wilderness, living in complete solitude "in a narrow place between the mountain and the lake", probably the area above the Upper Lake now known as Temple-na-Skellig. The story is told of the blackbird who lays her egg in the saint's hand as he stands in ascetic contemplation, his arms outstretched in the shape of the Cross, a posture he holds

"in the sun and rain for weeks
until the young are hatched and fledged and flown" (Seamus Heaney).

The two lakes at Glendalough were once one. They are set in a valley whose dramatic contours were shaped by an Ice Age glacier descending from the Wicklow Mountains. The splendidly wooded southern shore of the Upper Lake, the site of several features associated with St Kevin, is particularly striking, with cliffs (100ft/30m) dropping precipitously into the dark waters of the lake. For many years the area was the scene of mining activity, with the woods being cut to smelt lead, zinc, iron, copper and silver ores. The Miners' Road, which runs along the northern shore of the lake to a deserted mining village at the top of the valley, provides the best view of St Kevin's Bed and the ruins of Temple-na-Skellig.

Walking About

Visitor Centre

(Dúchas) (&) Visitor centre. Open daily, 9.30am-6pm (5pm mid-Oct to mid-Mar); last admission 45min before closing. Closed 24-27 Dec. €2.50. Audio-visual show (4 languages). Guided tour on request (6 languages). Parking. Picnic area. ☎ 0404 45325, 45352; Fax 0404 45626

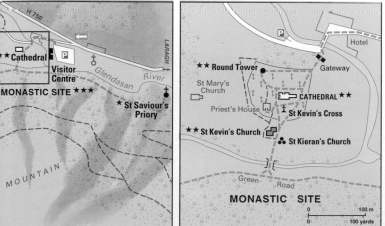

Glendalough

This spacious modern building has a number of displays including a fine model, based on Glendalough, of a typical monastery complex as it would have appeared in medieval times. Old photographs show the site as it was before restoration and reconstruction in the late 19C; an audio-visual show traces the monastic history of Ireland.

Monastic Site★★★

The ruins of the later monastic settlement, east of the Lower Lake, form the most important part of the Glendalough site. It is approached through the gateway, the only surviving example in Ireland of such an entrance to a monastic enclosure. Set in the wall just beyond the first of two arches is a great slab of mica schist with an incised cross, probably marking the point at which sanctuary would be granted to those seeking it.

Round Tower★★ – This fine example of a round tower (100ft/30m high) is the dominant feature of the site. Probably constructed in the early 10C, it would have served as landmark, storehouse, bell tower, lookout and refuge; its entrance is some way above the ground (12ft/4m). The thick walls (3ft/1m at the base) taper slightly towards the tip. Internally the tower was divided into six storeys, connected by ladders.

Cathedral★★ – This roofless structure, once the focal point of the communal life of the monastery, is still a substantial presence on the site, its nave one of the widest of early Irish churches. Built in stages, perhaps from the late 10C onwards, it consists of a nave and chancel with a small sacristy attached to the latter on the south side. The principal features of the nave are the corner pilasters, the west doorway and the south windows. A gravestone set against the north wall of the chancel bears carved crosses and inscriptions in Irish; an adjacent slab has outstanding scroll designs.

St Kevin's Cross – This early, undecorated Celtic high cross (12ft/3.5m high) is the best preserved of the many crosses on the site.

St Kevin's Church★★ – This early Irish oratory with its high-pitched roof of overlapping stones dates from the 11C. Its alternative popular name – St Kevin's Kitchen – is because of its unusual circular tower resembling a chimney or perhaps because of the scullery-like sacristy at its eastern end. The sacristy was once entered from a chancel, now demolished, whose outline can be traced in what remains of its foundations and in the line where its roof met the wall of the nave. Inside there is a sturdy barrel vault with a croft between it and the roof.

St Kieran's Church – The remains of a very small nave and chancel were discovered in 1875 close to St Kevin's Church but outside the stone wall surrounding the monastic enclosure.

St Saviour's Priory★

East of the Lower Lake by the Green Road. The Priory may have been founded by St Laurence O'Toole, Abbot of Glendalough, but is probably earlier in origin. The buildings (reconstructed in 1875), now enclosed within a forestry area, include a nave and chancel with a small group of domestic buildings on the north side. The chancel arch and the east window are impressive features in the Irish Romanesque style with much fine carving.

Glendalough

H Champollion/MICHELIN

Upper Lake★★

1.5mi/2.5km on foot W of the Visitor Centre by the Green Road – or 0.5mi/0.8km on foot from the Upper Lake car park. The approach to St Kevin's Cell is by a pathway which is steep and even muddy in places. There is no access to St Kevin's Bed or Temple-na-Skellig, which are best viewed from the far side of the lake.

Crosses – *East shore of Upper Lake.* The crosses, which originally marked the boundary of the monastic site, were later used as Stations of the Cross when Glendalough became an important pilgrimage centre.

Reefert Church★ – Traditionally the burial place of kings, and even perhaps of St Kevin himself, this roofless church is set among the oak and hazel woodland of the lower slopes above the lake. With a plain but beautiful chancel arch, round-headed windows in the south wall of the nave and an imposing granite doorway with sloping jambs, the building may date from the late 10C. In the graveyard are grave slabs and two crosses, one with fine interlaced carving.

St Kevin's Cell – Nothing remains of the cell where St Kevin dwelt alone save for a ring of foundation stones, colonised by three oak trees. His lonely abode was probably built with corbelled stones *(see ARCHITECTURE)* on the pattern of the beehive dwellings on Skellig Michael. The doorway faced eastwards down the valley and there may have been a window overlooking the lake.

St Kevin's Bed – This tiny cave in the rockface (30ft/9m above the lake) was probably a Bronze Age tomb. Believed to be the place where St Kevin would go to pray and fast, it used to be the focal point of a pilgrimage to Glendalough; having arrived at Temple-na-Skellig by boat, the pilgrims would make their way along the lake shore, climb steps hewn in the cliff and then be helped, one by one, into the "bone-rock bed of the austere saint" (Richard Hills).

Temple-na-Skellig – The first church on this site (about 20ft/6m above the lake) may date from the time of St Kevin himself, though the present ruined structure was probably a 12C rebuilding and was restored in the 1870s. It has an east window with narrow round-headed twin lights and a huge granite lintel above the incomplete west doorway. The huts of the earliest monastic community were probably built in the raised enclosure to the west of the church.

Poulanass Waterfall – From close to the cottage housing the National Park Information Centre, a path follows the miniature chasm of the Lugduff Brook steeply upstream to a lovely waterfall set among the oaks and holly trees of the surrounding forest.

Kells★

This little market town, a designated Heritage town, in the valley of the River Blackwater owes its fame to the wonderful illuminated manuscript now in the library of Trinity College. Of the monastery from which the Book of Kells was taken there remain some fascinating relics, while the town itself boasts a courthouse and a church designed by the Georgian architect Francis Johnston.

Location

Population 2 183 - Michelin Atlas p 92 and Map 712 – L 6 – Co Meath.
Kells *(Ceanannas Mór)* is situated in the Irish Midlands, NW of Dublin on N 3.
🅱 *Open May Sep, Mon-Sat, 10am-1pm and 2-6pm, Sun, 1.30-6pm; Oct-Apr, Tue-Sat, 10am-5pm, Sun and Bank Hols, 1.30-6pm.* ☎ *046 47840; Fax 046 47684; kellsheritagecentre@eircom.net; www.meathtourism.ie*
Adjacent Sights: See BOYNE VALLEY, CAVAN, DROGHEDA, DUNDALK, MULLINGAR, TRIM.

Directory

SHOPPING

Loughcrew Studio, Loughcrew Gardens *(see below)* – Furnishings, carpets, fabrics; showrooms and workshop

EVENTS AND FESTIVALS

Opera in Loughcrew Gardens *(see below)* – Two performances under canvas in late July.

O'Carolan Harp Festival – This festival of traditional music is held annually at Nobber *(9mi/15km NE by N 52 and R 162)* First Fri-Sun in Oct. Information from the Secretary, Keadew, Co Roscommon. ☎ *046 52115 or 52272*

Background

The Book of Kells

The monastery at Kells was founded by **St Columba** *(see p 208)* in the 6C. In the 9C his relics were brought here by monks fleeing from Viking raids on their monastery on Iona. Even here they were not secure and Kells itself was attacked by the Vikings on more than one occasion, as well as being sacked by the native Irish in the 12C and by the Scotsman Edward Bruce in the 14C. The great illuminated manuscript may have been produced at Kells or brought here from Iona. In 1007 it was stolen from the sacristy but found two months later minus its gold ornament. During Cromwell's campaigns, it was taken to Dublin for safe keeping, then presented to Trinity College in 1661.

Worth a Visit

Round Tower and High Crosses★★

Market Street. Open Jul-Aug, 10am-1pm and 2-5pm. Donation.
Parts of the monastery have survived in the churchyard of **St Columba's Anglican Church**.
The **round tower**, built before 1076, has lost its conical cap, but still rises to an imposing height of almost 100ft/30m. A number of well-weathered heads adorn the doorway.
Next to the tower stands the **South Cross**, probably dating from the 9C. The lively biblical scenes decorating it are not confined to the base but spread up the shaft and over the arms, intermingled with interlacing, foliage, and birds and animals. They depict Daniel in the Lions' Den, the Three Children in the Fiery Furnace, Cain and Abel and Adam and Eve *(south face)*, the Sacrifice of Isaac *(left arm)*, St Paul and St Antony in the desert *(right arm)*, David with his harp and the miracle of the loaves and fishes *(top)*, the Crucifixion and Christ in Judgement *(west side)*. Nearby stands the stump of a cross showing various biblical scenes and geometric decoration. South of the church stands an unfinished cross with raised panels ready to be carved and the Crucifixion on one face, while to the north of the church is a medieval church tower with grave slabs inserted at the base.
Detailed information about the monastery, the crosses, the Kells crozier *(in the British Museum)* and the Book of Kells is displayed in the gallery of the church.

St Columba's House★

Keys available at the house with the vehicle entrance in the lane beside the east churchyard gate.
Higher up the lane stands an ancient stone oratory with a steep corbelled stone roof. It probably dates from the 11C or 12C. The original entrance is visible in the west wall; the intervening floor is missing. Between the ceiling vault and the steep roof there is a tiny chamber *(access by ladder)*.

Kells Heritage Centre

Old Courthouse. Open May-Sep, Mon-Sat, 10am-1pm and 2-6pm, Sun, 1.30-6pm; Oct-Apr, Tue-Sat, 10am-5pm, Sun and Bank Hols, 1.30-6pm.
☎ *046 47840; Fax 046 47684; kellsheritagecentre@eircom.net; www.meathtourism.ie*
Artefacts on loan from the National Museum, touch screens, models and audio-visual presentations provide information about the Book of Kells, the high crosses, the life of the monastery and the history of the locality.

Book of Kells

Excursions

St Kilian's Heritage Centre

8mi/13km N of Kells by R 164 and R 194 to Mullagh. ♿ *Open Easter-Oct, Tue-Sun and Bank Hol Mon, 10am (2pm Sat-Sun) to 6pm. €3. Video (15min). Parking. Restaurant. Craft shop.* ☎/*Fax 046 42433*

The centre celebrates the life of **St Kilian** (640-689), the "Apostle of the Franks" who became the patron saint of Würzburg and died a martyr's death. North of Mullagh stands a ruined church known as Kilian's church (*Teampall Ceallaigh*). People still pray at his holy well, although formal observances ended early in the 19C.

St Kilian

Kilian was born in the 7C in Mullagh in Co Cavan and was educated at the monastic school in Rosscarbery (*see p 302*) in Co Cork. As a pilgrim for Christ, he went to Würzburg in Franconia to convert the people to Christianity. According to tradition he disapproved when the local ruler, Gozbert, whom he had converted, married his brother's wife and so she had St Kilian beheaded. In 782 his remains were moved to a round church on the Marienberg.

Castlekeeran High Crosses

5mi/8km W of Kells by R 163; after 3mi/5km turn right at the crossroads. Park beside the road. Through the farmyard and across the field and stile. Round the edges of the graveyard are three undecorated early crosses which pre-date the scriptural crosses at Kells. Beside the yew tree stands an **Ogham Stone**. They mark the site of an early monastery which grew up round the hermitage of Kieran, a monk from Kells.

Ballinlough Castle Gardens

3mi/5km W of Kells by R 163 to Ballinlough. Open May-Sep, Tue-Sat, 11am-6pm; Sun and Bank Hols, 2-6pm. Closed Aug, first two weeks. €5. ☎ 046 33344; Fax 046 33331
Surrounded by extensive parkland and reflected in the waters of one of its lakes, the castle *(not open to the public)* has been in continuous occupation by the O'Reilly/Nugent family since the Middle Ages, though its present romantic appearance is a reflection of late 18C ideas of what a castle should look like. It can be admired from woodland and lakeside walks, but the principal attraction of Ballinlough is its complex of walled gardens, rescued from dereliction and expertly planted as a series of contrasting compartments.

Loughcrew Historic Gardens

15mi/24km from Kells by R 163 and R 154 and a minor road W to Millbrook. Gardens: Open mid-Mar to Oct, daily, noon 6pm, Sun, noon-4pm; Nov and Jan to mid-Mar, Sun and Bank Hols, noon-4pm. €5. Opera: late-Jul, Fri-Sat (2 performances). ☎ 049 854 1922, 049 854 1356 (Loughcrew Garden Opera); Fax 049 854 1722, 049 854 1921 (Loughcrew Garden Opera); info@loughcrew.com; www.loughcrew.com
The gardens are an extraordinary palimpsest of ruins, earthworks, and ancient avenues, enhanced by imaginative recent additions. The estate was the home of the Plunkett family, its most renowned member Saint Oliver Plunkett, who may have been born here and who probably worshipped in the now roofless family church. Around

Mercury Gate, Loughcrew Gardens

the church extends the skeleton of an early 17C formal garden, its dominant feature an avenue of venerable yew trees leading to a medieval motte. Close by are the foundations of the original Loughcrew House, replaced in the early 19C by an imposing mansion designed by the great neo-Classical architect Charles Cockerell. It too has disappeared, though its portico has been re-erected in the countryside beyond the gardens as a very effective eye-catcher.

Loughcrew Passage Graves★

15mi/24km W of Kells by R 163. Beyond Ballinlough bear right onto R 154. After 3mi/4.6km turn left; after 0.5mi/0.8km turn left again onto narrow rough road. Car park. (Dúchas) Key available on payment of deposit from Loughcrew Gardens, same opening days, noon-4pm. Very steep climb to both sites; sturdy footwear required. ☎ 049 854 1356 (Loughcrew House); 041 988 0300 (Brú na Bóinne Visitor Centre); Fax 041 982 3071; www.heritageireland.com
Far less famous than the Neolithic tombs of the Boyne valley, the passage graves here are hardly less impressive, prominently sited as they are atop the Loughcrew Mountains. The cemetery covers two adjoining peaks, Cairnbane East and

Cairnbane West, on either side of the road, on Slieve na Calliagh (908ft/277m). It consists of at least 30 graves, some of which have been excavated. Most of them date from between 2500 and 2000 BC, although excavations in 1943 in Cairn H on Cairnbane West uncovered objects bearing Iron Age La Tène style decoration. **Cairn T** (120ft/37m in diameter), the largest grave on Cairnbane East, is decorated with concentric circles, zigzag lines and flower motifs.

Kenmare★

The small market town, a designated Heritage town, is charmingly set in a horseshoe of mountains at the point where the Roughty River widens into the long sea-inlet known as the Kenmare River. Kenmare is a popular tourist centre, with a wide range of hotels and restaurants and elegant shops (jewellery, linen, delicatessen, books and foreign newspapers) catering for visitors from many countries, many of whom use it as a starting point for explorations of the Beara and Iveragh peninsulas.

Location

Population 1 420 - Michelin Atlas p 76 and Map 712 – D 12 – Co Kerry.
Kenmare *(Neidín)* is located on N 71, a scenic road between Killarney and Glengarriff, and is a good place to stay while exploring Co Kerry.
🖪 *Heritage Centre, Kenmare. Open seasonally. 064 41233 and 31633*
🖪 *Glengarriff. Open Jul-Aug, Mon-Sat. ☎ 027 63084*
Adjacent Sights: See BANTRY, CORK, KILLARNEY.

Walking About

TOWN CENTRE

Kenmare is an 18C planned town, the work of the first Marquess of Lansdowne. Lined with neat stone houses and laid out in the form of a cross, its two streets meet at a triangular space intended to serve as a market-place but now a park. The town's origin goes back further, to the Marquess's ancestor, the energetic **Sir William Petty** (1623-87), organiser of the Down Survey *(see p 258)* who encouraged immigration from England and Wales, founded ironworks, and by astute land purchase ended up as owner of a quarter of Kerry.

Kenmare Heritage Centre

Main Street. 🖢 Open Easter-Sep, daily, 9.15am-6pm. ☎ 064 41233
The centre traces the history of Kenmare, originally called Nedeen *(Neidín* in Irish), and its buildings, its sufferings during the Famine and the story of the Nun of Kenmare, one of the community which established the lace-making industry in the 19C.

Kenmare

H Champollion/MICHELIN

Directory

GETTING ABOUT

Garinish Island Ferry – *Operates from Glengarriff Jul-Aug, daily, 9.30am (11am Sun) to 5pm (5.30pm Sun); Apr-Jun and Sep, daily, 10am (1pm Sun) to 5.30pm (7pm Sun); Mar and Oct, daily, 10am (1pm Sun) to 4.30pm (5pm Sun); last landing 1hr before closing time. Time 10min usually including Seal Island. €7.* ☎ *027 63333 (Blue Pool Ferry), 63555; Fax 027 63149*

Operates from Glengarriff Mar-Oct, daily, every 20min. €7.50. ☎ *027 63116 (Harbour Queen Ferry), 087 234 5861 (mobile); Fax 027 63298; www.garnishislandferry.com*

Dursey Island Cable Car – ♿ *Operates Mon-Sat, 9am-10.30am and 2.30pm-4.30pm, Sun, 9am-10.15am and noon-1pm; also return trip daily at 7pm. Return €3.17. Parking (mainland terminal).*

Bere Island Ferry – ♿ *Operates (10min; weather permitting) in summer, 7 times daily; in winter, 5 times daily (6 times Fri); Sun, reduced service. Return €20 (car+ 2 passengers), €5 (pedestrian). Also angling and diving trips. Parking. Refreshments.* ☎ *027 75009 (Bere Island Ferry), 086 242 3140 (mobile); Fax 027 75000; biferry@indigo.ie*

WHERE TO STAY

• Budget

Ceann Mara – *1mi/1.6km E on R 569 (Cork rd) -* ☎ *064 41220 - Fax 064 41220 - ceann.mara@eircom.net – Jun-Sep –* 🍽 🅿 *- 4 rm €40/64* 🛏. The driveway is shrouded in greenery, the garden spacious and the views of the Bay and surrounding hills are most impressive. The house itself has a reassuringly homely and cosy feel. Open only for four months in summer.

Mylestone House – *Killowen Rd - 0.25mi/0.4km E on R 569 (Cork rd) -* ☎ *064 41753 - mylestonehouse@eircom.net - Mar to 10 Nov -* 🅿 *- 5 rm €42/60* 🛏. Clean and affordable guest house accommodation just out of town. Guests are offered tea on their arrival; bedroom comforts are fairly simple but all are en-suite with shower rooms.

The Rosegarden – *0.75mi/1.2km W by N 71 on N 70 (Sneem rd) -* ☎ *064 42288 - Fax 064 42305 - rosegard@iol.ie - 18 Mar to Oct -* 🍽 *- 8 rm €55.50/79* 🛏 *- Meals €20/32.45.* Would be hard to find more immaculately kept accommodation. The Dutch owners provide old school hospitality and the bedrooms are colourful, bright and cheerful. A simple dinner menu is also provided.

Sea Shore Farm – *Tubrid – 1mi/1.6km W by 71 on N 70 (Sneem rd) -* ☎ *064 41270 - Fax 064 41270 - seashore@eircom.net – Mar-Oct -* 🅿 🍽 ♿ *- 6 rm €50/120* 🛏. With its 32 acres/13ha and views of the river and Caha mountains, one would be hard pressed to find a better spot than this farmhouse B&B. Comfortable bedrooms come in different colour schemes and bathrooms have power-showers.

• Moderate

Sallyport House – *0.25mi/0.4km S on N 71 -* ☎ *064 42066 - Fax 064 42067 - port@iol.ie – Easter-Oct -* 🍽 🅿 🍽 *- 5 rm €95/140* 🛏. One of the more expensive guesthouses but guests are assured of a warm welcome, an impressive breakfast and a particularly comfortable bedroom. Nicely decorated with antique pieces and there's a veritable mountain of local tourist information.

WHERE TO EAT

• Budget

An Leath Phingin – *35 Main St -* ☎ *064 41559 - Closed 15 Nov to 15 Dec and Wed -* 🍽 *- €18/29.40.* Hard to resist the winning combination of this high street restaurant; authentic Italian home cooking, sweet-natured service and rustic surroundings juxtaposed with modern art. Always, and understandably, busy.

• Moderate

Packies – *Henry St -* ☎ *064 41508 - 15 Mar to 15 Nov and closed Sun and Mon - €24/42.* One of the town's most established dinner spots, with its flagstone flooring adding to the character. The tried and tested menu features traditional Irish country cooking complemented by relaxed and welcoming service.

Mulcahys – *16 Henry St -* ☎ *064 42383 - Closed 15-30 Jan, 15-30 Nov, 24-26 Dec and Tue - €26/37.50.* The decoration of this modern restaurant testifies to a well-travelled owner. Asia is the theme with an assortment of banners and sculptures. This fusion, particularly Japanese, is further reflected in the eclectic menu.

The Lime Tree – *Shelburne St -* ☎ *064 41225 - benchmark@iol.ie – Apr-Oct -* 🅿 *- €28.40/37.40.* Converted from a former schoolhouse but with such warm hospitality and confident modern cooking, it means that truancy will never be a problem here. Local artists' work is for sale in the upstairs gallery.

SPORTS AND LEISURE

The Beara Way – This is a moderately easy walk (122m/196km) which rarely rises above 1115ft/340m and consists of old roads and tracks forming a loop round the Beara Peninsula.

EVENTS AND FESTIVALS

Queen of the Sea Festival – Held in Castletownbere *(early Aug)*

There is a display of wonderfully delicate antique **Kenmare Lace**. The **Lace and Design Centre** gives demonstrations of lace-making and sells lace made by a local cooperative working from the designs created by the nuns. *Open May-Sep, Mon-Sat, 10am-5.30pm. Lace-making demonstrations: Good Fri to mid-Jun and Sep, 10.15am-5.30pm; in winter on request.* ☎ *064 41491, 42636; Fax 064 42636; lacekenmare@eircom.net*

> **KENMARE LACE**
>
> Kenmare lace is needlepoint lace, a technique introduced from Italy in the 17C. It is the most difficult kind as it is worked in needle and thread without any supporting fabric. The design is drawn on parchment or glazed calico and outlined with skeleton threads which are later removed together with the backing. Its distinctive characteristics are braided outlines and the use of linen rather than cotton thread. Raised point is created by using buttonhole stitches over cords or horsehair.

Stone Circle

W off Market Street. On the edge of the town there is a prehistoric stone circle consisting of one central stone surrounded by 15 upright stones.

Excursion

Glen Inchaquin Park★★

8mi/14km SW by R 571 and left turn into a single-track lane (5mi/8km). ♿ *to waterfall. Open daily, 9am (later in winter) to 8pm (earlier in winter). 4. Parking. Refreshments.* ☎ *064 84235*

The lane leads into the lonely heart of the mountains with their lakes, tumbling streams, glorious sessile oak woodlands and richly varied wild flowers. At the head of the glen there is a farmhouse with tearoom and car park and a picnic site has been laid out at the foot of a spectacular braided waterfall cascading down the blackened rock face. The views down the glen to the Kenmare River and McGillycuddy Reeks are spectacular, even more so if the circular footpath (1hr 30min) leading around the top of the falls is followed.

Tour

RING OF BEARA★★

Round tour of 85mi/137km – 1 day

The Beara peninsula, a rocky spur projecting some 30mi/48km into the Atlantic, has some of the wildest and most beautiful mountain, moorland and coastal scenery in the southwest.

From Kenmare take N 71 S and turn left beyond the Kenmare River.

Sheen Falls

Here the Sheen River swirls and tumbles over rocks and boulders before joining the Kenmare River.

Caha Pass

Work on the Kenmare-Glengarriff road began around 1839, and tunnels had to be blasted in the rock to carry it over the rugged terrain of the Caha Mountains. South of the pass there is a fine **view** of Glengarriff and Bantry Bay.

Glengarriff (An Gleann Garbh)★

Little more than a main street with shops and pubs, hotels and guesthouses, Glengarriff has nevertheless been a resort of international renown since the mid-19C; as early as the 1830s visitors to the area were publishing their impressions of the exotic flora which flourish in the exceptionally mild and moist climate of southwest Cork. Queen Victoria stayed at the **Eccles Hotel**, which was built in 1833 as a coaching stage and has retained its original façade and some interior features. **George Bernard Shaw** wrote part of his play *St Joan* in the dining room and the remainder on Garinish Island.

There are pleasant walks along the wooded shore of the Blue Pool (*poll gorm* in Irish) in the northwest corner of Glengarriff Harbour. The best view of Glengarriff is from the top of **Shrone Hill** (919ft/280m – *SW*).

Ilnacullin★★

Garinish Island Ferry (see Directory). (Dúchas) ♿ *Open Jul-Aug, daily, 9.30am (11am Sun) to 6.30pm; Apr-Jun, Sep, 10am (11am Sun) to 6.30pm; Mar and Oct, 10am (1pm Sun) to 4.30pm (5pm Sun). Closed 25-26 Dec; last landing 1hr before closing time. €4; separate charge for ferry. Self-guiding trails. Guide book (6 languages). Coffee shop.* ☎ *027 63040; Fax 027 63149*

Garinish Island (37 acres/15ha), also known as **Ilnacullin**, lies in Glengarriff Harbour. Early this century it was turned by the English landscape designer Harold Peto into a meticulously planned garden for the Belfast-born MP Annan Bryce.

Italianate formality and Classical pavilions contrast wonderfully both with the austere mountain backdrop and with the lush planting of exotic species; flowers are in bloom all year because of the benign weather and the garden's protected position. A path leads to the **Martello Tower** (135ft/41m above sea level), the highest point on the island.

Bamboo Garden

Glengarriff. &. Open daily, 9am-7pm. €5. Parking. Plants for sale. ☎ 027 63 570; ☎ 027 63 975 (ticket office); Fax 027 63 255; bambooparkltd@eircom.net; www.westcork.com/bamboopark

The climate is ideally suited to the oriental bamboo; an exotic forest is being created of 30 different species of this plant and 12 different species of palm trees. The slim green leaves of the bamboo contrast with the darker green of the myrtle and hydrangeas; visitors can take a stroll in the old garden, enjoy the exotic flora of the new, or swim from the South Beach. There are fine views of Glengarriff Harbour and Bantry Bay from the Tower and from the waterfront, which is embellished with 13 stone pillars.

From Glengarriff take R 572 W; in Adrigole turn right (sign) to the Healy Pass.

Healy Pass★★

The road is particularly steep near Glanmore Lake. Opened only in 1931, the road climbs through a series of tortuous hairpin bends *(7mi/11km)* to the summit; on a clear day the **views**★★ of both shores of the peninsula are very impressive.

The **Healy Pass** was named after Tim Healy, who was born in Bantry in 1855. He was a Nationalist MP at Westminster from 1880 until 1916 and in 1922 he was appointed the first Governor-General of the Irish Free State. At a presentation in the Anchor Bar, Bantry, on his retirement as Lord Chief Justice of Ireland, he was invited to choose a leaving present; he asked for improvements to be made to what until then had been a mere bridleway over the mountains between Adrigole to Lauragh.

At the crossroads turn left to Derreen Gardens (sign).

Derreen Gardens★

Open Apr-Sep, daily, 10am-6pm. €4; garden map €.30. Parking. ☎ 064 83588

These lush gardens were planted 100 years ago by the 5th Lord Lansdowne beside Kilmakilloge Harbour, an inlet on the south shore of the Kenmare River. The woodland is richly underplanted with azaleas and rhododendrons; the most notable attraction is the grove of New Zealand tree ferns.

Take R 571 W for 8mi/12.9km to the Ballycrovane junction

Ballycrovane Ogham Pillar Stone

Donation to enter the field In a field stands the tallest pillar stone in Ireland (15ft/5m high); the Ogham inscription – MAQI-DECCEDDAS AVI TURANIAS (of the son of Deich descendant of Torainn) – was probably added later.

Continue W to Eyeries

Eyeries

This typical Irish mountain settlement, with four pubs, a couple of shops and brightly painted cottages, is the home of a famous, tangy soft cheese made from cow's milk. There is a beach *(1mi/1.6km W)*.

Take R 575 W along the coast to Allihies.

Allihies

The peninsula was known for its wealth of copper ores and their extraction by a largely Cornish workforce. In the 19C Allihies was a prosperous community; above the straggling village *(sign)* are the extensive remains of its **copper mines**★. Old engine houses and spoil heaps are visible among the many invisible but dangerous abandoned mineshafts. **Ballydonegan Strand** *(1mi/1.6km S)* is a magnificent beach composed of crushed stone from the mines.

Continue S on R 575; after 2.5mi/4.2km turn right onto R 572.

Garnish Bay

At low tide one can walk from the tiny hamlet of six houses and a post office to **Garnish Island**, a good vantage-point for **views**★ *(N)* of the Iveragh Peninsula and *(NW)* of the Skellig Islands.

Continue W to Dursey Island.

Dursey Island

Access by cable car (see Directory). Limited tourist accommodation.

The island's isolation ended when Ireland's only cable railway was strung across the strait in 1970; it can carry six passengers or a cow and its minder. Cliff-girt Dursey, 4mi/6km long, has one village, Kilmichael, and one road; its main attractions are its amazing bird life and the superlative views it offers of the mainland coast.

Return E; after 1.5mi/2.4km turn right to Crow Head.

Crow Head

The bleak headland provides a fine view of Mizen Head *(S)* and the Skellig Islands *(N)*. On 23 July 1943 a German bomber plane crashed into it in fog, killing all four crew *(plaque)*.

Continue E on R 572; after 6mi/9.7km turn left.

Slieve Miskish Mountains

After 2mi/3km the road becomes a track suitable only for climbers; 45min on foot to summit. The high climb into the mountains is rewarded with splendid **views★**; the summit commands the entire length of Bantry Bay.

Return to R 572 and continue E; after 1mi/1.6km turn right (sign) to Dunboy Castle (0.5mi/0.8km).

Dunboy Castle

Surrounded by Dunboy woods *(walks and picnic areas)* are the remains of this star-shaped castle, the last O'Sullivan stronghold to resist the English in 1602. Nearby is the vast shell of Puxley's Castle, part French château, part Italian villa, burned down by the IRA in 1921. It was built by the Puxley family, the local landlords, with the huge royalties produced by the Beara copper mines. The history of the family and the mines inspired Daphne du Maurier to write her novel *Hungry Hill*.

Continue E on R 572 to Castletownbere.

Castletownbere

This town was developed in the early 19C when rich copper deposits were discovered at Allihies. The area was particularly badly hit by the 19C potato famine. Later in the century Castletownbere became an important fishing port. Fish processing is now a substantial industry, and the harbour is often full of trawlers and factory ships flying a variety of flags.

Bere Island

Bere Island Ferry (see Directory). No tourist accommodation. The island was an important base for the Royal Navy, one of the three Treaty Ports given up to the Free State only in 1938. It is home to a dozen families and the headquarters of a sailing school.

Take R 572 E to return to Glengarriff and N 71 N to return to Kenmare.

Kildare★

The name of Kildare is intimately associated with the nearby Curragh, the extensive plain of short springy turf dotted with clumps of yellow gorse which is the headquarters of Irish horse racing and breeding. Neat little Kildare itself is a county and cathedral town and designated Heritage town, tracing its origins to the 5C religious community founded by St Brigid and St Conleth, which was one of the few convents for women in the Celtic period.

Location

Population 4 278 - Michelin Atlas p 86 and Map 712 – L 8 – Co Kildare.
Kildare *(Cill Dara)* is situated on the main road (N 7) leading SW from Dublin to Limerick.

🖪 *Kildare Tourist Information, Kildare. Open May, Mon-Fri; Jun-Sep, Mon-Sat.* ☎ *045 522 696; kildaretownheritagecen@ireland.com*

Adjacent Sights: See ABBEYLEIX, ATHY, MAYNOOTH, MULLINGAR, ROSCREA, TULLAMORE, WICKLOW MOUNTAINS.

Directory

SIGHTSEEING

Canal Barge trips in summer from the **Old Canal Hotel**, Robertstown; cruisers for hire from **Lowtown Marina** *(see below). Open Mon-Fri, 9am-5pm; Sat-Sun and Bank Hols, 12.30-6pm. Canal barge trips: Apr-Sep; €7.50 (1hr); €20.00 (3hr; min 20 people). Restaurant: Open Mon-Wed, 8.30am-6pm; Fri-Sat, 8.30am-10.30pm.* ☎ *045 870 005; Fax 045 870 313; robertstown@eircom.net*

SPORTS AND LEISURE

The **Curragh Racecourse** hosts all five Classic **horse races** including The Budweiser Irish Derby and 14 other race days. *Open Mar-Sep. For the Derby: Reserved enclosure €50. Classic and group meetings €16. Regular meetings, Sat-Sun and May Bank Hol Mon €13.* ☎ *045 441205 (Manager); Fax 045 441 442; info@curragh.ie; www.curragh.ie*

Worth a Visit

Cathedral★

Open Mon-Sat, 10am-1pm and 2-5pm, Sun, 2-5pm. Services: Sun, noon (Holy Communion). ☎ 045 441 654

The present cathedral building is a late-19C reconstruction, incorporating portions of a 13C structure. The plain unplastered interior is relieved by a medieval stone font, stained-glass windows, and a number of tombs with effigies, including the superb figure of Bishop Wellesly dating from around 1539.

Standing separately in the churchyard, the **round tower** (108ft/32m high) has been substantially restored in recent years; from the top there are **views** over the Curragh and the surrounding Midland counties.

A minor road opposite the cathedral leads to **St Brigid's shrine** and **well**.

Kildare Heritage Centre

Open May-Oct, Mon-Fri, 9.30am-5.30pm, Sun, 2-6pm; Oct-Apr, by appointment. €3. Public car park. Chairlift. ☎ 045 530 672; Fax 045 530 659; kildaretownheritagecen@ireland.com

The history and heritage of Kildare are clearly presented, using an audio-visual film (12min) and 18 storyboards, in the 18C market house, above the Tourist Information Office.

Excursions

Irish National Stud★★

1mi/1.5km SE of Kildare (sign) at Tully. ♿ Open mid-Feb to mid-Nov, daily, 9.30am-6pm. €8.50. Brochure (10 languages). Parking. Refreshments. Gift/craft shop. ☎ 045 521 617, 522 963; Fax 045 522 964; stud@irish-national-stud.ie; www.irish-national-stud.ie

Lord Wavertree, a wealthy Scotsman from a brewing family, began breeding horses at Tully in 1900; in 1915 he gave his stud to the British Crown and it continued as the British National Stud until it was handed over to the Irish Government in 1943. The stallion boxes, with their lantern roofs, were built in the 1960s. In the Sun Chariot yard, finished in 1975, pregnant mares

> **THE CURRAGH**
>
> The name is derived from the old Irish word *(cuir-rech)* meaning racecourse and the area has been associated with horse racing since the pre-Christian era. The first recorded prize is the Plate donated in 1640 by the Trustees of the Duke of Leinster. By the mid-19C there were some 25 courses at the Curragh ranging from a short course (2 furlongs/440yd/402m) for yearlings to "Over the Course" (4mi/6km). For many years the Curragh was an important British army base, notorious for the "Curragh Mutiny" of March 1914, when officers let it be known that they would disobey any orders to put down the planned uprising in Ulster against Home Rule.

are stabled during the stud season and yearlings are housed from July to October. Mares and foals can be seen in the paddocks from the Tully Walk *(2mi/3km long)*.

National Stud

The most intriguing exhibit in the **Irish Horse Museum** is the skeleton of Arkle, the Irish racehorse with an outstanding record of wins whose career ended in a fall at Kempton Park in England on 27 December 1966. The other exhibits, which include a 13C horse skull found at Christchurch Place in Dublin and harness made in Dublin between the 13C and 15C, trace the history of the horse, horse racing and steeple-chasing *(see p 318)*.

The grounds of the stud contain an extensive lake, created by Eida *(see below)*, and the ruins of the **Black Abbey**, founded as a preceptory of the Knights Hospitaller of St John after the Anglo-Norman invasion of Ireland in 1169. According to tradition it is connected by a tunnel (1mi/1.5km) to Kildare Cathedral. When the abbey was suppressed in the mid-16C, it passed into the possession of the Sarsfield family and it was here c 1650 that **Patrick Sarsfield** *(see p 307)*, leader of the Irish at the Siege of Limerick, was born.

Japanese Gardens★★ – *In the grounds of the National Stud (see above).* ♿ *Open same as Irish National Stud.*

Among the most ambitious of their kind outside Japan, the gardens were created for Lord Wavertree between 1906 and 1910 by the Japanese gardener Eida and his son Minoru. The main garden depicts the story of the life of man, beginning with the **Gate of Oblivion** and the **Cave of Birth,** continuing across the bridges of engagement and marriage to the **Hill of Ambition** and the **Well of Wisdom.** Formerly the concluding feature, the **Gateway to Eternity** now leads into the **Garden of Eternity** (1974) depicting the conflict of human nature. The **Zen meditation garden** (1976) is not designed to suggest any particular thought; visitors are encouraged to generate their own concepts.

Peatland World

12mi/19km N by R 401 and R 414 at Lullymore. (♿) Open Apr-Oct, Sun-Fri, 9.30am (2pm Sun) to 6pm, Sat, by appointment; Nov-Mar, Mon-Fri, 9.30am-6pm. €5. Parking. Refreshments. ☎ 045 860 133; Fax 045 860 481

The importance of peat in Irish life (its place in the landscape, its use as fuel, flavouring for whiskey, and in industry) is brought home in a vivid manner in this Centre, housed in the stables of an old estate. The displays explain peat cutting by hand for the home, and by machine to fuel the peat-powered electricity generating stations. Among the exhibits are bog wood and bog butter and a pre-Christian bog-oak canoe, turf cutting spades, cloth made from peat fibres, products derived from peat such as oil, wax, candles, toilet articles such as shampoo, toothpaste and soap from Germany. Upstairs the display illustrates the flora and fauna of the peat bogs and their conservation.

Hill of Allen

6mi/10km N by R 415. The summit of the 19C tower (676ft/206m) provides **views** of the vast Bog of Allen *(NW)* stretching westward to the Shannon.

Robertstown (Inis Robertaig)

10mi/16km N by R 415. The village is strategically located at the point where the Grand Canal divides, one arm eventually reaching Waterford, the other the Shannon. The waterfront is fascinating, dominated by the stately red-brick Grand **Canal Hotel**, built in 1803 to serve the passengers on the flyboats *(see p 48)*; it now houses an exhibition.

Kilcullen

7mi/11km E by R 413. The **Hide Out Bar**, designed in the style of a jungle hut, has a bizarre relic in the shape of the black and withered right arm of prize-fighter Dan Donnelly (1786-1820), who won a spectacular bout on the The Curragh on 13 December 1815. The pub also displays a collection of old maps, deer heads, hunting guns and knives.

Punchestown Standing Stone

15mi/24km east by N 7 to Naas and R 411. North of the famous racecourse *(Woolpack Road)* stands a granite long stone (20ft/6m high) which is thought to date from the early Bronze Age.

Kilkenny★★

Kilkenny is Ireland's outstanding medieval city, set on the banks of the River Nore and dominated by castle and cathedral facing each other across the city centre. Narrow alleys, known locally as slips, recall the medieval street pattern. The city's historical legacy, splendidly expressed in any number of well-restored ancient buildings, is matched by a strong cultural and artistic tradition.

Location

Population 8 507 - Michelin Atlas p 80 and Map 712 – K 10 – Co Kilkenny.
Kilkenny *(Cill Chainnigh)* is a good base for exploring the SE corner of Ireland, well served by good roads in all directions.

Directory

Sightseeing

Guided walking tour of the medieval town. *Operates from Kilkenny Tourist Office Apr-Oct, Mon-Sat, 6 times daily, Sun, 4 times daily; Nov-Mar, Tue-Sat, 3 times daily. €5. ☎/Fax 056 65929, 087 265 1745 (Tynan Tours); 087 265 1745 (mobile)*

Where to Stay

• *Budget*

Shilloger House – *Callan Rd – 0.6mi/1km from the town centre via the N76. - ☎ 056 63249 - Fax 056 64865 - 8 rm €45/50* ☕. Michael and Gorette Hennessy have made their house as attractive as possible for their guests. The perfectly kept rooms wouldn't disgrace a first-rate hotel.

Abbey House – 12mi/19km S by R 700 to *Thomastown, opposite the entrance to Jerpoint Abbey - ☎ 056 24166 - Fax 056 24192 - 7 rm €50/75* ☕. Flower-print curtains and Victorian furniture in a lovely old building surrounded by its garden. Excellent à la carte breakfast with fresh fruit juice and home-made scones.

Berkeley House – *5 Patrick St - ☎ 056 64848 - Fax 056 64829 - berkeleyhouse@eircom.net - Closed 23-27 Dec - P - 10 rm €55/98* ☕. Not only is this Georgian house in the very heart of the city but it also has a good size car park, which will ease the nerves of those who have ever spent time trying to park in this city. Bedrooms are spacious, with the quietest at the rear.

Where to Eat

• *Moderate*

Zuni – *26 Patrick St - ☎ 056 23999 - info@zuni.ie - Closed 23-28 Dec - P - €30.25/42.40.* Its origins as Kilkenny's first cinema are reflected in the original façade and contrast with the stylish and modern interior, following its conversion in 2000 into the city's trendiest restaurant. Cooking from the open-plan kitchen is equally à la mode.

Shopping

The **Kilkenny Design Centre** *(Castle Stables)*, housed in the monumental 18C stable buildings of the Castle, is a major retail outlet for high-quality souvenirs and provides accommodation for a variety of craftspeople; it was set up in the 1960s as a focal point for improvement in the design of ceramics, textiles, furniture and jewellery. ♿ *Open daily, 9am (10am Sun) to 6pm. Restaurant: Apr-Dec, daily, 9am (10am Sun) to 5pm; Jan-Mar, Mon-Sat, 9am-5pm. ☎ 056 22118; Fax 056 65905; info@kilkennydesigncentre.com; www.kilkennydesign.com*

A number of craft studios are grouped in **Bennetsbridge** *(7mi/11km south)*, including **Nicholas Mosse**, housed in an old flour mill, which offers a variety of craft work, including pottery made on the premises.

For hand-blown glass, where the craftsmen can be seen at work, visit **Jerpoint Glass Studio** *(south of Stoneyford on the Thomastown road).*

Sports and Leisure

The magnificent estate of **Mount Juliet** (1 400 acres/567ha) offers many sporting facilities including a golf course designed by Jack Nicklaus; the house (c 1780) is a luxury hotel, open only to residents. *Advance booking required for sporting facilities. ☎ 056 73000; Fax 056 73019; info@mountjuliet.ie; www.mountjuliet.com*

Greyhound racing.

R Holzbachova, Ph Benet/MICHELIN

Irish pipers

Events and Festivals

Kilkenny Arts Festival – One of the most important arts events in Ireland, featuring classical music, visual art, theatre, literature, children's arts and outdoor events *(mid-Aug)*

Shee Alms House, Rose Inn Street, Kilkenny. Open May-Sep, daily; Oct-Mar, Mon-Sat.
☎ 056 51500; Fax 056 63955; www.irelandsoutheast.travel.ie
Adjacent Sights: See ABBEYLEIX, CAHER, CASHEL, CLONMEL, ENNISCORTHY,
NEW ROSS, ROSCREA.

Background

Capital of the Kingdom of Ossory – The city is named after St Canice, who founded a church here in the 6C. From the 2C to the 12C Kilkenny was the capital of the Gaelic Kingdom of Ossory; the ruling MacGiolla Phadruig family was engaged in a constant struggle for the kingship of Leinster.

Statutes of Kilkenny – Following the Anglo-Norman invasion in the 12C Kilkenny quickly became strategically and politically important; it was a major venue for Anglo-Irish parliaments. Under Anglo-Norman rule the native clans and the invaders lived side-by-side in reasonable co-existence despite frequent incomprehension. Over the centuries many of the Anglo-Norman families, led by the dominant Butler family, tended to become absorbed into the native Gaelic culture, wearing their dress, speaking their language, and intermarrying. Not unnaturally, this process displeased the authorities in Dublin and England, who wished to maintain a proper distance between rulers and ruled; in 1366 a parliament in Kilkenny passed the **Statutes of Kilkenny** to prohibit the Anglo-Normans from intermingling with the Irish but the process was so far advanced that the new laws were ignored.

Confederation of Kilkenny – Kilkenny's outstanding period was from 1642 to 1648, when the Confederation of Kilkenny functioned as an independent Irish parliament, representing both the old Irish and the Anglo-Irish Roman Catholics.

KILKENNY

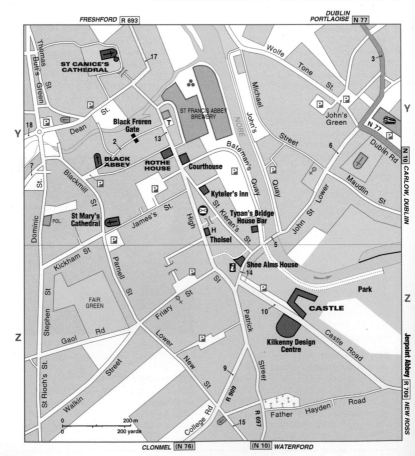

Kilkenny Castle

Later the Confederation split and the Anglo-Irish side supported the English Viceroy, while the Old Irish relied on the military support of Pope Innocent X. The Old Irish, led by Owen Roe O'Neill, were eventually defeated; following Cromwell's siege of Kilkenny in 1650 the Irish army was permitted to march out of the city.

Nationalist Tradition – Kilkenny has always had a strongly nationalistic tradition and played a key role in the movement for independence early in the 20C. **William T Cosgrave**, who, as the first president of the Executive Council, was a much-needed steadying hand in the early days of the Free State, was Sinn Féin member for Kilkenny, first at Westminster and then in the Irish Parliament (Dáil).

Special Feature

Kilkenny Castle and Park★★

(Dúchas) (& to ground floor) Castle: Guided tour Jun-Aug, daily, 9.30am-7pm; Sep, 10am-6.30pm; Apr-May, 10.30am-5pm; Oct-Mar, 10.30am-12.45pm and 2-5pm; last admission 45min before closing. Tour of park: Jul-Aug, Sun at 3pm. Closed Good Fri and Christmas, sometimes in winter for essential maintenance; telephone for details. €4.40. No photography. Tearoom (May-Sep). ☎ 056 21450; Fax 056 63488

The castle was built by William the Earl Marshal between 1192 and 1207 on a most imposing site overlooking the curving River Nore. Uniquely among Irish castles, it was a nobleman's residence, the main seat of the Butler family, Earls and Dukes of Ormond, who dominated the southeast of Ireland for many years. Much of the medieval fabric remains, including three of the four corner towers. The castle was extensively modernised in the 19C but fell into dereliction and was eventually taken over by the state in 1967. Since then, much restoration and refurnishing has taken place, and the great stronghold seems to fulfil the expectations of the many who visit it in the hope of experiencing something of the lifestyle of the Anglo-Irish aristocracy.

From the hall, paved with Kilkenny marble and hung with portraits, mahogany stairs installed in 1838 lead up to the Library and Drawing Room, restored to their Victorian appearance with some of the original furniture. The Dining Room is furnished in the style of the 18C.

The most imposing interior is the 19C Long Gallery hung with Gobelin tapestries and family portraits (on loan) and with a hammerbeam roof decorated in the Pre-Raphaelite style with neo-Celtic motifs. The bedrooms have hand-painted Chinese silk wallpaper and a mahogany bed with a horsehair mattress. In the 19C the castle was staffed by 93 servants who came and went through a tunnel under the road to the stables.

The **Butler Gallery** *(Basement)* displays a collection of 19C and 20C Irish art and visiting exhibitions of contemporary art.

The extensive **park** (50 acres/20ha) with its formal gardens and woodlands provides many beautiful walks.

Walking About

Shee Alms House

Open Jul-Aug, daily, 9am (11am Sun) to 7pm (5pm Sun); May-Jun, Mon-Fri, 9am-6pm, Sat-Sun, 11am-1pm, 2-5pm; Apr and Sep, Mon-Sat, 9am-6pm; Jan-Mar and Oct-Nov, Mon-Sat, 9am-1pm and 2-5pm. ☎ 056 51500; Fax 056 63955; info@southeasttourism.ie
The 16C building, once used as a hospice, now houses the tourist information office.
Walk up Rose Inn Street and turn right into High Street.

Tholsel

Open Mon-Fri, 9am-1pm and 2-5pm. ☎ 056 21076
The Tholsel (toll stall), built in 1761 (restored), contains examples of mayoral regalia dating back two centuries. The first tholsel was constructed around 1400, when the city walls were built.

Courthouse

The courthouse was built above Grace's Castle (1210) which was converted into a prison in 1568.

Rothe House★

Open daily, 10.30am (3pm Sun) to 5pm. Closed Good Fri. €3. Audio-visual show. Guided tour (45min) available. Leaflet (3 languages). ☎ 056 22893; rothehouse@aircom.com
With its splendid Tudor facade, this is a unique survival, the only remaining town house of the Renaissance period in Ireland. Built in 1594 by a local merchant, John Rothe, it was used in the 17C as a meeting place by religious and political leaders during the Kilkenny Confederation, then in the 19C by the nationalist Gaelic League. It now houses the local museum, which presents many historical curiosities, including letters written by Daniel O'Connell when he was MP for Kilkenny City in 1836-37, an 18C penal cross, and the Carlingford Screw, all that remains of the first Irish aeronautical patent, taken out in 1856 by Viscount Carlingford, a local landowner. There is a small costume collection on the top floor.
Continue N along Parliament Street over the bridge; cross Dean Street and take the steps up to the Cathedral.

St Canice's Cathedral★★

♿ *Open Mon-Sat, 9am (10am Oct-Easter) to 1pm and 2-6pm (4pm Oct-Easter); Sun, 2-6pm (4pm Oct-Easter). Closed Wed and Holy Days, 10-11am; Good Fri, 25 Dec to 1 Jan. Donation. Round Tower: Open (weather permitting) Easter to mid-Sep; €2. Guided tour (30min). Leaflet (9 languages). Guide book. Gift shop. ☎ 056 64971 (Cathedral), 056 21516 (Deanery); stcanicescathedral@eircom.net*
The cathedral stands upon a small hill, which may be the site of St Canice's 6C church, and is best approached by St Canice's Steps *(SE)* which date from the early 17C. It was built in the 13C in harmonious early Gothic style and has been periodically restored, firstly after 1650 when Cromwell damaged the monuments, destroyed the roof and stabled horses in the nave, secondly in the mid-18C and 19C, and again from 1959 to 1961 when the roof and organ were renovated.
The many architectural features of the interior of the cathedral, the second-longest in Ireland, are best appreciated from the west end of the nave. Among the many fine tombs the best known *(south transept)* is that in black Kilkenny marble of Piers Butler, Earl of Ormond and Ossory (died 1539) and his wife Margaret Fitzgerald; her effigy has a finely jewelled and embroidered girdle.
The oldest tomb (13C) *(north transept)* bears part of the original dog-tooth ornament. The oldest slab, found under the High Street in 1894, is the **Kyteler slab** *(north aisle)*, inscribed in Norman French in memory of Jose Kyteler, probably the father of Dame Alice Kyteler, who was tried for witchcraft in 1323.
In the graveyard stands a **round tower** (100ft/30m high), built between 700 and 1000, which gives an overall view of Kilkenny and its surrounding countryside.
Return along Parliament Street, turn right into Abbey Street.
The street passes through the medieval **Black Freren Gate**.

Black Abbey★

♿ *Open daily, 8.30am-7pm. No visiting during services. Donation. Brochure. ☎ 056 21279*
The church, one of the few **medieval churches** in Ireland still in use, was founded soon after 1226 for the Dominicans. The interior is decorated with fine early-14C window tracery in the south transept, particularly the five-light Rosary window. Although inscribed 1264, the lovely alabaster carving of the Most Holy Trinity beside the altar is thought to date from c 1400. In the graveyard are 10 stone coffins dating from the 13C and 14C.
Turn left into Blackmill Street.

St Mary's Cathedral

The Roman Catholic cathedral was built in the 19C of limestone with a high tower (200ft/61m).

Excursions

Thomastown

11mi/18km S of Kilkenny by R 700. Little twisting streets focus on the market-like main street close to the old bridge over the Nore, half-obliterated by its modern concrete deck. There are remains of the medieval town walls and castle. **Ladywell Water Garden** is an intricate mixture of trees, shrubs and aquatic plants. *Open Apr-Oct, daily, 10am-5pm; Nov-Mar, Mon-Fri. €1.30. Coffee shop (Tue-Fri; also Apr-Oct, Sun). ☎ 056 24690; Fax 056 54766; thewatergarden@camphill.ie; www.camphill.ie*

Jerpoint Abbey★★

12mi/19km S of Kilkenny by R 700 and N 9 S from Thomastown. (Dúchas) (&) Mar to Nov, daily, 10am (9.30am Jun to mid-Sep) to 5pm (6.30pm Jun to mid-Sep, 4pm Nov). Closed 25-26 Dec. €2.50. Guided tour (45min) by appointment. Leaflet (6 languages). Parking. ☎ 056 24623; Fax 056 54003; jerpointabbey@ealga.ie

The sturdy tower with its stepped Irish battlements rising over the Little Arrigle River signals the presence of one of the country's foremost Cistercian monasteries. Jerpoint is lovely even in ruin, with some fascinating medieval sculpture, and sufficiently intact to evoke the atmosphere of monastic life.

Cistercian monks from Baltinglass in Co Wicklow *(see ATHY)* came this way in 1180, founding their establishment on the site of an earlier Benedictine house. In the mid-13C the community numbered 36 monks and 50 lay-brothers. After the Dissolution in 1540 the monastery, with its farm buildings, fisheries, and extensive estates, passed into the hands of the Earl of Ormond.

Jerpoint is of sufficient importance to warrant a **Visitor Centre**, with a small exhibition devoted to medieval stone carving in the region.

The abbey **church** has the classic Cistercian cruciform plan. The aisled nave is supported on stout Romanesque pillars; the transepts, which belong to the original late-12C construction, have two chapels each. In the **chancel** are splendid effigies of two bishops, one believed to be

Jerpoint Abbey Cloisters

Bord Fáilte, Dublin

Felix O'Dulany, first abbot of Jerpoint and Bishop of Ossory (1178-1202). On the north wall are remains of a 15C-16C wall painting showing the heraldic shields of some of Jerpoint's main benefactors. A new flight of wooden steps follows the run of the night stairs, down which the monks of the choir once descended to sing the night office; it's worth climbing them for a view of the abbey's setting.

The columns of the 14C or 15C **cloisters** (restored) bear remarkable carvings of animals, saints, knights and ladies showing the clothing and armour worn in medieval Ireland .

Kilfane Glen and Waterfall★

14mi/23km S of Kilkenny by R 700 and N 9 N from Thomastown. Open Jul-Aug, daily, 11am-6pm; Apr-Jun and Sep, Sun, 2-6pm. €5.50. ☎ 056 24558; Fax 056 27491; susan@irishgardens.com; www.nicholasmosse.com

This is an unusual and fascinating garden, a romantic creation from the late 18C. Lost in its wooded ravine, it has been restored and linked in poetic counterpoint to more formal contemporary gardens and modern sculpture placed in the woodland. A barn-like structure among outbuildings, the work of the American artist, James Turrell *(see p 335)*, invites visitors to look anew at the heavens; modern sensibility is left far behind among the rock outcrops, deep shade and rushing stream of the ravine. Precipitous walks, steps and bridges, a winding stairway, a waterfall and, above all, a delightful thatched cottage orné, set in a grassy glen, all testify to the advanced taste of the Power family, in touch in this seemingly remote place with the latest trends in landscaping of the 1790s.

The ruined church in the village contains a famous effigy, the **Cantwell Knight★**, a fine carving of a Norman nobleman, placed upright in the roofless nave; he makes an awesome presence in this lonely spot.

Kells Priory★

8mi/13km S of Kilkenny by R 697. The remains of this priory in its quiet setting beside the Kings River are some of the most extraordinary ruins in Ireland. Founded in 1193 by Geoffrey de Marisco with four Augustinian canons from Bodmin in Cornwall, the priory suffered repeated attacks, which perhaps explains why it was fortified so impressively; the extensive (5 acres/2ha) site is enclosed by a curtain wall with towers and a gateway.

Edmund Rice Centre

10mi/16km SW of Kilkenny by N 76 to Callan. ⅙ *Open daily, 10am-1pm; also Apr-Oct, 2-6pm. Closed Good Fri, 25 Dec. Guided tour (approx 1hr) available. Parking.* ☏ *056 25141; westcourtkk@eircom.net*
Run by the Christian Brothers, the complex with its visitor centre and chapel is built around the the cottage **birthplace** of Edmund Ignatius Rice (1762-1844), founder of this teaching order which has played an important role in Irish education. The kitchen has a stone-flagged floor, open hearth and spinning wheel, as in Rice's day; the other rooms are similarly preserved with furniture of the period.
In the town of Callan there are substantial remains of a 15C Augustinian priory.

Bród Tullaroan

10mi/16km W of Kilkenny by a minor road. Open Jun-Aug, Mon-Fri, 10am-5pm, Sun, 2-6pm; Easter-May and Sep-Nov, Sun, 2-5pm. €3. ☏ *056 67107; info@ brodtullaroan.com; www.brodtullaroan.com*
This heritage centre, the "Pride of Tullaroan", set in deep countryside, is devoted to the memory of **Lory Meagher**, the "prince of hurlers" who dominated the sport in Co Kilkenny in the 1920s and 1930s. The thatched farmhouse where he was born and lived has been restored and furnished to evoke the period around 1884, the year in which the Gaelic Athletic Association *(see p 72)* was founded, by Lory's father among others. The adjoining **Museum of Hurling** presents the regional history of the sport in fascinating detail.

Kilcooly Abbey

21mi/32km NW of Kilkenny by R 693; from Urlingford take R 689 S for 3.5mi/5.5km; 500yd/0.5km on foot from parish church car park. The substantial ruins of this Cistercian abbey, which was founded around 1200, include a massive tower over the crossing and a cloister. Among a number of fine monuments is the carved effigy of a knight. The abbey is protected by a ha-ha and formidably buttressed. In the field stands a large dovecot.

Dunmore Cave★

7mi/11km N of Kilkenny by N 77 and N 78. (Dúchas) Guided tour (40min) mid-Mar to Oct, daily, 10am (9.30am mid-Jun to mid-Sep) to 5pm (4.30pm Sat-Sun, 6.30pm Mon-Fri mid-Jun to mid-Sep); Nov to mid-Mar, Sat-Sun, 10am-4.30pm; Bank Hols, 10am-4.30pm; last admission 45min before closing. Closed 25-26 Dec; also some lunchtimes. €2.50. Parking. ☏ *056 67726*
Running beneath the surface of the isolated Castlecomer limestone outcrop, this is one of the few large caves in Ireland, with fascinating formations, including stalagmites and stalactites. The rebuilt visitor centre is poised dramatically over the entrance to the cave, and has exhibits explaining the site's geology and history. The 10C tale of a horrible massacre by Vikings seemed confirmed when coins and human skeletons were found here in 1973. A later chance find, in 1999, revealed more Viking remains, including further coins as well as highly ornamental brass buckles and delicate silverwork of North African origin.

Castlecomer

11.5mi/19km N of Kilkenny by N 77 and N 78. The village was laid out in the Italian-village style in 1635 by Sir Christopher Wandesforde, whose family mined the coal in this region for three centuries. The coalmining industry is now defunct but in Reddy's Coalmine Lounge, where the main bar is decorated like a mine, lumps of Castlecomer coal are on show, together with items of mining equipment such as lamps, picks and shovels.

Killala★

Killala is a quiet seaside resort overlooking Killala Bay at the mouth of the River Moy, which is partially blocked by Bartragh Island, a narrow sandbank. It has a sandy beach, and land and water sports facilities; the harbour warehouses show that it was once a busy port. The remote little town enjoys a place of disproportionate importance in the history of Ireland, as it was here that the French first halted when they invaded in 1798.

To the west of the town lies North Mayo, one of the most remote and least inhabited regions of Ireland. In fine weather the bog gleams gold in the sun but when the sky is overcast the prospect is bleak like the entrance to the Underworld. This apparently unwelcoming land was nevertheless an important human habitat in Neolithic times, and fascinating traces of its occupation are still to be seen.

Directory

WHERE TO STAY
• *Budget*
Downhill Inn – *Sligo Rd, Ballina - 1mi/1.6km E off N 59 - ☎ 096 73444 - Fax 096 73411 thedownhillinn@eircom.net - Closed 21-30 Dec -* 🅿 ♿ *- 45 rm €65/110* ⌧ *- Restaurant €17.50/30.* This family-owned purpose-built hotel on the outskirts of town offers clean and comfortable accommodation. Bedrooms are warmly decorated and are uniform in size.

SPORTS AND LEISURE
Surfing, water-skiiing, windsurfing and sub-aqua in and around Killala Bay
Salmon fishing in the River Moy and in the Deel River at Crossmolina
Canoeing on the Moy River at Foxford
Boating on the lakes and rivers
Hot seaweed baths at Inishcrone *(see below)*

TRACING ANCESTORS
Enniscoe House – *Crossmolina.*

Location
Population 713 - Michelin Atlas pp 94-95 and Map 712 – E 5 – Co Mayo.
Killala *(Cill Ala)* is in a remote location on R 314 N of Ballina which is on N 59 W of Sligo.
🅱 *Ballina. Open Apr-Sep, Mon-Sat.* ☎ *096 70848*
Adjacent Sights: See KNOCK, SLIGO, WESTPORT.

Worth a Visit

St Patrick's Cathedral
Open during daylight hours. Services: Sun, 10.30am. ☎ *096 21654*
The present Anglican **cathedral** *(floodlit at night)* was erected in 1670 by Thomas Ottway, Bishop of Killala, using rubble and stones from the ruined medieval cathedral – south doorway and Gothic east window – and is furnished with box pews. In the graveyard stands a fine example of a 12C **round tower**, which is built of limestone (84ft/25m high); the cap is a 19C reconstruction. The tower is all that remains of the monastery founded by Muiredach, the first bishop of Killala, who was appointed by St Patrick in the 5C. There is also a 9C **souterrain** with many chambers *(unfenced)*.

THE YEAR OF THE FRENCH
In August 1798 a force of 1 067 French revolutionaries under General Humbert landed at Kilcummin, a hamlet on the west shore of Killala Bay. In Killala John Moore was appointed President of the Provisional Government of Connaught by General Humbert. As the French advanced inland they were joined by a growing number of enthusiastic but ill-equipped Irishmen.

The first place of importance to fall to them was Ballina, where their capture of the town is commemorated by the Humbert Monument.

Then came their first encounter with General Lake, who was in command of a vastly superior force of militia and yeomanry. Despite being outnumbered General Humbert routed his opponent and the ignominious retreat of General Lake's cavalry became known as the **Races of Castlebar**.

Another monument at Carrignagat *(S of Sligo on N 4 before Collooney, E side)* marks the site of their third victory over the English. Humbert then moved southeast in the hope of avoiding the English army and of joining up with the United Irishmen but the latter had already been defeated and he himself was overcome at Ballinamuck, near Longford. The French were taken prisoner; the Irish were hanged as traitors.

The events of the 1798 Rebellion were re-enacted in Killala in 1981 during the filming of Thomas Flanagan's historical novel, *The Year of the French.*

SLIDE FILE, Dublin

Killala Harbour

Tours

NORTH MAYO COAST

25mi/40km drive

The northern coast of Co Mayo is one of the most remote and least inhabited regions of Ireland, confronting the Atlantic with a line of dramatic sea cliffs, broken only by **Broad Haven**, a broad bay of sandy coves, narrow sea-inlets and tiny habitations, flanked by **Benwee Head** (829ft/253m – *E*) and **Erris Head** (285ft/87m – *W on the Belmullet Peninsula*). Inland the country is largely covered in Atlantic blanket bog (400sq mi/1 036km²), which is extensively exploited to generate electricity; the turf is harvested by machine to fuel the power station at Bellacorick, which is supplemented by wind turbines. *From Killala take R 314 N; after crossing the river turn right; climb the stile into the field (left).*

Breastagh Ogham Stone

The stone (8ft/2.5m high), probably a Bronze Age standing stone, is marked with the linear Ogham script but the inscription is only partially legible.

Continue to the crossroads; turn right.

Rathfran Abbey

Lying close to the shore, this 13C Dominican friary was burned down in 1590 by Sir Richard Bingham, the English Governor of Connaught, in the course of one of his destructive forays. Though little remains of the cloisters and conventual buildings, the long rectangular church is still largely intact, complete with a panel over the west door depicting the Crucifixion.

Return to the crossroads; turn right; continue N via Carrowmore, Killogeary and Rathlackan.

North of Killogeary the road follows the coast providing a fine view of the broad sands of Lackan Bay and then of Downpatrick Head projecting flat-topped and blunt into the sea against the backdrop of Benwee Head.

Downpatrick Head

Turn right to Downpatrick Head; 20min there and back on foot from car park to cliff. The projecting headland is undermined by the sea which appears at the bottom of a **blow hole** *(fenced off)*. Just offshore stands Dunbriste, a rock stack surmounted by a prehistoric earthwork, which was probably detached from the mainland in 1393. The views are superb, taking in *(E)* Benbulben and the Dartry Mountains north of Sligo, *(SE)* the Ox Mountains (Slieve Gamph), *(SW)* the Nephin Beg Mountains, *(W)* the cliffs to Benwee Head and the Stags of Broadhaven offshore.

Continue to Ballycastle; take R 314 NW.

Céide Fields★

(Dúchas) (&) Open mid-Mar to Nov, daily, 10am-5pm (6pm Jun-Sep); Dec to mid-Mar, telephone for details; last admission 1hr before closing. Closed 25-26 Dec. €3.10. Audio-visual show (20min). Guided tour (45min) by appointment. Leaflet (6 languages). Protective clothing and walking shoes advised. Tearoom. ☎ 096 43325; Fax 096 43261; ceidefields@ealga.ie

Most of North Mayo lies beneath a deep layer of blanket bog, a desolate and seemingly unwelcoming landscape which nevertheless has been shown to conceal fascinating evidence of settled and productive prehistoric occupation. Using iron probes and bamboo markers, archaeologists have mapped several square miles of fields laid out by the Neolithic people who lived near the Céide Cliffs over 50 centuries ago and who were contemporaries of the tomb builders of the Boyne Valley (see p 145).

The **Visitor Centre** explains the geological structure of the terrain, the development of the bog which now covers the site to a depth of 13ft/4m and the archaeological interpretation of the site. From the evidence found on the site – a primitive type of plough, postholes – deductions can be made about the lifestyle of the Stone Age farmers, who cleared the land of primeval forest and piled up the stones to create enclosed fields and houses. In the light of this knowledge and viewed from the roof gallery, the sombre landscape all around takes on an entirely different meaning.

Continue W on R 314 via Belderrig (sign).

Belderrig Prehistoric Farm

(& to visitor centre) Open Jun-Sep, 9.30am-6.30pm; mid-Mar to May and Oct-Nov, 10am-5pm (4.30pm Nov). €3.17. Audio visual show (20min). Guide book and leaflet (4 languages). Tearoom ☎ 096 43987

The centrepiece of the **visitor centre** is a large and twisted Scots pine 4 400 years old, which was found in the vicinity. In the prehistoric era this site was a farming estate; it is now reduced to a circle of earth marked with post stones and hearthstones.

MOY ESTUARY

20mi/32km drive

The coast road around the estuary of the salmon-rich River Moy passes close to the exceptionally picturesque ruins of two 15C Franciscan establishments, continues to North Mayo's largest town, Ballina, and goes on to the popular little resort of Inishcrone.

From Killala take the coast road S.

Moyne Abbey*

10min there and back on foot across the fields. The extensive remains of the Franciscan friary at Moy include cloisters, sacristy, chapter house, kitchen and refectory as well as the church, all dominated by a splendid six-storey tower. As elsewhere, Sir Richard Bingham, the English Governor of Connaught did his best to make the place uninhabitable but, despite his efforts, some of the friars contrived to remain in residence, the last of their number dying in about 1800.

Continue S; on reaching the Rosserk River turn left.

Rosserk Abbey*

On the Rosserk River, a tributary of the Moy, Rosserk Abbey was the first Franciscan house to be built in Ireland, and its ruins are some of the best preserved in the country. The decorative features of the church include the carved west door, the east window, the south transept window and the carved piscina in the chancel, which shows a round tower, angels and the instruments of the Passion. From the cloisters, stairs lead up to the dormitories and refectory above the vaulted rooms on the ground floor. Rosserk too suffered grievously at the hands of the ruthless Sir Richard Bingham.

Return to T-junction and turn left; continue S.

Ballina

Busy Ballina, the largest town in North Mayo and the seat of the bishop of the Roman Catholic diocese of Killala, straddles the River Moy. Lacking in distinction, it is nevertheless a good base for visitors, particularly for anglers attracted by the salmon in the Moy. The **Cathedral of St Muredach** on the east bank between the bridges was built in the 19C next to the ruins of a late-14C Augustinian **friary** founded by the O'Dowd family; the decorated west door and window of the friary church date from the 15C. *Open daily. Services: Sun, 8am, 9.30am, 11am, 12.30pm, 7.30pm.*

From Ballina drive along the E side of the estuary, via Castleconor, for 9mi/14km.

Inishcrone (Enniscrone)

This is a popular family seaside resort on the east coast of Killala Bay, with indoor water facilities at Waterpoint. *Open mid-Jun to late-Aug, daily, 10am-10pm (8pm Sat-Sun); late-Aug to mid-Jun, 4pm (11am Sun, 1pm Sat) to 10pm (8pm Sat-Sun). Heated swimming pool; fun pool; water slide; activity room; adult health suite with steam room, jacuzzi and sauna. Snack bar. ☎ 096 36999 or 00 800 60160160; Fax 096 36988; www.enniscrone.ie*

The local speciality is a traditional Irish **seaweed bath** in the elegant Edwardian bath house; the deliciously silky warm seawater is not only a fine way of relaxing but may also relieve the symptoms of rheumatism and arthritis. *Open Apr-Oct, daily, 10am-9pm (10pm Jul-Aug); Nov-Apr, Sat-Sun and Bank Hols, 10am-8pm. ☎ 096 36238; Fax 096 36895; bathhouse@eircom.net; www.enniscrone.ie/seaweedbaths.com*

Killaloe★

Killaloe is delightfully sited on the west bank of the Shannon, at a point where the river, emerging from Lough Derg, is forced into a relatively narrow channel, constricted by the Arra Mountains to the east and Slieve Bernagh to the west. It is a pretty village and designated Heritage town, with steep and narrow streets, a cathedral, and an ancient stone bridge.

Location

Population 972 - Michelin Atlas p 84 and Map 712 – G 9 – Co Clare.
Killaloe (Cill Dalua) is just off the main road (N 7) between Limerick and Nenagh, at the south end of Lough Derg.
🛈 The Bridge, Killaloe. Open May-Sep. ☎ 061 376 866
🛈 Connolly Street, Nenagh. Open mid-May to mid-Sep. ☎ 067 31610; Fax 067 33418
Adjacent Sights: See BIRR, CASHEL, ENNIS, LIMERICK, ROSCREA.

GETTING ABOUT
Holy Island Ferry – Operates (weather permitting) from Mountshannon May-Oct, daily, 9.30am-6.30pm. €8 per person.
☎ 061 921 615; Mobile 086 874 9710

SPORTS AND LEISURE
Killaloe is a water sports centre of international importance.

TRACING ANCESTORS
Tipperary North Genealogical Service is housed in the old prison (1842) in Nenagh. Open Mon-Fri, 9.30am-1pm and 2-5pm. Closed Bank Hols. Genealogy service.
☎ 067 33850; Fax 067 33586; tippnorthgenealogy@eircom.net; http//www.irishroots.net/NTipp.htm

Worth a Visit

St Flannan's Cathedral★

Open daily, during daylight hours. Guided tour of tower: usually Easter-Sep, 11am-4.30pm (when shop is open). Cathedral, donation; tower and bells €1.27. ☎/Fax 061 376 687

The austere, aisleless **cathedral**, which stands on the site of a monastery founded in the 6C by St Molua and dedicated to his successor, was begun by Dónall Mór O'Brien in 1185. By 1225 it had been rebuilt in the present mixture of Romanesque and Gothic. Its outstanding features include an elaborately carved 12C **Romanesque doorway**, a 12C high cross from Kilfenora in The Burren (see p 155), and a cross shaft carved c 1000 bearing a unique dual inscription in both **Ogham** and **Viking Runic script**.

St Flannan's Oratory

Beside the cathedral stands the vaulted nave of a little 12C Romanesque church incorporating a loft beneath its steeply sloping stone roof.

St Molua's Oratory

The oratory, which stands beside the Roman Catholic church at the top of the hill, was built c 1000 on Friar's Island in the Shannon; it was transferred stone by stone when its original location was submerged by the hydroelectric scheme in the 1920s.

Killaloe Heritage Centre

Open May-Sep, daily, 10am-6pm. €2.30; subject to change; check by telephone. ☎ 061 360 788 (Shannon Heritage central reservations); Fax 061 361 020; reservations@shannondev.ie; www.shannonheritage.com

The display traces in pictures and text the history of Killaloe from the birth of Brian Ború, High King of Ireland (1002-14), through many years of fishing and cruising to the Civil War and the building of the Ardnacrusha dam to provide electricity.

Tours

LOUGH DERG

From Killaloe take R 463 N; after 1mi/1.6km turn right (sign) into a track (0.5mi/0.8km); cross the fields.

Béal Ború Earthwork

This large circular earthwork surrounded by a deep ditch and a grove of beech and pine trees is set immediately above the Lough Derg shoreline. From its name, which means "Pass of the Tributes", Brian Ború took his title.
Continue N on R 463.

Tuamgraney

The village is known as the birthplace of the novelist, Edna O'Brien (see Letters). At the south end of the village stands a 15C tower house (restoration in progress). Beside it stands St Cronan's Church (Anglican), which is believed to be the oldest church in continuous use in Ireland or Great Britain. The west portion with its lintelled doorway dates from c 969; the east end of the building is 12C; note the Romanesque windows. It now houses the **East Clare Heritage Centre**, which documents the local history, including the life and times of Brian Ború. *Open Jun-Oct, daily. Audio-visual show (10min). €5. Guided tour (3 languages) by appointment. ☎ 061 921 351; eastclareheritage@eircom.net; www.eastclareheritage.com*

The **Memorial Park** *(330yd/300m W of the village)*, is planted with the indigenous trees and shrubs of Co Clare to commemorate the victims of the Great Famine of 1845-52.

Continue N on R 463 to Mountshannon.

Holy Island★

The island with its extensive and evocative remains of a 7C monastery makes a fascinating destination for a short trip on Lough Derg. As well as the remains of no fewer than six churches, there is a **round tower** (80ft/24m high) and a curious **bargaining stone**; it has a hollow channel through which, it seems, men would shake hands to seal an agreement.

MOUNTAIN DRIVE

From Killaloe take R 463 S, in O'Briensbridge cross the river; in Montpelier turn right to Castleconnell.

Castleconnell★

The well-kept small village by the Shannon offers excellent salmon fishing and riverside walks under the trees.

From Castleconnell drive E on a minor road (crossing N 7); turn left onto R 503, E of Newport turn right (sign); car parks both sides of the river.

Clare Glens★

The Clare River descends in a series of lovely **waterfalls** cascading through wooded glens.

Continue S on minor road to Murroe; turn in through the park gates.

Glenstal Abbey

Impressive grounds and lakes surround the castle which is now a Benedictine monastery and school *(private)*. The modern **church** is known for its surrealistic decor and for the Ikon Chapel in the crypt. *Open daily, 6.30am-9.30pm. ☎ 061 386 103; Fax 061 386 328; monks@glenstal.org; www.glenstal.org*

Return to R 503 and continue E. At the crossroads near Inch turn left onto R 497. Drive N via Dolla to Nenagh.

Nenagh Castle★

The colossal circular keep (100ft/30m high) is the finest in the country; together with the 13C hall (restored), it recalls the Anglo-Norman castle built c 1200.

Nenagh, a substantial garrison town in the 19C, is now the county town and commercial centre of Tipperary North Riding. The 13C Franciscan friary, one of the most important in Ireland, was dissolved during the reign of Queen Elizabeth I so that only the church walls still stand.

From Nenagh take R 494 W. Beyond Portroe turn left (sign) into minor road.

Graves of the Leinstermen

The group of prehistoric stones on the west face of Tountinna (1 512ft/461m) is probably one of the first inhabited places in Ireland. There are commanding **views★** over much of Lough Derg to Slieve Bernagh.

Continue along minor road. Turn left onto R 494. In Ballina turn right to Killaloe.

Killarney★★

Tourists have been coming to Ireland's foremost tourist town for more than two hundred years, entranced by its glorious setting of lakes, luxuriant vegetation, romantic ruins and meticulously managed desmesnes. All around are rugged mountains including Macgillycuddy's Reeks which culminate in the highest peak in Ireland, Carrauntoohill (3 414ft/1 041m). No visit to the area is complete without making the classic trip into the Gap of Dunloe, a formidable breach rammed by a glacier through the heart of the mountains.

Location

Population 8 809 - Michelin Atlas p 77 and Map 712 – D 11– Co Kerry.
Killarney *(Cill Airne)* is on N 22 between Cork and Tralee, not far from Farranfore Airport *(N by N 22)*, an ideal touring centre, with many hotels and restaurants.

Directory

GETTING ABOUT

Valentia Island-Renard Point Car Ferry – *Open daily, noon-9pm. €2.* ☎ *066 976 1353 (Patrick Houlihan).*

Skellig Islands Ferry – *Operates (weather permitting) by appointment. On Great Skellig only very experienced climbers should continue above the monastery ruins to the cross carved near the summit.* ☎ *066 947 3355 (Kerrry Skellig Region office); www.skellig.com*

Farranfore Airport – ☎ *066 976 4644.*

SIGHTSEEING

There are **information centres** at Muckross House and at Torc Waterfall *(summer only).* The **National Park** may be explored on land or by water. There are many miles of walks to suit all tastes at Ross Castle, Muckross House and through the Gap of Dunloe.

There are **boat trips** on Lough Leane from Ross Castle to Innisfallen Island or as part of the trip through the Gap of Dunloe. *Operate from Ross Castle (1hr; weather permitting) 5 times daily, on board Pride of the Lakes, €8,* ☎ *064 32638 (destination Killarney); Fax 064 36656; 6 times daily on board Lily of Killarney, €8,* ☎ *064 31068 (Dero's Tours); Fax 064 35583; Bus shuttle between Scott's Gardens and Ross Castle,* ☎ *064 31068 (Killarney Watercoach Cruises Ltd); Fax 064 35001*

Trips in a **jaunting car** are available from the southern end of the Main Street or at Muckross House. *Operate from Killarney (south end of Main Street) and from Muckross Abbey and Muckross House. €7.62. (1hr round the lake); €30.47 (6mi/10km).*

Jaunting car

WHERE TO STAY

• *Budget*

Naughton's Villa – *Muckross Rd -* ☎ *064 36025 - 17 Mar to 15 Nov -* 🅿 *- 5 rm €35/80* 🍽. Guests can take advantage of the balcony terrace at this pink-hued guesthouse, close to the centre. Bedrooms have a certain cottagey feel and the ensuite bathrooms are all a decent size.

Redwood – *Rockfield, Tralee Rd - 3mil/4.8km N on N 22 -* ☎ *064 34754 - Fax 064 34178 - rewd@indigo.ie -* 🅿 🍽 *- 6 rm €40/60* 🍽. Comfortable and well-priced bed & breakfast accommodation to the north of the town, surrounded by several acres of farmland. Spacious sitting room and conservatory, comfy bedrooms. A non-smoking house.

Kingfisher Lodge – *Lewis Rd -* ☎ *064 37131 - Fax 064 39871 - kingfisherguesthouse@eircom.net - Closed 14 Dec to 1 Feb -* 🅿 🍽 *- 8 rm €50/80* 🍽. Friendly and comfortable guesthouse, 3-min walk from the centre. Bedrooms are clean and neat, in co-ordinated pastel colours, with the quieter ones at the back of the house. All have large showers.

Hussey's Townhouse – *43 High St -* ☎ *064 37454 - Fax 064 33144 - husseys@iol.ie - 21 Mar to Oct -* 🅿 🍽 *5 rm €55/80* 🍽. Relax in the first-floor lounge, with its quiet reading area, or mix with the locals in the snug bar at the front of this town house. Bedrooms are compact, cosy and well kept and all have en-suite shower rooms.

• *Moderate*

Old Weir Lodge – *Muckross Rd -* ☎ *064 35593 - Fax 064 35583 - oldweirlodge@eircom.net - Closed 23-28 Dec -* 🅿 🍽 *- 30 rm €75/110* 🍽. The emphasis is on comfort and space at this purpose-built town centre property. There are two comfortable lounges and a roomy breakfast room with conservatory extension. Immaculate bedrooms in warming hues.

Fuchsia House – *Muckross Rd -* ☎ *064 33743 - Fax 064 36588 - fuchsiahouse@eircom.net - 15 March to 4 Nov -* 🅿 🍽 *- 9 rm €80/116* 🍽. A small hotel with the feel of a country house, from its antique furnished and individually designed bedrooms to the comfortable sitting room and well-tended back garden. Home-made breakfast produce.

Kathleen's Country House Hotel – *Tralee Rd - 2mil/3.4km N on N 22 -* ☎ *064 32810 - Fax 064 32340 - info@kathleens.net - Easter-Oct -* 🅿 🍽 *- 17 rm €80/140* 🍽. Neat, comfortable and well kept with pretty bedrooms overlooking the garden. The eponymous Kathleen, with her ebullient hospitality, is one of the main reasons why her guests keep returning each year.

• *Expensive*

Coolclogher House – *Mill Rd -* ☎ *064 35996 - Fax 064 309 933 - info@coolclogherhouse.com - Closed Dec -* 🅿 *- 4 rm €150/200* 🍽. Play Lord of the Manor by staying at this imposing Victorian Italianate mansion standing proudly in 68 acres/27ha of parkland. Sympathetically restored yet retaining a period charm. Noted feature is the 180 year-old camellia in its own conservatory.

WHERE TO EAT

• Budget

The Granary Restaurant & Bar –
The Pound, Touhills Lane, Beech Rd -
☎ *064 20075 - www.granaryrestaurant.com -*
🍴 *- €20.* Black and white photos of filmstars adorn the walls of this contemporary spot. The bar is open all day for light snacks with a more formal upstairs restaurant open for dinner. Trendy and popular.

• Moderate

The Laurels – *Main St -* ☎ *064 31149 -* 🍴 *- €30.* Probably one of the best of the town's myriad pubs. Live music, a bustling atmosphere and palpable sense of tradition. The menu offers an extensive selection of favourites from Irish stew to home-made burgers.

The Old Presbytery – *Cathedral Pl -*
☎ *064 30555 - oldpresbytery@eircom.net -*
Closed Good Fri, 25 and 26 Dec, 2 weeks Jan, Tue - 🅿 *- €29/40.50.* A more recent addition to the town's restaurant scene, opposite St Mary's Cathedral. Spread over two floors with a pianist who belts out the classics. Menu adds some modern touches to its traditional base.

TAKING A BREAK

O' Connor's – *7 High Street -*
☎ *064 31 115 -*
www.gapofdunloetours.com – Open daily from 8am. For those looking for that traditional Irish pub then head for the town centre and this recently restored family-owned watering hole. There's a welcoming atmosphere and traditional music twice a week. They also organise tours from here in a 1926 bus.

SHOPPING

High Street – This is the main shopping district of the town and where to find the majority of pubs and restaurants. There are a number of shops ideal for those looking for souvenirs; from jewellery to linen and glassware.

Quills Woollen Market – *High Street - Market Cross -* ☎ *064 32 277 - Mon-Sat, 9am-6pm, Sun, 11am-5pm.* A family business established in 1939. Spread over two floors, with a large collection of authentic, and typically Irish, goods, ranging from Donegal tweeds and Aran handknits to linen and individually designed pieces of jewellery.

Avoca Weavers – *Moll's Gap - 15mi/24km S by N 71* Fashionable woollen clothing.

Kerry Woollen Mills – *Beaufort; 5mi/8km W by N 72; 4mi/6km turn right at sign; after 1mi/1.6km turn left and then right -* ☎ *064 44122 - Fax 064 44556 - sales@kerrywoollenmills.ie - Open Apr-Oct, Mon-Sat, 9am-5pm, Nov-Mar, Mon-Fri, 9am-5pm.* Woollen goods have been produced here for over 200 years; showroom and retail shop - rugs and blankets for people and horses, tweeds for clothes and furnishings, scarves and shawls, knitwear and knitting yarn.

🖪 *Beech Road, Killarney. Open Jul-Aug, daily; Sep-Jun, Mon Sat.* ☎ *064 31633; Fax 064 34506; www.corkkerry.ie*

🖪 *Kerry County Airport, Farranfore* ☎ *Freephone in Arrivals Terminal*

🖪 *Waterville. Open Jun-Sep, Mon-Sat.* ☎ *066 947 4646*

Adjacent Sights: See DINGLE PENINSULA, KENMARE, TRALEE.

Background

The monastery founded on the little island of Innisfallen in the 7C became a centre of learning, later responsible for the *Annals of Innisfallen*, one of Ireland's earliest historical chronicles. The area was later ruled by the O'Donoghues, McCarthys and O'Sullivans, who were displaced by Elizabethan settlers like the Brownes and Herberts. It was an 18C Browne, Thomas, the 4th Viscount Kenmare (1726-95), who laid out the present street plan and created a neat town of slated houses and shops. He also introduced linen and woollen manufacturing and beautified the surroundings by tree planting and the provision of seats and belvederes. These were appreciated first by locals, then by an ever-swelling stream of visitors, among them many poets, painters and writers. Shelley found Killarney more impressive even than Switzerland; Macaulay thought Innisfallen "not a reflex of heaven, but a bit of heaven itself". On the other hand Charlotte Brontë had the misfortune to be thrown from her horse while exploring the Gap of Dunloe, and Thackeray was dismayed by the throngs of touts and guides. Killarney's tourist vocation was confirmed with the visit of Queen Victoria in 1861. In 1932 the Muckross estate was presented by its American owners to the nation as the Bourn Vincent Memorial Park, becoming the core of the present National Park, Ireland's first.

CINEMATIC HISTORY

The Dawn, a famous Irish film set in the War of Independence, was shot in Killarney between 1933 and 1934, with a cast of 250, mainly local amateurs; its initiator was Tom Cooper, a local cinema owner. Shooting usually took place on Thursdays, early closing day. Photographs of this production, of *The Quiet Man*, filmed in 1952 at Cong, and of *Ryan's Daughter*, shot at Banna Strand in 1968, can be seen in the bar of the Three Lakes Hotel.

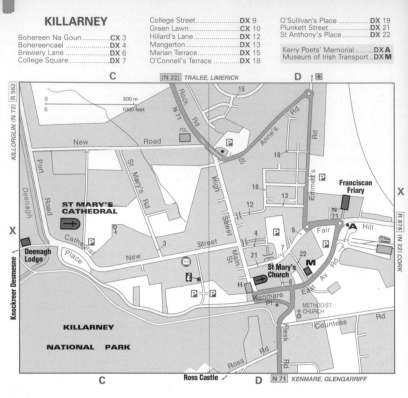

KILLARNEY

Bohereen Na Goun..............**CX** 3
Bohereencael ....**DX** 4
Brewery Lane ....**DX** 6
College Square ....**DX** 7

College Street....................**DX** 9
Green Lawn ....**CX** 10
Hillard's Lane......................**DX** 12
Mangerton ....**DX** 13
Marian Terrace....................**DX** 15
O'Connell's Terrace ....**DX** 18

O'Sullivan's Place ....**DX** 19
Plunkett Street....................**DX** 21
St Anthony's Place ....**DX** 22

Kerry Poets' Memorial ....**DX A**
Museum of Irish Transport ..**DX M**

Walking About

Being some distance from the lakes and undistinguished architecturally, Killarney town depends for its atmosphere on the visitors thronging its streets and the many busy bars, hotels and shops catering to their needs. Focal points include Market Cross, the intersection of Main Street, High Street and New Street, and Kenmare Place, where the jaunting cars wait for passengers.

St Mary's Cathedral★

&. *Open daily, 8.30am-8.30pm (7am-9pm Oct-Mar). If locked, apply to the Cathedral Office. Parking.* ☎ *064 31014*

The Roman Catholic cathedral with its prominent spire (285ft/87m high) was designed by Augustus Pugin; the austere unplastered interior reveals the various hues of the limestone. Although the foundation stone was laid in 1842, work was discontinued between 1848 and 1853 and the building used as a shelter for famine victims. The cathedral was consecrated in 1855 and adapted for the new liturgy in 1972-73.

St Mary's Church

Open daily, 10am-5pm.

The Anglican church, built in 1870 in the Early-English style on the site of an earlier 17C church, contains a stained-glass window, which reproduces Holman Hunt's *Light of the World*. Among the several interesting memorials is one *(north side of the nave)* to the Revd Arthur Hyde, great-grandfather of Douglas Hyde *(see p 345)*, first president of Ireland.

Museum of Irish Transport

Open May-Sep, daily, 10am-6pm; Apr and Oct, 11am-5pm. €4. Parking. ☎ *064 34677; Fax 064 31582*

The many veteran and vintage cars, posters and magazines on display make this museum a Mecca for motor enthusiasts. The Silver Stream, designed in 1907-09, is the only car of its type ever built; the 1910 Wolseley which belonged to Sir Jocelyn Gore Booth *(see p 342)* was driven by Countess Markievicz and William Butler Yeats. Mercedes produced the 540K (1938) and the 300SL (1955) gullwing models.

Kerry Poets' Memorial

The memorial, a personification of Ireland in the form of a beautiful woman *(speir bhean)*, was created in 1940 by Seamus Murphy to commemorate Co Kerry's four best-known Gaelic poets – **Pierce Ferriter**, a poet, soldier and musician from the Dingle Peninsula, who refused to submit to the Cromwellians in 1652 and was hanged in 1653 in Killarney; **Geoffrey O'Donoghue of the Glens** (1620-78), who was Chieftain of Glenflesk and lived in Killaha Castle, southeast of Killarney;

Egan O'Rahilly (1670-1728), the greatest of the four poets, who was educated in the bardic tradition and gave his allegiance to the Brownes, as the McCarthys were unable to act as his patrons; **Owen Roe O'Sullivan** (1748-84), who led a roving life as a hedge schoolmaster in winter and an itinerant labourer in summer, as well as serving in the British army and navy; to the delight of Admiral Rodney he wrote a poem in English about the Admiral's victory over the French at Dominica in 1782.

Franciscan Friary
The friary, built in 1860 in a style similar to Muckross Friary *(see below)*, contains a stained-glass window *(entrance hall)* by Harry Clarke.

Tours

GAP OF DUNLOE★★ 1

There are various ways of exploring the Gap.

By organised round trip from Killarney: by bus to Kate Kearney's Cottage, by pony or pony and trap to Lord Brandon's Cottage, by boat across the three lakes and by bus back to Killarney. Operates (weather permitting) Apr-Oct, daily, 10.30am-5pm (round tour (6 7hr). Bus and boat €20.50; pony €45.50; pony trap €38 (Deros Tours). Bus & Boat €25; boat only €12 (Gap of Dunloe Tours). ☎ 064 31633; Fax 064 34506 (Tourist Office); ☎ 064 30200; Fax 064 30201 (Gap of Dunloe Tours); ☎ 064 31052 (O'Connor); 064 31251, 31567; Fax 34077 (Deros Tours); ☎ 064 36666; Fax 36555 (Corcoran's); www.corkkerry.ie

By car: from Killarney take N 72 W; after 4mi/6km turn left and continue to the car park at the north end of the Gap near Kate Kearney's Cottage, hire a pony or pony and trap or continue on foot before returning to the car park. The route through the gorge is unsuitable for vehicular traffic and drivers attempting it risk the displeasure of pony traffic.

By bicycle: make a round trip by hired cycle either via the lakes (cycles are carried aboard a special boat), via the Kerry Way (involving some dismounting and pushing) or via Moll's Gap.

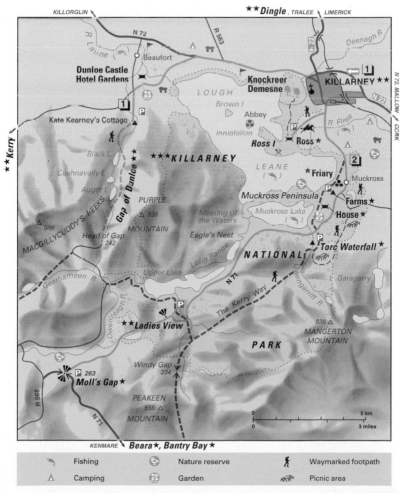

	Fishing		Nature reserve		Waymarked footpath
Λ	Camping		Garden		Picnic area

The jarvies plying for hire with their carriages throng the roadsides and the forecourt of **Kate Kearney's Cottage**, originally an old coaching inn kept by the beautiful Kate, who served *poteen* to 19C tourists. ᕃ *Open daily, 9am-11.30pm (11pm Dec-Apr). Live entertainment, including Irish dancing: summer months, Wed, Fri-Sun. Restaurant (6.30-9.30pm); bar food (11am-8pm). Craft shops. Parking.* ☎ *064 44146; Fax 064 44641; katekearneys@eircom.net*

The trip through the deep and narrow rock-strewn gorge is one of the highlights of a visit to Ireland, and deservedly so. The initial press of pony traps, riders, cyclists and walkers soon thins out, though lovers of solitude should either visit the Gap towards the end of the day or enter it from the Black Valley to the south. The U-shaped glacial breach (1 500ft/457m deep) is traversed by a narrow unsurfaced road which winds up a scries of hairpin bends, runs beside several mountain tarns, crosses a tumbling stream and passes the ruins of a Royal Irish Constabulary strongpoint. Most traffic turns back on reaching the Head of the Gap (794ft/242m). As the track descends into the Gearhameen Valley, where red deer graze, there is a fine view of the Upper Lake, bordered by native oakwoods and backed by Mangerton Mountain (2 756ft/838m).

KILLARNEY NATIONAL PARK★★★ ②

Tour of 30mi/48km. S of Killarney by N 71. (Dúchas) ᕃ *Visitor Centre: Open mid-Mar to Oct, daily, 9am-6pm (7pm Jul-Aug); Nov to mid-Mar by request; last admission 1hr before closing. Audio-visual show (20min). Leaflet (5 languages).* ☎ *064 31440; Fax 064 37565; killarneynationalpark@ealga.ie*

The park (39sq mi/101km²) embraces the three lakes – Lower (Lough Leane), Middle (Muckross Lake) and Upper, which are linked by the Long Range River – the foreshore and the mountain slopes south and west. The original nucleus of the Muckross Estate is now complemented by Knockreer, Ross Island and Innisfallen, formerly part of the Kenmare Estate. Blanket bog on the higher land contrasts with Ireland's largest remaining area of ancient oak woodland, and in addition there are yew woods, alder carrs and, most famously, many examples of arbutus, the strawberry tree, which flourishes in the exceptionally mild climate. The special character of the park was given international recognition in 1981 when it was designated as a UNESCO Biosphere Reserve.

Knockreer Demesne

Footpath to Ross Castle (see below). Open daily. Tearoom at Deenagh Lodge. ☎ *064 36274*

The grounds of Knockreer House extend westwards from Killarney to the shore of Lough Leane; the entrance from the town is marked by a thatched cottage, **Deenagh Lodge**.

Ross Castle★

1mi/1.6km S by N 71 and a minor road W (sign). Footpath to Knockreer Demesne (see above). Boat trips to Innisfallen Island (see Directory). (Dúchas) (ᕃ *to ground floor) Guided tour (40min) Apr-Sep, daily, 10am (9am Jun-Aug) to 6pm (5pm Apr, 6.30pm Jun-Aug); Oct, Tue-Sun, 10am-5pm; last admission 45min before closing. Closed 24-26 Dec. €2.50. Leaflet (5 languages). No photography. Parking nearby.* ☎ *064 35851; www.goireland.com*

The well-restored castle, the last in Munster to hold out against Cromwellian forces (1652), who captured it only by attacking it from armed boats, was built on the shore of Lough Leane in the 15C by one of the O'Donoghue Ross chieftains. A fortified bawn reinforced by circular flanking towers surrounded the rectangular keep. The four floors, containing the parlour, the bedchamber and the Great Hall, have been restored using medieval building techniques and furnished in the style appropriate to the early-15C to late-16C period.

The promontory, known as **Ross Island**, where there were active copper mines in the early 19C, extends into Lough Leane and is traversed by a profusion of tree- and flower-lined avenues. Shelley was particularly impressed by the strawberry tree during his visit in 1813. There are fine views of Lough Leane in its mountain setting and of the islands.

No trace remains on **Innisfallen** of the 7C monastery which was a famous centre of learning, but the luxuriantly wooded island harbours the evocative remains of a later abbey with a fine Romanesque doorway.

Muckross Friary★

5min on foot from car park; footpath to Muckross House. (Dúchas) (ᕃ) *Open mid-Jun to early-Sep, daily, 10am-5pm (4.15pm last admission). €5. Guided tour by appointment. Public parking nearby.* ☎ *064 31440*

The friary, also called Muckross Abbey, was founded for the Franciscans in 1448 and constructed over a period of 59 years; it features a mid-15C nave and choir – the latter lit by a widely splayed window of four lights crowned by intersecting bar tracery – a broad central tower and a south transept built about 1500. The 22-arch cloisters and the domestic offices were built in four different phases. The three-storey building north of the choir probably contained the Sacristy and the Sacristan's lodging.

Muckross House and Farms★

Car park; footpath to Muckross Friary. (Dúchas) ♿ *House: Open daily, 9am-6pm (7pm Jul-Aug, 5.30pm Nov to mid-Mar). Gardens: Open daily. Farms: Open May-Sep, daily, 10am (1pm May) to 7pm (6pm May); mid-Mar to Apr and Oct, Sat-Sun and Bank Hols, 1-6pm; last admission 1hr before closing. Closed one week at Christmas. House and farms €7.50; house or farms €5. Leaflet (6 languages). Audio-visual show. Parking. Licensed restaurant; coffee shop.* ☎ *064 31440; Fax 064 37565; killarneynationalopark@ealga.ie; mucros@iol.ie*

The Elizabethan-style mansion in Portland stone was built in 1843 for the Herbert family. Many of the rooms are furnished in the style of the early 20C: the **drawing room**, **library** and **dining room**, with their lavish decorations; the nursery containing dolls made c 1870; an old-fashioned bathroom; and a bedroom with a four-poster bed. The basement is devoted to regional crafts.

The beautiful **gardens** with their magnificent rhododendrons extend down to the lakeside.

SLIDE FILE Dublin

Muckross Gardens

The **Muckross Peninsula**, which divides Lough Leane from Muckross (Middle) Lake, contains one of the finest yew woods in Europe *(nature trails)*.

The **Traditional Farms** *(1hr on foot)* are a showpiece of early 20C Irish rural life. Live animals inhabit the yards and fields and the buildings, from large farmhouse to labourer's cottage, are appropriately furnished with dressers, presses and settle-beds. Indoors turf fires burn in the hearths and the staff, in period costume, demonstrate the work of a country housewife in the days before electricity and other modern amenities came to the Irish countryside.

Torc Waterfall★

Car park. The **cascade** (60ft/18m) in its lovely sylvan setting is one of the highest in Ireland. The adjacent viewpoint *(173 steps)* provides a fine view of the lakes.

Ladies View★★

Car park. Climbing over the hills to Kenmare, the road (N 17) enables visitors to enjoy some of the finest panoramas over the Killarney landscape without the need to scale a mountain. Queen Victoria was particularly impressed by the prospect of Macgillycuddy's Reeks and the island-studded Upper Lake from this roadside viewpoint when she and her entourage came this way in 1861.

Moll's Gap★

Car park. The pass (863ft/263m) provides *(N)* a striking view of the Gap of Dunloe in Macgillycuddy's Reeks and *(S)* a glimpse of the Kenmare River.

RING OF KERRY★★

126mi/203km – 1 day

The Iveragh peninsula is world famous for its spectacular combination of high mountains, rocky bays, sandy beaches and dramatic seascapes. Known as the **Ring of Kerry**, the road (N 70) skirting the entire coastline between Killorglin in the north and Kenmare in the south, is one of the world's great scenic drives; it is possible to go round it in a single day but only a more measured trip of several days is sufficient to do justice to the superlative quality of the ever-changing succession of landscapes.

From Killarney take N 72 NW. Most coach tours on this route travel from north to south; passing is difficult as the coast road is narrow.

Dunloe Castle Hotel Gardens

After 4mi/6km turn left. Open May-Sep, daily; groups by appointment. Catalogue €1.27.
☎ *064 44111; Fax 064 44583; www.iol.ie/khl*

From the modern hotel the luxuriant gardens, partly enclosed by grey stone walls, extend to the 13C tower house overlooking the **River Laune** and the River Loe with a clear view of the Dunloe Gap. The botanic collection consists of exotic specimens from all parts of the world – the Killarney strawberry tree, South African lilies, Australian gums, New Zealand cabbage trees and cherries, Japanese maples, North American dogwood, Chilean fir trees, South American fuchsias and such rare specimens as the Chinese swamp cypress and the "Headache" tree with its aromatic leaves.

Return to N 72 and continue NW to Killorglin.

Killorglin (Cill Orglan)

The town is best known for the **Puck Fair** *(August)*; a large local billy-goat is enthroned on a chair in the town square during three days and nights of revelry.

The **Puck Fair Exhibition**, displayed in the basement room of a private house *(turn right after crossing the bridge at the foot of the hill)*, consists of souvenirs, photos, press cuttings etc. *Open daily, noon-9pm. €2.* ☎ *066 976 1353 (Patrick Houlihan).*

Continue W on N 70; turn left to Caragh Lake, then right and left to Lickeen.

Lough Caragh★

The road along the west shore affords attractive views of the lake, which provides good salmon and trout fishing; southeast rise the Macgillycuddy's Reeks (3 414ft/1 041m).

Return to N 70 and continue W; in Caragh Bridge turn right.

Cromane Strand

The long spit of sand shelters the great stretch of shallow water known as Castlemaine Harbour.

Continue W on N 70; west of Glenbeigh take the minor road W across the bridge to Rossbeigh Strand.

Rossbeigh Strand

The long strand (3mi/5km) is backed by a small hamlet with a pub and a shop; there are extended walks in Rossbeigh Woods.

Continue W on N 70; in Kells turn right onto the minor road to Kells Bay (1mi/1.6km).

Kells Bay

This small secluded beach backed by trees is a popular bathing place.

Continue W on N 70.

Lough Caragh, Ring of Kerry

B. Kaufmann/MICHELIN

Beside the road *(right)* stand the gaunt ruins of **Daniel O'Connell's Birthplace**, Carhan House.

Cahersiveen (Cathair Saidhbhín)

Close to the south shore of the inlet known as the Valentia River, the native town of Daniel O'Connell is a relatively recent foundation, dating from the early 19C. The **O'Connell Memorial Church**, built in 1888 of Newry granite with dressings of local black limestone, lacks the intended tower. Although rejected at first by the church authorities as too elaborate, the plans were approved by Pope Leo XIII.

The old police headquarters by the bridge, burnt out in 1922, have been restored to house the **Barracks Heritage Centre** with displays on local history. *Old RIC Barracks, Cahersiveen. Open Jun-Sep, Mon-Sat ☎ 066 947 2589; Fax 066 947 6377*

Take the minor road N towards Cooncrome harbour; after crossing the river turn left (2mi/3.2km).

Cahergall Fort

The walls of this massive stone fort are stepped on the inside as at Staigue *(see below)*. They enclose two drystone buildings, a beehive hut and a rectangular house.

On foot continue W; turn right into a private road.

Leacanabuaile Fort

This partly reconstructed prehistoric drystone fort was inhabited during the Bronze and Iron Ages; from the top of the ramparts there are excellent **views**★★ of the coast.

Return to Cahersiveen and continue W on N 70.

To visit Valencia Island EITHER turn right to Renard Point and take the ferry to Knight's Town (see Directory) OR continue on N 70, turn right onto R 657 to Portmagee and cross the bridge over the Portmagee Channel.

Valencia Island

Although the island is small (7 x 2mi/11.3 x 3.2km), its name is well known to all who listen to the BBC shipping forecasts and in 1858, less than 2 000mi/3 219km from Newfoundland, Valencia was the eastern terminal for the first transatlantic telegraph cable.

Knight's Town, the quiet little port which is the island's main settlement consists of a single street ending at the weatherboarded clock tower by the harbour. A steep narrow road north of the church leads *(2.5mi/4km)* up to a grotto created in the mouth of a disused slate quarry; from the headland there is a view of Beginish Island and Doulus Head.

The western extremity of Valencia Island, Bray Head, is marked by **Bray Tower** *(30min on foot up a track from the end of the road)*, a 16C stone watchtower, which gives views *(S)* to the Skellig Islands and *(N)* to the Dingle Peninsula.

Skellig Experience

Valencia Island. ♿ *Open Mar-Nov, daily, 10am-7pm (6pm Sep-Nov); last admission 45min before closing. Exhibition €4.44. Skellig Islands Cruise available. Parking. Refreshments. ☎ 066 947 6306, Fax 066 947 76351; info@skelligexperience.com; www.skelligexperience.com*

The stone-clad, grass-roofed building by the bridge linking Valencia to the mainland houses imaginative displays which convey something of the extraordinary character of the Skellig Islands – the monastery, lighthouses, wildlife and a video of the local underwater sealife.

Skellig Islands★★

Access by ferry (see Directory).

These bare and rocky islands, 10m/16km out in the Atlantic, rise out of the waves like the peaks of drowned mountains, a truly astonishing sight. Little Skellig is a nature reserve, and no landing is allowed, leaving its colonies of kittiwakes, razorbills, guillemots, shearwaters and gannets undisturbed. The larger island, Skellig Michael, now a World Heritage Site, is sometimes accessible, depending on weather conditions and the whims of local boatmen. Its remote position on the westernmost edge of the known world was chosen as a monastic site in the 6C by St Finian; his monastery survived for 500-600 years before its inhabitants abandoned their austere surroundings for more congenial quarters at Ballinskelligs on the mainland. The well-preserved ruins – church, two oratories and six beehive huts – are still here, perched precipitously above the sea on a narrow platform at the top of a flight of several hundred steps.

From the island take the bridge over the Portmagee Channel to Portmagee (An Caladh); turn right to take the coast road S.

The road climbs behind Glanearagh (1 044ft/318m) and then plunges in steep narrow zigzags down to St Finan's Bay; in fine weather there is a view of the **Skellig Islands.**

Continue S on R 567.

Ballinskelligs (Baile an Sceilg)

This very small Irish-speaking village is noted for its minute harbour and long golden strand (4mi/6km).

Continue E on R 567; at the junction turn right onto N 70.

Waterville (An Coireán)

The little resort is built on an isthmus between **Lough Currane** and the sea; it boasts a long promenade (0.5mi/0.8km). Many photographs of Charlie Chaplin's frequent visits are to be found in the foyer of the Butler Arms Hotel, redolent of the 1950s in its decor.

Coomakesta Pass

The winding pass (700ft/213m) offers striking views of the coast.

Derrynane National Historic Park★★

(Dúchas) (&) Open May-Sep, daily, 9am (11am Sun) to 6pm (7pm Sun); Apr and Oct, Tue-Sun, 1-5pm; Nov-Mar, Sat-Sun, 1-5pm; last admission 45min before closing. €2.50. Guided tour (30min) by appointment. Parking. Coffee shop. ☎ 066 947 5113; Fax 066 947 5432; derrynanehouse@ealga.ie

The demesne formerly belonged to Daniel O'Connell (1775-1847), the great champion of Catholic emancipation, known as the Liberator.

The **park** (298 acres/121ha) which borders Derrynane Bay includes a bathing beach, a bird sanctuary, and Abbey Island which is accessible at low tide. There are walks through flower gardens and woodlands near the house.

The south and east wings of the slate-fronted **house** are presented as they were when built by O'Connell in 1825 – there are family portraits, original furniture and mementoes.

The centrepiece of the drawing room *(first floor)* is the elaborate **table** presented to O'Connell when he was an alderman of Dublin Corporation; the top is made of walnut and the base, made from Irish oak, features Irish wolfhounds and a harp; the carving took four years to complete. The chapel adjoining the house was built by O'Connell in 1844 in thanksgiving for his release from prison; the huge triumphal chariot, in which he was paraded through Dublin, has been restored to its full gilded magnificence.

From Derrynane take N 70 E; in Castlecove turn left at the Staigue Fort House hotel.

Staigue Fort★

Narrow approach road; 20p donation "for trespass". This restored 2 000 year-old drystone fort is one of the finest in Ireland. It was built as a centre of communal refuge probably before the 5C. The walls (18ft/5m high and up to 13ft/4m thick) are stepped on their interior face to provide access to the parapets. The entire fort is surrounded by a bank and ditch.

Continue E on N 70.

Sneem (An Snaidhm)★

This attractive village is set at the head of the Sneem Estuary. Monuments to Cearbhall O'Dálaigh (1899-1976), former President of Ireland, who lived in Sneem, have been erected in the two large grass-covered squares, which are linked by a narrow bridge.

The **Anglican Church** is a charming small building dating from 1810 with a tower and a small spire supporting a salmon-shaped weathervane. Among the few ornaments in the white-painted interior are a number of brass pew plates, bearing the names of former parishioners. *Open in summer, daily; in winter key available from café opposite. Services: Sun, 10am. ☎/Fax 064 41121; shawa@eircom.net*

Continue E on N 70 to Kenmare (see p 270) and then on N 71 N to return to Killarney.

Kilrush★

Overlooking the sheltered waters of the Shannon estuary, Kilrush is the second-largest town in Co Clare, still with something of the character it had when laid out by the Vandeleur family in the 18C. In the 19C it prospered as a port, and became the favourite summer resort of prosperous people from Limerick. Today it is a designated Heritage town and a gateway to the beaches and cliffs of the Loop Head peninsula. There is a modern marina and lively horse fairs are often held in the main square. In summer families of bottlenosed dolphins can be seen sporting in the Shannon Estuary.

Location

Population 2 740 - Michelin Atlas p 83 and Map 712 – D 10 – Co Clare.
Kilrush *(Cill Rois)* is SW of Ennis by N 68 and a few miles W of Killimer on the north bank of the River Shannon, which is the arrival and departure point for the Shannon Ferry.
🔋 *Moore Street, Kilrush. Open Jun-Sep, daily. ☎ 065 905 1577; www.kilrush.ie; www.shannondev.ie*
🔋 *O'Connell Square, Kilkee. Open Jun to early-Sep, daily. ☎ 065 905 6112*
Adjacent Sights: See ADARE, ENNIS, LIMERICK, TRALEE.

Directory

GETTING ABOUT

Shannon Car Ferry *(from Killimer; 5.5mi/8.8km E of Kilrush)* carrying vehicles and passengers to Tarbert on the south shore of the Shannon Estuary – *Operates (crossing time approx 20min) daily (except 25 Dec) from Killimer (north bank), hourly on the hour, Apr-Sep, 7am (9am Sun) to 9pm; Oct-Mar, 7am (10am Sun) to 7pm; from Tarbert (south bank) hourly on the half hour, Apr-Sep, 7.30am (9.30am Sun) to 9.30pm; Oct-Mar, 7.30am (10.30am Sun) to 7.30pm. Capacity 52 + 60 vehicles. Car €12.50 (single), €19 (return); pedestrian €3 (single), €5 (return). Visitor Centre at Killimer. Open daily, 9am-9pm (7pm Oct-Mar). Parking. Bureau de change.* ☎ *065 905 3124; Fax 065 905 3125 (Shannon Ferry Ltd); enquiries@shannonferries.com; www.shannonferries.com*

Ferry to Scattery Island – *Operates (subject to tide, demand and weather) from Kilrush Creek Marina May-Sep; daily. Telephone to confirm timetable. 1-2hr on the island. There and back €8.* ☎*/Fax 065 905 1327 (Griffins); shannondolphins@eircom.net; www.shannondolphins.ie*

SIGHTSEEING

Dolphin Watch Trip – *Operates from Kilrush Creek Marina (2hr 30min approx; subject to demand and weather conditions) May-Sep. €14.* ☎*/Fax 065 905 1327 (Griffins); shannondolphins@eircom.net; www.shannondolphins.ie*

Dolphin Watch Trip – *Operates from Carrigaholt Apr-Oct, daily. €17.* ☎ *065 905 8156; www.dolphinwatch.ie*

Boat Trips – Cruises and deep-sea fishing expeditions.

SPORTS AND LEISURE

Beaches at Cappa and Brew's Bridge.

Marina at Merchant's Quay in Kilrush with 120 berths, a boatyard and yacht hire.

Fishing in the Shannon Estuary and off the Atlantic coast

Worth a Visit

Vandeleur Walled Garden

Ferry Road. Open daily, 10am-6pm (4pm Nov-Mar). €2.5. Parking. Coffee shop; picnic sites. ☎ *065 905 1760; Fax 065 905 2821*

The magnificent woodlands (420 acres/168ha), the old walled garden, which is being imaginatively restored, and the stables, now a Visitor Centre, are all that remain of the Vandeleur family seat; the mansion (1803) was destroyed by fire in 1897. The Vandeleurs, a family of Dutch origin, settled in Kilrush in 1688 and were responsible for building the town in the 18C but they acquired an unenviable reputation as harsh landlords in the 19C.

Scattery Island Visitor Centre

W of Merchant's Quay. (Dúchas) (&) Open mid-Jun to mid-Sep, daily, 10.30am-1pm and 2-6.30pm (5.45pm last admission). Parking. ☎*/Fax 065 905 2139; scatteryisland@ealga.ie; www.heritageireland.ie*

The centre provides information about the history and wildlife of Scattery Island 2mi/3km out in the estuary *(see below)*.

Excursions

Scattery Island★

Accessible by boat from Kilrush (see Directory). In the 6C the island was chosen as the site of a monastery by St Senan. Legend relates that the saint had first to rid it of a terrible monster; more certain is the monastery's fate at the hands of the Vikings, who raided it on more than one occasion. There are evocative ruins of five medieval churches, but the most imposing structure is the tall (115ft/33m) **round tower**, which, most unusually, has its doorway at ground level.

West Clare Railway

4mi/6.4km NW of Kilrush by N 67 opposite Clancy's pub in Moyasta. Open May-Sep, daily, 10am-6pm; also Easter, 17 Mar, and 31 Oct. Guided tour (30min), every 30min. €6. Tearoom, picnic area. Shop. ☎ *065 9051 284*

Visitors may take a short ride on a restored section of the West Clare Railway, which originally ran between Ennis *(see p 251)* and Kilkee. There are plans to restore more of the line.

Kilkee (Cill Chaoi)

8.5mi/13.5km NW of Kilrush by N 67. This seaside resort is set deep in Moore Bay with a long promenade embracing a wide horseshoe-shaped sandy beach, where horse races are held at low tide *(last weekend in August)*. The Duggerna rocks at the entrance to the bay are accessible at low tide.

Kilrush

Kilkee Beach

Loop Head Peninsula

West of Kilrush and Kilkee the land forms a peninsula, terminating in Loop Head. The treeless landscape is divided into fields by earthbanks rather than the hedges or flagstones found further inland. It is a monotonous scene, a foil to the drama of the coastal cliffs and rocks.

On the south coast **Carrigaholt Tower House** stands beside the pier. It was built in the 16C by the McMahon family, who once controlled the peninsula, and was last besieged in 1649. From the top of the tower there are fine **views** south to the north Kerry coast *(3mi/5km)*.

The north coast is much wilder, with spectacular cliffs, stacks and puffing holes. Near Moneen a huge natural arch, the **Bridge of Ross★** *(sign)*, formed by the action of the sea, is visible from the edge of the cliffs.

Loop Head is surmounted by the lighthouse (277ft/84m above sea level) which was built on the headland in 1854. It is the third light on the site; the first, built in about 1670, was one of four stone-vaulted cottage lights which had a coal-burning brazier on a platform on the roof.

Kinsale★★

Pretty little Kinsale, a designated Heritage town, on the broad estuary of the River Bandon, has had a long history as a harbour town, then as a favoured resort, with charming narrow lanes and neat Georgian houses stepping up the hillside overlooking the water. In recent years Kinsale has become particularly fashionable, with a gastronomic reputation which is celebrated annually with a food festival.

Location

Population 2 007 - Michelin Atlas p 78 and Map 712 – G 12– Co Cork.
Kinsale *(Cionn Tsáile)* is situated south of Cork city and Cork Airport and easily reached by N 27 and R 600.
🚹 *Pier Road, Kinsale. Open Apr-Sep.* ☎ *021 477 2234; Fax 021 477 4438; user@cktourism.ie*
🚹 *Ashe Street, Clonakilty. Open Apr-Sep, Mon-Sat.* ☎ *023 33226*
Adjacent Sights: See COBH, CORK, SKIBBEREEN.

Directory

SIGHTSEEING

Historic Kinsale Walking Tours - *Operate at 9.45am, 11.15am, 2.30pm, 4pm; Sun and Bank Hols, 11.15am only. Start from outside the Tourist Office. Duration 1hr approx. €3.* ☎ 021 772 873 (Herlihy)

Kinsale Harbour Scenic Cruises – *Operate daily downstream past Summer Cove and Charles Fort to Middle Cove and Money Point and upstream past James Fort and under the road bridge, turning for home at the bend in the River Bandon.* ☎ 021 773 188

WHERE TO STAY

• Budget

Chart House – *6 Denis Quay -* ☎ *021 477 4568 - Fax 021 477 7907 - charthouse@eircom.net - Closed at Christmas -* ✕ *- 4 rm €52/104* ☑. Cosy and quaint little Georgian B&B. Ask for the Blue or the Green room; both have antique beds and jacuzzi baths. The extensive tea offered to all arrivals will refresh the most jaded of travellers.

Glebe Country House – *Ballinadee -* ☎ *021 477 8294 - Fax 021 477 8456 - glebehse@indigo.ie - Closed 21-28 Dec -* ☐ ✕ *- 4 rm €57/90* ☑ *- Meals €30.* The spacious gardens of this ivy-covered 17C former rectory provide many of the ingredients for the kitchen. A peaceful setting with the church steeple peeping over the trees. Individually decorated bedrooms with antiques aplenty.

Rivermount House – *Barrells Cross – 0.5mi/0.8km NE -* ☎ *021 477 8033 - Fax 021 477 8225 - rivermnt@iol.ie - Feb-Nov -* ☐ ✕ *- 6 rm €60/80* ☑. This bungalow guesthouse in a quiet hillside spot enjoys sweeping views over the garden and the River Bandon. The owner will gladly provide packed lunches for those off to the beach, just a short drive away.

Kilcaw Guesthouse – *1mi/1.6km E on R 600 -* ☎ *021 477 4155 - Fax 021 477 4755 - info@kilcawhouse.ie -* ☐ ✕ *- 7 rm €65/76* ☑. A custom-built guesthouse in seven acres/3ha of land. The breakfast room has a farmhouse feel while the sitting room, with its open fireplace, offers a restful sanctuary. The pine-furnished bedrooms are uniform in size.

• Expensive

Desmond House – *42 Cork St -* ☎ *021 477 3575 - Fax 021 477 3575 -*

Kinsale Harbour

J Malburet/MICHELIN

desmondhouse@compuserve.com – Mar-Nov - ✕ *- 4 rm €150/180* ☑. The owners of this centrally located Georgian town house are justifiably proud of the extensive breakfasts they lay on for their guests. Bedrooms are a good size and each comes in a different colour.

WHERE TO EAT

• Budget

Raftery's – ☎ *091 846 004 -* ☐ ☐ *- €15.* Seafood salads and assorted sandwiches are on offer at this well-kept family run pub in the high street. On colder days, take advantage of the snug bar with its own fireplace.

Max's – *Main St -* ☎ *021 477 2443 - Closed Nov-Mar and Tue -* ✕ *- €17/45.* Sweet and intimate with exposed beams, wood flooring and a small conservatory extension. The menu has a discernible French accent and features carefully sourced local produce with deft use of herbs.

Dalton's – *3 Market St -* ☎ *021 477 7597 - colmdalton@tinet.ie - Closed Good Fri, 25 Dec, Sat and Sun -* ✕ *- €17/24.* The purple painted exterior is the first clue that this is no ordinary pub. The emphasis is firmly on the food with a menu that blends international influences garnered from the owner's experiences abroad.

Fishy Fishy Cafe (at The Gourmet Store) – *Guardwell -* ☎ *021 477 4453 - Closed Sun Oct-Mar -* ☐ ✕ *- Bookings not accepted - €19.40/25.25.* It says it all in the name; fresh fish, fun and informality. It's also very popular so go early to avoid the queue. Choose your fish from an impressive selection behind the counter or from the menu and grab a seat inside or on the pavement terrace.

• Moderate

Crackpots – *3 Cork St -* ☎ *021 772 847 - Closed Nov, weekends only in winter -* ☐ *- €25.* Self-styled "ceramic restaurant" where pottery workshops are held, with all the original ceramic pieces for sale; you can even buy the tableware after your meal. Mildly eclectic menu in an atmosphere of candlelight and ambient music.

• Expensive

The Vintage – *Main St -* ☎ *021 477 2502 - info@vintagerestaurant.ie - Closed 1 Jan to 13 Feb, Sun and Mon in winter - €42/58.* The oak beams add to the palpable sense of history while the cosy bar and candlelight add to the intimate atmosphere. The traditional menu features local produce and oysters are something of a house speciality.

SHOPPING

There is a wide variety of shops, selling craftwork of all kinds.

SPORTS AND LEISURE

Good facilities for yachting and deep-sea fishing.

EVENTS AND FESTIVALS

A **good food festival** is held in October when visitors (maximum 300 for the whole 4 days) sample the delights created by the international chefs of the Kinsale Good Food Circle or buy a day ticket to enjoy the many other local restaurants and pubs; reservations are scarce.

Background

Kinsale was founded in the late 12C by the Anglo-Normans but really enters the history books only in 1601. In that year a Spanish force occupied the town, a long way from their ally Hugh O'Neill, fighting the English in far-off Ulster. Kinsale was besieged by an English army, who were besieged in their turn by O'Neill after an exhausting march from the north. The combined Irish/Spanish forces should have easily defeated their enemy but the Spaniards watched from the walls as O'Neill was routed. The disposition of the armies is explained on roadside panels. This defeat marked the beginning of the end of the old Gaelic order and clan system; until the end of the 18C no native Irish were to settle within its 13C walls. In 1641 the town declared for Cromwell and so was spared much damage.

Similar lack of success attended **James II** who landed at Kinsale in March 1689 in an attempt to regain his kingdom; after the Battle of the Boyne *(see p 148)* he returned to exile in France from Duncannon in Waterford Harbour.

During the 17C Kinsale flourished as a shipbuilding port for the Royal Navy, which constructed *HMS Kinsale* here in 1700. The 18C trend towards larger ships rendered the docks obsolete.

Worth a Visit

Kinsale Regional Museum★

Open summer, Mon-Sat, 11am-1pm; winter, daily, 2pm (3pm Sun and Bank Hols) to 5.30pm. Closed 25 Dec. €2.54. Guided tour (20min). Brochure (6 languages). ☎/Fax 021 47 77930
Housed in the late-17C town hall, which is surmounted by distinctive Dutch gables, the museum has many relics of old Kinsale, including several royal charters. In the loggia is the Toll Board listing charges on goods coming to market, and a gun from *HMS St Albans*, which foundered in Kinsale harbour on 8 December 1693. The great hall is associated with the famous inquest on the victims of the *Lusitania (see below)*. The exhibition room displays a variety of items: Kinsale-made lace which, like the Kinsale cloak, was popular for over a century; footwear and cutlery belonging to the Kinsale giant, **Patrick Cotter O'Brien** (1706-1806), who made a lucrative career on the English stage. There are additional displays at Desmond Castle and at Charles Fort *(see below)*.

St Multose Church (Anglican)★

Open when possible Easter-Sep, Mon-Sat, 10am-noon and 2-4pm. Donation. Guide book. Services: Sun, 8am, 11.30am. ☎ 021 4772 220 (Rectory); dhw@gofree.indigo.ie
The original church was built about 1190 and dedicated to St Multose or Eltin, the patron saint of Kinsale, who lived in the 6C. The massive square tower has a 12C Romanesque doorway with zigzag decoration. A statue of St Multose stands in a niche over the west door. The interior contains some fascinating 16C gravestones.

Desmond Castle

(Dúchas) Open mid-Apr to Oct, daily, 10am-6pm (5.15pm last admission). €2.50. Guided tour available. Leaflet. ☎ 021 477 4855

Kinsale at night

The three-storey tower house was built in the late 15C or early 16C by the Earls of Desmond as a custom house, as the site was then close to the harbour. During the siege of Kinsale it was used as a magazine and then reverted to being a custom house until 1641. Subsequently it was used as a jail for French and other foreign prisoners, hence its other name – the "French Prison". It now houses a **Museum of Wine** reflecting the days when Kinsale was a port, and traces the number of Irish families connected with winemaking in France, Spain, Australia and the USA.

Excursion

Kinsale Harbour★

There is a pleasant walk *(1.5mi/2.4km)* along the east bank of the Bandon estuary to **Summercove**; the single village street dips down to a minute harbour where English ships landed guns and supplies for their army during the siege of Kinsale (1601-02). From the graveyard of St Catherine's Anglican Church there are extensive **views**★ across the harbour.

Charles Fort★ *(up the hill; car park)*, was begun about 1670 and remained in use until 1922. The vast star-shaped stronghold is a typical example of Baroque fortification, and is the largest structure of its date in Ireland. Many of the buildings surrounding the quadrangle of greensward are derelict but the old ordnance-store houses a good interpretive exhibition. From the fort there are extensive **views** of Kinsale harbour. *(Dúchas)* (&) *Open mid-Mar to Oct, daily, 10am-6pm; Nov to mid-Mar, daily, 10am-5pm; last admission 45min before closing. Closed 25-26 Dec. €3.10. Guided tour (45min) available. Guide book (7 languages). Sturdy footwear advised. Parking. Tearoom.* ☎ *021 772 263; Fax 021 774 4347; charlesfort@ealga.ie*

The harbour was guarded on the west side by **James Fort** *(cross the bridge over the Bandon River and turn left; after 0.5mi/0.8km park; 0.5mi/0.8km on foot)* which was built in 1604 but is less well preserved than Charles Fort; only the central tower, blockhouse and portions of the defensive walls are still partially intact.

The harbour entrance is protected by the **Old Head of Kinsale** *(from the river bridge take R 600 W and R 604 S)*. On the top of the headland stand the ruins of a 15C De Courcy fort. The road stops just short of the modern lighthouse, which replaced one built in 1683.

LUSITANIA

On the seabed *(12mi/19km S)* lies the wreck of the great transatlantic liner *Lusitania*, torpedoed by a German submarine on 7 May 1915 on her way from New York to Liverpool; her sinking changed the climate of opinion in the United States and prepared the way for the American declaration of war on Germany two years later. Among the 1 500 who lost their lives was Sir Hugh Lane, the wealthy art collector who established the Hugh Lane Gallery of Modern Art in Dublin.

Tour

CARBERY COAST★

38mi/61km W of Kinsale by R 600

The south coast of Co Cork is penetrated by a number of sea-inlets, some framed by woodland, and offers many attractive views of land and sea.

Timoleague★

The village on the Argideen estuary is dominated by a ruined **Franciscan** friary★, founded in 1320 and plundered by Oliver Cromwell in 1642. The extensive ruins include the cloisters and the outer yard, and *(0.5mi/0.8km S)* the ruins of a 12C leper hospital.

Courtmacsherry★

3mi/5km detour E by R 601. This attractive village and family resort, overlooking the estuary, is a fine base for walking and deep-sea fishing; footpaths lead through the trees to Wood Point, or to a pebble beach at Broadstrand Bay.

From Timoleague take R 600 W. Before the junction with the main road (N 71) turn left (sign).

Lios na gCon

Closed for major work until 2003. Open previously summer, daily, 10am (11am Sat-Sun) to 5pm. €2.54. Guided tour. Brochure. Leaflet. Parking. ☎ *023 33302 (9.15am-5pm), 023 33279 (after 6pm); Fax 023 34449*

The 10C ring fort has been restored according to the evidence uncovered by a team of archaeologists who conducted an excavation in 1987-88. The souterrain is still intact and the enclosing ditch and bank are well preserved and give a wide **view** of the surrounding country.

Clonakilty (Cloich na Coillte)

The market town, founded in 1598, is renowned for its Gaelic traditions as well as for its **black puddings**, which were first produced in the 1880s by Philip Harrington at 16 Sovereign Street (now Pearse Street). The celebrated water pump, known as the Wheel of Fortune *(at the junction of Connolly Street and Lamb Street Lower)*, was provided by the Earl of Shannon in 1890.

The town centre is distinguished by **Emmet Square**, with its central garden and tall Georgian houses with pretty fanlights. Many of the renovated shopfronts have attractive Gaelic lettering.

The **West Cork Regional Museum★**, in the converted schoolhouse, traces local history with special emphasis on the War of Independence and on Michael Collins, who was born at Sam's Cross *(3mi/5km W)*. *Open May-Oct, daily, 10.30am-5pm, Sun, 2.30-5.30pm. €2.50. Guided tour by appointment. Parking.* ☎ 023 33115

The **West Cork Model Railway Village**, which is set in the 1940s, is a delight for children, who should enjoy following the trains round the track and reading the historical and environmental captions at each station and halt. *Open Feb-Oct, daily, 10am-5pm (6pm summer). €5. Parking. Tearoom.* ☎ 023 33224; *modelvillage@eircom net; www.clonakilty.ie*

The peninsula, Inchydoney Island *(3mi/5km S by the causeway road)*, is renowned for its sandy beaches; the large grass-covered spit of land jutting south into the sea is known as the "Virgin's Bank".

From Clonakilty take N 71 W.

Rosscarbery

This small village at the head of a narrow inlet has an enormous quadrangular square and a much-restored 12C Romanesque building, **St Fachtna's Cathedral** (Anglican), with an elaborately carved west doorway. That great evangeliser of the Germans, St Kilian *(see p 269)* was educated here at the monastic school, founded in AD 590 by St Fachtna, bishop and abbot, before setting out on his mission to Würzburg; two centuries later, that city repaid the compliment by sending one of its monks, St James, to found a Benedictine community in Rosscarbery.

From Rosscarbery take R 597 W towards Glandore; after 4mi/6.4km turn left to the Drombeg Circle (sign).

Drombeg Stone Circle★

This is probably the most impressive of the 60 stone circles built in prehistoric times in west Cork. It has 14 evenly spaced stones which form an enclosed circle (30ft/9m in diameter); usually the number of stones was uneven. Of similar antiquity is the nearby cooking pit *(see p 103)*.

Continue W on R 597 to Glandore.

Glandore★

The original Irish name for this small village, Cuan Dor meaning the "harbour of the oaks", recalls the extensive woods which covered much of west Cork 300 years ago.

The semicircular harbour faces two minute islands in the estuary called Adam and Eve; old sailing directions told sailors to "avoid Adam and hug Eve". A walk up the hill *(300yd/275m)* leads to Glandore's upper level.

Cross the river to Union Hall; take the road via Rineen to Castletownshend.

Castletownshend★

The steep main street of this tiny village descends to the water's edge where a small pier offers fine views across the lovely Castle Haven estuary.

St Barrahane's Church (Anglican) is attractively set at the top of four flights of steps *(50)* at the foot of the main street; the colourful Nativity Window was designed by Harry Clarke. *Open daily. Services: Apr-Sep, Sun, 9.45am; Nov-Mar, first Sun of the month, 9am.*

Knock

Until the late 19C Knock was a quiet little village set on a wind-swept ridge in the middle of a vast and inhospitable bog. Since then it has become one of the world's great Marian shrines, attracting up to a million pilgrims a year, many of them during Knock Novena week in August, when the Statue of the Virgin is carried in procession in the grounds to celebrate the anniversary of the Apparition.

Location

Population 575 - Michelin Atlas p 95 and Map 712 – F 6 – Co Mayo.
Knock *(An Cnoc)* straddles the crossroads of N 17 and R 323. Knock International Airport (8mi/13km N by N 17) provides quick access to this part of the west of Ireland.
🚹 *Linenhall Street, Castlebar. Open Apr-Sep, Mon-Sat.* ☎ *094 21207*
Adjacent Sights: See BOYLE, CONG, SLIGO, STROKESTOWN, WESTPORT.

Directory

Worth a Visit

Apparition Church
The south gable of the church where the apparition was seen has been glassed in to provide protection against the weather. Early pilgrims used to take away pieces of the wall plaster, believing it to have miraculous powers.

Basilica of Our Lady, Queen of Ireland★
The huge hexagonal church (48 687sq ft/4 524m²), which can hold 12 000 people, was consecrated in 1976 and designed by Dáithí P Hanly. A slender spire surmounts the tower which contains the Blessed Sacrament Chapel.
The external covered ambulatory is supported on 12 pillars of red Mayo granite, and 32 pillars of stone from each of the 32 counties of Ireland.
Inside, above the chapel entrance, hangs a large tapestry depicting the apparition, designed by Ray Carroll in the form of a hand-woven Donegal carpet. The centre of the church is occupied by the high altar.
The rest is divided into five chapels dedicated to the Sacred Heart, St John the Evangelist, Our Lady of Knock, St Joseph and St Columba, each represented by a statue. Each partition wall contains a replica of a church window from one of the four provinces of Ireland.

Folk Museum
♿ *Open May-Oct, daily, 10am-6pm (7pm July-Aug).* €4. *Guided tour (30min) by appointment. Brochure (English only). Guide book (French). Parking.* ☎ *094 88100; Fax 094 88295, info@knock-shrine.ie; www.knock-shrine.ie*

A modern building, bearing the shields of the four provinces of Ireland – Ulster, Connaught, Leinster, Munster – houses a well-presented display illustrating life in the west of Ireland in the 19C; the development of Knock shrine; the 15 witnesses, who are buried in the Knock cemetery, the Papal visit in 1979 and the life and achievements of Mgr James Horan, parish priest (1963-87).

Tour

INLAND MAYO
Round trip of 86mi/139km.
From Knock take R 323 N via Kiltimagh; in Bohola turn left into N 5.

Museum of Country Life★★
Turlough. Open Tue-Sun, 10am (2pm Sun) to 5pm. Guided tour (40min) at frequent intervals. ☎ 1890 687 386; Fax 094 31628; tpark@museum.ie; www.museum.ie
Providing a fitting home for 50 000 items from the National Museum's collections which had languished in storage for years, this new establishment is set in the restored grounds of Turlough Park, occupying both the Victorian Gothic mansion and a stunning, purpose-built structure cleverly blended with the terraced landscape.

On four levels, using every device of contemporary museum interpretation, the richly varied collections eschew any hint of sentimentality to present traditional life as lived in the Irish countryside until the second half of the 20C. The objects are endlessly fascinating, and the scope is comprehensive, dealing with the physical realities of the countryside and its resources, the unremitting cycle of work, the home, the role of women, the community, folklife and folklore. An introductory section invites visitors to reconsider the often romantic view of past rural life, a concluding section looks at the forces of change which have transformed the countryside in recent times.

The imposing ruin of a medieval Fitzgerald stronghold guards the approach to the park, while crowning a hilltop on the far bank of the Castlebar River is a fine example of a round tower next to a roofless church on the site of a monastery supposedly founded by St Patrick.
Continue W on N 5.

Castlebar
The county town and commercial centre of Mayo, is pleasantly sited on the Castlebar River. It was here in 1798 that French General Humbert and his Irish peasant allies put a far superior British force to ignominious flight, an event gleefully referred to subsequently as the "Castlebar Races". John Moore, who headed the short-lived "Republic of Connaught" and who died in prison, is buried by the 1798 memorial in the grassy town centre space known as **The Mall**.
From Castlebar take L 134 N; on the outskirts of the town turn left onto the minor road towards Burren and Windy Gap.

Windy Gap
The steep and narrow road through the pass provides **views** of Lough Conn and Castlebar.
Continue N and turn left onto R 315; 3mi/5km beyond Lahardaun turn right.

Errew Abbey★
20min there and back on foot across the fields. The abbey ruins stand on a lonely and picturesque **site** on the very end of a spit of land extending into Lough Conn. Little remains of the abbey, which was founded in 1413 for the Augustinian canons; the 13C church with its piscina and trefoil windows pre-dates the cloister buildings.
Return through Lahardaun and continue S on R 315; turn left in Pontoon.

Pontoon Bridge View★
From the bridge there is an extensive **view★** of **Lough Cullin** (S) and of **Lough Conn** (N), both known for angling (brown and white trout); Lough Cullin has safer sandy beaches for swimming.
Continue E and turn right onto R 318.

Foxford Woollen Mills
Guided tour (1hr) daily, 10am (2pm Sun) to 6pm, every 20min. €5. Guided tour and brochure (5 languages). Jewellery craft centre. Parking. Restaurant. Shop. Bureau de change. ☎ 094 56756; Fax 094 56794; foxfordwoollenmills@eircom.net
The Woollen Mills were set up by Mother Arsenius, of the Irish Sisters of Charity, who came to Foxford with a group of nuns in 1890 and established the thriving mill which has been independent of the nuns since 1987.

An audio-visual presentation about the history of the mill is followed by a tour of the obsolete machinery (1930s) and a view of the various processes – carding, spinning, weaving, mending, washing and drying – involved in the production of the famous Foxford blankets, rugs and tweeds, which are on sale in the shop.

Take N 58 S.

Strade

An annexe to the modern church houses the **Michael Davitt Memorial Museum**, devoted to the life of Michael Davitt (1846-1906), the founder of the Land League, who was born in Strade and is buried in the churchyard: letters, photographs, Land League sash, books by and about Davitt. & *Open daily, 10am-6pm. €3.20. Parking.* ☎ *094 31022; davittmuseum@eircom.net; www.museumsofmayo.com/davitt*

MICHAEL DAVITT (1846-1906)

Davitt was born in the middle of the Great Famine. When he was four years old his family was evicted for non-payment of rent and emigrated to Lancashire in England. At the age of nine he was employed in a woollen mill but three years later his right arm was amputated following an accident at work. The loss gave him time to attend a Wesleyan School and at 16, when he took up work in a printing business, he began to attend evening classes at the Mechanics' Institute and studied Irish history. He joined the Fenian movement and became organising secretary in Northern England and Scotland but was arrested and imprisoned for seven years for smuggling arms.

On his release in 1878 he returned to Co Mayo and helped to organise the tenants to obtain improvements from the landlords. Davitt persuaded Parnell to join the movement, and the Mayo Land League was formed in Daly's Hotel in Castlebar on 16 August 1879. The Irish National Land League was formed in October. During the ensuing Land War Davitt and others were arrested under the Coercion Act (1881). When the Land War ended in 1882 Davitt moved out of the limelight but continued to work as a reformer, teacher, writer and social thinker, with particular interest in the lot of the agricultural labourer and trade unionism; he was also involved in the formation of the Gaelic Athletic Association. He travelled widely and wrote several books – *Leaves from a Prison Diary* (1885), *The Fall of Feudalism in Ireland* (1904) and titles on working conditions in Australia and South Africa. He was elected to Parliament four times and used his position to advocate prison reform.

The ruined **friary** was founded in the 13C for the Franciscans but transferred to the Dominicans in 1252. Although most of the building seems to be 15C, the chancel is 13C; there are several cross-slabs against the south wall and a beautifully sculpted tomb in the north wall.

Continue on N 58, turn left onto N 5; in Bohola turn right onto R 321; in Kiltimagh take R 323 to return to Knock.

Limerick★★

Astride the River Shannon at its lowest fording point, Limerick is the main administrative and commercial centre of the mid west region and the fourth largest city in Ireland. Its three historic quarters are still quite distinct: medieval Englishtown on King's Island defended by one of the most formidable castles in Ireland; Irishtown, forming the modern city centre; and the Georgian district of Newtown Pery, laid out on a grid pattern during the 18C. The atmosphere created by a particularly turbulent past, with extremes of wealth and poverty, marked Limerick deeply but today the city, with its recently established (1972) university, modern industries and proximity to Shannon Airport is a much more welcoming place.

Location

Population 52 039 - Michelin Atlas p 84 and Map 712 – G 9, 10 – Co Limerick.
Limerick *(Luimneach)* on the River Shannon is the largest town in the west of Ireland and the point where N 7 from Dublin and N 24 from Waterford meet N 18 from Galway, N 20 from Cork, N 21 from Tralee and N 69 along the south shore of the Shannon Estuary.

🚩 *Arthur's Quay, Limerick, Co Limerick. Open daily.* ☎ *061 317 522; Fax 061 317 939; tourismInfo@shannondev.ie; www.shannondev.ie/tourism*
🚩 *Shannon Airport Arrivals Hall. Open daily.* ☎ *061 471 664; Fax 061 471 661*
Adjacent Sights: See ADARE, ENNIS, KILLALOE, KILRUSH.

Directory

GETTING ABOUT

Shannon International Airport –
☏ 061 712 000

SIGHTSEEING

Walking Tours – Historical tour and *Angela's Ashes* tour, based on the popular novel by Frank McCourt about the wretched life of the poor in Limerick during his childhood – *Depart from Arthur's Quay Mon-Fri, at 11am (Historical Tour) and 2.30pm (Angela's Ashes Tour); Sat-Sun apply to Tourist Information Office, Arthur's Quay. €6. ☏/Fax 061 318 106 (Mon-Fri), ☏ 061 327 108 (Sat-Sun; tour guide); smidp@iol.ie*

WHERE TO STAY

• **Budget**

Clifton House – *Ennis Rd – 1.25mil/2km NW on R 587 - ☏ 061 451 166 - Fax 061 451 224 - cliftonhouse@eircom.net - Closed 21 Dec to 2 Jan - ▣ - 16 rm €45/64 ⌸.* Simple but well-priced accommodation in this uniformly decorated house perched on an elevated position out of town. Guests can make use of the large garden and there are family rooms available.

Clonmacken House – *Clonmacken Rd, off Ennis Rd – 2.5mil/4km NW by N 18 turning right at Clonmacken roundabout - ☏ 061 327 007 - Fax 061 327 785 - clonmac@indigo.ie - Closed 21 Dec to 2 Jan - ▣ - 10 rm €50/70 ⌸.* Five minutes from the city centre and a useful modern guesthouse. Pretty little garden, a fairly quiet position and a well-kept house. Family rooms available.

Carrig House – *2 Meadowvale, Raheen – 2.75mil/4.4km SW by N 20 - ☏ 061 309 626 - Closed 24-26 Dec - ✉ ▣ ↦ - 3 rm €50/70 ⌸.* This affordable and immaculately kept, purpose-built guesthouse offers compact but colourfully decorated bedrooms, all with en-suite showers. The welcoming owner runs a friendly and welcoming house.

• **Moderate**

Jurys Inn Limerick – *Lower Mallow St - ☏ 061 207 000 - Fax 061 400 966 - jurysinnlimerick@jurysdoyle.com - Closed 24-26 Dec - ↦ ᕳ - 151 rm €79 - ⌸ €10 - Restaurant €23.* It may be a branded group hotel but it is in an excellent location and bedrooms are competitively priced and all a good size. Some even overlook the River Shannon while those at the rear are quietest.

WHERE TO EAT

• **Budget**

Brûlées – *Corner Mallow/Henry St - ☏ 061 319 931 - Closed Sun and Mon - €19.50/34.50.* Split between three floors of a Georgian house, with the aproned owner providing the attentive service and his wife the cooking, which emphasises local produce. Plenty of daily specials and local fish.

TAKING A BREAK

Dolans – *Dock Road - ☏ 061 314 483 - www.dolanpub.com – Open daily from 8am.* Probably the best-known pub in the region. It offers a fairly comprehensive menu of assorted seafood but what really draws the crowds is the live music at the end of the week, a variety of traditional and folk.

Schooners – *Steamboat Quay, Dock Road - ☏ 061 318 147 – Open daily from 8am.* Boasts a super location beside the Shannon; make use of the terrace in summer to watch the boats go by. The bar's a favourite with the locals and live concerts are held at the end of the week.

ENTERTAINMENT

Belltable Arts Centre – *- ☏ 061 319 866 - belltabl@iol.ie – Open daily, 9am-6pm.* Host to various theatre productions.

Royal Theatre – *Upper Cecil Street - ☏ 061 414 224.* Popular for music and other forms of entertainment.

Savoy Cinema – *Bedford Row - ☏ 061 311 900.* Five screens.

Greyhound racing.

SHOPPING

Arthur's Quay Shopping Centre – *Arthur's Quay - ☏ 061 419 888 - jjk@102.ie - Mon, Tue, Wed and Sat, 8.30am-8pm, Thu-Fri, 8.30am-10pm and Sun, 12am-6pm.* Arthur's Quay Shopping Centre, housing more than 30 stores, has several boutiques where you will find hand-knit and machine-made sweaters and clothing by Irish designers in linen, tweed and cotton.

Hunt Museum – *See below.* Good selection of high quality articles.

Limerick Lace is now rare but the traditional product is still hand-made by a few amateurs – *☏ 061 303 871 (Eileen Brown)*

Background

City of Sieges – In 922 Vikings from Denmark sailed up the Shannon and established a base on King's Island from which they plundered the rich agricultural hinterland. For over a century the town was repeatedly attacked by Irish forces until Brian Ború, High King of Ireland, sacked it and banished the settlers.

The Normans captured the place in 1194 and established themselves firmly in the city and its region; as well as raising the great fortress of King John's Castle and building city walls, they peppered the countryside around with hundreds of other strongholds.

In 1642 Limerick was besieged for six months by the Cromwellians, and a further, more momentous siege took place in 1690-91. After the Battle of the Boyne in July 1690 and despite the flight to France of James II, the defeated Jacobite forces

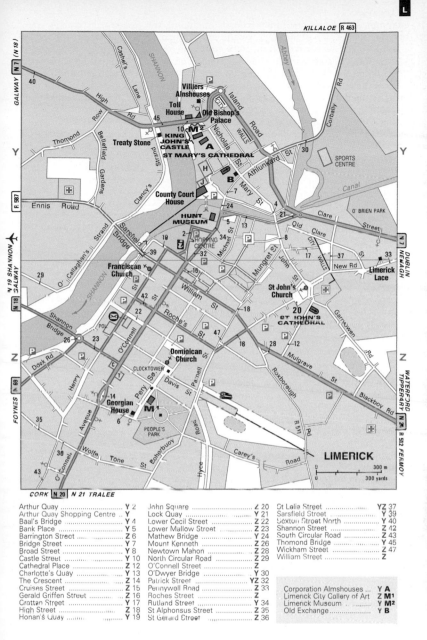

LIMERICK

CORK N 20 N 21 TRALEE

withdrew to Limerick where, under the bold leadership of Patrick Sarsfield they were besieged by William of Orange. William abandoned the siege at the end of August but the following year another Williamite army led by General Ginkel returned to the attack while an English fleet blockaded the Shannon. Sarsfield sued for peace, which was granted on surprisingly generous terms by the **Treaty of Limerick**; the Irish force was given safe conduct to France and Roman Catholics in general were

SARSFIELD'S RIDE

A gentleman of Old English, Catholic descent, Patrick Sarsfield showed daring and effective generalship during the wars of 1690-91. In early August 1690, acting on information from a deserter, he slipped out of the city with 600 cavalry. They headed north and then east, fording the Shannon upstream of Killaloe Bridge, which was held by the Williamites. After travelling south through the Silvermine Mountains, they intercepted the Williamite siege train at Ballyneety *(18mi/30km S of Limerick);* the noise of its destruction was heard in the city. With this coup Sarsfield had bought time but not victory. After negotiating the Treaty of Limerick he and 10 000 other Irish soldiers, the famous "Wild Geese", left for France, where many earned further military distinction. Sarsfield himself died in battle in the service of Louis XIV in 1693.

guaranteed many rights and privileges, including the freedom to practise their religion. Ratification of the treaty by the Irish Parliament was, however, only partial and the Penal Laws enacted from 1695 were seen by Roman Catholics as a betrayal.

18C to 20C – Despite considerable agrarian revolt in the region in the 18C, the City Corporation decided that Limerick no longer needed to be fortified and in 1760 most of the city walls were demolished. The 18C was also marked by the last flowering of the old Irish culture; after the Great Famine of the 1840s and subsequent emigration, Gaelic ceased to be the vernacular language of Limerick.

In the early 20C, Limerick and its county were strongholds of nationalism and of working-class radicalism. Three of the leaders of the 1916 Easter Rising came from the Limerick district; most famous was **Eamon de Valera** (1882-1975), later Prime Minister *(Taoiseach)* and then President of the Republic. In 1919, at the start of the three-year War of Independence, a general strike took place in Limerick in protest against British military rule, and a soviet was set up in the city.

> **LIMERICK LACE**
>
> The craft was introduced to Limerick in the 1820s by English lace makers and reached its peak in the 19C when 900 girls were employed locally. The elaborate Celtic patterns were outlined on machine-made cotton net in thin or thick thread and filled in with decorative stitches

Walking About

As King's Island was almost encircled by the Shannon and its tributary, the Abbey River, it was easily defended and an obvious site for the Vikings and Normans to establish their settlements. The street layout and some of the buildings recall the area's medieval origins.

The **County Court House** was built in 1809 to replace its 18C predecessor.

Walk up Bridge Street and turn left into Nicholas Street.

St Mary's Cathedral★

Open summer, Mon-Sat, 9.30am-5pm; otherwise by appointment. Donation €2. Leaflet (4 languages). ☎ 061 310 293; Fax 061 315 721; www.limerick.anglican.org

The Anglican cathedral, founded in 1168 by Dónall Mór O'Brien, King of Munster, is the oldest surviving building in Limerick. Parts of the king's palace were incorporated in the original cruciform church, which was built in the transitional Romanesque style; the west doorway may have been the palace entrance.

The black oak choir stalls and their splendidly carved misericords in the Jebb Chapel, both dating from the 15C, are the only surviving examples of their kind in Ireland. The reredos of the high altar was carved by the English father of Patrick Pearse. The north transept contains fine 15C carvings on the **Arthur Memorial** *(below the window)*, which commemorates Geoffrey Arthur (d 1519), the cathedral Treasurer, and a small rectangular lepers' squint *(right)*. In the south transept is the 15C Galway-Bultingfort tomb.

Continue along Nicholas Street. All that remains of the **Old Limerick Exchange** *(see Limerick Museum)*, built in 1673, is seven Tuscan columns, bricked up to form a wall.

Turn left into a side street.

The **Corporation Almshouses**, also known as the 40-shilling (£2) Almshouses or the Widows' Almshouses, were built for the use of 20 widows by Limerick Corporation in 1691.

Cross Castle Street.

The **Bishop's Palace**, the oldest-surviving dwelling in Limerick, was designed in the Palladian style by Francis Bindon (c 1690-1765), a native of Limerick. It now houses the Limerick Civic Trust. *Open Mon-Fri, 10am-4pm. ☎ 061 313 399 (Limerick Civic Trust); Fax 061 315 513; denismleonard@ireland.com*

Continue along Castle Street.

The **Villiers Almshouses**, designed by James Pain to form three sides of a courtyard and built in the Bishop's garden, were founded in 1826 for 12 poor Protestant widows, each to receive £24 per annum.

Return down Castle Street to Thomond Bridge.

The **Toll House**, a Gothic-style building with castellated parapets by the eastern bridgefoot, dates from 1839 when the Thomond Bridge was rebuilt.

Cross Thomond Bridge.

The **Treaty Stone**, a block of limestone on which the 1691 Treaty of Limerick *(see above)* was said to have been signed, was mounted on a pedestal and moved here in 1865. It used to stand on the opposite side of the road, in front of the Black Bull public house, where it was used as a mounting-block and despoiled by souvenir hunters.

Continue S along Clancy's Street and cross Sarsfield Bridge. Turn right into Henry Street.

Franciscan Church

It is difficult to obtain a full perspective of the impressive Corinthian portico owing to the narrowness of the street. The apse is lined with multi-coloured marble and mosaic work; the surrounding niches contain representations of many of the saints of the order; the shrine of St Anthony is a miniature of the chancel.

At the next junction turn left and then right into O'Connell Street and walk south to the Crescent.

The old Irish town which grew up on the south bank of Abbey River, outside the walls of the English town, now forms the centre of modern Limerick. Its extension to the south – a fine example of 18C town planning composed of broad parallel streets lined with **red-brick terraces** – was named **Newtown Pery** after Edmond Sexton Pery (1719-1806), Speaker of the Irish House of Commons from 1771 to 1785.

From the Crescent turn left into Barrington Street and left into Pery Square.

Overlooking the green space of People's Park are the **Georgian House** and **Limerick City Gallery of Art** *(see Worth a Visit).*

Walk to the end of Pery Square.

St Saviour's Dominican Church

The 17C statue of Our Lady of Limerick, brought from Flanders in 1640, was presented to the Dominicans as a mark of atonement by a Limerick merchant, whose uncle had sentenced Sir John Burke to death for allowing a priest to say Mass in his house during a time of severe religious persecution. The Kilmallock chalice dates from 1649. The Stations of the Cross and the fresco over the chancel arch were painted by Fr Aengus Buckley, a local priest in the Dominican order.

From Pery Square turn right into Davis Street, left into Parnell Street and bear right into Gerald Griffin Street.

John Square★, started in 1751, is bordered on three sides by terraces of three-storey houses, plain limestone buildings with shouldered architraves above the main doorways and plain architraves surrounding the red-brick niches. Originally the houses were occupied by the wealthy citizens of Limerick; now restored, they are mainly used by the legal and medical professions.

The fourth side of the square is closed by **St John's Church** (deconsecrated), built of limestone in 1843.

St John's Cathedral★

Cathedral Place, off the south side of John Square. & Open daily, 9am-6pm (8pm Sat-Sun). Brochure (6 languages). Guided tour available. Parking. ☎ 061 414 624; Fax 061 316 570; stjohnsparishlk@tinet.ie

The Roman Catholic cathedral on the southern fringe of what was the old Irish town was built in the neo-Gothic style in 1861. The spire (280ft/85m), completed in 1883, is the tallest in Ireland.

17C Italian mould-blown emerald green glass jug with gilt metal mounts, Hunt Museum

Worth a Visit

Hunt Museum★★

& Open Mon-Sat, 10am-5pm, Sun, 2-5pm. €5.70. Visitor guide (5 languages). Guided tour (1hr; book for foreign languages). Shop. Restaurant. ☎ 061 312 833; Fax 061 312 834; info@ huntmuseum.com; www.ul.ie/~hunt

The 18C Custom House designed by Italian architect Davis Duchart provides a fitting home for this outstanding collection of art and antiquities, the life's work of John and Gertrude Hunt, acknowledged experts in the field of medieval and religious art. The exhibits are sensitively displayed so that visitors may explore the collection and get to know something of the lives of this remarkable couple. The items span every age and include works of every scale, from the immense to the miniature. Highlights include the wooden carved *Apollo – Genius of the Arts*, a small bronze *Horse*, attributed to Leonardo da Vinci, and a startling self-portrait by Robert Fagan (c 1745-1816), a painter of the English school and dealer in antiquities in Rome. The archaeological collection embraces, the ancient civilisations of

Egypt, Greece and Rome, together with Irish treasures such as the Cashel Bell *(see p 162)* and Antrim Cross and a Jewellery Gallery where the Mary Queen of Scots Cross is exhibited. Religious art is dramatically displayed in the Treasury; here among the gleam of silver and precious stones is a Greek coin, traditionally thought to be one of the "Thirty Pieces of Silver".

Georgian House★

2 Pery Square. Open Mon-Fri, 10am-4pm (last admission), Sat-Sun by appointment. House and garden €2.54; Ashes exhibition €2.54; combined ticket €4.44. ☎ 061 314130; Fax 353 61 310130; georgianhouse@eircom.net

The terrace of six Georgian town houses facing People's Park, the focal point of the Newtown Pery district, was built by the Pery Tontine Company in 1838. One of the houses has been restored as a splendid example of Georgian architecture and decor; a unique feature is the basement mezzanine floor. The garden also has been faithfully recreated. The **Ashes Exhibition** in the coach house at the rear reflects the filming of the immensely popular novel *Angela's Ashes* by Frank McCourt and the wretched life led by the poor in the Limerick of his childhood.

King John's Castle★

(&) Open Jul-Aug, daily, 9am-6pm; Apr-Jun and Sep-Oct, daily, 9.30am-5.30pm; Nov-Mar, 10.30am-4.30pm; last admission 1hr before closing; subject to change; check by telephone. €6.65. Audio-visual show (20min). Audioguide and brochure (5 languages). Parking. Coffee shop. ☎ 061 411 201 (Castle), 061 360 788 (Shannon Heritage central reservations); Fax 061 361 020; reservations@shannon-dev.ie; www.shannonheritage.com

The castle on the east bank of the River Shannon guarding Thomond Bridge, is a fine example of a medieval fortification, a reflection of its role as the most important Norman stronghold in the west. The history of the castle and the city is traced through multi-media displays, including an audio-visual presentation, in the modern **Visitor Centre**, which is supported on piles to reveal the archaeological excavations below – pre-Norman fortifications and three houses.

The castle was built between 1200 and 1216 without a keep; massive round towers reinforce the gateway and the curtain walls, which were higher in those days to withstand the contemporary siege machines. In the 17C a diamond-shaped gun bastion (1611) was built at the southeast corner, and the other towers and the wall-walks were lowered to accommodate cannon. The repairs carried out after the structure was bombarded by General Ginkel in 1691 can still be seen from Thomond Bridge. In the mid-18C barracks, now demolished, were built within the castle walls, and c 1793 the east wall and part of the southeast bastion were dismantled to enlarge the parade ground.

In the courtyard are reproductions of war engines – mangonel, trebuchet and battering-ram. The sentry walk on the battlements between the Gate Tower and the Northwest Tower provides good views of the Shannon, the city and its surroundings.

Limerick Museum★

& Open Tue-Sat, 10am-1pm and 2.15-5pm. Closed Bank Hols. Parking. ☎ 061 417 826; Fax 061 415 266; lwalsh@limerickcity.ie; www.limerickcity.ie

The museum, named after Jim Kemmy TD *(see p 226)*, gives a comprehensive account of the city and its history, with particular emphasis on the later 19C and early 20C. An extensive collection of 18C silverware recalls a once-flourishing

King John's Castle

H Champollion/MICHELIN

Limerick craft. Limerick **lace** was of great delicacy and examples on show here include tambour, needlepoint and tape lace. The **Nail** from the Old Exchange *(see below)*, on which commercial transactions were settled, is made of limestone with a brass top; "paying on the Nail" was a common feature of English trading centres. Finds from excavations in the Abbey River are displayed on the upper floor.

Limerick City Gallery of Art

Pery Square. & Open daily, 10am-6pm (7pm Thu; 1pm Sat). Closed at Christmas, 1 Jan. ☎ 061 310 633; Fax 061 310 228; www.limerickcorp.ie

This two-storey building, once the Carnegie Library, now houses a permanent collection of leading Irish artists, such as Sean Keating, Jack B Yeats and Evie Hone. There are frequent visiting exhibitions.

Excursions

Cratloe Woods House

5mi/8km W by N 18 (&) Open Jun to mid-Sep, Mon Sat, 2-6pm; otherwise by appointment. Guided tour. €3.50. Tearoom. ☎ 061 327 028; Fax 327 031

A red gate-lodge marks the entrance to the estate, which provided the oak timber for the roof of Westminster Hall in London.

The house (1600) is a rare example of the Irish long house *(see p 108)*, *albeit later altered.* The interior displays furniture and fascinating souvenirs of the owners, direct descendants of Brian Ború and the O'Briens, the leading family of the region.

Cratloe Wood on the north side of the road covering the lower slopes of Woodcock Hill incorporates a lake and forest walks and a fine **view★** of the Shannon Estuary from the car park *(0.75mi/1.2km from the entrance).*

Bunratty Castle★★

7mi/11km W by N 18. & Open Jun-Aug, daily, 9am-6.30pm; Sep-May, daily, 9.30am-5.30pm; last admission 1hr before closing, subject to change; check by telephone. Closed Good Fri, 24-26 Dec. Castle and Folk Park €9.50; Folk Park €6.35 (after 4pm). Guided tour of castle available. Visitor map (8 languages). Brochure (4 languages). Medieval banquets: daily, 5.30pm and 8.45pm; €45.50. Medieval banquet with traditional Irish stories, music and song: Apr-Oct, daily at 7pm (subject to demand); €38. Parking. Refreshments. ☎ 061 360 788 (Shannon Heritage central reservations). Fax 061 361 020; reservations@shannondev.ie; www.shannonheritage.com

A formidable presence commanding the main road between Limerick and Ennis, this is perhaps the most splendid **tower house** in Ireland. Built in 1460 by the powerful O'Brien family, it stands on the site of earlier fortifications on the banks of the Bunratty River where it flows into the Shannon Estuary. It was restored in the 1950s to its 16C state and now displays the superb Gort collection of furniture and tapestries dating from the 14C to the 17C. In the evenings medieval-style banquets are held in the Great Hall which has a fine **oak roof**.

The **Folk Park** is a wonderful and very convincing re-creation of country life in Ireland at the turn of the 19C/20C when the old agricultural practices were giving way to the modern era. Some of the buildings in the park were transferred from their original sites and some are replicas: the blacksmith's forge, complete with bellows and iron-working tools; the flour mill with its river-driven horizontal wheel; the houses of many regional types including the mountain farmhouse with its settle bed and flagstone floor, and the more elaborate thatched Golden Vale farmhouse.

The **village** contains typical 19C shops, such as a pawnshop, a pub, a post office, a hardware shop, a grocery store, a draper's shop and a printer's workshop complete with hand-set type and a hand-operated printing press.

Bunratty House, built in 1804, is a local adaptation of the Georgian box house so common in Ireland. The **Talbot Collection of agricultural machinery** is displayed in the farmyard.

Tours

MAIGUE VALLEY

From Limerick take R 512 S; after 8.5mi/13.6km bear left.

Lough Gur Interpretive Centre★

& Open May-Sep, daily, 10am-6pm; subject to change; check by telephone. €4. Audioguide. Parking. Refreshments. ☎ 061 385 186 (site), ☎ 061 360 788 (Shannon Heritage central reservations); Fax 061 361 020; reservations@shannon-dev.ie; www.shannonheritage.com

Set among low hills, horseshoe-shaped Lough Gur is the largest water body in Co Limerick. The area around the lake is one of the longest-inhabited districts in Ireland, with an exceptional wealth of stone circles, standing stones, burial chambers and cairns; excavations have contributed much valuable information about life in the Stone Age. Many Stone Age and Bronze Age relics, as well as models of stone circles and burial chambers, are on display in the thatched hut housing the **visitor centre**, which also provides an audio-visual film illustrating the life of Neolithic people in this region.

Return to T-junction; turn left into R 512; continue S via Holycross and Bruff.

Kilmallock★

Its nucleus an abbey founded by St Mocheallog in the 7C, Kilmallock was the seat of the Fitzgeralds and one of the most important towns in the province of Munster, with town walls, a castle and four gates. In 1568 it was burnt down to prevent it from being taken by the English; a century later, after Cromwell's departure, its extensive walls had gone and many of its buildings lay in ruins; it suffered again in the Williamite wars and never regained its former status.

By the little River Loobagh stand the ruins of **Kilmallock Abbey★**, a 13C Dominican foundation. A fine transept window survives; the tower (90ft/27m high) is gracefully supported by narrow arches but a substantial part of one corner has collapsed. At the entrance to the abbey is a small town **museum**. *Open Mon-Sat, 2-5pm. Donation.* ☎ *063 98259*

In the 13C **Collegiate Church★** (Roman Catholic), dedicated to St Peter and St Paul, the walls and arches of the nave and south transept are largely intact; the tower is part of an ancient round tower.

A substantial portion of the **Town Walls** survives intact between Blossom's Gate and the vicinity of the Collegiate Church.

KILMALLOCK'S POET

In the 18C a rustic school of Gaelic poetry flourished along the banks of the River Maigue and its tributary the Loobagh. One of its number, Aindrias Mac Craith, was a hedge schoolmaster and a versatile versifier, in English as well as Gaelic. Mac Craith died in 1795 in the 15C house next to the bridge in Kilmallock and he is buried in the graveyard of the Collegiate Church. It is possible that he was jointly responsible for the invention of the limerick; in playful poetic conflict with a fellow-poet and tavern-keeper, one Seán Ó Tuama, he wrote

> O'Toomey! You boast yourself handy
> At selling good ale and brandy,
> But the fact is your liquor
> Makes everyone sicker
> I tell you that, I, your friend Andy.

Blossom's Gate, spanning the entrance to the town from the west, is the sole survivor of the five gates, which pierced the walls of the medieval town.

The **King's Castle**, a 15C tower house, occupies the site of an earlier fortress built to guard the Loobagh valley. During the Parliamentary Wars (1645-51) it was used as an arsenal by the Irish and later as a hospital by the Cromwellians.

From Kilmallock take R 518 west to Bruree.

De Valera Museum

Bruree. ♿ *Open daily, 10am (2pm Sat-Sun) to 5pm. €4. Audio-visual show (20min). Parking. Picnic area.* ☎ *063 90 900*

The museum and heritage centre, which celebrates the former President of the Republic, is housed in the old national school in **Bruree** between the ancient six-arch bridge over the River Maigue and the old mill with its perfectly preserved mill wheel. On display are De Valera's school copy-books and his desk with his initials carved into the top. De Valera walked to school from the **cottage** where he lived with his uncle (1.5mi/2.4km N on the road to Athlacca).

From Bruree take the minor road north; in Athlacca bear left to Croom.

EAMON DE VALERA

Eamon de Valera (1882-1975) was born in New York to a Spanish father and Irish mother but was largely brought up by his uncle near Kilmallock. De Valera suffered imprisonment, more than once by the British, who only refrained from executing him after the 1916 Rising because of his American birth, then by the Free State authorities after he had taken the Republican side in the Civil War. He founded the Fianna Fáil party in 1926, became Prime Minister (*Taoiseach*) in 1932, and kept Ireland neutral in the Second World War. Between 1959 and 1973 he served as President of the Republic. Steadfastly nationalist in political outlook, he was very conservative in his personal vision of how Irish society should develop, declaring: "Whenever I wanted to know what the Irish people wanted I had only to examine my own heart".

Croom Mills

Open daily, 9am-6pm (later in summer). Parking. Restaurant. ☎ *061 397 130; Fax 061 397 199 (Mary Hayes); croommills@eircom.net; www.croommills.com*
The watermill built by Denis Lyons in 1788 on the River Maigue now has hands-on exhibits, giving visitors experience of how its machinery worked, an exhibition and an audio-visual presentation. The restaurants have an attractive view over the mill race which drives the nearby waterwheel.

From Croom take the minor road east to Monaster.

> **"CROM ABU"**
> The battle cry of the Earls of Kildare derives from their castle at Croom on the River Maigue.

Monasteranenagh Abbey★

The impressive ruins, parts of which survive to roof level, lie beside the River Camoge. The Cistercian monastery, colonised by monks from Mellifont, was founded in the 12C by Turlough O'Brien, King of Thomond, as a mark of thanksgiving for defeating the Danes in the Battle of Rathmore in 1148.

Lismore★

No bigger than a village but a designated Heritage town, this idyllic little place on the banks of the salmon-rich River Blackwater was once a great centre of medieval learning. It still has a cathedral, but the dominant edifice is the romantically rebuilt castle overlooking the lovely wooded valley.

Location

Population 715 - Michelin Atlas p 79 and Map 712 – I 11 – Co Waterford.
Lismore *(Lios Mór)* is on the south bank of the River Blackwater on N 72 between Dungarvan and Fermoy.
🛈 *Lismore Heritage Centre, Lismore. Open seasonally.* ☎ *058 54975*
Adjacent Sights: See CAHER, CLONMEL, COBH, CORK, MALLOW, MIDLETON, YOUGHAL.

Background

The monastery founded by **St Carthach** in the 7C became one of Europe's most distinguished universities. In its heyday, Lismore had no fewer than 20 seats of learning and religion within its walls but in 978 the Danish Vikings raided the town and burned the monasteries. Nevertheless, the place was still sufficiently important for Henry II to receive the submission of Irish chiefs here soon after his landing in Ireland in 1171. A prosperous town grew up around the castle built by King John in 1185, which in 1589 passed into the hands of Sir Walter Ralegh, who sold it to Richard Boyle, the "Great" Earl of Cork. Like most of the town, it was destroyed by Cromwellian forces.

The castle was eventually rebuilt in the mid-19C in spectacular style by Sir Joseph Paxton, designer of the Crystal Palace in London and gardener to the Duke of Devonshire, the new owner of the castle. It rises dramatically, a magnificent neo-Tudor fantasy, over the park-like valley of the River Blackwater and its elegant bridge by the Dublin architect Thomas Ivory. In the mid-20C this lovely setting was enjoyed by Adele Astaire, sister of the great dancer and movie star, who had married the castle's then proprietor, Lord Charles Cavendish.

Worth a Visit

Lismore Castle Gardens★

Open late-Mar to Oct, daily, 1.45pm (11am Jul-Aug) to 4.45pm. €4. Leaflet (2 languages). ☎ *058 54424; Fax 058 54896; lismoreestates@eircom.net; www.lismorecastle.com*
The gardens, where Spenser is said to have composed part of *The Faerie Queene*, straddle the Riding Gate entrance to the castle *(not open to the public)*. The lower garden, known as the Pleasure Grounds, dates from c 1850 although the Yew Walk is much earlier; it is at its best in spring – camellias, rhododendrons and magnolias. The terraced upper garden was laid out in the 17C. The central grass walk is aligned on the spire of the cathedral, and flowers and vegetables grow in the plots screened by yew, beech and box hedges. Against the north wall are greenhouses (1858) designed by Paxton. The Broghill Tower *(SW corner)* provides a fine view.

St Carthage's Cathedral (Anglican)★

Open daily, 9am-6pm (4pm Oct-Mar). Information board (8 languages). Parking. ☎ *058 54137*

The present structure, now Lismore's parish church, is the successor to three previous edifices, and dates largely from a rebuilding ordered by Sir Richard Boyle in 1633, though the **ribbed ceilings** were built by Sir Richard Morrison about 1820 and the fine **tower** and **ribbed spire** were added in 1826 by the Payne brothers of Cork. Set in a charming graveyard shaded by yews and lime trees, it is a lovely building, somehow redolent of Lismore's long history. At the west end are fragments of 9C tombstones, and there is an enormous and elaborate **table-tomb** of 1548. Sir Edward Burne-Jones contributed the fine stained-glass window in the south transept, and pebbles from the Isle of Iona in Scotland are set into the floor of St Columba's Chapel.

St Carthach's Church (Roman Catholic)

Open daily, 9.30am-8pm (5pm winter). ☎ *058 54246*

Designed by WG Doolin in 1881, this is one of the most outstanding Lombardo-Romanesque churches in Ireland, richly detailed and built of red sandstone with white limestone dressings and a detached bell tower.

Facing the west entrance to the church is a fine row of 19C artisans' cottages.

Lismore Heritage Centre

Open Mar-Oct, daily, 9.30am-5.30pm; Nov-Feb, Mon-Fri, 9.30am-5.30pm. €4. Audio-visual show (30min) and brochure (4 languages). ☎ *058 54975; Fax 058 53009; lismoreheritage@eircom.net; lismore-ireland.com*

The Old Courthouse uses models and an audio-visual presentation to provide an introduction to the history of Lismore and the life and works of Robert Boyle, the father of modern chemistry, who was born in Lismore Castle.

Excursions

The Gap★

10mi/16km N by R 688. A splendid backdrop to the Blackwater valley, the Old Red Sandstone Knockmealdown Mountains rise to a peaty summit of 2 608ft/795m. The Lismore-Caher road runs through the lush valley landscape before climbing open slopes to the scenic V Gap with its magnificent **views★**. On the north slopes of Sugar Loaf mountain (2 144ft/653m) stands **Grubb's Grave**, the burial cairn of Samuel Grubb, a local Quaker who died in the 1920s. The sugar-loaf construction enabled him to be buried upright overlooking his estates.

Mount Melleray Abbey

8mi/13km NE by N 72, R 669 and a minor road right. Open 7.15am-8pm. ☎ *058 54404; Fax 058 52140; mountmellerayabbey@eircom.net*

This Cistercian monastery stands in an open setting on the lower slopes of the Knockmealdowns with fine views over the Blackwater valley to the south. It was founded in 1832 for Irish monks from Melleray in France; the community is devoted to prayer and pursues numerous crafts. Only part of the church, built in the early 20C in a somewhat anaemic neo-Gothic style, is open to the public.

Longford

The market centre for the surrounding agricultural area, Longford lies on the Camlin River amid the pleasant but undistinguished scenery of its county, a few miles from where the Shannon broadens out into Lough Ree.

Co Longford has important literary associations with Oliver Goldsmith (around Lough Ree) and with Maria Edgeworth (at Mostrim), and it was at Ballinamuck *(10mi/16km north)* that the last engagement of the 1798 rebellion *(see KILLALA)* was fought, when General Humbert's French troops and Irish volunteers were defeated by the English forces under General Lake.

DIRECTORY

Michael Casey – *Barley Harbour, Newtowncashel (13mi/21km SW by N 63, R 397 and R 398)* – Artist in bogwoods, tree roots uncovered during peat-harvesting; several of his works stand round the village green in Newtown Cashel on the east bank of Lough Ree.

Location

Population 6 393 - Michelin Atlas p 91 and Map 712 – I 6 – Co Longford.
Longford *(An Longfort)* is situated on the main road (N 4) linking Dublin and Sligo.
🛈 *Market Square, Longford. Open May, Mon-Fri; Jun-Sep, Mon-Sat.* ☎ *043 46566*
Adjacent Sights: See ATHLONE, CARRICK-ON-SHANNON, MULLINGAR, STROKES-TOWN.

Worth a visit

St Mel's Cathedral

Dublin Street. ♿ *Open daily, 7.45am-8pm (9pm Sat, 6pm Sun). Parking.* ☎ *043 46465*
Longford's otherwise modest townscape is enhanced by its monumental Roman Catholic cathedral in neo-Classical style. Designed by John Keane in 1840, it has a vast Ionic portico with a richly sculpted pediment and is dominated by a tall octagonal bell tower crowned by a dome. Construction was interrupted by the Famine and the cathedral was completed only at the end of the 19C. The interior is supported on a double row of Ionic columns

The greatest treasure of the **Diocesan Museum** *(right transept)* is **St Mel's Crozier** (10C), a stick of yew encased in bronze, inset with studs and decorated with animal motifs, foliage and interlacing; it was found at old St Mel's Church in Ardagh *(see below)* in 1860 and may originally have consisted of four sections. *Open Jun-Sep, Mon, Wed and Fri, 11am-2pm; Sat-Sun, 2-4.30pm.* ☎ *043 46465*

> **MARIA EDGEWORTH (1767-1849)**
>
> She is best known for her novels on Irish life – *Castle Rackrent* (1800), *The Absentee* (1812) and *Ormond* (1817) – in which she developed the regional and historical novel; she also wrote English novels and stories for children. In her day her influence was acknowledged by Jane Austen, Macaulay, Ruskin, Thackeray, Turgenev and Sir Walter Scott, who described her as "the great Maria" and visited her in 1825. Apart from some time in England at school, she lived all her life (1767-1849) at the family home in Mostrim, also known as Edgeworthstown *(8.5mi/14km E)*, where her circle included the Pakenhams of Tullynally and the Lefroys of Carrigglas. She was the eldest daughter of Richard Lovell Edgeworth; as well as marrying four times and producing 22 children, this wealthy but eccentric landlord was a prolific inventor, who installed a central heating system at Tullynally *(see p 327)*.

Excursions

Carrigglas Manor

3mi/5km E of Longford by R 194.♿ *Open May-Sep, Mon-Tue and Fri-Sat, 11am-3pm. Guided tour of house (45 min; 2 languages) at noon, 1pm, 2pm. Gardens and Costume/Lace Museum €5; House additional €3.80. Parking Tearoom.* ☎ *043 45165, Fax 043 42882; info@carrigglas.com; www.carrigglas.com*
This castellated Gothick mansion was designed in 1837 for Thomas Lefroy, Lord Chief Justice of Ireland and youthful admirer of Jane Austen, who may have used him as the model for Mr Darcy in *Pride and Prejudice*.
The outstanding feature of the interior (restored) is the **corniced and moulded ceilings** in the reception rooms. The house contains some fine early Dutch furniture, artefacts and pictures including many portraits of the Lefroy family, who are still in residence.
The **Costume Museum** *(stable buildings)* displays costumes worn by past generations of Lefroys and a collection of **lace**, some made by the ladies of Carrigglas.
The magnificent **double stable and farmyard** *(restoration in progress)* was designed by James Gandon in 1790; the stable yard is enclosed by four ranges of two storeys, with pedimented and rusticated arches, adjoining the farmyard where the lower storey is gradually absorbed into the rising ground.
The woodland garden with its rich and varied plant collection was inspired by the great Victorian designer, William Robinson.

Ardagh

7mi/11km SE of Longford by N 4 and R 393. The charming little estate village was largely rebuilt in the 1860s by Lady Fetherstone, who lived at Ardagh House.
The ruins of a simple stone church, St Mel's Cathedral, are said to stand on the site where the saint, a nephew of St Patrick, was buried.
The **Ardagh Heritage Centre** in the old schoolhouse traces the history of the locality from the pre-Christian era of folk tales, through the arrival of Christianity, the internal rivalries of the local O'Farrell tribe and the 1619 Plantation to the present. *Open daily, 9am-6pm (9pm Sun). €2. Video (15min). Restaurant.* ☎ *043 75277; Fax 043 75278; www.goireland.com*

Corlea Trackway

Corlea Trackway

10mi/16km S of Longford by N 63 and R 397; in Keen turn right (sign). (Dúchas) ♿ *Guided tour Apr-Sep, daily, 10am-6pm (5.15pm last admission). €3.10. Audio-visual show (20min). Parking. Tearoom (open Jun-Sep); picnic area.* ☎ *043 22386; Fax 043 22442*

The ancient trackway *(togher)*, discovered in the 1980s, dates from 147-8 BC. It consisted of oak planks secured by pegs and was wide enough to carry wheeled vehicles for the transport of animals and personal effects across the bog, although it lasted for only about 10 years as its weight caused it to sink below the surface. A section of it has been preserved and relaid under cover on its original site. Its excavation by an international team of archaeologists and its preservation are described in an audio-visual film; it is set in its Iron Age context by the accompanying exhibition.

GOLDSMITH COUNTRY

The country around Lough Ree is where Oliver Goldsmith (c 1731-74), poet, playwright, historian and naturalist, spent the first 20 or so years of his life, visiting relatives and going to school in Elphin, Mostrim, Athlone and Lissoy.

The road from Ardagh to Athlone (N 55) links a number of sites connected with his life and work.

In **Ardagh** he himself experienced the plot of his play *She Stoops to Conquer*, by mistaking the big house for the village inn.

The site of his first boyhood home at **Pallas** is marked by a statue by Foley.

Until 1731 Goldsmith's father was Rector of **Forgney** church, which contains a stained-glass window depicting "sweet Auburn".

After her husband's death in 1747, Goldsmith's mother lived in **Ballymahon** on the Inny River.

It was in **Tang** that Goldsmith first went to school near the mill.

The pub, known as **The Three Jolly Pigeons**, preserves the name of the inn in Goldsmith's play *She Stoops to Conquer*.

Lissoy Parsonage, now in ruins, was the house where the Goldsmith family lived from 1731 to 1747; **Lissoy** village is recalled as "sweet Auburn" in his poem *The Deserted Village*.

Mallow★

A busy crossroads and market town, Mallow is attractively sited above the River Blackwater, sometimes described as the "Irish Rhine". It is a historic place, still with faint traces of the atmosphere of the glory days when it was the foremost spa in Ireland, frequented by the notorious "Rakes of Mallow", who today would no doubt be keen patrons of the nearby racecourse.

Location

Population 6 434 - Michelin Atlas p 78 and Map 712 – G 11 – Co Cork.
Mallow *(Mala)* is on N 20 between Cork and Limerick at the junction with N 72, the Dungarvan to Killarney road.
Adjacent Sights: See COBH, CORK, LISMORE, MIDLETON.

A RAKISH RESORT

The curative properties of Mallow water – ranging in temperature from 66°F to 72°F and supposedly efficacious in purifying the blood – were discovered in 1724. The town soon became a popular spa with a fast reputation; its male patrons infamous as the **Rakes of Mallow**.

> *living short but merry lives,*
> *Going where the devil drives,*
> *Having sweethearts, but no wives...*

During the season, which lasted from April to October, visitors would take the waters before breakfast and during the afternoon; the evenings were spent in dancing and playing cards. Balls, music meetings and other diversions were held in the Long Room in emulation of the entertainment available in Bath, Tunbridge Wells and Scarborough. By 1828, when the Spa House was built in the Tudor style with a pump-room, a reading room and baths, the popularity of Mallow was in decline.

Background

Mallow had an Anglo-Norman castle, built towards the end of the 12C, perhaps by King John. Four hundred years later, after becoming the seat of Sir John Norreys, Lord President of Munster, it was replaced by a fine mansion, now ruined.

In the early 19C the spa declined and the town became a centre of considerable nationalistic political activity, helped by the fact that the Protestant patriot and unchallenged leader of the Young Ireland movement, **Thomas Davis** (1814-45), was born *(73 Main Street)* and brought up here. Another noted nationalist and MP was **William O'Brien** (1852-1928), who was born in what is now known as William O'Brien's House *(Bank Place, Main Street)*; he wrote the quotation – "Ireland has not in our time lost a more able or unselfish young patriot" – which is inscribed on the statue of JJ Fitzgerald (1872-1906) who was described as a scholar, patriot and champion of all oppressed.

Mallow has literary connections with **Anthony Trollope**, a resident for some years *(Davis Street – see p 141)*; with **Canon Patrick Sheehan**, one of Ireland's most prolific and popular authors in the late 19C and early 20C, who was born here in 1852 *(29 O'Brien Street)* and whose statue stands in Doneraile where he was parish priest from 1895 to 1913; and with Elizabeth Bowen.

ELIZABETH BOWEN (1899-1973)

For the first seven years of her life, Elizabeth Bowen used to spend the winter in Dublin, where she was born, and the summer at Bowen's Court (demolished), the family seat, built by Henry Bowen c 1775 near Kildorrery *(12mi/19km NE of Mallow)*. Although she spent her later childhood and married life in England, she entertained many guests at Bowen's Court during the summer months until 1959 when the expense of maintaining such a large house obliged her to sell. She is buried beside her husband in the graveyard of Farahy Church at the entrance to Bowen's Court on the western edge of Kildorrery.

She wrote of her early childhood days in *Seven Winters* (1942) and told her family history in *Bowen's Court* (1942). In *The Last September* (1929) she drew on her experience of country house life in Ireland. Her most widely read and best-known works are *The Death of the Heart* (1947) and *The Heat of the Day* (1949).

Walking About

Start at the junction of Main Street, Spa Walk and Bridge Street.
The **Clock House**, a four-storey timber-framed building with a clock tower, was built around 1855 by an amateur architect supposedly enthused by an Alpine holiday, and it certainly has something incongruously Swiss about it.
Walk along Spa Walk.

The **Spa House**, containing a pump-room, a reading room and baths, was erected in 1828 by Charles Jephson, in the Tudor style although its designer, George Pain, favoured a building in the classical style like a Greek temple. *Open Mon-Fri, 9am-1pm and 2-4.30pm.* ☎ *022 43610*

Return to the junction and walk along Main Street and turn left into St James's Avenue.

St James's Church★, Mallow's Anglican church, is a fine example of Gothic Revival architecture, built in 1824 by the English-born Pain brothers from Cork. It replaced the medieval church of St Anne's which had been badly damaged in the Williamite wars. In 1814 Thomas Davis was baptised in this older church, of which substantial ruins remain. *Open by appointment. Services: Sun, 11.30am.* ☎ *022 21473 (Rector)*

Return to the junction.

At the entrance to the demesne of **Mallow Castle** *(private)* stands the ruin of the mansion which replaced the earlier castle. The extensive grounds, including a deer park, extend to the River Blackwater with its impressive weir.

P. Thebault/MICHELIN

Church of the Resurrection, Mallow

Return to the junction, walk down Bridge Street, cross the river and turn right into Mill Street. The **Church of the Resurrection** (1966-69), designed by JR Boyd Barratt, is shaped like a fan focusing on the altar; the Stations of the Cross carved in Tyrolean oak and the vividly coloured stained glass is by the Murphy Davitt Studios of Dublin. *Open daily.* ☎ *022 21112*

Excursions

Buttevant Friary★

7mi/11km N of Mallow by N 20. The ruins of a Franciscan friary, built in 1251, stand beside the River Awbeg next to St Mary's Roman Catholic Church. The building, which was used until recently as a place of burial, has two crypts, one above the other; the chancel walls are still largely intact.

Doneraile Wildlife Park★

6mi/10km NE of Mallow by N 20 and R 581. (Dúchas) (&) Open mid-Apr to Oct,

> **STEEPLECHASING**
>
> The **steeplechase** had its origin in Ireland, when huntsmen set wagers with each other on who would be the first to reach a prominent landmark. The first such contest took place from Buttevant in 1752, with the steeple of the Anglican Church as the starting point of a race to St Leger Church near Doneraile (4.5mi/7km).

Mon-Sat, 8am (10am Sat) to 8.30pm, Sun and Bank Hols, 11am-7pm; Nov to mid-Apr, daily, 8am (10am Sat-Sun and Bank Hols) to 4.30pm. €1.20. Parking. Picnic areas. ☎ *022 24244; scrowley@ealga.ie*

The walled demesne (395 acres/160ha) is noted for its herds of red, fallow and sika deer. Clumps of trees in this rolling parkland are broken by ornamental lakes. Doneraile Court was built c 1700 and remodelled in its present form in the early 19C; its lawn is complemented by fine old larch trees.

A stone arched vault and spiral staircase are all that remains of **Kilcolman Castle**, once the residence of the English poet Edmund Spenser.

Annes Grove Gardens★

11mi/18km E of Mallow by N 72; in Castletownroche turn left onto the minor road. Open mid-Mar to Sep, daily, 10am (1pm Sun) to 5pm (6pm Sun); otherwise by appointment. €4. Leaflet and guided tour (3 languages). Parking. Picnic area. ☎ */Fax 022 26145; annesgrove@eircom.net*

The woodland gardens surrounding an 18C house and lawns overlooking the River Awbeg include a fine collection of rhododendrons and magnolias, as well as many rare trees and shrubs. Winding paths lead to the cliff garden overlooking the lily pond and the extensive river garden; in the walled garden with its 19C hedges there are herbaceous borders and water gardens.

Longueville House

3mi/5km W of Mallow by N 72; turn right at sign. This magnificent house (1720), now a hotel open to non-residents, features an imposing dual staircase. The interior is hung with political portraits, a virtual roll-call of the great men who influenced the course of Irish history from the 18C to the 20C.

In the courtyard at the back of the house there is a 150 year-old **maze**, the estate (500 acres/202ha) includes a **vineyard** (3 acres/1.2ha), the only one in Ireland; in a good year its grapes produce a Riesling-type wine.

Kanturk (Ceann Toirc)★

13mi/21km W of Mallow by N 72 and R 576. This small market town has three fascinating **bridges:** the six-arch humpback structure (1760) spanning the River Dalua; the nearby six-arch Greenane bridge (1745) over the River Allua; the four-arch Metal Bridge built in 1840 by Sir Edward Tierney over the River Dalua, at the western end of the town, near the Church of the Immaculate Conception built in the French Gothic style.

The **castle**★ ruin *(S by R 579)* is still substantial. According to legend, in about 1609 the local chieftain, MacDonagh MacCarthy, built the biggest mansion ever to belong to an Irish chief, the English Privy Council ordered the work to stop on the grounds that "it was much too large for a subject"; when MacCarthy heard the news, he was so enraged that he threw away the blue glass tiles destined for the roof.

Maynooth

The name of this town on the Royal Canal is almost synonymous with the great seminary which for more than two hundred years has educated priests for the Roman Catholic Church. For far longer Maynooth was the seat of the Fitzgeralds, descendants of a Norman-Welsh adventurer who arrived in Ireland in 1169, and who became one of the country's most powerful families. Today it is a growing commuter and university town, with rail and motor way connections to Dublin.

Location

Population 8 528 - Michelin Atlas p 93 and Map 712 – M 7 – Co Kildare.
Maynooth *(Maigh Nuad)*, only 15mi/24km from Dublin on the Grand Canal and formerly on one of the main roads radiating from the capital, is now bypassed by M 4.
Adjacent Sights: See DUBLIN, FINGAL, KILDARE, MULLINGAR, TRIM.

Worth a Visit

Maynooth Castle

At the west end of the broad main street stand the ruins of the 12C Fitzgerald castle, consisting of a massive keep surrounded by fragments of towers, walls and the entrance gate. At the height of the power of the Fitzgerald Earls of Kildare in the 15C and early 16C, it was effectively the political capital of Ireland. In 1535, following the Silken Thomas rebellion the previous year, it was successfully besieged by the royal forces and Thomas was led away to execution in London.

In 1656 the castle was abandoned in favour of a new residence at the east end of the main street; known as Carton House *(private)*, this structure was rebuilt by Richard Castle and Maynooth itself was extensively remodelled to provide a fit setting for the new Great House as well as accommodation for the army of estate workers. A fine avenue of limes links town and desmesne.

Maynooth College

The college, now part of the National University, is laid out around two spacious courtyards, the first dating from the early years of the 19C, the second, one of Pugin's finest Gothic Revival projects, completed in mid-century despite problems caused by the Great Famine and inadequate funding. Pugin's pupil, JJ McCarthy, designed the Chapel with its tall spire and splendid array of choir stalls carved in oak.

The college had a predecessor in the College of the Blessed Virgin Mary established by a Fitzgerald in 1518 but suppressed only 17 years later after town and castle had been taken by the royal forces. During the Penal period, Roman Catholic priests had to be educated abroad, but after the outbreak of the French Revolution, the situation changed; many Continental seminaries were suppressed and at the same time the government became anxious to propitiate local Catholic opinion by opening a seminary in Ireland. St Patrick's College was founded in 1795, some of its academic staff being refugee French priests. Since then it has educated more than 10 000 churchmen. Maynooth graduates served congregations throughout the British Empire, where Roman Catholics far outnumbered Protestants, and the college acquired a world-wide reputation, not least through missionary work in India, China and Africa.

The history of the college and of the town and district is presented in the **Visitor Centre**, which organises guided tours of the Chapel, Stoyte House, the Pugin building and the gardens. *Open May-Sep, Mon-Fri, 11am-5pm, Sat-Sun, 2-6pm. Guided tour.* ☎ *01 708 3576; Fax 01 628 9063*

Excursions

Castletown House★★

Celbridge; 4mi/6.4km SE of Maynooth by a minor road. (Dúchas) (&) Open Easter-Sep, daily, 10am (1pm Sat-Sun and Bank Hols) to 6pm; Oct, Sun-Fri, 10am (1pm Sun and Bank Hols) to 5pm; Nov, Sun, 1-5pm; last admission 1hr before closing. €3.80. No photography. Parking. Coffee shop. Lift to all floors ☎ 01 628 8252; Fax 01 627 1811; castletown@ealga.ie; www.heritageireland.ie

When built in 1722, this great Palladian mansion was the largest private house in Ireland, and helped set the fashion for the construction of similarly palatial residences throughout the country. Looking south over the Liffey valley to the Wicklow Mountains, it consists of a 13-bay central block by the Italian architect Alessandrio Galilei linked by curving colonnades to two pavilions designed by Sir Edward Lovett Pearce who supervised the construction work. The house was commissioned by William "Speaker" Conolly, reputedly the richest commoner in Ireland.

Long Gallery, Castletown House

House – Work on Castletown's sumptuous interiors went on for two generations. The original decorative scheme, using only local wood and stone, is preserved in the **Brown Study** with its coved ceiling, tall and narrow oak doors and pine panelling stained to resemble oak. In 1758, at the age of 15, Lady Louisa Lennox married into the family and her hand is evident almost everywhere. She employed the Lafranchini brothers to transform the staircase with their exuberant stuccowork, Sir William Chambers to remodel the ground-floor rooms in neo-Classical style, and decorated the **print room** with a selection of Old Master prints, which she had collected. The most magnificent room is the **Long Gallery**, with its Pompeian decor of vivid blue, red and green and its hand-blown chandeliers from Murano near Venice.

Castletown Follies – Closing the vista to the north of the house stands the extraordinary **Castletown Obelisk**, also known as the **Conolly Folly** *(visible from the windows of the Long Gallery and from the Maynooth–Castletown road)*; mounted on two tiers of arches, it was designed by Richard Castle and erected in memory of Speaker Conolly by his wife, in order to create employment during the severe winter of 1739.

The **Wonderful Barn** *(private)* which closes the northeast vista *(3mi/5km E by R 403 and R 404)* was built in 1743; it is a conical structure, with an external spiral staircase, containing four diminishing brick domes, used for drying and storing grain.

Steam Museum

5mi/8km S of Maynooth by R 406. (&) *Open Jun-Aug, Tue-Sun and Bank Hols, 2-5.30pm (last admission); Easter Sun to May and Sep, Sun and Bank Hols, 2.30-5pm (last admission). €4; garden only €3. Parking. Teahouse.* ☎ *01 627 3155; Fax 01 627 3477; info@steam-museum.ie; www.steam-museum.ie*

The Gothic Revival church in which the engineers of the old Great Southern & Western Railway used to worship has been removed from its original site among the workshops at Inchicore near Dublin and given a new vocation as a museum. Part of it is now the **Model Hall** with a fascinating collection of more than 20 fine models of locomotives from the late 18C onwards; part is the **Power Hall**, with an array of stately stationary engines which once provided power to mills, distilleries and breweries, as well as a triple-expansion marine engine from SS Divis of Belfast.

Coolcarrigan Gardens

10mi/16km SW of Maynooth by R 408 via Donadea to Timahoe; 1mi/1.6km S of Timahoe turn right (sign). Open by appointment Apr-Aug. €4. ☎ *045 863 512; Fax 01 834 1141*

The parkland laid out in the 19C has been much embellished by more recent planting of well-chosen **shrubs** and **trees**, all clearly labelled. Roses and herbaceous borders are arranged in the formal gardens near the handsome Victorian house. The **glasshouse** contains a vine, a passion flower, peaches and nectarines. At the end of the **woodland walk** *(30min)* through the forest there is a fine view across the Bog of Allen. The **church** (1881), which is surrounded by a moat and approached through a lych-gate, is in the Hiberno-Romanesque revival style and decorated with stained glass.

Midleton

Midleton is a pleasant-enough old market town set in the rich fertile plain of East Cork but the reason it attracts visitors from all over the world is the presence here of the distillery, where all the famous brands of Irish whiskey – except Bushmills *(see p 452)* – are produced.

Location

Population 3 266 - Michelin Atlas p 79 and Map 712 – H 12 – Co Cork.

Midleton *(Mainistir An Corann)* is situated on the main road (N 25) between Cork and Youghal.

🄱 *Jameson Heritage Centre, Midleton. Open Mar-Oct, daily.* ☎ *021 461 3702; user@cktourism.ie*

Adjacent Sights: See COBH, CORK, KINSALE, YOUGHAL.

Directory

SHOPPING

At the famous **Stephen Pearce Pottery** *(9mi/14.5km SE by R 630 and R 629)* visitors may watch the production process and buy the finished article.

SPORTS AND LEISURE

There are beaches and coves for bathing all along the coast south of Midleton from Roche's Point eastwards to Knockadoon Head.

Trabolgan recreation complex *(at Roche's Point)* offers an indoor swimming pool, plunge pool, sauna, solarium, fitness centre, tennis, 10-pin bowling and an indoor sports hall.

Sailing enthusiasts will find plenty of activity in Ballycotton Bay, at Roche's Point and in Cork Harbour.

Anglers may choose between shore and lake fishing.

For those who prefer dry land there are many golf courses and pleasant walks, particularly **forest walks** in **Rostellan Wood** on the shore of Cork Harbour in what was once the demesne of Rostellan House (demolished) *(6mi/9.7km SE by R 630)* and splendid **clifftop walks** from Roche's Point to Ballycotton overlooking Ballycotton Bay and the lighthouse on Ballycotton Island *(11mi/18km SE by R 630 and R 629)*.

Worth a Visit

Old Midleton Distillery

  Guided tour (60min) daily, 9am-6pm (4.30pm last tour); otherwise by appointment. €5.70. Guided tour and brochure (6 languages). Audio-visual show (15min). Tutored whiskey tasting in the bar. Parking. Restaurant. ☎ 0214 613 594; Fax 0214 613 642; dbyrne@idl.ie; www.whiskeytours.ie

The home of Jameson Irish Whiskey is a modern distillery built in 1975; it stands beside the original buildings, which were used as a woollen mill and barracks before becoming a distillery in 1825. The informative and entertaining tour begins with an audio-visual presentation on the history of the distillery and ends with a whiskey tasting. In between there is a guided tour of the old buildings and equipment – kiln where the malted barley was dried, five-storey storehouse where the grain was stored and turned, the waterwheel (1852) which operated five pairs of millstones, the **largest copper pot still** (1825) in the world (capacity 33 000 gallons/1 485hl), and the oak casks in which the spirit was matured to add tannin and vanillin for colour and taste.

SLIDE FILE, Dublin

Midleton Distillery

Excursions

Cloyne Cathedral★

5mi/8km S by R 630 and R 629. *Open May-Sep, daily, 10am-6pm; otherwise key available at the cottage. Donation. Guided tour by appointment. Service: Sun, noon. Parking.*
Three famous names are associated with the cathedral village of Cloyne. Christy King, the greatest ever hurler, is remembered by a more than life-size bronze statue, **George Berkeley** (1684-1753) was bishop of what was once a vast diocese,

and St Colman (522-604) founded a monastery here. Little is left of Colman's establishment, though a tiny edifice near the much restored 14C cathedral may be a reconstruction of his oratory and a 10C **round tower** (100ft/30m high) survives which can be climbed for a superb view. As well as being a highly regarded and original philosopher, Bishop Berkeley devoted himself to practical matters such as good farming practice and the benefits of drinking tar water. Though his attempt to found a college in America came to nothing, his line "Westward the course of empire takes its way" inspired the naming of Berkeley in California. There is a monument to him in his cathedral.

Barryscourt Castle

4mi/6.4km W by N 25 and R 624. Restoration in progress. (Dúchas) (&) Open Jun-Sep, daily, 10am-6pm; Oct-May, Fri-Wed, 11am-5pm; last admission 45min before closing. Closed 25-26 Dec. €1.90. Parking. Restaurant; tearoom. ✆ 021 488 2218, 021 488 3864 (Oct-May and Restaurant)

The ruined medieval castle, surrounded by a bawn, occupies a strategic site on the main route from Cork to Waterford. It takes its name from Philip de Barri of Manorbier in Wales, who established himself here c 1180 in the early days of Anglo-Norman Ireland. A more famous member of the De Barri family was **Gerald of Wales** (c 1146-1233), also known as Giraldus Cambrensis, who travelled in Ireland with Prince (later King) John and published accounts of the country and of its conquest by Henry II.

Monaghan

Monaghan is the commercial centre and the county town of Co Monaghan, which was part of the original province of Ulster and projects deep into Northern Ireland as far as the Blackwater River. Previously ruled by the McMahon clan, the area was settled by the British in the early 17C and the town was given its charter in 1613. Its mostly Scottish Presbyterian citizens established a thriving linen industry in the 18C; in the 19C the building of the Ulster Canal and the Ulster Railway brought further benefits, and the town still bears the imprint of these prosperous times, with dignified grey limestone buildings lining its narrow streets. Nowadays it is a popular angling centre.

Location

Population 5 628 - Michelin Atlas p 98 and Map 712 – L 5 – Co Monaghan.
Monaghan *(Muineachán)* is situated on N 2, one of the main roads north from Dublin, which runs close to the border before becoming the A 5 to Omagh.
🚹 *Market House, Monaghan. Open Apr-Oct, Mon-Sat. ✆ 047 81122*
Adjacent Sights: See CAVAN, ENNISKILLEN, NEWRY.

Walking About

Town Centre

The elegant **Market House** (1792), designed by Samuel Hayes, an amateur architect, in the local grey limestone with round-headed arches and decorative carved panels, now houses the Tourist Office.
Church Square *(E)* forms a dignified ensemble, with the **Courthouse** (1830), a handsome Classical building still bearing the scars of the Civil War, and **St Patrick's Anglican Church** (1831), a charming example of Regency Gothic style.
East of Church Square is the **Diamond**, the original market-place against the north wall of the 17C castle (demolished); the **Rossmore Memorial**, an elaborate neo-Gothic drinking fountain (1875) was erected to the 4th Baron Rossmore *(see below)*.
At the south end of Dublin Street stands the 17C **Market Cross** in the form of a sundial; the head is upside down and the indicators are missing.

> ### CHARLES GAVAN DUFFY (1816-1903)
> Duffy, who was born in Monaghan *(no 10 Dublin Street)*, became a journalist and co-founded *The Nation*. He worked through the Young Ireland movement to repeal the Act of Union, formed the Tenant Rights League and was elected as MP for New Ross. Disillusioned by the lack of response from Westminster, he emigrated to Australia where he became Prime Minister of the State of Victoria (1871) and worked for federation of the states.

Worth a Visit

St Macartan's Cathedral

Dublin Road. ᕼ *Open daily, 9am-6pm. Parking.* ☎ *047 82300; presbytery@eircom.net*
In a dominant position overlooking the town from the southeast stands the splendid Gothic Revival Roman Catholic cathedral, completed in 1892. Built from the local limestone and with a soaring spire (250ft/76m), it is one of the finest works of Ruskin's prolific pupil JJ McCarthy. The exterior is extravagantly decorated with Carrara marble statues of saints and bishops; the spacious interior spreads out beneath a splendid **hammerbeam roof** and has modern **tapestries** illustrating the Christian life and the life of St Macartan, one of the earliest Irish saints.

County Museum

Hill Street near the Tourist Office. (ᕼ) *Open Tue-Sat, 10am (11am Sat) to 1pm and 2-5pm. Closed Bank Hols.* ☎ *047 82928; Fax 047 71189; comuseum@monaghancoco.ie*
Occupying a pair of stately early-19C terrace houses, the museum has exceptionally well-presented displays on the region and its history. Linen and lace-making feature strongly, but the museum's greatest treasure is the 14C **Cross of Clogher**.

St Louis Heritage Centre

Open Mon-Tue and Thu-Fri, 10am-noon and 2.30-4.30pm, Sat-Sun, 2.30-4.30pm. €2. ☎ *047 83529; Fax 047 84907; stjohnsheritage@eircom.net*
The centre tells the story of the Order of St Louis, founded in France in 1842, and of its nuns who came to Ireland in 1859. There is a **crannóg** in Spark's Lake in the convent grounds.

Excursions

Rossmore Forest Park

2mi/3.5km S of Monaghan by N 54 and R 189. Gates open daily. Parking. €5 per day. Picnic area. ☎ *049 433 1046*
Of the residence of the Earls of Rossmore only the foundations remain, though their mausoleum still stands in the grounds of their desmesne, now a Forest Park, a delightful landscape of woods and water in the drumlin country of Co Monaghan.

Clones

12mi/19km SW of Monaghan by N 54.
Right on the border with Northern Ireland, Clones (pronounced as two syllables) is a pleasant market town and angling centre on the slope of a hill. A typical Ulster Plantation settlement, it nevertheless looks back on a long history, beginning with the monastery founded by St Tighernach in the 6C; its ruins include a **round tower**, a **monolithic shrine** and a 12C **church.** The **high cross** (c 10C) standing in the central Diamond, below the Anglican church (1822), probably comes from the monastery. Its carvings depict *(west face)* Daniel in the Lions' Den, Cain and Abel and Adam and Eve, and *(east face)* the Crucifixion, the Last Supper and the Adoration of the Magi.

Clones Lace

The **Ulster Canal Stores** building has been converted to house a display of **Clones lace**, a crochet lace, in which individual motifs are connected by areas of Clones knot. *Open Jun-Sep, daily, 9.30am (2pm Sun) to 5.30pm (6pm Sun); Oct-May, Mon-Fri, 9.30am-5.30pm. Café/teashop.* ☎ *047 52125 or 51718; Fax 047 51720; clonesdevelopment@eircom.net; www.clones.ie*

Lough Muckno Leisure Park

15mi/24km SE of Monaghan by N 2 to Castleblaney. The largest and loveliest of the lakes in Co Monaghan, studded with islands and with a highly diverse shoreline, Lough Muckno is surrounded by a wooded park (91 acres/37ha) laid out with **nature trails**. The park was originally the desmesne of Sir Edward Blaney, King James I's Governor of Monaghan, whose name lives on in Castleblaney, the little town laid out on the slope rising from the lake's western shore. A later Blaney built the Georgian **Courthouse** and, in 1808, the Anglican church. In the late 19C Blaney Castle was bought by Thomas Hope, a London banker, who renamed it Hope Castle; his name too lives on as the owner of the ill-omened Hope Diamond, now in the Smithsonian Institution.

Mullingar

The county town of Westmeath is an important agricultural market in the middle of prime cattle country. Unremarkable in itself, Mullingar is an excellent centre for anglers with easy access to the well-stocked waters of the Westmeath lakeland.

Location

Population 8 040 - Michelin Atlas p 91 and Map 712 – JK 7 – Co Westmeath.
Mullingar *(An Muileann Gcearr)* is situated on N 4, the major road from Dublin to Sligo in the northwest.
🏛 *Market House, Mullingar. Open Jul-Aug, Mon-Sat; Sep-Jun, Mon-Fri. ☎ 044 48650; Fax 044 40413; info@coast-midlandstourism.ie; www.ecoast-midlands.travel.ie*

Adjacent Sights: See ATHLONE, BIRR, KELLS, KILDARE, LONGFORD, TRIM, TULLAMORE.

SHOPPING
At **Mullingar Bronze and Pewter**
(5mi/8km E of Mullingar by N 4; after 4mi/6km bear left towards Killucan to The Downs) visitors may watch the moulding, soldering, turning, polishing and blackening, and admire and purchase the finished articles in the showroom. *Open Mon-Fri, 9.30am-6pm, Sat, 10am-5.30pm (12.30pm Fri last tour). Parking.* ☎ *044 48791; info@mullingarpewter.com; www.mullingarpewter.com*

SPORTS AND LEISURE
Fishing and sailing on Lough Ennell. Greyhound racing.

Background

In the 2C AD there was a royal residence on **Uisneach Hill** *(6mi/9.6km W by R 390)*, an ancient druidic sanctuary, where the Celts held ritual assemblies, particularly the Maytime festival. The **Catstone** marks the meeting point of the five provinces of ancient Ireland.

When the Normans arrived in the 12C, they constructed several mottes and baileys in the region as well as stone castles; a Corporation was established in Mullingar with a seal, discovered in 1880. In the 16C, under Henry VIII, Meath was divided in two and Mullingar became the county town of Westmeath. Its prosperity was assured by good communications with Dublin; the Royal Canal arrived in the 1790s, the Midland & Great Western Railway in 1848, and the main Dublin-Sligo road ran through the town until the the present dual carriageway bypass was built. In 1825 a prison and a handsome courthouse were erected in Mount Street, with the intervening space used for public hangings.

During his student days **James Joyce** spent some time in Mullingar, where his father was reorganising the electoral rolls; he had already begun to write and the town provided him with settings for scenes in *Ulysses* and *Stephen Hero*.

Worth a Visit

Cathedral of Christ the King
Mary Street. ♿ Open daily, 7.30am-8pm. Parking. ☎ 044 48338
At the end of the street, in parkland extending to the Royal Canal, rise the twin towers (140ft/43m), surmounted by crosses, of the Roman Catholic cathedral, by far the most prominent building in town. Designed by Ralph Byrne in a "last flamboyant fling ... of Classicism" (J Sheehy), it was dedicated in 1939. The portico above the main door has a tympanum with a **sculpture** in Portland stone by Albert Power, a pupil of Rodin. The ambitious **mosaics** in St Anne's and St Patrick's Chapels are by the Russian artist Boris Anrep.

The **cathedral museum** *(upstairs – ask the Verger)* displays a letter written by Oliver Plunkett *(see p 211)*, his vestments; catechisms in Irish; a model of the earlier cathedral (1834-1936); penal crosses; chalices and monstrances. *Open May-Sep, Thu and Sat-Sun, 3-4pm. €1.50. Parking.* ☎ *044 48338; mullcath@iol.ie; www.mullingarparish.org*

Excursions

Belvedere House and Gardens★
3.5mi/5.6km S of Mullingar by N 52 – half a day. Open daily, 10.30am (9.30am Apr-Aug) to 6pm (7pm Sat-Sun Apr-Aug; 4.30pm Nov-Mar); last admission 1hr before closing. €6. Parking. Restaurant. ☎ *044 49060; Fax 044 49002; info@belvedere-house.ie; www.belvedere-house.ie*

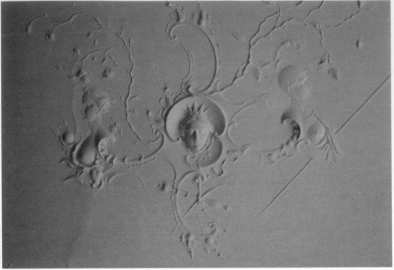

Belvedere House

The beautiful landscape park on the steep east bank of Lough Ennell is graced by an elegant villa (1740) which was probably designed by Richard Castle as a fishing lodge for Robert Rochfort, known locally as the Wicked Earl. Between 1912 and 1960 the house was the property of Col Charles Howard-Bury.

The **Visitor Centre**, housed in the old stables, gives a detailed history of the estate, its rebarbative creator and his long-suffering wife.

The house has been restored to its original appearance and is furnished in period. The elegant **interior** is embellished with finely carved woodwork and ceilings of Rococo plasterwork.

> ### EVEREST EXPEDITION
> In 1921 Col Charles Howard-Bury led an expedition to Everest. Dressed in Donegal tweed his party came within 2 000ft/600m of the summit, took the first photos of the mountain and brought back stories told by the local porters of "abominable snowmen" clad in their own hair.

The **gardens** include three terraces overlooking the lake, added by Charles Brinsley Marly, Robert Rochfort's great-great-grandson. The **walled garden** was started by Marly and developed by Col Bury. The **woodland walk** *(2mi/3km)* on the north side of the house takes in a fine array of romantic follies, including an **octagonal gazebo**, a **Gothick arch**, and an **ice house**, as well as two **stone bridges** over the stream. The 18C plantations of beech have been supplemented by exotic conifers and other rare and ornamental trees. The **jealous wall** (148ft/45m high), designed as a mock-Gothic ruin, was built in about 1760 by Robert either to hide the stables or to blot out the view of Tudenham House (now in ruins), the residence of his brother George, with whom he had quarrelled.

> ### THE WICKED EARL
> Robert Rochfort (1708-79), created 1st Earl of Belvedere in 1757, was a quarrelsome man. In 1736, following the death of his first wife, he married Mary Molesworth, aged 16; she was reluctant but her father was keen on the title and Robert's position at court; four children were born. As Robert spent more and more time at court, Mary turned in her need for company to her brother-in-law Arthur and his wife. Rumours of an affair between Mary and Arthur reached Robert. He brought an action against his brother for £20 000 damages; as Arthur was unable to pay, he went abroad. On his second visit to Ireland Robert had him arrested and he spent the rest of his life in prison. Mary was confined to Robert's gloomy residence at Gaulstown, seeing no one but the servants. Once she escaped but her parents in Dublin sent her back to Gaulstown, where she stayed until Robert's death in 1779 when she was released by her son. Robert's rare visits to Gaulstown ceased completely once he had built Belvedere.

Multyfarnham Franciscan Friary★

8mi/13km N of Mullingar by N 4; in Ballynafid turn right. The outdoor Stations of the Cross are composed of life-size figures set in a grove of evergreens beside a swiftly flowing stream.

Taghmon Church

7mi/11.5km N of Mullingar by N 4 and R 394; in Crookedwood turn right. Between the stream and the foot of the slope, on the site of a monastery founded by St Fintan Munna, stands a fortified church, which probably dates from the 15C; the four-storey tower contains living accommodation and has two sculpted heads incorporated in the north and west walls.

Tullynally★

15mi/24km N of Mullingar by R 394 to Castlepollard and R 395 W; ramped drive (0.75mi/1.2km) from gateway to house. Gardens: Open May-Aug, daily, 2-6pm. Castle: Guided tour mid-Jun to Jul, daily, 2-6pm. Castle and gardens €8; garden €5. Tearoom. ☎ 044 61159 or 62934; Fax 044 61856

Tullynally, the seat of the Pakenham family since 1655, is a great grey pile of turrets and crenellations rising over the oaks and other trees of its extensive parkland. The original fortress with its masonry walls (10ft/3m thick) was converted early in the 18C into a country house and later Gothicised by Francis Johnston and extended by Sir Richard Morrison.

The interiors reflect the 19C love of all things medieval, with a **Great Hall** rising through two storeys and an octagonal **dining room** which has wallpaper designed by Pugin for the House of Lords. Even more striking are the service wings displaying the equipment required to run a large country house – butler's room; **kitchen** splendidly equipped with ovens, copper pans, a great pestle and mortar and an ice chest; **laundry** fitted with lead-lined sinks, washing boards and a huge box mangle; **ironing room; drying room** with vertical racks; **boiler room**. The family coach (restored) is on display in the courtyard.

By 1760 the early-18C formal layout

with canals and cascades had been replaced by **gardens** designed in a more natural landscape style; the terraces were created in the Victorian era for tennis and croquet. The **woodland garden** contains a beech tree, that produces both cut-leaved and normal foliage. The **flower garden** dates from 1740; a "weeping pillar" embellishes the lily pond. Two Coad stone sphinxes (1780) flank the gate into the huge walled **kitchen garden** with its Regency glasshouses and avenue of Irish yews linked by a variegated hedge of box, yew and holly, so dense that moss can grow on its surface.

From the stretch of ornamental water a **forest walk** leads past a waterfall to the lower lake (herons, swans and wild duck) and a **view** of the castle.

Fore Abbey★

15mi/24km N of Mullingar by R 394 to Castlepollard and R 195 E; turn right to Fore.

The ancient monastic site in its valley setting is one of the loveliest in the country. The extensive ruins – church, cloisters, chapter house, refectory, kitchen and columbarium – are mostly those of the Benedictine abbey founded in 1200, though to the south stands **St Fechin's Church**, an 11C or 12C structure named after the saint who founded the original monastery and who died in 665. At the western limit of the Pale, in 1436 the monastery was fortified and enclosed by a wall to protect it from attack by the native Irish; there is a fine **view** from the top of the west tower *(75 steps)*.

Various features have traditionally been known as the **"Seven Wonders of Fore"** and described in miraculous terms. They comprise the "monastery in a bog", the **abbey** itself, raised on firm ground in the middle of marshland; "water that will not boil" from **St Fechin's Well** in the shade of a "tree that will not burn", the three branches of which represented the Trinity; the "stream that flows uphill" to drive the "mill without a race" appeared when the saint beat his crozier on the ground; the "hermit in the stone" was Patrick Beglen, the last anchorite in Ireland, who in the 17C languished in a medieval watchtower, later incorporated into a **chapel mausoleum** for the Nugent family; the "stone raised by St Fechin's prayers" is the huge lintel over the west doorway of his church, which proved too heavy for the masons to lift into place and had to be wafted aloft by the power of prayer.

New Ross

Far inland on the tidal River Barrow, this thriving place was once the country's principal port, and ocean-going ships still tie up at the broad quayside on the east bank of the river. Substantial warehouses and tall quayside houses give the town a 19C appearance but its history goes back to the 6C; narrow streets, many linked by footpaths incorporating flights of steps, rise steeply from the riverside to Irishtown, site of the ancient monastic settlement on the heights above. Very much a working town, New Ross is also a starting point for explorations upstream of the attractive valleys of the Barrow and Nore and downstream of the Hook Head Peninsula.

Location

Population 5 012 - Michelin Atlas p 80 and Map 712 – L 10 – Co Wexford.

New Ross *(Ros Mhic Treoin)* is situated on the road between Wexford and Waterford (N 25) and its junction with N 30 from Enniscorthy, R 705 from Graiguenamanagh on the River Barrow, the R 700 from Thomastown and Kilkenny on the River Nore and R 733 and R 734 which serve the Hook Head peninsula.

Ⓘ *The Quay, New Ross. Open Jun-Aug, Mon-Sat. ☎ 051 421 857; www.ireland-southeast.travel.ie*

Ⓘ *Hook Head Community Office, Hook Head. Open Apr-Sep. ☎ 051 397 502*

Adjacent Sights: See CLONMEL, ENNISCORTHY, KILKENNY, WATERFORD, WEXFORD.

Directory

GETTING ABOUT

Waterford Harbour Ferry – *Operates between Passage East and Ballyhack daily, 7am (9.30am Sun and Bank Hols) to 10pm (8pm Oct-Mar). Closed 25-26 Dec. Capacity 30 cars. Single €5.71 (car), there and back €8.25 (car); there and back €1.90 (pedestrian). ☎ 051 382 480, 382 488; Fax 051 382 598; passageferry@eircom.net; www.passageferry.com*

ENTERTAINMENT

Galley Cruising Restaurants – *Gourmet and ecological trips on the local rivers – Cruises from New Ross and Waterford Apr-Oct, 11am-7pm; check time and price when booking. Cruise only prices from €6;*

lunchtime cruise with lunch from €15; afternoon cruise €10 with afternoon tea; evening cruise with dinner from €25. ☎ 051 421723; Fax 051 421950; info@rivercruises.ie; www.rivercruises.ie

SPORTS AND LEISURE

Beaches at Duncannon; scuba-diving at Slade; riverside walks in Inistioge; birdwatching In spring and autumn on the Hook Head Peninsula, where over 200 species have been recorded.

TRACING ANCESTORS

Dunbrody – Computer database with records of more than two million emigrant journeys between 1846 and 1886 *(see below).*

Background

In the late 6C or early 7C St Abban founded a monastery on the heights near Irishtown. New Ross itself was founded in about 1200 by William le Marshall, Earl Marshal of Ireland, and his wife, Countess Isabelle de Clare, daughter of Strongbow. The first bridge across the River Barrow was built in 1211 and in 1265 the first town walls were constructed. New Ross flourished as a port but by the end of the 17C it had lost its place as Ireland's premier harbour to Waterford. In 1649, mindful of the massacre suffered by Wexford, the Catholic garrison prudently surrendered the town to Cromwell. In the 1798 rebellion the town was successfully defended against the insurgents, who suffered thousands of casualties. An even worse disaster occurred in 1832, when the cholera epidemic claimed three thousand lives. During the mid-19C New Ross had a substantial maritime trade; its ships sailed to the Baltic and crossed the Atlantic, some of them carrying emigrants fleeing the Famine.

Walking About

Dunbrody★

Open daily, 9am-6pm (10am-5pm Oct-Mar). €6. Parking. ☎ 051 425 239; Fax 051 425 240; www.dunbrody.com

Moored at the quayside, Dunbrody is a splendid achievement, a full scale reconstruction of a 458 tonne three-masted barque, 176ft/54m long. The original *Dunbrody*, built in Quebec in 1845 as a freighter by an Irish emigrant shipwright for a New Ross merchant family, served as a passenger vessel between 1845 and 1851, carrying people desperate to escape the Great Famine. Visitors boarding her are met by "emigrants", who bring to vivid life the conditions endured on a one-way trip to New York in 1849. A fascinating exhibition evokes the achievements of members of the Irish diaspora, epitomised by the story of John Fitzgerald Kennedy, and there is also a computer database with records of more than two million emigrant journeys.

From the bridge walk up Mary Street.

Tholsel

At the crossroads on the Corner of South Street and Quay Street (right). Open by appointment Mon-Fri, 9am-5pm. ☎ 051 421 284 (New Ross Town Council); Fax 051 421 605; townclerk@newrossudc.ie

This comely neo-Classical building, surmounted by a tower and a weather-vane, was built in 1749 and rebuilt in 1806, when the ground subsided. The front façade was designed by William Kent, pupil of Sir Christopher Wren, and a weekly market used to be held on the ground floor before the arches were closed. It houses the local council, which holds many volumes of corporation minutes dating from the 17C, as well as the mace of Charles II and the charter of James II (1688). Opposite the building is a statue of a **croppy boy**, a local term given to the insurgents in the 1798 rebellion because of their short hair; it commemorates the uprising and the subsequent battle of New Ross.

Continue up Mary Street.

St Mary's Church★

Services: Sun, 11.45am. ☎ 051 425 004; pmoon@esatclear.ie; www.rostapestry.cjb.net

The early-19C Anglican church was built on the site of the nave and crossing of what was probably the largest parish church in medieval Ireland, part of the abbey founded by William le Marshall and his wife Isabelle between 1207 and 1220. The extensive abbey ruins are surrounded by a large unkempt graveyard. The ruined chancel contains some striking late-13C and early-14C effigies.

Walk back down Mary Street a few steps; turn left into Bewley Street and right into Michael Street.

Roman Catholic Parish Church

From the front of the church there are fine views over the town and river. The design of the building with its high ceiling and Corinthian columns was inspired by that of St Mary's Church *(adjacent)*. Construction began in 1832 but was interrupted by the cholera epidemic in that year.

Leave by the rear entrance. Walk up Cross Lane; turn right into Neville Street.

Town Walls and Gates

At the junction stands the Three Bullet Gate *(left)*, through which Cromwell entered the town in 1649, and the Mural Tower; both date from the 14C. The substantial remains of the Maiden Gate are 15C.

Walk down William Street. Turn right into Priory Street and left into Marsh Lane to return to the Quay.

Excursions

UPSTREAM FROM NEW ROSS

Graiguenamanagh★

11mi/18km N of New Ross by N 30, R 700 and R 705. Its quaysides once the site of much commerical activity, Graiguenamanagh ("granary of the monks") stands on a particularly attractive stretch of the River Barrow, overlooked by the heather-covered summit of Brandon Hill (1 694ft/516m). The township is dominated by the restored ruins of Duiske (pronounced Dooishka) Abbey, established here in the early 13C by William le Marshall for the Cistercians, who characteristically chose to site their communities in harmonious settings such as this.

Duiske Abbey★★ – The abbey was suppressed in 1536 but the monks continued to occupy it for many years afterwards. The tower collapsed in 1774 and much of the area covered by the abbey was later built on. The outstanding feature of the restoration is the high-pitched church roof, constructed from unseasoned timbers of oak and elm with wooden pegs to secure the joints. The effigy of the Knight of Duiske, cross-legged, sword-seizing, dates from about 1300 and is one of the most impressive anywhere in Ireland; the knight's identity remains a mystery.

The Abbey Centre houses a museum, which displays some of the Abbey plate and other items relating to the abbey, and a gallery exhibiting the work of contemporary artists on Christian themes using a variety of media. *Open daily, 8am-7.30pm. Mass: Sun, 8.30am, 11am, 7.30pm (vigil). Abbey Centre: Mon-Fri, 10am-5pm; also Jun-Aug, Sat-Sun, 2-5pm. ☎ 0503 24238*

Inistioge★

10mi/16km N of New Ross by N 30 and R 700. Inistioge (pronounced Inisteeg), a famously picturesque village, is set on the west bank of the Nore which is spanned by a splendid 18C bridge with 10 arches As well as lovely riverside walks and plenty of places to picnic, Inistioge has some fascinating reminders of a long history which began when a priory was founded and a castle built early in the 13C.

The ruins of the **castle**, once the borough courthouse, stand between the river and the tree-lined **square**, which contains the remains of a cross erected in 1621 and damaged in 1798; on the west side next to the ruined Tholsel is a real curiosity, the **Armillary Sphere**, a device said to have been invented by Eratosthenes in 250 BC to demonstrate the movements of the earth and moon. The 19C almshouse was built by a member of the Tighe family, who resided at Woodstock *(see below)*.

The Roman Catholic church contains stone carvings *(near the entrance)* of uncertain date, said to illustrate the legend of the mermaid being taken from the River Nore in the village in 1118; up the lane is **St Colmcille's Well.**

Adjoining the Anglican Church are the tower, nave and Lady Chapel of the **Augustinian priory**, founded in 1210 and dedicated to St Mary and St Columba *(Colmcille)*. In the graveyard is the elaborate tomb erected in memory of Mrs Mary Tighe, a locally famous poet, who died in 1810.

Woodstock Forest Park *(1mi/1.6km SW of Inistioge)* is the former Tighe family demesne offering forest walks, an old tiled Japanese garden and a conical dovecot as well as the ruins of the house, which is claimed to have been the finest 18C mansion in Co Kilkenny and was burned down during the Civil War.

DOWNSTREAM FROM NEW ROSS

Kennedy Arboretum★

7.5mi/12km S of New Ross by R 733 and R 734; turn right (sign). (Dúchas) ♿ *Open daily, 10am-8pm (6.30pm Apr and Sep; 5pm Oct-Mar); last admission 45min before closing. Closed Good Fri and 25 Dec. €2.50. Audio-visual show (15min). Guided tour (1hr 15min) by appointment. Self-guiding trails. Parking. Tearoom (051 388 195); picnic area.* ☎ *051 388 171; Fax 051 388 172; jfkarboretum@ealga.ie; www.heritageireland.ie*

The arboretum (667 acres/252ha), opened in 1968 in memory of John F Kennedy, President of the USA, is divided into the plant collection, forest plots and mountain heathland. The many varieties of shrubs and trees are arranged in two circuits, one mainly conifers, the other broadleaf. When complete the collection should total 6 000 species. There are extensive walks through the arboretum, and a scenic road winds to the summit of Slieve Coillte. The views are superb, taking in the rich pattern of enclosed farmland, the Hook Peninsula and mountain ranges. Footpaths radiate from the car park, one of them leading to the **Mountain Viewpoint**, where a memorial stone commemorates the 1798 rebels who camped here.

Kennedy Homestead

Dunganstown; 4mi/6.4km S of New Ross by R 733 and the minor road W. Open May-Sep, 10am-5.30pm; Oct-Apr, by appointment. €4. ☎ *051 388 264; info@ kennedyhomestead.com; www.kennedyhomestead.com*

The birthplace in 1820 of the great-grandfather of John F Kennedy, President of the USA (1961-63) now displays photographs and mementoes of the President's visit in 1963, including the wreath he laid on the graves of the leaders of the 1916 Easter Rising at Arbour Hill in Dublin; family tree in Ireland and America.

Kilmokea Gardens★

10mi/15km S of New Ross by R 733 and a minor road W. (♿) Open Mar-Nov, Tue-Sun, 10am-5pm (6pm gardens). €5. Guided tour (1hr 30min) by appointment. Plants for sale. Refreshments in Georgian conservatory. ☎ *051 388 109; Fax 051 388 776; kilmokea@indigo.ie; www.kilmokea.com*

Within the earthern ramparts of what was probably an early Christian monastic foundation stands a handsome Georgian glebe house; its gardens, some of the most exquisite in Ireland, were developed over half a century; they offer a delightful contrast between formal areas close to the house and a luxuriant, carefully created and maintained jungle extending along the narrow valley of a tiny stream.

Dunbrody Abbey★

10mi/16km S of New Ross by R 733. Key at Furlong's cottage by the main road entrance. Open May-Sep, daily, 10am-6pm (7pm Jul-Aug). Abbey €1.90; maze €2.54. ☎ *051 388 603 or 051 389 104 (after hours)*

Close to the village of Clonmines, a deserted medieval borough with remains of tower houses, fortified church and Augustinian priory, are the handsome ruins of the abbey built in 1182 by Cistercian monks from St Mary's Abbey in Dublin. The roofless but well-preserved cruciform abbey church, pleasantly set above an inlet of the River Barrow, has a low turreted tower and six transept chapels with slender single-light windows. Slight traces exist of some of the outlying buildings.

After the Dissolution, the abbey passed into the hands of the Etchingham family; there are substantial remains of the fortified dwelling they erected around the Norman keep built to defend the abbey. In its grounds is a new-grown maze of yew.

Ballyhack Castle

(Dúchas) Open Jun-Sep, daily, 9.30am-6.30pm (5.45pm last admission). €2.50. Guided tour by appointment (booking essential). Public parking nearby. ☎ 051 389 468

Overlooking the ferry crossing to Passage East on the west bank of Waterford Harbour is an imposing tower house (15C or 16C); steep stairs in the thickness of the wall link the five floors, of which the ground and first floor are vaulted and the others now open to the sky. The site originally belonged to the Knights Templar, from whom it passed to the Knights Hospitaller and then came into the possession of the Earl of Donegall.

Duncannon Fort★

(&) Open Jun to mid-Sep, daily, 10am-5.30pm. €4. Guided tour available. Café. ☎/Fax 051 389 454; duncannonfort@hotmail.com; www.thehook-wexford.com/heritage/hert.htm

Duncannon Fort (3 acres/1.2ha) was first selected for defensive purposes by the Anglo-Normans in the 12C. In 1588, as part of the precautions against the Spanish Armada, the fortress was strengthened and assumed its present star-shaped form with a dry moat. In 1690 both James II and William III took ship from Duncannon following the Battle of the Boyne.

Tintern Abbey★

5mi/8km E of Duncannon by R 737, R 733 and R 374 to Saltmills. (Dúchas) (&) Restoration work in progress. Open mid-Jun to late-Sep, daily, 9.30am-6.30pm (5.45pm last admission); late-Sep to mid-Jun, telephone for opening hours. €1.90. Guided tour by appointment. Parking. Tearoom. ☎ 051 562 650, ☎ 056 24623 (winter)

The ruined Cistercian abbey, a daughter house of Tintern Abbey in Monmouthshire, whence its name, was founded in 1200 by William le Marshall in thanksgiving for his safe crossing from England in a violent storm. At the Dissolution of the Monasteries in the 16C the abbey was granted to the Colclough family, who took up residence in the nave and tower.

Hook Head Peninsula

A remote location, quiet beaches and distinctive landscapes have long drawn holiday-makers to the Hook Head Peninsula, bounded to the west by Waterford Harbour and to the east by Bannow Bay. **The pleasant little resort of Fethard**, the largest place on the peninsula, was originally founded by the Anglo-Normans, whose first expedition to Ireland landed in 1169 at Bannow Island.

Slade is a minute fishing village, with a small double harbour, and is a popular scuba-diving centre because of the clear water and the range of interesting sea formations. On the pier are the remains of 18C salthouses where sea water was evaporated to make salt. Beside them stand the ruins of **Slade Castle**, consisting of a tower house (15C-16C) and a house (16C-17C), built by the Laffan family.

Hook Head Lighthouse – *At the seaward end of the narrow promontory. Open Mar-Oct, daily, 9.30am-5.30pm; otherwise check by phone. €4.75. ☎ 051 397 055; Fax 051 397 056; thehook@eircom.net; www.thehook-wexford.com*

The lighthouse is one of the oldest lighthouses in Europe, where a light was maintained almost continuously for 1 500 years. The cylindrical keep (82ft/25m) with its vaulted chambers was built by the Normans in the early 13C to aid navigation up Waterford Harbour to their port at New Ross. It is topped by a more conventional structure erected early in the 19C.

Portumna★

This little township of Portumna, meaning the port of the oak, is a major crossing point on the River Shannon where it enters Lough Derg, the lowest and most attractive of the Shannon lakes. Occupying part of the shoreline, Portumna Forest Park has a deer herd, nature trails, a marina and an observation tower; the birdlife, both migratory and resident, is abundant.

Location

Population 984 - Michelin Atlas p 90 and Map 712 – H 8 – Co Galway.

Portumna *(Port Omna)* is situated at the north end of Lough Derg on N 65 between Borrisokane and Loughrea and R 489 and R 353 between Birr and Gort. The road bridge over the Shannon is raised at regular intervals to allow the passage of vessels on the river *(see Directory)*.

Adjacent Sights: See ATHENRY, BIRR, CLONMACNOISE.

Worth a Visit

Portumna Castle★

(Dúchas) Open Apr-Oct, daily, 10am-6pm (5.15pm last admission). €1.90. Guided tour. Parking. ☎ 0509 41658; Fax 0509 41889; portumnacastle@ealga.ie; www.heritageireland.ie

The early 17C castle, which stands in the northeast corner of its park, was for centuries the seat of the Burke family.

Long derelict but now well on the way to restoration, it is a handsome example of the kind of sophisticated, semi-fortified residence built to replace the tower houses and castles of medieval times. The house was accidentally burnt-out in 1826 and abandoned. Its replacement, designed by Sir Thomas Deane, was burned down during the Civil War.

The approach passes through a series of formal gardens divided by an Adam Gate (partially ruined), a Gothic Gate and a Tuscan Gate *(nearest the house)*. The Gothic Gate houses an exhibition telling the story of the castle and its occupants, and the 17C walled kitchen garden is planted with fruit trees, flowers, herbs and vegetables.

Dúchas, Dublin

Portumna Castle

Portumna Priory

South of the castle stand the ruins of a priory, originally a Cistercian chapel, which was granted to the Dominicans by O'Madden, the local chieftain. The north and south windows at the eastern end of the church, probably part of the Cistercian building, date from the 13C. The rest of the priory is 15C and contains some fine windows.

DE BURGO – DE BURGH – BURKE

The illustrious name of Burke derives from de Burgo, of Norman origin. In 1193 William de Burgo, who came to Ireland with Prince John in 1185, married the daughter of Donal Mor O'Brien, king of Thomond; his son was made Lord of Connaught; in 1265 Walter de Burgo was created Earl of Ulster. In the 14C the property passed to a descendant of Richard, Lord of Connaught, who adopted the name de Burgh by royal licence and was made Earl of Clanrickard in 1543. John, the 9th Earl, abandoned the family tradition of loyalty to the Crown and fought with the Jacobites; he was taken prisoner at Aughrim (1691) and his lands confiscated but they were redeemed 12 years later for £25 000. On the death of Hubert de Burgh Canning (1832-1916), who was a bachelor recluse, the title passed to the Marquess of Sligo and the land to Henry Lascelles, 6th Lord Harewood who married the Princess Royal, daughter of George V and Queen Mary.

Excursions

Clonfert Cathedral★

17mi/27km NE of Portumna by N 65, R 355, R 356 via Eyrecourt and a minor road E; key available at the lodge. Open (restoration work permitting) May-Sep, daily, 9am-dusk. Donation. If locked, key available at the lodge. ☎/Fax 0509 51269; clonfert@clonfert.anglican.org

The church was built in the 12C on the site of a monastery founded in 563 by St Brendan the Navigator *(see p 253)*. It is justly famous for its **west doorway★★**, a masterpiece of Hiberno-Romanesque decoration in red sandstone, aptly described as "the apogee of the Irish Romanesque mason's love of ornamentation" (P Harbison). It is surmounted by a triangular hood, containing alternating human heads and triangles above a row of arches, and is framed by six recessed orders decorated with a variety of fantastical motifs and animal heads. The sixth order was added in the 15C, at the same time as the tower, south transept and sacristy. The chancel arch, also 15C, is carved with angels, a rosette and a mermaid; the beautiful east windows are Romanesque. The Romanesque south transept is in ruins; the Gothic north transept has been demolished. The grounds *(through the rear churchyard gate, turn left)* contain an ancient **yew walk**, now suffering from storm damage and exposure; it was probably planted by the monks in the shape of a cross over 400 years ago. The ruined Bishop's Palace belonged to Sir Oswald Mosley from 1951 to 1954 when it was destroyed by fire. The charming circular oratory serves the Emmanuel Retreat House.

Meelick Franciscan Friary

7mi/11km NE of Portumna by N 65, R 355 and a minor road E.

The friary was built in the 15C on a slight rise overlooking the Shannon. In 1986 the ruins were restored and the church roofed and equipped for worship. Most of the walls, the west door and two arches in the south wall are original; between the arches is a small figure of St Francis, which was added later. During the restoration four quills were found in a chimney in the dwelling house, which dates from 1732. A short walk *(0.5mi/1km E)* leads to Meelick Weir and Victoria Lock, the largest lock on the Shannon.

Lorrha

6mi/10km E of Portumna by R 489 via Portumna Lifting Bridge and a minor road S.

The tiny village contains no fewer than three ruined churches. Part of one is used for Anglican worship; on the west front there are antae and a 13C doorway framing a 15C doorway carved with a pelican vulning (pecking at her breast). It stands on the site of a monastery founded by St Ruadhán (d 845), a disciple of St Finian of Clonard. **St Ruadhan's Church** is a 15C building with an ornate west doorway, handsome east and west windows and a vaulted sacristy; on the south side of the village, next to the Roman Catholic church, are the remains of a church belonging to a Dominican priory founded by Walter de Burgo c 1269.

Roscrea★

Laid out on the steeply sloping banks of the Bunnow River, this prosperous agricultural town lies in the gap between the Slieve Bloom Mountains to the north and Devils Bit Mountain to the south. Ancient roadways converged here; in the 7C St Cronan founded a monastery here and in the early 13C the Anglo-Irish recognised the strategic value of the site by erecting a castle.

Location

Population 4 170 - Michelin Atlas p 85 and Map 712 – I 9 – Co Tipperary.
Roscrea *(Ros Cré)* is situated at the junction of the main road (N 7) between Dublin and Limerick and (N 62) between Birr and Thurles.

Adjacent Sights: See ABBEYLEIX, ATHY, BIRR, KILKENNY.

> **DIRECTORY**
> **Roscrea Heritage Centre** – *Roscrea Castle (below)* – Computerised genealogical service.

Worth a Visit

Roscrea Castle

(Dúchas) (&) Open Apr-Oct, daily, 10am-6pm (5.15pm last admission). €3.10. Guided tour (45min) by appointment. Genealogy service. ☎ 0505 21850 or 21689; roscreaheritage@ealga.ie; www.elyocarroll.com/roscas.html

Dominating the centre of the town is the 13C **castle,** an irregular polygonal enclosure surrounded by curtain walls and two D-shaped towers. The medieval gatetower, embellished with 17C gables and chimneys, now houses the **Roscrea Heritage Centre**, which presents an exhibition on the history of Norman castles in Ireland.

Damer House* – Standing within the castle walls is an elegant 18C three-storeyed house containing a handsome pine staircase. It was started in 1715 by Joseph Damer, the richest man in the country when he died in 1720 and a member of a Plantation family which came to Ireland in 1661. The house was completed in the 1720s becoming the residence of the Anglican Bishop of Killaloe; in 1798 it was used as a military barracks. The rooms house exhibitions of local historical interest.

St Cronan's Church and Round Tower

Church Street. Sacked no fewer than four times in the course of the 12C, the monastery founded by St Cronan was quarried for building stone in the 19C, and suffered the indignity of having the main Dublin-Limerick road driven through it in the 20C (the town now has a bypass). The somewhat fragmented remains include the west façade of the 12C church, a 12C **high cross** and an 8C **round tower** (60ft/18m high) which lost its conical cap in 1135 and was further diminished by the fighting in 1798.

Franciscan Friary

The present Roman Catholic church of St Cronan, set on a slight incline, is approached through the bell tower of the original 15C friary. The east and north walls of the earlier chancel and part of the nave arcade have been incorporated into the modern church.

Excursions

Monaincha Abbey

1mi/1.6km W by N 7 and minor road from the roundabout. Embedded in trees, this exquisite 12C ruin with its finely carved doorway and chancel arch stands on a raised site which was an island until the surrounding bog was drained in the late 18C. In early Christian times the site was a famous place of retreat, associated with various saints including St Cronan, then in the Middle Ages developed into an important pilgrimage centre.

Devil's Bit Mountain

15mi/24km S of Roscrea by N 62. Legend has it that the gap at Devil's Bit Mountain was scooped out by the devil to form the Rock of Cashel. Reality is more prosaic; the hollow was created by glacial action. There is an easy climb to the summit of the mountain (1 577ft/479m), rewarding for the extensive views of the Golden Vale to the south and east.

Skibbereen

This busy little market town owes its existence to Algerian pirates, who raided the neighbouring settlement of Baltimore in 1631. Some of the English settlers were captured but the remainder fled inland and set up two settlements, one of which grew into Skibbereen. The town suffered severely during the 19C famine but has regained a certain vitality in the last 20 years and makes a useful centre for exploring the splendid coastal scenery of the region.

Location

Population 1 926 - Michelin Atlas p 77 and Map 712 – E 13 – Co Cork.
Skibbereen *(Sciobairín)* stands on the Cork coast road (N 71) where it crosses the River Ilen a few miles inland.
🅱 *North Street, Skibbereen. Open Jul-Aug, daily; Sep and Jun, Mon-Sat; Oct-May, Mon-Fri.* ☎ *028 21766; Fax 028 21353; skibbereen@corkkerrytourism.ie; www.corkkerry.ie*
Adjacent Sights: See BANTRY, CORK, KINSALE.

Worth a Visit

Skibereen Heritage Centre

Upper Street by the river. The exhibits displayed in the old Gas Works Building provide information on the Great Famine *(audio-visual show)* and Lough Hyne *(see below)* – formation, marine biology, fish tank.

Directory

SIGHTSEEING

Baltimore-Sherkin Island Passenger Ferry – *Operates (15min) from Baltimore Pier Jun-Sep, 8 times daily, 9am-8.30pm (7 times on Sun); Oct-May, 3 times daily, 10.30am-5.30pm; extra services at peak times. There and back €6.35.* ☏ *028 20125; 028 20218; www.sherkinisland.ie*

Baltimore-Cape Clear Island Ferry – *Operates daily (weather permitting); times available by phone. There and back €11.43.* ☏ *028 39135 (Capt O'Driscoll), 08626 62197 (mobile), 028 39119 (office); Fax 028 20442 (Booking Office)*

Baltimore-Skull Ferry – *Operates Jun-Aug, daily: from Baltimore to Hare Island (15min) to Skull (35min) at 10am, 1.45pm and 4.40pm; from Skull to Hare Island (35min) to Baltimore (15min) at 11.30am, 3pm and 5.30pm. €10.* ☏ *028 39153, 087 268 0760 (mobile); Fax 028 39164; westcorkcruises.com; www.westcorkcruises.com*

Skull Ferry – *Operates to Cape Clear Island: Jul-Aug, 3 times daily, from Schull at 10.30am, 2.30pm, 4.30pm, from Cape Clear at 11.30am, 3.30pm, 5.30pm; May-Jun and Sep, from Schull at 2.30pm, from Cape Clear at 5.30pm. Operates to Sherkin Island and Baltimore: Jul-Aug, from Schull at 10am, 1.45pm, 4.30pm, from Sherkin Island/Baltimore at 11am, 3pm, 5.30pm; Jun and Sep from Schull at 1.45pm, from Sherkin Island/Baltimore at 5.30pm. There and back €12 (bikes carried free). Trips to Fastnet Rock Lighthouse twice weekly at 7pm.* ☏ *028 28278; molloykieran@eircom.net*

WHERE TO STAY
• Budget

Fastnet – ☏ *028 20515 - Fax 028 20515 - fastnethouse@eircom.net - Feb-Nov - ⊁ - 4 rm €45/64* ⌨. Old stone walls, open fireplaces and wooden floors bear out the history of this old merchant's house, dating back to 1820 and located in the centre of town. Still very much a family home, with multilingual owners.

ENTERTAINMENT

West Cork Arts Centre *(North Street)* – Regular arts events – *Open Mon-Sat, 10am-6pm.* ☏ *028 22090; Fax 028 23237, westcorkarts@eircom.net*

SPORTS AND LEISURE

Sailing at Baltimore (temporary marina in summer) and Skull.

Excursions

The Liss Ard Foundation

2mi/3km S of Skibbereen by R 596. (&) *Open May-Oct, Mon-Fri, 10am-6pm, Sat Sun, noon-6pm; Nov-Mar, by appointment. €3.81. Parking.* ☏ *028 40186; Fax 028 40187; lissardfoundation@eircom.net, www.lissard.com*

The estate is tended so as to enhance the natural flora and fauna. Each element is isolated from the rest to create a series of open-air "rooms" where visitors are invited to linger long in contemplation of the colours, shapes and sounds – the subtle colours in the wild flower meadow, the rustle of leaves in the woodland walk, the ripples on the surface of the lake, the chuckling of the waterfalls or the silence of the grass arena and oval of sky in the Crater, created by James Turrell *(see p 281).*

> ### "KEEPING AN EYE ON THE CZAR OF RUSSIA"
>
> In the 1890s a leader in the *Skibbereen Eagle* remarked that the paper was "keeping an eye on the Czar of Russia". The comment, outrageously bombastic for a small provincial newspaper, was picked up by the international wire services and went around the world. Still quoted today, it turned out to be the most famous line ever written in an Irish newspaper. The files of the old *Eagle* may be inspected by appointment at the offices of the *Southern Star* newspaper in Ilen Street.

Lough Hyne Nature Reserve

6mi/10km SW of Skibbereen by R 595 and a minor road S. Extensive observation facilities in preparation. The presence of sea urchins makes barefoot paddling dangerous.

Set among low hills, this unpolluted saltwater lagoon is a marine nature reserve with a unique ecosystem; over 60 species have been recorded, including the red-mouth goby, otherwise found in Portugal. From the north side of the lough a track leads to a prominent viewpoint in the forest providing extensive panoramas of the area.

Baltimore

8mi/13km SW of Skibbereen by R 595. This attractive fishing village lies at the end of a road offering fine views of the myriad islands just offshore in Roaringwater Bay. Baltimore has some of the safest anchorages on the southwest coast and is the starting point for ferries to several of the islands. Overlooking the two piers – one old, one new – are the ruins of the early-17C fortified house built by the local lord, Sir Fineen O'Driscoll. On the breezy headland *(1mi/1.6km S)* stands **Lot's wife**, a medieval beacon, shaped like a rocket and painted white; from its immediate vicinity there are panoramic **views** of Sherkin Island.

Baltimore
Baltimore

SLIDE FILE, Dublin

Sherkin Island★

Access by ferry (see Directory). A full day is needed to explore the island; if the weather turns stormy visitors may be marooned for a night or more. As well as the remains of an O'Driscoll stronghold, a ruined friary and some lovely beaches, little Sherkin has a **marine research station**, which monitors the marine environment and organises courses on pollution.

Cape Clear Island

Access by ferry (see Directory). At least two days, more in bad weather, are needed to visit the island. Basic accommodation for visitors is provided by the bird observatory. The vast seabird colonies attract many ornithologists to remote and rocky Cape Clear Island, Ireland's southernmost inhabited island; there are countless guillemots, cormorants, shearwaters, petrels and choughs, while whales, turtles, sharks, seals and dolphins can be spotted in the waters around. The north and south harbours are divided by an isthmus; the one tiny village is called **Cummer**. The island is one of the last bastions of Irish in west Cork, and some of its summer visitors come here to learn the language. Many of the people living on the island are called O'Driscoll or Cadogan, which presents problems for the postman.

Tour

MIZEN PENINSULA
Tour of 35mi/56km W of Skibbereen – 1 day
The spectacular scenery of the peninsula reaches a climax in the wave-shattered cliffs of remote Mizen Head *(see below)*.
From Skibbereen take N 71 W. After 10mi/16km turn left.

Ballydehob
The main street with its brightly painted houses slopes down steeply to island-studded Roaringwater Bay. The 12-arch railway bridge, part of the Skull and Skibbereen light railway which closed in 1947, has been converted into a **walkway**.
Take the minor road N uphill bearing W and S to Mount Gabriel and Skull.

Mount Gabriel
This mountain (1 339ft/408m) offers a challenging climb, the reward being a fine panorama of the bay. Copper was mined here in the Bronze Age, and in the 19C the mines rivalled those of Cornwall; the abandoned workings contrast with the modern technology of the two globes near its summit which are aircraft tracking stations.
Take the road S to Skull.
Beyond the pass there is a fine **view**★★ of Skull and Roaringwater Bay.

Skull (Schull)★
Ferries to Baltimore and Cape Clear Island (see above). This pretty little market town and commercial fishing centre is popular with yachtsmen. Skull – its name meaning "school" after the monastic place of learning established here in the 10C - can also

claim two bookshops. The **planetarium** presents an exhibition, regular astronomy shows *(60 seats)* and holds telescope viewing nights. *(&)* *Open May and Sep, Sun, 3-5pm (Starshow at 4pm); Jun, Tue and Sat, 3-5pm (Starshow at 4pm), Thu, 7.30-9pm (Starshow at 8pm); Jul-Aug, Tue-Sat, 2-5pm (Starshow at 4pm), Mon and Thu, 7-9pm (Starshow at 8pm); also mid-Jul to mid-Aug, Wed-Fri, extra shows. Starshow (45min; €4.50). Parking.* 028 28315, 28552; *Fax 028 28467; www.homepage.eircom.net/-planetarium*
Continue W; in Toormore turn left into R 591 to Goleen and Crookhaven. Turn right (sign) at the entrance to the village of Goleen.

The Ewe Art Retreat
(&) *Open Jun-Aug or by appointment, daily, 10am-6pm. €2.50. Parking.* /*Fax 028 35492; courses@theewe.com; www.theewe.com*
This residential art centre welcomes visitors to its gallery and delightful sculpture garden overlooking the sea.

Crookhaven
The little resort of Crookhaven was once a place of some importance, a busy fishing harbour used as a stopping point for mailboats en route to America and the West Indies and with copper mines at nearby Brow Head, where Marconi set up his transatlantic telegraph station in 1902.
Take the minor road along the east side of Barley Cove.

Barley Cove
Popular with surfers, the deep inlet with its **sandy beach** between the cliffs makes a splendid holiday resort; the many chalets do not detract from the overall view.
After crossing the causeway at the head of Barley Cove turn left to Mizen Head.

Mizen Head Visitor Centre
10min steep descent on foot from car park. Open mid-Mar to Oct, daily, 10.30am (10am Jun-Sep) to 5pm (6pm Jun Sep); Nov to mid-Mar, Sat-Sun, 11am-4pm. €4.44. Parking. Restaurant. 028 35115 *(summer only); otherwise* 028 35591 *or 35225; Fax 028 35603, info@mizenhead.net; www.mizenhead.net*
The storm-battered cliffs of Mizen Head mark the southwesternmost tip of Ireland. In 1910 the Irish Lights fog signal station was built on Cloghnane Island, with access to it via a reinforced concrete footbridge constructed with some difficulty because of the extreme exposure. Crossing the chasm 150ft/46m above the Atlantic swell can be a thrilling experience in wild weather. The **Visitor Centre** presents the work of the station and of lighthouse keepers; local marine life – dolphins, seals, basking sharks and whales and seabirds – and wrecks; the Fastnet Race and the building of the Fastnet Rock Lighthouse *(SE – 9mi/14km)*.

Sligo★★

Sligo is a busy market town, an important shopping and cultural centre for much of the northwest of Ireland. It stands on the short River Garavogue which drains Lough Gill into the sea, and one of its greatest assets is the beautiful and varied landscape all around – green and wooded valleys, lofty mountains, sandy seashores, as well as an exceptional wealth of prehistoric monuments. Sligo and its surroundings are intimately associated with the Yeats family; with the portrait painter John B Yeats, the artist Jack B Yeats, and above all the poet William Butler Yeats (1865-1939).

Location
Population 17 786 - Michelin Atlas p 96 and Map 712 – G 5 – Co Sligo.
Sligo *(Sligeach)* is the hub of several major roads: N 4 E to Dublin ; N 59 W into Co Mayo; N 15 N into Donegal and N 16 over the border to Enniskillen.
🖪 *Aras Reddan, Temple Street, Sligo. Open Jun-Aug, daily; May and Sep, Mon-Sat; Oct-Apr, Mon-Fri.* 071 61201; *Fax 071 60360; ireland-northwest@eircom.net; www.ireland-northwest.ie*
Adjacent Sights: See BOYLE, DONEGAL, ENNISKILLEN, KILLALA, KNOCK.

Background

A Turbulent History – In 807 Sligo was plundered by the Vikings; following the Norman invasion in the 13C it was granted to Maurice Fitzgerald, who built a castle and the abbey; for 200 years its possession by the O'Conors was disputed by the O'Donnells. A fort was built by the Cromwellians; Patrick Sarsfield reinforced the defences so that Sligo was one of the last places to capitulate after the Battle of the Boyne (1690). The Battle of Carrignagat (1798) was fought south of the town.

Directory

GETTING ABOUT

Sligo Airport – ☎ 071 68280.

SIGHTSEEING

Walking Tour – Sligo town and the locations associated with the Yeats brothers – *Operates Jun-Sep.* ☎ 071 61201; Fax 071 60360

There are **waterbus trips** on **Lough Gill**, particularly to the Isle of **Innisfree**, from Doorly Park and Parke's Castle. *Wild Rose Water Bus: Operates mid-Jun to Sep, from Doorly Park (SE of Sligo town centre) daily, at 2.30pm (3hr round tour of Lough Gill stopping at Parke's Castle) and 5.30pm (to Parke's Castle); from Parke's Castle (NE corner of Lough Gill) daily, at 12.30pm (1hr to Innisfree), 1.30pm (to Doorly Park), 3.30pm (1hr to Innisfree), 4.30pm (to Sligo and back), 6.30pm (1hr to Innisfree); Fri, at 9pm (Irish music, bar); Apr, May, Oct, Sun only. Innisfree €6.35; Lough Gill €7.62. Refreshments.* ☎ 071 64266; 0882 598 8869 (mobile)

There are also boat trips offshore to **Inishmurray** from Rosses Point and from Mullaghmore *(N of Sligo). Boat trips (15 passengers minimum) from Mullaghmore* ☎ 071 66124 *(Rodney Lomax),* ☎ 072 41874 *(Brendan Merrifield), 088 277 3874; and Rosses Point* ☎ 071 42391 *(Tommy McCallion)*

WHERE TO STAY

• *Budget*

Benwiskin Lodge – *Shannon Eighter – 1.25mi/2km N of Sligo by N 15 -* ☎ 071 41088 - Fax 071 41088 - *pquigley@iol.ie - Closed 22 Dec to 7 Jan -* ▣ ⤬ *- 5 rm €40/64* ⛏. DIY enthusiasts can compare their handiwork with that of the owner; he handcrafted the majority of the furniture at this detached guesthouse. The decor is bright and cheery and the pitch n' putt close by.

Tree Tops – *Cleveragh Rd - 0.25mi/0.4km S of Sligo by Dublin road -* ☎ 071 60160 - *Fax 071 62301 - treetops@iol.ie - Closed 15 Dec to 15 Jan -* ▣ ⤬ *- 5 rm €40/62* ⛏. An unassuming house in a residential area but made special by the warmth and hospitality of the owner. She also has an impressive collection of Irish art which adorns many of the walls. Bedrooms are cosy and comfortable.

Ard Cuilinn Lodge – *Drumiskabole - 3mi/5km SE of Sligo by N 4 off R 284 -* ☎ 071 62925 - *ardcuiln@esatclear.ie - 16 Mar to Oct -* ▣ ⤬ *- 4 rm €40/54* ⛏. Notable for its quiet, semi-rural location with views of the surrounding hills, yet 5-min drive from the town centre. The three well-kept bedrooms overlook the garden. Local smoked salmon and scrambled egg are a breakfast speciality.

WHERE TO EAT

• *Moderate*

Montmartre – *Market Yard -* ☎ 071 69901 - *montmartre@eircom.net - Closed 5-21 Jan, 23-27 Dec and Mon - €29.40/42.70.* The menu offers a broad range of styles but the atmosphere and style of the room have a strong Gallic accent, from the pictures of French landmarks on the walls to the helpful mesdemoiselles providing the service.

ENTERTAINMENT

The **Hawk's Well Theatre** – ☎ 071 61526.

SHOPPING

Sligo Crystal – *10mi/16km N by N 15 at Grange – Open Jun-Sep, Mon-Fri, 9am-9pm, Sat-Sun, 10am to 7pm; Oct-May, Mon-Sat, 9am to 6pm.* ☎ 071 43440. Factory and showrooms with guided tours; see craftsmen using the oldest traditions known for producing hand-cut crystal.

SPORTS AND LEISURE

Strandhill is good for windsurfing but bathing can be dangerous.

Rosses Point *(An Ros)*, a sandy peninsula projecting into Drumcliff Bay, provides a championship golf course and two beautiful sandy beaches for bathing and windsurfing.

EVENTS AND FESTIVALS

Yeats Annual Winter School – Weekend in February of lectures and a tour of Yeats Country

---

A Prosperous Port – In the 18C and 19C Sligo developed into a busy trading port which saw many emigrants set out for the New World. Several buildings date from that period: warehouses by the docks; the Courthouse, built in 1878; the City Hall, built in 1865 in the Italian Renaissance style. The stone building with a roof-top lookout turret, now known as the **Yeats Watch Tower** *(no public access)*, was once a warehouse belonging to the family of WB Yeats's mother, the Pollexfen dynasty of Sligo merchants and sea traders.

Sligo Today – Sligo has a lively cultural scene, with theatres, concerts and high-profile art exhibitions at the greatly expanded Model Arts Centre *(see below)*. Festivals stud the calendar and at the Yeats Memorial Building there is a famous summer school devoted to the work of WB Yeats and his family.

YEATS COUNTRY

In their youth, the Yeats brothers spent many of their summer holidays with their Pollexfen cousins at Elsinore Lodge on Rosses Point, often watching their grandfather's ships in the bay from the top of the warehouse now known as the Yeats Watch Tower. Jack Yeats once remarked that he never did a painting without putting a thought of Sligo in it. Sligo and its surroundings, together with their rich mythical and legendary associations, continued to inspire William throughout his life; he is buried at Drumcliff *(see below)*, and he recorded in verse his visits to Lissadell House *(see below)* on Drumcliff Bay.

The town's many visitors seem to relish the contrast between its almost cosmopolitan atmosphere and the wild countryside around. Both they and local people profit from the proximity of the fine sandy beaches at Strandhill as well as at Rosses Point, where there is also a championship golf course.

Worth a Visit

Sligo Abbey★

South bank; Abbey Street. (Dúchas) Open late-Jun to mid-Sep, daily, 9.30am-6.30pm (5.15pm last admission). €2.50 Guided tour (45min) by appointment. Public parking nearby. ☎ 071 46406, ☎ 16 472 453 (opening times); sligoabbey@ealga.ie

The ruins standing on the south bank of the Garavogue River occupy the site of a Dominican friary, founded by Maurice Fitzgerald c 1252, which was accidentally damaged by fire in 1414; the refurbished buildings (1416), which were spared by Queen Elizabeth on condition that the friars became secular clergy, were deliberately set on fire in 1641 by the Parliamentary commander Sir Frederick Hamilton. The nave, which contains an elaborate altar tomb *(north wall)* belonging to the O'Creans (1506), is separated by a 15C rood screen (partially restored) from the 13C chancel, which contains the 17C O'Conor monument. North of the church are the 13C sacristy and chapter house and part of the 15C **cloisters** which have some fine carving.

Model Arts and the Niland Gallery★

The Mall. Open Apr-Oct, Tue-Sun 10am (noon Sun) to 5.30pm; Nov-Mar, Tue-Sat, 10am-5.30pm. ☎ 071 41405; Fax 071 43694; info@modelart.ie; www.modelart.ie

The forbidding-looking former Model School has been extended and transformed to give Sligo an arts centre of more than regional importance as well as a fine home for the **Niland Collection**, of **modern Irish art**. Displayed in rotation, the collection was assembled by the former county librarian Nora Niland and includes some 200 works by Jack B Yeats, including key paintings like *The Island Funeral*. In addition there are works by George Russell, Maurice McGonigal, Norah McGuiness, Estella Solomons, Paul Henry, Augustus John and Seán Keating.

County Museum

Stephen Street. Open Jun-Sep, Tue-Sat, 10am-noon and 2-4.50pm; Oct-May, Tue-Sat, 2-4.50pm. ☎ 071 42212 (Museum); 071 47190 (Central Library); Fax 071 46798, sligolib@shgococo.ie; sligolib@iol.ie

The old manse (1851) houses the **Yeats Memorial Collection** of manuscripts, photographs and letters connected with William Butler Yeats, as well as a pleasingly old-fashioned display of local antiquities and a large painting "1916", showing Countess Markiewicz and her fellow-insurgents surrendering outside the Royal College of Surgeons in Dublin.

St John's Cathedral

South bank; John Street. Open Sun, 8.30am and 10.30am; Jun-Aug, Mon-Sat, 10am-4pm. ☎ 071 62263 (The Dean, The Rectory, Strandhill Road, Sligo)

This unusual structure was designed in 1730 by Richard Castle; the apse and the windows were replaced during a not altogether fortunate remodelling in the Gothic style in 1812. A brass tablet *(north transept)* commemorates the mother of William Butler Yeats, Susan, who was married in the church; the tomb of her father, William Pollexfen, is near the main gates.

Cathedral of the Immaculate Conception

South bank; John Street or Temple Street. ♿ Open daily, 7am-9pm. Parking. ☎ 071 62670

The most interesting features of this uninspired neo-Romanesque building of 1874 are the 69 stained-glass windows, made by Loblin of Tours in France, best seen in the light of evening or early morning.

Excursion

SLIGO PENINSULA

The peninsula terminates at Strandhill, where the Atlantic breakers provide fine surfing (but hazardous bathing). Here too is Sligo's little airport, but the area's fame is mostly due to its outstanding prehistoric monuments.

Carrowmore Megalithic Cemetery★

3mi/5km SW of Sligo by a minor road. (Dúchas) (♿) Open early-April to mid-Nov, daily, 9.30am-6.30pm. €2.50/€8.80. Guided tour (45min). Sturdy footware advised. Parking. ☎ 071 61534

Carrowmore is the largest Stone Age cemetery in Ireland; it consists of over 60 passage graves – dolmens and stone circles and one cairn, which is the largest grave; the oldest dates from 3200 BC, 700 years earlier than Newgrange *(see p 146)*. The Visitor Centre contains an exhibition about Stone Age man and the excavations.

Knocknarea★

7mi/11km W of Sligo by R 292. After 6mi/10km bear left; after 1mi/1.6km park at the side of the road; 1hr 30min there and back on foot to the summit.

The approach road climbs up "The Glen", a natural fault in the limestone creating a special habitat in which rare plants thrive. On the summit of **Knocknarea** (1 076ft/328m) is a massive heap of stones (197yd/180m round), visible for miles, which probably contains a passage grave. Tradition and WB Yeats say that this

> *...cairn-heaped grassy hill*
> *Where passionate Maeve is stony-still*

is the tomb of Medb/Maeve, Queen of Connaught in 1C AD but it is more likely that she was buried at **Rathcroghan** near Tulsk *(see p 344)*. On a fine day the **view★★** from the top of the cairn is panoramic.

Tours

LOUGH GILL★★

Round tour of 30mi/48km E of Sligo – half a day

The lake is one of Ireland's loveliest, with islands, fine shoreline woodlands and with the looming presence of the limestone mountains to the northwest.

From Sligo take N 4 S; after 0.25mi/0.4km bear left (sign) to Lough Gill.

Tobernalt

Car park (right) at the road junction. The holy well shaded by trees marks an old Celtic assembly site where a festival was held in August (Lughnasa).

Continue on the shore road; at the T-junction turn left onto R 287.

Dooney Rock Forest

Car park. The top of Dooney Rock provides one of the best views of the lake, its islands, and Benbulben .

At the crossroads turn left; after 2mi/3.2km turn left; 2mi/3.2km to car park.

Innisfree

WB Yeats was especially drawn to the tiny island, immortalising it in his poem "Lake Isle of Innisfree". Only a few yards from the jetty on the mainland, it offers fine views of the lake and Parke's Castle *(see below)*.

Return to R 287 and continue E.

Dromahair

This attractive riverside village lies between the shell of Villiers Castle (17C) and a ruined abbey.

Creevelea Abbey

Park behind the Abbey Hotel (left); 6min there and back on foot across the bridge. An avenue of evergreens beside the Bonet River leads to the ruins of a Franciscan friary which was founded by Owen O'Rourke in 1508. The church presents well-preserved east and west windows and west door. Carved pillars in the cloisters on the north side show St Francis with the stigmata and with birds perched on a tree. In the 17C the tower was turned into living quarters.

Continue on R 287 (car park and viewpoint).

Parke's Castle★

(Dúchas) (& to grounds) Open mid-Mar to Oct, daily, 10am-6pm (5.15pm last admission). €2.50. Guided tour (40min) by appointment. Exhibitions. Audio-visual show (20min; 4 languages). Leaflet (6 languages). Tearoom. ☎ 071 64149; info@ heritageireland.ie; www.heritageireland.ie

The extensively restored castle is a fine example of a fortified Plantation mansion, its walls rising directly from the waters of the lough. It was built in 1609 by the Englishman Capt Robert Parke on the site of an earlier tower house, the home of Sir Brian O'Rourke, executed for treason in London in 1591. The bawn wall enclosing the yard supported the less substantial thatched outbuildings and there was a postern gate and a water gate to the lake; the water level was higher (10ft/3m) in the 17C. A **sweathouse** has been hollowed out in the wall by the shore. An audio-visual presentation gives an overview of the area's history.

Continue W on R 286 (car park and viewpoint); after 7mi/11.3km turn left.

Parke's Castle

Hazelwood

A nature trail explores the wooded peninsula which provides attractive views of the lake; the Palladian house *(private)* was designed by Richard Castle in 1731.

Continue W on R 286 to return to Sligo.

BENBULBEN

Round tour of 44mi/71km N of Sligo   1 day

The menacing silhouette of Benbulben, a limestone table mountain with a west-facing escarpment like the prow of a dreadnought, dominates the country for miles around.

From Sligo take N 15 N.

Drumcliff★

Car park. The many admirers of **William Butler Yeats** make the pilgrimage to his **grave** in the churchyard at Drumcliff *(left)*, where his great-grandfather had been rector. Yeats died in the south of France in 1939 but, in accordance with his wishes his body was later interred here. The gravestone carries the enigmatic epitaph he composed himself :

> Cast a cold eye
> On life, on death.
> Horseman, pass by!

Yeats' Tomb

The site beneath Benbulben (1 730ft/526m) by the Drumcliff River was also chosen by St Columba for the foundation of a monastery in about 575; the **round tower** was damaged by lightning in 1396; the **high cross**, which was probably erected c 1000, shows Adam and Eve, Cain killing Abel, Daniel in the Lions' Den and Christ in Glory on the east face, and the Presentation in the Temple and the Crucifixion on the west.

Make a detour left via Carney.

Lissadell House

Guided tour (40min) Jun to mid-Sep, Mon-Sat, 10.30am-1pm and 2-5pm (12.15pm and 4.15pm last admissions). €5. Parking. ☎ 071 63150; Fax 071 66906

Standing on the north shore of Sligo Bay surrounded by woods, this austere neo-Classical house is still lived in by the Gore-Booth family, descendants of the Englishman Captain Gore, who settled in the district in the reign of Elizabeth I. Sir Robert Gore-Booth, for whom the house was built in 1830, later nearly bankrupted himself attempting to relieve the distress of his tenants during the Famine. WB Yeats was a visitor here, enchanted by the atmosphere and half in love with the daughters of the family, Eva and Constance.

The interior has an appealing character of somewhat faded grandeur. The oval gallery, which is hung with paintings collected on the Grand Tour, was designed as a music room and visitors may be invited to test the excellent acoustics at the grand piano. More paintings, by and of the family, hang in the rooms overlooking the garden.

Leave the grounds by the north gate; turn left; after 1mi/1.6km turn left to Raghly (sign – 3mi/5km).

> ### COUNTESS MARKIEVICZ
> The most remarkable member of the Gore-Booth family was Constance (1868-1927), who married the Polish artist, impresario and boulevardier Casimir Markievicz and lived with him in Dublin and Paris. The couple drifted apart, not least because of Constance's passionate devotion to the Nationalist cause. While Casimir fought on the Allied side in the First World War, Constance took part in the Easter Rising. She was condemned to death, but reprieved two years later. She then became the first woman elected to the House of Commons in Westminster but never took her seat.

Ardtermon Castle

Standing within its bawn wall is the restored fortified dwelling built by a member of the Gore family in the early 17C. The entrance is flanked by two round towers; the staircase is contained in a semicircular projection at the rear facing the road.

Return to N 15 and continue N.

The road passes **Streedagh Point**, a sand bar (3mi/5km) lying parallel with the shore, where three ships from the Spanish Armada – *Juliana*, *La Levia* and *La Santa Maria de Vision* – were wrecked; over 1 300 men are thought to have died, those surviving drowning being put to death by the English soldiery.

In Cliffony turn left to Mullaghmore.

Mullaghmore

Sandy beaches flank the approach to the rocky headland pointing north into Donegal Bay. The village on the sheltered east side is grouped round the stone-walled harbour, built in 1842 by Lord Palmerston, who also built the splendidly picturesque neo-Gothic **Classiebawn Castle** (1856) which rises on the exposed west shore. The castle later became the holiday home of Lord Mountbatten, who, with several members of his family, was blown up in his sailing boat in 1979 by the IRA.

Inishmurray

11mi/18km offshore; access by boat from Mullaghmore pier and from Rosses Point near Sligo (see Directory). St Molaise founded a settlement on this little island in the 6C, and within its small compass is a surprising array of early monuments. The remains of Molaise's monastery include the Women's Church *(Teampall na mBan)*; rectangular and "beehive"-style dwellings; the main or Men's Church; souterrains and stone altars. Elsewhere on the island are pillar stones which may be pre-Christian, 57 inscribed stone slabs and 16 Stations of the Cross, spaced around the rocky perimeter. The island has a long history of human habitation – a decorated container found here dates back to 2000 BC – and not until 1948 did the last people leave, defeated by postwar fuel restrictions, which ended the regular supply-boat trips from Killybegs *(see p 201)*.

From Mullaghmore return inland bearing left at the first fork and right at the second. At the crossroads turn left onto N 15; car park opposite.

Creevykeel Court Cairn*

Car park. The well-preserved court tomb, which dates from the Late Stone Age (c 2500 BC), consists of an open court leading into a double burial chamber surrounded by a wedge-shaped mound of stones. Two other chambers, entered from the side, were probably made later.

At the crossroads turn left inland.

Gleniff Horseshoe Scenic Drive

This short loop road *(6mi/10km)* makes a fascinating incursion into the upland landscapes of the Dartry Mountains between the western face of their highest summit, **Truskmore** (2 120ft/644m), and Benbulben itself.

Turn left onto the minor road. After 6mi/9.5km turn left onto N 15; before reaching Drumcliff turn left onto a minor road.

Glencar Waterfall★

Car park left; access path right; 5min there and back on foot. The waterfall tumbles over layers of rock to a sheer drop (50ft/15m) into a round pool. The wind howling in from the Atlantic sometimes blows its waters upwards, an effect noted by WB Yeats:

...the cataract smokes upon the mountain side... that cold and vapour-turbaned steep.

Continue E. At the junction turn right into N 16 to return to Sligo.

Strokestown★

A particularly fine example of an estate village and now a Heritage town, Strokestown has a broad main street running up to the fanciful Gothick arches of the entrance to Strokestown Park House. Lived in by its founding family until 1979, the house gives an intriguing picture of the life led by a prominent family of the Anglo-Irish Ascendancy. The surrounding district is rich in relics of earlier Irish society.

Location

Population 568 - Michelin Atlas p 90 and Map 712 – H 6 – Co Roscommon.
Strokestown *(Béal Na Mbuilli)* is on N 5, the main road leading northwest from Longford, in the north part of Co Roscommon.

🄱 *Harrison Hall, Roscommon. Open Jun-Aug, Mon-Sat.* ☎ *0903 26342*

Adjacent Sights: See ATHLONE, BOYLE, CARRICK-ON-SHANNON, KNOCK, LONGFORD)

> **TRACING ANCESTORS**
> County Roscommon Heritage
> Centre – Genealogical research service –
> *See below*

Background

Confiscated from its original owner, O'Connor Roe, part of whose bawn survives in the building now housing the restaurant, land at Strokestown was granted to Capt Nicholas Mahon (d 1680), a Cromwellian officer, and the estate was later extended to secure his support for Charles II. As they prospered, successive members of the Mahon family rebuilt or extended the house begun by Nicholas Mahon. In 1800, Maurice Mahon accepted a Union peerage, becoming Baron Hartland of Strokestown, despite his father having been a bitter opponent of the Act of Union. In 1845, as the Great Famine began, the property passed to Major Denis Mahon, who acquired an unenviable reputation as a heartless evictor of his destitute tenants, more than 3 000 in total, many of whom perished aboard the notorious "coffin ships". On 2 November 1847 in broad daylight, while riding in an open carriage, he was shot dead by two assassins; that evening, bonfires were lit in celebration on the nearby hills.

Worth a Visit

Famine Museum★

♿ *Open mid-Mar to Oct, daily, 10am-5.30pm. Museum €5; museum, house and garden €12. Leaflet (3 languages). Restaurant.* ☎ *078 33013; Fax 078 33712; info@ strokestownpark.ie; www.strokestownpark.ie*

The museum, which is housed in the stable yard, presents a comprehensive, detailed and balanced account of the Great Famine, based on State archives and the Strokestown estate records for the famine years, which were used by Cecil Woodham-Smith in compiling her book *The Great Hunger.*

The exhibition traces the history of the family and the estate, explains the political, economic and natural events in the mid-19C which produced the Great Famine and Emigration, and makes telling comparisons between conditions in Ireland in the 19C and the Third World today.

Strokestown Park House★

(&) *Guided tour (40min) Apr-Oct, daily, 10am-5.30pm. House €5; house, garden and museum €12. Leaflet (3 languages). Restaurant. ☎ 078 33013; Fax 078 33712; info@strokestownpark.ie; www.strokestownpark.ie.*

The house, a fine Palladian mansion designed by Richard Castle in the 1730s, consists of a central three-storey block with a pillared portico, linked by curving corridors to the service wings.

The well-preserved interiors give an impression of a comfortable and sociable rather than ostentatious life. There are many fascinating touches,

Famine pot, Strokestown Famine Museum

from the bowed window in the ballroom to accommodate the musicians, to the children's quarters upstairs, with bedroom, schoolroom and a display of toys. As well as spits and a trio of ovens for baking, roasting and smoking, the great **kitchen** has a dresser filled with Belleek pottery *(see p 425)* and is overlooked by a gallery from which the housekeeper could supervise her underlings.

Both **Walled Gardens** have been fully restored to their original splendour. The larger pleasure garden (4 acres/1.6ha) is embellished with a magnificent Edwardian pergola and an immensely long herbaceous border; the smaller Georgian fruit and vegetable garden contains the original glasshouses for growing grapes, peaches and figs, as well as an elegant gazebo with two Venetian windows providing fine views of the gardens and estate.

Roscommon County Heritage Centre

& *Open Mon-Fri, 2.30-4.30pm. Closed Bank Hols. Genealogical service. Parking. ☎ 078 33380; Fax 078 33398; www.roscommonroots.com.*

At the north end of the village stands St John's Church (Anglican – deconsecrated), an octagonal structure designed in 1820 to resemble a medieval chapter house; it presents a historical interpretation of Strokestown.

Tour

CRUACHAN DISTRICT

6.5mi/10km from Strokestown by R 368 N to Elphin; follow signs.

Elphin Windmill

(&) *Guided tour daily, 10am-6pm. €2.50. Picnic area. ☎ 086 838 2118 or 078 35695*

The early-18C windmill is the only one of its kind in the west of Ireland and has been restored to full working order. It is an imposing and unusual structure, its conical thatched roof and sails made to face the wind by means of cartwheels running on a circular track.

From Elphin take R 369 W; turn left onto N 61; in Tulsk turn right onto N 5 to Rathcroghan.

Cruachan Aí Visitor Centre

& *Open daily, 10am-6pm (5pm Oct-Mar). Guided tours by appointment: Visitor Centre (1hr approx; €4.50); site tour (1hr approx; €3.50). Café. ☎ 078 39268; Fax 078 39060; info@cruachanai.com; www.cruachanai.com*

On the banks of the little Ogulla River, this sensitively designed structure and its fascinating displays offer the key to understanding the area's extraordinary complex of field monuments which have long fascinated archaeologists and antiquarians but whose precise function and meaning is only now being unravelled.

The Centre abuts a ring fort and the motte of an Anglo-Norman style castle, but the majority of the monuments – Bronze Age tumuli, ring-barrows (one over 65yd/60m in diameter, souterrains, field systems and ceremonial avenues – are spread widely over a broad and and fertile landscape which has been grazed since Neolithic times and which features in some of the country's most compelling myths and legends as well as in its actual history. According to the *Táin Bó Cúailgne* saga, it was from here that Queen Medb/Maeve set out on the great Cattle Raid of Cooley, and it was here that the kings of Ireland were buried before Tara became the royal cemetery in the first century AD. The kings of Connaught were inaugurated on the summit of the hill at Carnfree, the last such ceremony taking place as late as 1641. The inauguration stone is now at Clonalis House *(see below)*.

Continue NW on N 5 for 9mi/14km.

Douglas Hyde Centre

&. *Open May-Sep, Tue-Sun, 2-5pm (6pm Sat-Sun); otherwise telephone for details. Donation. Parking. Picnic area.* ☎ *0907 70016*

The Anglican Church in Tibohine, where his father was Rector, is now devoted to the life of Douglas Hyde (1860-1949), first President of the Irish Republic (1938-45), who is buried here. Unusually for one of Anglo-Irish origin, Dr Douglas Hyde was an Irish scholar and a passionate collector of Irish poetry and folk tales. As president of the Gaelic League, his efforts were directed to the preservation of Gaelic as the national language of Ireland and the promotion of Irish literature.

Take the minor road S via Cloonfad and Fairymount and R 361 to Castlerea. Turn right onto N 60, then right again.

Clonalis House*

(&. to ground floor) Guided tour (45min) Jun to mid-Sep, Mon-Sat, 11am-5pm. €5. Parking. Refreshments ☎*/Fax 0907 20014; clonalis@iol.ie*

Clonalis is the seat of the O'Connor Don (Don means king or leader), one of the most ancient of Irish dynasties, who trace their ancestry back to Federach the Just in AD 75. The present house, overlooking the River Suck, is of rather less antiquity, an Italianate structure designed in 1878 by the English architect Pepys Cockerell.

Beside the front door *(left)* stands the inauguration stone of the O'Connor clan which was formerly at **Rathcroghan** *(see above)*.

The well-furnished house is full of mementoes of the O'Connors, who played a prominent role not just in the life of Ireland but abroad, one of them founding the city of Tucson in Arizona. There are portraits, costumes, uniforms, and the standard borne at the coronation of George V in 1911 by Denis O'Connor, the first member of an Irish Gaelic family to be so honoured. Over the centuries, the O'Connors assembled vast and valuable archives, a library of more than 5 000 books and over 100 000 documents and letters, some of them on display in the billiard room; their signatories include Louis XIV, Samuel Johnson, Daniel O'Connell, Gladstone and Douglas Hyde. Also here is the harp belonging to the blind bard Turlough Carolan, who often played for the O'Connors.

Two relics from the Penal Period are displayed in the **chapel** : an altar from a secret chapel, and a chalice which unscrews for easy concealment.

Take N 60 SE; after 2.5mi/4km turn left to Ballintober.

Ballintober Castle

The ruined castle was inhabited as recently as the 19C. The high walls, fortified by a polygonal tower at each corner and originally surrounded by a moat, enclose a large rectangular courtyard. Two projecting turrets guard the entrance gate. In 1652 the castle was captured by the Cromwellians but in 1677 it was returned to the O'Connor Don *(see above)*, by whose ancestors it was built c 1300.

Take R 367 S; turn right onto N 60. In Ballymoe turn left and left again onto the minor road to Glinsk.

Glinsk Castle

The four-storey ruin is roofless and gutted but the windows and chimneys and projecting towers suggest a fine fortified house, built by the Burkes c 1618-30.

Continue SE through Creggs and on R 362. Before joining N 63, turn left and left again onto a private drive.

Castlestrange Stone*

In a field *(right)* is a rounded granite boulder decorated with curvilinear designs in the Celtic style of ornament known as La Tène which dates from 250 BC.

Turn left onto N 63 towards Roscommon.

Roscommon Dominican Friary

The ruined friary, established in 1253, still has an effigy of its founder, Felim O'Connor, his feet resting on a dog; below is a panel with vigorous carvings of mail-clad and well-armed gallowglasses, the fearsome mercenary warriors imported from the west of Scotland in the 14C.

Continue on N 63 to Roscommon.

Roscommon

The county town, an important market in the middle of rich cattle and sheep country, is named after St Comán, first Bishop of Roscommon and abbot of Clonmacnoise. He founded a monastery of Augustinian canons in Roscommon; traces of it may have been incorporated into the Anglican church. The history of the monastery, the town and the district is illustrated in the endearingly old-fashioned **Roscommon County Museum**, housed in a former Presbyterian chapel. &. *Open Mon-Fri, 10am-3pm. €2.* ☎ *0903 25613*

N of the town on N 61; From the car park 2min on foot over a stile and across a field.

Roscommon Castle★

On rising ground stands the impressive ruin of an enormous Norman castle, built in 1269 by Robert de Ufford and originally protected by a lake or swamp. Its massive walls, which are defended by round bastions at each corner, enclose a vast rectangular area. The mullion windows were inserted by Sir Nicholas Malby, Governor of Connaught, who probably occupied the castle in 1578. In 1645 it was captured by the Confederates under Preston but he surrendered in 1652 to the troops of Cromwell, who ordered its destruction.

Tralee

At the head of its bay, the county town of Kerry is a flourishing, workaday place with a range of traditional and modern industries. Not particularly oriented to tourism, it is nevertheless an important gateway to the Dingle peninsula, treating its visitors to an ambitious and informative evocation to the region, the "Kingdom of Kerry". It is also the home of the country's National Folk Theatre, and hopefuls come here from all over the Irish diaspora for the annual "Rose of Tralee" festival.

Directory

GETTING ABOUT

Tarbert Pier is the departure point for the **Shannon Ferry** which carries cars and passengers to Killimer on the north bank – *Operates (crossing time approx 20min) daily (except 25 Dec) from Killimer (north bank), hourly on the hour, Apr-Sep, 7am (9am Sun) to 9pm; Oct-Mar, 7am (10am Sun) to 7pm; from Tarbert (south bank) hourly on the half hour, Apr-Sep, 7.30am (9.30am Sun) to 9.30pm; Oct-Mar, 7.30am (10.30am Sun) to 7.30pm. Capacity 52 + 60 vehicles. Car €12.50 (single), €19 (return); pedestrian €3 (single), €5 (return). Visitor Centre at Killimer: Open daily, 9am-9pm (7pm Oct-Mar). Parking. Bureau de change.* ☎ *065 905 3124; Fax 065 905 3125 (Shannon Ferry Ltd); enquiries@shannonferries.com; www.shannonferries.com*

ENTERTAINMENT

National Folk Theatre of Ireland (Siamsa Tíre) – The performances of this theatre, founded in 1974, draw on the rich local Gaelic tradition to evoke in music, song, dance and mime the seasonal festivals and rural way of life in past centuries. The past is also reflected in the ultra-modern theatre building which is shaped like a ring fort; a round tower gives access to the upper catwalks. &. *Opening times according to performances, telephone for details. Closed Good Fri, 25-26 Dec. Gallery no charge; Theatre productions from €15.24. Refreshments. Audio loop.* ☎ *066 712 3055; Fax 066 712 7276; siamatire@eircom.net; www.siamsatire.com*

SHOPPING

Crafts – Visit the Blennerville craft workshops *(see below).*

SPORTS AND LEISURE

Beaches – West and north in Tralee Bay. There are indoor water facilities at the **Aqua Dome** – *Open Jun-Aug, daily, 10am-10pm; Sep-May, phone for times. €8 (Apr-Aug); €7 (Sep-Mar). Parking.* ☎ *066 712 8899 (Reception), 066 712 8755 (Administration), 066 712 9150 (24hr information); Fax 066 712 9130; aquadome@eircom.net; www.discoverkerry.com/aquadome* Seaweed baths at Ballybunnion. Greyhound racing.

EVENTS AND FESTIVALS

Listowel Writers' Week – Celebration of the exceptional literary reputation of Listowel held annually in May.

Location

Population 19 056 - Michelin Atlas p 83 and Map 712 - C 11 - Co Kerry.
Tralee *(Trá Lí)* is situated at the neck of the Dingle Peninsula on the main roads (N 21 and N 69) between Dingle and Limerick. It is only 20mi/32km N of Farranfore Airport.

🖪 *Ashe Memorial Hall, Tralee. Open daily.* ☎ *066 712 1288; Fax 066 712 1700; TourismInfo@shannondev.ie; www.shannondev.ie/tourism*
Adjacent Sights: See ADARE, DINGLE PENINSULA, KENMARE, KILLARNEY.

Background

Desmond Stronghold and Denny Fief

Tralee grew up around the castle built in 1243 by the Anglo-Norman, John Fitzgerald; his descendants, the Earls of Desmond became one of the most powerful Old English clans, "more Irish than the Irish" and deadly rivals of the Ormonds. The Geraldine (ie Fitzgerald) line came to an end in 1583 when the 15th Earl, who had rebelled with Spanish and Papal help, was betrayed and executed; his head was displayed on a spike at the Tower of London Tralee and the Desmond estates were granted to Sir Hugh Denny, who had helped defeat the Spanish; the Denny family held sway here for 300 years.

> **ROSE OF TRALEE**
> Every August the town is host to the International Rose of Tralee Festival which attracts visitors, particularly emigrants, from many parts of the world; all girls of Irish descent are eligible for the title In the Town Park stands a statue of William Mulchinock (1820-64), who wrote the song *The Rose of Tralee*, of which this is the refrain:
> "She was lovely and fair as the rose of the summer
> Yet 'twas not her beauty alone that won me
> Oh no 'twas the truth in her eye ever dawning
> That made me love Mary, the Rose of Tralee."

The town suffered badly in the wars of the 17C and now has a mostly 18C and 19C character, its most distinguished edifice being the Greek Revival Courthouse designed by Sir Richard Morrison in the mid-19C. Strongly nationalistic in outlook, Tralee became an important centre of opposition to British rule in the late 19C-early 20C.

Tralee Bay

Worth a Visit

Kerry – The Kingdom★

Ashe Memorial Hall. ⮾ *Open mid-Mar to Oct, daily, 9.30am-5.30pm; Nov-Dec, daily, 11am-4.30pm. Closed 24-27 Dec. €8. Audioguide (3 languages). Commentary (8 languages). Museum brochure (6 languages). Guided tour available. Parking. Café.* ☎ *066 712 7777; Fax 066 712 7444; kcmuseum@indigo.ie.*

This popular visitor attraction has three sections. In **The Geraldine Experience** the sights, sounds and even the smells of the medieval town are recreated for visitors who are carried through a partial reconstruction of Tralee in time cars equipped with multi-lingual commentary. **Kerry in Colour** is an exciting multimedia presentation of the history of the region from Mesolithic times onwards, complemented by the **Kerry County Museum**, with a wealth of artefacts, scale models and stimulating displays. The surrounding **town park** contains the ruins of the **Geraldine castle**.

Tralee–Blennerville Light Railway

 & *Operates June to early-Oct, daily, 11am-5.30pm, on the hour from Ballyard Station in Tralee, on the half hour from Blennerville. €4. Parking. Restaurant at Blennerville.* ☎ *066 712 1064*

The Tralee & Dingle Light Railway meandering over the hills of the Dingle peninsula was the westernmost railway in Europe. It closed in 1953 but the centenary year of its construction was marked in 1991 by the re-opening to passenger traffic of the first stretch *(1.5mi/2.4km)* of the narrow-gauge (3ft/1m) line between Tralee and Blennerville *(see below)*. The train is composed of three original carriages drawn by No 5, last of the original steam locomotives.

Excursions

Blennerville Windmill*

2mi/3.2km S of Tralee by R 559. & *Open Apr-Oct, daily, 10am-6pm. €4. Audio-visual show (8min). Brochure. Guided tour (30min) available. Parking. Restaurant. Craft centre.* ☎ *066 712 1064*

The exceptionally tall, white-painted five-storey windmill (60ft/18m high), built by the local landlord, Sir Rowland Blennerhassett, c 1800 and derelict by 1880, is again in working order; an electric engine takes over when the wind fails.

The **Emigration Exhibition** in the adjoining building illustrates the experience of the many thousands who left Ireland for America in the 19C – embarkation, the sea voyage, food, medical matters, quarantine on arrival. Work began here in 1998 on the construction of a 540 tonne replica of an emigrant ship, the *Jeannie Johnston*, and she was officially launched at nearby Fenit in 2002.

In the **craft workshops** visitors can see artists at work and buy the finished product – pottery, enamels etc.

Blennerville Windmill

Crag Cave*

11mi/18km E of Tralee by N 21 to Castleisland (Oileán Ciarraí); take the minor road N for 1mi/1.6km (sign). & *Open Apr-Oct, daily, 10am-6pm. €4. Audio-visual show (8min). Brochure. Guided tour (30min) available. Parking. Restaurant. Craft centre.* ☎ *066 712 1064*

The complex of limestone caves (4 170yd/3 813m), discovered in 1983, is thought to be over a million years old. A short descent *(62 steps)* leads to the tunnels and chambers of the show cave (383yd/350m); lighting enhances the natural beauty of the many calcite formations – stalactites, stalagmites, columns, curtains, drip stones and flow stones. The myriad shimmering white straw stalactites in the **Crystal Gallery** provide a magical climax.

Tour

NORTH KERRY

Drive of 87mi/140km
From Tralee take R 551 N and R 558 W.

Fenit Sea World

Park on the pier. & *Open Mar-May, daily, 11am-5.30pm; Jun-Aug, 10am-6pm; €5.50. Parking.* ☎/*Fax 066 713 6544*

Every few minutes a wave of water crashes into the **aquarium**. All the myriad species of fish displayed are named and identified. The touch-tank presents cockles, mussels, urchins, crabs, limpets and starfish.

Take a minor road N to Ardfert.

Ardfert★

(Dúchas) (&) Open early-May to late-Sep, daily, 9.30am-6pm (5.15pm last admission). €1.90. Leaflet (5 languages). Guided tour (45min) by appointment. Parking. Wheelchair access to exhibition area and viewing point. ☎ *066 713 4711*

Ardfert was established as a missionary base as early as the 5C. The stone church, founded in the 6C by **St Brendan** the Navigator *(see p 253)* as part of a monastery, was destroyed by fire in 1089. Under the Normans Ardfert became a borough, far more important than Tralee, though the lack of a harbour led to its eventual eclipse; two major ecclesiastical ruins have survived from this period.

The **cathedral** was built c 1150 and destroyed by fire in the 17C but its walls still rise to the eaves and its east end has a trio of elegant lancet windows. The south transept (15C) contains an exhibition on the history of the building and the two adjacent small churches, which are decorated with interesting sculptures.

Standing among the fields, **Ardfert Friary**, a Franciscan house, was founded in 1253 and substantially rebuilt in 1453; much of the tower and of the chancel with its nine lancets in the south wall and five-light lancet in the east wall are still intact.

Continue N on R 551.

Banna Strand★

The vast stretch of sandy beach (5mi/8km) was used for the filming of *Ryan's Daughter* in 1968. A memorial at the entrance commemorates Sir Roger Casement (1864-1916), who landed on the beach on 21 April 1916 from a German submarine with a consignment of arms for the Easter Rising; he was recognised and arrested almost at once and subsequently executed.

Continue N on R 551.

Rattoo Round Tower★

The exceptionally well-preserved round tower and the ruined 15C church mark the site of an abbey founded in 1200 for the Knights Hospitaller of St John the Baptist. In 1202 it became an Augustinian house, which was burned in 1600.

The **Rattoo-North Kerry Museum** at Ballyduff *(2mi/3.2km N)* displays relics illustrating the history of the locality – Bronze Age (2000 BC) ferry boat carved from a split oak trunk. & *Open Apr-Sep, daily, 10am (2pm Sun) to 6pm. €2.50. Guided tour available.* ☎/*Fax 066 713 1000*

Continue N on R 551; make a detour along the coast road via Kilcoly, Beal and Astee.

Ballybunnion

This rather old-fashioned little seaside resort has amusement arcades and several fine beaches; it is also noted for its outdoor baths, where seaweed is used for therapeutic purposes.

Continue N and E on R 551; just before Ballylongford turn left into a minor road.

Carrigafoyle Castle★

Once the principal seat of the O'Connor clan, who ruled most of north Kerry, the castle, originally on an island, was finally destroyed by Cromwellian forces in 1649. One of the flanker towers is fitted out as a dovecot. A spiral staircase leads to the top of the tower (80ft/24m high) for extensive **views** of the Shannon estuary.

Return to R 551 and continue E; in Ballylongford turn left to Saleen.

Lislaughtln Abbey

This Franciscan foundation dates from the 15C; the church has an attractive west window and three well-preserved sedilia; traces of the refectory and dormitory remain on the east side of the cloisters; the lavatories were housed in the tower at the north end.

Continue E on minor road to Tarbert.

Tarbert

Tarbert Bridewell, built 1828-31, has been converted into a museum describing, through wax tableaux in the courtroom and cells, the legal and penal systems in force in Ireland at that time. *Open Apr-Oct, daily, 10am-6pm; Nov-Mar, by appointment. €5. Guide book (5 languages).* ☎ *068 36500; Fax 068 36500*

The **woodland walk** *(starting from the car park)* leads through the grounds of **Tarbert House** (17C), which has seen such notable guests as Benjamin Franklin, Charlotte Brontë and Daniel O'Connell, and continues along the wooded shore to Tarbert Old Pier. *Open May to mid-Aug, 10am-noon and 2-4pm. €3.17.* ☎ *068 36198, 36500*

From Tarbert take N 69 S.

Listowel (Lios Tuathail)

17mi/27km N of Tralee by N 69. The literary reputation of the market town and Heritage town of Listowel and of north Kerry is celebrated in **Writers' Week**, which is held annually in May and attracts world-wide participation. In the huge central square stands **St John's Art and Heritage Centre**, formerly the Anglican parish church, which offers live performances of music and theatre, film shows and various exhibitions about art, literature, history; the permanent display, consisting of collected texts, archive recordings and audio-visual presentations, covers the work of John B Keane, Brian McMahon, Brendan Kennelly and other local writers. & *Open daily, 10am-6pm. Closed Good Fri; 23 Dec to 2 Jan. Monthly programme of theatre, music and dance; films and exhibitions. Parking. Refreshments.* ☎ *068 22566; Fax 068 23485; stjohnstheatre@eircom.net; www.stjohnstheatrelistowel.com*

In the northeast corner of the square is the striking **plasterwork façade** of the Central Hotel.

Continue S on N 69 to return to Tralee.

Trim★

Straddling the Boyne by an ancient ford, little Trim, a designated Heritage town, is dominated by the ruins of its castle, the largest in Ireland, a medieval monument to match the great prehistoric structures further down the valley. Other imposing remains recall Trim's important role as a stronghold and ecclesiastical centre on the outer edge of the Pale established by the Anglo-Normans.

Location

Population 1 740 - Michelin Atlas p 92 and Map 712 – L 7 – Co Meath.
Trim *(Baile Átha Troim)* is situated on the River Boyne, a little SW of Navan, on a minor road (R 154) which forks off the N 3 Dublin-Navan road.
🚩 *Trim. Open May-Sep, Mon-Sat.* ☎ *046 37111*
Adjacent Sights: See BOYNE VALLEY, FINGAL, KELLS, MAYNOOTH, MULLINGAR.

Worth a Visit

Trim Castle★★
South bank; access through the Town Gate or along the river bank from the bridge. (Dúchas) Castle and keep: Open May-Oct, daily, 10am-6pm (5.15pm last admission). Keep: Guided tour (45min). Castle €2.50. Very busy site; access cannot be guaranteed during the summer. Leaflet/guide booklet. Parking nearby. ☎ *046 38618; 046 38619;* ☎ *041 988 0300 (reservations for keep tour mid-Sep to mid-June); Fax 041 982 3071; www.heritageireland.ie*

The magnificent ruins of this medieval castle rise over the meadows flanking the Boyne, whose waters fed the now-dry moat. An outer curtain wall with gatehouses and several towers encloses a broad grassy space dominated by the formidable **keep** (1225) with its two great halls and sleeping accommodation above.

The first stronghold here was built in 1172, in the early days of the Anglo-Norman conquest by Hugh de Lacy, but was soon attacked and destroyed by the native Irish. Rebuilt, it served as King John's headquarters on his sojourn in Ireland and is often called King John's Castle. Protected by two drawbridges and a barbican, the Dublin Gate served as a prison, where the young prince who was to become Henry IV was held prisoner by Richard II. The castle was attacked by Cromwell's troops, who left a breach in the river wall; an adjacent stretch of wall collapsed in 1839, in the course of a storm known as the Big Wind.

Across the river stands a stone arch, the medieval **Sheep Gate, a fragment of the town's medieval walls**; tolls were levied here on flocks bought and sold at the great sheep fairs.

Yellow Steeple

North bank; access from the High Street.
The ruined late-14C tower, which gleams in the sun, marks the site of **St Mary's Abbey**, an Augustinian community, founded by St Malachy of Armagh in the 12C near the point where St Patrick landed in the 5C and converted Foitchern, the son of the local chieftain and later first Bishop of Trim. Many pilgrims were attracted to the abbey by Our Lady of Trim, a wooden statue with a reputation for effecting miracles, which disappeared in the Cromwellian period.

In 1425 the west cloisters of the abbey were converted by Lord Lieutenant Talbot into a fortified house, **Talbot's Castle**, which bears the Talbot coat of arms on the north wall. After the Reformation the house became a Latin School, later attended by the young Duke of Wellington, sometime MP for Trim, whose family home was at Dangan (SE). Unlike many other members of the Ascendancy, the Iron Duke was not particularly proud of his origins, famously denigrating his Irishness by declaring "because a man is born in a stable, it does not make him a horse".

Cathedral

North bank; 1mi/1.6km E at Newtown Trim. Among the graves of Newtown Cemetery is a **tomb** bearing the recumbent figures of Sir Luke Dillon, in his Renaissance armour, and his wife, Lady Jane Bathe, in an Elizabethan gown. Separated by a sword, they are referred to as "the jealous man and woman", Lady Jane supposedly having deceived her husband with his brother. People leave pins on the tomb in the belief that their warts will disappear.

Further west are the lovely ruins of a **cathedral**, built early in the 13C to replace the church at Clonard (SW), which was burned by the Irish at the end of the 12C. To the southwest, further remains are those of a priory, two walls of its refectory still standing next to the 14C kitchen.

Crutched Friary

South bank; 1mi/1.6km E at Newtown Trim. On the south bank of the Boyne are the ruins of a 13C hospital built by the Crutched Friars, an order of mendicant friars who wore a cross on their habit. The buildings consist of a keep with several fireplaces, a ruined chapel with a triple-light window and the hospital and stores beside the river.

Trim Castle

Bective Abbey★

5mi/8km NE by R 161 (T 26); after 4mi/6.4km turn right. Park beyond the abbey near the bridge. The impressive and extensive ruins stand in a field on the west bank of the Knightsbrook River. The abbey, one of the earliest Cistercian houses in Ireland, was founded in 1150 by the King of Meath, Murcha Ó Maolsheachlainn, and dedicated to the Blessed Virgin; its abbot was a member of the Parliament of the Pale and Hugh de Lacy was buried here in 1195. Little remains of the 12C buildings. The **cloisters**, the tower and the great hall in the south wing date from the 15C when the buildings were altered and fortified.

The film *Braveheart* (1996) was shot among these ruins and also at nearby Dunsoghly Castle.

Tullamore

Once known as King's County after Mary Tudor's Spanish husband, Co Offaly forms the very heart of southern Ireland, with the Shannon to the west, the great Bog of Allen to the east, and the Slieve Bloom Mountains to the south. Bustling Tullamore has been the county town since 1833. Otherwise undistinguished, the place still has something of its late-18C/early-19C character, when much rebuilding took place and when the construction of the Grand Canal brought the town a measure of prosperity.

Location

Population 9 221 - Michelin Atlas p 91 and Map 712 – J 8 – Co Offaly.
Tullamore *(Tulach Mhór)* is due west of Dublin, on the Grand Canal, just south of the Dublin-Athlone road (N 6).
🖪 *Tullamore Dew Heritage Centre, Tullamore. Open daily.* ☎ *0506 52617*
Adjacent Sights: See ABBEYLEIX, ATHLONE, ATHY, BIRR, KILDARE, TRIM.

DIRECTORY
Irish Midlands Ancestry, *Bury Quay, Offaly – Open Mon-Fri, 9am-1pm and 2-4pm. Public Reading Room: Open 10am-4pm.* ☎ *0506 21421l; Fax 0506 21421; ohas@iol.ie; www.offalyhistory.com*

Worth a Visit

Tullamore Distillery Heritage Centre

& *Open daily, 9am (10am Oct-Apr; noon Sun) to 6pm (5pm Oct-Apr). Closed 25 Dec. €4.45. Lift. Parking.* ☎ *0506 25015; Fax 0506 25016; tullamoredhc@eircom.net; www.tullamore-dew.org*

A golden drop of *Tullamore Dew* or *Irish Mist* awaits in the bar but first it is worth discovering the history of Tullamore, particularly of the distillery, founded in 1829 by Michael Molloy. In 1887 Daniel E Williams, who had been steeped in whiskey production since joining the staff at the age of 15, became general manager and gradually acquired overall control of the business. He used his own initials to provide a brand name – *Tullamore Dew* – for the distillery's pot still whiskey and from that flowed the advertising slogan – *Give every man his Dew*. In the 1950s, when sales were low, the distillery began to produce *Irish Mist*, a whiskey-based liqueur, inspired by a traditional Irish recipe for heather wine made with pot still whiskey, herbs and heather honey.

Excursions

Locke's Distillery

Kilbeggan; 7.5mi/12km N of Tullamore by N 52. (&) *Open Apr-Oct, daily, 9am-6pm; Nov-Mar, daily, 10am-4pm. Closed 23-30 Dec. €4.13. Guided tour including complimentary whiskey sampling (in summer; 3 languages). Self-guided tour (7 languages). Parking. Restaurant/*

A MELANCHOLY ACCIDENT
This was the term used at the time to describe what was one of the world's first air disasters. In 1785, only two years after the Montgolfier brothers had launched their hot air balloon into the skies over Paris, a Tullamore gentleman was showing off his balloon to the townsfolk. Unfortunately it crashed and exploded, severely damaging a hundred of the town's buildings. The Great Balloon Fire turned out to be a blessing in disguise; under the leadership of the Moore/Bury family, the town was largely rebuilt in a dignified late Georgian style.

coffee shop. Very limited wheelchair access. ✆/Fax 0506 32134; lockesmuseum@iol.ie; www.lockesdistillerymuseum.com
On the west bank of the River Brosna stand the extensive buildings of the distillery (1757-1953) established by John Locke, possibly the oldest licensed distillery. In the **cooperage** craftsmen make the oak casks in which whiskey, produced at Cooley, is matured. The process of distilling whiskey is explained and much of the original equipment is still in place: three sets of millstones for grinding barley; the mash tuns (known as kieves) for making wort; the huge wooden vats (washbacks) for fermentation; the hogsheads for maturing the whiskey; coopers' tools; the undershot waterwheel, and the steam engine which replaced it when the water level was too high or too low.

Locke's Distillery

Clara Bog

7mi/10km NW of Tullamore by N 80, in Clara take a minor road S; car park at the end of a short causeway; visitors should not stray from this causeway unless accompanied by a knowledgeable guide. This raised bog (1 640 acres/665ha; 23ft/7m maximum depth) is one of the finest and largest of its kind remaining in Ireland and is of international interest. In 1987 it was designated a National Nature Reserve. It has a diverse flora, including at least 10 different bog mosses; in wet areas carnivorous plants, like sundews and bladderworts, entrap unwary insects.

DURROW HIGH CROSS

The *Book of Durrow,* an illuminated manuscript now in Trinity College Library in Dublin, is the most famous relic of the abbey founded in 556 by St Columba at Durrow *(4mi/7km N of Tullamore by N 52).* In 1186 the abbey church was pulled down by the Anglo-Norman Hugh de Lacy, an act of sacrilege which so outraged a local man that he cut off the intruder's head. The Book survived despite being used by a farmer to cure his sick cattle, touching them with it after soaking it in water. The site of the abbey *(private property)* is a gloomily romantic place, with a ruined 18C church, a holy well, a cemetery with 9C to 11C grave slabs, and above all a fine 10C **high cross**. Its east face shows the Sacrifice of Isaac together with Christ in Glory flanked by David with his harp *(left)* and David killing the Lion *(right)*; the west face shows the Crucifixion and associated events.

Waterford★

The harbour city of Waterford continues to benefit from its superb location on the tidal River Suir inland from its confluence with the River Barrow and the vast stretch of sheltered water known as Waterford Harbour. With glassware which has become a global brand, the city enjoys a prosperity which has deep roots in a mercantile and manufacturing tradition going back to its foundation by the Vikings in the 9C.

Many memories of this long history are preserved in the mile-long quayside, the close-packed streets and the surviving sections of the once extensive City Walls★ which enclosed the town. The watchtower (35ft/10m high) surveys a well-preserved section on the south side near John's River. As well as the Norman extensions, which are mostly 13C, there are traces of the 9C and 10C Danish walls, including the sally-ports in Reginald's Bar near Reginald's Tower.

Location

Population 42 540 - Michelin Atlas p 80 and Map 712 – K 11 – Co Waterford.
Waterford *(Port Láirge)* is situated on the country boundary with County Wexford on the major coast road between Wexford and Cork (N 25) and at the junction of N 9 to Carlow, N 24 to Limerick.

Directory

GETTING ABOUT

Passage East Car Ferry – There is a ferry across Waterford Harbour from Passage East (SE of Waterford by R 683) to Ballyhack – *Operates between Passage East and Ballyhack daily, 7am (9.30am Sun and Bank Hols) to 10pm (8pm Oct-Mar). Closed 25-26 Dec. Capacity 30 cars. Single €5.71 (car), there and back €8.25 (car); there and back €1.90 (pedestrian).* ☎ *051 382 480, 382 488; Fax 051 382 598; passageferry@eircom.net; www.passageferry.com*

SIGHTSEEING

Walking Tours – Tours of the city are organised by the Tourist Board – *Depart Mar-Oct, daily at 11.45am and 1.45pm from Waterford Treasures at the Granary; noon and 2pm from Granville Hotel on the Quay. €5.08.* ☎ *051 873 711; Fax 051 850 645 (Jack Burtchaell)*

WHERE TO STAY

• *Budget*

Three Rivers – *Cheekpoint - 7mil/11km E of Waterford by R 683 -* ☎ *051 382 520 - Fax 051 382 542 - mail@threerivers.ie - Closed 20 Dec to 7 Jan -* 🅿 ✖ *- 14 rm €38/76* ☺. If eating at McAlpin's Suir Inn (see below), this purpose-built house offers worthy local accommodation. It has a peaceful setting, with the garden overlooking the estuary. Bedrooms are uniformly decorated and are all en suite.

Blenheim House – *Blenheim Heights – 3.4mil/5.5km E of the city on the Passage East road. -* ☎ *051 874 115 - 6 rm €40/50* ☺. The parkland surrounding this lovely Georgian house is inhabited by deer who have no inhibitions about making guests welcome. The rooms are not large but comfortable and furnished with care.

Coach House – *Butlerstown Castle, Cork Rd -* ☎ *051 384 656 - Fax 051 384 751 - coachhse@iol.ie - Closed 20 Dec to 5 Jan and restricted opening Feb and Nov -* 🅿 ✖ *- 9 rm €60/95* ☺. Large stone-built house of Victorian origins that lies in the grounds of the ruins of Butlerstown Castle. Attractive and warmly decorated with period furniture sitting alongside modern facilities.

The Anchorage – *9 The Quay -* ☎ *051 854 302 - Fax 051 856 979 - anchors@indigo.ie -* ✖ *- 14 rm €38/78* ☺. Simple, clean and straightforward accommodation on the edge of the city and priced fairly. The rooms at the front have the views of the quay and the river while those at the back tend to be quieter.

Diamond Hill – *Slieveroe -* ☎ *051 832 855 - Fax 051 832 254 - diamondhill29@hotmail.com - Closed at Christmas -* 🅿 ✖ *- 18 rm €45/80* ☺. Away from the town centre, Diamond Hill boasts delightful mature gardens for which the owners have won awards. As it is purpose built, the bedrooms are bright and modern and the house is ideal for those happier in a village atmosphere.

Avondale – *2 Parnell St, Dunmore East -* ☎ *051 852 267 - info@staywithus.net - Closed 23-29 Dec €45/75* ☺. Personally run, clean and friendly terraced town house, two minutes walk from the town centre. Bedrooms are tidy, come in a variety of shapes and sizes and are sensibly priced.

• *Moderate*

Brown's Townhouse – *29 South Parade -* ☎ *051 870 594 - Fax 051 871 923 - 6 rm €70/75* ☺. In a residential street in the city centre, this Victorian house may not look like much but it offers all the comforts of a good hotel.

WHERE TO EAT

• *Budget*

Wine Vault – *High St -* ☎ *051 853 444 - info@waterfordwinevault.com - Closed 25 Dec and Sun - €10.75/28.35.* Amateur oenologists need look no further. Wine is the theme at this converted 15C warehouse and features weekly wine specials and an impressive number available by the glass. The menu mixes the classic with the more modern.

McAlpin's Suir Inn – *Cheekpoint -* ☎ *051 382 220 - cheekpoint@eircom.net - ⊘ - €15.* This pretty and immaculately-kept inn on the harbourfront has served the local fishermen for almost 300 years. The hand-written daily changing menu may include mackerel salad or large seafood platters.

• *Moderate*

The Ship – *Dock Rd, Dunmore East -* ☎ *051 383 141 - Closed Sun and Mon Nov-Mar and Christmas - €22.15/32.25.* With chairs fashioned from barrels, fishing nets covering the ceiling and local seafood on the menu it is little wonder this ivy-clad pub is the first port of call for hungry sea dogs in this picturesque fishing village.

ENTERTAINMENT

Waterford Show – *City Hall. Open early-May to Sep, Tue, Thu, Sat at 9pm. €8 inc pre-show drink at 8.45pm and glass of wine during the show. Booking at Waterford Tourist Office or the Waterford Crystal Visitor Centre.* ☎ *051 358 397 or 875 788 (credit card bookings), 051 381 020 or 087 681 7191 (after 5pm).* Irish music, stories, singing and dancing in a historical setting.

Garter Lane Arts Centre – Regular art exhibitions, recitals and theatrical productions – ♿ *Open Mon-Sat, 10am-6pm. No charge gallery and some events; other events €2-16.* ☎ *051 855 038; Fax 051 871 570; boxoffice@garterlane.ie; www.garterlane.ie*

SHOPPING

The main shopping streets are Barronstrand Street, which runs inland from the Clock Tower in the Quay, and the neighbouring streets.

SPORTS AND LEISURE

Beaches and bathing at Tramore and at Woodstown south of Passage East and south of Duncannon Fort on east shore of Waterford Harbour.

Splashworld – ☎ *051 390 176* – Ireland's premier water leisure centre.
Greyhound racing.

EVENTS AND FESTIVALS

Waterford Light Opera Festival – *Held annually in September* in the Theatre Royal.
www.waterfordfestival.com

TRACING ANCESTORS

Waterford Heritage Genealogical Service – *St Patrick's Church, Jenkin's Lane – Open Mon-Fri, 9am-5pm (2pm Fri). b 051 876 123; Fax 051 850 645; mnoc@iol.ie; www.iol.ie/~mnoc*

🚹 *The Granary, Merchants' Quay, Waterford. Open Sep-May, Mon-Sat; also Jul-Aug, Sun. ☎ 051 875 823; Fax 051 381 572, 876 720; info@southeasttourism.ie; www.southeastireland.com*
🚹 *Waterford Crystal Visitor Centre. Open Feb-Dec, daily; Jan, Mon-Fri. ☎ 051 358 397*
🚹 *Tramore. Open Jun-Aug, Mon-Sat. ☎ 051 381 572; Fax 051 281 572*
Adjacent Sights: See CLONMEL, NEW ROSS, WEXFORD, YOUGHAL.

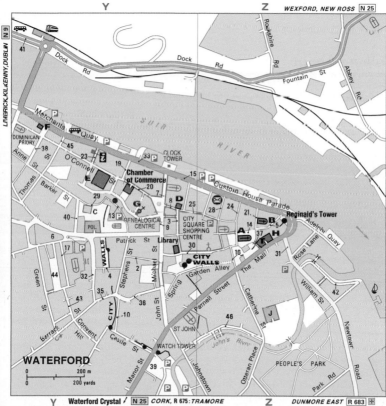

Background

The Danish Vikings sailed up the Suir in 853, establishing a settlement which they called *Vadrefjord* (meaning weather-haven). Despite constant warfare with the local Irish, the Danes retained control of Vadrefjord until 1169 when the Anglo-Norman Earl of Pembroke (Strongbow) fought his way into the town, subsequently marrying the King of Leinster's daughter in Reginald's Tower.

Under Anglo-Norman rule Waterford became the second most important town in Ireland after Dublin with a reputation of fierce loyalty to the English king. In 1649 Waterford was unsuccessfully besieged by Cromwell but it fell to his general, Ireton, the following year.

Waterford Crystal

Terry Murphy Photography

Walking About

French Church

(Dúchas) Access via Reginald's Tower Museum (see Worth a Visit).
Many of the most distinguished families of Waterford are buried within the precincts of the now ruined church. Originally a Franciscan foundation, built in 1240, then a hospital, this was where the Huguenots of Wexford worshipped between 1693 and 1815.

City Hall and Theatre Royal

Open (functions permitting) Mon-Fri, 9am-5pm; telephone for details. Guided tour. ☎ 051 309 900 (Waterford Corporation); www.waterfordcorp.ie

> **FAMOUS SONS**
> **Thomas Francis Meagher** (1822-67) was a wealthy lawyer, who joined the Young Ireland Uprising. For his part in the rising at Ballingarry in Co Tipperary he received a death sentence, which was commuted to transportation to Tasmania. From there he escaped to the USA where he founded the Irish Brigade and fought in the American Civil War.
> **William Hobson** (1783-1842), who was born in Lombard Street near The Mall, became the first Governor of New Zealand.

The **City Hall**, originally the city exchange, is a stately edifice designed by John Roberts in 1788. The first-floor council chamber displays a complete dinner service of 18C Waterford crystal, a cut-glass chandelier of similar vintage and a painting of Waterford city in 1736 by a Flemish artist, William van der Hagen.

The building incorporates the **Theatre Royal** (1876); its Victorian decor is rare in Ireland. The three-tier horseshoe design (seating capacity 650) rises to an impressive dome; the specially designed Waterford Crystal chandelier was presented by Waterford Crystal in 1958. *Open for theatrical performances all year; details by telephone. Tour of theatre by appointment. Coffee shop. ☎ 051 874 402 (box office); 051 853 626 (General Manager); Fax 051 856 900; theatreroyal@eircom.net; www.theatreroyalwaterford.com*

Christ Church Cathedral

Open (restoration work permitting) daily, 10am (noon Sun) to 1pm, and 2-5pm; check times by telephone. Donation. ☎/Fax 051 858 958; info@thesurefoundation.com; www.thesurefoundation.com

The present building was designed in the 18C English Classical style by John Roberts (1714-96), a noted 18C Waterford architect; and completed in 1779. In 1891 the galleries and square pews were removed. Within is a model of the original Viking church, which stood on the site from 1050 to 1773, and also several monuments from the medieval church – the tomb of James Rice showing his body a year after his death with signs of decay and vermin; two monuments by John van Nost to the Fitzgeralds and to Susanna Mason.

Medieval Waterford

First level below the City Square Shopping Centre.
Waterford's thousand-year history was dramatically revealed when, during construction of the modern shopping centre, 12 layers of housing were found resting on Viking foundations. Stones mark the site of St Peter's church (12C), the earliest example of an apsed church in Ireland. The mural depicts the area c 1100.

St Patrick's Church

As it was built during the Penal Period, the church was deliberately constructed to resemble a house from the outside.

Chamber of Commerce

Open Mon-Fri, 9am-5pm. Leaflet (2 languages). ☎ *051 872 639; Fax 051 876 002; info@waterfordchamber.ie; www.waterfordchamber.ie*
The fine Georgian building (1795) was designed by John Roberts; over the door are the words Waterford Harbour Commissioners; the interior contains a well-preserved dome, staircase and carvings.

Worth a Visit

Waterford Treasures★

The Granary. ♿ *Open daily, 9.30am (10am Oct-Mar) to 6pm (9pm Jun-Aug, 5pm Oct-Mar).* €5. *Public parking nearby.* ☎ *051 304 500; Fax 051 304 501; mail@waterfordtreasures.com; www.waterfordtreasures.com*
The old grain store houses a fascinating display of Viking and medieval finds from local excavations – coins, leatherwork, jewellery, woven cloth, pottery, bone needles, wooden bowls and spoons and a plan of a Viking house. Also on display are the city charters and regalia.

Waterford Treasures

Reginald's Tower Museum

Custom House Parade. (Dúchas) (♿) *Open late-Mar to Oct, daily, 10am (9.30am Jun-Sep) to 5pm (6.30pm Jun-Sep). Closed 25-26 Dec.* €1.90. *Guided tour (45min) by appointment. Public parking nearby.* ☎ *051 304 220; regionaldstower@ealga.ie*
This stone fortress, in a commanding location overlooking the River Suir, was built by the Vikings in 1013 as part of the town's defences, then strengthened by the Anglo-Normans. Its three floors, linked by a stair built within the thickness of the walls, contain displays on towers and fortifications and coinage.

Waterford Crystal★

1.5mi/2.5km S of city centre by N 25. ♿ *Visitor Centre: Open Mar-Dec, daily, 8.30am-6pm; Jan, Mon-Fri, 9am-5pm; Feb-Mar, daily, 9am-5pm. Factory: Guided tour (1hr) Mar-Oct, daily, 9am-4pm; Nov-Feb, Mon-Fri, 9am-3.15pm.* €6. *Brochure (major European languages). Audio-visual show. Parking. Restaurant.* ☎ *051 373 311; Fax 051 378 539; visitorreception@waterford.ie; www.waterfordvisitorcentre.com*
Waterford Glass in the original style was first produced in 1783; the factory is now the largest glassworks in the world.
The factory tours begin with a film on the story of glass in Ireland and then take in all aspects of production, starting with the moulding of the molten glass and concluding with the delicate polishing. A collection of crystal is on display; there are videos of the production process for sale.

WATERFORD COAST
From Waterford take R 683.

Passage East
Car ferry across Waterford Harbour to Ballyhack (see Directory). Formerly a fort, the fishing village is built beneath a high escarpment with small squares and streets and brightly painted houses; there are no fewer than three quays: Boathouse Quay, Hackett's Quay and Middle Quay.
Continue S on R 685.

Geneva Barracks
On the west shore of Waterford Harbour stand the impressive remains of an extraordinary project undertaken by the government in 1793. The four walls (each 0.25mi/0.4km long) enclosed a new town intended to house Swiss immigrants, who would set a good example with their metalworking skills and their Protestant work ethic. The project failed, and the buildings became a barracks, notorious in 1798 for the atrocities committed against the rebels held here.
Continue S on R 685; turn left into a minor road.

Dunmore East★
The fishing village, built in the Breton style, has several thatched cottages and a number of attractive little coves, including Badger's Cove and Ladies' Cove. There are forest walks beside the Ballymacaw Road *(0.25mi/0.4km W).*
Take R 684 and R 685 W via Clohernagh.

Tramore (Trá Mhór)
9mi/14.5km S of Waterford by R 675. Tramore is one of Ireland's main holiday resorts, built on a steep slope descending to a large amusement park (50 acres/20ha) and a long sandy beach (3mi/5km) overlooking Tramore Bay.
There are fine walks, with extensive sea views, along the Doneraile cliffs *(S)*. Great Newtown Head *(W)* across the bay is crowned by three early-19C navigational pillars, one of which is surmounted by the **Tramore Metal Man**, an extraordinary cast-iron figure (14ft/4m high), with pale blue jacket and white trousers, erected in 1823 as a warning to shipping.
Take R 675 N to return to Waterford.

Westport★★

With more than a touch of Georgian elegance and charm, Westport was planned and built c 1780 for the local landlord, John Denis Browne, of Westport House, one of Ireland's great country houses. Until the arrival of the railway in the 19C, Westport Quay on the estuary was a busy port lined with imposing 18C warehouses.

Location
Population 4 253 - Michelin Atlas p 94 and Map 712 – D 6 – Co Mayo.
Westport *(Cathair Na Mart)*, a designated Heritage town, occupies an attractive site on the meandering Carrowbeg River and is an excellent centre for touring the west coast of Mayo. The town is at the western extremity of N 5, part of the national road network, and about 30mi/48km from Knock International Airport.
🛈 *Westport Quay, Westport. Open Mon-Fri. ☎ 098 25711; Fax 098 26709; info@ irelandwest.ie*
🛈 *Newport. Open Jun-Aug, Mon-Sat. ☎ 098 41895*
🛈 *Achill. Open Jul-Aug, Mon-Sat. ☎ 098 45384*
Adjacent Sights: See CONG, CONNEMARA, KNOCK.

Walking About

Town Centre★
The focal point of the neatly laid out Georgian town is the **Octagon**, where the weekly market is held round a Doric pillar once crowned by a statue of George Glendinning, a local banker and benefactor. From here James Street descends to the river past the **Heritage Centre**, with informative displays and splendid models of the town and the nearby holy mountain of Croagh Patrick. ♿ *Open daily, 9am-6pm (4pm winter). 3. Parking. ☎ 098 25711; Fax 098 26709; www.visitmayo.com*

Directory

SIGHTSEEING

Clare Island Ferry *(see below)* – *Operates from Roonagh Quay (20min) Jul-Aug, 8 times daily; Jun and Sep, 4 times daily; May, 3 times daily. There and back €15. Capacity 96 passengers; sundeck; bar; video and commentary.* ☎ *098 26307; Fax 098 28288;* ☎ *087 241 3783 (mobile);* *098 25265/25212/28288;* *clareislhotel@hotmail.com*

WHERE TO STAY

• Budget

Augusta Lodge – *Golf Links Rd – 0.5mi/0.8km N off N 59 –* ☎ *098 28900 - Fax 098 28995 - info@augustalodge.ie - Closed 1 week at Christmas -* 🅿 ✕ *- 10 rm €55/80* ⌐. *There is a clue in the name. Not only is this guesthouse close to the local course but the owner has his golfing memorabilia displayed in the lounge along with a wall mounted map highlighting all of Ireland's courses. He even has his own putting green next door.*

Ashville House – *Castlebar Rd - 2mi/3.2km E on N 5 -* ☎ *098 27060 - Fax 098 27060 - ashvilleguesthouse@eircom.net - Mar-Oct -* 🅿 *- 9 rm €60/70* ⌐. *This guesthouse is a couple of miles outside of town but is worth it for the tennis court, large garden and suntrap terrace. Wood floored throughout with two of the bedrooms on the ground floor. A warm welcome is assured.*

• Moderate

The Wyatt Hotel – *The Octagon -* ☎ *098 25027 - Fax 098 26316 -* ✕ ♿ *- 49 rm €75/100* ⌐ *- Restaurant €32. Contemporary comfort in the very centre of the town. Its busy bar is a popular local spot and the restaurant provides a menu featuring assorted influences from around the world. Bedrooms are modern and comfortable.*

• Expensive

Delphi Lodge – *Leenane   8.25mi/ 13.2km NW by N 59 on Louisburgh rd -* ☎ *095 42222 - Fax 095 42296 - delfish@iol.ie - Closed 20 Dec to 6 Jan -* 🅿 *- 12 rm €135/240* ⌐ *- Restaurant €45. Dwarfed by the surrounding mountains and nestling by the lake, this Georgian sporting lodge boasts an unrivalled setting and is much loved by holidaying fishermen. Communal dinner around the large polished table allows guests the chance to discuss the one that got away.*

Atlantic Coast – *The Quay - 1mi/1.6km W by R 335 -* ☎ *098 29000 - Fax 098 29111 - reservations@atlanticcoasthotel.com - Closed 24-Dec -* 🅿 ✕ ♿ *- 84 rm, 1 suite €140/240* ⌐ *- Restaurant €25/36. Originally an 18C mill, converted into a modern and well-equipped hotel and overlooking Clew Bay and Croagh Patrick. Bedrooms are roomy and stylish while the top floor restaurant offers contemporary cuisine. Up-to-the-minute leisure club.*

WHERE TO EAT

• Budget

Matt Molloy's – *Bridge St -* ☎ *098 26655 -* ✉ *- €15. The eponymous Matt Molloy is a member of the celebrated Irish folk band, The Chieftains, and live music plays a big part in this town centre pub. It is a smoky, lively, noisy and the authentic Irish pub experience.*

• Moderate

Lemon Peel – *The Octagon, Leenane -* ☎ *098 26929 - robbie@lemonpeel.ie - Closed 24-26 and 31 Dec and Mon - Booking essential - €21.50/28.25. Klimt prints and appropriately lemon-hued walls decorate this narrow little restaurant in the town centre. The chef owner often comes out of his kitchen to greet the regulars. Lively, informal feel with an eclectic mix of influences on the menu.*

Linenmill – *The Demesne - Off Newport Rd -* ☎ *098 29500 - www.linenmill.ie - Closed Good Fri , 25-26 Dec, Mon, Tue, Sun dinner -* 🅿 *- €25/39. Part of a new development to the west of town, comprising a museum of the textile industry, a shop selling fabrics and home decoration and a roomy, bright restaurant. Accomplished modern cooking; try the daily changing seafood dishes.*

SHOPPING

Linen Mill & Museum   *See above.*

SPORTS AND LEISURE

Sailing, fishing, walking and horse riding; sandy beaches to the southwest (Silver Strand).

Flanked by the leafy North and South Malls, the tamed river runs between stone retaining walls and is crossed by a trio of bridges.

The most prominent building in South Mall is **St Mary's Church**, rebuilt in the 20C as a spacious, basilica-like structure, with stained glass by Harry Clarke and Patrick Pye. By contrast, **Holy Trinity Church** is a neo-Gothic building, with a pencil spire and an interior enhanced by ornate mosaics depicting scenes from the Gospels. *Open Jul-Aug, daily. If locked, ask at the Rectory.*

Worth a Visit

Westport House★★

House: Open Jul to late-Aug, daily, 11.30am (1.30pm Sat-Sun) to 5.30pm; Jun and late-Aug to early-Sep, daily, 1-5.30pm; Easter, Apr-May and early to late-Sep, 2-5pm. Outdoor attractions: Jun to early-Sep, same hours as house. Antique shop: as house. House and attractions €12; house €9. Brochure (3 languages). Time: 1hr-2hr. Parking. Refreshments. ☎ *098 25430; Fax 098 25206; info@westporthouse.ie; www.westporthouse.ie*

The house is the work of several architects: Richard Castle who designed the east front in 1730, Thomas Ivory who was responsible for the south elevation (1778), and James Wyatt who added the west front c 1780; the replica Greek columns on the south front were erected in 1943. It replaces an earlier house built in 1650 on the site of an O'Malley castle. Originally the sea came right up to the house; the lake was created in the 18C by damming the Carrowbeg River. The garden terraces were built in the early 1900s.

The **tour** of the main rooms and bedrooms reveals the elegant decor and a number of distinctive items – the Pompeian frieze and cloud-painted ceiling in the drawing room commissioned by the 2nd Marquess in about 1825; a collection of **family portraits** in the Long Gallery; doors made of mahogany from the family estates in Jamaica for the dining room; the sideboards and wine coolers made for the 2nd Marquess; Waterford glass finger bowls; 18C silver dish rings and a unique **centrepiece** of bog oak and beaten silver; the **Mayo Legion Flag** brought to Mayo in 1798 by General Humbert *(see p 283)*; the **oak staircase** by James Wyatt; the **marble staircase** installed for the 3rd Marquess by Italian workmen; chalk drawings of the children of the 2nd Marquess by F Wilkin and *The Holy Family* by Rubens on the landing; 200 year-old wallpaper in the **Chinese Room**. The **basement** includes the dungeons of the O'Malley castle, now furnished with attractions for children.

Bord Fáilte, Dublin

Westport House Staircase

The old **walled garden**, containing a mulberry tree planted in 1690, now houses a small zoo. A **craft shop** is located in the Farmyard Buildings Holiday Centre, there are fishing and rowing boats on the lake and a diesel train in the grounds.

Clew Bay Heritage Centre

Westport Quay. Open Apr-Oct, Mon-Fri, 10am-5pm; also Jul-Aug, Sun, 3-5pm. €3. Parking; westportheritage@eircom.net

The small museum is endearingly cluttered with items giving an insight into local history and some of the prominent personalities associated with the area, like Grace O'Malley *(see below)*, John MacBride (1868-1916), executed in Kilmainham Gaol for his part in the Easter Rising, and William Joyce, who broadcast from Germany as Lord Haw-Haw during the Second World War.

THE BROWNES OF WESTPORT

Twelve generations of Brownes have lived at Westport and their activities are recorded in the family archives which cover 400 years. The family is descended from Sir Anthony Browne of Cowdray Castle in Sussex, whose younger son John came to Mayo in the reign of Elizabeth I. The first house was built by his great-grandson, Col John Browne (1638-1711), a Jacobite, who was made bankrupt by the Williamite victory; his wife was the great-great-granddaughter of **Grace O'Malley** *(see p 362)*. His grandson, John Browne (1709-76), was brought up as an Anglican to avoid the sanctions of the Penal Laws and ennobled as Earl of Altamont. Two generations later, John Denis (1756-1809) was made Marquess of Sligo at the time of the Act of Union in 1800. The 2nd Marquess, Howe Peter (1788-1845), a friend of Lord Byron, returned from a tour of Greece in 1812 with the two columns from the doorway of the Treasury of Atreus in Mycenae; in 1906 they were discovered in the basement, identified and presented to the British Museum.

Excursion

Ballintubber Abbey★★

13mi/20km SE of Westport by R 330; after 11mi/18km turn left. Open May-Sep, daily, 10am-5pm. Donation. Guided tour (1hr) available. Brochure. Parking. Coffee shop. ☎ 094 30934 and 30709; Fax 094 30018. btubabbey@eircom.net

The abbey, one of the few medieval churches where Mass has been celebrated continually for over 750 years, is a fine example of the Romanesque school of the West of Ireland.

Founded in 1216 by Cathal O'Conor, King of Connaught, for a community of Augustinian canons, the abbey lost most of its conventual buildings when sacked in 1653 by the Cromwellians who destroyed its timber roof.

A mid-20C restoration has enhanced the appreciation of its many fine details and furnishings, among them the 13C west door and window and the 13C piscina with a carved head in the Lady Chapel. The de Burgo chapel (now the Sacristy) contains the tomb of Theobald Burke, Viscount Mayo *(see p 362)*, who was murdered in the locality in 1629.

The **Cloisters** are in ruins but elements have survived of the 13C Treasury and Chapter House and of the warming room with under-floor heating ducts and an external fireplace. The abbey is the starting point for a revived pilgrimage *(20mi/32km)* to Croagh Patrick *(see below)*.

Tours

MURRISK PENINSULA★★

Drive of 51mi/82km S of Westport – 1 day
From Westport take R 335 W.

On leaving Westport Quay the road skirts the wooded shore, crossing the Owenee River at Belclare where the O'Malley chiefs *(see below)* had their seat
After 5.5mi/9km turn right.

Murrisk Abbey

By the shore are the ruins of an Augustinian Friary founded by the O'Malleys in 1457 and suppressed in 1574, although a chalice was made for the monastery by Grace O'Malley's son Theobald in 1635.
Return to R 335.

Croagh Patrick★

Car park; 2hr on foot to the summit. The distinctive conical mass of Ireland's sacred mountain (2 503ft/763m) dominates Clew Bay and its countless islands. According to legend all the snakes in Ireland plunged to their death when **St Patrick** rang his bell above the mountain's steep southern face. In his honour up to 100 000 pilgrims, some of them barefoot, climb the stony slopes to the summit on the last Sunday in July (Reek Sunday); they used to climb by torchlight, possibly an echo of the old Celtic festival of Lughnasa. Recent excavations have shown that the narrow plateau of the summit was occupied by a pre-Christian hillfort, then by an early Christian oratory. The present oratory dates from 1905. The superlative panorama of sea and mountains is ample reward for the rigour of the climb, best begun from the attractively designed **Croagh Patrick Information Centre**, which gives essential background information on the mountain as well as useful tips on the ascent. ♿ *Open daily, 9am-6pm. Parking. Restaurant. Shop. ☎ 098 64114; Fax 098 64115; info@croach-patrick.com; www.croagh-patrick.com*

On the opposite side of the road to the Centre, John Behan's startling modern sculpture of a "cofffin ship" constitutes the **National Famine Monument**, unveiled by former President Mary Robinson in 1997.
Continue W on R 335.

Louisburgh

The central octagon of this charming little 18C town on the Bunowen River was laid out by the 1st Marquess of Sligo, whose uncle Henry had fought against the French at the Battle of Louisburgh in Canada.
Turn right at the central crossroads.

Folk and Heritage Centre

Louisburgh. Open Jun-Sep, daily, 11am-6pm; Oct-May, by appointment. €3.17. Parking. ☎ 098 66341

The centre traces the family tree of the O'Malleys, the history of the clan and their territory, and the life of Grace (1530-1603), the most famous member of the family.
Take the road S towards Killadoon. Make a detour W to Roonagh Quay for the ferry to Clare Island.

Clare Island

Clare Island Ferry (see Directory). Bicycles for hire at the island harbour; bus tour and accommodation available.

Bounded by 300ft/90m cliffs and rising to 1 512ft/461m at the summit of Mount Knockmore, the massive bulk of Clare Island commands the entrance to Clew Bay. Grace O'Malley spent her childhood in the castle by the quay; she may be buried in the Carmelite friary which was founded on the island by the O'Malleys in 1224, although the ruins are of later date. The sandy beach near the harbour is safe for bathing and water sports. Traditional Irish music is played in the island pubs.

Return to the road to Killadoon and continue S.

Killeen

A cross-inscribed stone stands in the northwest corner of the graveyard.

Turn right at the crossroads; after 0.5mi/0.8km turn right and park.

Bunlahinch Clapper Bridge★

Beside a ford stands an ancient stone footbridge of 37 arches constructed by laying flat slabs on stone piles.

Return to the crossroads. EITHER go straight across OR turn right to make a detour (10mi/16km there and back) to Silver Strand.

Beside the road *(left)* stands a **cross-inscribed stone.**

Silver Strand

The vast sandy beach (2mi/3.2km) is sheltered by dunes.

Return to the crossroads and turn right.

Altore Megalithic Tomb

Beside the road *(left)* overlooking Lough Nahaltora are the remains of a wedge-shaped gallery grave.

At the T-junction turn right onto R 335.

Doo Lough Pass★

The road, which was constructed in 1896 by the Congested Districts Board *(see Historical Perspective)*, descends from the pass to **Doo Lough** (2mi/3.2km long), which is enclosed by the **Mweelrea (Muilrea) Mountains** (2 668ft/817m) *(W)* and the **Sheeffry Hills** (2 504ft/761m) *(E)*; at the southern end of the lake rises Ben Gorm (2 302ft/700m).

Bunlahinch Clapper Bridge

W

H Champollion/MICHELIN

Killary Harbour

Delphi
The 2nd Marquess of Sligo renamed his fisheries on the Bundorragha River near Fin Lough after visiting Delphi in Greece.

Aasleagh Falls★
Car park left and right. At the narrow head of the fjord the Erriff River gushes over a broad sill of rock. The fight in *The Field* was filmed at Aasleagh.
Turn right onto N 59.

Killary Harbour★
The harbour is a magnificent fjord, a narrow arm of the sea (13 fathoms/23.4m deep) extending inland (8mi/13km) between high rock faces; it broadens out opposite Leenane on the south shore. *(See also p 184).*

CLEW BAY
Drive of 25mi/40km — half a day
From Westport take N 59 N.

Newport
This charming little angling resort is dominated by the disused railway viaduct (1892), which has been converted into an unusual walk spanning the Newport River. The broad main street climbs the north bank of the river to St Patrick's Church, built in the Irish-Romanesque style in pink granite (1914) and containing a fine **stained-glass window** by **Harry Clarke**, a particularly spectacular example of his work.
Continue N on N 59; after 1mi/1.6km turn left.

Burrishoole Abbey★
By a narrow inlet where the waters of Lough Furnace drain into the sea lie the ruins of a **Dominican friary**, founded in 1486. A squat tower rises above the church, which consists of a nave, chancel and south transept. The east wall is all that remains of the cloisters. In 1580 the friary was fortified and garrisoned by the English under **Sir Nicholas Malby**.
Burrishoole was an important port even before the arrival of the Normans but was abandoned as Westport harbour was developed.
Continue N on N 59; after 2.5mi/4km turn left.

Carrigahowley (Rockfleet) Castle
The 15C or 16C four-storey tower house is built on a most attractive site on flat rocks beside a sea-inlet commanding Clew Bay. The living room was on the fourth floor separated from the lower storeys by a stone vault. In 1566 the owner, Richard Burke, became the second husband of Grace O'Malley *(see p 362).*
Take N 59 E; after 1mi/1.6km turn left.

Furnace Lough★
A narrow switchback road loops north between Lough Furnace and Lough Feeagh. At the salmon leap where the waters of Lough Feeagh tumble, golden and foaming, over the rocks into Furnace Lough, census work on the numbers of fish moving up- and down-stream is conducted by the Salmon Research Trust of Ireland. There is a **view** north to Nephin Beg (2 065ft/628m).
Continue W on N 59 and R 319.

Achill Island★

The island approached by a bridge from the Corraun peninsula is Ireland's largest (36 223 acres/14 659ha), a wonderful mixture of sandy bays and spectacular cliffs dominated by two peaks – Slievemore (2 204ft/671m) and Croaghaun (2 192ft/667m). Once poor and remote, its economy dependent on emigrants' remittances, it attracted artists and writers like the painter Paul Henry and the German Nobel Prize winner Heinrich Böll, and nowadays prospers on tourism, with summer visitors drawn by its excellent surfing, boating and sea-angling.

On the shore of Achill Sound south of the bridge stand the ruins (restored) of **Kildavnet (Kildownet) Church** (c 1700), which contains Stations of the Cross in Gaelic. The name means the church of **Dympna**, an Irish saint who sought shelter on Achill in the 7C.

Kildavnet (Kildownet) Castle, a square four-storey 15C **tower house**, commanding the southern entrance to Achill Sound, was one of the strongholds of the redoubtable **Grace O'Malley** *(see p 362)*; there are traces of a boat slip and the original bawn.

Trawmore Strand has a splendid sandy beach backed by cliffs. **Keel** is the main resort; at the southeastern end of its long beach the cliffs have been sculpted into bizarre forms. **Keem Strand** too has a lovely sandy shore, sheltered by the great mass of Croaghaun, whose northwestern face plunges spectacularly seaward forming one of the most awesome sea-cliffs in Europe, best viewed by boat.

Between Keel and the little north coast resort of **Doogort** are the remains of abandoned settlements. One was a 19C Anglican mission founded to woo the islanders from Roman Catholicism, the other consists of the ruins of summer dwellings known as booleyhouses; this seems to have been the last place in the British Isles where the ancient practice of transhumance was carried out, finally ceasing in the 1930s.

Wexford★

The county town and the commercial centre of the southeast region, Wexford is a place of great antiquity and a designated Heritage town – it was first granted a charter in 1317 – with narrow streets and alleyways, set on the south bank of the River Slaney where it enters Wexford Harbour. The town has a strong cultural tradition and is known internationally for its annual opera festival. It is also a popular place for family holidays.

Location

Population 9 533 - Michelin Atlas p 81 and Map 712 – M 10 – Co Wexford.

Wexford *(Loch Garman)* in the southeast corner of the country is linked to Dublin by N 11 and to Waterford by N 25. The **ferry terminal** at Rosslare Harbour *(5mi/8km SE)* provides passenger and car ferry services from Ireland to South Wales and the ports of northern France.

🛈 *Crescent Quay, Wexford. Open Jul-Aug, daily; Apr-Jun and Sep-Oct, Mon-Sat; Nov-Mar, Mon-Fri.* ☎ *053 23111; Fax 053 41743; www.irelandsoutheast.travel.ie*

🛈 *Kilrane, Rosslare. Open Apr-Sep, daily.* ☎ *053 33622*

Adjacent Sights: See ENNISCORTHY, NEW ROSS, WATERFORD, WICKLOW MOUNTAINS.

Background

The site of Wexford was noted by Ptolemy in his 2C AD map but the town's history really began when the Vikings arrived in 950, naming their settlement *Waesfjord* (the harbour of the mud flats).

When the Anglo-Normans invaded in 1169 Wexford was captured and the first Anglo-Irish treaty was signed at Selskar Abbey. In the 13C the earthen ramparts of the Norse town were replaced by a stone wall.

In 1649 Cromwell entered Wexford; Selskar Abbey was destroyed and hundreds, possibly thousands of citizens were massacred in the market place by Cromwell's forces.

During the rebellion of the United Irishmen in 1798 Wexford was held for a month by the insurgents, some of whom treated their opponents with extreme cruelty. It was then recaptured with even more bloodshed by the Crown forces.

In the 19C, led by local shipping companies, Wexford built up a strong maritime trade. Silting of the harbour and competition from Waterford led to its decline in the early 20C but the town's proximity to the harbour at Rosslare and its vibrant cultural life have more than compensated for this.

Directory

GETTING ABOUT

Trips to the Saltee Islands from Kilmore Quay – *Operate Apr-Oct (max 12). Environmental and sightseeing trips around Saltee Islands. Reef and wreck fishing. Scenic trip €1.50; Fishing trip €3 per day.* ☏ 053 29704, Fax 053 29975; Mob 087 254 9111 *(Dick Hayes)*

SIGHTSEEING

Walking Tours – Enquire at the Tourist Information Office.

WHERE TO STAY

• *Budget*

The Blue Door – *18 Lower George St* - ☏ *053 21047* - ⌗ - *4 rm €50/55* ⌣. A good place to stay in the middle of town. Hanging baskets and window boxes full of flowers, plus well-kept and pleasantly decorated rooms. The landlady has lots of useful tips about the area.

McMenamin's Townhouse – *3 Auburn Terr, Redmond Rd* - ☏ *053 46442* - Fax *053 46442* - mcmem@indigo.ie - *Closed 20-29 Dec* - ▣ ⌁ - *6 rm €50/80* ⌣. Sympathetic decoration, antiques and original fireplaces add to the charm and period feel of this late Victorian townhouse. The bedrooms have original washstands and wrought-iron or half tester beds.

• *Moderate*

Whitford House – *New Line Rd 2.25mil/3.6km W on R 733* - ☏ *053 43444* - Fax *053 46399* whitford@indigo.ie - *Closed 23 Dec to 7 Jan* - ▣ - *36 rm €69.84/165.06* ⌣ - *Restaurant €20.65/33.65.* Particularly comfortable bedrooms, many with private balconies or patios, at this family-owned and run purpose-built hotel. The spacious dining room often features live music and the menu makes good use of local seafood.

ENTERTAINMENT

Wexford Arts Centre – Concerts, plays and art exhibitions are held throughout the year. (⌖) *Open Mon-Sat, 10am-6pm. Closed Sun and Bank Hols. No charge for exhibitions. Guided tour (15min) available. Restaurant. Disabled visitors must telephone in advance.* ☏ *053 23764; Fax 053 24544; wexfordartscentre@eircom.net; www.wexfordartscentre.ie*

SHOPPING

The majority of shops are in Main Street – North and South

SPORTS AND LEISURE

Beaches at Rosslare (south) and Curracloe (north)

EVENTS AND FESTIVALS

Wexford Festival Opera – *High Street* - ☏ *053 22400* - info@wexfordopera.com - *www.wexfordopera.com* – Box Office: open mid-Oct to early-Nov, Mon-Fri, 9am-5pm; performances: also Sat-Sun. The **Opera Festival** was inspired by a long-established love of opera in Ireland and provides many young singers with an opportunity to start a career. It is an annual event, lasting 18 days in late October; during this time it puts on three productions and over 50 events. It has gained an international reputation for the quality of its performances and for its policy of specialising in rare or unjustly neglected operas. The company of artists and the audiences are truly international, being drawn from all over the world. The productions are staged in the **Theatre Royal**.

Walking About

Crescent Quay

Wexford's long quayside and promenade, facing the broad and tidal River Slaney, is relieved by the curve of Crescent Quay, which is graced with a statue of John Barry, a native of Co Wexford, who became Senior Commodore of the US Navy in 1794. *From Crescent Quay walk inland along Henrietta Street and turn right into Main Street.*

Main Street★

The commercial centre of Wexford is a long and winding street, mainly pedestrianised, so narrow that the shops and houses on each side, fronted in the grey slate characteristic of the area, almost seem to touch. Many of the small shops retain the traditional 19C design and style of country town establishments; the once-proud boast of O'Connor's bakery – "Bread is still the Staff of Life" – appears above the premises, while Kelly's bakery features window displays of traditional Irish loaves, such as wheatsheaves and ducks.

St Iberius' Church★

Open Mon-Sat, 10am-5pm. Donation €1.27. When closed, key available from The Rectory. Brochure (8 languages). ☏ *053 43013; Fax 053 43013; helpcentre@eircom.net* The Anglican church stands on an ancient Christian site dating back 1 500 years, at that time at the water's edge. The present church was built in 1760 in the Georgian style, with an Ionic reredos and two Corinthian columns screening the sanctuary. The Venetian-style façade was added in the mid-19C.

Bull Ring

The scene of Cromwell's exemplary massacre in 1649, the **Bull Ring** was originally used for bull baiting, a popular sport among the Norman nobles of 12C and 13C Wexford. The 1798 **memorial** shows the bronze figure of a pikeman, a dramatic work by Oliver Sheppard (1864-1941), designer of many patriotic monuments.

Continue along Main Street North.

Selskar Abbey

Only the outer walls and square tower remain of the abbey, founded c 1190 by the Anglo-Norman nobleman Sir Alexander de la Roche on his return from the Crusades. In 1170-71 Henry II, king of England, spent time in Ireland, partly to assert his authority over the ambitious Strongbow, partly perhaps to escape the opprobrium following the murder of Thomas Becket, and it was at Selskar that he passed the whole of Lent 1171 doing penance for the assassination of his archbishop.

West Gate Heritage Centre

& *Open May-Dec, Mon-Sat, 9.30am-1pm and 2-5pm; also Jul-Aug, Sun 2-6pm; Jan-Apr, telephone for details. €1.50.* ☎ *053 46506*

The West Gate is the only one of the five original fortified gates still standing; it was built by Sir Stephen Devereux c 1200 and closed to traffic in the late 16C. The Norman rooms in the tower give access to a battlement walk to Selskar Abbey; the cosmopolitan history of Wexford is traced in an audio-visual presentation.

Walk S along Abbey Street and High Street; turn right into Rowe Street Upper.

Twin Churches★

The **Church of the Immaculate Conception** *(Rowe Street)* and the **Church of the Assumption** *(Bride Street – further S)* were both designed by Augustus Welby Pugin in an almost identical Gothic style; their towers are the same height (230ft/70m) and their foundation stones were laid on the same day in 1851.

From Rowe Street Upper turn left into School Street.

Franciscan Friary★

(&) *Open Mon-Sat, 9.30am-1.30pm and 2.30-6pm. Closed Sun and Bank Hols. Parking for the disabled; wheelchair access to church and friary.* ☎ *053 22758; Fax 053 21499*

The church founded by the Franciscans in 1230 was confiscated in 1540 at the Dissolution of the Monasteries but returned in 1622. The present church (restored) has an attractive stucco ceiling and works by contemporary Irish artists, including a striking modern sculpture – **The Burning Bush Tabernacle** – created by Brother Benedict Tutty of Glenstal Abbey *(see p 287)*.

Continue S via School Street and Roches Road; turn left into Bride Street. From Bride Street turn left into Main Street South.

Excursions

Rosslare (Ros Láir)

10mi/16km S of Wexford by N 25 and R 740. The pleasant and popular seaside resort of Rosslare boasts a most attractive long beach (6mi/9.5km) and various sporting facilities.

Lady's Island

11mi/18km S of Wexford by N 25 and minor road from Killinick. A place of pilgrimage, the island has the ruins of an Augustinian friary and a Norman castle; the tower of the latter leans at a greater angle than that at Pisa.

Tacumshane Windmill

11mi/18km S of Wexford by N 25 and minor road from Killinick. (Dúchas) Key available from Gerry Meyler (pub next door). Admission charge.

The windmill, which was built in 1846, was restored complete with sails in the 1950s.

Kilmore Quay★

15mi/24km SW of Wexford by N 25 and R 739. This fishing village retains much of its 19C atmosphere, as about 15 houses still have thatched roofs. The *Wooden House* pub has an extensive collection of historic photographs.

The **maritime museum** in the former *Guillemot* lightship, moored in the harbour, contains many relics of the Wexford seafaring tradition, including old maps and a 200 year-old compass and binnacle, a whale's backbone and a large-scale model of HMS *Africa*, sister ship to Nelson's *Victory*. *Open Jun-Aug, daily; Sep-May, Sat-Sun, noon-6pm. €4. Audioguide (3 languages). Guided tour by appointment.* ☎ *0532 1572 and 051 561 144; wexmar@hotmail.com*

Saltee Islands★

Boat trips from Kilmore Quay (see Directory); 3mi/4.8km offshore. The Great and Little Saltee Islands (each about 0.5mi/0.8km long), normally uninhabited, form Ireland's largest bird sanctuary, home for many thousands of gannets, guillemots and puffins (200 000 birds) as well as seals and dolphins.

Irish Agricultural Museum, Johnstown Castle★★

5mi/8km SW of Wexford by N 25; after 4mi/6.4km turn right (sign). (& to ground floor) Open Jun-Aug, daily, 9am (11am Sat-Sun and Bank Hols) to 5pm; Apr-May and Sep to early-Nov, Mon-Fri, 9am-12.30pm and 1.30-5pm, Sat-Sun and Bank Hols, 2-5pm; early-Nov to Mar, Mon Fri, 9am-12.30pm and 1.30-5pm. €4. Parking. Refreshments (summer). Parking for the disabled. ☎ 053 42888 (weekdays); Fax 053 42213

The Johnstown estate was donated to the Irish State in 1945. **Johnstown Castle** *(not open)*, designed by Daniel Robertson, now houses an agricultural research centre.

The park (50 acres/20ha) contains **ornamental grounds** with over 200 species of trees and shrubs, three ornamental lakes, walled gardens, hothouses and a picnic area.

The old farmyard buildings now house a well-presented museum displaying many examples of obsolete agricultural machinery. The transport section includes tub traps, widely used in rural Ireland until the arrival of the motor car in the 1920s, a jaunting car made in Gorey, Co Wexford, about 1880, carts, traps and harness; corn winnowing machines and old tractors, which heralded the revolution in farming. There are sections on dairying, haymaking and poultry keeping; reconstructions of a cooperage, a harness-maker's workshop, a blacksmith's forge and a carpenter's shop, a re-creation of 19C Irish rural living and a display of fine Irish country furniture.

The **Famine Exhibition** is a thorough, science-based interpretation of the causes, effects and aftermath of the Great Famine (1845-49), with re-creations of a rural home and the lazy-beds in which potatoes were grown, as well as explanations of how life could be surprisingly well sustained on a monotonous diet of potatoes and dairy products and how the disaster affected different regions of the country. A reconstruction of a soup kitchen evokes relief work, and a reconstruction of a field laboratory demonstrates how the fight against disease was conducted.

Irish National Heritage Park★

2.5mi/4km NW of Wexford by N 11 going N across the River Slaney to Ferrycarrig. & Open daily, 9.30am-6.30pm (subject to seasonal changes). €7. Guided tour and Audiovisual show (5 languages). Parking. Restaurant. ☎ 053 20733; Fax 053 20911; info@inhp.com; www.inhp.com

Nine thousand years of Irish history are brought to life very convincingly by 16 separate sites, mostly reconstructed, linked by a visitors' trail and a nature trail. The **Stone Age**, 7000-2000 BC, is represented by a Mesolithic camp site, an early Irish farmstead and a portal dolmen. The **Bronze Age** is illustrated by a cist burial chamber and a stone circle. The Celtic and early Christian ages, the most extensively reconstructed, are represented by an early Christian monastery, an **Ogham stone** showing the earliest form of writing in Ireland, and a **crannóg**, an artificial island protected by a palisade. The horizontal watermill is a reconstruction of one dating from 833 in Co Cork. The round tower is a replica, built in 1857 to commemorate Wexford men killed in the Crimean War (1854-56).

The only real historic relic is the Norman earthworks and fortifications, built by Robert FitzStephen in 1169.

Other exhibitions cover the Great Potato Famine (1845-47) and Harry Ferguson, of tractor fame, and his system.

Curracloe Beach

Wexford Wildfowl Reserve

3mi/4.8km N of Wexford by R 741; turn right along the coast. (Dúchas) (&) Open (circumstances permitting) daily, 9am-6pm (10am-5pm Oct to late-Mar). Closed 25 Dec. Guided tour on request. Lectures. Parking. Picnic area. ☎ 053 23129; Fax 053 24785

For eight months of the year most of the world's population of Greenland white-fronted geese winters on the north shore of Wexford Harbour.

Curracloe★

6mi/9km N of Wexford by R 741 and R 742.

Thatched cottages, glorious sand dunes and seemingly endless sandy beaches (7mi/12km) overlook Wexford Bay.

Wicklow Mountains★★

A wonderful asset to the capital city and its inhabitants, the Wicklow Mountains south of Dublin provide high peaks and spectacular views, lakes, reservoirs and waterfalls, open moorland and verdant valleys, some landscaped into elegant gardens. The rolling heights are covered in peat bog where the rivers form broad shallow treeless corridors; on the harder schist they create deep and narrow wooded gorges, like Dargle Glen, Glen of the Downs and Devil's Glen. In the past the mountains were even wilder and far less accessible than today and served as a refuge for outlaws and rebels; some of the 1798 insurgents found sanctuary here for several years, prompting the construction by the British of the Military Road (see below). The mountains fall eastward to the shingle ridge and sand dunes of the coast, with its string of resorts: Bray, Greystones, Wicklow and Arklow.

Location

Michelin Atlas p 87 and Map 712 – M, N 8, 9 – Co Wicklow.

The Wicklow Mountains extend S from Dublin for about 30mi/48km as far as Arklow. Between the coast road (N 11) and the inland road (N 81) there is a network of steep and narrow country roads providing magnificent views of the lakes and moorland.

🛈 *Rialto House, Fitzwilliam Square, Wicklow. Open Jun-Sep, Mon-Sat; Nov-May, Mon-Fri. ☎ 0404 69117; Fax 0404 69118; wicklowtouristoffice@eircom.net; www.ecoast-midlands.travel.ie*

🛈 *Arklow. Open May-Sep, Mon-Sat; Oct-Apr, Mon-Fri. ☎ 0402 32484*

🛈 *(Dúchas) (&) Open May-Aug, daily, 10am-6pm; Sep-Apr, Sat-Sun, 10am-6pm. Closed 25-26 Dec. Guided walks, telephone for details. ☎ 0404 45425; Fax 0404 45306; www.heritageireland.ie*

Adjacent Sights: See ATHY, DUBLIN, ENNISCORTHY, KILDARE, MAYNOOTH.

Powerscourt Gardens

Directory

GETTING ABOUT

Bus Service from Dublin to Glendalough –
*Operates 11.30am, 6pm, from Dublin (west
side of St Stephen's Green - in front of the
Royal College of Surgeons) via Bray and
Roundwood. Single P9; return P15.
bus@glendalough.com;
www.glendaloughbus.com*

SIGHTSEEING

**Wicklow Mountains National Park
Information Point** at the Upper Lake in
Glendalough *(see p 264) – (Dúchas) (&) Open
May-Aug, daily, 10am-6pm; Sep-Apr, Sat-Sun,
10am-6pm. Closed 25-26 Dec. Guided walks,
telephone for details. ☎ 0404 45425; Fax
0404 45306; www.heritageireland.ie*

WHERE TO STAY

• Budget

Beechwood House – *Manor Kilbride -
5.75mi9.25km NE of Blessington by N 81 off
R 579, turning left past Mooney's pub -
☎ 01 458 202 -
amcann@beechwoodhouse.ie - 2 Jan to
23 Dec - ⌁ ▣ ✕ - 6 rm €44/64 ⌑ -
Meals.* Imposing country house in two acres
of well-tended gardens. Board games in the
sitting rooms, home baking a speciality of the
owner; it's all very relaxing. Bedrooms at the
front have the best views of the Wicklow
mountains.

Keppel's Farmhouse – *Ballanagh -
2mi/32.km S of Avoca by unmarked road -
☎ 0402 35168   Fax 0402 30950 -
keppelsfarmhouse@eircom.net – May-Oct -
▣ ✕ - 5 rm €50/70 ⌑* The farmhouse,
with its surrounding dairy farm, dates back to
1880 and provides far-reaching views of the
surrounding countryside. The atmosphere is
relaxed and tranquil and breakfast a
predictably hearty affair.

Glendalough River House – *Rathdrum -
0.5mi/0.8km S of Laragh off R 755 -
☎ 0404 45577 -
glendaloughriverhouse@hotmail.com - Closed
15 Nov to 3 Jan - ▣ ✕ - 4 rm €60/90 ⌑.*
This late 17C farmbuilding beside a
meandering river provides quiet and cosy
accommodation. Surrounded by 10 acres of
woodland so plenty of choice for walkers.
Simple but spotless pine-furnished bedrooms.

• Moderate

Ballyknocken House – *Glenealy -
3mi/4.8km S of Ashford by N 11 -
☎ 0404 44627 - Fax 0404 44696 -
cfulvio@ballyknocken.com - Mar-Nov - ▣
✕ - 7 rm €80/105 ⌑ - Meals €26.50.*
A Victorian farmhouse providing the ideal
getaway for jaded cosmopolitans.
Sympathetically restored to a good standard
yet retaining a homely charm, with many
Victorian antiques. Menus feature plenty of
home produce.

WHERE TO EAT

• Budget

Avoca Handweavers – *Avoca -
☎ 0402 35105 - info@avoca.ie - €16.* Learn
the art of weaving at reputedly Ireland's

oldest mill, see the finished article in
the shop then stop for a light bite to
eat. Simple formula; queue up at the
servery then find a table. Salad, quiches,
even local wild salmon available.

• Moderate

Ballymore Inn – *Ballymore
Eustace ☎ 045 864 505 -
theballymoreinn@hotmail.ie - Closed
Sun and Bank Hols - ▣ - €25.* A
characterful pub in the middle of town. On
one side there's an informal café offering a
range from coffees and salads to sausages
and puddings. Adjacent is a more formal
restaurant specialising in Wicklow lamb.

SHOPPING

Avoca Weavers – Fashionable woollen
goods available at the mill in Avoca or at
the shop in Kilmacanogue *(see below) – &
Kilmacanogue: Open daily, 9.30am-6pm
(5.30pm winter). Parking. Restaurant. Café
and Garden Terrace. ☎ 01 286 7466,
01 286 7402; Fax 01 286 2367,
01 276 0458.*
& *Avoca Mill: Open daily, 9.30am-6pm
(5.30pm winter). Guided tour of the weaving
process. Parking. Tearoom. ☎ 0402 35105,
35284; Fax 0402 35446; info@avoca.ie,
www.avoca.ie*

SPORTS AND LEISURE

**Blessington Lakes Land and
Watersports Centre**, *Poulaphouca Reservoir,
Blessington – (&) Open daily, 10am-6pm.
€6-20 according to activity.
Parking. ☎ 045 865 092;
Fax 045 865 024;
www.blessingtonsports.com*

Clara Lara Fun Park, *Vale of Clara* – Variety
of activities for children – assault course,
adventure playgrounds, radio-controlled
boats, bathing, boating and fishing, picnic
meadows – *(&) Open May-Aug, daily,
10.30am-6pm. €6 (some extra charges).
Parking. Refreshments. ☎ 0404 46161;
claralara@eircom.net*

Wicklow Way, a long-distance footpath
(82mi/132km), starts in Marlay Park in
Rathfarnham, in the southern suburbs
of Dublin, passes near Powerscourt,
Lough Tay and Lough Dan, Glenmacnass,
Glendalough, Glenmalur and Aghavannagh
and finishes in Clonegal in Co Carlow
(access at Moyne, Bridgeland and Kilquiggin);
the trail, consisting of forest tracks, bog
roads and mountain paths, crosses
mountains, switches back and forth
through river valleys and presents
glorious views.

Tiglin Adventure Centre – *Devil's Glen
(see p 52).*

TRACING ANCESTORS

Wicklow Family Heritage Centre,
Wicklow's Historic Gaol, Wicklow – *Open
Mon-Fri 9am-5pm (4pm Fri) ☎ 0404 20126;
Fax 0404 61612; wfh@tinet.ie;
www.wicklow.ie*

Inland

North to south

Powerscourt★★

(&) *Open daily, 9.30am-5.30pm/dusk. Closed 25-26 Dec. Gardens and house exhibition €8; house exhibition €2.50. Brochure (5 languages). Parking. Terrace café. Garden Centre. ☎ 01 204 6000; Fax 01 204 6900; visitor@powerscourt.ie; www.powerscourt.ie*

Partly restored after a terrible fire in 1974, the Palladian mansion designed by Richard Castle in 1730 looks out over a magnificent prospect which seamlessly combines all the elements of landscape architecture: grassy terraces and stone stairways descending steeply to a lake, antique statuary, formal and informal gardens, fountains, woodland and specimen trees, together with the "borrowed scenery" of the mountains beyond, crowned by the near-perfect cone of Great Sugar Loaf (1 654ft/503m). No scene in Ireland rivals this masterly synthesis of artifice and nature.

MILITARY ROAD

After the 1798 Rebellion the British Government built a military road running south from Dublin through some of the most rugged and isolated parts of the Wicklow Mountains. The original barracks in Glencree now house **St Kevin's**, an organisation which seeks to promote reconciliation between people of different religious traditions on both sides of the border.

The estate takes its name from Eustace le Poer, a Norman knight. In 1609 the land was granted to Sir Richard Wingfield by James I, who made him Viscount Powerscourt. In 1961 the estate was sold to Mr and Mrs Slazenger.

The **gardens** may have first been laid out by Richard Castle. They were then added to by successive viscounts, mostly in the course of the 19C. In 1843 the 6th Viscount employed the architect Daniel Robertson to design the terraces; this gouty eccentric directed the work from a wheelbarrow, usually with a bottle of sherry to hand. The 7th Viscount added the superb wrought-iron gates and much of the statuary, some of it brought from Europe, some of it specially commissioned, like the Triton Fountain in the lake, which spews a 100ft/30m jet of water into the air. Many of the ornamental trees were planted at this time, among them numerous superb conifers. New features continued to be added in the early 20C, among them the Pepper Pot Tower and the jungle-like Japanese Gardens, created in 1908 on reclaimed bogland.

The fire which gutted the mansion in 1974 broke out in the course of a party celebrating the completion of a lengthy restoration programme. Reconstruction has incorporated craft outlets and a terrace café overlooking the gardens, and there is an exhibition with a video on the history of the estate and its owners.

Take R 760 S; after 2mi/3.2km turn right (sign); at the crossroads drive straight on for 2mi/3.2km to Valclusa.

Powerscourt Waterfall★★

5min on foot from car park to foot of waterfall; climbing the rock face is dangerous. (&) *Open daily, 9.30am-7pm/dusk. Closed 2 weeks before Christmas. €3.50. Nature trail. Play area for children. Parking. Refreshments. ☎ 01 204 6000; Fax 01 204 6900; visitor@powerscourt.ie; www.powerscourt.ie*

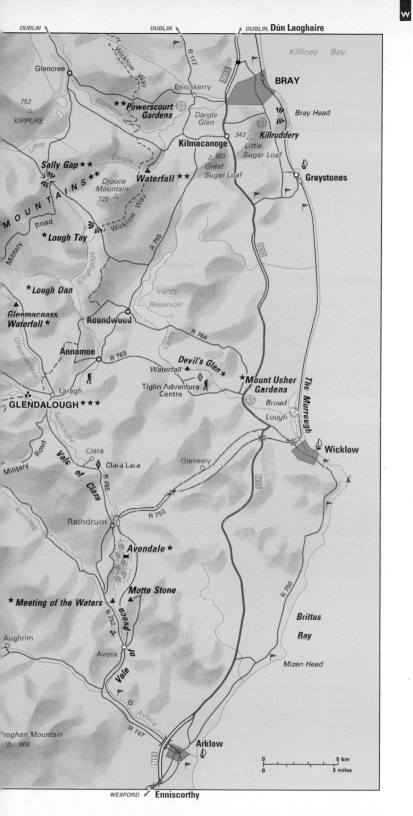

DUBLIN   DUBLIN   DUBLIN, **Dún Laoghaire**

Killiney   Bay

BRAY

Glencree

R 117

Enniskerry

**★★Powerscourt
Gardens**

Dargle
Glen

Bray Head

752
△
KIPPURE

Killruddery

Liffey

342

Kilmacanoge

Little
Sugar Loaf

△ 503
Great
Sugar Loaf

Sally Gap ★★

Waterfall ★★

Greystones

M O U N T A I N S ★★

Djouce
Mountain
725 △

Wicklow Way

Road

★ Lough Tay

Military

★ Lough Dan

Vartry
Reservoir

**Glenmacnass
Waterfall ★**

Roundwood

R 764

Annamoe   R 763

Devil's Glen ★

Waterfall ▲

**★Mount Usher
Gardens**

Tiglin Adventure
Centre

Laragh

Broad
Lough

GLENDALOUGH ★★★

The Murrough

Clara

Clara Lara

Glenealy

Wicklow

Military   Road

Vale of Clara

R 755

R 752

Rathdrum

R 750

Avondale ★

Motte Stone ▲

*Brittas
Bay*

★ Meeting of the Waters

R 752

Mizen Head

Aughrim

Avoca

Vale   of   Avoca

'roghan Mountain
△ 606

R 747

Arklow

0 _____ 5 km
0 _____ 3 miles

WEXFORD   **Enniscorthy**

The highest waterfall in Ireland is formed by the Dargle River which plunges (400ft/122m) in a spray of thick white spume down a jagged grey rock face in a horseshoe of hills. There are pleasant walks and nature trails by the river, and swings and slides for children at the visitor centre.

Killruddery*

(&) Gardens: Open Apr-Sep, daily, 1-5pm. House: Open May-Jun and Sep, daily, 1-5pm. Garden €4.50; house and garden €6.50. Parking. ☎ 01 286 3405, ☎/Fax 01 286 2777; info@killruddery.com; www.killruddery.com

The **formal gardens** at Killruddery were designed by a Frenchman in 1682 for the Earl of Meath, whose descendants still inhabit the house. The gardens are a fascinating rarity, a particularly complete example of the kind of formality which went out of fashion in the following century, when most desmesnes were landscaped (or re-landscaped) in an informal, naturalistic manner.

The major features are a pair of parallel canals (550ft/168m long), the **Long Ponds**, prolonged by the **Lime Avenue** leading uphill to the 18C park. The **Angles** consists of a number of intersecting walks lined with high hedges; the wilderness of trees is bisected by broad walks; a bay hedge encloses the **sylvan theatre**, while the **beech hedge pond** consists of two concentric circular beech hedges, surrounding a round pond (60ft/18m in diameter) and a fountain.

The **house**, which dates from the 1650s, was considerably remodelled in the 1820s in neo-Tudor style by Richard and William Morrison. The west front is enhanced by a lovely conservatory with a domed roof and an ornamental octagonal dairy. Above the stableyard entrance is a clock and striking mechanism, both operated by water power and built by members of the family in 1906-09.

Kilmacanogue

The shop and factory of **Avoca Weavers** stand on the site of a house, Glencormac, built in 1864 by James Jameson of the famous whiskey family. The grounds contain many rare species – a weeping cypress, Blue Atlantic cedars, several Wellingtonias, various types of eucalyptus and pine and 13 yew trees which are said to be 700 to 800 years old and originally formed part of an avenue leading to Holybrook Abbey.

Russborough***

Guided tour (including 5min film) May-Sep, daily, 10.30am-5.30pm; Apr and Oct, Sun and Bank Hols, 10.30am-5.30pm. Booklet (5 languages). €6. Children's playground. Craft workshops. Restaurant. ☎ 045 865 239; Fax 045 865 054; russborough @eircom.net

Bord Failte, Dublin

Drawing Room, Russborough

This is one of the grandest country houses in Ireland, a Palladian palace in Wicklow granite facing a lake which mirrors the mountains rising to the east. Commissioned in 1742 by Joseph Leeson, heir to a brewing fortune, it is the masterpiece of the architect Richard Castle, its central block reaching far out into the landscape via curving colonnades, side pavilions, walls, archways and minor buildings.

Leeson – later Earl of Milltown – is depicted in stucco over the door linking the staircase and entrance halls; he was a great traveller and collector and, when his line died out at the end of the 19C, his paintings passed into the ownership of the National Gallery in Dublin.

Today Russborough is home to another fine collection, assembled by Alfred Beit (1853-1906), co-founder with Cecil Rhodes of the De Beers diamond mining company; in 1952 his heir, also an Alfred Beit, bought the great house in order to provide a home for his uncle's **Old Master paintings**★★ by Goya, Murillo, Velasquez, Gainsborough, Rubens, Vermeer and Frans Hals.

The setting in which the Old Masters are hung is superb – with ornate mantelpieces, extensive use of carved mahogany and satinwood inlay, fine furniture and displays of porcelain and silverware – but the outstanding features are the almost incredibly rich **stucco ceilings** by the Lafranchini brothers and their pupils. The thick

RUSSBOROUGH'S STOLEN TREASURES

Russborough's magnificent painting collection has proved too great a temptation to thieves not once, but twice. In 1974 a gang including the British heiress Rose Dugdale broke in and took 19 pictures worth £8m, using them in a vain attempt to get IRA prisoners in England transferred to Belfast. On this occasion all the paintings were swiftly found by the police. In 1986 another raid, this time by professional criminals, netted £30m worth of pictures. Their fame made them almost impossible to sell and most, but not all, have been subsequently recovered.

and heavy stuccowork on the staircase is by a less accomplished hand. Gorgeous stucco panels frame exquisite seascapes by Vernet, now back in place after being sold in 1926.

Sally Gap★★
The crossroads on the Military Road gives splendid views of the surrounding blanket bog on the Wicklow Mountains.

Loughs Tay and Dan★
Scree slopes plunge directly into the dark waters of Lough Tay, which is linked to Lough Dan by the Cloghoge River.

Roundwood
The village (780ft/238m above sea level) consists of little more than a broad main street with several pubs and craft shops; a pub and a café both claim the honour of being the highest in Ireland.

Annamoe
There are pleasant walks beside the Annamoe River. It was here at the age of seven that Laurence Sterne (see p 173) fell into the mill race and emerged unscathed.

Glenmacnass Waterfall★
Car park. The mountain river streams dramatically down an inclined rock face.

Glenmacnass

Wicklow Gap★★
The road west from Glendalough (see p 264) to Hollywood follows the course of the medieval pilgrims' path, **St Kevin's Road**, through the Vale of Glendasan. Where the modern road loops northeast, hikers may follow the old direct route (2mi/3km) closer to Lough Nahanagan. The motor road rejoins the old route to pass through the Wicklow Gap between Tonelagee (2 686ft/816m *N*) and Table Mountain (2 302ft/700m *W*).

Devil's Glen★
The Vartry River makes a spectacular **waterfall** (100ft/30m) by cascading into the Devil's Punchbowl, a deep basin in the rock. There are **walks** in the immediate vicinity and good views of the coastline.

Mount Usher Gardens★
&. *Open mid-Mar to Oct, daily, 10.30am-6pm. €5. Guided tour (1hr) by appointment. Brochure (2 languages). Parking. Tearoom. ☎/Fax 0404 40205; mount_usher.gardens@indigo.ie; www.mount-usher-gardens.com*
Set on the outskirts of Ashford village, the natural-style gardens (20 acres/8ha), which are planted with over 5 000 species, many subtropical, are renowned for the collections of eucryphia and eucalyptus. They were laid out in 1868 by Edward Walpole, a member of a Dublin linen-manufacturing family, and totally restored following severe flood damage in 1986.
Two suspension bridges lead to the woodland walks on the east bank of the River Vartry, which has been attractively developed with the addition of weirs.

Vale of Clara

The road, which follows the lushly wooded course of the Avonmore River, a trout stream, links Laragh, a meeting point of many roads and glens, to the attractive village of Rathdrum.

Glenmalur★

The road beside the upper reaches of the Avonbeg River ends in a remote and desolate spot at the northeast foot of Lugnaquilla, Ireland's second-highest mountain (3 039ft/926m high).

Avondale★

(&) *Park: Open daily. House: Open mid-Mar to Oct, daily, 11am-6pm (5pm last admission). Closed Good Fri. Grounds €5 per car; house (extra) €4.45. Audio-visual show (25min). Leaflet (7 languages). Guided tour available. Children's play area. Parking. Restaurant, coffee shop, picnic areas. ☎ 0404 46111; Fax 0404 46111; costelloe_j@coillte.ie; www.coillte.ie;*

The Avondale estate was the home of the Parnells, a prosperous Protestant landlord family, and it was here that **Charles Stewart Parnell**, the ill-fated Nationalist leader was born and lived .

The two-storey neo-Classical **house** has been restored to its appearance during Parnell's lifetime when it was much used for social occasions. It was designed in 1759 by Samuel Hayes; there is Coade stone ornamentation by the **Lafranchini brothers** in the dining room. The life of Charles Parnell, the history of his family in Ireland, his role in 19C Irish politics, are traced by a video. Among the furniture and memorabilia are Parnell's stick and chair (he was 6ft 3in/1.9m tall), photos of Parnell and Kitty O'Shea, her wedding ring of Avonmore gold mined by Parnell, a set of folding library steps made of Irish bog oak.

CHARLES STEWART PARNELL (1846-91)

After an unpromising school career Parnell entered Parliament in 1875 and soon attracted the attention of the Nationalists. He became Vice-President of the Home Rule Confederation of Great Britain. As President of the Land League he campaigned for the tenants to keep a firm grip on their homesteads and went on a fund-raising trip to America and Canada; he was so well received that he was dubbed the "uncrowned king of Ireland". In September 1880 he proposed the policy of "moral Coventry" which advocated what came to be known as boycotting, after Capt Boycott who was the first to feel its effect. Parnell used his own newspaper *United Ireland* to attack government policy. In 1882 he founded the National League to campaign for Home Rule. In 1886 he took up residence with Mrs Kitty O'Shea, whom he had met in 1880, and in 1889 Captain O'Shea won an uncontested case for divorce, citing Parnell as co-respondent. Parnell was called upon to resign but he refused and his party split. His career destroyed, he died in October 1891 four months after marrying Kitty O'Shea.

The **forest park** (512 acres/207ha) covers a steep slope facing east across the Avondale River. The oldest surviving trees – two gigantic silver firs by the river as well as oaks, beeches and larches – were planted by Samuel Hayes in the 18C. The stump of a beech tree, planted nearly 250 years ago, has its rings delineated in relation to subsequent historical events. There are several trails and woodland walks ranging from the **Pine Trail** (0.5mi/0.8km), which is suitable for disabled people, to the **River Walk** (4mi/6.4km), which passes through the massed conifers on the banks of the Avonmore River and along the Great Ride.

Meeting of the Waters★

The confluence of the rivers Avonbeg and Avonmore is set amid the forests of south Co Wicklow; nearby stands the tree beneath which Thomas Moore (1779-1852) is said to have celebrated the "valley so sweet" in his poem *The Meeting of the Waters* of 1807.

SAMUEL HAYES

Avondale was inherited by the Parnell family from Samuel Hayes, a plantsman, whose Chippendale bureau is on display in the house. In 1788 Hayes presented a bill to Parliament "for encouraging the cultivation of trees" and in 1904 Avondale became the national forestry training centre.

Motte Stone

The name of the large glacial boulder is derived from the French word for half *(moitié)*, as it used to mark the halfway point on the Dublin-Wexford road before the advent of mileposts.

Vale of Avoca

The village of Avoca has attracted visitors in great numbers, since it was chosen as the setting for the hugely popular television series, *Ballykissangel*. There are forest walks in the wooded river valley.

At the **Avoca Weavers Mill**, founded in 1723 and therefore the oldest surviving business in Ireland, visitors may watch the production of textiles by traditional methods.

On the Coast

North to south

Bray

Bray is an old-established resort with a sand and shingle beach at the south end of Killiney Bay; it is also the southern terminus of the DART suburban railway line and in recent years has become a dormitory town for Dublin. The public park on Bray Head provides a fine **view** of the coastline. The local history is traced through photographs, maps and artefacts in the **Heritage Centre** in the Town Hall. *Open Jun-Aug, Mon-Fri, 9am-5pm, Sat, 10am-3pm; Sep-May, Mon-Fri, 9.30am-4.30pm, Sat, 10am-3pm. €3. Audioguide. ☎ 01 286 6796*

The **National Sea-Life Centre**, on the seafront, presents more than 30 displays populated by an array of marine and freshwater creatures. ♿ *Open mid-Mar to Oct, daily; Nov to mid-Mar, Sat-Sun, 10am-5pm. €7.50. ☎ 01 286 6939*

Greystones

The resort has developed from a fishing village with a harbour flanked by shingle beaches.

The Murrough

0.5mi/0.8km N of Wicklow on the east bank of the estuary.

A long shingle beach (3mi/5km) backed by a broad grass bank is flanked by the sea and the **Broad Lough**, a lagoon noted for its wildfowl and golden plover.

Wicklow

At the eastern foot of the mountains, the harbour town of Wicklow is the main commercial centre for the area as well as the county town and a Heritage town. Its Irish name *(Cill Mhantáin)* recalls St Mantan, a missionary who established a church in the 5C, while its English name is derived from *Wyking-alo*, Viking-meadow in Danish; the Vikings came here in the 9C, establishing a port which developed into an important trading centre.

The statue of a pikeman in the Market Square represents all those who fought in nationalist uprisings. The **Halpin Memorial**, an obelisk of polished granite, commemorates Captain Robert C Halpin (1836-94), a native of the town, who commanded the *Great Eastern*, the ship built by Brunel which laid the first transatlantic telegraph cable; mementoes are displayed at his residence, Tinakilly House, now a hotel *(2mi/3km NW by N 11)*.

Black Castle, which stands on a rocky promontory immediately south of the harbour, was built in 1176 by Maurice Fitzgerald, to whom the district had been granted after the 12C Anglo-Norman invasion, and was the subject of frequent attacks by local clansmen, the O'Byrnes and the O'Tooles, until the 16C. The ruins form a fine vantage point for **views** over the town and the coast of north Co Wicklow.

The 18C **Anglican Church** has an onion-shaped copper cupola, donated in 1777, and incorporates a 12C Irish-Romanesque doorway. The interior contains a fine king-post roof, a 12C font, an organ, transferred in the late 18C from the Anglican cathedral in Cashel, and a memorial tablet to Captain Halpin *(see above)*. The title "the Church of the Vineyard" recalls the vines planted by the Normans on the "Vineyard Banks" which descend to the River Vartry. *Open daily, 9.30am-dusk.*

In the grounds of the parish priest's house are extensive ruins of a **Franciscan friary**, founded by the Fitzgerald family in the 13C.

Wicklow's Historic Gaol – The formidable stone-built prison dates from 1702, the time of the Penal Laws, and was used as a prison until 1924. It now houses elaborate exhibits which bring to life some of the more dramatic aspects of Ireland's history. A warder inducts visitors into the ghastly conditions suffered by prisoners in the 18C; British soldiers ponder how to crush the 1798 Rebellion (many of the participants were tried in this building); local gentleman-rebel Billy Byrne awaits his execution; the life of convicts in the 19C, both here and in Australia, is evoked; stern Captain Betts shows how to deal with recalcitrant prisoners on board the transportation vessel *Hercules.* (♿) *Open mid-Mar to Oct, daily, 10am-6pm (5pm Mar and Oct); last admission 1hr before closing. €5.70. Café. ☎ 0404 61599; Fax 0404 61612; wccgaol@eircom.net; www.wicklowshistoricgaol.com*

Brittas Bay

The long sandy beach (3mi/5km), backed by dunes, is one of the most popular resorts on the east coast.

Arklow

The seaside resort, founded by the Vikings on the south bank of the Avoca estuary, is also an important east-coast fishing harbour and a base for Ireland's main fleet of coastal trading ships. The most famous product of the local boatyards is

Gypsy Moth III, the yacht in which Sir Francis Chichester sailed around the world in 1967. There are attractive walks by the harbour and along the south bank of the river.

The **Maritime Museum** displays about 200 exhibits connected with Ireland's maritime history and traces the development of local commercial shipping since the 1850s; a video, *Eyes to the Sea*, tells the maritime history of Arklow. *Open Mon-Fri, 10am-1pm and 2-5pm; also May-Sep, Sat. €5. Parking.* ☎ *0402 32868; Fax 0402 32868*

Arklow Rock *(2mi/3.2km south)* provides a fine **view** of the coastline.

Youghal★

Nowadays an attractive seaside resort with miles of fine beaches along the lovely estuary of the River Blackwater, this ancient harbour town looks back on a long and colourful history, attested to by a fine array of old buildings and the country's most extensive system of defensive walls, enough to merit the title Heritage town.

Location

Population 5 630 - Michelin Atlas p 79 and Map 712 – I 12 – Co Cork.
Youghal *(Eochaill)* – pronounced yawl – is situated on the coast road (N 25) between Cork and Waterford.
🛈 *Heritage Centre, Market Square, Youghal. Open May-Sep.* ☎ *024 923 90; Fax 20170; youghal@eircom.net; www.homepage.tinet.ie/~youghal*
🛈 *Sea Front Car Park, Ardmore. Open May-Sep.* ☎ *024 94444*
🛈 *Dungarvan. Open all year.* ☎ *058 41741*
Adjacent Sights: See COBH, CORK, CLONMEL, LISMORE, MIDLETON, WATERFORD.

Directory

SIGHTSEEING
Guided walking tour of Youghal – *Operates Jun-Aug, Mon-Sat at 10.30am (90min; 2 languages).* ☎ *024 20170 or 92447; Fax 024 20170; youghaltourism@eircom.ie*

WHERE TO STAY
• Budget
Acacia Cottage – *2 Foxfield, Dooradoyle Rd - 2.5mil/4km SW off Ballykeefe roundabout -* ☎ *061 304 757 - Fax 061 304 757 - acaciacottage@iolfree.ie -* 🄿
⚒ *- 4 rm €40/60* ⚏. Found in a residential cul-de-sac, away from the town centre. Cosy, cottagey-style bedrooms that lend the house a warm and homely feel which is further enhanced by the hospitable owner.

• Moderate
Glenally House – *Copperalley - 1mi/1.6km N by N 25 -* ☎ *024 91623 - Fax 024 91623 - enquiries@glenally.com - Mar to mid-Dec -* 🄿

⚒ *- 4 rm €70/110* ⚏ *- Meals €35.*
The owners have successfully combined contemporary styles and bold, rich colours with the original features of this peaceful Georgian house. Guests can enjoy carefully prepared meals 'en famille'.

WHERE TO EAT
• Moderate
Aherne's Seafood Restaurant and Bar (at Aherne's Hotel) – *163 North Main St -* ☎ *024 92424 - Closed at Christmas -* 🄿 *- €40/56.* Lovers of seafood have made this family-run business something of a landmark since its opening in the 1960s. The art work in the dining room is available to buy and the bedrooms are all thoughtfully decorated.

SPORTS AND LEISURE
Beaches at Ardmore
Greyhound racing

Background

The name Youghal comes from the Irish for yew tree, a reminder that the town's hinterland was once richly wooded. In the 9C the site was occupied by the Danish Vikings, who used it as a base to plunder the rich lands along the River Blackwater and to raid other settlements along the south coast. The Anglo-Normans arrived at the end of the 12C; strategically placed for the landing of forces from England and always vulnerable to the threat of invasion from France and Spain, Youghal became one of Ireland's most strongly defended seaports, enclosed by impressive town walls..

In the late 16C, while mayor of Youghal, **Sir Walter Ralegh** introduced the tobacco and potato plants into Ireland. He later sold his extensive estates to another Englishman, Richard Boyle (1566-1643), an unscrupulous speculator in confiscated lands who became the richest individual in Ireland and was ennobled as the 1st "Great" Earl of Cork. In 1649 Youghal's garrison prudently went over to Cromwell, who overwintered here with his army. Despite its prosperity as one of Ireland's leading ports, for much of the 18C the town was riven by conflict between the dominant Protestant minority and the underprivileged Roman Catholic majority. In the latter part of the 19C some 150 sail-powered schooners traded from here; sailors from Youghal could recognise one another throughout the ports of the world by their distinctive whistle. This once-strong tradition began to decline early in the 20C with the silting-up of the estuary and the building of steam-powered freight ships.

Walking About

Start from the Tourist Information Office.

Youghal Heritage Centre
Open Mon-Fri, 9am-5.30pm (6.30pm summer), Sat-Sun, 9.30am-5pm (6.30pm summer).
☎ 024 20170 or 92447; Fax 024 20170; youghal@eircom.net
The old Market House now houses the Tourist Information Office and an exhibition on the history of the walled port of Youghal.

H Champollion/MICHELIN

Youghal Harbour

In the Market Square stands a memorial commemorating the *Nellie Fleming*, the last of the old Youghal sailing vessels.

The pub on the corner, **Moby Dick's**, displays many photographs taken during the filming of *Moby Dick* on location in Youghal during the summer of 1954.

Walk inland along one of the side streets; turn right into South Main Street.

Clock Gate★
The unusual four-storey building straddling the Main Street was constructed by the corporation in 1777 to replace the Iron Gate, also known as Trinity Castle, part of the walls. The new tower was used as the town jail until 1837; such was the state of insurrection in the late 18C that it soon became overcrowded; rebels were hanged from the windows as an example to the rest of the populace.

Walk though the Clock Gate and continue N along South Main Street.

Benedictine Abbey
Left side of the street. All that remains of the abbey is the east gable wall pierced by a moulded Gothic doorway with ornamental spandrels; in the passageway are the arched piscina and square aumbry from the original church. The abbey was founded in 1350 and used by Cromwell as his winter headquarters in 1649-50.

The Red House
Left side of the street. This fine example of early-18C Dutch domestic architecture creates a marked contrast with its neighbours. The red-brick façade with white stone quoins is surmounted by a triangular gable and a steep mansard roof. It was designed in 1710 for the Uniacke family by a Dutch architect-builder Claud Leuvethen.

Tynte's Castle

Right side of the street. This 15C battlemented building has a device over the front door for pouring boiling oil on rebels and other unwelcome visitors. Once on the waterfront, it is now some distance (200yd/182m) from the river.

Almshouses

Left side of the street. The Elizabethan almshouses, still used for residential purposes, were erected in 1610 by the Earl of Cork, who provided "five pounds apiece for each of ye six old decayed soldiers or Alms Men for ever".

Turn left into Church Street.

Also used for residential purposes is the neighbouring former Protestant **asylum**, dated 1838 and now called Shalom House.

St Mary's Collegiate Church★★

Open mid-May to mid-Sep, daily, 9am-1pm and 2-5pm. Brochure (5 languages). ☎ 024 91014

It is probable that the first church on the site, a wooden building, was erected by followers of St Declan of Ardmore in c 400. The present early-13C edifice was pronounced "one of Ireland's most impressive churches" by the late Claud Cockburn, writer and long-time Youghal resident; it replaced an 11C Danish-built church destroyed in a great storm soon after its construction. During the late-15C wars, the forces of the Earl of Desmond occupied the building and removed the roof of the chancel. Large-scale restoration, including the remodelling of the chancel, took place between 1851 and 1858.

The church contains a large collection of **grave slabs** and **effigies**, including some from the 13C and 14C with Norman-French inscriptions. None remotely match the monument in the south transept erected to himself by the 1st Earl of Cork, a superbly pretentious house-size structure showing him reclining nonchalantly beneath his family tree, surrounded by his wives, children and mother-in-law.

Town Walls★

Partially accessible from the churchyard. Youghal has the best-preserved town walls in Ireland, their extent even greater than the city walls of Londonderry. They were built in the 13C and extended in the 17C; large sections are still in excellent condition, although only three of the 13 medieval towers remain. The portion restored in the 19C with a turret and a cannon is accessible from the churchyard; the sentry walk provides a fine **view** of the town and the harbour. The full length of the walls is best seen from the outside *(Raheen Road)*.

Tour

Drive of 30mi/48km

From Youghal take N 25 E; beyond Kinsalebeg turn right into a minor road via Moord to Ardmore.

Whiting Bay★

The bay, which is flanked by Cabin Point and Ardoginna Head, is very isolated but offers fine **views** *(SW)* across Youghal Bay to Knockadoon Head.

Ardmore★

The many attractions of this pleasant little resort include a lovely sandy beach, wonderful cliff walks, and a fascinating architectural heritage evoking the era of St Declan, a predecessor of St Patrick.

Declan, who died early in the 5C, seems to have studied in Wales and to have sailed across St George's Channel to Ardmore in the company of a large stone carrying his bell; the stone (in fact a glacial boulder) stands on the beach and offers a cure for rheumatism to anyone agile enough to crawl beneath it. There is also a holy well associated with the saint. The site of his original monastic foundation overlooking the sea is marked by the exceptionally fine **round tower★** (97ft/29m) which is among the best preserved of its kind; probably dating from the 12C; it has a conical cap, projecting string courses marking each of its four storeys and corbels carved with human and other ornaments. The outstanding feature of the ruined **cathedral★** (10C-14C) is the exterior **arcade★** of sunken panels on the west gable; nearly all the panels are filled with vigorously carved but much weathered sculptures similar in style to those found on high crosses dating from the 10C, the best known being the one depicting the Weighing of Souls. Nearby, a small building probably dating from the 5C settlement of Ardmore by Declan is known as **St Declan's Oratory**.

The long distance footpath called St Declan's Way runs from here to Cashel (62mi/100km) but a shorter local walk offering superb sea views, is from the Cliff House Hotel to Ram Head.

Take the coast road E to Mine Head.

Mine Head

Mine Head provides impressive **views** of the cliffs.

Take the coast road E to Helvick Head.

Ringville (An Rinn)

This small village is the centre of an Irish-speaking area, the **West Waterford Gaeltacht**; there are excellent **views★** across Dungarvan harbour.

Helvick Head★

1mi/1.6km E of Ringville. Helvick Harbour, a small but busy port backed by a row of fishermen's cottages, shelters below the headland which, despite its modest height (230ft/82m), provides outstanding **views★** of the coastline.

Cunnigar Peninsula

1mi/1.6m W of Ringville. The sandy spit of land extending into Dungarvan harbour shelters a wealth of birdlife and may be walked from end to end *(1.5mi/2.4km).*

Dungarvan

18mi/30km E by N 25. The thriving seaside resort occupies an attractive **site** astride the Colligan estuary overlooking the broad bay known as Dungarvan Harbour and flanked by the Drum Hills *(S)* and the Monavullagh and Comeragh Mountains *(N).* **King John's Castle**, built by the king in 1185 not long after the Anglo-Norman invasion, consists of a large circular **keep** surrounded by fortified walls, much modified in subsequent centuries.

The **Dungarvan Museum**, housed in the Municipal Library, has a nautical theme; local shipwrecks are well documented, especially the *Moresby* which went down in Dungarvan Bay on 24 December 1895 with the loss of 20 lives. *Open Mon-Fri, 9.30am-1pm and 2-5pm.* ☎ *058 45960; www.dungarvanmuseum.org*

On the east bank of the river are the ruins of a 13C **Augustinian priory** which was founded by the McGraths, who also built the 12C or 13C **castle**, of which only the west wall still stands. The walk on the seaward side of the graveyard provides fine **views★** across Dungarvan Harbour south to Helvick Head.

MASTER McGRATH MONUMENT

In a career of 37 races, Master McGrath, a locally bred greyhound, was beaten only once. Between 1868 and 1871 he won the Waterloo Cup in England three times and is commemorated in the only monument in Ireland to a dog *(2mi/3.2km NW of Dungarvan by R 672).*

Giant's Causeway

Northern Ireland

Antrim

The former county town of Co Antrim, traditionally known for its linen-spinning, is linked to Belfast by rail and motorway and was subjected to rapid expansion in the last decades of the 20C. Located on the Six Mile Water, a fine trout stream, the town's greatest asset is its proximity to the broad waters of Lough Neagh (see p 446); there are cruises from the lakeside marina and a championship golf course is laid out on the shore. Antrim was attacked during the 1798 Rebellion by a force of 3 500 United Irishmen under Henry Joy McCracken, a Belfast cotton manufacturer, who was defeated and subsequently hanged.

Location
Population 20 878 - Michelin Atlas p 103 and Map 712 – N 3 – Co Antrim.
Antrim *(Aontroim)* is situated on the shore of Lough Neagh, 20mi/32km NW of Belfast by M 2.
🚪 *16 High Street, Antrim BT41 4AN. Open May-Sep, Mon-Sat; Oct-Apr, Mon-Fri.*
☎ *028 9442 8331; Fax 028 9448 7844; abs@antrim.gov.uk; www.antrim.gov.uk*
Adjacent Sights: See ANTRIM GLENS, BELFAST, CARRICKFERGUS, LOUGH NEAGH.

Directory

ENTERTAINMENT
Clotworthy Arts Centre, *Antrim Castle Grounds (see below)* - Theatrical and musical performances, exhibitions of painting, photography and sculpture; talks and lectures; courses and workshops – *Open Mon-Fri, 9.30am-9.30pm, Sat, 10am-5pm; also Jul-Aug, Sun, 2-5pm.*

☎ *028 9442 8000; Fax 028 9446 0360; clotworthy@antrim.gov.uk*

SPORTS AND LEISURE
Antrim Forum Leisure Centre – (♿) *Open Mon-Fri, 9am-10pm, Sat, 9.30am-5.30pm, Sun, 2-5.30pm. Lift.* ☎ *028 9446 4131*

Walking About

Pogue's Entry
East end of the main street. ♿ Open May-Sep, Thu-Fri, 2-5pm, Sat, 10am-1pm and 2-5pm. Guided tour (15min). ☎ *028 9442 8996 (May-Sep),* ☎ *028 9442 8000 (Clotworthy Arts Centre); Fax 028 9446 0360*
In a picturesque alleyway stands the simple cabin where **Alexander Irvine** (1863-1941), the son of a cobbler, spent his childhood. Irvine became a missionary in the Bowery in New York; his book, *My Lady of the Chimney Corner*, is about his mother's struggle against poverty.

Antrim Castle Gardens
West end of the main street. Open Mon-Fri, 9.30am-9pm, Sat-Sun, 10am (2pm Sun) to 5pm. ☎ *028 9442 8000 (Clotworthy Arts Centre); Fax 028 9446 0360*
Beyond the Market Place and the Court House (1726), a magnificent Tudor gate leads to what used to be the desmesne of the Clotworthy family, ennobled as Lords Massarene in the 17C. Their castle burned down accidentally in 1922 but their formal garden survives, best viewed from the top of the Norman motte. The garden is a rare, and in Ulster unique, example of a Dutch-style landscape, with ornamental canals connected by a cascade, flanked by geometric parterres and screened by high pleached hedges of lime and hornbeam.

Round Tower★
From the High Street 10min on foot N along Railway Street and Station Road; beyond the school turn left into Steeple Park. Among the trees stands a fine example of a round tower (90ft/27m), one of the best preserved in Ireland; the conical cap has been restored. It was probably built c 900 and is all that remains of an important 6C monastery, abandoned in 1147.

Excursions

Patterson's Spade Mill
5mi/8km SE by A 6 via Templepatrick. (NT) ♿ Guided tour Jun-Aug, daily, 2-6pm; Apr-May and Sep, Sat-Sun and Bank Hol Mon; Mar, certain days. £3.25. Wheelchair available; ramps. ☎ */Fax 028 9443 3619*
The only surviving water-powered spade mill in Ireland was founded in 1919; five generations of Pattersons worked at the mill until 1990. The tour includes all the

Finishing Shop, Patterson's Spade Mill

stages involved in producing spades in the traditional way – the forge for heating the metal billet, the huge tilt hammer for shaping the blade which is then sharpened and tempered, the riveting of the blade to the shaft, and the painting – all done by two men. Beside the mill are the ruins of associated industrial buildings.

Ballance House

11mi/17km S by B 101, A 26 and A 30 via Glenavy. (&) Open Apr-Sep, Tue Sun and Bank Hol Mon, 11am (2pm Sat-Sun) to 5pm. £3. Parking. Refreshments. ☎ 028 9264 8492; Fax 020 9204 8098
The house was the birthplace of John Ballance (1839-93), who emigrated to Birmingham and thence to New Zealand, where he became a journalist and then entered politics, becoming the first Liberal Prime Minister. Partly furnished in mid-19C style, the house is also a fascinating museum devoted to the Ulster-New Zealand connection.

Templetown Mausoleum

Templepatrick; 5mi/8km E of Antrim by A 6. Park at the end of the drive. (NT) Open daily, 11am-6pm. ☎ 028 9751 0721 (Regional Office)
A walled graveyard encloses the mausoleum, a triumphal arch designed by Robert Adam in the Palladian style c 1770 for Sarah Upton in memory of her husband Arthur. It contains tablets to later generations of Uptons who received the title Viscount Templetown.
The name Templepatrick derives from an earlier church dedicated to St Patrick who is supposed to have baptised converts at a nearby Holy Well in about 450.

Slemish

16mi/26km NE by A 26 to Ballymena, A 42 E and B 94; after 1mi/1.6km turn left; after 3mi/4.8km turn right (Carnstroan Road); after 0.25mi/0.4km turn right. From the car park 1hr there and back on foot. The distinctive bare silhouette of Slemish (1 437ft/438m), an extinct volcano, rises abruptly from the flat landscape of the Ballymena plain. On St Patrick's Day (17 March) it is a place of pilgrimage, since tradition has it that **St Patrick** spent six years here in captivity herding swine for the local chieftain Miluic. From the top there is a fine **view** including the ruins of Skerry Church *(NW)*, the burial place of the O'Neills, supposed to be founded by St Patrick himself.

Arthur Cottage

17mi/27km NW by A 26 to Ballymena and B 62 to Cullybackey. Cross the river and turn sharp right onto a narrow lane. & Open Easter-Sep, Mon-Sat, 10.30am-5pm (4pm Sat). £2. Craft demonstrations: Jun-Aug, Tue, Fri-Sat, 1.30pm. Guided tour (30min). Parking. ☎ 028 2588 0781 (May-Sep), 028 2563 8494; Fax 028 2563 8495; ballymenatice@ hotmail.com; devel.leisure@ballymena.gov.uk; www.ballymena.gov.uk

At the end of the lane stands an isolated one-storey cottage with the traditional split door, clay floor and roof of flax-straw thatch. From here the father of Chester Alan Arthur, 21st President of the USA, emigrated in 1816 to Vermont where he became a Baptist clergyman. His son was one of more than a dozen US Presidents with Ulster roots. The furniture is in period; in summer there are demonstrations of traditional domestic crafts. The large outbuilding contains collections of local agricultural and domestic implements from the past, and a display on Chester Alan Arthur's family and 19C emigration from Ireland.

Gracehill

11mi/18km NW by A 26 to Ballymena and A 42. The Georgian architecture and attractive layout of this village are the work of the Moravians, who came via London from Bohemia where their church was persecuted. Their settlement, started in 1759 and, grouped round a central square, included a church, the minister's house and communal houses for single men and women. The boarding schools for girls and boys acquired an enviable reputation far outside their locality. Men and women sat on separate sides in church and were buried in separate sections of the graveyard.

Randalstown Presbyterian Church

5mi/8km W by A 6. The charming oval church was built of dark stone with pointed windows in 1790. The porch, containing curved flights of steps to the internal gallery, was added in 1829 and the row of oval oculi was inserted in 1929 when the height of the walls was raised.

Antrim Glens★★★

A drive up the Antrim Coast offers a great variety of scenery and a sense of expectancy at each approaching headland. Seaward are attractive villages, long flat strands, steep basalt or limestone cliffs, and a distant prospect of the Mull of Kintyre in Scotland. Inland are the glens created by the tumbling mountain streams which descend from the uplands of heath and bog, now punctuated by forestry plantations. In the glens, where the underlying sedimentary rocks are exposed, the farms are arranged like ladders climbing the valley sides so that each has a share of the good land near the river and of the poorer upland pasture.

Location

Michelin Atlas p 103 and Map 712 – N, O 2, 3 – Co Antrim.
The A 2 runs along the Antrim coast between Larne and Ballycastle at the foot of the nine Glens of Antrim which descend from the Antrim Plateau to the sea.
🗓 *Narrow Gauge Road, Larne. Open Apr-Sep, Mon-Sat; Oct-Mar, Mon-Fri.*
☎/Fax 028 2826 0088
🗓 *7 Mary Street, Ballycastle BT54 6QH. Open Jul-Aug, daily; Sep-Jun, Mon-Fri.*
☎ *028 2076 2024; Fax 028 2076 2515*
Adjacent Sights: See CARRICKFERGUS, GIANT'S CAUSEWAY, PORTRUSH.

Background

For many years this was the most isolated and least anglicised part of the country owing to the difficult terrain. There had always been a track along the coast, which still makes a good walk, but the first all-weather road dates from 1832 when the Grand Military Road from Carrickfergus to Portrush was built under the supervision of the Scottish engineer William Bald. A true corniche, it had to be laid out along an ancient raised beach, and involved the blasting away of vast quantities of basalt and chalk and protection from landslides.
Two narrow-gauge railway lines (3ft/1m) were laid in the 19C to carry the increasing output of the Glenariff

DIRECTORY

Rathlin Island Ferry – *Operates (weather permitting) Jun-Sep, daily, from Ballycastle (45min) at 10am, noon, 4.30pm, 6.30pm; from Rathlin at 8.30am, 11am, 3.30pm, 5.30pm; Oct-May, telephone for details. There and back £8.40. ☎ 028 2076 9299*
In case of bad weather, overnight accommodation available on the island at Rathlin Guesthouse (☎ 028 2076 3917) and at The Manor House (☎ 028 2076 3964).
Larne Lough Ferry to Island Magee *(see p 412) – Operates (weather permitting) hourly, 7.30am-5.30pm. ☎ 028 2827 4085*

mines, which opened in the late 1860s. One, the railway built by the Glenariff Iron Ore & Holding Co, ran from Inverglen down Glenariff to the southeast end of Red Bay, where the bed of the track is still visible. The other ran from Ballymena up the Clogh Valley to Retreat (1876) but was never extended further, owing to the steep gradient down Glenballyemon to the coast; it turned to carrying passengers and opened up the glens to the tourist trade before ceasing operations in 1930.

Tour

LARNE TO BALLYCASTLE
70mi/113km – 1 or 2 days

Larne
The town, the southern gateway to the Glens of Antrim, is a busy port with a regular ferry service to Cairnryan in Scotland and another ferry to Island Magee *(see Directory)*. Larne has long been an entry point to northern Ireland: landings were made in the 9C and 10C by the Vikings; in 1315 Edward Bruce sailed over from Scotland in the course of his doomed attempt to secure an Irish crown; in April 1914, in open defiance of British authority, 25 000 German rifles and 3 million rounds of ammunition were unloaded and rapidly distributed to the Ulster Volunteers, clear evidence of their determination to resist Home Rule by all possible means.
South of the harbour on the spit of land called Curran Point stand the ruins of **Olderfleet Castle**, a square four-storey tower house, one of three protecting the entrance to the lough in the early 17C.
The **Chaine Memorial Tower**, a modern replica of the traditional Irish round tower, erected in honour of James Chaine, a local MP and benefactor, stands on the shore at the northern entrance to the harbour.
From Larne take A 2 N.

Carnfunnock Country Park
Open Apr-Sep, daily, 10am-6pm (8pm Jul-Aug; 9am-4.30pm Oct-Mar). Maze (Apr-Sep). Miniature railway. Crazy ball, putting and 9-hole golf course: prices by telephone. Parking. Refreshments. ☎ *028 2027 0541, 2826 0088 (Larne TIC); Fax 028 2827 0852; mcwilliama@larne.gov.uk; www-larne.gov.uk.*
In a lovely setting of green hills dropping down to the sea north of Drains Bay village, the Park (173 acres/190ha) was once a private demesne. Set among the flowers and shrubs in the walled garden are 12 sundials showing GMT, Summer Time or local time. A viewing platform overlooks the interior of the **maze**, which reflects the shape of Northern Ireland. The **limekiln walk** *(1hr)* includes the old ice house and the Look Out; there is also a walk through the forest. There is a 9 hole golf course and putting green. Opposite the park entrance on the shore are a marine promenade and boat slip.
Continue N on A 2.
Ballygally Castle, now a hotel, was built in 1625 by James Shaw; the twin bartizans are original but the sash windows were introduced later. Inland rises a natural amphitheatre, Sallagh Braes; the fine walk above the Braes along the plateau edge *(access via Carncastle and Ballycoose Road)* forms part of the Ulster Way.
Continue N on A 2.

Glenarm Village
This attractive little port, which wears a light coating of white dust from the local limestone quarries, is the oldest village in the Glens. The main street runs inland past the 19C barbican gateway of **Glenarm Castle** *(private)*, the seat of the Earl of Antrim, which was begun in 1606 and remodelled in the Elizabethan style by William Vitruvius Morrison early in the 19C.
The **Forest Park** at the top of the street *(car park)* provides a view of the castle, and there are pleasant walks by the stream in the upper woodlands beyond the belt of conifers.
Return to A 2; turn left onto B 97.
The road runs up **Glenarm**, the southernmost of the Antrim Glens, passing through open farmland with views of Glenarm Forest on the far side of the valley. At the top of the glen, the unmistakable outline of Slemish *(see p 383)* comes into view to the south.
At the T-junction turn right onto A 42.
In **Glencloy** the road descends through gently sloping pastures to the coast.
Turn left into A 2.

Carnlough
The large sandy bay makes this an attractive resort. Until the 1960s, limestone from the quarries above the town was transported by rail to the tiny harbour which is now full of pleasure boats. The line was carried across the main road by a low

bridge which, together with the adjoining clock tower and former courthouse, was built by the Marquess of Londonderry *(see p 439)* in 1854.

Beyond Garron Point, the beautiful expanse of **Red Bay** comes into view, backed by the distinctive steep-sided, flat-topped silhouette of Lurigethan (1 154ft/352m). The bay takes its name from the colour of the sandstone washed down by the mountain streams.

Glenariff (also Waterfoot)

The village lies at the mouth of the Glenariff River. On the headland, above the road tunnel, stand the ruins of Red Bay Castle, built by the Norman Bisset family.

From Glenariff take A 43 inland.

In **Glenariff▲**, justly named the **"Queen of the Glens"**, the broad lush pastures are enclosed between steep hanging crags.

Glenariff Forest Park★★

  ♿ *Open daily, 10am-dusk. £3 car; £20 coach; £1.50 pedestrians. Parking. Restaurant; picnic area.* ☏ *028 2955 6000; Fax 028 2955 7162; www.forestserviceni.gov.uk*

The forest (2 298 acres/930ha) consists of woodland, peat bogs, rocky outcrops and several small lakes and rivers.

The visitor centre beside the garden and aviary is probably the best place to find out more about the Antrim Glens, and has excellent displays on forestry, local wildlife, the 19C iron ore and bauxite mines and their railways.

The **waterfall★★** known as Ess na Larach *(1hr there and back on foot from the north side of the car park)* tumbles through a wooded gorge created by the Glenariff River; from the Fog House the waterfall can be viewed through panels of tinted glass which impart a sun-lit glow, a moonlit chill or a luminous green light.

Continue SW on A 43; at the junction turn right onto B 14.

In **Glenballyemon**, after emerging from an evergreen forest into open moorland, the road passes through Retreat on the north slopes of Lurigethan.

Waterfall, Glenariff Forest Park

Cushendall

Urbane little Cushendall stands at the meeting point of three glens, and is as good a base as any for local exploration. Its principal sight is the red sandstone tower, known locally as the Curfew Tower, which was built as a watchhouse in 1809 by Francis Turnly of the East India Company.

Take Layde Road, the steep coast road going N to Cushendun.

Layd Old Church

The ruins of the church stand in a graveyard romantically sited by a swiftly flowing stream which plunges directly into the sea. The church is thought to have been founded by the Franciscans but from 1306 to 1790 it was a parish church. There are MacDonnell memorials in the graveyard.

As the coast road continues uphill there is a fine panoramic view – even to Scotland.

At the T-junction in Knocknacarry turn left onto B 92 and left again onto A 2.

The name of **Glencorp** translates as the glen of slaughter.

After 1.5mi/2.4km turn right onto Glenaan Road. Turn left onto a lane (sign "Ossian's Grave"); car park beyond the farmhouse; 20min there and back on foot.

Ossian's Grave

The figure of Ossian appears in a number of guises, one of them as an early Christian warrior-bard, the son of Finn McCool, whose legendary feats are recounted in the Ossianic Cycle. Revived in the work of the 18C poet James McPherson, Ossian enjoyed a great vogue among the Romantic writers of the late 18C/early 19C, particularly in continental Europe. Whoever he was, it was not here that he found his last resting place; Ossian's Grave is a Neolithic court tomb, with a semicircular forecourt opening into a bi-cameral burial gallery, enclosed in an oval cairn. But this is nevertheless an evocative spot, with fine views all around.

Continue W up the glen.

In **Glenaan** the Glenaan River flows down from the slopes of Tievebulliagh *(S)* where Neolithic men made axeheads from the hard porcellanite rock.

At the crossroads turn right onto Glendun Road to Cushendun.

Glendun★, the Brown Glen is the wildest of the nine glens; its river, which is noted for sea trout and salmon fishing, flows under the viaduct designed by Charles Lanyon in 1839 to carry the main coast road.

Cushendun

The houses of this picturesque village, which is now preserved by the National Trust, cluster at the southern end of a sandy beach flanked by tall cliffs. The village owes its distinctive and rather fey character to Sir Clough Williams-Ellis, the playful architect of Portmeirion in North Wales, who worked here for Ronald McNeill, the first (and last) Lord Cushendun. There are terraces of small white houses around a square, a number of slate-hung cottages, and a neo-Georgian mansion, Glenmona Lodge, which stands in a pine grove facing the sea.

From Cushendun take the coast road, a winding, steep and narrow road N. After 5mi/8km fork right onto Torr Road.

Torr Head *(car park)* is a low promontory, crowned by a lookout post – the nearest point to the Scottish coast (12mi/19km).

Continue NW along the coast road; after 2.5mi/4km turn right.

Murlough Bay National Nature Reserve★★★

1mi/1.6km to the upper car park; smaller car park lower down the cliff face. This is the most beautiful bay on the Antrim coast, set in the lee of **Fair Head** (Benmore) at the foot of steep and towering cliffs. From the shore, grassy slopes dotted with birch and rowan trees climb steeply to the escarpment. The stone cross is a memorial to Sir Roger Casement *(see p 118)*. From the lower car park there are two fine walks *(waymarked)*: one path leads north to some long-abandoned coal mines before returning along the shore past the remains of the miners' cottages and the ruins of Drumnakill Church; the other leads south past an old lime kiln, bears inland through the wood to avoid Murlough Cottage *(private)* and ends at Benvan farmhouse.

From the upper car park there is a path *(waymarked)* along the clifftop to wind-blown **Fair Head**. From here there are glorious **views★★★** of Rathlin Island *(N)* and the Mull of Kintyre *(NE)*. To return to the car park the path swings inland across the rough and often wet ground of the plateau, past a **crannóg** in Lough na Cranagh *(right)*, the farm buildings *(car park)* at Coolanlough and Lough Fadden *(left)*.

Return to the coast road; turn right to Ballycastle.

Bonamargy Friary

Well sited beside a stream stand the remains of a Franciscan friary *(c 1500)*, now surrounded by Ballycastle golf course. The ruined church has a vault containing remains of several MacDonnells. These descendants of the Scottish MacDonalds engaged in bitter rivalry with the McQuillan clan for possession of this part of Ireland, and were known for their treachery and lack of scruple, fighting now for, now against the English. By contrast, the McQuillans produced a nun, Julia, known for her piety; the round-headed cross in the nave is thought to mark her grave, placed here so that even in death she could practise humility, walked on by the feet of worshippers.

On the edge of Ballycastle turn left onto B 15; after 0.25mi/0.4km bear right uphill onto Dunamallaght Road.

Glenshesk

The road overlooks the Glenshesk River and skirts the southern edge of Ballycastle Forest. From Breen Bridge, at the foot of the south face of Knocklayd Mountain, a waymarked footpath, the **Moyle Way**, a spur of the Ulster Way, leads north over the summit of Knocklayd (1 695ft/514m) to Ballycastle *(4mi/6.4km)*.

From Breen Bridge take B 15 W.

Armoy Round Tower

In the graveyard of St Patrick's Church stands the base of a round tower (30ft/9m), which dates from 460 and was part of a monastery founded by Olcan, a disciple of St Patrick.

From the crossroads take the minor road N to Ballycastle.

Glentaisie

The glen skirts the west face of Knocklayd.

Turn right onto A 44 to Ballycastle.

Ballycastle

This attractive little resort and market town is situated at the foot of Knocklayd Mountain with a view over Ballycastle Bay to Rathlin Island. Among its many amenties are a long sandy beach, salt- and fresh-water angling, golf links and other sports facilities, while in June there is a well-attended Irish Music and Dance Festival. In August the Ould Lammas Fair combines livestock sales with street stalls selling two traditional sweet confections – **Yellowman**, a sort of toffee, and **Dulse**, a dried edible seaweed. A stone memorial, symbolising aerials and radio waves, standing at the west end of the harbour, recalls the wireless link between Ballycastle and Rathlin Island set up in 1898 by Marconi *(see p 191)* and his assistant George Kemp.

The town centre is graced by **Holy Trinity Church**, an elegant 18C building with a balustraded tower and steeple. *Open daily, 9am-5pm.* ☎ *028 2076 2461 (Rector); www.ramoan.connor.anglican.org*

On the cliffs east of the town is the **Corrymeela Centre**, which works for reconciliation between the two cultural traditions in Northern Ireland; it contains a semi-underground heart-shaped oratory,

From Ballycastle take B 15 W. After 5mi/8km turn right to Larry Bane Bay and Carrick-a-rede Rope Bridge.

Carrick-a-rede Rope Bridge★★★

From the car park 30min there and back on foot. People cross the rope bridge at their own risk; dangerous in a high wind; remember the return journey. (NT) Open mid-Mar to Sep, daily (weather permitting), 10am-6pm (8pm Jul-Aug). Guided tour by appointment. Parking (£3). Information point. Tearoom. ☎ *028 2073 1159 or 1582; Fax 028 2073 2963; carrickarede@ntrust.org.uk*

The rope bridge is put up every spring for the fishermen who operate the island salmon fishery. As the migrating salmon swim west along the shore seeking their freshwater spawning grounds in the River Bush or River Bann, they are deflected north by the island (*Carrick-a-rede* means Rock-in-the-Road) straight into the nets which are always set in the same place. The bridge (66ft/20m long) bounces and sways as one ventures gingerly along the planks above the rock-strewn water (80ft/25m below). In the past there was only one handrail but accidents seem to have been few during the bridge's 200 years of existence. There are superb views of the coast.

Rathlin Island★

Access by boat from Ballycastle (see Directory). The island lies north of Ballycastle across Rathlin Sound (5mi/8km), often a rough and dangerous crossing. L-shaped, treeless, pitted with shallow lakes and divided into fields by drystone walls, Rathlin is almost entirely surrounded by high white cliffs where in early summer the seabirds congregate in their thousands. From the sheltered harbour, where seals sometimes bask on the rocks, three roads radiate to the outlying homesteads and the lighthouses. The traditional occupations are fishing and farming, supplemented in the past by smuggling and now by tourism.

In the 6C St Columba nearly lost his life off Rathlin when his boat was trapped in a whirlpool. In 1306, according to tradition, it was while taking refuge in one of the island's many caves that Robert the Bruce received his famous lesson in perseverance from a spider *(accessible only by boat).*

Carrick-a-rede Rope Bridge

H Champollion/MICHELIN

Armagh★★

Built on hills like Rome, Ireland's ecclesiastical capital stands in a pleasant and prosperous countryside of fruit orchards. The town with its many fine Georgian buildings is dominated by its two cathedrals, the seats of Ireland's Anglican and Roman Catholic archbishops. For long a county town, in 1994 Armagh was given city status, a tribute to its unique significance in the religious life of the whole country.

Location

Population 14 265 - Michelin Atlas p 98 and Map 712 – L, M 4 – Co Armagh.
Armagh (Ard Macha) is situated between Lough Neagh and the border, 50mi/80km SW of Belfast by M 1.
🚩 *40 English Street, Armagh BT61 7BA. Open daily.* ☎ *028 3752 1800; Fax 028 3752 8329*
Adjacent Sights: See DUNGANNON, MONAGHAN, LOUGH NEAGH, NEWRY, SPERRIN MOUNTAINS.

Directory

WHERE TO STAY
• *Moderate*
Armagh City Hotel – *2 Friary Rd, BT56 8BN* - ☎ *028 3751 8888* - Fax 028 3751 2777 info@armaghcityhotel.com - Closed 25 Dec - 🅿 & - 82 rm £75/90 ☑ - Restaurant £15/20.20. This purpose-built group hotel opened in 2002 and is next door to Armagh Golf Club. Boasts an up-to-the-minute leisure club, modern facilities in all the bedrooms and a large split-level dining room with an Irish theme to the menu.

TRACING ANCESTORS
Armagh Ancestry – *42 English Street. Open Mon-Sat, 9am-5pm.* ☎ *028 3752 1802; Fax 028 3751 0033*
St Patrick's Trian *(see below)*

Background

Armagh, derived from Ard Macha meaning Macha's Height, is named after a legendary pagan queen who built a fortress on the central hill of Armagh. Although the major pre-Christian power centre of Ulster was nearby Navan Fort *(see below)*, the settlement of Armagh grew in prominence after Navan's destruction in AD 332. In his mission to convert Ireland to Christianity, c 445, St Patrick arrived in Armagh and chose it as the centre of the new religion, building his church on the cathedral hill; he declared that it should take precedence over all other churches in Ireland and from that time it has been the ecclesiastical capital of the whole country.

In the following centuries Armagh developed into an important centre of learning under teachers such as the great 12C Archbishop St Malachy; its reputation was such that in 1162 an ecclesiastical Synod decreed that only those who had studied at Armagh could teach theology elsewhere in Ireland. The famous 9C manuscript, the *Book of Armagh*, now in Trinity College Library *(see p 233)* was written and illuminated here.

Its famous orchards originally laid out by English settlers from the Vale of Evesham, the county of Armagh formed part of the early-17C Plantation of Ulster, though the native Irish population was far from being wholly displaced; the city of Armagh has long had English, Scotch and Irish Streets, and today the county consists of a largely Protestant north and a predominantly Catholic south.

ARCHITECTURAL ELEGANCE
In the peaceful conditions of the 18C and early 19C, farming and commerce flourished; Armagh acquired some of its finest architecture under the benevolent patronage of its Anglican Primate: Richard Robinson, later Lord Rokeby, who became Archbishop in 1765. Robinson restored the cathedral, built himself a fine palace, constructed a library and other public buildings, founded an observatory, and beautified the city's famous Mall. He was the patron of Francis Johnston (1761-1829), a native of Armagh, helping him establish himself as one of the country's foremost architects. but he failed in his ambition for Armagh to become a university city and the capital of Ulster.

Walking About

The Mall★

The Mall is a most attractive urban feature, a long stretch of grass with a pavilion and cricket pitch bordered by elegant terraces. In the 8C it was common grazing land, as its former name, The Commons, implies, and it was used for horse racing, bull-baiting and cock-fighting until these gambling activities were stopped by Archbishop Robinson in 1773 and the land converted to public walks.

At the north end stands the Classical-style **Courthouse**, designed in 1809 by Francis Johnston.

The remaining stone was used to build the **Sovereign's House**; the office of Sovereign was equivalent to that of Mayor but the title ceased to be used in 1850. It now houses the **Royal Irish Fusiliers Museum★**, with a splendid array of flags and standards, uniforms, medals, weapons, silver, portraits and paintings evoking the story of this unit, originally raised in 1793 to fight the French. *Open Easter-Aug, Mon-Sat and Bank Hols, 10am-12.30pm and 1.30-4pm; Sep-Easter, Mon-Fri. £1.50. Guided tour (30min).* ☎ *028 3752 2911; www.armagh.gov.uk*

Continue along the east side.

Beresford Row was designed by John Quinn between 1810 and 1827 and named after Lord John Beresford; the houses have elegant iron balconies.

Charlemont Place, one of the finest Georgian terraces, was designed by Francis Johnston in 1827.

Set back from the street behind a lawn, stands a building with a handsome Ionic portico, designed by Francis Johnston as a school. It houses the rich and varied collections on local history of the **Armagh County Museum★**. ♿ *Open Mon-Fri, 10am-5pm, Sat, 10am-1pm and 2-5pm. Closed 12-13 Jul, 25-26 Dec.* ☎ *028 3752 3070; Fax 028 3752 2631; acm.um@nics.gov.uk; www.magni.org.uk*

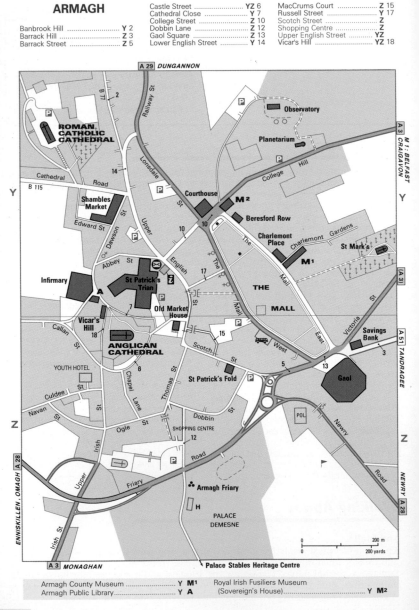

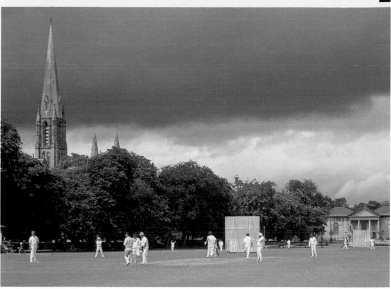

Cricket in the Mall

A long tree-lined drive leads up to **St Mark's Church**, also designed by Francis Johnston in 1811.

His nephew, William Murray, designed the small **Savings Bank** building with an unpedimented portico in 1838.

The south end is closed by the old **Gaol**, erected in 1780 on the site of the barracks. *Walk along Barrack Street and at the roundabout bear right into Scotch Street.*

St Patrick's Fold

The house, which is thought to stand on the site of St Patrick's first church in Armagh, was designed in 1812 for Leonard Dobbin, MP for Armagh from 1833 to 1838, by Francis Johnston to whom the houses (1811) in nearby Dobbin Street are also attributed.

Old Market House

A technical school now occupies the Market House, which was commissioned in 1815 by Archbishop Stuart from Francis Johnston, and originally consisted of only two storeys. *Walk up the hill to St Patrick's Cathedral (Anglican).*

St Patrick's Cathedral★

  Open daily, 9.30am-5pm (4pm Sun and winter). Guided tour (20min) available (charge). Leaflet (3 languages). Pilgrimage to Hill of Patrick: 17 Mar (St Patrick's Day). Parking. ☎ 028 3752 3142; Fax 028 3752 4177

The core of the **Anglican cathedral** on its hilltop site is medieval, but the building was very thoroughly restored by Archbishop Robinson in 1765, and again by Archbishop Beresford between 1834 and 1837, when it was faced with a cladding of sandstone and the steeple demolished. It is now a plain structure in the Perpendicular Gothic style with a squat crenellated central tower.

The **exterior** is decorated with a series of grotesque medieval stone heads and a sundial which dates from 1706. When King Brian Ború and his son, Murchard, were killed at the Battle of Clontarf (1014), on the north side of Dublin Bay, they were buried according to the king's wishes at Armagh *(plaque on W wall of N transept)*.

The **interior** contains an outstanding collection of 18C monuments by masters of this particular art, among them Roubiliac, Rysbrack, Nollekens and Chantrey. There are also fragments of an 11C market cross.

Vicar's Row

The terrace of small houses on the west side of the cathedral close was begun in about 1720 as accommodation for female clergy dependants.

Armagh (Robinson) Public Library

Open Mon-Fri, 10am-1pm and 2-4pm. Closed Bank Hols. Guided tour (charge). Parking. ☎ 028 3752 4177; armroblib@aol.com; www.armaghrobinsonlibrary.org

The library, which was founded by Archbishop Robinson in 1771, is housed in a building designed by Thomas Cooley; the Greek inscription on the façade means "the healing of the mind". The library contains a copy of *Gulliver's Travels* annotated by Swift and many other ancient books and manuscripts; it also contains the Rokeby Collection of 18C engravings as well as maps of historical interest, including a complete set of the 1838 edition of the Ordnance Survey Maps of the 32 counties of Ireland.

Infirmary

The infirmary, another of Archbishop Robinson's foundations, was designed by George Ensor *(see below)* and completed in 1774; it is still in use.

Turn right into Abbey Street to visit St Patrick's Trian (see Worth a Visit).

Shambles

As is written over the entrance, the building was erected in 1827 by Archbishop Beresford; it was designed by Francis Johnston and is still used as a meat market.

From Dawson Street turn left into Cathedral Road and cross over to St Patrick's Cathedral (Roman Catholic).

St Patrick's Cathedral★

Closed for repair work until Easter 2003. Open (previously) daily, 10.30am-5pm. Services: Sun, 9am, 10.30am, noon. Guided tour by appointment with the Sacristan. Parking. ☎ 028 3752 2638

The twin-spired 19C **Roman Catholic cathedral** stands on a hill approached by a monumental flight of 44 steps, flanked at the top by statues of Archbishop Crolly and Archbishop McGettigan, under whom it was built. It is a striking Gothic Revival structure, occupying the most prominent position available, an expression of growing Catholic confidence as well as faith, built with the proceeds of countless collections and raffles as well as with contributions from royalty and the Pope himself.

Construction began in 1840 in the Perpendicular style of Thomas J Duff but the Great Famine brought work to a halt until 1854; the cathedral was completed in 1873 in the Decorated style favoured by JJ McCarthy. The statues in the niches on the west front represent the Apostles.

The **interior** is lavishly and colourfully decorated with a painted vaulted roof, stained-glass windows and mosaics on the walls; the spandrels frame the heads of Irish saints. The sanctuary was renovated in 1981-82 under the architect Liam McCormick.

St Patrick's Roman Catholic Cathedral

Worth a Visit

Palace Demesne

Friary Road – S of the city centre. ⓖ *Open Jul-Aug, Mon-Sat, 10am-5.30pm, Sun, 1-6pm; Sep-Jun, daily, 10am (2pm Sun) to 5pm. Closed at Christmas. Guided tour (90min). £3.50. Sensory gardens. Adventure playground. Parking. Licensed restaurant.* ☎ *028 3752 9629; Fax 028 3752 9630; stables@armagh.gov.uk; www.armagh.gov.uk*

From the 17C to the 20C the estate was the residence of the Anglican Archbishop of Armagh.

The buildings surrounding the stable yard now house the **Palace Stables Heritage Centre**. The display presents a typical day in the life of the palace, in fact 23 July 1776 when Arthur Young, the famous agricultural improver, and other guests were entertained by Archbishop Richard Robinson. Costumed interpreters ensure that visitors enjoy a lively experience.

The **Primate's Chapel**, a superb example of Georgian neo-Classical architecture, was commissioned by Richard Robinson, begun in 1770 by Thomas Cooley and completed in 1786 by Francis Johnston. It contains some very fine carved oak panelling and an ornamental plaster ceiling .

Nearby are the conservatory, an ice house and a tunnel providing access to the house for the servants. There is an eco-trail through the park, while close to the entrance are the ruins of the 13C **Armagh Friary**, a Franciscan establishment distinguished by its extremely long and narrow nave.

St Patrick's Trian

Abbey Street. Open daily 10am (2pm Sun) to 5pm. Closed 25-26 Dec. £3.75. Genealogy service. ☎ 028 3752 1801; Fax 028 3751 0180; info@saintpatrickstrian.com; www.armagh-visit.com

As well as housing the Tourist Information Centre, this modern visitor centre has a series of fascinating displays, dealing first with the religious and architectural history of the city, then, in the *Land of Lilliput*, with the adventures of the hero of Jonathan Swift's *Gulliver's Travels*. Children are intrigued by the giant figure of Gulliver bound to the ground by the pigmy Lilliputians. Swift was a frequent visitor to Co Armagh, where he had several friends.

Armagh Planetarium

College Hill – NE of the city centre. ♿ Open daily, 10am (1.15pm Sat-Sun) to 4.45pm. Closed Good Fri, 12 Jul, 24-27 Dec. Show (45min) at 2pm, 3pm, 4pm. £3.75; exhibition only £1. Astropark (20min walk). ☎ 028 3752 3689; Fax 028 3752 6187; www.armagh-planetarium.co.uk

Observatory: not open to the public; www.star.arm.ac.uk

The planetarium is housed under a dome (50ft/15m in diameter) which serves as a hemispherical screen for the projection of films of the sky at night. The Hall of Astronomy contains 12 computer stations presenting information on planets, constellations and space flight. The Planetarium was set up in 1968 by Dr Lindsay, Director of the Observatory (1937-74), who invited Patrick Moore to be its first director.

In the grounds stands the **Observatory**, founded and endowed in 1789 by Archbishop Robinson; it is one of the oldest meteorological stations in the British Isles.

Road Bowls

The ancient Irish sport of road bowling is still played on Sundays in Co Armagh and Co Cork. A heavy iron ball (28oz/794g; 7in/18cm) is hurled along a stretch of quiet winding country road in as few throws as possible; the ball may hurtle through the air at shoulder height. Betting is heavy.

Excursions

Navan Fort*

2mi/3.2km W of Armagh by A 28. ♿ Site: Open daily. Visitor Centre: Open daily, 10am (11am Sat, noon Sun) to 5pm; last tour 1hr 30min before closing. Closed at Christmas. £3.95. Guided tour of site (30min) by appointment. Parking. Restaurant. ☎ 028 3752 5550; Fax 028 3752 2323; navan@enterprise.net; www.armagh-visit.com

The fort is an impressive earthwork, surrounded by sacred places and settlement sites; in the late Bronze Age it was the most important place in Ulster, thought to be synonymous with Emain Macha, the capital of legendary Ulster, mentioned in the *Ulster Cycle* *(see MYTHS AND FAIRIES)*.

Navan Fort Excavations

Excavations carried out between 1961 and 1971 showed traces of human activity as early as 2000 BC; in c 400 BC a round wooden house and yard was built, which was replaced many times during the next 300 years. In c 100 BC a huge wooden structure (125ft/40m in diameter) was erected consisting of an outer timber wall and five concentric inner rings of large posts; the remains of a very large central post made it possible to date the structure, which was probably roofed. Soon after it was built it was filled with limestone boulders and set on fire and the remains covered with earth to form a mound, probably as part of a religious ritual. Navan Fort seems to have been part of a religious complex. The four Iron Age bronze trumpets (one is now in the National Museum in Dublin), which were found in the 18C in the water at the edge of Lough na Shade *(NW of the Fort beyond the quarries)*, may have been deposited in the lake as an offering to the gods. Excavations carried out in 1975 show that the King's Stables *(NW of the Fort)* was an artificial pool used for ritual deposits in the Late Bronze Age.

The multi-media displays in the sensitively designed **Visitor Centre** evoke the world of the Celts and pre-Christian Ireland, bring to life the heroes and events of the legends, and trace the archaeological study of the fort and its associated sites and shows how they were used by their Neolithic builders.

Navan Centre

The fort itself *(5min on foot from the Visitor Centre or by road; car park)* consists of a massive bank and inner ditch enclosing a circular area. Within is a high mound on the highest point of the hill, flanked by a low circular mound surrounded by an infilled ditch.

The Argory★

10mi/16km N of Armagh by A 29 and a minor road right. (NT) (♿)
Grounds: Open daily, 10am-8pm (4pm Oct-Apr). House: Guided tour (1hr) Jun-Aug, daily, noon (1pm Mon-Fri in Jun) to 6pm; mid-Mar to May, Sat-Sun and Bank Hol Mon, noon-6pm; Sep, Sat-Sun, noon-6pm. House and parking £4; parking only £2. Tearoom; picnic area. Wheelchair available; wheelchair access to ground floor, walks, tearoom. ☎ 028 8778 4753; Fax 028 8778 9598; uagest@smtp.nrust.org.uk

This handsome country house built around 1824 in neo-Classical style beside the River Blackwater remained for many years in the ownership of the McGeough-Bonds. The family decorated their home with loving care, filling it with fine furniture and much bric-a-brac and paying unusual attention to matters of heating and lighting, with an acetylene gas plant installed in the yard. Little has changed here since the early years of the 20C, and a tour of the house is a fascinating evocation of the comfortable life lived at the time. The most extraordinary single object is the cabinet **barrel organ** of 1820, still in full working order.

The **Gardens**, which extend to the Blackwater River, comprise old roses set in box-lined beds, a sundial dated 1820, yew tree arbours, Pleasure Grounds, a Garden House, a Pump House and a lime tree walk.

Ardress House

7mi/11km NE of Armagh by B 77. (NT) (♿) House: Open Jun-Aug, Wed-Mon, Bank Hol; mid-Mar to May and Sep, Sat-Sun, 2-6pm. Farmyard: Open as above. House £2.70; farmyard £2.40. Guided tour (30min). Parking. Picnic area. Wheelchair access to ground floor and picnic area. ☎/Fax 028 3885 1236; vagest@smtp.ntrust.org.uk

Ardress is a simple 17C manor house, of five bays, enlarged and embellished in the 18C. It was inherited by the architect, George Ensor, on his marriage in 1760.

The house displays glass from Dublin, Cork and Belfast, and some fine furniture, including Irish Chippendale chairs. The symmetry and proportions of the elegant **drawing room** are enhanced by the delightful stuccowork by Michael Stapleton on the walls and ceiling.

The cobbled **farmyard** with its central pump is surrounded by farm buildings – a milking shed, a dairy with pottery and wooden skimming dishes, churns and measures, a forge, a threshing barn and a display of old farm implements including baskets and bee skeps.

Orange Order Museum

6mi/10km NE of Armagh by A 29 and B 77 to Loughgall; halfway up the west side of the main street; caretaker's house on the right of the museum. Open by appointment Mon-Sat. ☎ 028 9070 1122

On 21 September 1795, following the affray later called the "Battle of the Diamond" at a nearby crossroads *(3mi/5km NE)*, the victorious Protestant Peep O'Day Boys retired to celebrate their triumph at Jim Sloane's pub. It was here that the Orange order was instituted, dedicated to sustaining the "glorious and immortal memory of King William III". The pub's long and narrow room is overflowing with mementoes of the Order: sashes, caps, waistcoats, banners, the table on which the first warrants were signed, guns and pikes used in 1795.

Tayto Potato Crisp Factory

11mi/18km E of Armagh by A 51; factory entrance next to the police station on entering Tandragee. Guided tour by appointment (1hr 30min; max 45 people) Mon-Thu, at 10.30am, 1.30pm, Fri, at 10.30am. Closed Easter, 12-13 July, and Christmas week. Brochure (3 languages). Parking. ☎ 028 3884 0249, ext 256/248; Fax 028 3884 0085

The factory is housed in Tandragee Castle, which dominates the town; it was built in 1837 by the 6th Duke of Manchester.

The tour *(1hr)* starts in the warehouse in which great cliffs of potatoes are stored; it then passes the washing, peeling and slicing machines to where the raw white wafers enter a tunnel of hot sunflower oil and emerge as wavy golden crisps. At the next stage the crisps acquire a flavour and are packed by ingenious machines, one of which swathes stacks of cardboard boxes in polythene film like mummies.

Gosford Forest Park

7mi/11km SE of Armagh by A 28 to Markethill; two car parks: one near the entrance and the other between the Castle and the Walled Garden. ⚬ *Open daily, 10am-dusk. £1.50; £3 (car). Guided tour (2hr) by appointment. Pony trekking. Parking. Café, barbecue area.* ☎ *028 3755 2169 (Forest Ranger), 028 3755 1277 (office).*

The Forest Park was formerly the demesne of the Acheson family, the Earls of Gosford. Contemporary with the building of the present castle, a huge pseudo-Norman pile designed by Thomas Hopper in 1819, are the **arboretum**, which contains many magnificent mature trees from all over the world, and the **walled gardens**, which are beautifully laid out with flowers and shrubs, and contain a brick **bee house** with niches to protect the straw skeps from the damp.

Jonathan Swift was a privileged but frequently irritating guest here, altering the gardens without his hosts' permission and forcing Lady Acheson into long and exhausting country walks. There is a waterfall called Swift's Well, while the **Dean's Chair** is an artificial sun trap created by making a semicircular hollow protected by a yew hedge in a south-facing bank.

The **Gosford Heritage Poultry Collection** aims to conserve in their natural surroundings the native poultry breeds that would have been found in the 18C poultry yard of a large estate.

Bangor

Looking out over Belfast Lough at the northern end of the Ards Peninsula, Bangor is Northern Ireland's foremost seaside resort, with all the usual seaside amenities and an array of Victorian hotels and guesthouses. The town has a long history, firstly as one of Ireland's most important monastic settlements and then as a 17C Plantation town; today it serves as a dormitory for Belfast commuters.

Location

Population 52 437 - Michelin Atlas p 99 and Map 712 – O, P 4 – Co Down.
Bangor *(Beannchar)* is situated 15mi/24km E of Belfast by A 2 - Local map see p 465
🚩 *34 Quay Street, Bangor BT20 5ED. Open Jun-Sep, daily; Oct-Mar, Mon-Sat.*
☎ *028 9127 0069; Fax 028 9127 4466, bangor@nitic.net; www.northdown.co.uk*
Adjacent Sights: See BELFAST, MOUNT STEWART, STRANGFORD LOUGH.

Background

Bangor Abbey, founded by St Comgall in 558, became one of the most famous abbeys in western Christendom, sending its missionary monks to found other monasteries in Ireland and abroad. In the 9C Comgall's tomb was desecrated in Viking raids; Malachy, appointed abbot in 1124, built a stone church and introduced the Augustinian Order; in 1542 the abbey was dissolved.

On the accession of James I in 1603, Bangor was granted to Sir James Hamilton, later Viscount Clandeboye, who created a town with settlers from his native Ayrshire. In 1620 he was granted a warrant to establish a maritime port including the nearby creeks.

In 1689 the Duke of Schomberg landed at Groomsport; his army of 10 000 men probably came ashore at Bangor or Ballyholme; the Duke spent the first night as a guest of the Hamiltons, before proceeding south to the Battle of the Boyne, where he was killed.

In 1710 Sir James' estates passed by marriage to the Ward family of Castle Ward on the south shore of Strangford Lough. Two generations later Col Robert Ward improved the harbour, promoted the textile industry and founded a boys' school. Bangor's role as a seaside resort, complete with pier, really started with the arrival of the railway in 1865; the pier was demolished in 1981 but the railway still brings day trippers as well as daily carrying thousands to their places of work in Belfast.

Directory

SIGHTSEEING

There are **boat trips** in Bangor Bay, cruises to the Copeland Islands in the afternoon and deep-sea fishing trips from Donaghadee *(see below)* in the morning or evening.

Bangor Bay Cruise – *Operates from Bangor seafront (20-30min) Jul-Aug, daily, 2pm; May-Jun and Sep-Oct, Sat-Sun, 2pm. Also birdwatching, angling and longer pleasure cruises. £2.50.* ☎ *028 9145 5321 (Bangor Harbour Boats)*

Belfast Lough Cruise – *Operate from Donaghadee (2–3hr) (weather permitting) Jun-Sep, daily; May and Sep, Sat-Sun. Fishing tackle provided. Licensed.* ☎ *028 9188 3403 (Nelson's Boats), 07811 230 215 (boat); quintonnelson@btconnect.com; www.nelsonsboats/co.uk*

Copeland Islands Ferry – *Operates Jul-Aug, daily; May-Jun and Sep-Oct, by appointment from Groomsport or Donaghadee.* ☎ *028 9188 3403 (Nelson's Boats); 07811 230 215 (boat); quintonnelson@btconnect.com, www.nelsonsboats.co.uk*

WHERE TO STAY
• *Budget*

Shelleven House – *59-61 Princetown Rd, BT56 8BN -* ☎ *028 9127 1777 - Fax 028 9127 1777 - shellevenhouse@aol.com -* 🅿 ✕ *- 11 rm £33/54* ☞ *- Meals £25.*
A large Victorian terraced house with the bedrooms at the top of the house enjoying views over the town. Clean, tidy and traditionally decorated bedrooms, with home-cooked meals available if booked in advance.

Cairn Bay Lodge – *278 Seacliffe Rd, BT56 8BN – 1.25mi/2km E by Quay St -* ☎ *028 9146 7636 - Fax 028 9145 7728 - info@cairnbaylodge.com - Closed Sun dinner -* 🅿 ✕ *- 5 rm £35/60* ☞ *- Meals £18.* A detached Edwardian house, sympathetically decorated with plenty of wood panelling. The sitting room is particularly attractive while the dining room overlooks the garden. Listless guests can take advantage of the owners' beauty therapy business.

WHERE TO EAT
• *Moderate*

Shanks – *150 The Blackwood, Crawfordsburn Rd, Clandeboye, BT56 8BN – 3.25mi/5.2km SW by A 2 and Dundonald Rd following signs for Blackwood Golf Centre -* ☎ *028 9185 3313 - www.shanksrestaurant.com - Closed 2 weeks Jul, 25-26 Dec, 1 Jan, Sat lunch, Sun, Mon and Easter Tue -* 🅿 *- £21/57.* Part of a modern golfing complex, this effortlessly well-run restaurant attracts diners from miles around. Stylish interior with the restaurant spread over two floors. The modern menu changes with the seasons and lunch represents particularly good value.

SPORTS AND LEISURE

Safe sandy beaches, sea-water swimming pool, marina (560 berths), waterfront fun park, golf course.

Walking About

Old Custom House and Tower

On the seafront stands the Custom House (now the Tourist Information Centre) built by Sir James Hamilton in 1637 with financial assistance from the Crown, in the Scottish Baronial style with flanking watchtowers, a crow-stepped gable and a quarter-round corbelled turret.

Walk up Main Street.

Bangor Abbey Church

Abbey Street. Open Mon, Wed, Fri, 10am-noon; apply to the Parish office beside church; otherwise by appointment. ☎ *028 9145 1087*

The 14C tower is the only structure to survive the Dissolution of Bangor Abbey in 1542.

North Down Heritage Centre★

Castle Park. ♿ *Open Tue-Sun and Bank Hol Mon, 10.30am (2pm Sun) to 5.30pm (4.30pm Sep-Jun). Guided tour (45min) by appointment. Leaflet (4 languages). Parking. Refreshments.* ☎ *028 9127 1200; Fax 028 9127 1370; bangor_heritage_centre@yahoo.com; www.northdown.gov.uk/heritage*

The Centre is housed in part of Bangor Castle, a fanciful mid-19C exercise in Elizabethan-Jacobean revival style, which is now the Town Hall. It does justice to the town as a resort, with displays evoking the cheerful heyday of seaside holidays, and brings home Bangor's surprisingly long and eventful past, with absorbing displays on the prehistoric era (local finds), the early Christian heritage (superb model of the abbey, rare 9C bronze handbell), Viking attacks and the Plantation, with special emphasis on the local landed family, the Wards. There is also an informative display on the attractions of the 15mi/26km coastal walk.

Excursions

Crawfordsburn Country Park

7mi/11km W of Bangor by B 20. & Open daily, 9am-8pm (4.45pm Oct-Easter). Visitor Centre: Open Mon-Fri, 10am-5pm; Sat-Sun, 10am-6pm (5pm Oct-Easter). Closed one week at Christmas. Grey Point Fort: Open Easter-Oct, Wed-Mon, 2-5pm; Oct-Easter, Sun, 2-5pm. Parking. Restaurant. Braille leaflet and audioguide. ☎ *028 9185 3621; Fax 028 9185 2580*

This coastal country park, like the picturesque village, takes its name from the Crawford family from Scotland who bought the estate in 1674 and landscaped and planted it with rare species.

The history of the estate and its flora and fauna are comprehensively illustrated in the **Park Centre**, which also has a 3-D show on bees and wasps, a colony of leaf-cutter ants, and an array of brightly coloured interactive exhibits.

The **glen walk** *(30min there and back on foot)* passes the old salmon pool and then goes under the handsome viaduct of 1865 which carries the railway across the glen on five arches. Upstream is the waterfall, a rushing torrent after heavy rain, which formerly drove corn, flax and saw mills and as early as 1850 generated electricity to light the glen.

Grey Point Fort *(accessible by footpath – 1hr there and back – within the Country Park or by residential roads (Coastguard Avenue)* commands the sea approaches to Belfast and was manned during both World Wars by the Royal Artillery. Panels outline its history (1907-63) and a solitary six-inch gun, a gift from the Government of the Republic of Ireland, is mounted in one of the massive reinforced concrete gun emplacements.

Ulster Folk and Transport Museum★★

8mi/13km W of Bangor by A 2. & Open daily, 10am (11am Sun) to 6pm (5pm Mon-Fri Mar-Jun; 5pm Sat-Sun Oct-Feb; 4pm Mon-Fri Oct-Feb). Closed at Christmas. Combined ticket £5. Brochure (5 languages). Parking. Refreshments. ☎ *028 9042 8428; Fax 028 9042 8728; www.nidex.com*

Set in the grounds of Cultra Manor, this is one of the most extensive and interesting museums in the whole of Ireland. The grounds are bisected by the busy coast road (A 2), with the folk section on the south side, while on the north the transport section extends as far as the seashore.

Folk Museum – This is an excellent example of a skansen, a vast open-air array of buildings brought here from the Irish countryside and re-erected to form a museum of traditional life. Convincingly attired occupants tell the story of each structure or give fascinating demonstrations of the activities that went on in or around them (weaving, spinning, agricultural work, cooking).

The dwellings, which are furnished as they would have been at the end of the 19C, range from a one-room farmhouse, shared by the family with the cattle, to a substantial 17C farmhouse with panelled walls. Working premises include a flax-scutching mill and a spade mill, a weaver's house and a bleach green watchman's hut; the duty of this person was to guard the webs of linen spread out on the grass from theft or damage by animals. The **village** is composed of a school, a market-cum-courthouse, a church and a rectory, together with two terraces of urban cottages including a shoemaker's workshop and a bicycle repair shop.

In the **Gallery** *(three floors)* the traditional Ulster way of life is illustrated with original domestic, industrial and agricultural implements.

Transport Museum – With examples of virtually every kind of wheeled vehicle used in Ireland over the last 200 years, the museum has made great efforts to put them in their social context, and this is far from being a sterile collection of hardware of interest only to enthusiasts.

Rectory and Church, Ulster Folk Museum

NITB, Belfast

In the **Irish Railway collection**, fascinating wall panels evoke the sometimes idiosyncratic history of the island's railways, but it has to be admitted that here at least it is the beautifully restored hardware which compels most attention; the undoubted star is *Maeve (Maebh)*, named after an ancient Celtic deity, one of the 4-6-0 800 Class locomotives built in 1939 and the most powerful ever to run on Irish rails.

The **Road Transport Galleries**, richly furnished with all types of transport memorabilia, display two-wheelers of all kinds, from the draisiennes and velocipedes of early days to the stylish scooters of the 1960s or the massive mounts of tattooed ton-up bikers. Buses include a 1973 Daimler Fleetline, burnt out but lovingly rebuilt, while the most extraordinary vehicle is perhaps No 2 of the Bessbrook and Newry Tramway Co, built in 1885 and still carrying passengers in the 1940s.

In the final gallery, devoted to *The Car in Society* – from the 1898 Benz Velo Confortable, the oldest petrol vehicle in Ireland, to one of the glamorous cars produced in 1981 by the short-lived De Lorean company – the emphasis is as much on car culture as on the vehicles themselves; many tentative answers are provided as to why a nominally functional object should play such a dominant part in people's lives.

The **Dalchoolin Transport Galleries** present a miscellany of exhibits – shoulder creels and wooden sledges, carts and jaunting cars; horse-drawn vehicles from a dogcart to a dress chariot; and ships. The **Flight Experience** is a hands-on exhibition on flight and the aerospace industry giving fascinating facts about flight through archive film footage, CDRom, aircraft models, engineering interactive displays, and the Short SC1, a pioneering VTOL (Vertical Take-off and Landing).

The **Titanic Gallery** describes how the great liner, built at the famous Harland and Wolff shipyard in Belfast, sank on her maiden voyage after being holed by an iceberg, and shows pictures of the wreck obtained by divers in 1985.

Somme Heritage Centre

3mi/5km S of Bangor by A 21. Open Apr-Sep, Mon-Thu, 10am-4pm, Sat, noon-4pm. £3.75. Parking. ☎ *028 9182 3202; sommeassociation@dnet.co.uk; www.irishsoldier.org*
With the outbreak of the First World War in 1914, many Irishmen put aside the differences which seemed to be leading inevitably to civil war and volunteered for service in the British army. Irish units suffered terribly in the Somme offensive of 1916, the Ulster Division losing 5 000 men in the first two days alone. The Centre commemorates the sacrifices made in battle, with a "time tunnel" and uncannily realistic reconstructions of the trenches and their terrible sights and sounds.

Groomsport

1.5mi/2.5km E by coast road. Groomsport is an attractive little seaside resort, flanked by sandy beaches and modern bungalows and caravan parks. In the harbour, yachts ride the water beside the fishing boats. Fishing is still an important activity but only two fishermen's cottages, one thatched, still stand beside the harbour; they now house an **art gallery**.

Donaghadee

7mi/11km E of Bangor by B 21. The picturesque, winding streets lead to the **parish church** which dates from 1641. The huge harbour, now full of pleasure boats, was built in 1820 to accommodate the mail ships, which were transferred to Larne in 1849. From the 16C to 19C Donaghadee–Portpatrick was the most popular route between Ireland and Scotland as it is the shortest crossing (21mi/34km). The Norman **motte** near the shore was probably raised by William Copeland, a retainer of John de Courcy; it is crowned by a stone building (1818) providing a fine **view** of the Copeland Islands and the coast of Galloway across the North Channel.

Copeland Islands

Accessible by boat from Groomsport or Donaghadee (see Directory). The nearest and largest island was inhabited until the 1940s, when the last residents moved to the mainland and the island was left to the sheep and weekend cottages. A modern lighthouse was built on Mew Island in 1884. Lighthouse Island is now a wildlife sanctuary in the care of the National Trust – buzzards, golden eagles, resident seals, dolphins, porpoises, basking sharks, minke whales, killer whales.

Ballycopeland Windmill

Ballycopeland Windmill★

10mi/16km SE of Bangor by B 21 and A 2; in Millisle turn right. Car park. The mill is not open to the public when the machinery is working owing to the risk of accident. (HM) Open Apr-Sep, Tue-Sun and Bank Hol Mon, 10am (2pm Sun) to 6pm. £1. ☎ *028 9186 1413 (windmill); Scrabocp@doeni.gov.uk; www.ehsni.gov.uk*

Syndication International

In the late 18C, when grain was grown extensively in the Ards Peninsula, the landscape was thickly dotted with windmills. The rare survivor at Ballycopeland was probably built in 1780 or 1790 and worked until 1915. It is again in working order; the neighbouring miller's house provides an explanatory display. Beside the mill is a dust-house and the kiln where the grain was dried before being milled.

Ards Peninsula

The peninsula is a long narrow tongue of land *(23 x 3-5mi/37 x 5-8km)* enclosing the broad waters of Strangford Lough *(see p 464)* and extending south from Bangor to Ballyquintin Point. Favourable soils and a relatively dry and warm climate make this low-lying land one of the best grain-producing regions of Ireland.

The east coast is swept by bracing sea breezes; the **coast road**, which follows the bare shoreline, skirting frequent sandy beaches and occasional rocky outcrops, is almost constantly in sight and sound of the sea. **Portavogie** is the home base for one of Northern Ireland's three fishing fleets, where fish is sold on the quayside when the fleet is in port. The southern end of the peninsula presents an austere landscape of marsh and heath.

Belfast★

One of the great industrial and commercial cities of the Victorian era, the capital of Northern Ireland has survived 30 years of Troubles to flourish again, with a wave of new building and a vibrant cultural life without equal in the rest of the province. Half a million people live within a few miles of the city centre, a third of Northern Ireland's population. Few cities have such a splendid natural setting; Belfast stands at the mouth of the River Lagan at the point where it discharges into the great sea inlet of Belfast Lough which is sheltered on both sides by hills; to the west rises the formidable basalt escarpment of Cave Hill and Black Mountain.

Location

Population 279 237 - Michelin Atlas p 99 and Map 712 O 1 Co Antrim.

Belfast *(Béal Feirste)* is set on the shores of Belfast Lough which opens into the North Channel a narrow strait between Ireland and Scotland. It is served by 2 motorways – M 1, running W via Craigavon and Dungannon to Enniskillen, and M 2, running NW via Antrim and Dungiven to Londonderry.

🛈 *47 Donegall Place, Belfast BT1 5AD. Open Jun-Sep, daily; Oct-May, Mon-Sat. ☎ 028 9024 6609; Minicom 028 9024 6407; Fax 028 9031 2424; belfastwelcomecentre@nitic.net; www.gotobelfast.com*

🛈 *Belfast City Airport TIC, Sydenham Bypass, Belfast BT3 9JH. ☎ 028 9045 7745; Fax 028 9045 9198*

🛈 *Belfast International Airport TIC, Belfast BT29 4AB. ☎ 028 9442 2888; Fax 028 9445 2084*

Adjacent Sights: See ANTRIM, BANGOR, CARRICKFERGUS, LISBURN.

Background

Norman Castle to Industrial City – Belfast takes its name from a ford by a sandbank *(bealfeirste* in Irish) where the Anglo-Norman John de Courcy built a castle during his invasion of Ulster in 1177. The development of the town really began only in the early 17C when a quay was built and trade diverted from Carrickfergus further down the lough. The city was settled by Scottish Presbyterians, whose industrious attitudes to work were reinforced by the Huguenot refugees who came later in the century and brought new techniques to the burgeoning linen industry. Cotton spinning was introduced in 1777, shipbuilding in 1791. By the early 19C, these activities had created the conditions for industrial lift-off, and in the course of the century the population multiplied 15-fold, from under 25 000 to 350 000. General engineering flourished, as did distilling, rope-making and tobacco products, but it was the great shipyards that gave the city its distinctive industrial character, with Harland and Wolff – builders of the *Titanic* - becoming the United Kingdom's largest construction and repair yard. In the 20C, Short Brothers produced the Sunderland flying boat and the first VTOL jet; their airstrip in the docks now doubles as Belfast City Airport.

Dissent and Division – Owing to the predominance of the Presbyterian Church, its cultural links with Scotland and its commercial wealth, Belfast early became a centre for intellectual activity and sometimes dissent. Belfast had the first printing press in Ireland (c 1690) and published the first Irish newspaper, the *Belfast News Letter*, in 1737; it is the oldest morning paper in the British Isles.

Directory

GETTING ABOUT

Citybus – For travel within the city of Belfast – *Citybus kiosk, Donegall Square West: Open Mon-Sat, 8am-6pm.*
☏ *028 9024 6485 (24hr information),*
☏ *028 9033 3000; www.translink.co.uk*

Ulsterbus – For travel outside Belfast – *Ulsterbus, Europa Bus Centre, Glengall Street, Belfast BT12 5AH.* ☏ *028 9066 6630 (enquiries),* ☏ *028 9033 7003 (bus station),* ☏ *028 9033 7004; Fax 028 9024 6926; information.ulsterbus@translink.co.uk; www.translink.co.u*
Bus service between the Europa Bus Centre and Belfast International Airport.

SIGHTSEEING

Citybus Tours – *Operate (subject to demand) from Castle Place, late-May to early-Sep. Belfast City Tour (3hr; £9) Mon-Sat at 1.30pm; Belfast Living History tour (2hr 30min; £9) Tue, Thu and Sun at 1pm; Lagan Experience (2hr 30min; £10) Wed, 1pm; City Hopper tour (55min; £5) Tue-Sat, 10am-4pm, hourly. Commentary. Refreshments.*
☏ *028 9045 8484 (tours), 9024 6485 (gen enquiries); Fax 028 9064 1629; feedback@translink.co.uk; www.translink.co.uk*

Black Taxi Service – Guided tours with commentary – *Operate daily. £25 per hr or £8 per person (minimum 3). Tours of central Belfast including the murals in the Shankhill Road and the Falls Road; the Giant's Causeway; Londonderry; Northern Ireland.*
☏ *028 9064 2264; freephone 0800 052 3914; Mobile 07860 127 207; Fax 028 9064 7700; michael@belfasttours.com; www.belfasttours.com*

There are various **themed walking tours** of the city, including:

Belfast – The Old Town of 1660-1685 – *Easter-Oct, Sat at 2pm from the Tourist Information Centre, NITB, 59 North Street*
☏ *028 9024 6609.*

Bailey's Historical Pub Tour of Belfast – *Sat at 4pm and Tue at 7pm from Flannigan's (upstairs in the Crown Bar), Great Victoria Street* ☏ *028 9268 3665 (Judy Crawford)* or ☏ *028 9088 2596.*

Belfast Town and Gown Tour – *Jun-Sep, Sat at 10.30am from the Wellington Park Hotel* ☏ *028 9049 1469 (Kathleen Chandler) for group bookings.*

Belfast City Centre and Laganside Walk – *Jun-Sep, Fri at 2pm from the front gates of City Hall* ☏ *028 9049 1469 (Kathleen Chandler) for group bookings.*

Laganside Walk – Towpath walk beside the River Lagan from the **Lagan Lookout** (see below) upstream to Lisburn (7mi/12km).

WHERE TO STAY

• *Budget*

Roseleigh House – *19 Rosetta Park – 1.5mi/2.4km S of Belfast by A 24 Ormeau Rd -* ☏ *028 9064 4414 - Fax 028 9064 2983 - roseleighhouse@ukonline.co.uk - Closed 25 Dec -* ⊠ ✝= *- 9 rm £35/50* ⌁ *- Meals £17.50.* A guesthouse that enjoys a very good

location; it is in a fairly quiet residential area close to Belvoir Park, provides easy access to the city centre and also has its own off-street parking. Bedrooms are well equipped and the welcome is always warm.

The Old Rectory – *148 Malone Rd -* ☏ *028 9066 7882 - Fax 028 9068 3759 - info@anoldrectory.co.uk - Closed 24 Dec to 1 Jan and Easter -* ⊠ ☐ ✝= *- 5 rm £36/60* ⌁ *- Rest £20.* A very nice little place in the middle of nowhere. Nice garden.

Greenwood Guest House – *25 Park Rd -* ☏ *028 9020 2525 - Fax 028 9020 2530 - info@greenwoodguesthouse.com - Closed Christmas and New Year -* ✝= *- 7 rm £37.50/55* ⌁. A family-run Victorian house, overlooking Ormeau Park, decorated in an attractive contemporary style. A daily changing three-course dinner is offered in the wooden floored dining room at the front of the house.

• *Moderate*

Ash Rowan Town House – *12 Windsor Ave -* ☏ *028 9066 1758 - Fax 028 9066 3227 - ashrowan@hotmail.com - Closed 23 Dec to 7 Jan -* ☐ ✝= *- 5 rm £48/86* ⌁ *- Meals £20.* Bed and breakfast with the emphasis on breakfast; guests are offered a huge choice from the fried to the healthy. A Victorian house with a traditional feel and period charm. It was once home to Thomas Andrews, designer of the *Titanic*.

Madison's Hotel – *59-63 Botanic Ave -* ☏ *028 9050 9800 - Fax 028 9050 9808 - info@madisonshotel.com -* ⚒ ⚐ *- 35 rm £70/80* ⌁ *- Restaurant £13.55/22.85.* Its proximity to the university ensures a lively local atmosphere and this hotel contributes by having its own nightclub. Bedrooms are brightly coloured to help you rise the morning after and the restaurant provides a varied menu for all tastes.

The Crescent Townhouse – *13 Lower Cres -* ☏ *028 9032 3349 - Fax 028 9032 0646 - info@crescenttownhouse.com - Closed 11-12 Jul, 25-26 Dec and 1 Jan - 11 rm £80/125* ⌁ *- Restaurant £13.95/24.40.* In a vibrant area of the city, this Regency house has been converted into a stylish and comfortable hotel. The bar has a distinctive Gothic feel with oak panelling and the brasserie offers imaginative dishes in a lively atmosphere.

WHERE TO EAT

• *Budget*

The Wok – *126 Great Victoria St -* ☏ *028 9023 3828 - Closed 25-26 Dec and 1 week July - £6.50/20.60.* In the vanguard of modern Chinese restaurants; stylish and contemporary interior with efficient service. The menu combines the classics with the less commonly seen dishes, and many regions of China are represented.

Cayenne – *7 Lesley House, Shaftesbury Sq -* ☏ *028 9033 1532 - reservations@ cayenne-restaurant.com - Closed 12-13 Jul, 25-26 Dec, 1 Jan, Sun and lunch Sat - Booking essential - £13.50/26.50.* Emphatically stylish and the place to see and be seen, with some impressive pieces of modern artwork. Its lively atmosphere is complemented by the well-priced menu featuring contemporary cuisine with an Asian twist.

• Moderate

Ginger – 271 Ormeau Rd - ☏ 028 9049 3143 - Closed 2 weeks Jan, 2 weeks July, Sun and Mon - Booking essential - £18/27. This unpretentious little place, tucked away in a parade of shops, is forever busy. There's ample choice from the daily changing blackboard menu, with influences from all around the world. It's unlicensed so take your own wine.

Oxford Exchange – First floor, St George's Market, Oxford St - ☏ 028 9024 0014 - oxfordexchange@mountcharles.com - Closed 1 week Jul, 25 Dec, 1 Jan, Sun and Sat lunch - £18.50/23.50. First-floor location overlooking the recently restored St George's market. The glass roof ensures the room is bright and airy. The kitchen is open plan and the house speciality is chargrilled fish and meats.

Nick's Warehouse – 35-39 Hill Street - ☏ 028 9043 9690 - nicks@warehouse.dnet.co.uk - Closed 2 days Easter, 1 May, 12 Jul, 25-26 Dec, 1 Jan, Sat lunch, Mon dinner and Sun - £20.50/28.15. This former Bushmills warehouse on a cobbled street is one of the city's best known restaurants. Downstairs has the "buzz", upstairs is slightly more formal. The eponymous Nick oversees a busy kitchen producing carefully prepared modern cooking.

• Expensive

Restaurant Michael Deane – 36-40 Howard Street - ☏ 028 9033 1134 - michaeldeane@deanesbelfast.com - Closed Easter, 1 week July, Christmas, New Year and Sun-Tue - £38.50. The city's premier restaurant provides original and accomplished cooking, enhanced by discreet and professional service. The rich burgundy colours, leather armchairs, mirrors and candlelight all create a mood of refined tranquillity.

TAKING A BREAK

Bittle's Bar – 103 Victoria Street - ☏ 028 903 11 088 – Open daily from 11.30am. Well worth a drink here as it is something of an architectural oddity. This bar is housed in a peculiarly triangular shaped building dating back to 1861. It was originally called The Shakespeare and the Bard is celebrated in the decoration.

Kelly's Cellar – 30 Bank Street - ☏ 028 9032 4835 – Open daily from 11am. As an antidote to the homogeneous modernity of the city's development, this pub in the financial district, keeps tradition well and truly alive. It first opened its doors in 1720 and there's a palpable sense of history in its mottled decoration.

Kitchen Bar – 16-18 Victoria Street - ☏ 028 903 24 901 - Open Mon-Sat from 11.30am. Reputedly opened in 1859, this bar is most celebrated for its live traditional Irish music and for many years was associated with the neighbouring music hall, the Empire.

A comprehensive choice of beers is available.

La Bodega – 4 Calender Street - ☏ 028 902 43 177 – Open Mon-Sat, 11.30am-9pm. It's another world when you pass through the doors of this well-known pub. The current Spanish theme was adopted in the 1960s but it has been a pub for over 100 years. A great place to drop in for a beer if you're in the centre of town.

Madden's – Berry Street. - ☏ 028 9024 4114 – Open Mon-Sat, 11am-1am. Fits the bill for those looking for that authentic pub experience. Whether it's blues night or folk, there's always a spontaneity to the atmosphere and the musical roots of the pub are emphasised by the assorted instruments that adorn the walls

Pats Bar – 19-22 Princes Dock Street - ☏ 028 9074 4524 – Open Mon-Sat from 11am. Juxtaposed with the contemporary cafés, which reflect the recent developments of the docks area of the city, lies this century-old pub. Inside, it's cosy and characterful. Wednesday is traditional music night.

Robinson's – 38-40 Great Victoria Street - ☏ 028 902 47 447 – Open Mon-Fri, 11.30am, Sat, 11.30am 2am. Worth making the effort to find this Victorian pub which was rebuilt in the 1990s. Individual rooms have various themes so there is an upstairs lounge decked out like an 18C ship, a library on the ground floor, and the back bar resembles a country grocery.

Rotterdam Bar – 54 Pilot Street - ☏ 028 907 46 021 – Open daily from 11.30am. During the day it's an oasis of calm with the warm glow of the open fire. In the evening the pace is far livelier with live music ranging from blues and salsa to folk and jazz. Noted for its huge display of spirits behind the bar.

The Crown Liquor Saloon – 46 Great Victoria Street - ☏ 028 9024 9476 – Open Mon-Sat, 11.30am-1am, Sun, 12.30am-10pm. Featured in the James Mason film "Odd Man Out" and rightly celebrated for its highly ornate Victorian style with original Italian influences. Its heritage is such that it is now owned by the National Trust. Try to grab one of the panelled snugs.

The Empire – 40-42 Botanic Avenue - ☏ 028 902 49 276 – Open Mon-Fri and Sun, 11.30am-1am. Those in search of more youthful surroundings and contemporary music should head for The Empire, housed in a once derelict Presbyterian church which may explain the existence of a resident ghost. It is also home to a popular comedy club.

The Garrick – 29 Chichester Street - ☏ 028 903 33 875 – Open daily from 11.30am. Apparently named after David Garrick, the Shakespearean actor, although there is some dispute as to whether he ever visited. Now a well-kept family-owned pub, where the walls are adorned with portraits of celebrated golfers.

The John Hewitt – 51 Donegall Street - ☏ 028 902 33 768 – Open daily from 11.30am. Found in the Cathedral District, this pub has a genuine community feel. It holds exhibitions by local artists, it often features local musicians and, with its log fire and long counter, ensures that the art of conversation is alive and well.

Whites Tavern – *2-4 Winecellar Entry -* ☎ *028 9024 3080 – Open daily from 11.30am.* Lays claim to being the oldest tavern in the city and there is evidence to suggest that there has been drinking at this site for 400 years; colourful 17C life is depicted in the vivid mural. Traditional folk music and honest "pub grub" are on offer.

ENTERTAINMENT

Belfast Civic Arts Theatre – *Botanic Avenue -* ☎ *028 9031 6900.* Musicals, contemporary drama and concerts.

Crown Liquor Saloon

Ph Hurlin/MICHELIN

Belfast Waterfront Hall – *2 Lanyon Place -* ☎ *028 903 34 400 - www.waterfront.co.uk.* Opened in the late 1990s at a cost of £32 million and seating 2 500, the Waterfront plays host to a variety of art forms throughout the year. With its bars and restaurants, it has also become a popular choice for an evening out.

Cultúrlann Macadam Ó Fiaich – *Falls Road -* ☎ *028 9023 9303.* Irish Language arts centre featuring concerts and exhibitions.

The Crescent Arts Centre – *University Road -* ☎ *028 9024 2338.* Various workshops in what was originally a Victorian school.

The Grand Opera House – *Great Victoria Street, BT2 7BA -* ☎ *028 9027 7705 (24hr information),* 028 9024 1919.

The Odyssey – *2 Queen's Quay -* ☎ *028 9045 0055 - www.theodyssey.co.uk.* All the entertainment you need under one roof. This millennium project features a 10 000 seater stadium and is home to the "Belfast Giants" ice hockey team. It also holds a 12-screen multiplex, an interactive centre and a myriad of bars and restaurants.

Ulster Hall – *Bedford Street -* ☎ *028 9032 3900.* Pop concerts, sporting events and a regular venue for the Ulster Orchestra.

GOING OUT FOR THE EVENING

Benedicts of Belfast – *7-21 Bradbury Place - Shaftsbury Sq -* ☎ *028 9059 1999 – Open daily from 11.30am.* The mock Gothic interior of this bustling bar has been created using reclaimed pieces from churches, from arches to stained-glass windows. This monastic feel contrasts with the nightly scene of revellers enjoying the live music.

SHOPPING

National Trust Gift Shop – *57 Fountain Street -* ☎ *028 9032 0645 – Open Mon-Wed, Fri-Sat, 9am-5.30pm, Thu, 9am-7pm.* Plenty of choice for those wishing to take home a top quality piece of Irish craftsmanship. Embroidery, crystal, ceramics and original gifts featuring traditional Celtic designs are all on offer. What better memento than Irish Whiskey marmalade!

St George's Market – *12-20 East Bridge Street – Open Fri, 8am-2pm, Sat, 8am-2pm.* This covered market is over 100 years old and has been recently renovated. Market day is every Friday, where the atmosphere is colourful and the crowds considerable. On Saturday mornings there is a small farmers market.

EVENTS AND FESTIVALS

Belfast Festival at Queen's – *One of Ireland's major international arts festivals. It is based on the campus of Queen's University but events take place in all the major venues of Belfast, including the Waterfront Hall, the magnificent Grand Opera House and several other historic buildings which are specially converted into performance spaces. The Festival offers the best of international classical and popular music, theatre and dance, jazz, folk, comedy, literature, film and visual arts, commissioned works, world premieres and the UK debuts of many of the world's most exciting performers; it also provides a showcase for the work of Irish artists. – Takes place annually Oct-Nov, for three weeks. Full programme and tickets available from mid-Sep from The Belfast Festival at Queen's, Festival House, 25 College Gardens, Belfast BT9 6BS.* ☎ *028 9066 7687; festival@qub.ac.uk; www.belfastfestival.com*

It was in Belfast in 1791 that Wolfe Tone helped to found the Society of United Irishmen; in 1792 they published the *Northern Star*, a newspaper which expressed radical opinion and first promoted the idea of the Irish nation, which, in Tone's words, would "substitute the common name of Irishman in place of....Protestant, Catholic, and Dissenter". To the dismay of the United Irishmen, their ideals did not survive the failure of the 1798 Rebellion, which had only sharpened existing divisions. Until the end of the 18C, Belfast had been an overwhelmingly Presbyterian city. In the 19C its spectacular industrial growth drew in a new Catholic population from all over Ireland; the newcomers tended to settle in the Falls Road area of the city, between the predominantly Protestant working-class districts of Sandy Row and Shankill Road, the outcome being the sectarian geography familiar today.

Walking About

CITY CENTRE

Donegall Square★

The hub of Belfast is Donegall Square, a vast rectangle of grass and flower beds formally laid out round the City Hall *(see below)*; here all the buses converge on the edge of the pedestrian shopping precinct.

The gardens at the centre of the square contain several statues: Queen Victoria is flanked by two bronze figures representing shipbuilding and spinning; a group commemorates the *Titanic*, which was built in Belfast by Harland and Wolff and sank on her maiden voyage in 1912 after colliding with an iceberg; in front stands Sir Edward Harland.

Bordering the square are *(south side)* **Yorkshire House**, which is decorated with roundels containing low-relief heads of famous men and gods and goddesses; *(west side)* an office block (1899-1902), designed by the Belfast architects Young and Mackenzie for Scottish Provident; *(north side)* an old linen warehouse (1869) built of pink stone in the Venetian style.

Also on the north side is the **Linen Hall Library**, which was founded in 1788 as the Belfast Library and Society for Promoting Knowledge and has retained its old-fashioned interior – good collection of material relating to the Troubles. *Open Mon-Sat, 9.30am-5.30pm (4pm Sat). Closed Bank Hols. Guided tour (20min) by appointment. Refreshments. ☎ 028 9032 1707; Fax 028 9043 8586; info@linenhall.com; www.linenhall.com*

City Hall★

 ♿ *Guided tour (1hr) Jun-Sep, Mon-Fri at 10.30am, 11.30am and 2.30pm, Sat at 2.30pm; Oct-May, Mon-Sat at 2.30pm. Brochure (3 languages). Closed 17 Mar, Easter Mon and Tue, May Day and late Spring Bank Hol, 12-13 July, late summer Bank Hol, 25-26 Dec, 1 and 3 Jan. ☎ 028 9027 0456, 028 9032 0202 ext 2346, 028 9027 0405 (minicom); civicbuildings@belfastcity.gov.uk, www.belfastcity.gov.uk*

This huge neo-Renaissance edifice in Portland stone with its copper-covered dome and corner towers dominates Donegall Square. Designed by Sir Brumwell Thomas and completed in 1906, it was a triumphant expression of Belfast at its zenith of industrial and commercial might as well as a celebration of the city status granted by Queen Victoria in 1888.

The guided tour of the **interior** includes the grand staircase; a mural of the founding of the city and its principal industries painted by John Luke, a Belfast artist; a sculpture by Patrick MacDowell (1790-1870), a native of Belfast, of the Marquess of Donegall (1827-53), who devoted the proceeds of his music and poetry to good works; the Council Chamber, panelled in hand-carved Austrian oak; the Reception Hall displaying the original Charter of Belfast granted by James I on 27 April 1613; the Banqueting Hall; portraits of sovereigns who have visited Belfast and the shields of the Provinces of Ireland in the stained glass in the Great Hall.

From the NW corner walk W along Wellington Place.

Belfast City Hall

Ph Hurlin/MICHELIN

Royal Belfast Academical Institute

College Square. The inter-denominational boys' school, commonly known as "Inst", is set back from the street behind pleasant gardens. The main block – a long three-storey brick façade relieved by four pairs of plain pilasters and a recessed doorcase at the back of a Doric porch – was probably designed by Sir John Soane and completed in 1814.

Turn left into Fisherwick Place.

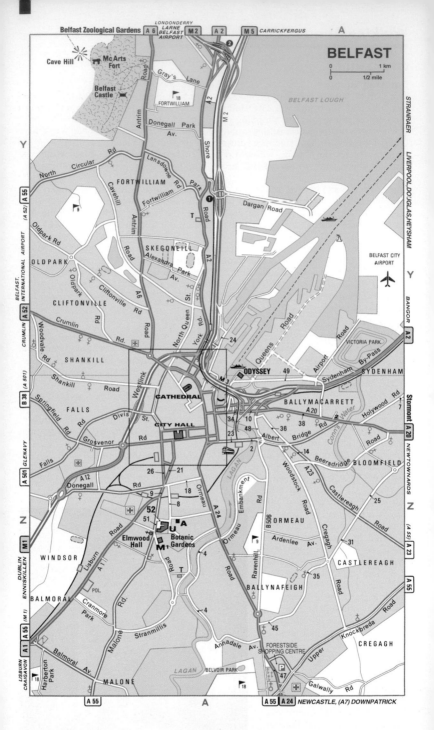

Church House

The headquarters of the Presbyterian Church in Ireland was designed by Young and Mackenzie (1905), Belfast architects, in the 15C Gothic style. The massive corner tower, which derives from St Giles' Cathedral in Edinburgh, contains a peal of bells. The semicircular Assembly Hall with its two galleries (refurbished in 1991) can seat about 1 500 people.

The **Presbyterian Historical Society Museum** contains old communion plate, pitch pipes and communion tokens, originally lead, now card. The Society keeps records and information about the Presbyterian Church in Northern Ireland but has little information from the 17C and 18C. &. *Open Mon-Tue and Thu-Fri, 10am-12.30pm, Wed, 10am-12.30pm and 1-3.30pm. Closed Bank Hols and other times.* ☏ *02890 322 284*

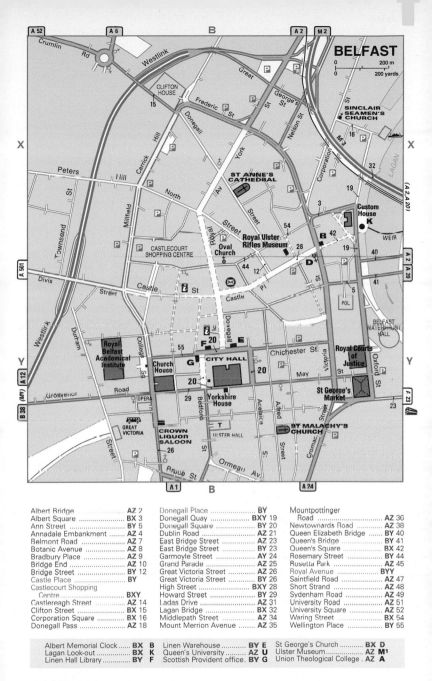

Grand Opera House

Designed by the theatre architect Frank Matcham and opened in 1894, this gorgeous building has a gilt-and-red-plush interior more than matching its exuberant facade. Like its famous neighbour, the Europa Hotel, it was badly damaged during the Troubles, but has been lavishly restored; as well as regular concerts it is the venue for the Northern Ireland Opera spring and autumn seasons.

Crown Liquor Saloon★

(NT) ♿ *Open Mon-Sat, 11.30am-midnight; Sun, 12.30-10pm. Full bar and snack lunches.* ☎ *02890 249 476; www.nationaltrust.org.uk*

The Victorian interior is richly decorated with coloured glass and brightly coloured and moulded tiles, reflected in the arcaded mirrors behind the long curved marble bar. Carved animals top the doorposts of the panelled snugs. The ornate ceiling is supported on hexagonal wooden columns with feathered ornament. Inspired by his travels in Spain and Italy, Patrick Flanagan built the public house as a railway hotel in 1885; it is now owned by the National Trust.

Turn left into Amelia Street and walk E along Franklin Street. Turn right into Alfred Street.

St Malachy's Church★

Open daily, 8am-5.30pm approx; otherwise by appointment. Services: Sun, 9.30am, 11.30am, 5pm. ☎ 028 9032 1713; 028 9023 3241 (Caretaker); Fax 028 90 333 224; stmalachys.belfast@ukgateway.net

The austere fortified exterior of this red-brick crenellated Roman Catholic church (1844) gives no hint of the ornate interior, which is dominated by white stucco fan vaulting inspired by Henry VII's Chapel in Westminster Abbey.

Return to the junction; turn right into Sussex Place; walk along Hamilton Street and into East Bridge Street; turn left and walk N along Oxford Street past St George's Market (see Directory).

The **Royal Courts of Justice** (1929-33), a massive building of Portland stone was designed by JG West.

Continue N along the waterfront.

Belfast's waterfront along the River Lagan is undergoing a spectacular refurbishment.

The centrepiece of an array of development projects is the glittering **Waterfront Hall**, a vast circular structure in Postmodern style which hosts all kinds of entertainments as well as serving as a prestigious conference centre.

Lagan Lookout

& *Open Apr-Sep, daily, 11am (noon Sat, 2pm Sun) to 5pm; Oct-Mar, Tue-Sun, 11am (1pm Sat, 2pm Sun) to 3.30pm (4.30pm Sat-Sun). £1.50. ☎ 028 9031 5444; Fax 028 9031 1955; lookout@laganside.com; www.laganside.com*

This glass lookout gives views of the waterfront and the modern weir, which regulates the water level in the river, and has fascinating displays on the history of Belfast's river, its shipbuilding industry and its flora and fauna.

Custom House

The building was designed by Charles Lanyon and erected in 1857 on the west bank of the River Lagan near the docks; the two wings and central porch make an E-shape facing the city.

South of the Custom House turn away from the river into Queen's Square.

Albert Memorial Clock

Owing to subsidence the tower has inclined slightly from the vertical since it was built in 1865 by WJ Barre; a statue of the Prince Consort stands in a niche facing up the High Street.

Continue along the High Street.

On the corner stands **St George's Church**, designed by John Bowden in 1816; the Classical portico comes from the palace which the Earl Bishop *(see p 454)* started to build at Ballyscullion after 1787.

Turn right into Skipper Street and left into Waring Street past the Royal Ulster Rifles Museum (see Worth a Visit). Continue to Rosemary Street.

Oval Church

(&) *Open Sun, Wed, 10.30am-12.30pm; otherwise by appointment. Musical recital: Jul-Aug, Wed at 1.15pm. ☎ 028 9084 3592 (Minister); www.firstchurchbelfast.co.uk*

The First Presbyterian Church, the oldest church in Belfast, opened in 1783. Its elliptical plan was designed by Roger Mulholland. The line of the box pews echoes the curve of the galleries, which are supported on columns with Corinthian capitals. The Lewis organ (1907) retains its tubular pneumatic action and is of special interest to visiting musicians.

Turn left into Royal Avenue to return to Donegall Square.

Worth a Visit

CITY CENTRE

St Anne's Cathedral★

(&) *Open daily 10am-4pm (4.30pm Sun); restricted movement during services (at 10am, 11am and 3.30pm). Leaflet (5 languages). Donations welcome. ☎ 028 9032 8332; Fax 028 9023 8855; admin@belfast.cathedral.org; www.belfastcathedral.com*

Begun in 1899 by Sir Thomas Drew in Hiberno-Romanesque style and built in white stone, Belfast's Anglican Cathedral suffered many delays in construction, not least because, like much of the city, it is built on waterlogged and unstable ground; it was completed only in 1981. Unremarkable externally, inside it has a fine Chapel of the Holy Spirit, consecrated in 1932 on the 1 500th anniversary of St Patrick's mission to Ireland; colourful mosaics evoke the event and there is an altar in early Christian style. The capitals of the south transept and nave depict an extraordinary range of aspects of Belfast life, including temperance and shipbuilding. As well as a chapel dedicated to Irish regiments, there is an ecumenical chapel where people from other denominations gather regularly to pray.

Sinclair Seamen's Church★

Open Sun, 11am-1pm and 6.30-8.30pm; also Mar-Oct, Wed, 2-4pm. ☎ 028 9077 2429 (Mrs Carole Davis)

The church's service to the maritime community is reflected in its position near Belfast docks and its interior decoration. The ship's bell from *HMS Hood* is rung at the beginning of the evening service; the collection is taken up in model lifeboats instead of the pole boxes which now hang on the walls; a ship's wheel and a capstan stand in front of the pews; a ship's binnacle once served as a font; the reading desk is shaped like the prow of a ship; the pulpit and organ are adorned with port and starboard lights, a masthead light, a ship's clock and a barometer.

Royal Ulster Rifles Museum

5 Waring Street. Open Mon-Fri, 10am-12.30pm and 2-4pm (3pm Fri); otherwise by appointment. Closed Bank Hols. £1. Guided tour (30min). ☎ 028 9023 2086; rurmuseum@yahoo.co.uk; www.rurmuseum.tripod.com

The small museum celebrates the military exploits of the regiment through weapons, sporting and shooting trophies, medals, 19C uniforms, and a collection of drums including the Lambeg *(see p 432).*

UNIVERSITY DISTRICT

South of the city centre is the area around Queen's University. The linking axis (Queen Victoria Street or Dublin Road, Bradbury Place and University Road) is at its liveliest in the evening, and with its many pubs, bars and places to eat is known as the "Golden Mile". Clustered around the university are pleasant Georgian and Victorian suburban streets, together with the Botanic Gardens and the province's most important museum.

Ulster Museum★★

& Open daily, 10am (1pm Sat, 2pm Sun) to 5pm. Closed Christmas, New Year. Café. ☎ 028 9038 3000; www.ulstermuseum.org.uk

The national museum and art gallery of Northern Ireland is housed in a modern building (1972), added to the previous premises built in 1929 in the Botanic Gardens. Its variegated and well-presented collections give an excellent overview of the province, its capital and their place in Ireland.

Visitors are advised to take the lift to the fourth floor and descend through the galleries which are linked by ramps.

Art Galleries – The small collection of pre-1900 British and Continental painting includes works by JMW Turner (1775-1851) and portraits of local gentry by Sir Joshua Reynolds (1723-92), George Stubbs (1724-1806) and Pompeo Batoni (1708-87). The two charming views of the Giant's Causeway *(see p 427)* by Susanna Drury (c 1740) were largely responsible for bringing this extraordinary natural phenomenon to the attention of the public.

Works by Irish artists – portraits, landscapes and watercolours – or on Irish subjects are periodically presented together with Irish furniture in the **Irish Gallery:** among the artists represented are Hugh Douglas Hamilton (1740-1808), Joseph Peacock (c 1783-1837), Sir John Lavery (1856-1941), Roderic O'Conor (1860-1940), Sir William Orpen (1878-1931), Andrew Nicholl and Richard Dunscombe Parker.

Craft Galleries – The collections cover glass (pieces commemorating personalities and incidents in Irish history), ceramics (Belleek pottery – *see p 425*), the work of Irish silversmiths (17C-19C), jewellery (16C-20C), costume and textile collection (18C-20C) as well as lace, embroidery and household linen.

Geology of Ireland – A skeleton of the extinct Giant Irish Deer dominates this excellent gallery – sections on Irish Flora and Fauna and the Living Sea giving a comprehensive view of the landscape of Ireland.

Antiquities – Human activity from the Prehistoric Era to the Middle Ages is traced through artefacts excavated from archaeological sites: the **Shrine of St Patrick's Hand★**, a 14C or 15C silver-gilt hand studded with glass and rock crystal and stamped with animal figures; a Bronze Age cauldron and a pair of horns which still produce a musical note; early Iron Age sword scabbards decorated in the "Celtic" style; an early Christian brooch. Pride of place goes to the **Spanish Armada treasure★★**, excavated from shipwrecks on the Irish coast: cannon and shot, a gold salamander set with rubies, gold chains, rings and crosses and coins.

Local History (16C-20C) – The "Made in Belfast" gallery is devoted to the history of industry in the city and the northeast of Ireland. There is also a section on coins minted in Ireland up to 1690 and another on the Post Office displaying the portable desk used by **Anthony Trollope** *(see p 141)* to write his novels.

Botanic Gardens, Belfast

Textile Gallery –The process of turning flax into linen, the traditional industry most intimately associated with Ulster, is explained by means of texts and diagrams and 11 of the original machines.

Botanic Gardens

Open daily, 7.30am-dusk. Palm House and Tropical Ravine: Open daily, 10am-noon and 1-4pm (5pm Apr-Sep). Guided tour (charge) by appointment. Parking. ☎ 028 9032 4902, ☎ 028 9032 0202 (guided tour); maxwell@belfastcity.gov.uk; www.parks.belfastcity.gov.uk
At the entrance to the Botanic Gardens stands a statue of Lord Kelvin (1824-1907), a native of Belfast, who invented the absolute scale of thermodynamics, the Kelvin Scale. The gardens (28 acres/11ha), consisting of a bowling green, sweeping lawns, shrubberies, flower beds and a rose garden with pergola, slope gently to the River Lagan. Although the gardens were originally laid out for the study of plants by the Botanic and Horticultural Society, founded in 1827, many other activities and entertainments were organised to meet the constant need for funds. In 1895 the Gardens became a public park.

Palm House★ – This beautiful cast-iron and curvilinear glass structure, one of the earliest of its type, was designed by Charles Lanyon and completed in 1840. It was constructed by Richard Turner, who later collaborated with Decimus Burton on the construction of the Great Palm House at Kew. The dome was added in 1852.

Queen's University, Belfast

Tropical Ravine House – The present house is an extension of the older Fernery established in 1887 by the curator, Charles McKimm. In 1900 a stove section was added; two years later the lily pond was created over the boiler house. An internal gallery enables the plants to be viewed from both above and below.

Queen's University

Queen's College, Belfast, was incorporated in 1845 and established as a university in 1908. The red-brick Tudor-style building by Charles Lanyon is reminiscent of Magdalen College in Oxford.

Opposite stands **Elmwood Hall**, now an examination hall, an Italianate building with an arcaded façade in polychromatic freestone which was designed in 1862 by John Corry as a Presbyterian Church.

University Square is an attractive mid-Victorian terrace, now occupied by the Faculty of Arts, with fanlights over the front doors and magnolia trees in the gardens.

Excursions

Belfast Zoological Gardens★★

5mi/8km N of Belfast by A 6. Car park; footpath to McArts Fort (see below). & *Open daily, 10am-5pm (2.30pm Oct-Mar). Closed 25 Dec. £6. Parking. Café.* ☎ *028 9077 6277; Fax 028 9037 0578; strongej@belfastcity.gov.uk; www.belfastzoo.co.uk*

The Zoo, which opened in 1934, lives up to its full name since the animal enclosures are set in the former Hazlewood Gardens, surrounded, where possible, by dry ditches or water-filled moats. There are spacious green areas for the big cats, the various types of deer and the kangaroos; an aquatic complex is subdivided to house penguins, sea lions and polar bears; waterfowl and flamingoes congregate round the large lake. A large walk-through aviary enables visitors to see free-flying birds at close quarters. The zoo is in a state of continuous development; recent additions include an otter park and buildings housing groups of chimpanzees and gorillas.

Belfast Castle

1mi/6.4km N of Belfast by A 6. Turn left into Innisfayle Park to Belfast Castle. & *Open (functions permitting) daily, 9am-10pm (6pm Sun). Closed 25 Dec. Lift.* ☎ *028 9077 6925; bcr@belfastcastle.co.uk; www.belfastcastle.co.uk*

In a superb location on the lower slopes of Cave Hill, this great mansion in Scottish Baronial style was built for the Donegall family in 1867-70 by WH Lynn; the external Baroque staircase was added to the east front in 1894. The interior now houses a restaurant and reception rooms, as well as a **Heritage Centre** on the top floor, with displays on the history of the castle and its surroundings. The commanding views over the city in its setting can be enjoyed by use of a remote camera with a powerful zoom lens. The castle has formal gardens and is one of a number of starting points for the waymarked trails through **Cave Hill Country Park**.

Cave Hill

4mi/6.4km N of Belfast by A 6. Accessible on foot from several car parks, including those at Belfast Castle and at the Zoological Gardens; various waymarked paths lead to the summit.

North of Belfast rears the black basalt cliff, known as Cave Hill (1 182ft/360m), which marks the southern end of the Antrim plateau and is said to resemble the profile of Napoleon. The headland, which is separated by a deep ditch from the rest of Cave Hill, is marked by an ancient earthwork, known as **McArts Fort**, after a local 16C-17C chieftain who was probably killed by the Elizabethans; it has served as a watchtower and place of refuge for the native Irish against Vikings and Anglo-Normans. In 1795 Wolfe Tone and his fellow United Irishmen *(see Historical Perspective)* spent two days and nights in the fort planning the independence of Ireland. There's a fine view of Belfast city and Belfast Lough and, on a clear day, of County Down and Strangford Lough *(SE)*, Lough Neagh and the Sperrin Mountains *(W)*, and Scotland *(NE)*.

Stormont

4mi/6.4km E of Belfast by A 20. Grounds: Open daily during daylight hours.

The Northern Ireland Parliament, a plain white Classical building with a central portico, which was designed by A Thornley, stands prominently on a hill approached by a broad avenue (1mi/1.6km long) through rolling parkland. A statue of Sir Edward Carson (1854-1935) stands at the centre of the roundabout. Parliament met regularly from 1932, when the building was opened, until 1972 when direct rule from Westminster was imposed. In 1999 it became the meeting place of the new Northern Ireland Assembly. Other government offices are housed in Stormont Castle *(right)*, built in the Scottish Baronial style.

Fernhill House People's Museum

4mi/6.4km W of city centre by Shankhill Road, Woodvale Road, Ballygomartin Road, Forthriver Road and Glencairn Road to Glencairn Park. &♿ *Open daily, 10am (1pm Sun) to 4pm. £2.* ☎ *028 9071 5599; Fax 028 9071 5582; historydetective@hotmail.com*

The People's Museum is set in a mid-Victorian butter merchant's mansion, with wide views across Glencairn Park to the city centre. It includes an exhibition on the social history of the Shankhill area, with fascinating photographs of residents and their houses, and *(upstairs)* a history of Unionism.

Carrickfergus

Atop its basalt promontory, the largest and best-preserved Norman castle in Ireland dominates this pleasant seaside town on the north shore of Belfast Lough. A broad promenade runs along the front, between the bathing beach and the Marine Gardens; and a marina packed with yachts and fishing boats now occupies the harbour where, until the development of Belfast, there was a thriving port.

The district has nurtured three literary figures: Jonathan Swift wrote his first book at nearby Kilroot; William Congreve and Louis MacNeice both lived in Carrickfergus as children.

Location

Population 22 786 - Michelin Atlas p 103 and Map 712 – O 3 – Co Antrim.

Carrickfergus *(Carraig Fhearghais)* is situated on the north shore of Belfast Lough, 10mi/15km from Belfast by A 2.
🅱 *Heritage Plaza, Antrim Street, Carrickfergus BT38 7DG. Open Jul-Aug, daily, 9am (10am Sat, noon Sun) to 6pm; Apr-Jun and Sep, Mon-Sat, 9am (10am Sat) to 6pm; Oct-Mar, Mon-Fri, 9am-5pm.* ☎ *028 9336 6455; Fax 028 9335 0350; touristinfo@carrickfergus.org; www.carrick.fergus.org*
Adjacent Sights: See ANTRIM, ANTRIM GLENS, BELFAST.

> **GETTING ABOUT**
> Larne Lough Ferry to Island Magee *(see p 385)* – Operates *(weather permitting)* hourly, 7.30am-5.30pm. ☎ *028 2827 4085*
>
> **SIGHTSEEING**
> Rowing boats for hire at the harbour
>
> **ENTERTAINMENT**
> Medieval banquets and the annual Lughnasa Fair *(Aug)* in the castle.

Background

The name Carrickfergus, meaning the Rock of Fergus, recalls the ruler of the ancient kingdom of Dalriada, Fergus Mór, who was drowned in a shipwreck off the coast c 531.

The town grew up in the shadow of the castle and shared its history. The castle was built late in the 12C by the Anglo-Norman, John de Courcy, and completed by Hugh de Lacy c 1240. Its strength and its strategic position made it appear the key to Ulster, indeed to Ireland. In 1315 it was captured after a year-long siege by Lord Edward Bruce from Scotland. The English recaptured it and held it for the next 300 years, withstanding many attacks by the local Irish and by invading Scots troops.

In 1688 the castle and the town were held for James II by Lord Iveagh but were captured in 1689 by Schomberg. On 14 June the following year William of Orange landed in Carrickfergus harbour *(plaque)* on his way to the Battle of the Boyne *(see p 148)*.

In February 1760 the town was briefly occupied by a French naval detachment, then in 1778 the American privateer John Paul Jones in his vessel *Ranger* attacked *HMS Drake* in an offshore engagement; Belfast folk, many of whom sympathised with the American Revolution, gathered in boats to watch the spectacle.

Worth a Visit

Castle★★

(HM) ♿ *Open Apr-Sep, Mon-Sat, 10am-6pm, Sun, 2pm (noon Jun-Aug) to 6pm; Oct-Mar, daily, 10am (2pm Sun) to 4pm. Closed 25-26 Dec. £2.70. Brochure (5 languages). Parking.* ☎ *028 9335 1273; Fax 028 9336 5190; janis.smith@doeni.gov.uk; www.ehsni.gov.uk*

Rising over the waters of lough and yacht harbour and commanding the seaward approach to Belfast, the great stronghold makes a splendid picture. To begin with, it occupied just the tip of the basalt promontory but was extended over the years to cover the whole of the promontory, which was originally protected by the sea on all but the landward side.

The **gatehouse towers**, which were completely circular when they were built at the same time as the Outer Ward, were cut back some time after the Elizabethan period. The room over the entrance passage contains the portcullis winding-gear and a "murder hole". The so-called Chapel on the first floor of the east tower gained its name because of its elaborate east window.

The **outer ward** was probably built by Hugh de Lacy between 1228 and 1242, to enclose the whole promontory and make the castle less vulnerable to attack from the land. Originally it probably contained living quarters but these were replaced in the 19C by ordnance stores supporting gun platforms.

The wall enclosing the **middle ward**, now partly reduced to its foundations, was built to improve the castle's defences soon after it had been successfully besieged by King John in 1210. The northeast angle tower is a fine example of 13C defensive work with an impressive array of arrow slits.

The castle's nucleus was the **inner ward**, enclosed by a high curtain wall, built by De Courcy between 1180 and 1200. The **keep** provided living accommodation for the lord of the castle. The life led here is evoked in a variety of ways; a large model of the castle at the time of Schomberg's siege in 1689; an audio-visual show, *Feasts and Fasts*, in the Banqueting Hall, and, on the banner-hung top floor, the opportunity to dress up in period costume.

St Nicholas' Church*

☎ 028 9336 3244 *(The Vicarage)*
John de Courcy provided Carrickfergus with a church as well as a castle. Centuries of turbulence left the building in a poor state; in 1614 it was heavily restored, leaving only the late-12C pillars in the nave to give an idea of the original structure. The west tower, begun in 1778, was completed in 1962 as a memorial to both World Wars. In the north transept is a fine marble and alabaster monument to Sir Arthur Chichester (1563-1625), an energetic Englishman who as Governor of Carrickfergus played a prominent and particularly ruthless role in the subjugation of Ulster and was the founder of the great landowning Donegal dynasty.

Carrickfergus Castle

P. Thebault/M CHELIN

North Gate and Town Walls

Between 1607 and 1610 Carrickfergus was enclosed with defensive walls and ditches by Sir Arthur Chichester, who by this time had been elevated to the rank of Lord Deputy of Ireland. The big arch of the North Gate is still largely 17C work but the structure has been repaired and altered many times; the pedestrian arch and crenellations are a 19C addition. A good stretch of wall survives to the east in Shaftesbury Park.

Excursions

Andrew Jackson Centre

2mi/3.2km N of Carrickfergus by A 2; turn right onto Donaldsons Avenue. Open Apr-May and Oct, Mon-Fri, 10am-1pm and 2-4pm, Sat-Sun, 2-4pm; Jun-Sep, Mon-Fri, 10am-1pm and 2-6pm, Sat-Sun, 2-6pm. £1.20. Parking. ☎ 028 9336 6455 (Tourist Information Centre); touristinfo@carrickfergus.org; www.carrickfergus.org

The Jackson family emigrated from Carrickfergus in 1765; their son, Andrew, born two years later, went on to become the 7th President of the United States, one of many with Ulster connections. The Jackson homestead has long since disappeared but close to where it stood between the road and the sea, this restored 17C single-storey cottage with its earthern floor preserves the family memory and traces the Ulster-American connection.

The adjoining **US Rangers Centre** presents the story of this American force which was formed in Northern Ireland in June 1942, with the task of acting as a spearhead for the invasions of the Second World War.

Dalway's Bawn

6mi/10km N of Carrickfergus by A 2, B 149 and B 90. South of Ballycarry beside the road *(left)* stand the remains of a bawn, with three flanker towers built by John Dalway c 1609 and now part of a farm.

Whitehead

5.5mi/9km NE of Carrickfergus by A 2. This little seaside resort is sheltered between the cliffs of White Head and Black Head. It has a pebble beach backed by a promenade and two golf courses.

The town is also one of the bases of the **Railway Preservation Society of Ireland** which owns a unique collection of steam locomotives and coaches, and operates steam rail tours to all parts of Ireland during the summer season *(see p 47).*

Island Magee

6mi/10km N of Carrickfergus by A 2. Although not an island, the peninsula (7mi/11km long), which separates Larne Lough from the North Channel, feels quite detached from the mainland. The road *(B 90)* along the west side of the peninsula provides fine views across Larne Lough. At the northern end of the peninsula, standing incongruously in the front garden of a private house, is the **Ballylumford Dolmen***, a Neolithic burial monument, consisting of four stones supporting a capstone. From **Brown's Bay**, a sandy beach sheltered between low headlands on the north coast, there is a view of the shipping entering and leaving the port of Larne, and in clear weather the coast of Scotland *(N).* **Portmuck** is a small bay and harbour. Further south are **The Gobbins**, precipitous cliffs (2mi/3.2km) from which the local inhabitants were flung into the sea in 1641 by the soldiers from the garrison in Carrickfergus.

Glenoe Waterfall

12mi/20km N of Carrickfergus by B 58 and B 99; car park (right) in Waterfall Road halfway down the hill. The gorge is so deep and so well screened by trees that this well-known waterfall is audible before it is visible. The river falls in a double cascade into a deep pool before flowing on under an old stone bridge through the village, attractive enough to merit preservation by the National Trust.

Downpatrick

Historic Downpatrick owes the first part of its name to a pre-Christian fort (*dún* in Irish), built on the prominent site now occupied by the cathedral, but the town is famous above all for its associations with the patron saint of Ireland. Traditionally held to be St Patrick's burial place, it developed into an ecclesiastical city with many religious foundations. Despite losing its status as a county town in 1973, Downpatrick is still a busy market centre serving the surrounding agricultural area, which to the south is known as the Lecale Peninsula.

Location

Population 10 113 - Michelin Atlas p 99 and Map 712 – O 4, 5 – Co Down.
Downpatrick *(Dún Pádraig)* is situated between the Mourne Mountains and Strangford Lough, 23mi/37km S of Belfast by A 7. Local map see p 465.
🄱 *74 Market Street, Downpatrick BT30 6LZ. Open Mon-Sat.* ☏ *028 4461 2233; Fax 028 8776 7911*
Adjacent Sights: See LISBURN, MOURNE MOUNTAINS, STRANGFORD LOUGH.

Background

AS well as the hill now crowned by the cathedral, there is a second great Iron Age earthwork, known as the **Mound of Down**, which rises from the marshy levels north of the town. The tree-covered mound sheltered an urban settlement destroyed by the Norman knight De Courcy in 1177 as a first step in his conquest of east Ulster. In the 18C, when Downpatrick was the administrative centre for the whole county, great improvements were made to the physical appearance of the

Directory

town by the Southwell family, who had acquired the demesne of Down through marriage to Lady Betty Cromwell, the last of the line to whom the land had been granted by James I in 1617. Until modern times Downpatrick was almost entirely surrounded by water and marshy ground, its narrow medieval thoroughfares – English, Irish and Scotch Streets – converging on the town centre where the market house once stood.

Walking About

Start at the junction of Irish Street, Scotch Street and English Street; turn into Market Street.

Saint Patrick Centre

Open Jun-Aug, Mon-Sat, 9.30am-7pm, Sun, 10am-6pm; Apr-May and Sep, daily, 9.30am (10am Sun) to 5.30pm; Oct-Mar, Mon-Sat, 10am-5pm. £4.50. Restaurant. Craft shop. ☎ *028 4461 9000, Fax 028 4461 9111; info@saintpatrickcentre.com; www.saintpatrickcentre.com*

The fascinating story of the patron saint of Ireland is retold in graphics, sculpture, video and Patrick's own words, accompanied by illustrations of beautiful early Christian artwork and the impact of Irish missionaries in Europe.

Return to the junction and walk up English Street.

English Street

At the lower end of the street are the red-brick Assembly Rooms designed in the Venetian Gothic style in 1882 by William Batt of Belfast. The **Customs House** *(no 26)* was built in 1745 by Edward Southwell. The Clergy Widows' Houses *(nos 34-40)* date from 1730 and 1750 although their appearance was altered early in the 19C. A low two-storey building *(right)*, originally designed with vaulted cells on the ground floor to hold prisoners, was converted in 1798 into the **Downe Hunt Rooms**; the Hunt has unbroken records dating from 1757. The Courthouse (1834) is the sole relic of a new prison constructed behind it in 1835; it has been immaculately restored after a bomb attack in 1971.

Down County Museum★

The Mall. (&) *Open daily, 10am (1pm Sat-Sun) to 5pm. Guided tour (1hr 30min) by appointment. Brochure (4 languages).* ☎ *028 4461 5218*

The museum is housed in the old Down County prison, which was built between 1789 and 1796; Thomas Russell, the United Irishman, was hanged in the gateway in 1803. When a new prison was built in the 1830s the old buildings were occupied by the South Down Militia and then by the army until the mid-20C. Surviving **cells** form part of the museum display.

The **gatehouse** contains the **St Patrick Heritage Centre** which tells the saint's history in words and pictures, and illustrates *(video)* the many local sites connected with St Patrick.

The display in the former **Governor's House** in the centre of the courtyard traces the history of Co Down from 7000 BC and describes the local wildlife.

The Mall

To avoid the deep dip between the Cathedral and English Street the road was raised (15ft/5m) in 1790.

Well below road level stands the **Southwell Charity**, which was founded in 1733 as a school and almshouses by Edward Southwell, the Secretary of State for Ireland, who by his marriage in 1703 became Lord of the Manor of Down.

The two teachers' houses are set well forward and linked to the main block by low quadrant walls. Opposite are the **Judges' Lodgings** *(nos 25 and 27)*, two late Regency-style houses built soon after 1835.

Down Cathedral★

♿ Open daily 9.15am (2pm Sun) to 5pm. Closed Good Fri, 25-26 Dec. Donation. Guided tour available. Brochure (4 languages). Parking. Bookshop. ☎ 028 4461 4922; Fax 028 4461 4456; www.cathedral.down.anglican.org

The present building is largely a 19C reconstruction, though it incorporates the chancel of the original abbey church. For many years the hilltop site attracted aggressors as well as pilgrims, and was attacked successively by Vikings, Scots and English. It also suffered damage in an earthquake. Not surprisingly, there is no trace of the monastery which grew up over the centuries since the time of St Patrick, although a round tower survived until 1780.

St Patrick's Tomb

The most influential attacker was probably the Anglo-Norman adventurer John de Courcy, who used the hilltop as a base for his (unauthorised) venture into Ulster in 1177. Seeking to consolidate his position, he replaced the incumbent Augustinians with a community of Benedictine monks from Chester, rebuilt the abbey church, changed the dedication to St Patrick, to please the native Irish, and renamed the town Downpatrick. He claimed he had found the bodies of Patrick, Colmcille and Brigid and reburied them in his new church.

The interior has a number of intriguing, in part unique features. There is a granite font originally used as a watering trough (narthex), two very unusual figures in ecclesiastical robes (Chapter Room), a choir screen which is the only one of its kind remaining in Ireland, and a splendid Georgian Gothick organ given by George III. But first on the list of most visitors to Downpatrick is the supposed site of St Patrick's Grave in the cathedral graveyard. A stone used to stand here bearing the names of Brigid and Columba (Columcille) as well as Patrick. The long-standing pilgrims' habit of carrying off handfuls of earth hollowed out a great cavity, which was covered up early in the 20C by the present massive slab of granite – which carries only the name of Patrick.

Excursions

From Downpatrick take a minor road E for 2mi/3.2km to Saul.

St Patrick's Memorial Church

2mi/3.2km E of Downpatrick. Open daily, 8am-dusk. Service: Sun, 10am. ☎ 028 4461 3101

The hilltop site, where St Patrick is said to have made his first Irish convert, is now crowned by a church built in 1932 to commemorate the 1 500th anniversary of St Patrick's landing near Saul in 432. It was designed in Celtic Revival style by Henry Seaver of Belfast and is built of Mourne granite, with a characteristic Irish round tower incorporated as the vestry.

There are few traces of the original medieval abbey, but its graveyards has two cross-carved stones and two small **mortuary houses**.

Slieve Patrick

3mi/4.8km E of Downpatrick. Car park. 15min there and back on foot to the top of the hill. A statue of St Patrick was erected on the top of the hill in 1932 to commemorate the 1 500th anniversary of St Patrick's landing near Saul. The path up to an open-air altar is marked by the Stations of the Cross. From the top there is a fine **view** over the surrounding countryside and the drumlin islands of Strangford Lough.

St Tassach's (Raholp) Church

4mi/6.4km E of Downpatrick. The ruins of this 10C or 11C church stand on the spot where Bishop Tassach is said to have administered the last sacrament to St Patrick.

ST PATRICK

When St Patrick returned to Ireland in 432 to convert the population to Christianity, his ship was carried by the wind and tide into Strangford Lough and he landed near Saul after sailing up the River Slaney, now a mere stream. He converted the local chief, Dichu, who gave him a barn (*sabhal* in Irish, pronounced Saul) to use as a church. St Patrick was very attached to Saul and returned there to die in 461. Some records state that he was also buried in Saul, rather than in Downpatrick. Many sites around Downpatrick are associated with St Patrick's life, work and death.

Struell Wells★

2mi/3.2km SE of Downpatrick. The site, in a secluded rocky hollow by a fast-flowing stream, comprises five buildings: an unfinished 18C church; a circular Drinking Well with a domed roof built on a wicker supporting arch; a rectangular Eye Well with a pyramidal corbelled roof; a Men's Bathhouse, with a stone roof and a dressing room with seats next to the bath; and a Women's Bathhouse without a roof – its dressing room is in the men's bathhouse.

Although the oldest of these buildings dates only from c 1600, there is written reference to a chapel on the site in 1306. A strong tradition associates the site with St Patrick. Struell has probably attracted pilgrims since the pre-Christian period, since streams and springs were important in Celtic pagan religion, but it was most popular from the 16C to 19C.

Ardglass★

7mi/11km S of Downpatrick by B 1. Little Ardglass is attractively located on the south side of a natural harbour, a fine haven for one of the province's fishing fleets. In the 15C it was an Anglo Norman enclave, the busiest port in Ulster, protected from the native Irish by numerous fortified buildings, several of which still stand. The finest of these is **Jordan's Castle**, an early-15C tower house in the middle of the town overlooking the harbour. In the Elizabethan period it withstood a three-year siege under its owner, Simon Jordan, until relieved by Mountjoy *(see Historical Perspective)* in June 1601. It was restored in 1911 by FJ Bigger, a solicitor and antiquarian from Belfast, and now houses his collection of antiquities. *(HM) Open Apr-Sep, Tue-Sun and Bank Hol Mon, 10am (2pm Sun) to 6pm. 75p.* ☎ *028 9181 1491; Fax 028 9182 0695; Scrabocp@doeni.gov.uk; www.ehsni.gov.uk*

Two other castles, King's Castle and Isabella's Tower, are mainly 19C structures. A row of fortified warehouses on the south side of the harbour has been converted into the clubhouse of the local golf course.

Ardglass Harbour

C HII

Killough

7mi/11km S of Downpatrick by B 176. A broad central avenue runs through this quiet but attractive village on the south side of a deep sea-inlet. In the 17C it was known as Port St Anne after Anne Hamilton, whose husband, Michael Ward of Castle Ward *(see p 467)*, developed the port to facilitate the export of lead and agricultural products from his estates.

St John's Point

10mi/16km S of Downpatrick by B 176, A 2 and a minor road. Near the point are the ruins of a 10C or 11C church built on the site of an early monastery. One of the most fascinating pre-Romanesque structures in Northern Ireland, it has a little west door with characteristic sloping jambs, while the high gable carried a roof supported on antae. The lighthouse stands on the southernmost point of the Lecale Peninsula; there is a fine **view** across Dundrum Bay.

Ballynoe Stone Circle

3mi/5km S of Downpatrick. Park opposite the old railway station (E); 6min there and back on foot by the track (W) between the fields.
The large circle is composed of low close-set stones round an oval mound which contained a stone cist at either end in which cremated bones were found during excavations in 1937-38. Nothing certain is known about its date but it was probably built by the late Neolithic Beaker people c 2000 BC.

Clough

6mi/10km SW of Downpatrick by A 25. North of the crossroads stands a stone tower (13C with later medieval additions) surmounting an Anglo-Norman earthwork castle, which in the late 12C or early 13C was surrounded by a wooden palisade.

Loughinisland Churches

5mi/8km W of Downpatrick by A 2 and a minor road N.
Three ruined churches stand on what was originally an island overlooking the lake. The oldest church (13C) stands in the middle. The larger church dates from the 15C and was in use until 1720. The smaller church bears the date 1636 over the door but it may be earlier; the initials PMC stand for Phelim MacCartan, whose family held land in the district and probably used the graveyard for their burials.

Seaforde Garden

9mi/14.5km W of Downpatrick by A 25 and A 2 N. Open Mon-Sat, 10am-5pm, Sun, 1-6pm. Butterfly House: Open Easter-Sep. £4.30; garden or butterfly house £2.50. Parking. ☎ 028 4481 1225; Fax 028 4481 1370; plants@seafordegardens.com; www. sea fordegardens.com
The old walled garden at Seaforde has been revived with a large hornbeam **maze.** Beyond is the Pheasantry, a deep dell dominated by great rhododendrons and exotic trees. Even more exotic is the **tropical butterfly house**, where brilliantly coloured specimens flutter among the vegetation and other creatures lurk in the lush undergrowth.

Dungannon

On its hilltop, Dungannon was for centuries a main residence of the O'Neill clan, one of the great families of Gaelic Ulster. Nowadays it is the busy hub of a rich dairying and fruit-growing district as well as a manufacturing centre of some importance; one of its oldest industries, textiles, has brought international fame to the name of Moygashel (founded in 1875).

Location

Population 9 190 - Michelin Atlas p 98 and Map 712 – L 4 – Co Tyrone. Dungannon *(Dún Geanainn)* is situated not far from Lough Neagh, 11mi/18km N of Armagh on A 29.
🚩 *Killymaddy Centre, Ballygawley Road (M1 extension), Dungannon BT70 1TF. Open Jul-Aug, daily; Sep-Jun, Mon-Sat. ☎ 028 8776 7259; Fax 028 8776 7911*
Adjacent Sights: See ARMAGH, LOUGH NEAGH, SPERRIN MOUNTAINS.

Directory

Shopping	Tracing Ancestors
Tyrone Crystal – *See below.*	**Heritage World**, *Main Street.* – Genealogical research centre, with extensive computerised archives – *Open Mon-Fri, 9am-1pm and 2pm-5pm* ☎*/Fax 028 8776 1306; wok@heritagewld.com; www.heritagewld.com*
Sports and Leisure	
Greyhound racing.	

Background

Plantation Town

Under the O'Neill clan Dungannon was little more than a collection of huts grouped round Castle Hill but early in the 17C English and Scottish settlers began to build a modern town. A charter was granted in 1612; in 1614 the Royal School was founded. When the native Irish rebelled in 1641 they were at first successful; the settlers' buildings were burned and their farms and orchards destroyed; the population dropped to 130. A new plantation followed the restoration of peace in 1653. After the Battle of the Boyne (1690) Dungannon expanded rapidly; in 1692 the town was purchased by Thomas Knox, whose expansionary regime coincided with the development of the coalfields at Drumglass and the digging of the local canal.

> ### VICTORIOUS O'NEILL
> Two important military engagements involving the O'Neills took place south of Dungannon. At the **Battle of the Yellow Ford** on the River Callan in 1598 Hugh O'Neill defeated the English forces under Sir Henry Bagnall; only about 1 500 Englishmen out of over 4 000 survived. In 1646 at the **Battle of Benburb**, fought at Derrycreevy west of Benburb on the north bank of the River Blackwater, the Scottish army of General Monroe was outmanoeuvred by Owen Roe O'Neill and 3 000 Scots were killed.

Worth a Visit

Tyrone Crystal

NE in Killybrackey Road (A 45). & *Guided tour of factory (40min) Mon-Fri. £2. Shop: Open Mon-Sat, 9am-6pm (Sun 1-5pm). Audio-visual show. Parking. Restaurant. Wheelchair available.* ☎ *028 8772 5335; Fax 028 8772 6260; tyrcrystal@aol.com; www.tyronecrystal.com*

Tyrone Crystal opened in 1971, exactly 200 years after an earlier glass factory had started production under Benjamin Edwards at Drumreagh, Newmills *(N)*. The nascent enterprise faced closure in the late 1970s' recession but local financial support was found and the factory moved into its present premises in 1990.

The **tour** covers the various stages in the process of producing hand-blown glass: preparing the molten glass, shaping the pieces by blowing, cooling, inspection for faults, bevelling, marking, cutting and polishing.

Excursions

Cornmill Heritage Centre

Coalisland; 4mi/7km NE of Dungannon by A 45. & *Open Mon-Fri, 10am-4pm (3pm last admission), Sat-Sun by appointment. £1.50. Parking. Lift.* ☎ *028 8774 8532; Fax 028 8774 8695*

The landscape around Coalisland is still marked by the extractive and other industries which once flourished here. Coal was being dug from bellpits as early as the 17C but severe faulting problems led to the closure of the last mine in 1970. Other industries included weaving, milling and a fireclay works; the Coalisland Canal had the first inclined plane to be built in the British Isles. The big brick corn mill, which dominates the centre of the town, was built in 1907 and has been extensively refurbished to serve as a community and heritage centre. The "Coalisland Experience" brings to life the past of this industrial area, unique in Ireland.

Donaghmore

Donaghmore; 5mi/8km N of Dungannon by B 43. In the centre of this quiet village stands an ancient sandstone cross (AD c 700-1000), associated with a former abbey; it is composed of the base and shaft of one cross and the shaft and head of another, decorated with motifs and biblical scenes: New Testament on the east face and Old Testament on the west. Originally it belonged to a nearby monastery said to have been founded by St Patrick.

Castlecaulfield

5mi/8km NW of Dungannon by A 4 and a minor road N. On the southeast edge of the village stand the stark ruins of a Jacobean **mansion** built (1611-19) by an ancestor of the Earls of Charlemont, Sir Toby Caulfield, who commanded Charlemont Fort *(see Moy below)* and whose arms appear over the gatehouse, an earlier structure defended with murder holes above the main door. The house was burned by the O'Donnells in 1641 but occupied for another 20 years by the Caulfields.

Moy

5.5mi/9km S of Dungannon by A 29. "The Moy" is an attractive Plantation town laid out in the 1760s by James Caulfield, Earl of Charlemont *(see p 239, 378)*, on the model of Marengo in Lombardy, which he had seen while making the Grand Tour. Horse chestnut trees line the main road where it passes through the broad central green, once the site of the great monthly horse fairs which lasted a whole week.

The road slopes down to the Blackwater River past the screen and entrance gates to Roxborough Castle (destroyed by fire in 1921), the 19C seat of the Earl of Charlemont. The boundary between Armagh and Tyrone, the Blackwater formed the front line in 1602 between territory held by the rebellious Hugh O'Neill and his English opponents, who fortified it with a great star-shaped stronghold on the south bank. Most of the fort was burned down in 1922, though the gatehouse still stands at the end of a short avenue of trees.

Benburb

7mi/11km S of Dungannon by A 29 to Moy and W by B 106. The ruins of **Benburb Castle** *(access on foot from priory grounds or just inside priory entrance)* occupy a dramatic site, a rocky ledge above the River Blackwater, which tumbles through the tree-lined gorge (120ft/37m below). The castle, which was built by Sir Richard Wingfield in 1611, replaces an earlier O'Neill stronghold. The entrance is flanked by two rectangular towers containing rooms with fireplaces; the walls, which are pierced by musket-loops, enclose an irregular rectangular bawn containing a 19C house *(private)*; the round tower overlooking the river contains a stair leading to a postern gate.

Parkanaur Forest Park★

7mi/11km W of Dungannon by A 4. ♿ *Open daily, 8am-dusk. Guided tour (1hr) by appointment. Parking.* ☎ *028 8775 9311*

The herd of **white fallow deer** at Parkanaur are direct descendants of a white hart and doe given by Elizabeth I in 1595 to her goddaughter, Elizabeth Norreys, who married Sir John Jephson of Mallow Castle *(see p 318)*.

Formerly the property of the Burgess family, Parkanaur is an old estate with several unusual specimen trees; two parasol beeches with branches like corkscrews grow beside the front drive. The woodland is being developed as an oak forest. The walks and nature trail include the formal Victorian Garden, the stone archway, the wishing well and the stone bridge and weir on the Torrent River. The farm buildings (1843, later restored) contain a display of forestry machinery.

Simpson-Grant Homestead

11mi/18km W of Dungannon by A 4; just before Ballygawley turn left to Dergenagh. ♿ *Open Easter-Sep, Tue-Sat, noon-5pm, Sun, 2-6pm. £1.50. Guided tour by appointment. Parking. Refreshments.* ☎ *028 8555 7133*

On the west side of the road stands the 17C homestead of the ancestors of Ulysses S Grant, President of the USA (1869-77).

The **Visitor Centre** tells the story of the Ulster-Scots Plantation, the Simpson family and the Ulster-American connection .

The house has been restored to its mid-19C state, the yard has hens and a duck-pond, and the smallholding on the far side of the road has fields for crops and grazing.

Fallow Deer

C Hill

Errigal Keerogue Cross

16mi/25km W of Dungannon by A 4; 1mi/1.6km W of the Ballygawley roundabout turn right to Errigal Keerogue (sign); at the crossroads in Ballynasaggart continue W; after 2mi/3.2km turn right.

In the graveyard stands a **high cross;** the carving is unfinished, probably owing to a fault in the stone. Two yew trees grow in the ruins of the medieval church, thought to be a Franciscan foundation (1489) which replaced an earlier monastery associated with St Kieran.

Augher

18mi/29km W of Dungannon by A 4. The village is set on one of the most beautiful stretches of the Blackwater River which provides good fishing. On the north side of the lake stands Spur Royal, now a hotel; it began as a bawn on the site of an earlier stronghold in 1615, was restored after a fire in 1689 and enlarged in 1832 .

Clogher Cathedral★

20mi/32km W of Dungannon by A 4. Open by appointment. Guided tour by appointment. ☎ *028 8554 8288 (Mr Jack Johnston, Ratory, Clogher).* ☎ *028 8554 8946 (Mr W Taggart, 35 Main Street, Clogher).* ☎ *028 8554 8235 (The Deanery, Augher Road, Clogher)*

Clogher claims to be the oldest bishopric in Ireland, supposedly founded in the 5C by St Macartan or Macartin, a disciple of St Patrick. The present cathedral, dominating the village from its hilltop, is an austere mid-18C Classical structure with a squat tower, but it preserves a number of relics from a much earlier age. Two **stone crosses** dating from the 9C and 10C stand in the graveyard outside the west door. A 7C **stone cross** *(outer porch)*, which is also thought to be a sundial for timing the services of the Celtic church, has a fish, an early Christian symbol, carved on the base. The **Golden Stone** *(inner porch)*, which was a famous oracle in pagan times, is known in Irish as **Clogh-Oir**, which may be the origin of the name Clogher.

Knockmany Passage Grave★

21mi/34km W of Dungannon by A 4 and N by B 83; 1.5mi/2.4km N of the crossroads turn right onto a track. Car park; 20min there and back on foot.

The cairn on its hilltop site commands a superb view south over Knockmany Forest into the Clogher Valley. In 1959 a concrete bunker and skylight were built to protect it from the weather but the stones of the burial chamber are visible through the grill: the decoration of circles, spirals and zigzags is typical of passage grave art.

Enniskillen

The principal town of Co Fermanagh is a lively commercial and cultural centre, occupying a strategically important island site between Lower and Upper Lough Erne. In the 17C it was one of the main strongholds of the 17C Plantation of Ulster; nowadays it makes an ideal base for exploring Lough Erne, for embarking on the Shannon–Erne Waterway *(see p 160)*, for fishing the Fermanagh lakes or for touring the Sperrin Mountains. Nearby are two of Ireland's most magnificent country houses, Castle Coole and Florence Court.

Location

Population 11 436 - Michelin Atlas p 97 and Map 712 – J 4 – Co Fermanagh.
Enniskillen *(Inis Ceithleann)* is situated between Upper and Lower Lough Erne, 50mi/80km W of Dungannon by A 4 and 12mi/19km from the border.
🄱 *Wellington Road, Enniskillen BT74 7EF. Open Apr-Sep, daily; Oct-Mar, Mon-Fri.* ☎ *028 6632 3110; Fax 028 6632 5511; tic@fermanagh.gov.uk; www.fermanagh-online.com*
Adjacent Sights: See CAVAN, DONEGAL, SLIGO, SPERRIN MOUNTAINS.

Walking About

Start from the East Bridge and walk up the main street to the West Bridge.
In 1688 the **East Bridge**, which has almost disappeared under later alterations, replaced the drawbridge built by the planters on the site of an old ford in 1614.
The **Courthouse** *(left)*, with its Classical portico, was radically remodelled in 1821-22 by William Farrell of Dublin.

Directory

GETTING ABOUT

Devenish Island Ferry – *Operates (capacity 28) from Trory Point Easter-Sep, daily at 10am, 1pm, 3pm and 5pm. £2.25. Parking.* ☎ *028 6862 1588; Fax 028 6862 1375; CastleArch@doeni.gov.uk; ww.ehsni.gov.uk*

White Island Ferry – *Operates (weather permitting) from Castle Archdale Marina (15min) Apr-Jun, Sun, 2-6pm, hourly; Jul-Aug, daily, 11am-6pm, hourly (except 1pm); check with the Marina at Castle Archdale. £3. Maximum 12 passengers. Parking.* ☎ *028 6862 1333, 028 6863 2159, Mob 07836 787123; Fax 028 6862 1176*

SIGHTSEEING

Lough Erne Waterbus Cruises – From the **Round 'O' Jetty** in Brook Park on the west bank of the River Erne *(NW of the town centre)* – *Operates Jul-Aug, daily at 10.30am, 2.15pm, 4.15pm (also 7pm Sat dinner cruise to Moorings Restaurant at Bellanaleck); May-Jun, Sun, 2.30pm and extra Bank Hols sailings; Sep, Tue and Sat-Sun at 2.30pm. Time 1hr 45min (stopping for 30min at Devenish Island). £7; dinner cruise £13 (€ accepted). MV Kestrel, all-weather vessel (covered deck); capacity 56; refreshments, bar. All-weather day boats for hire. Coffee shop.* ☎ *028 6632 2882, Mob 07753 936 692;* ☎ *evening/Fax 028 6632 4822; www.discovernorthernireland.com/m.v.kestrel*

Upper Lough Erne Cruises *(1hr 30min)* – From the Share Centre in Lisnakea *(east shore of Upper Lough Erne)* – *Operate Jul-Aug, Thu-Sun at 2.30pm; Easter-Jun and Sep, Sun at 2.30pm. £7.50.* ☎ *028 677 22122; Fax 028 677 21893; celia@sharevillage.org; www.sharevillage.org*

The principal marinas are on Lower Lough Erne at **Kesh** *(east shore)* and on Upper Lough Erne at **Bellanaleck** *(west shore)* and **Carrybridge** *(east shore)*.

WHERE TO STAY

• *Budget*

Rossahilly House – *BT56 8BN – 4.5mi/7.2km N by A 32 off B 82 -* ☎ *028 6632 2352 - Fax 028 6632 0277 - info@rossahilly.com -* 🅿 ✖ *- 3 rm £40/70* ☕ *- Meals £25.* Built in 1930, a superbly located and personally run house in a quiet

and elevated position with terrific views of Lower Lough Erne, where guests can fish. Dinner uses produce from local suppliers as well as from the owners' garden.

WHERE TO EAT

• *Budget*

Gallery – *139 Irvinestown Rd, Cross, Ferndale, BT56 8BN – 2.5mi/4km N by A 32 -* ☎ *028 6632 8374 - Closed Sat and Mon lunch and Sun -* 🅿 ✖ *- £13.95/24.* Country restaurant where the chef owner combines robust Irish cooking with subtle modern influences picked up from his Antipodean travels. Attractive room with marble flooring and handpainted murals. Good value, modern bedrooms also available.

SHOPPING

Belleek Pottery – *See below.*

SPORTS AND LEISURE

Day boats for **fishing** – Enniskillen ☎ *028 6632 2882, Fax 028 6638 7954 (Erne Tours Ltd, Round 'O' Jetty, Brook Park, Belleek Road); Killadeas* ☎ *028 6862 8100 (Manor House Marine);* ☎ *028 6862 1557 (B Ternan, The Beeches, Killadeas); Kesh* ☎ *028 6863 2328, 028 6632 2666 (G Keown, Erinona Boats, Boa Island Bridge); Belleek* ☎ *028 6865 8181 (Belleek Angling Centre, The Thatch, Main Street); Newtownbutler* ☎ *028 6773 8118 (Crom Estate); Teemore* ☎ *028 6774 8893 (Shannon-Erne Country Cottages & Cruisers); Garrison* ☎ *028 6865 8194 (Sean Maguire); Derrylin* ☎ *028 383 44993 (Carrick Craft Knockninny Quay)*

Lakeland Canoe Centre, Castle Island, Enniskillen.

Lakeland Forum – For swimming, squash, volleyball, basketball, badminton, table tennis, bowls, archery, soccer, judo and keep-fit.

EVENTS AND FESTIVALS

Lady of the Lake festival in Irvinestown in July.

TRACING ANCESTORS

Roslea Heritage Centre, Monaghan Road, Roslea – *Open by appointment Apr-Sep, Mon-Fri, 10am-4pm; Oct-Mar, Mon-Fri, 9am-5pm, Sat-Sun. £2.* ☎ *028 6775 1750*

At the centre of the town The Diamond is graced by the **Town Hall** *(right)*, which was designed by William Scott in 1898 and given a splendid neo-Renaissance clock. In the **Buttermarket** *(turn right along Church Street)* the 19C courtyard buildings have been converted into a fascinating craft and design centre.

St Macartin's Anglican Cathedral, standing in its graveyard *(right)*, was completed in 1842 although the tower was part of the earlier 17C church.

St Michael's Roman Catholic Church *(opposite)*, completed in 1875, is a French Gothic Revival building by John O'Neill lacking the spire which was intended to crown the tower; more impressive is the external view of the apse rising above the substructure, supported by flying buttresses (1921).

The street descends towards the **West Bridge** (completed in 1892); to the right are the Old Militia Barracks (1790) and to the left is Enniskillen Castle.

P. Trebault/MICHELIN

Lough Erne

Worth a Visit

Enniskillen Castle

(&) *Open Jul-Aug, daily, 10am (2pm Sat-Sun and ordinary Mon) to 5pm; May-Jun and Sep, Mon-Sat, 10am (2pm Sat and ordinary Mon) to 5pm; Oct-Apr, Mon-Fri, 10am (2pm ordinary Mon) to 5pm; subject to variation at Christmas and New Year. £2. Guide and information (3 languages). Parking. Lift. ☎ 028 6632 5000; Fax 028 6632 7342; castle@fermanagh.gov.uk.*

Until the 18C Enniskillen castle stood on its own island and is still best seen from the far bank, with its famously picturesque Watergate reflected in the waters of the Erne. The castle was first built in the 15C as a stronghold of the powerful Maguire family, the then rulers of Fermanagh, to command the strategic route between Ulster and Connaught across the formidable barrier of the Erne. In 1607 it was granted to the planter Captain William Cole, whose family later moved to nearby Florence Court. Cole laid out the town and made good damage to the castle; Enniskillen held out against the native Irish uprising in 1641 and against Jacobite attacks in 1689.

The castle houses an array of exhibitions evoking the region and its often unsettled past. The **Heritage Centre** has displays on the history, landscapes and wildlife of the county, while the keep, which incorporates parts of the original 15C fortress, deals with the evolution of the castle and the fortunes of the Maguires; it is also the home of the **Regimental Museum of the Royal Inniskilling Fusiliers**, the prestigious regiment formed in the late 17C together with the Inniskilling Dragoons. (&) *Open Jul-Aug, daily, 10am (2pm Mon, Sat-Sun) to 5pm; May-Jun and Sep, Mon-Sat, 10am (2pm Mon and Sat) to 5pm; Oct-Apr, Mon-Fri, 10am (2pm Mon) to 5pm. £2. ☎ 028 6632 3142; www.inniskilling.com.*

Exhibitions in the Watergate cover the ancient monuments and castles of Fermanagh, and the pilgrim's trail to Devenish Island *(see p 424).*

> ### PORTORA ROYAL SCHOOL
> This famous school was founded in 1608 by James I at Lisnakea *(S)*. In 1643 it moved to Enniskillen and in 1777 to a site near **Portora Castle** (17C), which was partially destroyed by an explosion caused by schoolboys in 1859. Among its pupils were Oscar Wilde and Samuel Beckett.

Forthill Park

SE of the town centre. Enniskillen's town park is named after the star-shaped fort built here in 1689 during the Williamite Wars. It has a delightful Victorian **bandstand**, an oriental-looking cast-iron structure with an octagonal canopy, supported on eight slender columns and surmounted by a clock. The centre of the fort is now occupied by **Cole's Monument**, erected between 1845 and 1857, in memory of General the Hon Sir Galbraith Lowry Cole (1772-1842), brother of the 2nd Earl of Enniskillen of Florence Court; he was a close friend of the Duke of Wellington and fought in the Peninsular Wars. Within the fluted Doric column a spiral stair *(108 steps)* climbs to a platform: extensive **view** of Enniskillen and the surrounding countryside. *Open mid-May to mid-Sep, daily, 2-6pm. 70p. Brochure (3 languages).*

Excursions

Castle Coole★★★

SE of the town centre by A 4. (NT) (&) Parkland: Open daily, 10am-8pm (4pm Oct-Mar). House: Open Jul-Aug, daily, noon-6pm (5.15pm last tour); Jun, Wed-Sun; Sep and mid-Mar to May, Sat-Sun and Bank Hols. £3.50. Parking. Tearoom. ☎ 028 6632 2690; Fax 028 6632 5665; castlecoole@ntrust.org.uk.

Crowning a gentle rise among great oaks and beeches and overlooking its lake, this superb neo-Classical house is perhaps the finest building of its kind in the whole country. It was completed to designs by James Wyatt in 1798 for the Corry family, Earls of Belmore, who lived here until the house passed into the hands of the National Trust in 1951. Built, decorated and furnished without apparent regard to expense, it has been comprehensively restored to something like its original glory.

> ### THE CORRYS OF COOLE
> John Corry, a Belfast merchant, originally from Dumfriesshire, purchased the manor of Coole in 1656 and in 1709 built a new house near the lake incorporating parts of an early-17C castle. In 1741 the estate passed to Armar Lowry-Corry, created 1st Earl of Belmore in 1797, who commissioned Wyatt to design the present house; his son, the 2nd Earl of Belmore, was responsible for the interior decoration and the Regency furnishings.

In the 1980s it was restored to something like its early-19C appearance by the recladding of the exterior and the redecoration of the interior, in accordance with the original intentions of Wyatt or of Preston, one of the leading Dublin upholsterers of the period, who refurbished the interior between 1807 and 1825.

The exterior consists of a central block containing the formal rooms, flanked by single storey colonnaded wings with the family accommodation. The pale Portland stone which lends the facade its particular distinction was imported from the far-off Dorset quarry via Ballyshannon, where a special quay had to be built. So as not to interfere with the harmony of the composition, the stable yards added in 1817 by Richard Morrison were built out of sight below the level of the house and linked to it by tunnel.

The whole of the interior has a wonderful spaciousness and sense of proportion. Wyatt's masterly scheme of decoration is best seen in the library and the dining room, while the oval saloon, the most important room in the house, has elaborate plasterwork and curved mahogany doors veneered with satinwood. Between 1807 and 1825 some interiors were refurbished by Preston, one of the leading upholsterers of the period; his more flamboyant style is evident in the porphyry colour used in the hall, on the staircase, and in the lobby on the first-floor landing. He provided the hangings and furniture in the drawing room and saloon, decorated the first floor Bow Room which was used by the ladies of the house, and created the sumptuous gold and scarlet State Bedroom in anticipation of George IV's visit to Ireland in 1821.

State Bedroom, Castle Coole

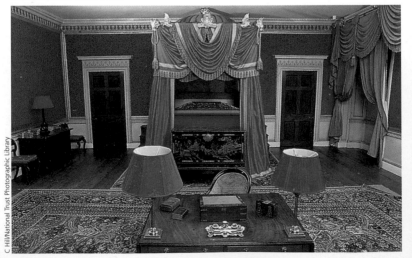

Florence Court★★

8mi/13km S of Enniskillen by A 4, A 32 and W by a minor road. (NT) (& to ground floor and garden) Grounds: Open daily, 10am-8pm (4pm Oct-Mar). House: Guided tour Jun-Aug, daily, noon (1pm Mon-Fri in June) to 6pm; Mar 17, Apr-May and Sep, Sat-Sun and Bank Hols. House £3.50; grounds £2.50 per car. Parking. Restaurant, tearoom, picnic area. ☎ 028 6634 8249; Fax 028 6634 8873; florencecourt@ntrust.org.uk; www.nationaltrust.org.uk

County Fermanagh's second great country house stands in parkland in a dramatic setting at the foot of Cuilcagh Mountain. Faced in attractive greyish-gold stone, the original three-storey house, probably designed in the 1740s, is flanked by seven-arched colonnades and canted pavilions, which were probably designed in the 1770s by Davis Ducart, a Sardinian, who spent most of his working life in Ireland. The property was transferred, largely unaltered, to the National Trust in 1955.

The interior is charmingly decorated with family portraits, photographs, drawings and other memorabilia, but the glory of **Florence Court** is the exuberant **Rococo plasterwork**, some of it restored after a fire in 1956.

It is seen to advantage in the ceiling of the **Dining Room** which has an exquisite surround of trailing foliage enclosing the central panel, where the four winds, represented by puffing cherubs, encircle an eagle. However, it is at its most exuberant on the **staircase,** where wall panels overflow with scrolls of foliage between a horizontal band of scrolls and a cornice formed of pendants.

The **Pleasure Grounds** were mostly planted by the 3rd Earl early in the 19C. In the walled garden the original ornamental section has been retained whereas the vegetable plot has been laid out as lawn with shrubs and ponds. An 18C summerhouse has been meticulously rebuilt and there is a fascinating brick-lined ovoid ice house as well as a working sawmill (restored).

> ### THE COLE FAMILY
> The Coles came to Ireland from Devonshire, in the reign of Elizabeth I. They lived first at Enniskillen Castle and then at Portora Castle *(see p 421)*. It was Sir John Cole (1680-1726) who settled at Florence Court, named after his wife, Florence Wrey, a wealthy heiress from Cornwall. Their son, also John Cole (1709-67), made Lord Mount Florence in 1760, built the present central block; the wings were added by his son, William Willoughby Cole (1736-1803), later Viscount and then Earl of Enniskillen, who made the Grand Tour in 1756-57.

Florence Court Forest Park – *For walkers. Open daily. For cars: Open daily except 25 Dec, 10am-7pm (4pm Oct-Mar). £2.50 (per car) during busy periods. Parking. ☎ 028 6634 8497*

Since 1975 the estate grounds have been developed as a forest park. In the woodlands southeast of the house stands the famous **Florence Court Yew**, also known as the Irish Yew, a columnar-shaped freak, which can be reproduced only by cuttings as seedlings revert to the common type. There are several trails of different lengths signposted with coloured indicators; the most challenging and rewarding extends to the moorland to the southwest and gives access *(9hr there and back on foot)* to the top of Cuilcagh Mountain (2 198ft/670m).

Marble Arch Caves ★★

11mi/18km S of Enniskillen by A 4, A 32 and W by a minor road. (&) Caves: Guided tour (1hr 15min; rain permitting) Easter-Sep, daily, 10am-4.30pm (5pm Jul-Aug last tour). £6; booking recommended (from 9am). Audio-visual show (20min). Tour translations (5 languages). Stout shoes and warm clothes advisable. Parking. Refreshments. Wheelchair access: telephone for details. ☎ 028 6634 8855; Fax 028 6634 8928; richard.watson@fermanagh.gov.uk; www.fermanagh-online.com

This spectacular cave system was formed in a bed of Dartry limestone by three streams on the northern slopes of Cuilcagh Mountain; they converge underground to form the Cladagh River which emerges at the Marble Arch and flows into Lough Macnean Lower.

The **reception centre** presents an exhibition on caving and a video *(20min)*, which covers the same ground as the tour and is a good substitute for those who cannot manage the many steep slopes and steps involved in the tour itself.

The **cave tour** includes a short boat trip on an underground lake which opens the way into a fantastic subterranean decor of stalactites, stalagmites, columns, flow stones, cascades, draperies and curtains, with picturesque names such as the Porridge Pot, Streaky Bacon, Cauliflowers, Tusks and Organ Pipes. The skilful illumination of these superb geological features is sometimes enhanced by reflection in pools of water. The longest stalactite (7ft/2m) is named after Edouard Martel, a famous French cave scientist who explored the caves in 1895.

The **nature reserve** *(car park at the cave entrance and on the Blacklion-Florence Court road)* consists of the wooded Cladagh gorge created by the collapse of caves eroded by the river. A path *(1hr there and back on foot)* along the east bank links the **Marble Arch**, a natural limestone arch, where the turbulent brown stream emerges from the ground, and the **Cascades**, where more water gushes forth. The forest is composed of ash, oak and beech and some conifers; in the spring the floor is a sea of bluebells.

LOUGH ERNE★★

Wet and wooded, the Fermanagh Lakeland was once the remotest part of a remote province, described by an early-16C traveller as "full of robbers, woods, lakes and marshes". Nowadays it is more accessible, much frequented by fishermen and increasingly popular for water-based activities, though its vast extent is such that it rarely feels crowded. Fed by the River Erne (50mi/80km long), Lough Erne is divided into two by the narrows around Enniskillen; the Upper Lough is a watery labyrinth of myriad islands and twisting channels, while the glorious expanse of Lower Lough Erne with its more orderly assemblage of islands and generally greater share of attractions broadens out to a maximum width of 5mi/8km.

The attractiveness of the Lough as a cruising centre was greatly enhanced in 1994 by the re-opening of the **Shannon-Erne Waterway** *(see p 160).*

Lower Lough Erne

Round tour of 66mi/106km – 1 day

Mysterious antiquities and planters' fortified houses enhance the natural allure of the lough, its islands and wooded banks.

From Enniskillen take A 32 N; after 3mi/5km turn left to Trory Point.

Devenish Island★

Access by ferry (see Directory).

Arrayed around a fine example of a round tower, the island's medieval remains have an appeal which is greatly increased by their lovely lakeside setting.

Devenish was chosen as the site for a monastery in the 6C by St Molaise. Devastated by the Vikings, frequently caught up in local feuds, and burnt down in the 12C, it nevertheless survived until early in the 17C.

The **museum** traces the history of the monastery, with models illustrating the seasonal activities of the monks. *Open Apr-Sep, daily, 10am-6pm. Guided tour (90min) available. Tower 75p.* ☎ *028 6862 1588; Fax 028 6862 1375; CastleArch@doeni.ogv.uk; www.ehsni.gov.uk*

Nearest to the jetty are the ruins of the **Lower Church** (Teampull Mór), begun in the early 13C and later extended. The mortuary chapel to the south was built for the Maguire family; their arms are visible near the entrance and on the east wall. The oldest gravestone is a long flat slab with a two-armed cross in the southeast corner. The smallest and oldest building, **St Molaise's House**, dates from the 12C although it is based on an earlier wooden church.

The **round tower** dates from the 12C (81ft/25m high). The view from the top floor *(key from the Caretaker)* is limited by the narrowness of the four windows.

St Mary's Priory dates from the 15C although the tower is later. The two doorways at first-floor level gave access to a rood screen dividing the monks' chancel from the laymen's nave; bell ropes passed through the holes in the vault. A most unusual 15C **high cross** stands in the graveyard.

Continue N by B 82 along the east shore of the lake.

Ancient crosses stand in **Killadeas** churchyard.

Devenish Island

Castle Archdale Country Park★

♿ Open daily. Visitor centre and Exhibition: Open Jul-Aug, daily, 11am-7pm; Easter-Jun, Sun, noon-6pm; also Sat preceding Easter Sun and Easter Sun and May Bank Hol Mon, 11am-6pm; Sep, by appointment. Parking. ☎ 028 686 21588, Fax 028 686 21375; www.ehsni.gov.uk

The fortified residence built in the early 17C by the Archdales, an English planter family from East Anglia, has long since been abandoned, but other relics of their presence remain in the form of a fine arboretum, 19C pleasure grounds, a cold bath and sweathouse and an old walled garden. The former outbuildings house a Visitor Centre with a display of agricultural implements, while modern additions include a butterfly garden and a Japanese garden. A caravan park occupies the site of the Second World War base used by the British and Canadian flying boats which patrolled the North Atlantic sea lanes, overflying neutral Ireland on the way.

The park has extensive and wonderfully diverse woodlands harbouring a variety of wildlife, while the ruins of **Old Castle Archdale** near the northeast entrance *(car access from the road)* include the original gateway of the bawn, a rare survival.

White Island★

Open Jun-Sep, Tue-Sun, 10am (2pm Sun) to 7pm. Guided tour available. £2.25.

Within a large pre-Norman monastic enclosure stand the remains of a 12C church with a handsome Romanesque doorway. The eight **stone figures** set up against the north wall and probably dating from the 9C or 10C have been the subject of much speculation; while definitely Christian, they have something of the pagan about them and include a particularly lewd example of a *Sheela-na-gig* (see Irish Art).

Continue N by the scenic route; N of Kesh hear left onto A 47. Near the W end of Boa Island park beside the road and follow sign to cemetery (about 550yd/500m there and back on foot).

Janus Figure★

In the appropriately sombre setting of an overgrown graveyard, this squat and ancient stone figure with two faces, staring eyes and crossed arms probably dates from the Iron Age.

Continue W on A 47.

Castle Caldwell Forest Park

♿ Open daily. Parking. Café (summer).

An important bird sanctuary, the forest covers two long fingers of land at the western end of Lough Erne. The ruined planter's castle was built in 1612 and later passed into the hands of the Caldwells. In 1770, family members were being enter-

Janus Figure, Boa Island

B. Kaufmann/MICHELIN

tained aboard their boat by a fiddler whose inebriated state caused him to fall overboard and drown. He is commemorated by the **Fiddler's Stone** at the park entrance.

Continue W on A 47.

Belleek

The village stands at the point where the waters of the Erne flow swiftly westward in a narrow channel to enter the sea in Donegal Bay.

Belleek Pottery – *Pottery: Guided tour (30min), Mon-Fri, every 30min (3.30pm Fri last tour). £2.50. Audioguide (4 languages). Brochure (4 languages). Visitor Centre: Open Apr-Sep, Mon-Sat, 9am (10am Sat) to 6pm; Sun 2pm (11am Jul-Aug) to 6pm; Oct, Mon-Sat, 9am-5.30pm, Sun 2-6pm; Nov-Mar, Mon-Fri, 9am-5.30pm. Museum. Showroom. Parking. Restaurant. ☎ 028 6865 8501; Fax 028 6865 8625; visitorcentre@belleek.ie; www.belleek.ie*

The pottery, which has an international reputation for its distinctive highly decorated Parian ware, takes its name from the small border village of Belleek.

> ### BELLEEK PARIAN WARE
> The pottery in its handsome building was founded in 1857 by John Caldwell Bloomfield, who had just inherited Castle Caldwell and needed to increase his income. He was a keen amateur mineralogist and realised that the estate contained the necessary ingredients to make pottery – feldspar, kaolin, flint, clay, shale, peat and water power. At first only earthenware was produced; the first Parian ware was the result of 10 years of experiment. Belleek won its first Gold Medal in Dublin in 1865.

The **tour** begins where the slip, a mixture of feldspar, china clay, frit (glass) and water, is moulded and trimmed. Gum arabic is added to produce the extruded raw material used to make the ornaments and the basketware which is woven by hand. By individual choice this is men's work; the women prefer to do the hand painting. All serve a five-year apprenticeship. The results of their craftsmanship are on show and for sale in the Visitor Centre.

ExplorErne – & *Open May-Sep, daily, 11am-5pm. Exhibitions £1. Parking.* ☎ *028 6865 8866; Fax 028 6865 8833; www.fermanagh-online.com*

The exhibition, which is housed in the purpose-built Tourist Information Centre, introduces visitors to the history, landscapes and ecology of the Lough, from legendary beginnings to the harnessing of its waters to generate hydroelectric power and control the capricious changes in level, which once meant that "in the summer Lough Erne is in Fermanagh, and in the winter Fermanagh is in Lough Erne".

Leave Belleek by A 46 going E.

The road skirts the southern shore of Lough Erne beneath the high Cliffs of Magho. *After 10mi/16km turn left to Tully Castle.*

Tully Castle★

(HM) Open Apr-Jun and Sep, Sat-Sun and Bank Hols, 10am-6pm. £1. ☎ *028 6862 1588; Fax 028 6862 1375; CastleArch@doeni.gov.uk; www.ehsni.gov.uk*

The ruined castle, a fine example of a fortified planter's house, was built in 1613 by Sir John Hume from Berwickshire but captured and abandoned in the rising of 1641.

The partially paved bawn is protected by walls and corner towers with musket loops; each corner tower was also a house. A 17C-style garden has been made inside the bawn. The three-storey house has a vaulted room on the ground floor containing the kitchen fireplace, an unusually large staircase leading to a reception room on the first floor and a turret stair to the floor above. The projecting turrets are best seen by walking round the outside.

Return to A 46 and immediately turn right onto B 81 and then second right to the Lough Navar Scenic Drive. After 3mi/5km turn right opposite Correl Glen.

Cliffs of Magho Viewpoint★★★

Open daily, dawn-dusk. Car £2.50, motorcycle £1.50, minibus £5 (during busy periods). Fishing. Parking. Picnic area. ☎ *028 6864 1256; Fax 028 6864 1743*

A scenic drive *(one way)* winds for 7mi/11km through the trees of **Lough Navar Forest** to a viewpoint *(car park)* on the top of the Cliffs of Magho. The panorama is immense, taking in the whole of the north end of Lower Lough Erne and extending to the far-off Blue Stack Mountains in Donegal.

Return to A 46 and continue S.

There are trails along the shore through the mixed woodland of **Ely Lodge Forest** *Continue S on A 46; turn right to Monea Castle.*

Monea Castle

Proceed up the drive; after 0.25mi/0.4km turn right at the gates of the house. The ruined castle, one of the largest and best preserved of the 17C tower houses, was built on a rocky bluff in 1618 by the planter Malcolm Hamilton, who later became Bishop of Cashel. Crow-stepped gables and corbelling on towers and turrets give it a Scottish look, but despite its formidable appearance it fell to the rebels of 1641 and to the Jacobite forces in 1689.

On leaving turn left; in Monea turn left onto B 81 to return to Enniskillen.

Upper Lough Erne

Crom Estate

21mi/34km S of Enniskillen by A 4 and A 34; in Newtownbutler turn right onto a minor road. (NT) & *Visitor Centre: Open late-Mar to Sep, daily, 10am (noon Sun) to 6pm (8pm Jul-Aug). £4 by car or boat. Guide book. Guided walks by arrangement. Check with property for events. Parking. Tearoom.* ☎*/Fax 02867 738 118; crom@ntrust.org.uk; www.nationaltrust.org.uk*

A visit to this estate, now a National Nature Reserve with oak woodland, reedbeds, meadows and heronry, gives an opportunity to experience something of the otherwise somewhat inaccessible Upper Lough. The desmesne and its planter's castle once belonged to the Creighton family from Scotland, who were later ennobled as the Earls of Erne and who built themselves a more spacious castle *(private)* in the 19C. Their story and that of the estate is told in the Visitor Centre. Trails lead through woodland and along the lakeshore, taking in the old castle, remains of a formal garden, and features like the boathouse, summer house, riding school and stable yards.

Giant's Causeway★★★

Perhaps the strangest of Ireland's scenic attractions, the 40 000 basalt columns of the Giant's Causeway have inspired legend, intense scientific debate and endless wonder and curiosity. Today the Causeway is a World Heritage Site, the annual destination of hundreds of thousands of visitors. It is the focal point, but by no means the only attraction of the "Causeway Coast" which stretches eastward from the resort of Portrush.

Location

Michelin Atlas p 102 and Map 712 –M 2 – Co Antrim.

The Giant's Causeway is on the coast road, A 2, between Portrush and Ballycastle on the north Antrim coast.

🏠 *44 Causeway Road, Bushmills BT57 8SU. Open daily. ☎ 028 2073 1855; Fax 028 2073 2537; causewaytic@ hotmail.com; www.northantrim.com*

Adjacent Sights: See ANTRIM, GLENS OF ANTRIM, LOUGH NEAGH, PORTRUSH

Background

The Giant's Causeway is the most dramatic of a whole series of similar geological features to be found all along this coastline. They were the result of a huge volcanic eruption some 60 million years ago which affected not only northeast Ireland but also western Scotland (Fingal's Cave), the Faroes, Iceland and Greenland. A succession of lava flows exuded from fissures in the chalk mantle covering the area, solidifying into layers of hard basalt which cracked as they contracted, forming masses of adjoining columns; the majority are hexagonal in shape although some have four, five, seven, eight and even nine sides.

Most of the legends associated with the Causeway depict it of course to be the work of giants, in particular of the Ulster warrior Finn McCool. One version has him falling passionately in love with a Scottish giantess and constructing a land bridge in order to make his way across the sea to claim her. In another he builds the causeway to facilitate a trial of strength with another giant from the far side of the water, the fierce Benandonner; Finn soon defeats his rival, and as the latter flees home, the causeway sinks beneath him.

The Causeway was brought to the attention of a wider world by the publication in 1693 of a description of it by the Royal Society. In the middle of the 18C it was depicted in a pair of charming views, now in the Ulster Museum, by the Dublin artist Susanna Drury. Her works were engraved and circulated widely abroad, arousing intense speculation among British and French geologists about the origins of this extraordinary natural phenomenon.

Walking About

Giant's Causeway★★★ ①

The modern Visitor Centre has an excellent video and exhibition about the Causeway and the coast generally. *(NT) (&) Causeway: Open daily. Wear appropriate outdoor footwear. Bus shuttle to Causeway (15min): & Operates during the season every 15min; £1.20; minibus with hoist available. Visitor Centre: Open daily, 10am-5pm. Audio-*

EARLY TOURISM

In the early days visitors to the Causeway travelled by boat or on horseback. Not everyone was impressed; in 1814 Walter Scott objected to being plied with "souvenirs", and in 1842 Thackeray longed to escape and be back in Pall Mall! Numbers greatly increased with the advent of the railway line from Belfast to Portrush. In 1883 a hydroelectric narrow-gauge tramway, powered by the River Bushmills, was built from Portrush to Bushmills and extended to the Causeway in 1887; it closed in 1949 unable to compete with road transport.

Some people came on day trips from Belfast; others stayed in one of the two hotels or the nearby boarding-houses.

The Causeway swarmed with unofficial guides who repeated fantastic legends about the formation of the Causeway and invented fanciful names for the different features.

*visual show (12min; 5 languages; £1).
Guided tour of Causeway: May-Aug;
otherwise by appointment. Parking
(£5). Tearoom. Tourist information, accommodation booking service and Bureau de Change.* ☎ *028 2073 1582/1159
(Visitor Centre);* ☎ *028 2073 1582
(NT office); Fax 028 2073 2963;
causewaytic@hotmail.com;
giantscauseway@ntrust.org.uk;
www.nationaltrust.org.uk*

The Causeway proper extends from
the foot of the cliffs into the sea like
a sloping pavement. Its mass of
hexagonal columns has been divided by the action of the waves into
three sections: the Little Causeway,
the Middle Causeway and the
Grand Causeway. The columns
themselves are split horizontally,
forming concave and convex sur-
faces. The individual features have
been given fanciful local names :
the **Wishing Well** (1) was a natural
freshwater spring in the Little
Causeway; the **Wishing Chair** (2)
on the Middle Causeway is formed
by a single column, the seat, backed
by a semicircle of taller columns;
the **Giant's Gate** is the natural gap
carrying the coastal path through
the **Tilted Columns** (3).

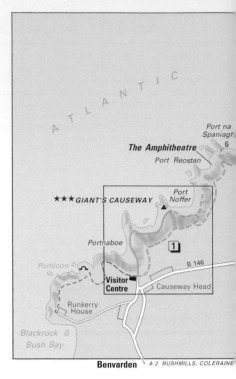

East across Port Noffer the columns (40ft/12m) of the **Organ** (4) are visible in the
cliff face; the **Chimney Tops** (6) are silhouetted against the skyline.

Causeway Coast Way ②

From the headland known as Weir's Snout, there is a view across Port Ganny
(E) to the Causeway and down into Portnaboe *(W)* where a volcanic dike, known
as the Camel's Back, is visible in the sea beyond the slipway where early visitors to the Causeway used to land. Aird Snout gives a bird's-eye view of the
Causeway.

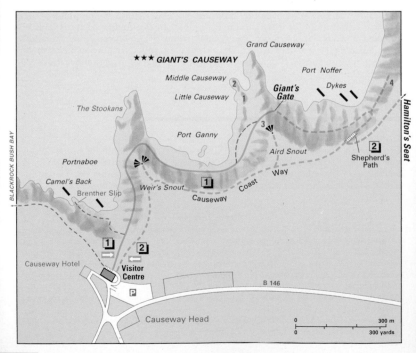

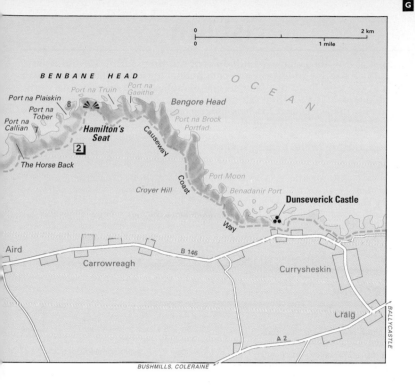

After Port Noffer comes Port Reostan, where the curved columns of the **Harp** (5), a product of the first lava flow, are set in a natural **amphitheatre**. The next headland is distinguished by the **Chimney Tops** (6), three rock stacks formed by the second lava flow. Through a passage in the rocks the path enters Port Na Spaniagh where the *Gerona*, a galleass of the Spanish Armada, was wrecked in 1588 with no survivors; the treasures recovered by diving on the wreck in 1968 are now in the Ulster Museum in Belfast. Beyond the next headland, the Horse Back, lies Port na Callian; the further promontory consists of the **King and his Nobles** (7), a file of figures apparently riding in from the sea.

Above the **Horseshoe** (8) in the rocks is **Hamilton's Seat** on Benbane Head. It is named after Dr William Hamilton who published his *Letters concerning the Northern Coast of Antrim* in 1786, and is a perfect place from which to survey the geological formations and admire the **view★★**, which on a clear day reaches to the mountains of Donegal *(W)*, and to Rathlin Island and in Scotland the Mull of Kintyre *(E)*.

The clifftop path continues east to **Dunseverick Castle** *(also accessible by road (B 146) from Bushmills)*. On their craggy promontory, separated from the mainland by two defiles, the scanty ruins of Dunseverick belie their past importance. The ancient kingdom of Dalriada, which encompassed not only Antrim but also Argyll in Scotland, was ruled from here, and this was the point at which one of the great roads radiating out from the Hill of Tara reached the sea.

The Giant's Causeway *painted c 1740 by S Drury*

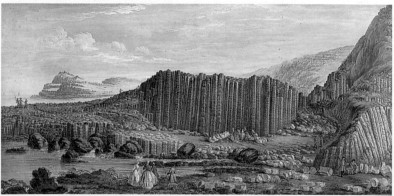

429

Lisburn

Forming part of the extensive built-up area running southwest from Belfast, Lisburn is a sizeable industrial and commercial town. It stands on the River Lagan at the very heart of Ulster's linen-manufacturing district, and in the 19C produced half the linen woven in the province. The Huguenot Louis Crommelin made Lisburn his headquarters when he was appointed Linen Overseer of Ireland by William III.

In 1707 most of the town was destroyed by fire, except for the Assembly Rooms at the top of the market square.

Location

Population 42 110 - Michelin Atlas p 99 and Map 712 – O, N 4 – Co Antrim.
Lisburn (Lios Na Gcearrbhach) is on the Belfast to Armagh road, A 3, and skirted to the S by M 1.
🅑 Irish Linen Centre, Lisburn BT28 1AG. Open Mon-Sat, 9.30am-5pm. ☎ 028 9266 0038; Fax 028 9260 7889; lisburn@nitic.net; www.lisburn.gov.uk; www.discovernorthernireland.com
🅑 The Courthouse, The Square, Hillsborough BT26 6AG. Open daily, 9am (2pm Sun) to 5.30pm (6pm Sun). ☎ 028 9268 9717; Fax 028 9268 9773; hillsborough@nitic.net.
Adjacent Sights: See BELFAST, NEWRY, DOWNPATRICK, STRANGFORD LOUGH.

Directory

SIGHTSEEING

Irish Linen Tour – *Guided tour (group bookings only) all year (Jul, limited availability). Prices on request. Booking essential. Full tour includes McConvilles in Dromore, a traditional flax farm and water-powered scutching mill (demonstration of scutching), the Irish Linen Centre in Lisburn and a local linen factory.*
☎ 028 4062 3322; Fax 028 4062 3114; banbridge@nitic.net; www.banbridge.com.tourism

Walks – *Lagan Canal towpath walk from Lisburn to Belfast (9mi/14.5km).*

Worth a Visit

Irish Linen Centre and Lisburn Museum★

 ♿ Open Mon-Sat, 9.30am-5pm. Leaflet (3 languages). Audioguide available. Speciality linen and crafts shop. Coffee shop. Loop system. ☎ 028 9266 3377; Fax 028 9267 2624; www.irishlinencentre@lisburn.gov.uk

Linen hand-loom

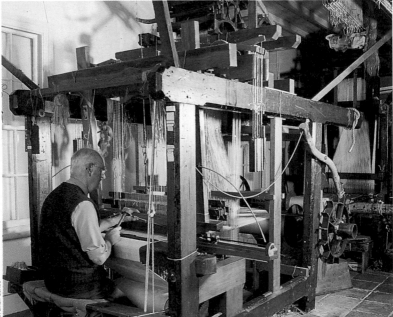

Irish Linen Centre

Lisburn's Assembly Rooms have been adapted and extended to house the town's museum as well as extensive and attractive displays, which tell the story of the area's linen industry from its origins in the 17C to the present. The emphasis is not only on technique, but on the beauty and adaptability of the product and on the lives of the people involved in its manufacture. There are reminders of the role of linen in the ancient world in the form of material from Tutankhamun's tomb. In the Middle Ages Irish flax was exported to England to be woven into cloth. Then in the 17C English and Scottish weavers helped establish the weaving industry, eventually under the direction of Crommelin, whose portrait hangs in the main hall of the Assembly Rooms. There are live demonstrations of spinning and weaving, a re-creation of a family at work in a late 18C to early 19C spinner's cottage, and a vivid reconstruction of the weavers' toil in "Webster's", a hypothetical 19C mill, where conditions, however harsh, were nevertheless preferable to life on the farm –

'I'll ne'er despise the weaving trade,
The shuttle's lighter than the spade".

John Dicky (1818).

Christchurch Cathedral

Services: Sun, 9.30am, 11am, 6.30pm. Key available from the Sexton's House in the church grounds. ☎ 028 9260 2400 (Office), 028 9266 2865 (Rectory); sam@lisburncathedral.org.uk; www.lisburncathedral.org.uk

The town is dominated by the cathedral, a fine example of the Gothic style adopted by the Planters (1623, reconstructed in 1708); in the graveyard *(south side)* is the Crommelin tomb.

Lisburn Castle Park

North of the cathedral is the site of the **castle**, now a small public park enclosed within the surviving walls; from the parapet there is a good view of the Lagan winding past below.

> **SIR RICHARD WALLACE**
> From 1873 to 1885 the MP for Lisburn was Sir Richard Wallace, owner of the Wallace Collection in London, whose mansion, built in imitation of Hertford House in London, stands opposite the entrance to the Castle Park.

Excursions

Hillsborough★

2.5mi/4km S of Lisburn by minor roads

This charming little town acquired its Georgian aspect under Wills Hill (1718-92), created Marquess of Downshire in 1789. Visitors stroll its sloping main street, attracted by cafés, craft shops and boutiques.

Hillsborough Castle, begun in 1760 by Wills Hill, stands at the top of the hill on the west side of the square. It is a neo-Classical red-brick edifice whose most outstanding feature is its magnificent 18C wrought-iron screen with gates, brought here from Richill Castle in Co Armagh. The building is, however, less famous for its architecture than for the role it plays in the life of the province; formerly the residence of the Governor of Northern Ireland, it is now used for state functions, its name associated particularly with the Anglo-Irish Agreement of 1985.

Court House – *(HM) Open Apr-Sep, Mon-Sat, 9am-5.30pm (also Jul-Aug, Sun, 2-6pm); Oct-Mar, Mon-Sat, 9am-5.30pm ☎ 028 9268 3285; liz.dennison@doeni.gov.uk, www.ehsni.gov.uk*

The 18C courthouse, which also served as a market, now contains the Tourist Information Centre and a fascinating exhibition on justice and law, which makes thought-provoking comparisons between ancient Brehon Law and modern penal policy.

Hillsborough Fort★ – *(HM) Open Apr-Sep, Tue-Sun and Bank Hol Mon, 10am (2pm Sun) to 7pm; Oct-Mar, Tue-Sun, 10am (Sun 2pm) to 4pm. Parking. ☎ 028 9268 3285; liz.dennison@doeni.gov.uk; www.ehsni.gov.uk*

The gates on the east side of the square open into a drive leading to the fort, which was begun c 1630 to command the chief roads in Co Down. Its builder and first commander was Col Arthur Hill, who gave his name to the town. The fort is laid out as a square (270 x 270ft82 x 82m) with a spear-shaped bastion at each corner to provide flanking fire from heavy cannon. Colonel Hill's descendant Wills Hill was responsible for the delightful gazebo over the northeast entrance and for the miniature Gothic fort in the northwest rampart.

The central ditch is part of a circular trench revealed by excavations (1966-69) which suggest that the site had been occupied since c 500-1000.

St Malachy's Church – The Anglican church, built in 1662 on the site of its predecessor (1636-41), was enlarged (1760-73) by Wills Hill, who added the main tower and spire and the two subsidiary towers, and furnished the interior with Irish oak Gothic woodwork and box pews which are raised in the transepts. Sir Hamilton Harty (1879-1941), the conductor, whose father was church organist, is buried in the churchyard.

Rowallane Gardens*

10mi/16km E of Hillsborough by B 178 towards Carryduff, B 6 to Saintfield and A 7 S. (NT) & Open daily, 10am-8pm (4pm Oct-Apr). Closed Christmas to New Year. £3. Dogs on leads only. Parking. Wheelchair available. ☎ 028 9751 0131; Fax 028 9751 1242; rowallane@ntrust.org.uk; uroest@smtp.ntrust.org.uk

The gardens (52 acres/21ha), which are famous for the spectacular spring colours of their massed azaleas and rhododendrons, are the work of a master plantsman, Hugh Armitage Moore, who inherited the estate in 1903. During the next half-century he turned the drumlins with their light acid soil into a natural garden: a rock garden on a natural outcrop of stone; patches of wild flowers to attract butterflies; a spring ground and a stream ground; walled garden with fuchsias and shrub roses. In the old wood the stone walls between the original fields are still standing. The pleasure grounds behind the house (National Trust headquarters) extend in a great grass sweep to a small pond.

Walled Garden, Rowallane

Tour

LAGAN VALLEY

9mi/14.5km – half a day

The River Lagan follows a winding course between Lisburn and Belfast, before discharging into Belfast Lough. It is one of the most fertile areas in Northern Ireland, and its banks, with their woods and their succession of landscaped estates now form a fine Regional Park, a great asset to the people of the surrounding built-up areas. Parallel to the river runs the **Lagan Canal**, which was built to bring coal from Coalisland via Lough Neagh to Belfast; ironically it was mostly used to carry coal imported through Belfast. Under the Lagan Navigation Company, founded in 1843, it became Ulster's most successful waterway but its use declined in the 1930s; it was closed in 1958 and its course west from Lisburn to Moira turned into a motorway.

From Lisburn take A 1 N; in Hilden turn right (sign).

Hilden Brewery Visitor Centre

Open daily, 10am-5pm. Guided tour of brewery (40min) daily at 11.30am; also May-Sep, daily at 2.30pm. £4.50 including tasting. Audio-visual show. Tap Room restaurant. Parking. ☎ 028 9266 3863; Fax 028 9260 3511

The brewery, one of the last real-ale establishments in Ireland, occupies a Georgian house once visited by William Wordsworth. An exhibition in the restaurant covers the history of beer-drinking and brewing, Hilden Village and the brewery building. The guided tours of the brewery take place before and after lunch.

Continue N on A 1 and turn right under the railway bridge onto B 103 to Lambeg.

Lambeg

This attractive village with its delightful suspension bridge over the river has given its name to the huge drums (over 30lb/14kg) which are played in the Orange Day parades. Brightly painted, almost as big as the drummers themselves, and with an intimidatingly loud beat, they were introduced to Ireland from the Netherlands by William III's army.

Continue on B 103 to Drumbeg. Car park (left) opposite the church.

Drumbeg Church

Grounds: Open daily, 9am-5pm. Church: Open by appointment.

Another picturesque village, little Drumbeg has a church on a knoll, reached via a magnificent lych gate and arches of yew trees. The present church (1870) is cruciform with a shallow apsidal chancel and an interesting wooden roof. The entrance porch contains a stone, marked "A Free Howse 1675", to which is attached a touching love story retold alongside.

Continue N on B 103.

Dixon Park

Car park. With woods, meadows and a tranquil Japanese garden, the park is nevertheless most famous for the rose trial grounds (11 acres/4ha) which contain about 30 000 roses. The final judging of the trial roses takes place during **Belfast Rose Week** (mid-July) which attracts breeders from many parts of the world.

Continue N on B 103. At the roundabout turn right onto the dual carriageway and right again.

Malone House

Car park. ♿ *Open Mon-Sat, 9am-5pm. Closed 25 Dec. Parking. Restaurant.* ☎ *028 9068 1246; Fax 028 9068 2197; mhreception@malonehouse.co.uk; www.malonehouse.co.uk*

In 1603 James I granted the Barnett demesne to the Sir Arthur Chichester, whose descendants became the Earls of Donegall, one of the country's great landed families, owners, among much other valuable property, of Belfast itself. Since Sir Arthur's day, three houses have occupied the hilltop overlooking the Lagan crossing. The present house, restored after a bomb attack in 1976, was built in the late 1820s and was probably designed by William Wallace Legge, who later bought the lease of the whole demesne. It is now owned by the City of Belfast, and is used for meetings, conferences and lectures.

The plain and unpretentious exterior belies the elegant and spacious interior. From the upper windows there is a magnificent view over the garden to the sloping wooded grounds

In the valley, beside the modern road bridge spanning the Lagan, are the five stone arches of **Shaw's Bridge** (1711), which replaced an oak bridge built by Captain Shaw in 1655 so that Cromwell's cannon could cross the river.

On leaving the park turn right; after crossing the bridge turn right; take the road along the south bank to Edenderry (sign).

Edenderry

The road ends beside the river among five terraces of red-brick cottages and a chapel. This fascinating example of a 19C industrial village was built for the workers in the now-derelict weaving mill.

Return to the last T junction; turn right onto Ballynahatty Road; after 1mi/1.6km turn right (sign "Giant's Ring").

Giant's Ring

Car park. The Ring is a huge bank of gravel and boulders enclosing a circle (600ft/183m in diameter) with a megalithic chambered grave in the middle. Its purpose is unknown but it may have been a place of assembly or worship; in the 18C it found a new vocation as a racecourse.

Londonderry ★

Northern Ireland's second city stands close to the border with the Republic in a fine setting on the broad River Foyle, the rounded Sperrin Mountains to the southeast, the wild heights of Donegal to the west and north. Almost uniquely in the British Isles, it has kept its defensive walls, erected in the early 17C when the ancient Irish settlement of Derry became a key stronghold in the English Plantation of Ulster and was renamed Londonderry. One of the flashpoints of the North's Troubles, the scene of the "Bloody Sunday" events of 1972, the city has since undergone something of a revival, with renewed economic growth, vibrant commercial activity, and original visitor attractions.

Location

Population 72 334 - Michelin Atlas p 101 and Map 712 - K 3 - Co Londonderry. Londonderry *(Doire)* is situated on the River Foyle, at the junction of A 2, A 5 and A 6, close to the border and Co Donegal.

Directory

GETTING ABOUT

City of Derry Airport – *At Eglinton.*
Tel 028 7181 0784; Fax 028 7181 1426;
dtierney@coda1.fsnet.co.uk;
www.cityofderryairport.com

SIGHTSEEING

Walled City Guided Walk – *Operates (1hr
30min) Jul-Aug, Mon-Fri at 11.15am and
3.15pm; Sep-Jun, Mon-Fri at 2.30pm. £4.*
☎ *028 7126 7284; Fax 028 7137 7992;*
info@derryvisitor.com;
www.derryvisitor.com

ENTERTAINMENT

Millennium Forum – *Newmarket Street,
BT48 6EB* – ☎ *028 7126 4455,
028 7126 4426 (admin);
Fax 028 7127 2799;
info@millenniumforum.co.uk;
www.millenniumforum.co.uk* –
Drama to dance, comedy to musicals
and light entertainment
to children's shows.

The Playhouse – *5-7 Artillery Street,
BT48 6RG* – ☎ *028 7126 8027;
Fax 028 7126 1884;
thederryplayhouse@hotmail.com* – Local,
national and international theatre, dance,
visual arts.

SHOPPING

Craft Village – *Off Shipquay Street.* A
web of picturesque alleyways, centred on a
little square and lined with a variety of
traditionally styled buildings housing cafés
and specialist shops.

SPORTS AND LEISURE

Greyhound racing.

EVENTS AND FESTIVALS

**Scoil Samhraidh Cholm Cille Summer
Schools** – Irish history, arts and culture, Irish
language classes, traditional music workshops,
poetry, storytelling, painting, walking tours, bus
tours and visit to Donegal Gaeltacht *(early June)*

Hallowe'en in Derry City – Spectacular
fireworks display against the backdrop of the
River Foyle and other special events centred
around the Hallowe'en Carnival *(31 October)*

TRACING ANCESTORS

Research service (fee-paying) for those tracing
their roots in County Derry and the
Inishowen Peninsula in Co Donegal –
*Genealogy Centre, Heritage Library, 14
Bishop Street, Londonderry BT48 6PW. Open
Mon-Fri, 9am-5pm. Tel 028 7126 9792; Fax
028 7136 0921; niancestors@btclick.com;
www.Irishroots.net*

🛈 *44 Foyle Street, Londonderry BT 48 6AT. Open Jul-Sep, daily; Apr-Jun, Mon-Sat;
Oct-Mar, Mon-Fri.* ☎ *028 7126 7284; Fax 028 7137 7992; info@derryvisitor.com;
www.derryvisitor.com*
*Adjacent Sights: See BUNCRANA, DONEGAL COAST, DONEGAL GLENS,
PORTRUSH, SPERRIN MOUNTAINS.*

Background

Monastic Foundation – According to tradition, the monastery at Derry (whose
Irish name *Doire* means "oak grove") was founded in 546 by St Columba. Derry was
occupied by the English in 1565 and 1600. During the four-month rebellion of Sir
Cahir O'Doherty in 1608, his forces attacked and captured Derry but could not sus-
tain their momentum after his death at Kilmacrenan in Donegal.

The Irish Society – Under the scheme for the colonisation of Ulster *(see p 461)* with
settlers from Britain, The Honourable The Irish Society was constituted by Royal
Charter in 1613 to plant the County of Coleraine, which was renamed County
Londonderry. Most of the land was parcelled out to the 12 main livery companies
of London but the towns of Derry and Coleraine were retained by the Society,
which still uses its income from fisheries and property to support projects of
general benefit to the community.

Siege of Londonderry – In the uncer-
tainty created by James II's flight to
France and William of Orange's landing
in Devon, 13 Derry apprentices locked
the city gates against a Jacobite regiment
under the Earl of Antrim sent to garrison
the town in December 1688. The citizens
declared for William and received an
influx of supporters although food supplies were low. In March James II landed
in Ireland with an army of 20 000 and in
April besieged the city, erecting a boom
across the river which held the relief
ships at bay for seven weeks.

The Scottish commander of the city,
Robert Lundy, favoured capitulation to
what seemed an overwhelming force

LUNDY

With a military man's eye to the likely outcome of
a battle, the Scottish Colonel Lundy advised the
citizens of Londonderry to avoid bloodshed and
destruction and surrender to the superior Jacobite
army. In this he utterly underestimated their fighting spirit; he was relieved of his command and
fled the city in disguise. His successors, Major
Henry Baker and the Reverend George Walker,
rallied their fellow-Protestants and organised the
resistance which was to prove so effective. Ever
after, the term "Lundy" has been synonymous
with cowardice and treachery, and the wretched
colonel's effigy is ceremoniously burned during
the Apprentice Boys' annual parade in August.

LONDONDERRY

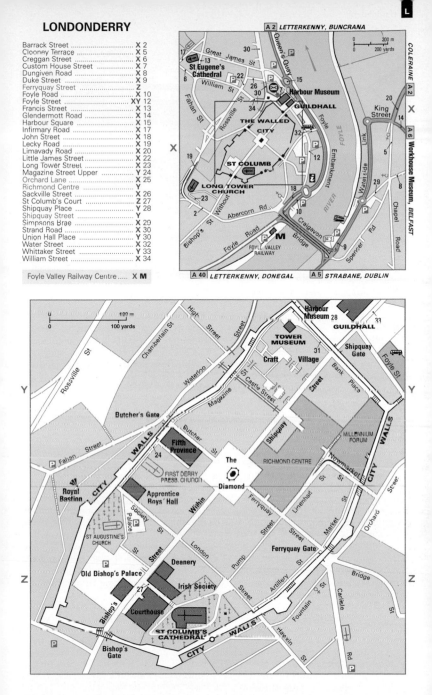

but advocates of resistance deposed him and took command *(see below)*. On 10 July a shell bearing terms for surrender was fired into the town by the besiegers; the defenders raised a crimson flag on the Royal Bastion to signify "No surrender", a slogan which continues to resonate with Northern Ireland's Protestant population. The siege lasted 15 weeks during which the 30 000 people crammed within the walls were reduced to eating cats, dogs, mice, rats and leather; thousands of them died of starvation. On 28 July 1689 the boom was broken and the relief ships sailed through to the quay. Three days later the Jacobite army retreated.

Sectors of the City – The character of the Plantation city changed drastically in the 19C. Migrants flocked here from all over Catholic Ireland, and by 1900 Protestants were a minority, though careful management of the boundaries of electoral districts and the allocation of public housing continued to deny Catholics control of the city council. While the traditional industry of shirt-making employed many women, male unemployment was rife, and housing conditions – notably in the Catholic

Ferryquay Gate

Bogside district – were among the worst in the United Kingdom. The city erupted into riot in 1968, the "Battle of the Bogside" was fought in 1969, and on 30 January 1972, "Bloody Sunday", paratroopers shot dead fourteen civilians in the violent aftermath of a banned protest march. In the years since, despite relative calm, sectarian boundaries have become more pronounced, with Protestants tending to withdraw from the west bank of the Foyle and settle in the Waterside district on the east bank.

Walking About

City Walls and Gates★★

(& *except at Bishop's Gate) Open daily. Information panels. Guided walking tour available.* ☎ *028 7126 7284 (Tourist Information Centre); Fax 028 7137 7992; info@ derryvisitor.com; www.derryvisitor.com.* The walls (1mi/1.6km long) enclosing the Plantation town were built from 1613 to 1618 by The Irish Society. Their survival in a near-perfect state of preservation is remarkable, but despite their effective role in more than one siege, they are no masterpiece of military engineering, being potentially far too exposed to gunfire from warships in the Foyle. It is now possible to complete the circuit of the walls on foot, admiring the various gateways, bastions, watchtowers and artillery pieces, as well as the splendid views.

The easiest point at which to join the wall walk is on the east side where the walls are pierced by Newmarket Street; walk clockwise.

Ferryquay Gate was the gate slammed shut by the 13 Apprentice Boys in the face of the Jacobite troops at the beginning of the 1688/89 siege.

The wall walk provides a good view of St Columb's Cathedral *(see Worth a Visit).*

The present **Bishop's Gate** was built on the site of the original gate as a triumphal arch on the 100th anniversary of the siege in 1789.

From here there is a fine view down **Bishop's Street Within**, the city's most distinguished thoroughfare with its cluster of fine late-18C to early-19C buildings: the red-brick Bishop's Palace (now the Freemasons' Hall), built by the Earl Bishop *(see p 454)*, which stands on the site of Colonel Henry Baker's house; the Greek Revival Courthouse in pale sandstone; the Irish Society's headquarters (1764); and the elegant Deanery.

The Royal Bastion is the point where Col Michelburn hoisted the crimson flag to signify "No Surrender" at the beginning of the great siege. The bastion commands an extensive view over the Bogside.

The **Apprentice Boys' Hall** stands on the site of the original Shambles.

The **Butcher's Gate** opening into Butcher Street leads into **The Diamond**, the characteristic focal point of a Plantation town, where the four main thoroughfares meet. Once the site of the Town Hall, Derry's Diamond is now graced by a war memorial. The city is laid out on a (slightly bent) grid and the street pattern is well preserved. Near the Butcher's Gate on the right is the Fifth Province *(See Worth a Visit).* The northernmost corner is marked by the entrance to the Tower Museum *(See Worth a Visit).*

The **Shipquay Gate** is surmounted by five of the cannon which defended the city during the siege. From here the street mounts steeply towards the Diamond, lined with several imposing buildings and basement bars.

Worth a Visit

WITHIN THE WALLS

St Columb's Cathedral★

Open summer, Mon-Sat, 9am-5pm; winter, 9am-1pm and 2-4pm. £1. Audio-visual shows. Brochure (5 languages). ☎ *028 7126 7313; dean@derry.anglican.org; www.stcolumbscathedral.org*

The fortified Plantation city was provided with a formidable battlemented cathedral within a few decades of its foundation. The decision to build was taken in 1613, construction started in 1628 and the late-Perpendicular edifice was completed in 1634, the first cathedral to be built in the British Isles since the Reformation. The 191ft/58m spire was added in the early 19C.

The outstanding architectural feature is the superb open-timbered **nave roof**, which is supported on corbels carved to represent the Bishops of Derry from 1634 to 1867. The Revd George Walker, city governor during the Siege, is also honoured in this way, and there is much else in the cathedral of local historical interest.

The **mortar shell** containing terms for surrender which was fired into the city during the Siege is preserved in the porch. The window in the Choir Vestry *(right)* depicts the Closing of the Gates in 1688, the Relief of the City in 1689 and the Centenary Celebrations in 1789.

The **bishop's throne** is a splendid 18C mahogany Chinese Chippendale chair, probably given by the flamboyant Earl Bishop *(see p 454)*.

On the chancel arch above the pulpit is a **Cross of Nails**, a gift from Coventry Cathedral signifying peace and reconciliation.

The **chapter house** *(for access ask the Verger)* was built in 1910 and contains further fascinating items including the padlocks and keys of the original city gates, Governor Walker's sword, fragments of Col Michelburn's crimson flag, and a pair of duelling pistols belonging to the Earl Bishop.

Tower Museum★

Open Jul-Aug, daily, 10am (2pm Sun) to 5pm, Sep-Jun, Tue-Sat and Bank Hol Mon, 10am-5pm. £4.20. ☎ *028 7137 2411; Fax 028 7137 7633; tower.museum@ derrycity.gov.uk*

The medieval-style modern building houses an excellent display about the history of the city of Derry using historical artefacts, wall panels and audio-visual and theatrical devices. Visitors are put in a receptive frame of mind by entering the museum along a brick-built tunnel paved with cobblestones, a convincing replica of the underground passageways which connected the city's buildings in the 17C. The exhibits deal comprehensively with Derry's monastic origins, the 17C Plantation, the Siege and its aftermath, 19C emigration, the Partition of Ireland, the Second World War and the post-war Troubles.

Children's Street Parade

Fifth Province

Butcher Street.   *Open Mon-Fri. Show: at 11.30am and 2.30pm. £3. Public parking.*
028 7137 3177

Embedded in the modern Calgach conference and office centre is this ambitious and imaginative evocation of the history and culture of the Celts. A wide variety of contemporary techniques, including exciting voyages by module and space shuttle, give magical life to the past and demonstrate its relevance to present-day people of Irish descent.

BEYOND THE WALLS

Long Tower Church★

Open Mon-Sat, 7.30am-9pm, Sun, 8am-6.30pm; longtower@aol.com; www.longtower parish.com

This is the oldest Roman Catholic church in Derry (1784-86). The present building has a lovely Rococo interior with extensive steeply sloping galleries. It stands on the site of Templemore, a great medieval church built in 1164, and its name recalls the Long Tower (10C), all that remained when the medieval church was destroyed by an explosion in 1567. From the churchyard there is a fine view of the Royal Bastion.

Guildhall★

  Open Mon-Fri, 9am-5pm. Closed Bank Hol Mon. 028 7137 7335; Fax 028 7137 7964

The Guildhall, which has twice been severely damaged – in 1908 by fire and in 1972 by bombs – was erected in 1890 in the late-Gothic style with a loan from the Irish Society. The river façade is richly ornamented; the corner tower contains a large four-faced clock. A reproduction of Follingby's painting of the Relief of Derry decorates the marble-faced vestibule. The numerous stained-glass windows, the work of Ulster craftsmen, make up a more or less complete visual history of the city, with London scenes on the stairs and early views of Derry in the Great Hall, which is panelled in oak and has a richly decorated ceiling.

The Guildhall from the City walls

NITB, Belfast

Harbour Museum

Open Mon-Fri, 10am-1pm and 2-4.30pm.   *028 7137 7331; Fax 028 7137 7633; museums@ derrycity.gov.uk*

The grandiose 19C building, which once housed the meetings of the Londonderry Port and Harbour Commissioners, is now a museum with paintings, models and all kinds of maritime memorabilia. The dominant exhibit is the largest curragh ever built, constructed in 1963 to re-create the legendary voyage of St Columba to Iona.

St Eugene's Cathedral

Open Mon-Sat, 7.30am (8.30am Sat) to 9pm, Sun, 6.30am-7pm.   *028 7126 2894, 7136 5712; Fax 028 7137 7494; steugenesderry@uk.online.uk*

Northwest of the city centre, between a district of elegant Georgian terraces and the green peace of Brooke Park, stands the Roman Catholic Cathedral, which was dedicated to St Eugene in 1873 by Bishop Keely, to whom the great east window is a memorial. The building was designed in the Gothic Revival style by JJ McCarthy in 1853 and finally completed with a cross on the top of the spire in 1903.

Foyle Valley Railway Centre

  Telephone for times. Train excursion £3. Parking. Refreshments.   *028 7126 5234; info@foylevalleyrailway.co.uk; www.foylevalleyrailway.co.uk*

Londonderry was once the focal point of no fewer than four railway companies, including the Londonderry and Enniskillen, "possibly the least efficient if not the most dangerous railway ever to operate in Ireland". Here too was the terminus of the County Donegal Railway, which was the most extensive of all the Irish narrow-gauge systems (125mi/200km). The Centre has steam engines, coaches, an old goods wagon, signals, signs and luggage. Excursion trains drawn by diesel car (1934) operate on a stretch of narrow-gauge line (2mi/3.2km) beside the Foyle. It is proposed to extend the line upstream to St Johnston (9mi/14.5km).

Workhouse Museum★

23 Glendermott Road, Waterside. Open Mon-Thu and Sat, 10am-4.30pm; also Jul-Aug, Fri, same times. ☎ 028 7131 8328 (James Coyle).

The city workhouse, designed by George Wilkinson and opened in 1840 with 800 inmates, now houses a library on the ground floor and a museum on the two floors above. The first floor has excellent displays and film footage about the important role played by the city in the Second World War, and particularly in the Battle of the Atlantic. On the upper floor, the grim 19C workhouse conditions have been re-created; an original display compares the 1845-49 Irish famine with the modern famines of the Horn of Africa.

Mount Stewart★★★

The combination on the eastern shore of Strangford Lough of magnificent formal gardens, extensive parkland, and the palatial mansion which was the home of one of the most eminent and politically influential families of the Ascendancy, make Mount Stewart one of Ireland's premier visitor attractions.

Location

Michelin Atlas p 99 and Map 712 – P 4 – Co Down.
Mount Stewart on the eastern shore of Strangford Lough is 5mi/8km SE of Newtownards by A 20.
🚹 *31 Regent Street, Newtownards BT23 4AD. Open Mon-Sat. ☎ 028 9182 6846; Fax 028 9182 6681; tourism@ards-council.gov.uk; www.kingdomsofdown.com*
Adjacent Sights: See BANGOR, DOWNPATRICK, STRANGFORD LOUGH.

SOLDIERS AND STATESMEN

Mount Stewart owes its name to the Stewarts, a Scottish family granted land in the Inishowen peninsula at the time of the Ulster Plantation, who settled on the banks of Strangford Lough in 1774. They acquired vast fortunes, not only through landed property but through ownership of immensely profitable coal mines in northern England. Robert Stewart was made Marquess of Londonderry in 1816 but the best-known member of the family is his elder son, Lord Castlereagh (1769-1822), who became leader of the House of Commons and as Foreign Secretary represented the United Kingdom at the Congress of Vienna in 1815. Entertaining the British Establishment in a great town mansion in Park Lane in London and a string of country houses in England as well as at Mount Stewart, the family's political influence flourished throughout the 19C and into the 20C, when they were staunch leaders of the Unionist cause. As well as creating Mount Stewart's incomparable gardens, Edith, the 7th Marchioness, was one of the great political hostesses of the interwar period.

Walking About

(NT) ♿ House: Open Jun-Aug, daily, noon-6pm; May and Sep, Wed-Mon; April and Oct, Sat-Sun, Bank Hol Mon; Mar, certain weekends. Guided tour (45min). Formal gardens: Open Mar, same as house; Apr-Sep, daily, 11am-6pm; Oct-Dec, Sat-Sun, 11am-5pm. Lakeside garden and walks: May-Sep, 10am-8pm (4pm Oct-Apr). House and gardens £4.75; gardens only £3.75. Parking. Restaurant. Wheelchairs and powered buggy, sympathetic hearing scheme. ☎ 028 4278 8387, 8487; Fax 028 4278 8569; mountstewart@ntrust.org.uk; www.nationaltrust.org.uk

Gardens

The old desmesne acquired by the Stewarts was soon planted up with fine parkland trees, creating the sheltered conditions favourable to the growing in the 20C of the exotic trees and shrubs favoured by Edith, Lady Londonderry. In linking the house to its surroundings with a series of inspired formal gardens, she took the advice of the great architect Sir Edwin Lutyens and his garden designer, Gertrude Jekyll, but was a confident planner and knowledgeable horticulturalist in her own right. She began work in 1921, an additional motive being to provide work for the unemployed in the aftermath of the First World War.

The huge Irish yews near the house look down on the **Italian Garden**, its straightforward geometrical layout a splendid foil for a superb array of herbaceous plants; it is enclosed at the east end by the **Dodo Terrace**, which is decorated with droll stone animals, recalling the nicknames, not always complimentary, given by Lady Londonderry to some of her London set. To the south is the **Spanish Garden** designed after a ceiling pattern in the Temple of the Winds (*see below*). The **Sunk Garden** honours Gertrude Jekyll with its subtle blending of orange, blue and yellow flowering plants. The theme of the **Shamrock Garden**, named for its shape, is Ireland: it has an ingenious topiary harp and a bed in the shape and colour of the Red Hand of Ulster.

Beyond the formal gardens, paths lead through the parkland which Lady Londonderry enhanced with trees and shrubs from all over the world, particularly Australasia; the eucalyptus collection is one of the finest anywhere. The hill which overlooks the **lake**, created in 1846-48, provides a superb **view** over Strangford Lough. A genuine but miniature Japanese pagoda stands beside the **Ladies' Walk**, an old path to the dairy and kitchen gardens.

J Cornish/National Trust Photographic Library

Italian Garden

House

The Londonderrys' sumptuous residence was built in two stages. George Dance was responsible for the west wing, completed in 1805, while the main part of the house, constructed between 1825 and 1835, was the work of William Vitruvius Morrison, who produced a symmetrical design in the same dark stone with lighter dressings and added a balustrade at roof level to create a sense of unity. A giant Ionic portico wide enough to take a carriage screens the entrance.

The interior is richly decorated with portraits of the family, Irish and English furniture, collections of porcelain, and Classical sculpture. Mount Stewart has one of the finest paintings in Ireland, *Hambletonian* by George Stubbs, which shows this prize-winning racehorse being rubbed down after a triumph at Newmarket; it hangs in Morrison's galleried entrance hall with its stained-glass dome, one of the house's outstanding spaces. Others include Dance's magnificent stairway, also domed, and the Music Room with its inlaid wooden floor in oak, mahogany and bog-fir. The Dining Room has portraits of William of Orange and his general, Schomberg; lining its walls are the 22 Empire-style chairs used by the delegates to the 1815 Congress of Vienna and subsequently presented to Lord Castlereagh, who is honoured by an array of memorabilia in another room. The spacious Drawing Room was redecorated by the 7th Marchioness, and is much as she left it, with a rich and varied mixture of furniture of different periods.

Temple of the Winds

30min there and back on foot from the house or 200yd/183m SE by road to the car park and 4min there and back on foot.

Inspired by the Temple of the Winds in Athens, this pleasure pavilion stands on a mound with a fine prospect of Strangford Lough. The view extends over the water to Scrabo Hill, topped by its tower commemorating the 3rd Marquess of Londonderry. The Temple was designed by James "Athenian" Stuart in 1783, and its banqueting room has a superb inlaid wooden floor matching the coffers, scallops and scrolls of the ceiling. The gloomy servants' quarters where meals were assembled are kept well out of sight underground.

Mourne Mountains★★

The highest range in Northern Ireland, rising dramatically from the sea and from the plain of Co Down, these granite mountains reach their summit in Slieve Donard (2 796ft/852m) and extend westwards to Carlingford Lough and north into rolling foothills. The Kingdom of Mourne was the name given to the strip of land between the mountains and the sea, a region of small fields divided by drystone walls where for centuries a life of farming and fishing continued largely undisturbed by external events. Nowadays the mountains and coast are one of the North's favourite holiday areas, with some good beaches and plenty of opportunities for hill walkers and climbers.

Location

Michelin Atlas p 99 and Map 712 – N, O 5 – Co Down.
The Mourne Mountains are bounded by the Newry–Downpatrick road, A 25, and the coast road, A 2.
🖪 *10-14 The Promenade, Newcastle BT33 0AA. Open daily.* ☎ *028 4372 2222; Fax 028 4372 2400; newcastle@nitic.ne; www.newcastle.org*
🖪 *6 Newcastle Street, Kilkeel BT34 4AE. Open Mon-Sat.* ☎ *028 4176 2525; Fax 028 4176 9947*
Adjacent Sights: See DOWNPATRICK, DUNDALK, NEWRY.

Worth a Visit

INLAND

Murlough National Nature Reserve

2mi/3.2km E of Newcastle by A 2. Car park. (NT) Open daily, dawn-dusk. Information Centre: Open (weather permitting) May-Sep, daily, 10am-6pm. Parking £3. ☎ *028 4375 1467; www.nationaltrust.org.uk*
An important site for migratory birds, and with a surprisingly varied plant life, this nature reserve is based on the magnificent sand dunes which have developed between the Carrigs River and Dundrum Bay, and which in places reach a height

Directory

SIGHTSEEING

Mourne Countryside Centre – *91 Central Promenade, Newcastle* – Provides information and organises a programmme of hill walks in the summer months, including the Mourne International Walking Festival *(see below)* – Open Mon-Fri, 9am-5pm; via adjoining offices of Mourne Heritage Trust.
☎ *028 4372 4059; Fax 028 4372 6493; mht@mourne.co.uk;*

WHERE TO STAY

• *Budget*
Drumgooland House – *29 Dunnanew Rd, Seaforde, Downpatrick, BT56 8BN - 2mi/3.2km N by A 24 -* ☎ *028 4481 1956 - Fax 028 4481 1265 - frank.mc_leigh@virgin.net -* 🖪 ✱ *- 3 rm £33.50/57* ☲. This attractive country house stands in a quiet spot in mature grounds. The traditionally furnished, large bedrooms have pleasant views. Many of the guests take advantage of the equestrian centre next door.
Slieve Croob Inn – *119 Clanvaraghan Rd, Castlewellan, BT56 8BN – 5.2mi/8.4km N by A 25 off B 175 -* ☎ *028 4377 1412 - Fax 028 4377 1162 - info@slievecroobinn.com - Closed 25 Dec -* 🖪 *- 7 rm £35/60* ☲ *- Meals £11.40/24.95.* Take the winding road up the mountain and you'll be rewarded with sweeping vistas down to the sea. The bar is the centrepiece of this rustic inn with its

exposed timbers. The bedrooms are simple yet pleasantly decorated.

SPORTS AND LEISURE

There are bathing beaches at Newcastle and Cranfield.
Castle and Islands Park, *Newcastle.* – Swings, slides, Slippery Dip, crazy golf, miniature golf, 9-hole pitch and putt course, tennis courts, boating lake.
Tropicana, *Newcastle.* – Heated outdoor seawater fun pools, giant water slides, bouncy castle, adventure playground, supervised crèche and kiddies' club.
Coco's Indoor Adventure Playground, *Newcastle.* – Snake slides, free fall, an assault course and a soft play activity area.

EVENTS AND FESTIVALS

The **Boley Fair**, a traditional sheep fair, takes place in Hilltown *(Tuesday after 12 July).*
The **Maiden of Mourne Festival** takes place in Warrenpoint with fireworks in the evening *(several days in early August).*
Fiddlers' Green Festival – Folk festival at the picturesque town of Rostrevor – ☎ *028 4173 8738; fiddlers.green@dnet.co.uk; www.fiddlersgreenfestival.com*
Mourne International Walking Festival – *Starting from Newcastle or Warren Point. Last weekend in June, Fri-Sun; £8 per day.*

of 100ft/30m. There are traces of early human habitation as well as a tripod **dolmen** (8ft/2.5m high), which is about 4 000 years old.

Dundrum Castle★

4mi/6.4m E of Newcastle by A 2; in Dundrum turn left uphill to car park. (HM) Open Apr-Sep, Tue-Sun, 10am (2pm Sun) to 7pm; Oct-Mar, Sat-Sun, 10am (2pm Sun) to 4pm. 75p. Guided tour (30min). Parking. ☎ 028 9181 1491; Fax 028 9182 0695; Scrabocp@doeni.gov.uk; www.chsni.gov.uk

The ruins of the castle stand on an attractive grassed and wooded site on a hilltop north of the town, its natural defences supplemented by an impressively deep rock-cut ditch. The castle was begun around 1177, probably by John de Courcy, to command the approach to the Lecale peninsula and Strangford Lough, and from the parapet of the unusual circular keep there are superb **views** of the sea and the surrounding country. The Lower Ward was added between the 13C and 15C; it contains the ruins of a once-grand house built by the Blundell family in the 17C. In place of the usual well, a cistern, cut into the rock and fed by seepage, supplied the castle with water.

Tollymore Forest Park★

♿ *Open daily, 10am-dusk. £2, car £4. Guided tour by appointment. Parking. Café; picnic areas. Fishing.* ☎ *028 4372 2428*

The mansion which was the focal point of this vast landscaped desmesne straddling the salmon-rich River Shimna has long since disappeared, but many of the follies, bridges and other features of the estate, which was opened as the province's first Forest Park in 1955, have been conserved. They include a hermitage, the extravagantly decorated Gothic and Barbican Gates and the church-like Clanbrassil Barn, now the information centre. There are splendid specimen trees, an avenue of Himalayan cedars, an azalea walk, and conifer plantations which provide a habitat for foxes, otters, badgers, red squirrels and pine martens, moths, butterflies and many species of birds including woodcock.

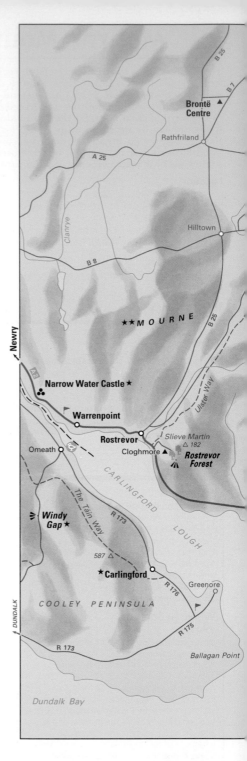

Castlewellan

4mi/6.4km N of Newcastle by A 50. This spacious and elegant little market town was laid out in 1750 around its two squares by the Earl of Annesley. The Annesleys, descendants of an Elizabethan army captain, were successors in this part of Ulster to the Magennis clan, who had been dispossessed after the 1641 rising. One of Castlewellan's squares is lined with trees, the other has the market house of 1764 at its centre.

Clough

★ **Dundrum Castle**

Murlough Reserve

Dundrum Bay

NEWCASTLE

★★ **Castlewellan Forest Park**

Lough Island Reavy

○ **Castlewellan**

Drumena Cashel and Souterrain

★ **Tollymore Forest Park**

Shimna

Ulster Way

Mourne Wall

M O U N T A I N S

Slieve Donard △ 850

★ **Spelga Pass and Dam**

670 △ Slieve Muck

Ben Crom Reservoir

Bloody Bridge

626 △

★ **Silent Valley Reservoir**

Slieve Binnian

Mourne Wall

Crocknafeola Forest

Sally Lough

Mullartown

▲ **Annalong Marine Park and Cornmill**

Kilkeel J.

Kilkeel ○

Greencastle

○ Cranfield

Cranfield Point

I R I S H   S E A

| 0 | | | | | 10 km |
| 0 | | | 5 miles | |

Castlewellan Forest Park★★

4mi/6.4km N of Newcastle by A 50. ♿ Open daily, 10am-dusk. £4 per car. Guided tour by appointment. Parking. Café; barbecue site. Fishing. ☎ 028 4377 8664; Fax 028 4377 1762

The forest park is based on the desmesne developed by the Annesley family from the mid-18C, its splendid tree collection forming the basis of the national **arboretum**. The core of the estate is not so much the castle, a Scottish Baronial style edifice built in granite and now used as a conference centre, but the superb

NITB, Belfast

Mourne Mountains

Annesley Gardens, enclosed by a wall and embellished by two fountains. The mile-long lake provides excellent fishing, while along its shores a fascinating 3mi/5km **Sculpture Trail** features pieces created from natural materials mostly gathered in the park. An ice-house stands on the south shore and there is a pagan standing stone, now covered with Christian symbols, on the north bank. What is claimed to be the world's largest maze, the Peace Maze, was opened in 2001.

The highest point of the park is Slievenaslat (896ft/273m), from where there are magnificent views southward to the Mourne Mountains.

Legananny Dolmen

11mi/18km N of Newcastle by A 50 and side roads (signed) from N of Castlewellan. One of the country's most-photographed prehistoric burial monuments, the dolmen consists of a huge slanting capstone delicately balanced on three unusually low supporting stones. It stands in a theatrical setting on the southern slope of Slieve Croob (1 745ft/532m) with a magnificent view of the Mourne Mountains.

Brontë Centre

1.5mi/2.5km N of Rathfriland, off B 25 in Drumballyroney (sign). (&) Open Mar-Sep, Tue-Fri, 11am-5pm, Sat-Sun, 2-6pm. £2. Guide book (3 languages). Parking. Picnic sites. Wheelchair access to church and school. ☎ 028 4063 1152

The little white schoolhouse and church in this hamlet have been turned into an interpretative centre which makes the most of the area's connections with the Brontë family. The occasion of the first sermon preached by Patrick Brontë, father of the famous literary sisters, is re-created in the adjoining deconsecrated church.

A **tour** *(signed 10mi/16km)* leads to other sites associated with the family.

BRONTË COUNTRY

Among the rolling northern foothills of the Mourne Mountains stands the ruined cottage *(plaque)* where Patrick Brontë, the father of the famous literary sisters, Charlotte, Emily and Anne, was born in 1777. In 1802 he went to study theology at St John's College, Cambridge. He was ordained in 1811 and moved to Haworth in Yorkshire in 1820.

He seems to have changed his name from Brunty (O'Pronitaigh), which is a local one, to Brontë before leaving Ireland; three years earlier in 1799 Lord Nelson had been made Duke of Brontë, a place in Sicily, by Ferdinand, King of Naples, in recognition of Nelson's assistance in recapturing Naples from the French.

Drumena Cashel and Souterrain★

A good number of the early Christian farm enclosures called cashels have survived in the Mourne Mountains. This well-preserved example consists of an oval area enclosed by a drystone wall containing the foundations of a house and a T-shaped underground tunnel, called a souterrain, which can be entered.

Silent Valley Reservoir★

Car park at the end of the drive. & Open daily, 10am-6.30pm (4pm Oct-Apr). £3 per car. Information Centre: Open as above. Parking. Bus shuttle between car park and Ben Crom Reservoir: Jul-Aug, daily; May-Jun and Sep, Sat-Sun; £1.20. Refreshments (summer). ☎ *0845 744 0088; waterline@waterni.gov.uk; www.waterni.gov.uk*

The Mourne Mountains have few natural lakes, and most people would agree that the landscape has been enhanced by the reservoirs which supply Belfast and Co Down with plentiful soft water. Opened in 1933, the Silent Valley scheme on the Kilkeel River took 10 years to complete and gave employment to as many as 2 000 workers; the reservoir holds 136 million cubic metres of water. The catchment is protected by the **Mourne Wall**, beautifully constructed in rough stone; snaking up and down the slopes, this extraordinary 22mi/35km linear structure was built from mountain granite between 1910 and 1922 and provided seasonal relief work for local men.

There is a pleasant walk *(2hr there and back on foot)* to the dam which provides a superb **view★** of the still waters of the reservoir at the foot of the west face of Slieve Binnian (2 441ft/744m). From the east end of the dam the path continues north to **Ben Crom Reservoir** *(3mi/4.8km)*. From the west end of the dam the path returns down the valley past **Sally Lough**, an attractive natural lake, through a grove of conifers and back over a wooden footbridge spanning the Kilkeel River.

Spelga Pass and Dam★

From the dam there is a superb **view** north over the foothills of the Mourne Mountains to the rolling hills of Co Down. The still waters of the reservoir, which provides fine angling for brown trout, cover the Deer's Meadow, formerly summer pasture which was inundated in 1959.

Crocknafeola Forest

Picnic areas. The small coniferous forest stands beside the road which traverses the Mourne Mountains from north to south skirting the west face of Slieve Muck (2 198ft/670m).

Tour

ALONG THE COAST

Newcastle

The town "where the mountains of Mourne sweep down to the sea", immortalised in verse by Percy French *(see p 169)*, began to develop in the early 19C when seaside holidays became fashionable. From the tiny harbour a long promenade of hotels, shops and amusement arcades extends northeast beside a long sandy beach overlooking Dundrum Bay. Beyond the red-brick bulk of the Slieve Donard Hotel, built by the railway company in 1898, lie the championship links of the Royal County Down Golf Club.

The town's Roman Catholic church, **Our Lady of the Assumption**, is a modern (1967), circular structure, the outstanding feature of which is its strikingly bold and colourful stained glass. *Open daily, 8am-8pm.*

On the banks of the Glen River, attractive **Donard Park** is the starting point for the path leading steeply but steadily to the summit of **Slieve Donard**. The mountain is named in honour of Donard, a local chieftain supposedly converted to Christianity by St Patrick.

From Newcastle take A 2 S.

Bloody Bridge

In the course of the 1641 uprising, a group of government prisoners was being conducted from Newry to Downpatrick to be exchanged for captured rebels. But the man in charge, one Russell, fearful of being overpowered, murdered them all at this fateful spot.

From A 2 turn S by the Police Station towards the shore.

Annalong Marine Park and Cornmill★

(&) Open Feb-Nov, Wed-Sun, 11am-5pm. £1.30. Parking. Wheelchair access to Marine Park only ☎ 028 4376 8736

A marine park has been laid out by the harbour of this little seaside town. On the banks of a stream stands an early-19C **cornmill** (restored), driven by a back-shot breast-shot water-wheel. It is the last of some 20 mills which existed in the Kingdom of Mourne in the late 17C and 18C for grinding wheat and oats or scutching flax. The Exhibition Room describes the history of milling, and a tour of the mill and its functioning machinery is a fascinating experience.

Kilkeel

In its attractive setting at the mouth of the Kilkeel River, this harbour town is the home of Northern Ireland's largest fishing fleet, at its liveliest when the boats are in port and the catch is being sold on the quayside. The townscape is full of interest, with stepped pavements and many changes of level.

Greencastle

(HM) Open Apr-Sep, Tue-Sun and Bank Hol Mon, 10am (2pm Sun) to 6pm. 75p. Parking. ☎ 028 9181 1491; Fax 9182 0695; Scrabocp@doeni.gov.uk; www.ehsni.gov.uk

The ruins of an Anglo-Norman stronghold, probably built in the mid-13C, are set on a low outcrop of rock extending into Carlingford Lough. The castle consisted of a large rectangular keep within a four-sided walled enclosure with D-shaped corner towers, which was surrounded by a moat cut in the rock.

From the top of the keep there is a fine view. Cranfield Bay *(SE)* has a sandy beach which is ideal for bathing.

Narrow Water Castle

Rostrevor Forest Park

Forest Drive to car park. The pine forest covers the south bank of the Kilbroney River and the steep northwest slopes of Slieve Martin (597ft/182m) beside a mountain stream. There are several walks – to the **Cloghmore**, a great glacial boulder, and to the **viewpoint★** high above Rostrevor Bay; on the opposite shore of Carlingford Lough rise the mountains of the Cooley Peninsula in the Republic.

Rostrevor

This attractive little town extends from its central square to the waterfront on Carlingford Lough. Even palm trees and mimosa thrive in its sheltered position at the foot of Slieve Martin.

Warrenpoint

Ferry and cruises. The town is both a port, equipped to take container traffic, and a pleasant resort, with a vast central square, used for markets and festivals, and a promenade facing south down Carlingford Lough between the Mourne Mountains and the Cooley Peninsula.

Narrow Water Castle★

2mi/3.2km N of Warrenpoint on A 2. (HM) Open Apr-Sep, Tue-Sun and Bank Hol Mon, 10am (2pm Sun) to 6pm. 75p. Parking. ☎ 028 4271 1491; ☎ 028 9182 0695; Scrabocp@doeni.gov.uk; www.ehsni.gov.uk
The castle occupies an attractive and strategic site on a promontory commanding the narrows at the mouth of the Newry River where it enters Carlingford Lough. It was built in the 1650s as an English garrison at the cost of £361 4s 2d. Although restored, it is an excellent example of a **tower house**, complete with its **bawn**. The contemporary British garrison suffered one of its worst losses here in 1979, when a bomb killed 18 soldiers.

Lough Neagh★

Ten rivers converge on the broad and tranquil lough, the largest body of fresh water in the British Isles (153sq mi/396km²) but it is drained by only one, the Lower Bann, which flows north to discharge into the sea just downstream from Coleraine. The vastness of the lake surface belies its depth, never more than 50ft/12m, and despite its size, the lough has little impact on the surrounding flat countryside. Only in Antrim Bay is the shore lined with woodland; elsewhere it is low and marshy, virtually roadless, and sometimes infested with (non-biting) midges. Together with its tiny northern neighbour, Lough Beg, Lough Neagh is a site of international importance for wintering wildfowl, and nature reserves have been established on many of its islands.

Location

Michelin Atlas p 102 and Map 712 – M, N 3, 4 – Co Antrim, Co Armagh, Co Tyrone and Co Londonderry.

Lough Neagh lies about 15mi/24km W of Belfast between M 1 and M 22. There is no continuous shore road, only a few points where minor roads reach the water's edge.

🚩 *The Warden, Lough Neagh Warden's Office, Lurgan BT66 6NJ. ☎ 028 3832 2398; Fax 028 38 329027; stephen.foster@doeni.gov.u*

Adjacent Sights: See ANTRIM, ARMAGH, BELFAST, LISBURN, SPERRIN MOUNTAINS.

THE EMPIRE OF THE EEL

The waters of Lough Neagh and its tributaries teem with every kind of freshwater fish. There are rudd, roach and pike, as well as the pollan (freshwater herring) and the rare dollaghan (a kind of salmon-trout); giant pike lurk in Lough Beg; there are bream in the Blackwater and trout and salmon in the Bann and other rivers. The lough is famous above all for its eels. Having hatched in the far-off Sargasso Sea, millions of elvers make their way across the Atlantic and swim up the Bann into the lough, where they stay for 12 to 14 years before attempting to return to their birthplace to die. Many of them are frustrated in this ambition; they are caught, not to be eaten locally but to be exported from the cooperative fishery at Toome to connoisseurs abroad, who relish them both smoked or unsmoked.

Worth a Visit

In clockwise order starting from the SE corner

Lough Neagh Discovery Centre

South shore; Oxford Island; sign at Junction 10 on M 1. ♿ Open Apr-Sep, daily, 10am-7pm; Oct-Mar, Wed-Sun, 10am-5pm. Exhibition £1.50. Birdwatching hides. Exhibition guide sheet (4 languages). Parking. Café. ☎ 028 3832 2205; Fax 028 3834 7438; oxford.island@craigavon.gov.uk; www.craigavon.gov.uk

This modern visitor centre, set among lakeside meadows and reached across a moat, is one of the best places to make the acquaintance of the lough. It presents an exhibition about the wildlife, history and management of the lake through audio-visual shows and touch-screen computers; there are five birdwatching hides and footpaths *(4mi/7km)* along the shoreline – reedbeds, wildflower meadows, woodland – and marina in Kinnego Bay.

Peatlands Park

South shore; sign at Junction 13 on M 1. ♿ Park: Open daily (except 25 Dec), 9am-9pm/dusk. Visitor Centre and Narrow-gauge railway: Open Jun-Aug, daily, 2-6pm; Easter-May and Sep, Sat-Sun and Bank Hols, 2-6pm. Guided tour by appointment. Parking. Picnic area. ☎ 028 3885 1102; Fax 028 3885 1821; peatlandspark@doeni.gov.uk

This old hunting park is the best place in the North to experience something of Ireland's long relationship with peat, one of the country's few natural resources. The peat has long since been cut over but the **narrow-gauge railway** installed by the Irish Peat Development Company is still in place, and visitors can enjoy a scenic tour of the site aboard a train hauled by the original diesel engines, as well as watching demonstrations of **turf cutting** by hand and machine at the outdoor turbary station. In addition there is a **bog garden**, two small lakes, an orchard and woodland, and about half the area has been designated a National Nature Reserve to protect the unusual flora and fauna.

Maghery

South shore. Sited at the point where the River Blackwater enters the lough, the village has a lakeside country park from which Coney Island, a densely wooded island, can be visited by boat.

Lough Neagh

Lough Neagh Discovery Centre

Directory

GETTING ABOUT

The **Loughshore Trail**, a relatively flat route, ideal for cycling and walking, is composed of 128mi/206km miles of quiet lanes, which run alongide or close to the lough shore. It forms Route 94 of the National Cycle Network and incorporates a short section of Route 96 by Lough Beg. *www.loughshoretrail.com*

SIGHTSEEING

Lake Cruises are available from **Kinnego Marina** on the south shore. *Operates (weather permitting) Sat-Sun, every 30min; Mon-Fri from Kinnego Marina (south shore) to Lough Neagh Discovery Centre (30min). Fares from £4.* ☎ 028 3832 7573

There are cruises from **Sixmilewater Marina** in Antrim. Occasionally there is also a **Bann cruise** between Antrim and Castlerock *(35mi/56km – 6/7hr).*

SPORTS AND LEISURE

Water sports are available at the marinas at Antrim, Ballyronan and Kinnego and at the Craigavon Watersports Centre.

There is an **RSPB reserve** at Portmore Lough (SE) and **nature reserves** at Reas Wood in Antrim, at Oxford Island, at Peatlands Park, at Washingbay Wetlands near Dungannon and at Randalstown Forest.

Fishing Permits for Lough Neagh are available from tackle shops and from the Fishery Conservancy Board in Portadown. *Permits available from Fisheries Conservancy Board, 1 Mahon Road, Portadown. Open Mon-Fri, 9am-1pm and 2-5pm. Licence for game and coarse fishing £4 for 1 day, £10.50 for 8 days, £21.50 per annum. Licence for coarse fishing (rod and line) under £4 for 3 days, £4 for 8 days, £8 per annum.* ☎ *028 3833 4666; Fax 028 3833 8912; info@fcbni.org; www.fcbni.com*

Permits and **gillie services** for the Lower Bann are available from Bann Systems, Coleraine. *Permits available from Bann System Ltd, 54 Castleroe Road, Coleraine, BT51 3RL. From £15 per day to £350 per annum.* ☎ *028 7034 4796; Fax 028 7035 6527; ed@irishsociety.freeserve.co.uk; www.bannsystem.com*

Ballyronan

West shore. With a little marina and a beach enhanced by pleasant walks, this is another of the few places where the lake shore is easily accessible.

Mountjoy Castle

West shore. A ruined early-17C castle with gun loops, built of stone and well-weathered brick.

Kinturk Cultural Centre

West shore. ♿ *Open Jun-Sep, daily, 10am-4.30pm, (8pm Sat-Sun); Oct-May, Sun-Fri, 11am (10am Sun) to 4.30pm (6pm Sun). £1.50. Audio-visual show. Lough Neagh Exhibition. Guided walks and boat trips. Parking. Licensed restaurant.* ☎/*Fax 028 8673 6512*
A lavish new community centre contains a fascinating exhibition dealing comprehensively with the long-established Lough Neagh eel fishery.

Ardboe Cross★

West shore, E of Cookstown by B 73. This is the finest high cross of its kind in Ulster, indeed one of the finest in all Ireland. It stands in an evocative spot at the entrance to a graveyard laid out around the ruins of a 17C church and is extensively carved with biblical scenes: Old Testament on the east side and New Testament on the west. The cross probably dates from the 10C and marked the site of Ardboe Abbey, probably a 6C foundation, which was associated with St Colman.
From Ardboe Point there is an extensive **view★** of Lough Neagh surrounded by distant mountains: Slieve Gallion and the Sperrin Mountains *(NW)*, Slemish *(NE)*, Divis Mountain *(E)*, the Mourne Mountains *(SE)*.

Bellaghy Bawn

North shore; in Bellaghy, 4mi/7km N of A 6. (HM) Open Easter-Aug, daily, 10am-6pm; Sep-Easter, Tue-Sat, 9am-5pm. Closed 25 Dec to 1 Jan. £2. ☎ *028 7938 6812/6186; Fax 028 7938 6556; bellaghy.bawn@doeni.gov.uk; www.ehsni.gov.uk*
The 17C bawn (restored) in the village of Bellaghy was built by the Vintners' Company in 1619; its exhibits pay tribute to Seamus Heaney and his writing. As well as books and manuscripts, there is the opportunity to see a film introduced by Heaney and listen to recordings of his broadcasts.

SEAMUS HEANEY
The poet and Nobel Prize winner Seamus Heaney (b 1939) was born at his family's farm near Bellaghy. Much of his work, in particular his Lough Neagh cycle, reflects the influence of the landscapes and people of his youth. His feeling for the land of Ireland and his respect for those who, like his father, were bound to it by hard physical work, is carried over into his own physical act of writing:

> "Between my finger and my thumb
> The squat pen rests.
> I'll dig with it."
> *Digging (1966)*

Churchtown Point

North shore. A low promontory marked by a holy well and the ruins of Cranfield Church, which probably dates from the 13C and attracted many pilgrims in the past.

Newry

Newry occupies a commanding position in the "Gap of the North", also known as the Moyry Gap, between the line of hills which separates Ulster from the plains of Meath. This strategic position has brought the town destruction as well as a degree of prosperity, as armies marched through on their way north or south. In the 18C Newry was linked by canals to Lough Neagh and to the sea at Carlingford Lough, becoming for a while the busiest port in the North. Those days are long gone but, owing to its situation on the main Belfast–Dublin road and railway, the town thrives as a modern commercial centre serving shoppers from both sides of the border.

Location

Population 21 633 - Michelin Atlas p 98 and Map 712 – M, N 5 – Co Armagh and Co Down.

Newry *(An Tiúr)* is situated on the main road (A 1/N 1) between Belfast and Dundalk, just north of the border.

🚹 *200 Newry Road, Banbridge BT32 3NB. Open Jun-Sep, daily; Oct-May, Mon-Sat.* ☎ *028 4062 3322; Fax 028 4062 3114*

Adjacent Sights: See ARMAGH, DUNDALK, MONAGHAN, MOURNE MOUNTAINS.

Background

Newry's history began with the foundation in 1157 of a Cistercian abbey. Thanks to the town's turbulent history, no trace of it remains, neither does anything survive of the castle built here by the Anglo-Norman John de Courcy, nor of the strongholds that succeeded it. The abbey still stood in the 16C, when it was used as a residence by Sir Nicholas Bagenal, Marshal of Ireland. In 1578 Bagenal built St Patrick's Church on the hill to the east of the town centre; it was the first Anglican church to be built in Ireland, and sports its founder's coat of arms in the porch.

In 1731 work began here on the first inland canal in the British Isles, linking Newry via 14 locks to Lough Neagh. Thirty years later, a ship canal was dug to provide the town with an outlet to Carlingford Lough and the Irish Sea. The town did well on trade in linen, coal, building stone and emigrants; a number of Georgian town houses and multi-storey quayside mills testify to the buoyant economic conditions of this era. The inland canal was closed in 1956. The ship canal became redundant when modern port facilities were provided downstream at Warrenpoint but it was reopened in 1987 for recreational use.

Worth a Visit

Newry Cathedral

Town Centre. Open daily, 8am-6pm. ☎ *028 3026 2586; Fax 028 3026 7505; office@newrycathedral.org; www.newrycathedral.org*

Newry has been the seat of the Roman Catholic diocese of Dromore since about 1750. Its cathedral, designed by Thomas Duff in 1825 and dedicated to St Patrick and St Colman, was the first Roman Catholic cathedral to be built in Ireland following the Act of Emancipation. It is less interesting for its Tudor-Gothic exterior than for its 20C interior decor of vivid stained glass and colourful mosaics.

Newry and Mourne Museum

(♿) Open Mon-Fri, 10.30am-1pm and 2-5pm. Café. Wheelchair access to Arts Centre but not museum. ☎ *028 3026 6232*

The museum is housed in the modern Arts Centre beside the Town Hall, which straddles the river and thus has one foot in Co Armagh and one in Co Down. It deals competently with the archaeology and history of the area; the prize exhibit is probably the lovely early-18C panelled room which evokes the town's most prosperous period, while a real curiosity is Nelson's cabin table from *HMS Victory*.

Excursion

Cardinal O'Fiaich Centre

Cullyhanna; 15mi/24km W of Newry by B 30 and N by A 29 and a minor road (left). Open Mon-Fri, 10am-5pm (6pm Bank Hols), Sat, by appointment; Sun, 2-6pm; ☎ *02830 868 757; Fax 02830 868 352; info@ofiaichcentre-cullyhanna.com; www.ofiaichcentre-cullyhanna.com*

The centre is devoted to the life story of Tomás O'Fiaich (d 1990), a local boy, who became Cardinal-Primate of all Ireland. It reviews his career as student, priest, professor and scholar, using audio-visual presentations of interviews and conversations, personal memorabilia, panels depicting life and times, archaeological models and artefacts.

Tour

SLIEVE GULLION★

Round tour of 27mi/43.5km – 1 day

This "enchanted mountain" (B Kiely), together with its attendant circle of lesser heights known as the Ring of Gullion, dominates the countryside to the west of Newry. It is intimately associated with the legendary Cuchulain, hero of the epic *The Cattle Raid of Cooley (Táin bo Cuainlge)* and is rich in prehistoric remains. Offering superlative views, the mountains were designated an Area of Outstanding Natural Beauty in 1991.

From Newry take A 25 W; after 1.5mi/2.4km turn right onto B 133 to Bessbrook.

Bessbrook

Bessbrook is an early and fascinating example of a planned industrial village, its terraces of granite-built, slate-roofed cottages neatly ranged round three sides of two grassy squares. It was built in 1845 by the Quaker linen manufacturer John Grubb Richardson for the workers in his flax mill; he also provided them with churches, schools, shops and a community hall but no pub. Bessbrook later inspired the Cadbury family to build the far larger model settlement of Bournville near Birmingham.

From Bessbrook take B 112; turn right onto A 25. W of Camlough village turn left onto B 30.

Cam Lough

From the road there is a fine view of the narrow lake in its deep trough between Camlough Mountain (1 417ft/423m) and Slieve Gullion.

At the crossroads turn left onto a narrow road along the west side of Cam Lough.

Killevy Churches

An ancient graveyard, overhung with beech trees, surrounds the ruins of two churches, standing end to end. The eastern church is medieval and its east window dates from the 15C. The western building is earlier (12C) although the west wall, which is pierced by a doorway below a massive lintel, may be 10C or 11C. A granite slab in the northern half of the graveyard is said to be the grave of St Monenna (also known as Darerca and Bline) who founded an important early nunnery at Killevy in the 5C; later it became a convent of Augustinian nuns until it was suppressed in 1542. A path north of the graveyard leads to a holy well.

Continue S for 1.5mi/2.4km; turn right onto B 113.

Slieve Gullion Forest Park★

Car park and picnic area. 8mi/13km Scenic Drive; steep gradients and difficult bends. Open daily until dusk. ☎ 028 3755 1277 (enquiries); Fax 028 3755 2143

The pines, larches and spruce of the Forest Park clad the lower slopes of the southwest face of Slieve Gullion. Before embarking on the panoramic route up the mountain it is worth while calling at the visitor centre housed in old farm buildings to learn more about the park and admire the old hand tools on display.

After climbing through the forest, the Scenic Drive emerges on the open slopes of Slieve Gullion and runs northwest skirting the trees; on the left is an extensive view over the treetops; on the

Kilnasaggart Stone

P Thebault/MICHELIN

right is the path, waymarked in white, to the top of the south peak of Slieve Gullion (1 894ft/573m) where there is a cairn; another cairn crowns the lower north peak. The Drive swings left downhill and doubles back along the southwest slope, through the trees and rocks, to a **viewpoint**★ *(car park)* overlooking a section of the **Ring of Gullion**, the ring-dike of smaller volcanic hills which encircle Slieve Gullion.

At the exit turn right onto B 113 and immediately turn left. After 1.5mi/2.4km turn right; after 1mi/1.6km park at the T-junction.

Kilnasaggart Stone

6min there and back on foot across two fields and stiles. Most of Ireland's cross-decorated pillar-stones are in the west of the country but this granite example (7ft/2.15m high) in its hedged enclosure is the earliest dateable one of its kind, its crosses carved around AD 700. The pillar itself, which marks the site of an early Christian cemetery, may in fact be much older, a prehistoric standing stone converted to a new use. It also bears an inscription in Irish stating that the site was dedicated under the patronage of Peter the Apostle by the son of Ceran Bic, Ternohc, who died c 715.

Return to B 113; turn right towards Newry; after 5mi/8km turn left to Ballymacdermot Cairn (sign).

Ballymacdermot Cairn

Beside the road *(right)* on the south slope of Ballymacdermot Mountain are the remains of a Neolithic court grave, which consisted of two burial chambers preceded by an antechamber and a circular forecourt enclosed in a trapezoidal cairn. From the site there is a fine **view** southwest across the Meigh plain to Slieve Gullion and the Ring of Gullion.

Continue for 1mi/1.6km.

Bernish Rock Viewpoint★★

Car park. One of the finest panoramas in the whole of Ireland, the view extends from Newry in the valley below to the glorious outline of the Mourne Mountains on the horizon to the east.

Return downhill to Newry.

Portrush

Easily accessible by road and rail from Belfast, Portrush has been one of the North's most popular seaside resorts since early Victorian times, the natural qualities of its sandy beaches and the nearby coastline supplemented by a host of man-made attractions. The town is laid out on a little peninsula which ends in Ramore Head, a notable haunt of birdwatchers.

Location

Population 5 703 - Michelin Atlas p 102 and Map 712 – M 2 – Co Antrim.
Portrush is situated north of Coleraine, between Portstewart and Ballycastle, on the coast road, A 2.
🛈 *Dunluce Centre, Sandhill Drive, Portrush BT56 8BF. Open Apr-Sep, daily; Mar and Oct, Sat-Sun afternoons.* ☎ *028 7082 3333; Fax 028 7082 2256; portrush@nitic.net; www.colerainetic.gov.uk*
🛈 *Railway Road, Coleraine BT52 1PE. Open Mon-Sat.* ☎ *028 7034 4723; Fax 028 7035 1756; coleraine@nitic.net*
Adjacent Sights: See GIANT'S CAUSEWAY, LONDONDERRY, LOUGH NEAGH, SPERRIN MOUNTAINS.

CONTROVERSY AND CONSERVATION

West of Portrush the coast is broken by the estuary of the River Bann and ends in a long sand dune extending into Lough Foyle. There are more dunes to the east of the town, which give way to strangely weathered and cave-riddled limestone cliffs, then to the extraordinary volcanic rock formations of the Giant's Causeway. The great geological importance of the north Antrim Coast is recognised by its designation as a National Nature Reserve; it was at Portrush that the evidence was found which settled a long-standing controversy about the origin of many of the Earth's rocks, including such features as the Giant's Causeway.

Worth a Visit

The **Dunluce Centre** which is housed in the same prominent pavilion as the Tourist Information Centre, contains such lavish revisions of traditional end-of-the-pier entertainments as Turbotours and Earthquest. (&) *Open Jul-Aug, daily, 10am-8pm; Jun, daily, 10am (noon Sat-Sun) to 5pm (7pm Sat-Sun); Sep-May, Sat-Sun, noon-5pm (7pm Apr-May). £7. Parking. Café.* ☎ *028 7082 4444; Fax 028 7082 2256; dayout@dunlucecentre.freeserve.co.uk; www.touristnetuk.com/ni/dunluce*

Directory

SIGHTSEEING

Excursions by open-top bus – Along the Causeway Coast between the Giant's Causeway and Portstewart. *Operates (weather permitting, otherwise normal single-decker bus) Jul-Aug, Mon-Sun (check at depot for 12-13 Jul); from Coleraine at 9.10am, 11.30am, 1.50pm, 4pm, 6.15pm; from Giant's Causeway at 10.20am, 12.40pm, 2.55pm, 5.10pm, 6.55pm. Journey may be broken at Portstewart, Portrush, Portballintrae, Bushmills. North Region Bus Timetable (Service 177) available from Ulster Bus depots and TICs. Single £2, there and back £3.60.* ☎ 028 7032 5400

Excursions by boat – To visit the caves in the limestone cliffs at **White Rock** *(E)*, and to **The Skerries**, a chain of offshore islands densely populated by seabirds.

WHERE TO STAY

• *Budget*

Glenkeen Guest House – *59 Coleraine Rd, BT56 8BN -* ☎ *028 7082 2279 - Fax 028 7082 2279 - glenkeen@btinternet.com - Closed 17 to 31 Dec -* 🅿 *- 10 rm £30/50* 🍽. Well-priced guest house accommodation on the main road into town. Personally run by the welcoming owner, the house is neat and well kept while the bedrooms are a generous size, all with shower rooms.

WHERE TO EAT

• *Moderate*

The Harbour Bar – *The Harbour, BT56 8BN -* ☎ *028 7082 2430 - Closed 25 Dec and Mon -* 🍽 🅿 *- £18.* This rustic, quayside pub is an ever-popular spot for lunch. Orders for food are taken at the bar but are then brought to the table. It certainly has character and the menu features all the popular classics.

Ramore Wine Bar – *The Harbour, BT56 8BN -* ☎ *028 7082 4313 - Closed 25 Dec - £20.* In an elevated position overlooking the harbour and the bay, the wine bar boasts a contemporary design while still retaining a relaxed and informal feel. There's a large bar, low tables and a blackboard menu offering plenty of choice.

SPORTS AND LEISURE

Sandy beaches at Portballintrae, Portrush, Portstewart, Castlerock and Magilligan Strand (Benone).

The **Countryside Centre** is located in an old Victorian bathhouse, converted to accommodate this introduction to the ecology and marine life of the locality; visitors can observe the denizens of the seabed from within the "wreck" of the *Nautilus. Open Apr-Sep, daily, 10am-6pm. Audio-visual room; exhibition. Parking.* ☎ *020 7082 3600; www.nics.gov.uk/ehs*

Tours

EAST OF PORTRUSH

7.5mi/12km
From Portrush take A 2 E.

Dunluce Castle★★

Car park. (HM) Open Apr-Sep, Mon-Sat, 10am-6pm, Sun, 2pm (noon Jun-Aug) to 6pm; Oct-Mar, Tue-Sun and Bank Hol Mon, 10am (2pm Sun) to 4pm. £1.50. Audioguide (foreign languages). Parking. ☎ *028 2073 1938; Fax 028 2073 2850; RoeVally2@doeni.gov.uk; www.ehsni.gov.uk*

There can be few more romantic sights than the jagged outline of ruined Dunluce Castle, perched on its isolated rock stack 100ft/30m above the sea and separated from the mainland by a deep defile. For years it was the seat of the Irish branch of the Scottish MacDonnell clan, "Lords of the Isles". In the 16C their most notable leader was Sorley Boy MacDonnell, a constant thorn in the flesh of both the native Irish and the English. Despite the use of artillery, the latter failed to expel him permanently from Dunluce, and his descendants were eventually made Earls of Antrim. In the 17C they modernised the castle to provide more comfortable accommodation but, no doubt discouraged by the disastrous collapse into the sea of the kitchen area, soon abandoned it altogether, leaving it to fall into its present pleasing state of decay. Beyond the drawbridge spanning the defile and the late-16C gatehouse with its Scottish-style turrets and crow-step gables, the earliest, 14C part of the stronghold consists of the two east towers and the south wall. The upper yard is dominated by the 17C **great hall**, built in grandiose style with bay windows on the west front. The cobbled **lower yard** is surrounded by service buildings including the bakery. From here there is a superb **view** of the Causeway Coast.

Continue E on A 2.

Bushmills Distillery

Car park. (♿) Guided tour (1hr 30min) Apr-Oct, Mon-Sat, 9.30am-5.30pm, Sun, noon-5.30pm (4pm last tour); Nov-Mar, Mon-Fri at 10.30am, 11.30am, 1.30pm, 2.30pm, 3.30pm; Sat-Sun at 1.30pm, 2.30pm, 3.30pm. £3.95. Parking. ☎ *028 2073 1521; Fax 028 2073 1339; scroskery@idl.ie; www.whiskeytours.ie*

Dunluce Castle

The most prominent feature in the village of Bushmills is the distinctive caps of the kilns in the **distillery**. The original licence to distil was granted to Sir Thomas Phillips in 1608, although the earliest mention of distilling on the site goes back to 1276. Using its own supply of water from St Columb's Rill, a tributary of the River Bush which rises in peaty ground, the distillery produces two blended whiskeys and one malt. The tour includes the main stages in the production of whiskey: mashing, fermentation, distillation, maturing in oak casks, blending and bottling. Tasting takes place in the Potstill Bar, a small museum has been created in the old malt kilns.

INLAND FROM PORTRUSH
15mi/24km
From Portrush take A 29 inland to Coleraine.

Coleraine
At the head of the Bann estuary, Coleraine is Co Londonderry's second largest town. Its main function is as important shopping and commercial centre for the area, though its character was enlivened by the siting here, rather than in Londonderry itself, of the province's second university (1968). Otherwise its greatest asset is the river and its estuary, with an interesting quayside, occasional regattas, a large-scale marina, and a bird sanctuary.
From Coleraine take B 67 E via Ballybogy for 5.5mi/9km.

Benvarden★
Open Jun-Aug, Tue-Sun and Bank Hol Mon, 1.30-5pm. No dogs. £2.50. ☎ 028 2074 1331; henvarden@onetel.net.uk
Benvarden House, home of the Montgomery family since 1798, opens its garden and grounds to the public every summer. One of Ireland's most attractive walled gardens (2 acres/0.8ha), parts of which may date back to the original fortified enclosure, features rose beds, a formal hedged garden, a vinery and a pergola walk. Beyond are the neatly laid out kitchen gardens, with Victorian hothouses and the old gardener's bothy. A wild garden and azalea walk lead down to the River Bush, which is spanned by a Victorian stone and cast-iron bridge, rare of its type in Ireland.
Return to Ballybogy. Turn left onto B 62 towards Ballymoney; from the by-pass roundabout follow the sign.

Leslie Hill Open Farm
(&) Open Jul-Aug, Mon-Thu and Sat-Sun, 11am (2pm Sun) to 6pm; Jun, Sat-Sun, 2-6pm; Easter-May, Sun and Bank Hols, 2-6pm. £2.90. Tearoom. ☎ 028 2766 6803
This mixed-farming estate has been in the ownership of the same family since the mid-18C, and the array of buildings and implements dating from most periods of the farm's existence give a vivid picture of its evolution. The cathedral-like Bell Barn contrasts with the modest two-room cabin lived in by the coachman's family. A little museum contains a fascinating collection of farm and family memorabilia. A track, hidden from view from the imposing Georgian house by a ha-ha, leads to the walled garden with its pit-house, hot wall, and the remains of the heating arrangements for growing peaches.

WEST OF PORTRUSH

20mi/32km

From Portrush take A 2 W.

Portstewart

Less exuberant than its larger neighbour, Portstewart was a fashionable watering place in the 19C and has kept something of its Victorian atmosphere. It has a picturesque harbour and the very prominent O'Hara's Castle, a Gothic-style mansion (1834), which is now a Dominican college. From the promenade, paths lead west along the cliffs to Portstewart Strand *(2mi/3.2km)*. Regular exhibitions are held at the Flowerfield Arts Centre.

Continue W on A 2 via Coleraine (see above); 1mi/1.6km beyond Articlave at the Liffock crossroads turn left into the car park.

Hezlett House

Castlerock, on the NW corner of the crossroads. (NT) (& to ground floor) Guided tour (40min; max 15 people) Jun-Aug, Wed-Mon; mid-Mar, Apr-May and Sep, Sat-Sun and Bank Hol, noon-5pm. £2.50. Parking. ☎/Fax 028 7084 8567; hezletthouse@ntrust.org.uk

Hezlett House, which was built in 1691 probably as a clergyman's residence, is a long, single-storey thatched cottage with battered, rough-cast walls, an attic and cruck truss roof. It was taken over by the Hezlett family in 1761 and acquired by the National Trust in 1976.

Visitors are led through the tiny kitchen, pantry, dining room, bed-sized bedrooms and parlour and up into the attic, where the servants slept. Furnishings date from the 19C and include balloon chairs (with holes for women's bustles) and prayer chairs, allowing women to kneel in hoop skirts while retaining their dignity. A small museum in the outbuildings shows Victorian farming implements.

Continue W on A 2.

EARL BISHOP

Known as the Earl Bishop, Frederick Augustus Hervey, Bishop of Derry (1730-1803), became the 4th Earl of Bristol on the death of his brother. A flamboyant character, fabulously rich, a passionate builder, traveller and collector of art and antiquities, he was also an unusually enlightened prelate, an advocate of church reform and a supporter of emancipation for Dissenters. Ill health meant that he spent much time on the Continent, where many a Hotel Bristol is named in his honour. On one occasion Napoleon's police arrested him as a spy. A ladies' man, he enjoyed a particularly scandalous affair with the mistress of the King of Prussia. An enemy characterised him as "a bad father, a worse husband, very blasphemous in his conversation, and greatly addicted to intrigue and gallentry".

The Earl Bishop's construction projects included the highly original Ickworth Place in Suffolk and another palatial residence in Ireland, at Ballyscullion on the shores of Lough Beg, never completed; its portico now graces St George's Church in Belfast.

He commissioned the house at Downhill, known as **Downhill Castle**, in 1772 from Michael Shanahan, his favourite architect, to house his huge collection of sculpture and paintings; most of it was destroyed in a fire in 1851.

Downhill★

(NT) Grounds: daily, dawn-dusk. Mussenden Temple: Open Jun-Aug, daily, 11am-6pm; mid-Mar to May, Sep, Sat-Sun and Bank Hols. Parking £3 per car. Picnics welcome. ☎ 02870 848 728; downhillcastle@ntrust.org.uk

The Earl Bishop's building activities still mark this stretch of the Co Londonderry coast, though his castle, rebuilt after the fire of 1851, is now a roofless shell. From the imposing **Bishop's Gate** a charming glen planted with flowers and shrubs, many presented by visitors, leads up to the clifftop.

The castle may be a shadow of its former self but convincing evidence of the Earl Bishop's efforts remains in the form of the **Mussenden Temple★**. This elegant Classical rotunda, based on the Temple of Vesta at Tivoli, is built of local basalt faced with sandstone from Ballycastle, and perches precariously on the very edge of the high cliffs. It was erected in 1785 as a memorial to Mrs Mussenden, the Bishop's cousin; he used it as his library and allowed the local Roman Catholic priest to say Mass in the basement. From here there is a splendid **view** of the coast in both directions and of the railway entering a tunnel *(below)*.

Continue W on A 2.

Beyond the Lion Gate there is a fine view of the sea and the strand where the Bishop held horse races and the present generation indulges in surfing.

Bear left into the Bishop's Road.

The Bishop's Road was driven across the Binevenagh Mountain to shorten the great man's journey between Limavady and his residence.

Mussenden Temple

Gortmore Viewpoint★★

Car park. The road climbs steeply up the northeast slope of Binevenagh Mountain. There is a superb **view** of Magilligan Strand extending across the mouth of Lough Foyle towards the Inishowen Peninsula; in the 19C it was used as the base line for the Ordnance Survey of Ireland.
Return downhill; turn left onto A 2.

Magilligan Strand★★

The long stretch of golden sand dunes (6mi/10km) is equipped with sports facilities at Benone. Much of the land is reserved for military purposes. The Point, where a Martello Tower (1812) was built during the Napoleonic Wars to guard the narrow approach to Lough Foyle, is now a Nature Reserve.

Sperrin Mountains★

These lonely smooth-topped mountains dividing the Londonderry lowlands from northeastern Ulster rise to their highest point in Sawel Mountain (2 224ft/678m). Composed of schist and gneiss, they were once covered in magnificent forests but their upper slopes are now grazed by sheep and clad in blanket bog and purple heather, and woodland is confined to the deep gorges worn by mountain streams. Over the moorland hover birds of prey; the rare hen harrier is sometimes seen, and the Sperrins are the only site in Ireland where the cloudberry grows. The rocks contain minute deposits of gold, the extraction of which gives rise to periodic controversy about the future of these mountains which have largely remained outside the mainstream of modern life.

Location

Michelin Atlas p 101-102 and Map 712 – J, K, L 3 – Co Tyrone and Co Londonderry.
The Sperrin Mountains are bounded to the W by A 5 between Londonderry and Armagh and bisected by A 29 between Armagh and Coleraine, and by A 6 between Londonderry and Belfast.
🚹 *The Burnavon, Burn Road, Cookstown BT80 8TA. Open Jul-Aug, daily; Sep-Jun, Mon-Sat.* ☎ *028 8676 6727; Fax 028 8676 5853*
🚹 *Council Offices, 7 Connell Street, Limavady BT49 0HA. Open Apr-Sep, Mon-Sat, Oct-Mar, Mon-Fri.* ☎ *028 7776 0307; Fax 028 7772 2010*
🚹 *1 Market Street, Omagh BT78 1EE. Open Apr-Sep, Mon-Sat; Oct-Mar, Mon-Fri.* ☎ *028 8224 7831; Fax 028 8224 0774; info@nitb.com; www.discovernorthernireland.com*
🚹 *Abercorn Square, Strabane BT82 8AE. Open Apr-Oct, Mon-Sat.* ☎ *028 7188 3735; Fax 028 7138 1348*
Adjacent Sights: See DUNGANNON, LONDONDERRY, LOUGH NEAGH.

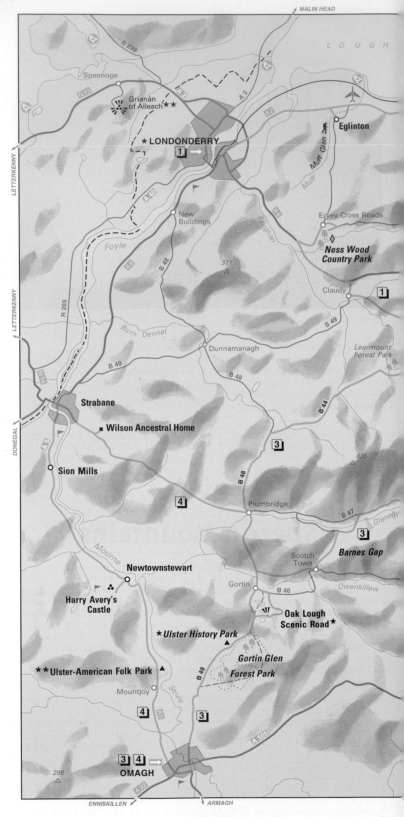

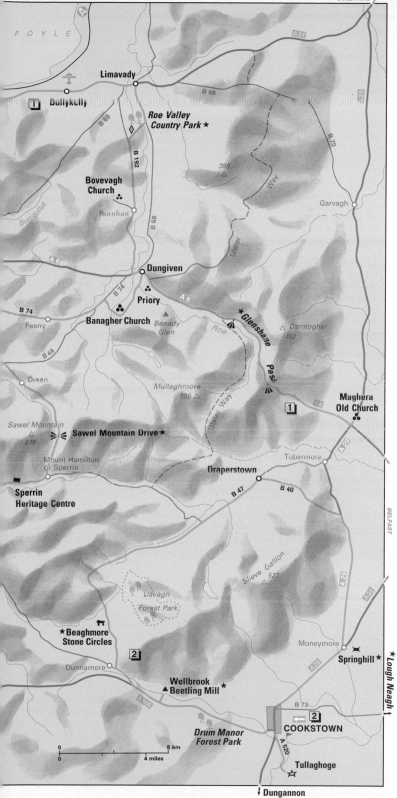

COLERAINE

F O Y L E

A 37

Limavady

B 66

Ballykelly

*Roe Valley
Country Park ★*

B 69

B 192

△ 399

*Ulster
Way*

Bovevagh
Church

Burntollet

Burnfoot

B 68

Garvagh

B 70

B 74

A 6

Dungiven

Priory

Banagher Church

*Benady
Glen*

Feeny

B 44

B 74

Roe

△ Carntogher
462

★Glenshane
Pass

Dreen

Mullaghmore
555 △

Ulster Way

Maghera
Old Church

1

Sawel Mountain
△
678

✳ **Sawel Mountain Drive ★**

*Mount Hamilton
or Sperrin*

Tobermore

A 29

**Sperrin
Heritage Centre**

Draperstown

B 47

B 40

BELFAST

Slieve Gallion
△ 527

*Davagh
Forest Park*

A 29

A 31

**★Beaghmore
Stone Circles**

2

Dunnamore

Moneymore

Springhill ★

★ *Lough Neagh*

**Wellbrook
▲ Beetling Mill ★**

A 505

B 73

2

COOKSTOWN

*Drum Manor
Forest Park*

A 520

0   8 km
0   4 miles

Tullaghoge
☆

↓ **Dungannon**

Directory

WHERE TO STAY

• Budget

Hawthorn House – *72 Old Mountfield Rd, Omagh - 0.75mi/1.2km N by B 48 - ☎ 028 8225 2005 - Fax 028 8225 2005 - info@hawthornhouse.co.uk -* 🄿 *- 5 rm £40/60* ☲ *- Restaurant £8/22.50.* A pretty pink-hued period house, 10min walk from the town centre. There's a cosy bar and first floor-lounge while the bedrooms are tidy and well equipped. The dining room is divided into three rooms and a conservatory.

• Moderate

Tullylagan Country House – *40B Tullylagan Rd, Sandholes, Cookstown - 4mi/6.4km S by A 29 - ☎ 028 8676 5100 - Fax 028 8676 1715 - reservations@tullylagan.fsnet.co.uk - Closed 24-26 Dec -* 🄿 ♿ *- 15 rm £49.95/90* ☲ *- Restaurant £16.80/22.90.* The Tullylagan river flows through the substantial grounds that surround this peaceful country house. The interior has a Georgian feel and the bedrooms, two of which have four-poster beds. all have an individual personality.

Streeve Hill – *1mi/1.6km NE on A 2, turning right immediately after the estate wall finishes - ☎ 028 7776 6563 - Fax 028 7776 8285 - p.jwelsh@yahoo.co.uk - Closed Easter, Christmas and New Year -* ⤫✕ *- 3 rm £55/90* ☲ *- Meals £30.* Striking Palladian façade to this fine 1730s house surrounded by a vast estate. The house is full of antiques; and guests enjoy a lavish dinner around a single table. The tranquillity and countryside views add to the air of relaxation.

WHERE TO EAT

• Moderate

Lime Tree – *60 Catherine St, Limavady - ☎ 028 7776 4300 - info@limetreerest.com - Closed 1 week Feb, 1 week July, 1 week Nov, 25-26 Dec, Sat lunch, Mon and Tue - £19.50/28.50.* Popular spot with the locals at lunchtime. Has a traditional feel and a good value menu featuring local produce. Those willing to eat early can take advantage of the inexpensive "early bird" menu.

SPORTS AND LEISURE

The **North Sperrin Trail**, a long-distance footpath, passes through the eastern slopes,between Castlerock on the north coast and Dungiven.

The Owenkillew and the Glenelly are both good trout streams. The many good angling streams flow north and west down the River Roe and the Foyle tributaries into the Foyle estuary or southeast into Lough Neagh.

TRACING ANCESTORS

Ulster-American Folk Park – *See below.*

Background

In the 17C some of the area was granted to the London city livery companies – Drapers *(see below)*, Skinners, Grocers and Fishmongers – who brought in new settlers mainly from Scotland, settling them in numerous new, planned towns and villages. Initially the land was let through local landlords on the rundale system *(see Landscape)*; by the early 19C it was overpopulated. Traces remain of the direct management which was then adopted in some areas. Assisted emigration was introduced; the land was reallocated in holdings of 20-30 acres/8-12ha of neatly-hedged fields; model farms were established to promote modern methods; roads and bridges, churches, schools and dispensaries were built.

Tours

The Sperrin Mountains cover an extensive area which has been divided into four tours – a northern tour starting from Londonderry, an eastern tour starting from Cookstown and a southern and a western tour starting from Omagh.

UPLANDS AND COAST 1

From Londonderry take A 2 E; turn right.

Eglinton

This elegant little village with its **Courthouse** was developed by the Grocers' Company between 1823 and 1825 round a tree-shaded green beside the Muff River. Upstream the river tumbles through **Muff Glen**, a narrow tree-lined valley of pleasant walks.

Ballykelly

The village was established early in the 17C by the Fishmongers' Company, who built a model farm which still stands on the north side of the road; a two-storey block is linked to two one-storey pavilions by curtain walls enclosing a farmyard. Opposite is the Presbyterian Church (1827). The Anglican Church of 1795, which stands on a slight hill screened by beech trees on the east side of the village, was one of several built by the Earl Bishop of Derry.

Limavady

The town takes its name from the Irish for Dogleap since the original settlement was further upstream (2mi/3.2km) by the 13C O'Cahan castle in what is now the Roe Valley Country Park. It was re-founded as Newtown-Limavady in the 17C by Sir Thomas Phillips, Chief Agent of the City of London in Ulster. It is now a pleasant Georgian market town where the famous song, *Danny Boy*, also known as *The Londonderry Air*, was noted down in 1851 by Jane Ross (1810-79) who lived at 51 Main Street *(plaque)*.

Take B 68 south.

Roe Valley Country Park★

Open daily. Visitor Centre: Open summer, daily, 10am-6pm; winter, Mon-Fri, 10am-5pm. ☎ *028 776 7532 (environmental educator),* ☎ *028 77 2 2074*

The country park extends along a stretch *(3mi/4.8km)* of the wild thickly wooded valley, where the peaty red River Roe tumbles over rocks and through gorges on its way north to the sea. The **Visitor Centre** at the Dogleap Bridge provides information on the local flora and fauna, old industries and on the 17C Plantation. As well as great natural beauty and scenes of the O'Cahans' legendary exploits, the park preserves evidence of early industrial activity: bleach greens, weirs and mill races, and 18C water-powered mills for sawing wood, scutching flax, weaving and beetling linen. An unusual feature is the stone-built **Power House** (1896), the site of early success in generating hydroelectric power.

Take B 192 S to Burnfoot.

Bovevagh Church

In the churchyard of a ruined medieval church stands a **mortuary house** similar to the one at Banagher *(see below)*; its ruined state reveals the cavity, which contained the body, and the hand hole in the east end through which the faithful could touch the relics.

Continue S; turn left onto A 6 and make a detour E.

Glenshane Pass★

The pass between **Mullaghmore** (1 818ft/555m – S) and **Carntogher** (1 516ft/462m – N) carries the main Belfast-Londonderry road through the Sperrin Mountains. The northern approach through dramatic mountain scenery overlooks Benady Glen on the River Roe; the southern approach *(viewing point)* provides a **panoramic view★★** across Lough Neagh in the mid-Ulster plain to Slemish *(see p 383)*.

Continue E on A 6.

Maghera Old Church

At the N end of the main street turn right into Bank Square, then left to the car park. (IIM) Key from the Recreation Centre (reception) in St Lurach's Road, E of Bank Square. ☎ *028 9054 3037; connor.jordan@doeni.gov.uk; www.ehsni.gov.uk*

This little town at the foot of the Glenshane Pass *(see above)* has a ruined church, probably dating from the 10C. Its outstanding feature is its splendid west door, added around 200 years later, with inclined jambs, wonderful floral and animal decoration and a lintel carved with an elaborate Crucifixion scene. In the graveyard stands a rough pillar stone, carved with a ringed cross, which, according to tradition, is the grave of St Lurach, who founded an important monastery on this site in the 6C.

Return W on A 6.

Dungiven Priory

(HM) Open daily. ☎ *028 9054 3037; connor.jordan@doeni.gov.uk; www.ehsni.gov.uk*

Before being handed over for development to the Skinners' Company, the little town of Dungiven was the base of the fierce O'Cahan clan. Just outside the town is an imposing natural strongpoint above the River Roe, the site of a pre-Norman monastery and of the ruins of the Augustinian priory which replaced it. The church remains are impressive in their own right, but their great treasure is the magnificent **tomb** of an O'Cahan chieftan, Cooey-na-Gal, who died in 1385. The tomb is designed in the tradition of 15C western Scotland, and as well as the effigy under a traceried canopy it has six robust carvings of "gallowglasses", heavily armed Scottish mercenaries in kilts.

In the 17C Sir Edward Doddington, who constructed the walls of Londonderry, built himself a house in the cloister; its foundations were excavated in 1982.

North of the path is a **bullaun**, a hollowed stone which was originally used for grinding grain but now collects rainwater; it is visited by people seeking cures for warts who tie rags on the overhanging tree.

In Dungiven turn left into a minor road.

Banagher Church

The ruined church dates from the late 11C or early 12C. In the graveyard stands a **mortuary house**, built of dressed stone early in the 12C, probably to house some relics disturbed by the addition of a chancel to the church. The panel on the west gable depicts a figure with a hand raised in blessing and bearing a crozier. According to tradition it is the tomb of St Muiredach O'Heney and sand from his tomb brings good luck.

Return to A 6 or take B 74 W through Feeny and Claudy to rejoin A 6.

Ness Wood Country Park

From the car park walk through the picnic area into the wood. The waterfall (30ft/9m) is unfenced; children should be accompanied. Woodland walk along both sides of the stream meeting at a bridge about 600yd/5508m from the car park.

The spectacular waterfall (*an eas* in Irish) was created, together with a series of gorges, potholes and rapids, by the River Burntollet eroding a channel through the metamorphic schist rock since the end of the last Ice Age.

EASTERN FOOTHILLS ②

Cookstown

Once an important linen centre, Cookstown is now the market centre for the surrounding agricultural countryside. Its most notable feature is the extraordinarily long and very broad main street which, under 10 different names, extends north from the River Ballinderry towards the silhouette of Slieve Gallion (1 732ft/528m). The result of one of the most ambitious attempts at urban planning ever imposed on the Irish landscape, it was laid out around 1750 by James and William Stewart, after the original Plantation settlement of Cookstown had been destroyed in the rebellion of 1641. The new street extended south to their own property at Killymoon Castle (*private*) which was redesigned by John Nash in 1803; its grounds are now a golf course.

The nondescript, mostly 20C buildings lining the Stewarts' grand avenue hardly measure up to its creators' aspirations.

From Cookstown take A 29 S; bear left into B 520. Turn left on a blind corner into the car park; 10min there and back on foot.

Tullaghoge Fort

The tree-crowned earthworks of this hillfort are replete with memories of the ancient rulers of Ulster; they enclosed the residence of the O'Hagans, who were the chief justices of the old kingdom of Tyrone, and it was here that the rulers of Tyrone were inaugurated, the last of them being Hugh O'Neill (*see DUNGANNON*) in 1593. Their stone throne was broken up by Lord Mountjoy in 1602.

The **view** is extensive: southwest to the circular walled graveyard at Donaghrisk where the O'Hagans were buried; east towards Lough Neagh; north to Slieve Gallion with the River Ballinderry in the foreground and Killymoon Castle in the trees by the river.

Return to Cookstown; take A 505 W for 2.5mi/4km.

Drum Manor Forest Park

&. *Open daily, 8am-dusk (4.30pm winter). £1; £3 car. Guided tour by appointment. Parking. Caravan and camping site. Refreshments.* ☎ *028 8775 9311*

The old country house of Drum Manor has long been a ruin, but its walled gardens and open parkland still exist and form the basis of this lovely Forest Park. One of the gardens has lent itself perfectly to conversion into a **butterfly garden**, where butterflies live naturally without restraint among the plants – buddleia, sweet rocket, Michelmas daisies, lavender and aubretia – which provide them with nectar. A most attractive **flower garden** has been created in the ruins of the manor house.

Continue W on A 505; turn right (sign).

Wellbrook Beetling Mill★

(NT) Guided tour Jul-Aug, daily, 12-6pm; mid-Mar to Jun and Sep, Sat-Sun and Bank Hol Mon. £2.50. Parking. ☎ *028 8674 8210 or 028 8674 1735; wellbrook@ntrust.org.uk*

Beetling is the last stage in the production of linen where the cloth is beaten to close up the weave and give it a smooth sheen. The first mill at Wellbrook came into operation in September 1767; eventually there were six and the present mill, known as no 6, dates from about 1830. It continued in operation until 1961 and is maintained in working order by the National Trust.

The drying loft contains an excellent display on the production of linen and the history of the Irish linen industry, while the lower floor houses the seven **beetling machines** turned by an external wooden waterwheel, which is fed by water carried from the mill race in a wooden flume. The amount of noise produced by two beetling engines operating for a few minutes explains why deafness was common among beetlers, who worked from early morning to nine at night.

Continue W on A 505; at Dunnamore Bridge turn right across the river.

Beaghmore Stone Circles

Beaghmore Stone Circles★

Mid-Ulster is particularly rich in prehistoric stone circles. Here there are seven, of Bronze Age date, overlaid on a site first used in Neolithic times. They are formed of quite small stones set on, rather than in, the ground. Six of the circles are arranged in pairs, with a cairn and a row of stones near the point of intersection. The area enclosed in the seventh unattached circle is studded with close-set stones, known as "Dragons' Teeth". The stones may well have been used to calculate the rising and setting of the sun and moon.

Continue N; turn right into minor road which joins B 47.

Draperstown

This pleasant little town is a busy market centre in the heart of Sperrin Mountain country. A classic settlement from the time of the Ulster Plantation in the early 17C, it makes an appropriate home for an establishment dealing with this and other aspects of local history.

In the **Ulster Plantation Centre** visitors move through a series of different settings to watch videos of costumed actors relating the defeat and **Flight of the Earls** of Ulster *(see p 206)*, and Tudor and Stuart plans to settle the area with English and Scottish planters. Further exhibits trace the history of the Plantation from the 17C to the present day, with fascinating displays on the Great Famine and emigration, and the influence of the London Drapers' Company on the life and architecture of Draperstown itself. *Open Jul-Aug, daily, 10am (1pm Sun) to 5pm; Oct-Jun, Mon-Fri, 10am-5pm;* ☎ *028 7962 7800; Fax 028 7962 7732; info@theflightoftheearls.com; www.theflightoftheearls.com*

From Draperstown take B 40 E; turn right onto A 29 to Moneymore.

Springhill★

(NT) (🚻 *to ground floor) Open Jul-Aug, daily, 12-6pm; late Mar and Jun-Sep, Sat-Sun and Bank Hol Mon. £3.50. Parking. Refreshments. Sympathetic hearing scheme.* ☎ */Fax 028 8674 8210; springhill@ntrust.org.uk; uspest@smtp.ntrust.org.uk*

This attractive seven-bay country house with its steeply-pitched roof house was the family home of the Conynghams, who came to Ulster from Ayrshire early in the 17C. Built around a deep courtyard flanked by service buildings, it is a rare survivor of the kind of comfortable residence built by Plantation families at this time, despite the difficult and sometimes dangerous conditions in which they lived. The property was altered and enlarged by subsequent generations of Conynghams, who usually followed military careers, and was transferred to the National Trust in 1957.

There are family portraits throughout the house and much **fine 18C and 19C furniture.** The splendid oak **staircase** is an outstanding feature, with oak stairs and a yew handrail. The older rooms contrast with the more spacious interiors added later like the drawing room (18C) and the dining room (early 19C), which is graced by an Italian marble chimney piece presented to the family by the notorious Earl Bishop of Londonderry *(see p 454)*. The collection of weapons in the gun room includes flintlocks used during the Siege of Derry and a pair of pikes from the Battle of Vinegar Hill *(see p 254)*.

The courtyard buildings housed staff quarters, stables, laundry, brewery, slaughterhouse and turf shed. They are now home to a **costume collection** consisting of about 2 300 articles of men's and women's dress from the 18C, 19C and 20C, which are displayed in rotation and include many rarities. The **barn**, built of the same rough-hewn local oak for the timberwork as was used in the house, is surmounted by a bell which could be rung to warn of approaching danger; a circular **dovecot** stands between the house and the road.

From Moneymore take A 29 S to return to Cookstown.

CENTRAL HEIGHTS ③

From Omagh (see below) take B 48 N.

Ulster History Park★

  Open Apr-Sep, daily, 10am-5.30pm (6.30pm Jul-Aug); Oct-Mar, Mon-Fri, 10am-5pm; last admission 1hr before closing. £3.75. Guided tour (2hr). Brochure (5 languages). Parking. Refreshments; cafeteria; picnic area. ☎ 028 8164 8188; Fax 028 8164 8011; uhp@omagh.gov.uk; www.omagh.gov.uk/historypark.htm.

The theme of the park (35 acres/14ha) in its lovely setting of wooded hills is the history of settlement in Ireland. The displays in the modern visitor centre serve as an excellent introduction to the topic, but the real attraction is the open-air park with its evocative, full-scale reconstructions of various kinds of habitat lived in by the people of Ireland, from the arrival of Mesolithic hunters to the 17C Plantation. There is a Mesolithic encampment (c 7000-4000 BC) and two Neolithic houses (c 4000-2000 BC), a court tomb and a wedge tomb, a standing stone and a stone circle, an early-Christian rath *(see ARCHITECTURE)* containing several round thatched huts, a cooking pit where the water was heated with hot stones *(fulacht fiadh)*, a crannóg, an early-Christian complex of round tower and church, a Norman motte and bailey, and a 17C Plantation house and bawn with a watermill.

Ulster History Park

Gortin Glen Forest Park

Open daily, 10am-dusk. Car £2.50. Guided tour (1hr) by appointment. Parking. Play area for children. Picnic areas; barbecue by arrangement. Campsite £1.70 per person/night. ☎ 028 8164 8217; Fax 028 8164 8070

The park, which was opened in 1967, is part of the larger Gortin Forest, a coniferous woodland planted to produce timber for commercial purposes. The forest drive *(5mi/8km – one direction only)* offers a number of beautiful vistas over the Sperrin Mountains. Detailed information is supplied in the Nature Centre and on the forest trails. The deer enclosure provides a close-up view of the Sika deer, and the pond attracts wildfowl.

From B 48 turn right.

The **Oak Lough Scenic Road★** loops round a cluster of lakes, the delight of canoeists, and provides a fine **view** of Gortin on the Owenkillew River.

Turn left onto B 46. In Gortin turn right onto B 48; after crossing the river turn right onto a minor road; in Scotch Town turn left.

The **Barnes Gap** carries the road through a narrow cleft in the hills between the valleys of the Owenkillew and Glenelly Rivers.

At the T-junction turn right; at the next T-junction turn left; cross the river at Clogherny Bridge; turn right; turn right onto B 47.

Sperrin Heritage Centre

Open Apr-Oct, daily, 11.30am (2pm Sun) to 5.30pm (6pm Sat-Sun); last admission 45min before closing. £3.73. Audioguide (3 languages). Parking. Refreshments. ☎ 028 8164 8142 (Strabane District Council); Fax 028 7138 1348; tourism@strabanedc.com; www.strabanedc.com

The Centre is conveniently sited on the B 47 linking Strabane with Draperstown via the lovely Glenelly Valley through the heart of the mountains. It is a sensitively designed building in vernacular style which harmonises well with the three adjoining cottages. Videos, computers and exhibitions enable visitors to explore the local flora and fauna, history and culture, and consider future management options. The Centre's symbol is the hen harrier, the otherwise rare bird of prey which still flourishes in the Sperrin uplands.

Continue E on B 47; in Sperrin / Mount Hamilton turn left.

The **Sawel Mountain Drive**, a narrow unfenced road along the east face of Sawel Mountain (2 229ft/678m), the highest peak, passes through the wild and austere beauty of the open moorland; the **views★★** are spectacular.

Continue E on B 47; in Sperrin / Mount Hamilton turn left. Beyond Dreen turn left onto B 44; turn left onto B 48 to return to Omagh via Plumbridge.

WESTERN VALLEYS 4

Omagh

The former county town of Co Tyrone, Omagh is normally a quiet market town, built on a steep slope overlooking the point where two rivers, the Camowen and the Drumragh, join to form the Strule. Sadly, the place won international notoriety in 1998 as the site of the greatest single atrocity of Northern Ireland's Troubles, when an intransigent republican grouping exploded a bomb in the town centre, killing 29 people.

From Omagh take A 5 N.

Ulster-American Folk Park★★

&. *Open Easter to late-Sep, Mon-Sat, 10.30am-6pm, Sun and Bank Hols, 11am-6.30pm; Oct-Easter, Mon-Fri, 10.30am-5pm; last admission 90min before closing. £4. Brochure (3 languages). Parking. Café; picnic area.* ☎ *028 8224 3292; Fax 028 8224 2241; uafp@iol.ie; www.folkpark.com*

Of all the establishments in Ireland celebrating the country's intimate links with America, this extensive open-air museum is perhaps the most evocative. Opened in 1976 as part of the American bicentennial celebrations, it is laid out around the ancestral cottage from which **Thomas Mellon**, of the banking dynasty, emigrated with his family at the age of five in 1818. There is also a Centre for Migration Studies, with a library, extensive database, and facilities for research.

A tour of the park, which is laid out in chronological order, begins with the Matthew T Mellon Information Centre and the **Emigrants' Exhibition**, which gives the historical context for the whole process of emigration, bringing it to vivid life by telling the stories of particular individuals who left their ancestral homes for the New World. Beyond is an extensive array of buildings; while some are carefully reconstructed replicas, many have been removed from their original sites in Ulster or America and re-erected here. They are laid out in chronological order, beginning with typical **Ulster buildings** of the 18C and 19C, like a humble cabin from the Sperrins, a complete "Ulster Street" with shops, workplaces and Reilly's pub-cum-grocery. The cottage in which Thomas Mellon was born in 1813 was built by his father with his own hands; it was transported here in 1976 to form the nucleus of the park. The **Ship and Dockside Gallery** marks the transition to America, and features the brig Union moored at the Belfast quayside. After pondering the crammed conditions endured by most emigrants during a voyage lasting up to 12 weeks, visitors move to the **American Street** with its all-important General Store and a replica of the 1870 First Mellon Bank of Pittsburgh. Beyond the street are log cabins and a complete mid-18C stone dwelling, brought here from what was then frontier territory in Pennsylvania, where it was built by an emigrant from Co Donegal.

In the workshops and cottages local people in **period costume** demonstrate the old crafts: cooking, spinning, weaving, basket weaving; making candles and soap; working in the forge and the carpenter's shop. Turf fires burn on the hearths throughout the year filling the air with their sweet fragrance.

Conestoga Wagon, Ulster American Folk Park

N.T.B. Belfast

Newtonstewart

The village is set near the confluence of the River Mourne and the River Strule. On a nearby hilltop stands **Harry Avery's Castle**, two D-shaped towers from a 14C O'Neill stronghold. There are fine views of the surrounding countryside.

Sion Mills

Broad grass verges, beech and chestnut trees line the main street of this model village, which was established by the three Herdman brothers, who in 1835 started a flax-spinning operation in an old flour mill on the Mourne. Twenty years later they built a bigger mill which is still working. The buildings are an appealing mixture of Gothic Revival terraced cottages in polychrome brick, black and white half-timbered edifices, of which the most striking is Sion House, and the Church of the Good Shepherd, a splendid Italianate Romanesque building (1909). By contrast, the Roman Catholic church, St Teresa's, is an uncompromisingly modern structure (1963) with a striking slate mural of the Last Supper running the whole width of the main facade.

Strabane

This small town has developed where the River Finn and the Mourne River flow into the Foyle, which forms the border between Co Londonderry and Co Donegal. In the 18C **Strabane** was a lively publishing centre. Two local apprentices made their mark in the USA: John Dunlap (1747-1812), an apprentice in Gray's Printery, printed the American Declaration of Independence in his newspaper the *Pennsylvania Packet*; James Wilson became editor of a Philadelphia newspaper after leaving for America in 1807.

The town's printing tradition is celebrated behind the bowed Georgian shopfront of **Gray's Printery** *(49 Main Street)*, where a 19C printing shop has been preserved with its 19C hand- and foot-operated presses. *(NT)* &. *Open Apr-Sep, Tue-Sat and Bank Hols, 2-5pm; other times by arrangement. £2.50. Audio-visual show. Guided tour (1hr) by appointment.* ☎ *028 7188 4094*

On the south side of Strabane turn E into a minor road.

The **Wilson Ancestral Home** is a whitewashed thatched cottage, where James Wilson is honoured less than his grandson, **President Woodrow Wilson**. The house contains some of the original furniture, including a cupboard bed by the kitchen fire and curtained beds in the main bedroom. Wilsons still live in the modern farmhouse behind the cottage. *Open daily, 1-6pm; ring the bell and wait.*

Continue on this road; in Plumbridge turn right onto B 48 to return to Omagh.

Strangford Lough★

This inland sea, 18mi/29km long with its 80mi/142km coastline, has a tranquillity and unspectacular beauty which is disturbed only when the tides rip through the narrow channel linking it to the Irish Sea. Strangford Lough was formed when the sea level rose at the end of the Ice Age, drowning the drumlins which are the most characteristic features of its landscape or converting them into countless whale-backed islands. The lough lends itself to sailing and boating and supports an exceptional wealth of birdlife, while its shores and islands are rich in historical remains

Location

Michelin Atlas p 99 and Map 712 – P 4 – Co Down.
Strangford Lough lies SE of Belfast and is ringed by the A 20, A 21, A 22 and A 25.
🛈 *31 Regent Street, Newtownards BT23 4AD. Open Mon-Sat.* ☎ *028 9182 6846; Fax 028 9182 6681; tourism@ards-council.gov.uk; www.kingdomsofdown.com*
🛈 *The Stables, Castle Street, Portaferry BT22 1NZ. Open Apr-Sep, daily.* ☎ *028 4272 9882; Fax 028 4272 9822; tourism@ards-council.gov.uk; www.kingdomsofdown.com*
Adjacent Sights: See BANGOR, DOWNPATRICK, LISBURN, MOUNT STEWART.

Background

The old Irish name for the lough was Lough Cuan but the name which has prevailed is the name bestowed by the Vikings – "violent fjord" – which refers to the regular spectacle of 350 million tonnes of sea water racing through the strait between Portaferry and Strangford village as the tide changes. Conditions in the lough itself vary between the eastern shore on the Ards Peninsula *(see BANGOR)* and the western shore; the eastern littoral is more exposed, and here the drumlins have been eroded by wave action and the prevailing westerly wind, while to the west an archipelago of intact drumlin islands runs the whole length of the lough.

The whole of the lough is a **Marine Nature Reserve**, the first to be designated in Northern Ireland. Some islands, stretches of the foreshore and neighbouring areas

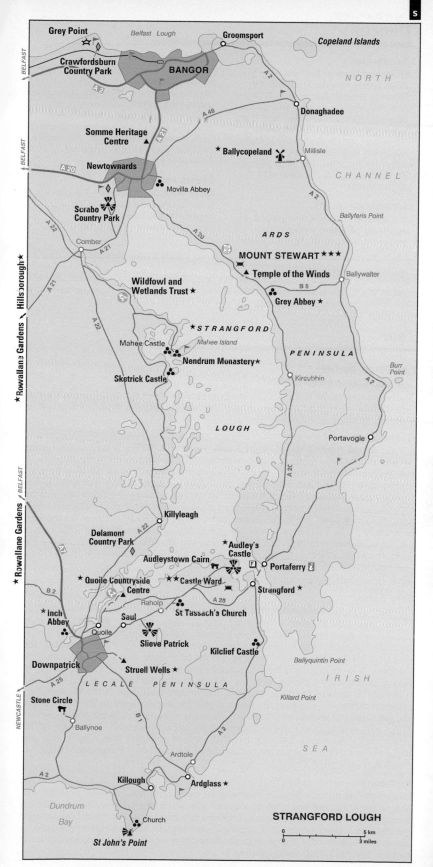

Grey Point

Belfast Lough

Groomsport

Copeland Islands

BELFAST

Crawfordsburn
Country Park

A 2

BANGOR

N O R T H

A 48

A 2

Donaghadee

Millisle

BELFAST

Somme Heritage
Centre

A 21

★ Ballycopeland

C H A N N E L

A 20

Newtownards

A 2

★ Movilla Abbey

Ballyferis Point

Scrabo
Country Park

A 22

Comber

A 21

A 20

A R D S

MOUNT STEWART ★★★

▲ Temple of the Winds

Ballywalter

Hillsborough ★

Wildfowl and
Wetlands Trust ★

B 5

Grey Abbey ★

A 22

★ *STRANGFORD*

★ Rowallane Gardens

Mahee Castle

Mahee Island

P E N I N S U L A

Nendrum Monastery ★

Sketrick Castle

Kircubbin

Burr
Point

A 2

L O U G H

Portavogie

A 20

BELFAST

★ Rowallane Gardens

Killyleagh

A 22

Delamont
Country Park

★ Audley's
Castle

Audleystown Cairn

F

Portaferry i

A 7

Quoile Countryside
Centre

★★ Castle Ward

Strangford ★

★ Inch
Abbey

B 2

Raholp

A 25

Saul

St Tassach's Church

Quoile

Slieve Patrick

Kilclief Castle

Ballyquintin Point

Downpatrick

Struell Wells ★

L E C A L E   P E N I N S U L A

I R I S H

A 25

Killard Point

NEWCASTLE

Stone Circle

B 1

A 2

Ballynoe

Ardtole

S E A

A 2

Killough

Ardglass ★

*Dundrum
Bay*

Church

STRANGFORD LOUGH

St John's Point

0 ——— 5 km
0 ——— 3 miles

Directory

SIGHTSEEING

Strangford Narrows Car Ferry –The ferry carries vehicles between Strangford and Portaferry. *Operates daily (except 25 Dec); from Strangford (on the hour and half-hour) Mon-Fri, 7.30am-10.30pm, Sat, 8am-11pm, Sun, 9.30am-10.30pm; from Portaferry (15min past and 15min to the hour) Mon-Fri, 7.45am-10.45pm, Sat, 8.15am-11.15pm, Sun, 9.45am-10.45pm. Car £4.50; passenger £1; motorcycle £3.* ☎ *028 4488 1637; Fax 028 4488 1249*

SPORTS AND LEISURE

The Tourist Information Centre in Portaferry presents an exhibition on places to visit around Strangford Lough, flora and fauna, local history and a film about tower houses; also local activities and what's on, eating out and accommodation.

There are many places where wild flowers, nesting birds, flocks of wildfowl, seals and other marine animals can be seen – Castle Espie, Delamont, Quoile Countryside Centre, Castle Ward and Mount Stewart. The marine life of the Lough can be viewed at the aquarium in Portaferry.

EVENTS AND FESTIVALS

Castle Ward Opera Festival – The festival is held in June in the grounds of this beautiful country house *(see below)*. *Information from* ☎ *028 661 090*

are protected as National Nature Reserves or as Areas of Special Scientific Interest. Most of the shore is managed by public bodies, the National Trust or the Royal Society for the Protection of Birds.

Tour

LAKESIDE DRIVE

Clockwise from Newtownards.

The tour explores the shores of the lough, giving plenty of opportunities to view its rich wildlife, its attractive villages and its early Christian and medieval heritage as well as a most unusual country house.

Newtownards

Set just inland from the head of the lough, Newtownards has a long history going back to the establishment of a priory in the 13C, though, as its name suggests, it was refounded in Plantation times. Today it is mainly interesting as a modern shopping centre and dormitory town for Belfast, though it has a spacious market square with a handsome Georgian town hall in Scrabo stone *(see below)* and, at the east end of the High Street, a distinctive market cross erected in 1635 and badly damaged a few years later. The priory ruins are unremarkable except for the burial vault of the Londonderry family *(see p 439)*, whereas there is a fine collection of 13C **cross slabs★** inscribed with foliage crosses at **Movilla Abbey**, once one of the most important abbeys in Ulster *(2mi/3.2km NE by A 48, B 172 and Old Movilla Road (right); entry through the graveyard)*.

From Newtownards take A 20 along the east shore of the lough.

Grey Abbey★

Car park. (HM) Open Apr-Sep, Tue-Sun, 10am (2pm Sun) to 7pm; Oct-Mar, Sat-Sun, 10am (2pm Sun) to 4pm. £1. Guided tour (30min). Parking. ☎ *028 4278 8585 (Supervisor); Fax 028 4278 8585; Scrabocp@doeni.gov.uk; www.ehsni.gov.uk*

Ruined Grey Abbey was a Cistercian foundation, established in 1193 by Affreca, the wife of John de Courcy, who brought monks here from Holm Cultram Abbey in Cumbria. Like many Cistercian monasteries, it stands in lovely surroundings in what was originally a remote spot. Its church, one of the first in Ireland to exhibit traces of the dawning Gothic style, has a magnificent **west door** (1220-30) with elaborate moulding and dog-tooth decoration. After being damaged in the Elizabethan wars the abbey church was restored and for many years served as the parish church. There is a small visitor centre with displays on monastic life and the building of the abbey, and a re-created herb garden with over 50 different medicinal plants and herbs of the kinds the Cistercian monks may have used in practising medicine.

Continue S on A 20.

Portaferry

Strangford Narrows car ferry. A busy coastal town until the mid-19C, Portaferry is now a yachting and sea angling centre. The attractive long waterfront, facing Strangford across the narrow strait, includes two handsome Georgian houses, now the marine biology centre of Queen's University, Belfast. **Portaferry Castle**, a tower house with only one projection flanking the entrance, was probably built early in the 16C by the Savage family.

S

Exploris★ – Much more than just an aquarium, Exploris presents the marine life of Strangford Lough and the Irish Sea in all its richness and complexity, with convincing re-creations of many underwater and shoreline habitats. There are Touch Tanks, a Marine Discovery Lab, and an Open Sea Tank, one of the largest of its kind in the United Kingdom, which visitors can view from above or from the depths of an underwater cave. ♿ *Open daily, 10am (11am Sat, 1pm Sun) to 6pm (5pm Sep-Mar). £5.40. Visitor map and guide. Parking. Café. Ramp; lifts.* ☎ *028 4272 8062; Fax 028 4272 8396. info@exploris.org.uk; www.exploris.org.uk*

Take the car ferry across the strait to Strangford.

Strangford Tower House

(HM) Key from the house opposite. ☎ *028 9054 3037; connor.jordan@doeni.gov.uk; www.ehsni.gov.uk*

In the middle of this charming little port, which dates from the Middle Ages, stands a **tower house**, which was begun in the 15C but is chiefly 16C in style. An internal wooden stair climbs the three storeys to a very narrow roof walk which provides a fine **view** of the ferry making its way across the Narrows to Portaferry on the opposite shore.

Make a detour (2.5mi/4km) S by the coast road (A 2).

Kilclief Castle

(HM) Open Apr-Sep, Tue-Sun and Bank Hol Mon, 10am (2pm Sun) to 6pm. 75p. ☎ *028 9181 1491; Fax 028 9182 0695; Scrabocp@doeni.gov.uk; www.ehsni.gov.uk*

The **tower house**, which is in the gatehouse style, with two projections to protect the entrance, was built, probably by the Bishop of Down between 1413 and 1441, to guard the entrance to the Narrows.

From Strangford take A 25 W.

Castle Ward★★

(NT) ♿ Estate and Grounds: Open daily, 10am-8pm (4pm Oct-Apr). House: Open: Jun-Aug, daily, noon-6pm; Sep-Oct, Sat-Sun; Mar, 16-18, 23-24, 29-31; Apr, first week and Sat-Sun; May, Wed-Mon. Grounds £3 per car; House £2. Braille guide. Parking. Tearoom. ☎ *028 4488 1204; Fax 028 4488 1729; castleward@ntrust.org.uk; www.nationaltrust.org.uk*

In its superb parkland setting overlooking Strangford Lough, this Great House built between 1760 and 1775 is unique, an odd but endearing architectural compromise between the conflicting tastes of Bernard Ward, later the first Lord Bangor, and his wife Anne. The master favoured building in the cool Classical manner while his wife was influenced by the first stirrings of the Romantic movement. The result was a Palladian main facade complemented by a garden front in the Gothick style pioneered by Horace Walpole at Strawberry Hill. The interiors exhibit a similar dichotomy.

The car park near the house is linked by a drive to another by the lake shore next to Old Castle Ward.

WARD FAMILY

Late in the 16C Bernard Ward from Capesthorne in Cheshire bought the Castle Ward estate from the Earls of Kildare. In 1610 Nicholas Ward built a tower house, Old Castle Ward, on the shore of Strangford Lough. In the 18C the Ward estates stretched all the way from Castle Ward to the coast of Dundrum Bay, but no trace remains of the 18C house built in the sixth generation by Michael Ward, a notable improving landlord, who promoted the linen trade, developed the lead mines on his estate, built the new town and harbour of Killough and became a Justice of the Court of the King's Bench in Ireland. In 1812 the property passed to Robert Ward, who abandoned it in favour of his other house, Bangor Castle. In 1827 the 3rd Viscount Bangor (the title was bestowed in 1781) began to restore the house and estate. On the death of the 6th Viscount Bangor in 1950 the house was received by the state in lieu of death duties and presented to the National Trust.

House – The original entrance in the southwest Classical front opens into the **hall** which is exuberantly decorated with stuccowork – partly the work of Dublin plasterers and partly in a more robust style by local workmen – and now in what is thought to be the original colour scheme.

The rooms on the northeast side of the house are decorated in the Gothick style favoured by Lady Bangor – the boudoir with **fan vaulting** based on that in Henry VII's Chapel in Westminster Abbey; the **saloon** with glass window panels thought to be 17C Flemish; and the **morning room** containing a landscape of Castle Ward in 1785 by William Ashford. By contrast, the **dining room** on the Classical side of the house has 18C panelling which was painted, grained and parcel-gilt in 1827; the dining chairs (c 1760) are in the Chippendale style.

A tunnel leads from the basement to the **stable yard** where the ground level was lowered to hide the service buildings from the house. Among them is the **laundry**, an 18C building with 19C equipment: wash tubs, a copper boiler, a stone mangle.

A von Einsiedel/National Trust Photographic Library

Gothick Boudoir, Castle Ward

Grounds – When the new house was built in the 1760s, a naturalistic landscape with broad sweeps of grass and clumps of trees and a deer park was substituted for the earlier formal landscape, of which the chief feature, the **Temple Water**, remains; this canal (1 800ft/550m) was created in 1724 and aligned on the tower of Audley's Castle *(see below)*. An **ice house** on the east bank stands close to the site of the long since demolished early 18C house. Opposite on a hill stands the **Temple**, a Classical summer house with a Doric portico (1750), next to the Walled Garden, which originally produced flowers, fruit and vegetables for the house and now contains pens for the **Wildfowl Collection**, reflecting the wildfowl to be found on Strangford Lough.

By the lough shore stands the 17C **tower house**, known as Old Castle Ward, the first dwelling built on the estate by a Ward. It is now surrounded by the farmyard buildings, most of which were built in a matching castellated style in the mid-19C. The original 18C mill, which was a tidal mill, was later driven by water from the Temple Water. Another building houses the **Strangford Lough Wildlife Centre**.

On foot from the north entrance to Castle Ward estate or by minor road W of Castle Ward estate. Drive through the gate to the car park.

Audley's Castle★

The ruins of this 15C **tower house**, which was designed in the "gatehouse" style, stand on a spit of land projecting into Strangford Lough. It was built by the Audley family, who held land in the area in the 13C, and sold in 1646 to the Wards of Castle Ward. There is a fine view of the wooded shores. The hamlet of Audleystown was demolished in the 1850s and the inhabitants are thought to have emigrated to the USA.

Audleystown Cairn

Walk across the fields. The cairn, which is revetted with drystone walling, is a dual court tomb with a forecourt at each end opening into galleries. Excavations in 1952 discovered 34 partly burned skeletons, Neolithic pottery and flint implements.

Continue W on A 25.

Quoile Countryside Centre★

& *Open Apr-Aug, daily, 11am-5pm; Oct-Mar, Sat-Sun, 2-5pm. Closed 25-26 Dec, 1 Jan. Parking. Wheelchair access to new bird hide. ☎ 028 4461 5520; Fax 028 4461 3280; quoilecc@doeni.gov.uk; www.ehsni.gov.uk*

In 1957 a barrage was built at Hare Island excluding the sea from the Quoile estuary, which had formerly been tidal, and turning the last few miles of the river into a freshwater lake with sluice gates to control flooding. This area (494 acres/200ha) is now a Nature Reserve with woodland, rushy grassland and reedbeds, providing a habitat for many woodland and wetland birds and several species of waterfowl, as well as otters.

From **Quoile Quay**, which was built in 1717 by Edward Southwell and served as a port for Downpatrick until 1940, the road reaches **Quoile Castle**, a late-16C tower house inhabited by the West family until the mid-18C; the south corner collapsed in 1977 revealing two vaulted rooms with gun loops on the ground floor. The **Visitor Centre** gives details of the local and natural history. The road ends at the Steamboat Quay, which was built in 1837 by David Ker as part of an unsuccessful attempt to establish a paddle-steamer service to Liverpool.

From Downpatrick (see p 412) take A 7.

Inch Abbey*

2mi/3.2km NW of Downpatrick by A 7; after 1mi/1.6km turn left; car park. (HM) Open daily. Parking. 028 9054 3037; *connor.jordan@doeni.gov.uk; www.ehsni.gov.uk*
The attractive site of the abbey ruins was originally an island in the marshes on the north bank of the Quoile River, approached by a causeway which carries the modern road. The abbey, a daughter house of the Cistercian abbey at Furness in Lancashire, was founded c 1180 by John de Courcy. The remains of the 13C church include a characteristic triple-lancet window. The detached buildings near the river were probably an infirmary *(SE)*, a bakehouse and well *(SW)* and a guesthouse.

From Downpatrick take A 22 N.

Delamont Country Park

Open daily, 9am-dusk. Tearoom. /Fax 028 4482 8333; *www.delamontcountrypark.co.uk*
The park, which contains a walled garden laid out with formal beds of shrubs, extends to the shore of Strangford Lough. In spring the woodlands are bright with wild flowers, and young lambs gambol in the meadows. One can see foxes, stoats and badgers; by the water, otters and seals. The bird population includes herons, which nest and rear their young between February and midsummer, treecreepers, owls, wrens, finches, wildfowl, guillemots, curlews, oystercatchers and several sorts of terns. Among the facilities are a spacious bird hide, the longest miniature railway in Ireland, boat trips, an adventure playground and orienteering.

Continue N on A 22.

Killyleagh

Killyleagh is an attractive sailing centre on the west shore of Strangford Lough, dominated by its romantically turreted **castle**, which was redesigned in 1850 by Charles Lanyon, and incorporates two circular towers dating from the 13C and 17C. The original castle, which was built by De Courcy, came into the possession of the O'Neills, was destroyed by General Monk in 1648 and then rebuilt by the Hamiltons, Earls of Clanbrassil and Viscounts Clandeboye.
Killyleagh was the birthplace of **Sir Hans Sloane**, whose collection of curios, books and manuscripts formed the nucleus of both the Natural History Museum and the British Museum in London.

Continue N on A 22; bear right into minor road along the shore.

Sketrick Castle

Car park. The approach to Sketrick Island is guarded by the ruins of a massive four-storey tower house, which collapsed in a storm in 1896. The ground floor was divided into four rooms; the largest, which is vaulted, was probably the kitchen; the one in the centre may have been a boat bay. At the rear a tunnel leads to a spring covered by a corbelled vault.

Drumlins in Strangford Lough

Continue N on minor road along the shore.

Nendrum Monastery★

At the north end of Mahee Island; car park. (HM) Open Apr-Sep, Tue-Sun, 10am (2pm Sun) to 7pm; Oct-Mar, Sat-Sun, 10am (Sun 2pm) to 4pm. 75p. Parking. ☎ 028 9181 1491; Scrabocp@doeni.gov.uk; www.ehsni.gov.uk

This inspiring early Christian site stands on an island in the lough ; once reached by boat or by crossing fords, it is now approached along a narrow twisting road and across causeways linking a chain of islands. Commanding the crossing of the final causeway are the ruins *(dangerous)* of **Mahee Castle**, a tower house built in 1570 by an Englishman, Captain Browne.

Nendrum was excavated and partly restored in the 1920s. A visitor centre tells the story of the site, which consists of three concentric enclosures (cashels) defined by drystone walls. The monastery seems to have been founded in the 5C in this well-protected location by St Mochaoi (Mahee); it was sacked by the Vikings and re-established in the 12C by the Anglo-Norman John de Courcy, who staffed it with Benedictine monks from Cumbria. But by the 14C it was no longer functioning.

The remains of the monastic church stand in the innermost enclosure; the east end was built by the Benedictines in the 12C but the west end is probably earlier, possibly 10C in date. Around the church is the graveyard and close by is the stump of a round tower. The second enclosure contained the school and monastic workshops, while the extensive outer enclosure was given over to the guesthouse, dwellings, gardens, orchards, pastures and arable fields. A tide mill was driven by the waters of the lough.

Continue N on minor road along the shore.

Wildfowl and Wetlands Trust (Castle Espie Centre)★

♿ Open Mar-Oct, daily, 10.30am (11.30am Sun) to 5pm (6pm Sun); Nov-Feb, daily, 11.30am-4.15pm (4.30pm Sat, 5pm Sun). Closed 23-25 Dec. £3.90. Bird hides. Parking. Coffee room. ☎ 028 9187 4146; Fax 028 9187 3857; www.wwt.org.uk

The centre occupies an attractive site on the west shore of Strangford Lough. Its freshwater lakes, formerly clay and limestone workings belonging to a brick, tile and pottery factory, make ideal breeding grounds and wintering habitats for both wild birds and endangered species bred in captivity. It is at its most interesting in winter, when thousands of wildfowl arrive here from the Arctic.

Continue N on A 22; in Comber take A 21; turn left up steep minor road.

Scrabo Country Park

Car park at the top of the hill; 5min on foot to the tower. Second car park in Killynether Wood. (♿) Country park: Open daily. Scrabo Tower: Open Easter-Sep, Sat-Thu, 10.30am-6pm. Parking. ☎ 028 9181 1491; Fax 028 9182 0695 (Warden); Scrabocp@doeni.gov.uk

The upper end of Strangford Lough is dominated by **Scrabo tower** rising from the top of Scrabo Hill. It is the centrepiece of a popular country park offering breezy walks, beech and hazel woodland, and fine views. The hill's topping of dolerite, volcanic lava extruded here at the same time as the Giant's Causeway was formed, has protected the underlying sandstone from the erosion which has stripped it from the surrounding countryside. Both rocks have been quarried in the past, the dark dolerite for Mount Stewart, the light sandstone for many Belfast buildings. Both were used in the 135ft/41m high tower, which was built in 1857 to commemorate the 3rd Marquess of Londonderry (1778-1854) *(see p 439)* and his concern for his tenants during the Great Famine. It now houses a small exhibition about the country park and an audio-visual presentation *The Story of Strangford Lough.*

The **view**★★ from the top *(122 steps – viewing maps)* is panoramic, extending as far as the Scottish coast *(N)* and the Isle of Man *(SE)* as well as over the lough and its myriad drumlin islands.

Index

Travel Publications

Hannay House, 39 Clarendon Road
Watford, Herts WD17 1JA, UK
☏ 01923 205 240 - Fax 01923 205 241
www.ViaMichelin.com
TheGreenGuide-uk@uk.michelin.com

Manufacture française des pneumatiques Michelin
Société en commandite par actions au capital de 304 000 000 EUR
Place des Carmes-Déchaux – 63 Clermont-Ferrand (France)
R.C.S. Clermont-Fd B 855 200 507

No part of this publication may be reproduced in any form
without the prior permission of the publisher

Based on Ordnance Survey Ireland by sanction of the Government
Permit No 7534 © Government of Ireland
Based on Ordnance Survey of Northern Ireland with the sanction
of the Controller of Her Majesty's Stationery Office, Permit No 1800

© Michelin et Cie, Propriétaires-éditeurs, 2003
Dépôt légal mars 2003 – ISBN 2-06-100728-7 – ISSN 0763-1383
Printed in France 05-03/5.2

Typesetting: NORD COMPO, Villeneuve d'Ascq
Printing-Binding: Imprimerie I.M.E., Baume-les-Dames